BEST OF THE Pillsbury Bake-Off COOKBOOK

RECIPES FROM
AMERICA'S FAVORITE
COOKING CONTEST

WILEY

Wiley Publishing, Inc.

Published by John Wiley & Sons, Inc., Hoboken, New Jersey

Published simultaneously in Canada

For general information on our other products and services or for technical support, please contact our Customer Care Department within the United States at (800) 762-2974, outside the United States at (317) 572-3993 or fax (317) 572-4002.

Wiley also publishes its books in a variety of electronic formats. Some content that appears in print may not be available in electronic books. For more information about Wiley products, visit our web site at www.wiley.com.

Library of Congress Cataloging-in-Publication Data:

Pillsbury best of the bake-off contest cookbook : recipes from America's favorite cooking contest / Pillsbury editors.—2nd ed.
    p. cm.
  Includes index.
  ISBN 978-0-470-19442-3 (cloth)
  1. Baking. 2. Desserts. 3. Cookery, American. I. Pillsbury Company.
  TX765.P525 2008
  641.7'1—dc22

                    2007041574

Printed in China

10 9 8 7 6 5 4 3 2 1

Cover photos: Jalapeño-Chicken Crescent Pinwheels (page 148); Chicken Fajita Pizza (page 76); Apple Berry Pie (page 290)

Interior Sidebar Art: Chapter 1: GMI Photo—Stock Photography Digistock; Chapter 2: ©Photodisc; Chapter 3: ©Photodisc; Chapter 4: ©Photodisc; Chapter 5: ©istockphoto.com/Juan Monino; Chapter 6: ©istockphoto.com/elena moiseeva; Chapter 7: ©Photodisc; Chapter 8: ©istockphoto.com/Sascha Burkard; Chapter 9: ©Photodisc; Chapter 10: ©istockphoto.com/MistikaS; Chapter 11: ©Photodisc

General Mills

Publisher, Cookbooks: Maggie Gilbert/ Lynn Vettel

Manager and Editor, Cookbook Publishing: Lois Tlusty

Recipe Testing: Pillsbury Test Kitchens

Photography and Food Styling: General Mills Photography Studios and Image Library

Photographer: Andy Swarbrick

Food Stylist: Sharon Harding; Carmen Bonilla

Wiley Publishing, Inc.

Publisher: Natalie Chapman

Executive Editor: Anne Ficklen

Senior Editorial Assistant: Charleen Barila

Senior Production Editor: Amy Zarkos

Cover Design: Suzanne Sunwoo

Art Director: Tai Blanche

Interior Design and Layout: Tai Blanche and Holly Wittenberg

Photography Art Direction: Lynne Dolan

Prop Stylist: Michele Joy

Manufacturing Manager: Kevin Watt

For more great recipes visit pillsbury.com

TABLE OF CONTENTS

"The newest $1 million Pillsbury Bake-Off® Contest winner is. . . ."

With that dramatic announcement, another talented amateur cook earns a place of honor in America's most prestigious culinary competition. Since it began in 1949, long before today's reality TV shows and chef competitions, the Pillsbury Bake-Off® Contest has been giving real people a chance to be recognized and rewarded for their unique skill—cooking creativity. The rest of America wins, too, with innovative and delectable new recipes to make meal times special for family and friends.

The Experience of a Lifetime

For every Bake-Off® Contest grand prize winner, the experience starts with the spark of a creative cooking idea, a new recipe innovative enough to earn them a trip to the contest finals. With tens of thousands of entries for each Bake-Off® Contest, the competition for one of the 100 coveted finalist spots is intense. Once those 100 best recipes are chosen, the 100 talented cooks who submitted them are off on an amazing adventure.

Each of the 100 finalists wins an expense-paid trip to the Bake-Off® Contest finals, held in appealing destinations around the country, like Orlando, Hollywood, Phoenix or Dallas. While the location changes, every contest finals offers fun-filled activities, the camaraderie of 99 other cooking enthusiasts and the thrill of the competition and awards ceremony.

Let the Contest Begin!

First items on the agenda for finalists are a contest orientation and enjoying the local sights. Then the cooking contest itself kicks off with a lively grand march of all the finalists onto the competition floor. Within minutes, the first whiffs of sautéing garlic and onions start to fill the air. The sound of chopping knives provides a counterpoint to the whirr of mixers, as the temperature in the room (which had been chilled in advance) rises from the heat of 100 ranges and overhead banks of camera lights.

Contest sponsors have transformed a hotel ballroom into the competition arena, with 100 mini kitchens set up in rows across the floor. Each finalist has a range and a small countertop area to prepare their recipe, with ingredients and utensils to make their recipe three times—once for the judges, once for photography, and the third, just in case. While the contest work station may not have all the conveniences of a home kitchen, it does have an extra benefit, a "runner." That's what contest sponsors call the floor assistants who aid Bake-Off® Contest finalists, running to bring ingredients from the refrigerators and freezers at the edge of the competition floor, escorting finalists to the judges or photography area, whisking away dirty dishes and generally helping to make the contest day go smoothly. Runners help with lots of things, but one thing they don't do is help the contestants prepare their recipes.

Visitors in the Kitchen

Bake-Off® Contest finalists also share their mini kitchens with guests, like food reporters curious about the recipe and what inspired its creation, supermarket representatives and sponsor hosts. Photographers and video crews maneuver their way through the work stations, trying to capture all the action of 100 cooks in the midst of the competition.

Often famous faces are spotted on the competition floor, too, as the celebrity host or another well-known guest stops to get a cooking tip from a finalist or nibble a finished dish. The roster of Bake-Off® Contest attendees includes celebrities from each decade of its history, ranging from Art Linkletter and Eleanor Roosevelt to Ronald Reagan, Bob Barker, Dick Clark, Willard Scott, Alex Trebek, Marie Osmond and Joy Behar.

Of course, the 100 finalists are the most important stars at each competition, because their creative genius makes the contest possible. While there were three men competing at the first contest in 1949, most of the 100 finalists were homemakers, reflecting the predominant role of women in the years following World War II. As more women joined the work force, the number of Bake-Off® Contest finalists who worked outside the home grew also. The list of professions from recent contests reflects the diversity of women's jobs today, with college professor, physician, business owner, portrait photographer and financial controller among the many career choices of finalists. With more men cooking in the home, more males have captured a finalist slot, too, with as many as twelve men among the 100 finalists at one competition.

Judging the Contest

One group of important Bake-Off® Contest guests isn't ever spotted on the competition floor—the official contest judges. To protect the contest's integrity, they are sequestered behind closed doors near the cooking area, to ensure that they do not know which finalist has created any of the recipes. As the finalists deem their dish ready for judging, they deliver their food to the judging room door, where it's quickly whisked from sight and to the judges. The panel of food expert judges score the recipes using the official judging criteria, then work in jury-room secrecy to deliberate on their final selection of the prize-winning recipes. How can they choose from among 100 spectacular dishes? As one newspaper food editor exclaimed about her judging role, "We're looking for something that makes you say 'Wow!' when you bite into it."

While the judges continue their deliberation—often for hours after the competition's end—contest sponsors dismantle the mini kitchens and wash mountains of dirty dishes. As the contest staff finishes last-minute preparations for the exciting awards ceremony the next day, the 100 finalists wait in suspense to learn which recipes have earned prize money.

The Winner Is...

The Bake-Off® Contest has always had a lucrative prize pool, awarding a grand prize plus additional category prizes. For the first contest, originally called the Grand National Recipe and Baking Contest, the grand prize was $25,000. Then it grew to $40,000, then $50,000. In 1996, the grand prize jumped to an amazing $1 million dollars.

As the contest's celebrity host announces each of the category prize winners, the tension builds for the final announcement. Traditionally, the grand prize-winning recipe is revealed by lifting a large silver dome to show a prepared dish hidden underneath—the dish that has earned the latest $1 million prize. Imagine the thrill for the finalist who sees their recipe in that place of honor!

For the finalist who earns the top prize, the next days are a whirlwind of activity. Recent grand prize winners like Denise Yennie of Nashville, Tennessee; Suzanne Conrad of Findlay, Ohio; and Anna Ginsberg of Austin, Texas, were whisked to New York City for appearances on one of the network morning shows, then later prepared their recipe for the country's most popular daytime talk show. Their recipe and photo appeared in newspapers around the country, and local television news shows shared video of the cooking action and dramatic awards announcement.

Everyone Wins!

Whether or not finalists win prize money, they all take home great memories of the event. Some leave having made cherished new friends from among the other finalists after sharing the Bake-Off® Contest experience. Finalists often become celebrities in their home cities, too, as a result of their Bake-Off® Contest participation. They report being recognized in the grocery store by someone who's seen news coverage of the Bake-Off® Contest. Others enjoy being able to use their notoriety to help gain attention for local charitable activities. Finalists may even hear from people around the country who have tried their winning recipe and want to share their pleasure with the dish.

What's Cooking in America's Kitchens

The recipes in each competition reflect what's cooking in contemporary American kitchens. While the early contests featured "from scratch" ideas, today's contest offers quicker, easier recipes. As more convenience products made their way into shopping carts, creative

cooks used them as the starting point for Bake-Off® Contest entries. Bake-Off® Contest recipes also introduced America's cooks to new flavors and ingredients, helping to broaden the reach of emerging cooking trends.

Today's Bake-Off® Contest recipes often pack more flavor punch than cooking did in the '50s and '60s, reflecting the growing diversity of America's cuisine and a new interest in spicier flavors. Contestants are using the wealth of choices in today's supermarkets, like an expanded variety of ethnic ingredients, new produce selections and shortcut convenience items, to add originality to their entries.

You Can Be a Bake-Off® Contest Finalist!

Home cooks who'd like to become a Bake-Off® Contest finalist can look to some of these new cooking ideas for inspiration for their entries. The official contest rules provide all the requirements for each event, including recipe categories that define what kinds of creations should be entered and eligible products that must be included in entries. For the first contest, all recipes had to use Pillsbury® flour; now eligible products include a long list of ingredients, including many items that allow for quick-to-prepare recipes. Rules also include the judging criteria—appropriate use of eligible products, taste, appearance, creativity and consumer appeal—which are used in selecting the 100 final recipes and by the judging panel at the event. Reading and following the contest rules are an important first step in preparing to enter the contest.

Bake-Off® Contest hopefuls submit their complete recipe online. All recipe entries first go to an independent judging agency, where the entrants' identifying information is removed. Recipes are screened to check that they meet the contest requirements, and then home economists read them to select the most appealing. These are forwarded to the Bake-Off® Contest kitchens, where they are prepared for evaluation by taste panels of home economists. Additional kitchen testing to ensure recipes will work consistently in home kitchens and a search process to verify originality further narrow the field of entries. Then the Bake-Off® Contest home economists complete the difficult task of choosing just 100 recipes to compete at the finals.

What does it take to become one of the elite 100? Some entrants, like grand prize winner Suzanne Conrad of Findlay, Ohio, make it to the competition the first time they submit a recipe. Others, like Michael Weaver of San Francisco, tried for 30 years before finally winning a trip to compete in 2006. But essential for any Bake-Off® Contest hopeful is a great-tasting original recipe.

A Collection of Memorable Bake-Off® Recipes

You can try some of the many wonderful Bake-Off® Contest recipes in this collection that spans nearly 60 years of American cooking traditions. Within this cookbook, you'll find favorites from throughout the contest's history. All the million-dollar grand prize winners are here, along with many of the Bake-Off® Contest classics and newer recipes destined to become favorites in home cooks' recipe repertoires. As you enjoy making dishes you've prepared in the past or trying new ideas, remember that behind each dish is a home cook, just like you and your neighbors, who was inspired to try something new.

The Bake-Off® Through the Years
1950s

The first Pillsbury Bake-Off® Contest spurred a phenomenon that many copied but few have perfected over the years. Throughout the '50s, the annual Bake-Off® Contest showcased the creativity of America's best home cooks and their favorite new flavors in the kitchen. The fictitious everywoman Ann Pillsbury—aka the Pillsbury Lady—presided over the contest and its innovative magazines. Ann encouraged cooks young and old to share a "love of good baked things that is so very strong in our country." Reflecting mid-century interest in the glamorous home, the contest was held at New York City's Waldorf-Astoria Hotel, where it resided for many years. The contest showcased kitchen innovations, including a white General Electric four-burner, double-oven. By the late '50s, electric mixers, another labor- and time-saving device, were introduced in each cook's "kitchen" at the contest. In the early years, every recipe included Pillsbury BEST® enriched flour.

Bake-Off® Recipes from the 1950s

Bake-Off® Contest 01, 1949
Old Plantation Rolls **Mrs. William Edwin Baker** Page 187
Starlight Mint Surprise Cookies **Laura Rott** Page 227

Bake-Off® Contest 02, 1950
Cherry Winks **Ruth Derousseau** Page 235
Orange Kiss-Me Cake **Lily Wuebel** Page 261

Bake-Off® Contest 03, 1951
French Silk Chocolate Pie **Betty Cooper** Page 35
Starlight Double-Delight Cake **Helen Weston** Page 263

Bake-Off® Contest 04, 1952
Brazilian Jubilee Cookies **Mrs. F. H. Speers** Page 225

Bake-Off® Contest 05, 1953
Caramel Pear Upside-Down Cake **Margaret Faxon** Page 261
"My Inspiration" Cake **Lois Kanago** Page 274

Bake-Off® Contest 06, 1954
Creole Gumbo **Elaine Thornton** Page 51

Bake-Off® Contest 07, 1955
Ring-a-Lings **Bertha Jorgensen** Page 208

Bake-Off® Contest 08, 1956
California Casserole **Margaret Hatheway** Page 89
Olive Cheese Nuggets **Johnnie H. Williamson** Page 157
Nutmeg Cookie Logs **Julia Woods** Page 225
Cheesecake Cherry Pie **Mrs. Henri L. J. deSibour, Jr.** Page 302
Ruby-Razz Crunch **Achsa Myers** Page 342

Bake-Off® Contest 09, 1957
Peanut Blossoms **Freda Smith** Page 33
Caramel Apple Pudding **Clifton G. Mandrell** Page 337

Bake-Off® Contest 10, 1958
Graham Cracker Brown Bread **Grace M. Kain** Page 172

Bake-Off® Contest 11, 1959
Mardi Gras Party Cake **Eunice G. Surles** Page 273
Lemon Cloud Pie **Jerry Ordiway** Page 298
Vienna Chocolate Pie **Dorothy Wagoner** Page 311

1960s

In the 1960s, the "Busy Lady" was a Bake-Off® theme. Bake-Off® recipes were "shortcutted, streamlined and up-to-dated for you" by Pillsbury. Although the heart of the home was still the kitchen in the 1960s, the fact that many women led busy lives outside of the kitchen meant everyday cooks created easy but delicious meals for their families. While it "used to take all day to make bread," the prizewinning Chicken Little Bread promised a great homemade loaf in less time. In 1967, the official Bake-Off® magazine featured shortcuts to prize recipes and offered "homemade goodness with hurry-up timing" to the average family cook. At the Bake-Off® Contest, the self-cleaning oven made its debut, and fresh refrigerated biscuit and crescent roll doughs were used as key ingredients for the first time. In 1969, the contest changed forever when it introduced "three divisions"—flour, mix and fresh refrigerated dough—each with a $10,000 Grand Prize. The best recipe won a $25,000 cash prize.

Bake-Off® Recipes from the 1960s

Bake-Off® Contest 12, 1960
Dilly Casserole Bread **Leona Schnuelle** Page 26
Aloha Banana Bread **Sharron Kollmeyer** Page 171
Chocolate Dream Pie **Lirene Alexander** Page 316

Bake-Off® Contest 13, 1961
Candy Bar Cookies **Alice Reese** Page 228
Peach-Berry Cobbler **Oliver C. Duffina** Page 341

Bake-Off® Contest 14, 1962
Cake 'n Cheese Cake **Imogene Noar** Page 266
Apple Pie '63 **Julia Smogor** Page 293
Cherry Cream Crunch **Joyce Herr** Page 342

Bake-Off® Contest 15, 1963
Hungry Boys' Casserole **Mira Walilko** Page 88
Kentucky Butter Cake **Albert G. Lewis, Jr.** Page 268
Melba Streusel Pie **Elaine Stoeckel** Page 294

Bake-Off® Contest 16, 1964
Cheese-Crusted Flatbread **Lois Mattson** Page 183
Chocolate Buttersweets **Vance Fletcher** Page 224
Peacheesy Pie **Janis Risely** Page 303
Strawberry Devonshire Pie **Grayce Berggren** Page 302
Mystery Pecan Pie **Mary McClain** Page 308
Royal Marble Cheesecake **Isaac Feinstein** Page 333

Bake-Off® Contest 17, 1966
Tunnel of Fudge Cake **Ella Rita Helfrich** Page 38

Bake-Off® Contest 18, 1967
Lickity Quick Lemonade Bread **Mrs. Joseph Pellecchia** Page 172
Praline Ice Cream Cake **Mrs. Thomas Griffin** Page 272
Almond Brickle Dessert **Louise Bork** Page 348
Oatmeal Carmelitas **Erlyce Larson** Page 240

Bake-Off® Contest 19, 1968
Poppin' Fresh® Barbecups **Peter Russell** Page 25
Crafty Crescent Lasagna **Betty Taylor** Page 87
Easy English Muffins **Julia Hauber** Page 186
Speedy Brioche **Mrs. Darrell L. Henderson** Page 188
Buttercream Pound Cake **Phyllis Lidert** Page 268
Cookie Cheesecake Squares **Grace M. Wold** Page 330

Bake-Off® Contest 20, 1969
Magic Marshmallow Crescent Puffs **Edna M. Walker** Page 23
Swiss Ham Ring-Around **Mrs. Lyman Francis** Page 63
Very Berry Lemon Cake **Alice Wyman** Page 256
Quick Crescent Blintzes **Mrs. Robert H. Levine** Page 324
Peanut Butter Cookie Pizza **Adeline Carr** Page 348

1970s

By 1972, Ann Pillsbury had disappeared from the Bake-Off® Contest, but a new icon had taken her place. The Pillsbury Doughboy, in a cowboy hat, graced the cover of the 1972 Bake-Off® recipe collection. His friendly face would remain a standing symbol of the contest for some time to come. The Doughboy's cowboy hat symbolized more than a friendly demeanor. It signaled the Bake-Off® Contest was on the move. Houston, New Orleans, San Diego and San Francisco were new sites for the contest and reflected America's growing diversity and shifts in population away from the East Coast. Celebrity hosts and judges awarded prizes on Bake-Off® day. By the early 1970s, the "health" food craze was recognizable in the Bake-Off® Contest. Many recipes featured apples, carrots, whole wheat, oats, and granola, but most contestant recipes reflected a lack of time for cooking. In the mid-1970s, the Bake-Off® recipe collection cost around a dollar and included recipes developed for the newest kitchen innovation, the microwave oven.

Bake-Off® Recipes from the 1970s

1980s

In the mid-1980s, the Bake-Off® Contest offered a fast-forward cuisine of quick and easy recipes, snacks and a new entrant to the arena, ethnic recipes. Competitors brought a wide variety of ethnic backgrounds to the contest. Wontons and Mexican-style recipes popped on the Bake-Off® scene for the first time. The microwave acquired a place in almost every home in the '80s, and many finalists used a microwave to prepare part or all of their entries in a matter of minutes. A microwave category was a new category at the contest. High-spending style was a hallmark of the '80s, and the Bake-Off® Contest followed suit. The Grand Prize increased to $40,000, and first-place winners in each of five categories won $15,000 for their favorite family recipes. Celebrities continued to be featured hosts, and in 1983, Bob Barker, longtime host of the TV show *The Price is Right*, awarded more than $130,000 in cash prizes in San Diego.

Bake-Off® Recipes from the 1980s

1990s

Although the theme "quick and easy" had been a staple at past Bake-Off® Contests, for the first time in 1998, Quick & Easy was its own category in the contest, increasing the number of Bake-Off® categories to five. The categories—30-Minute Main Dishes, Simple Side Dishes, Fast and Easy Treats, and Quick Snacks and Appetizers—all reflected the changing nature of the American kitchen. What changed in the kitchen? Time, more than ever, was in short supply for families with jobs, hobbies and kids, but a desire to give families the best food that mom—or dad—could make was never compromised by Bake-Off® contestants. The contest entered the modern era on February 26, 1996, when more than $1,054,000 in cash and prizes were awarded for the first time. The first million-dollar winner was Macadamia Fudge Torte, a recipe developed by Kurt Wait of California, one of 14 men whose recipes were chosen for the contest.

Bake-Off® Recipes from the 1990s

2000s

At the turn of the century, the Bake-Off® Contest turned 50! After all these years, the contest is still about creating great food while reflecting the changing nature of American society. In the first decade of the new century, the Bake-Off® Contest offered adventurous flavors that blurred ethnic boundaries. For the first time, recipes could be entered in the contest in Spanish. Bolder, even exotic, flavors came to the forefront as American cooks encountered a variety of cooking styles both at home and in travels around the world. In the 2000s, the number of Bake-Off® categories increased to six. Dinner Made Easy, Wake Up to Breakfast, Simple Snacks, Weekends Made Special, the empty-nest direction of Cooking for Two and a healthy cooking category, Brand New You, reflected a trend set by health-conscious American cooks.

Bake-Off® Recipes from the 2000s

1 | THE BEST OF THE BEST

Magic Marshmallow Crescent Puffs (page 23)

Million-Dollar–Grand Prize and Hall of Fame

Million-Dollar Winners

In 1996, the 37th Pillsbury Bake-Off® Contest got a million-dollar makeover—literally. The grand prize was increased to a million dollars, the largest prize ever awarded in a consumer cooking competition at that time. Kurt Wait was the first million-dollar winner and also the first male to win the grand prize.

Macadamia-Fudge Torte (page 22) by Kurt Wait, Bake-Off® Contest 37, 1996

Salsa Couscous Chicken (page 30) by Ellie Mathews, Bake-Off® Contest 38, 1998

Cream Cheese Brownie Pie (page 36) by Bobbie Sonefeld, Bake-Off® Contest 39, 2000

Chicken Florentine Panini (page 26) by Denise Yennie, Bake-Off® Contest 40, 2002

Oats 'n Honey Granola Pie (page 38) by Suzanne Conrad, Bake-Off® Contest 41, 2004

Baked Chicken and Spinach Stuffing (page 31) by Anna Ginsberg, Bake-Off® Contest 42, 2006

Hall of Fame

To celebrate its 50th Anniversary in 1999, the Bake-Off® Contest created a Hall of Fame to recognize some of the competition's most popular recipes. Contest home economists pored over nearly 4,000 recipes to select those that should be honored. They considered classic Bake-Off® Contest recipes and the ones most requested by consumers, finally narrowing their choices to the best ten recipes. Four more recipes won a place of honor through special consumer voting.

Black and White Brownies (page 35) by Penelope Weiss, Bake-Off® Contest 35, 1992

Broccoli-Cauliflower Tetrazzini (page 25) by Barbara Van Itallie, Bake-Off® Contest 33, 1988

Chocolate Praline Layer Cake (page 40) by Julie Bengtson, Bake-Off® Contest 33, 1988

Crescent Caramel Swirl (page 34) by Lois Ann Groves, Bake-Off® Contest 27, 1976

Dilly Casserole Bread (page 26) by Leona Schnuelle, Bake-Off® Contest 12, 1960

French Silk Chocolate Pie (page 35) by Betty Cooper, Bake-Off® Contest 3, 1951

Ham and Cheese Crescent Snacks (page 29) by Ronna Sue Farley, Bake-Off® Contest 26, 1975

Italian Zucchini Crescent Pie (page 30) by Millicent (Caplan) Nathan, Bake-Off® Contest 29, 1980

Magic Marshmallow Crescent Puffs (page 23) by Edna M. Walker, Bake-Off® Contest 20, 1969

Peanut Blossoms (page 33) by Freda Smith, Bake-Off® Contest 9, 1957

Poppin' Fresh Barbecups (page 25) by Peter Russell, Bake-Off® Contest 19, 1968

Salted Peanut Chews (page 33) by Gertrude M. Schweitzerhof, Bake-Off® Contest 29, 1980

Tunnel of Fudge Cake (page 38) by Ella Rita Helfrich, Bake-Off® Contest 17, 1966

Zesty Italian Crescent Casserole (page 29) by Madella Bathke, Bake-Off® Contest 28, 1978

Macadamia-Fudge Torte

Kurt Wait   Redwood City, CA
Bake-Off® Contest 37, 1996
$1,000,000 Grand Prize Winner

Prep Time: 30 Minutes
Start to Finish: 3 Hours
12 servings

FILLING
½ cup semisweet chocolate chips
⅓ cup low-fat sweetened condensed
milk (not evaporated)

CAKE
1 box (18.25 oz) Pillsbury® Moist
Supreme® devil's food cake mix
1½ teaspoons ground cinnamon
⅓ cup vegetable oil
1 can (15 oz) sliced pears in light syrup,
drained
3 eggs
⅓ cup chopped macadamia nuts or pecans
2 teaspoons water

SAUCE
1 jar (17 oz) butterscotch-caramel-fudge
topping
⅓ cup milk

SERVE WITH AND GARNISH,
IF DESIRED
Vanilla ice cream or frozen yogurt
Chocolate curls

Double the Distinction

When Bake-Off® contest judges awarded Macadamia-Fudge Torte the grand prize in 1996, winner Kurt Wait earned himself two places in the contest's record book: as the first $1 million winner in the contest's history and as the first man to capture the grand prize. Kurt, a single dad, gave some of the credit for his success to his then eight-year-old son: "Cy's the best tester there is because he's brutally honest about what he likes."

1   Heat oven to 350°F. Spray 9- or 10-inch springform pan with cooking spray. In 1-quart saucepan, cook filling ingredients over medium-low heat, stirring occasionally, until chocolate is melted.

2   In large bowl, beat cake mix, cinnamon and oil with electric mixer on low speed 30 seconds or until crumbly (mixture will be dry). In blender or food processor, place pears; cover and blend until smooth.

3   In large bowl, beat 2½ cups of the cake mix mixture, the pureed pears and eggs with electric mixer on low speed until moistened; beat on medium speed 2 minutes, scraping bowl occasionally. Spread batter evenly in pan. Spoon and spread filling over batter to within ½ inch of edges. Stir nuts and water into remaining cake mix mixture. Sprinkle over filling.

4   Bake 45 to 50 minutes or until top springs back when touched lightly in center. Cool 10 minutes. Remove side of pan. Cool completely, about 1 hour 30 minutes.

5   In 1-quart saucepan, cook sauce ingredients over medium-low heat 3 to 4 minutes, stirring occasionally, until well blended. To serve, spoon 2 tablespoons warm sauce onto each serving plate; top with wedge of torte. Serve with ice cream; garnish with chocolate curls.

High Altitude (3500–6500 ft): No change.

1 Serving: Calories 460; Total Fat 15g (Saturated Fat 4.5g; Trans Fat 0.5g); Cholesterol 55mg; Sodium 510mg; Total Carbohydrate 75g (Dietary Fiber 3g) Exchanges: 1½ Starch, 3½ Other Carbohydrate, 3 Fat; Carbohydrate Choices: 5

LONGEVITY. That describes how some Bake-Off® Contest recipes stand the test of time, remaining popular years after they first win at the competition.

Magic Marshmallow Crescent Puffs, the 1969 Grand Prize winner and one of the Hall of Fame recipes, has longevity. So does its creator, Edna Walker, who in her 90s enjoys what she calls "a new phase in my life" in a retirement community in Minnesota.

Her work career had longevity as well. Edna had always worked—first as a city clerk and then as a bookkeeper for her home-owner's association. "I was still working on my 90th birthday," Edna says, though she modestly points out, "but it was only part-time."

Her contest winnings have had longevity, too. "The $25,000 I won was first shared with Uncle Sam," Edna noted. After buying some new furniture, she invested the rest. The earnings from that initial cash prize have bought her special treats, like a cruise and a trip to Israel. But that initial investment remained untouched for more than three decades, paying interest for Edna to enjoy.

When encouraged to reflect on her achievements, Edna says she figures she's just as ordinary as any other Bake-Off® Contest winner. "Most of the winners are just like me," she says. "The finalists at the Bake-Off® Contest are like your next-door neighbors."

Magic Marshmallow Crescent Puffs

Edna M. Walker   Eden Prairie, MN
Bake-Off® Contest 20, 1969
$25,000 Grand Prize Winner

Prep Time: 20 Minutes
Start to Finish: 35 Minutes
16 rolls

ROLLS
¼ cup granulated sugar
2 tablespoons Pillsbury BEST®
   all-purpose flour
1 teaspoon ground cinnamon
2 cans (8 oz each) Pillsbury®
   refrigerated crescent dinner rolls
16 large marshmallows
¼ cup butter or margarine, melted

GLAZE
½ cup powdered sugar
½ teaspoon vanilla
2 to 3 teaspoons milk

1   Heat oven to 375°F. Spray 16 regular-size muffin cups with cooking spray. In small bowl, mix granulated sugar, flour and cinnamon.

2   Separate dough into 16 triangles. For each roll, dip 1 marshmallow in melted butter; roll in sugar mixture. Place marshmallow on shortest side of triangle. Roll up, starting at shortest side and rolling to opposite point. Completely cover marshmallow with dough; firmly pinch edges to seal. Dip 1 end in remaining butter; place butter side down in muffin cup.

3   Bake 12 to 15 minutes or until golden brown (place sheet of foil or cookie sheet on oven rack below muffin cups to guard against spills). Cool rolls in pan 1 minute. Remove from muffin cups; place on cooling racks set over sheet of waxed paper.

4   In small bowl, stir glaze ingredients until smooth, adding enough milk for drizzling consistency; drizzle over warm rolls. Serve warm.

High Altitude (3500–6500 ft): No change.

1 Roll: Calories 190; Total Fat 9g (Saturated Fat 4g; Trans Fat 1.5g); Cholesterol 10mg; Sodium 250mg; Total Carbohydrate 25g (Dietary Fiber 0g) Exchanges: 1½ Other Carbohydrate, 2 Fat; Carbohydrate Choices: 1½

Broccoli-Cauliflower Tetrazzini

Broccoli-Cauliflower Tetrazzini

Barbara Van Itallie   Poughkeepsie, NY
Bake-Off® Contest 33, 1988

Prep Time: 30 Minutes
Start to Finish: 50 Minutes
8 servings (1 cup each)

8 oz uncooked spaghetti, broken into thirds
1 bag (1 lb) frozen broccoli, carrots & cauliflower or 4 cups frozen cut broccoli
2 tablespoons butter or margarine
3 tablespoons Pillsbury BEST® all-purpose flour
2 cups fat-free (skim) milk
½ cup grated Parmesan cheese
Dash pepper
1 jar (4.5 oz) sliced mushrooms, drained
2 tablespoons grated Parmesan cheese

1   Cook spaghetti as directed on package. Drain; rinse with hot water. Cover to keep warm; set aside. Cook vegetables until crisp-tender as directed on bag; drain.

2   Meanwhile, heat oven to 400°F. Grease 13 × 9-inch (3-quart) glass baking dish. In 2-quart saucepan, melt butter over medium heat. Stir in flour until smooth. Gradually add milk, cooking and stirring until well blended. Cook 6 to 10 minutes or until mixture boils and thickens, stirring constantly. Stir in ½ cup Parmesan cheese and the pepper.

3   Spoon cooked spaghetti into baking dish. Top with cooked vegetables and sliced mushrooms. Pour milk mixture over mushrooms. Sprinkle with 2 tablespoons Parmesan cheese.

4   Bake 15 to 20 minutes or until bubbles around edges and is hot.

High Altitude (3500–6500 ft): Bake 20 to 30 minutes.

1 Cup: Calories 240; Total Fat 6g (Saturated Fat 3.5g; Trans Fat 0g); Cholesterol 15mg; Sodium 350mg; Total Carbohydrate 34g (Dietary Fiber 3g) Exchanges: 2 Starch, 1 Vegetable, ½ Lean Meat, ½ Fat; Carbohydrate Choices: 2

Poppin' Fresh® Barbecups

Peter Russell   Topanga, CA
Bake-Off® Contest 19, 1968
$2,000 Winner

Prep Time: 20 Minutes
Start to Finish: 35 Minutes
10 servings

1 lb ground beef
½ cup barbecue sauce
1 tablespoon dried minced onion or ¼ cup chopped onion
1 to 2 tablespoons packed brown sugar
1 can (12 oz) Pillsbury® Golden Layers® refrigerated flaky biscuits
½ cup shredded Cheddar or American cheese (2 oz)

1   Heat oven to 400°F. Lightly spray or grease 10 regular-size muffin cups. In 10-inch skillet, cook beef over medium-high heat, stirring frequently, until thoroughly cooked; drain. Stir in barbecue sauce, onion and brown sugar. Cook 1 minute, stirring constantly, to blend flavors.

2   Separate dough into 10 biscuits. Place 1 biscuit in each muffin cup; firmly press in bottom and up sides, forming ¼-inch rim. Spoon about ¼ cup meat mixture into each cup. Sprinkle each with cheese.

3   Bake 10 to 12 minutes or until edges of biscuits are golden brown. Cool 1 minute; remove from pan.

High Altitude (3500–6500 ft): Bake 12 to 17 minutes.

1 Serving: Calories 230; Total Fat 11g (Saturated Fat 4g; Trans Fat 2g); Cholesterol 35mg; Sodium 550mg; Total Carbohydrate 21g (Dietary Fiber 0g) Exchanges: 1 Starch, ½ Other Carbohydrate, 1 Medium-Fat Meat, 1 Fat; Carbohydrate Choices: 1½

It Was Fate

Peter Russell was just thirteen when his simple idea of filling refrigerated biscuits with a savory ground beef mixture won him a trip to the 19th Bake-Off® Contest and a $2,000 prize. Fast forward, and an adult Peter is dating an attractive young woman. In one of those conversations where a new couple exchanges some of their life stories, Peter tells about his Bake-Off® Contest experience. Much to the surprise of both, his girlfriend exclaims that she grew up eating Poppin' Fresh® Barbecups—never dreaming that one day she'd be dating the recipe's creator. Perhaps the popular adage should say that the way to a woman's heart is through a Bake-Off® recipe.

Hometown Celebrity

When Leona Schnuelle captured the Grand Prize in the 12th Bake-Off® Contest, she suddenly found herself a celebrity in her small town of Crab Orchard, Nebraska. "Everyone seems happier when I arrive, even at the square dances. They say, 'Hi, Mrs. Pillsbury!' Even though I miss a do-si-do now and then—they think I can bake a dilly of a bread! And all the fan mail I receive! It's exciting to hear from all the different people who come from various walks of life, yet all seem so interested in a bread recipe." Not surprising with a loaf like Dilly Casserole Bread to pique their interest.

Dilly Casserole Bread

Leona Schnuelle   Crab Orchard, NE
Bake-Off® Contest 12, 1960
$25,000 Winner

Prep Time: 20 Minutes
Start to Finish: 3 Hours
1 loaf (18 slices)

2 to 2⅔ cups Pillsbury BEST®
    all-purpose flour
2 tablespoons sugar
2 to 3 teaspoons instant minced onion
2 teaspoons dill seed
1 teaspoon salt
¼ teaspoon baking soda
1 package regular active dry yeast
¼ cup water
1 tablespoon butter or margarine
1 cup small-curd cottage cheese
1 egg
2 teaspoons butter or margarine,
    softened
¼ teaspoon coarse salt, if desired

1   In large bowl, mix 1 cup of the flour, the sugar, onion, dill seed, 1 teaspoon salt, the baking soda and yeast.

2   In 1-quart saucepan, heat water, 1 tablespoon butter and the cottage cheese until very warm (120°F to 130°F). Add warm liquid and egg to flour mixture; beat with electric mixer on low speed until moistened. Beat 3 minutes on medium speed.

3   By hand, stir in remaining 1 to 1⅓ cups flour to make a stiff batter. Cover loosely with greased plastic wrap and cloth towel. Let rise in warm place (80°F to 85°F) 45 to 60 minutes or until light and doubled in size.

4   Generously grease 1½- or 2-quart casserole. Stir down batter to remove all air bubbles. Turn into casserole. Cover; let rise in warm place 30 to 45 minutes or until light and doubled in size.

5   Heat oven to 350°F. Uncover dough; bake 30 to 40 minutes or until loaf is deep golden brown and sounds hollow when lightly tapped. If necessary, cover with foil to prevent excessive browning. Remove bread from casserole; place on cooling rack. Brush with 2 teaspoons softened butter. Sprinkle with coarse salt. Cool 15 minutes. Serve warm or cool.

High Altitude (3500–6500 ft): Heat oven to 375°F. Bake 35 to 40 minutes.

1 Slice: Calories 80; Total Fat 2g (Saturated Fat 1g; Trans Fat 0g); Cholesterol 15mg; Sodium 210mg; Total Carbohydrate 13g (Dietary Fiber 0g) Exchanges: 1 Starch; Carbohydrate Choices: 1

MILLION-DOLLAR WINNER

Chicken Florentine Panini

Denise Yennie   Nashville, TN
Bake-Off® Contest 40, 2002
$1,000,000 Grand Prize Winner

Prep Time: 10 Minutes
Start to Finish: 35 Minutes
4 servings

1 can (13.8 oz) Pillsbury® refrigerated
    classic pizza crust
1 box (9 oz) frozen spinach in a pouch
¼ cup light mayonnaise
2 cloves garlic, finely chopped
1 tablespoon olive oil
1 cup chopped red onion
1 tablespoon sugar
1 tablespoon vinegar (cider, red wine
    or balsamic)
2 boneless skinless chicken breasts
½ teaspoon Italian seasoning
4 (4-inch) slices provolone cheese

1   Heat oven to 375°F. Unroll dough; place in ungreased 15 × 10 × 1-inch pan. Starting at center, press out dough to edges of pan. Bake 10 minutes. Cool completely, about 15 minutes.

2 Meanwhile, cook spinach as directed on box. Drain well; squeeze dry with paper towels. In small bowl, mix mayonnaise and 1 of the cloves of garlic. Refrigerate.

3 In 1-quart saucepan, heat oil over medium-high heat until hot. Cook and stir onion in oil 2 to 3 minutes or until crisp-tender. Add sugar and vinegar. Reduce heat to low; simmer 3 to 5 minutes, stirring occasionally, until most of liquid has evaporated.

4 To flatten each chicken breast, place boned side up between 2 pieces of plastic wrap or waxed paper. Working from center, gently pound chicken with flat side of meat mallet or rolling pin until about ¼ inch thick; remove wrap. Sprinkle chicken with Italian seasoning and remaining clove of garlic.

5 Spray 10-inch skillet with cooking spray. Heat over medium-high heat until hot. Add chicken; cook about 8 minutes or until browned, fork-tender and juices run clear, turning once.

6 Cut cooled pizza crust into 4 rectangles. Remove rectangles from pan; spread each with 1 tablespoon mayonnaise mixture.

Top 2 rectangles with chicken, spinach, onion mixture, cheese and remaining crust rectangles, mayonnaise side down.

7 Heat 10-inch skillet or cast-iron skillet over medium heat until hot. Place sandwiches in skillet. Place smaller skillet on sandwiches to flatten slightly. Cook 1 to 2 minutes or until crisp and heated, turning once. Cut each warm sandwich into quarters.

High Altitude (3500–6500 ft): No change.

1 Serving: Calories 520; Total Fat 19g (Saturated Fat 6g; Trans Fat 0g); Cholesterol 55mg; Sodium 1070mg; Total Carbohydrate 58g (Dietary Fiber 2g) Exchanges: 2 Starch, 2 Other Carbohydrate, 3 Very Lean Meat, 3 Fat; Carbohydrate Choices: 4

meet denise yennie

DENISE YENNIE confesses a lifelong passion for food, inspired by her mother, her aunts and her German grandmother, all good cooks. Still to many acquaintances, Denise is known as a business consultant. Her consulting firm challenges clients' conventional wisdom in doing business, and Denise carries a bit of that renegade spirit into her cooking.

"Everything I do has to be quick and easy," Denise says. "My mom and grandmother used to cook things slowly, all day. Not me. I turn on the heat and crank it up." For the contest, "I wanted to create something special enough to get recognized," she says. And her recipe for Chicken Florentine Panini did just that, winning the $1 million Grand Prize at the 2002 Bake-Off® Contest.

Denise herself was a standout at the competition. Amid the quiet preparation of other finalists, she turned heads as she noisily pounded chicken breasts with a mallet. "I pounded so much chicken that I have 'chicken-pounding elbow,'" she joked.

After the contest finals, Denise made several television appearances. "I had to practice getting the preparation of the sandwich done in five minutes for *Oprah* and in two minutes for the *Today Show*," she says. "The best part has been the impact and effect on all the people who know me—how they go and tell their friends. They get to live this joy with me."

Contest Jitters

When television cameras follow your every shake, stir and move, it's hard not to be nervous. Finalists are often asked questions by roving reporters while they're competing.

- "What was the most interesting thing that ever happened to you?" was the question for one finalist who quipped, "Being chased out of my kitchen by an angry moose."

  - When asked the name of her prize-winning recipe, one flustered finalist stared at the camera and said, "I forgot."

Zesty Italian Crescent Casserole

Madella Bathke   Wells, MN
Bake-Off® Contest 28, 1978

Prep Time: 25 Minutes
Start to Finish: 50 Minutes
6 servings

1 lb ground beef
¼ cup chopped onion
1 cup tomato pasta sauce
1½ cups shredded mozzarella or Monterey Jack cheese (6 oz)
½ cup sour cream
1 can (8 oz) Pillsbury® refrigerated crescent dinner rolls
⅓ cup grated Parmesan cheese
2 tablespoons butter or margarine, melted

1   Heat oven to 375°F. In 10-inch skillet, cook beef and onion over medium heat 8 to 10 minutes, stirring frequently, until beef is thoroughly cooked; drain. Stir in pasta sauce; cook until hot.

2   In medium bowl, mix mozzarella cheese and sour cream.

3   Pour hot beef mixture into ungreased 12 × 8-inch (2-quart) glass baking dish, or 9½- or 10-inch deep-dish pie plate. Spoon cheese mixture over beef mixture.

4   Unroll dough over cheese mixture. (If using pie plate, separate dough into 8 triangles; arrange points toward center over cheese mixture, crimping outside edges if necessary.) In small bowl, mix Parmesan cheese and melted butter. Spread evenly over dough.

5   Bake 18 to 25 minutes or until deep golden brown.

High Altitude (3500–6500 ft): Bake 22 to 25 minutes.

1 Serving: Calories 500; Total Fat 33g (Saturated Fat 15g; Trans Fat 3g); Cholesterol 90mg; Sodium 800mg; Total Carbohydrate 25g (Dietary Fiber 1g) Exchanges: 1 Starch, ½ Other Carbohydrate, 3½ Medium-Fat Meat, 3 Fat; Carbohydrate Choices: 1½

Ham and Cheese Crescent Snacks

Ronna Sue Farley   Rockville, MD
Bake-Off® Contest 26, 1975

Prep Time: 15 Minutes
Start to Finish: 40 Minutes
24 snacks

1 can (8 oz) Pillsbury® refrigerated crescent dinner rolls
2 tablespoons butter or margarine, softened
1 teaspoon yellow mustard
1 cup cubed cooked ham
⅓ cup chopped onion
⅓ cup chopped green bell pepper
1 cup shredded Cheddar or American cheese (4 oz)

1   Heat oven to 375°F. Onto ungreased cookie sheet, unroll dough. Press or roll to form 13 × 9-inch rectangle; press perforations to seal. Pinch edges to form rim.

2   In small bowl, mix butter and mustard. Spread mixture over dough. Sprinkle ham, onion, bell pepper and cheese over mixture.

3   Bake 18 to 25 minutes or until edges are golden brown. Cut into squares. Serve warm. Store in refrigerator.

High Altitude (3500–6500 ft): No change.

1 Snack: Calories 70; Total Fat 5g (Saturated Fat 2.5g; Trans Fat 0.5g); Cholesterol 10mg; Sodium 200mg; Total Carbohydrate 4g (Dietary Fiber 0g) Exchanges: ½ Starch, 1 Fat; Carbohydrate Choices: 0

Zesty Italian Crescent Casserole

Italian Zucchini Crescent Pie

Millicent (Caplan) Nathan Boca Raton, FL
Bake-Off® Contest 29, 1980
$40,000 Grand Prize Winner

Prep Time: 30 Minutes
Start to Finish: 55 Minutes
6 servings

2 tablespoons butter or margarine
4 cups thinly sliced zucchini
1 cup chopped onions
2 tablespoons parsley flakes
½ teaspoon salt
½ teaspoon pepper
¼ teaspoon garlic powder
¼ teaspoon dried basil leaves
¼ teaspoon dried oregano leaves
2 eggs, well beaten, or ½ cup fat-free egg product
2 cups shredded Muenster or mozzarella cheese (8 oz)
1 can (8 oz) Pillsbury® refrigerated crescent dinner rolls or reduced-fat crescent dinner rolls
2 teaspoons yellow mustard

1 Heat oven to 375°F. In 12-inch skillet, melt butter over medium-high heat. Cook zucchini and onions in butter 6 to 8 minutes, stirring occasionally, until tender. Stir in parsley flakes, salt, pepper, garlic powder, basil and oregano.

2 In large bowl, mix eggs and cheese. Add cooked vegetable mixture; stir gently to mix.

3 Separate dough into 8 triangles. Place in ungreased 10-inch pie plate, 12 × 8-inch (2-quart) glass baking dish or 11-inch quiche pan; press over bottom and up sides to form crust. Firmly press perforations to seal. Spread crust with mustard. Pour egg mixture evenly into crust-lined pan.

4 Bake 18 to 22 minutes or until knife inserted near center comes out clean. If necessary, cover edge of crust with strips of foil during last 10 minutes of baking to prevent excessive browning. Let stand 10 minutes before serving.

High Altitude (3500–6500 ft): Bake 30 to 35 minutes, covering edge of crust with foil after first 15 minutes of baking.

1 Serving: Calories 370; Total Fat 25g (Saturated Fat 13g; Trans Fat 2.5g); Cholesterol 115mg; Sodium 800mg; Total Carbohydrate 21g (Dietary Fiber 2g) Exchanges: 1 Starch, 1 Vegetable, 1½ High-Fat Meat, 2½ Fat; Carbohydrate Choices: 1½

MILLION-DOLLAR WINNER

Salsa Couscous Chicken

Ellie Mathews Seattle, WA
Bake-Off® Contest 38, 1998
$1,000,000 Grand Prize Winner

Prep Time: 30 Minutes
Start to Finish: 30 Minutes
4 servings

1 cup uncooked couscous or rice
Water
1 tablespoon olive or vegetable oil
¼ cup coarsely chopped almonds
2 cloves garlic, finely chopped
8 chicken thighs, skin removed
1 cup salsa
¼ cup water
2 tablespoons dried currants or raisins
1 tablespoon honey
¾ teaspoon ground cumin
½ teaspoon ground cinnamon

1 Cook couscous in water as directed on package. Cover to keep warm.

2 Meanwhile, in 10-inch skillet, heat oil over medium-high heat until hot. Cook almonds in oil 1 to 2 minutes, stirring frequently, until golden brown. With slotted spoon, remove almonds from skillet; set aside.

Front Page News

Home cooks looking for great new recipes often turn to cookbooks, food magazines, or the food section of their local newspaper. But the front page section of the *Wall Street Journal*? Several years after Millicent Nathan's recipe took the top prize at the Bake-Off® Contest, a *Journal* reporter decided to write a feature story about the competition, its history, and the experiences of a contest winner. The reporter flew to Millicent's home in Florida to interview her and sample her zucchini pie. When the front-page story appeared in the business-focused newspaper, Millicent's recipe was also included, adding the venerable *Wall Street Journal* to the list of places to find Italian Zucchini Crescent Pie.

3 Add garlic to skillet; cook and stir 30 seconds. Add chicken; cook 4 to 5 minutes or until browned, turning once.

4 In medium bowl, mix remaining ingredients. Add to chicken; mix well. Reduce heat to medium; cover and cook about 20 minutes, stirring occasionally, until chicken is fork-tender and juices run clear. Stir in almonds. Serve chicken mixture with couscous.

High Altitude (3500–6500 ft): No change.

1 Serving: Calories 510; Total Fat 19g (Saturated Fat 4.5g; Trans Fat 0g); Cholesterol 85mg; Sodium 470mg; Total Carbohydrate 48g (Dietary Fiber 4g) Exchanges: 2 Starch, 1 Other Carbohydrate, 4 ½ Lean Meat, 1 Fat; Carbohydrate Choices: 3

MILLION-DOLLAR WINNER

Baked Chicken and Spinach Stuffing

Anna Ginsberg   Austin, TX
Bake-Off® Contest 42, 2006
$1,000,000 Grand Prize Winner

Prep Time: 35 Minutes
Start to Finish: 1 Hour
2 servings

3 tablespoons maple-flavored syrup
2 tablespoons peach preserves
½ teaspoon Worcestershire sauce
2 bone-in skin-on chicken breasts (1 lb)
¼ teaspoon salt
¼ teaspoon pepper
4 squares frozen homestyle or
    buttermilk waffles
1 tablespoon butter or margarine
½ cup chopped onion (1 medium)
¼ cup chicken broth
½ teaspoon poultry seasoning
½ teaspoon chopped fresh sage
1 tablespoon beaten egg white
1 box (9 oz) frozen spinach, thawed,
    drained (about 1 cup)
1 tablespoon chopped pecans

Bake-Off® Winner…and Blogger

Anna Ginsberg won the 2006 Bake-Off® Contest million-dollar prize with her family-pleasing main dish. With its maple glaze and spinach-accented stuffing, the dish brings the usual—baked chicken—to new heights. But Anna's passion remains baking cookies. Nearly every day, Anna experiments with a new cookie recipe, testing and tinkering, then tasting to see if it meets her standards. Then Anna posts a photo of the day's cookie, along with her opinion of it, on her blog. Just as early Bake-Off® Contest finalists swapped recipe cards with their neighbors over the backyard fence, Anna is sharing recipes with friends, too, in today's style—around the world through the Internet.

1 Heat oven to 350°F. Spray 9-inch glass pie plate or 8-inch square pan with cooking spray. In small bowl, mix syrup, preserves and Worcestershire sauce. Place chicken, skin side up, in pie plate; sprinkle with salt and pepper. Spoon syrup mixture over chicken.

2 Bake uncovered 40 to 45 minutes. Meanwhile, toast waffles until golden brown. Cool slightly, about 2 minutes. Cut waffles into ¾-inch cubes; set aside. Spray 1-quart casserole with cooking spray (or use 9 × 5-inch nonstick loaf pan; do not spray). In 10-inch nonstick skillet, melt butter over medium heat. Add onion; cook and stir about 2 minutes or until tender. Stir in waffle pieces and broth, breaking up waffle pieces slightly to moisten. Sprinkle with poultry seasoning and sage. Remove from heat; cool about 5 minutes. Stir in egg white and spinach. Spoon stuffing into

casserole. Sprinkle pecans over top.

3 Twenty minutes before chicken is done, place casserole in oven next to chicken in pie plate. Spoon syrup mixture in pie plate over chicken. Bake chicken and stuffing uncovered 20 to 25 minutes longer or until juice of chicken is clear when thickest part is cut to bone (170°F) and stuffing is hot. Spoon remaining syrup mixture in pie plate over chicken. Serve chicken with stuffing.

High Altitude (3500–6500 ft): In step 3, after adding stuffing to oven, bake chicken and stuffing 20 to 30 minutes longer.

1 Serving: Calories 630; Total Fat 21g (Saturated Fat 8g; Trans Fat 2g); Cholesterol 90mg; Sodium 1130mg; Total Carbohydrate 74g (Dietary Fiber 5g) Exchanges: 2½ Starch, 2 Other Carbohydrate, 1 Vegetable, 4 Lean Meat, 1½ Fat; Carbohydrate Choices: 5

Salted Peanut Chews

Salted Peanut Chews

Gertrude M. Schweitzerhof Cupertino, CA
Bake-Off® Contest 29, 1980

Prep Time: 35 Minutes
Start to Finish: 1 Hour 35 Minutes
36 bars

BASE
1½ cups Pillsbury BEST® all-purpose flour
⅔ cup packed brown sugar
½ teaspoon baking powder
½ teaspoon salt
¼ teaspoon baking soda
½ cup butter or margarine, softened
1 teaspoon vanilla
2 egg yolks
3 cups miniature marshmallows

TOPPING
⅔ cup corn syrup
¼ cup butter or margarine
2 teaspoons vanilla
1 bag (10 oz) peanut butter chips (1⅔ cups)
2 cups crisp rice cereal
2 cups salted peanuts

1   Heat oven to 350°F. In large bowl, beat all base ingredients except marshmallows with electric mixer on low speed until crumbly. Press mixture firmly in bottom of ungreased 13 × 9-inch pan.

2   Bake 12 to 15 minutes or until light golden brown. Immediately sprinkle marshmallows evenly over base; bake 1 to 2 minutes longer or until marshmallows just begin to puff. Cool while making topping.

3   In 3-quart saucepan, mix all topping ingredients except cereal and peanuts. Heat over low heat, stirring constantly, just until chips are melted and mixture is smooth. Remove from heat. Stir in cereal and peanuts. Immediately spoon warm topping over marshmallows; spread to cover. Refrigerate until firm, about 45 minutes. For bars, cut into 6 rows by 6 rows.

High Altitude (3500–6500 ft): Heat oven to 375°F.

1 Bar: Calories 200; Total Fat 11g (Saturated Fat 3.5g; Trans Fat 0g); Cholesterol 20mg; Sodium 130mg; Total Carbohydrate 22g (Dietary Fiber 1g) Exchanges: 1½ Other Carbohydrate, ½ High-Fat Meat, 1½ Fat; Carbohydrate Choices: 1½

Peanut Blossoms

Freda Smith Gibsonburg, OH
Bake-Off® Contest 9, 1957

Prep Time: 1 Hour
Start to Finish: 1 Hour
4 dozen cookies

1¾ cups Pillsbury BEST® all-purpose flour
½ cup granulated sugar
½ cup packed brown sugar
1 teaspoon baking soda
½ teaspoon salt
½ cup shortening
½ cup peanut butter
2 tablespoons milk
1 teaspoon vanilla
1 egg
Granulated sugar
48 Hershey®'s Kisses® milk chocolates, unwrapped

1   Heat oven to 375°F. In large bowl, beat flour, ½ cup granulated sugar, the brown sugar, baking soda, salt, shortening, peanut butter, milk, vanilla and egg with electric mixer on low speed, scraping bowl occasionally, until stiff dough forms.

2   Shape dough into 1-inch balls; roll in granulated sugar. On ungreased cookie sheets, place 2 inches apart.

3   Bake 10 to 12 minutes or until golden brown. Immediately top each cookie with 1 milk chocolate candy, pressing down firmly so cookie cracks around edge. Remove from cookie sheets.

High Altitude (3500–6500 ft): No change.

1 Cookie: Calories 100; Total Fat 5g (Saturated Fat 1.5g; Trans Fat 0g); Cholesterol 5mg; Sodium 70mg; Total Carbohydrate 11g (Dietary Fiber 0g) Exchanges: 1 Other Carbohydrate, 1 Fat; Carbohydrate Choices: 1

Hershey's and Kisses trademarks and associated trade dress are registered trademarks of The Hershey Company used under license.

Bake-Off® Grand Prize Grows

From 1949 through 1980, the Grand Prize Winner was awarded $25,000. For the first contest in 1949, however, Theodora Smafield was able to double her winnings by enclosing a special token with her entry. The grand prize grew to $40,000, then $50,000 since 1980 and is now worth a million dollars!

Crescent Caramel Swirl

Lois Ann Groves
Greenwood Village, CO
Bake-Off® Contest 27, 1976
$25,000 One of Two Grand Prize Winners

Prep Time: 20 Minutes
Start to Finish: 55 Minutes
12 servings

½ cup butter (do not use margarine)
½ cup chopped nuts
¾ cup packed brown sugar
1 tablespoon water
2 cans (8 oz each) Pillsbury®
    refrigerated crescent dinner rolls

1 Heat oven to 350°F. In 1-quart saucepan, melt butter. With 2 tablespoons of the melted butter, coat bottom and sides of 12-cup fluted tube cake pan; sprinkle pan with 3 tablespoons of the nuts. To remaining melted butter, stir in remaining nuts, the brown sugar and water. Heat to boiling, stirring occasionally. Boil 1 minute, stirring constantly. Remove from heat.

2 Remove dough from both cans; do not unroll. Cut each long roll into 8 slices. Arrange 8 slices, cut side down, in nut-lined pan; separate layers of each pinwheel slightly. Spoon half of brown sugar mixture over dough. Place remaining 8 dough slices alternately over bottom layer. Spoon remaining brown sugar mixture over slices.

3 Bake 23 to 33 minutes or until deep golden brown. Cool 3 minutes. Place heatproof serving platter upside down over pan; turn pan and platter over. Remove pan. Serve warm.

High Altitude (3500–6500 ft): No change.

1 Serving: Calories 300; Total Fat 19g (Saturated Fat 8g; Trans Fat 2.5g); Cholesterol 20mg; Sodium 350mg; Total Carbohydrate 29g (Dietary Fiber 0g); Exchanges: 1 Starch, 1 Other Carbohydrate, 3½ Fat; Carbohydrate Choices: 2

meet lois ann groves

CREATIVITY IS ONE of the keys to coming up with a winning recipe—but so is following through with your inspiration. Just ask Lois Ann Groves.

Lois Ann's mother would occasionally create a successful recipe and comment about entering the contest. "However, I guess my mother was so busy rearing her family that she never got her recipes written down and sent," says Lois Ann.

Years later, Lois Ann came across a Bake-Off® Contest entry blank on the very day of the deadline. After her young children were in bed, she tested her recipe for the first time, as her husband helped type the directions. At 11 p.m., they loaded the children into the car and drove 20 miles to have it postmarked before the entry deadline, a requirement in the days before online entry.

That entry won Lois Ann a trip to Hawaii for the 1971 Bake-Off® competition, and her experience inspired her to become even more creative in the kitchen. Her best creation—easy and spectacular Crescent Caramel Swirl—earned Lois Ann $25,000 in 1976 and later, a place in the contest Hall of Fame.

Her Bake-Off® Contest success also inspired Lois Ann to a new avocation. After finding she enjoyed talking to local groups about her experience, Lois Ann became a successful public speaker, sharing her personal story and inspirational message with thousands of women.

Black and White Brownies

Penelope Weiss   Pleasant Grove, UT
Bake-Off® Contest 35, 1992

Prep Time: 15 Minutes
Start to Finish: 2 Hours 30 Minutes
36 brownies

BROWNIES
1 box (19.5 oz) Pillsbury® Brownie
   Classics traditional fudge
   brownie mix
¼ cup water
½ cup vegetable oil
2 eggs
1½ cups chopped pecans
1 cup semisweet chocolate chips (6 oz)
1 bag (12 oz) white vanilla baking chips
   (2 cups)

FROSTING
2 cups powdered sugar
¼ cup unsweetened baking cocoa
3 to 4 tablespoons hot water
¼ cup butter or margarine, melted
1 teaspoon vanilla
½ to 1 cup pecan halves

1   Heat oven to 350°F. Grease bottom only of 13 × 9-inch pan with shortening or spray with cooking spray. In large bowl, beat brownie mix, ¼ cup water, the oil and eggs 50 strokes with spoon. Stir in chopped pecans, chocolate chips and 1 cup of the vanilla baking chips. Spread in pan.

2   Bake 28 to 34 minutes or until center is set. Immediately sprinkle with remaining 1 cup vanilla baking chips. Let stand 1 minute to soften chips; spread evenly over brownies.

3   In small bowl, beat all frosting ingredients except pecan halves with electric mixer on medium speed until smooth (mixture will be thin). Spoon over melted vanilla baking chips; spread to cover. Arrange pecan halves on frosting. Cool completely, about 1 hour 30 minutes. For brownies, cut into 6 rows by 6 rows.

High Altitude (3500–6500 ft): Add ½ cup Pillsbury BEST® all-purpose flour to dry brownie mix. Increase water in brownies to ⅓ cup.

1 Brownie: Calories 260; Total Fat 14g (Saturated Fat 5g; Trans Fat 0g); Cholesterol 15mg; Sodium 75mg; Total Carbohydrate 29g (Dietary Fiber 1g) Exchanges: 2 Other Carbohydrate, 3 Fat; Carbohydrate Choices: 2

French Silk Chocolate Pie

Betty Cooper   Kensington, MD
Bake-Off® Contest 3, 1951
$1,000 Winner

Prep Time: 50 Minutes
Start to Finish: 2 Hours 50 Minutes
10 servings

CRUST
1 Pillsbury® refrigerated pie crust (from
   15-oz box), softened as directed on
   box, or pastry for one-crust pie

FILLING
3 oz unsweetened baking chocolate,
   cut into pieces
1 cup butter, softened (do not use
   margarine)
1 cup sugar
½ teaspoon vanilla
4 pasteurized eggs* or 1 cup fat-free
   egg product

TOPPING
½ cup sweetened whipped cream
Chocolate curls, if desired

1   Heat oven to 450°F. Make and bake pie crust for One-Crust Baked Shell, using 9-inch pie plate. Cool completely, about 30 minutes.

2   In 1-quart saucepan, melt chocolate over low heat; cool. In small bowl, beat butter with electric mixer on medium speed until fluffy. Gradually add sugar, beating until light and fluffy. Add cooled chocolate and vanilla; beat well.

3   Add eggs 1 at a time, beating on high speed 2 minutes after each addition. Beat until mixture is smooth and fluffy. Pour into cooled baked shell. Refrigerate at least 2 hours before serving. Top with whipped cream and chocolate curls. Store in refrigerator.

High Altitude (3500–6500 ft): No change.

1 Serving: Calories 460; Total Fat 34g (Saturated Fat 19g; Trans Fat 1g); Cholesterol 150mg; Sodium 250mg; Total Carbohydrate 34g (Dietary Fiber 1g) Exchanges: 1 Starch, 1½ Other Carbohydrate, 6½ Fat; Carbohydrate Choices: 2

Pasteurized eggs are uncooked eggs that have been heat-treated to kill bacteria that can cause food poisoning and gastrointestinal distress. Because the eggs in this recipe are not cooked, be sure to use pasteurized eggs. They can be found in the dairy case at large supermarkets.

Cream Cheese Brownie Pie

Bobbie Sonefeld Hopkins, SC
Bake-Off® Contest 39, 2000
$1,000,000 Grand Prize Winner

Prep Time: 15 Minutes
Start to Finish: 4 Hours 5 Minutes
8 servings

CRUST

1 Pillsbury® refrigerated pie crust (from 15-oz box), softened as directed on box

CREAM CHEESE LAYER

1 package (8 oz) cream cheese, softened
3 tablespoons sugar
1 teaspoon vanilla
1 egg

BROWNIE LAYER

1 box (15.1 oz) Pillsbury® Fudge Supreme hot fudge swirl brownie mix
¼ cup vegetable oil
1 tablespoon water
2 eggs
½ cup chopped pecans

TOPPING

Reserved hot fudge from brownie mix
1 tablespoon water

1   Heat oven to 350°F. Place pie crust in 9-inch glass pie plate as directed on box for One-Crust Filled Pie.

2   In medium bowl, beat cream cheese layer ingredients with electric mixer on medium speed until smooth; set aside.

3   Reserve hot fudge packet from brownie mix for topping. In large bowl, place brownie mix and remaining brownie layer ingredients; beat 50 strokes with spoon.

4   Spread ½ cup brownie mixture in bottom of crust-lined pie plate. Spoon and carefully spread cream cheese mixture over brownie layer. Top with remaining brownie mixture; spread evenly. Sprinkle with pecans. Cover crust edge with

meet bobbie sonefeld

When most people hear about Bobbie Sonefeld's Bake-Off® Contest win, they immediately focus on the $1 million Grand Prize she earned for her decadent Cream Cheese Brownie Pie. But Bobbie says a rich part of the experience was the Bake-Off ®Contest weekend itself, a dazzling trip she and her husband, Steve, have christened their "second honeymoon."

The 2000 Bake-Off® Contest took place in a luxurious hotel in downtown San Francisco. "Neither of us had ever been to the West Coast," recalled Bobbie. "The way Pillsbury treated us was just great: three gourmet meals a day plus all kinds of tours and sightseeing." Didn't she get nervous? "Well, yes," she admits, "but I didn't get the butterflies bad until the night before. The next morning—once I was done baking and there wasn't anything I could do about it—I was fine. Then I thought, 'Wow, I already feel like a winner; it doesn't matter what happens next.'"

What happened next is part of history: Bobbie's pie won the grand prize. The Sonefelds' second honeymoon became even more exciting, as they jetted to New York City for a whirlwind of television and radio appearances and even more great meals.

After an amazing week, Bobbie and Steve returned home to Hopkins, South Carolina. That's when the honeymoon turned into a homecoming, as Bobbie was welcomed back by her very excited sons.

2- to 3-inch-wide strips of foil to prevent excessive browning; remove foil during last 15 minutes of bake time.

5 Bake 40 to 50 minutes or until center is puffed and crust is golden brown (pie may have cracks on surface).

6 In small microwavable bowl, microwave hot fudge from packet uncovered on High 30 seconds. Stir in 1 tablespoon water. Drizzle topping over pie. Cool completely, about 3 hours, before serving. Store pie in refrigerator.

High Altitude (3500–6500 ft): Add 3 tablespoons Pillsbury BEST® all-purpose flour to dry brownie mix.

1 Serving: Calories 610; Total Fat 37g (Saturated Fat 13g; Trans Fat 1.5g); Cholesterol 115mg; Sodium 360mg; Total Carbohydrate 64g (Dietary Fiber 2g) Exchanges: 1 Starch, 3 Other Carbohydrate, ½ High-Fat Meat, 6½ Fat; Carbohydrate Choices: 4

Oats 'n Honey Granola Pie

Suzanne Conrad   Findlay, OH
Bake-Off® Contest 41, 2004
$1,000,000 Grand Prize Winner and a set
of GE Profile™ kitchen appliances

Prep Time: 15 Minutes
Start to Finish: 1 Hour 35 Minutes
8 servings

CRUST
1 Pillsbury® refrigerated pie crust
(from 15-oz box), softened as
directed on box

FILLING
½ cup butter or margarine
½ cup packed light brown sugar
¾ cup corn syrup
⅛ teaspoon salt
1 teaspoon vanilla
3 eggs, slightly beaten
4 oats 'n honey crunchy granola bars
(2 pouches from 8.9-oz box),
crushed (¾ cup)*
½ cup chopped walnuts
¼ cup quick-cooking or old-fashioned
oats
¼ cup chocolate chips

SERVE WITH, IF DESIRED
Whipped cream or ice cream

1   Heat oven to 350°F. Place pie crust in 9-inch glass pie plate as directed on box for One-Crust Filled Pie.

2   In large microwavable bowl, microwave butter uncovered on High 50 to 60 seconds or until melted. Stir in brown sugar and corn syrup until blended. Beat in salt, vanilla and eggs. Stir in remaining filling ingredients. Pour into crust-lined pie plate. Cover crust edge with 2- to 3-inch-wide strips of foil to prevent excessive browning; remove foil during last 15 minutes of bake time.

3   Bake 40 to 50 minutes or until filling is set and crust is golden brown. Cool at least 30 minutes before serving. Serve warm, at room temperature or chilled with whipped cream. Store pie in refrigerator.

High Altitude (3500–6500 ft): No change.

1 Serving: Calories 540; Total Fat 29g (Saturated Fat 12g; Trans Fat 0g); Cholesterol 115mg; Sodium 320mg; Total Carbohydrate 64g (Dietary Fiber 1g) Exchanges: 1½ Starch, 3 Other Carbohydrate, 5 Fat; Carbohydrate Choices: 4

To easily crush granola bars, do not unwrap; use rolling pin to crush bars.

The Most Famous Bake-Off® Recipe

This divine chocolate cake that mysteriously develops a tunnel of soft fudgy filling as it bakes is likely the recipe most closely identified with the Bake-Off® Contest. Its creator, a Houston, Texas, homemaker named Ella Rita Helfrich, spent days of "trial-and-error baking" to come up with the distinctive treat. When the recipe took a $5,000 prize in 1966, bakers rushed to stores to find the then little-known Bundt pan, creating a rush of orders for its manufacturer.

Ella Rita's original recipe called for a box of dry frosting mix, a product discontinued after consumers began buying ready-to-spread frostings instead. Determined Bake-Off® home economists worked in the test kitchen until they came up with the current version that substitutes "from scratch" ingredients for the frosting mix, yet makes the same wonderful cake with its surprise filling.

Tunnel of Fudge Cake

Ella Rita Helfrich   Houston, TX
Bake-Off® Contest 17, 1966
$5,000 Winner

Prep Time: 35 Minutes
Start to Finish: 4 Hours 55 Minutes
16 servings

CAKE
1¾ cups granulated sugar
1¾ cups butter or margarine, softened
6 eggs
2 cups powdered sugar
2¼ cups Pillsbury BEST® all-purpose
flour
¾ cup unsweetened baking cocoa
2 cups chopped walnuts*

GLAZE
¾ cup powdered sugar
¼ cup unsweetened baking cocoa
4 to 6 teaspoons milk

1 Heat oven to 350°F. Grease 12-cup fluted tube cake pan or 10-inch angel food (tube) cake pan; lightly flour. In large bowl, beat granulated sugar and butter with electric mixer on medium speed until light and fluffy. Add 1 egg at a time, beating well after each addition. On low speed, gradually beat in 2 cups powdered sugar until blended. With spoon, stir in flour and remaining cake ingredients until well blended. Spoon batter into pan; spread evenly.

2 Bake 45 to 50 minutes or until top is set and edge begins to pull away from side of pan.** Cool upright in pan on cooling rack 1 hour 30 minutes. Turn cake upside down onto serving plate; cool at least 2 hours.

3 In small bowl, mix glaze ingredients, adding enough milk for desired drizzling consistency. Spoon glaze over top of cake, allowing some to run down sides. Store cake tightly covered.

High Altitude (3500–6500 ft): Increase Pillsbury BEST® all-purpose flour to 2¼ cups plus 3 tablespoons.

1 Serving: Calories 570; Total Fat 33g (Saturated Fat 15g; Trans Fat 1g); Cholesterol 135mg; Sodium 170mg; Total Carbohydrate 61g (Dietary Fiber 3g) Exchanges: 1 Starch, 3 Other Carbohydrate, ½ High-Fat Meat, 6 Fat; Carbohydrate Choices: 4

*Nuts are essential for the success of this recipe.

**Since this cake has a soft filling, an ordinary doneness test cannot be used. Accurate oven temperature and baking times are essential.

Tunnel of Fudge Cake

Chocolate Praline Layer Cake

Julie Bengtson   Bemidji, MN
Bake-Off® Contest 33, 1988
$40,000 Winner

Prep Time: 25 Minutes
Start to Finish: 2 Hours 15 Minutes
16 servings

CAKE
½ cup butter or margarine
¼ cup whipping cream
1 cup packed brown sugar
¾ cup coarsely chopped pecans
1 box (18.25 oz) Pillsbury® Moist
    Supreme® devil's food cake mix
1⅓ cups water
½ cup vegetable oil
3 eggs

TOPPING
1¾ cups whipping cream
¼ cup powdered sugar
¼ teaspoon vanilla
12 to 16 pecan halves, if desired
12 to 16 chocolate curls, if desired

1   Heat oven to 325°F. In 1-quart heavy saucepan, cook butter, ¼ cup whipping cream and brown sugar over low heat, stirring occasionally, just until butter is melted. Pour into 2 (9- or 8-inch) round cake pans.* Sprinkle evenly with chopped pecans.

2   In large bowl, beat cake mix, water, oil and eggs with electric mixer on low speed 30 seconds or until moistened. Beat 2 minutes on medium speed, scraping bowl occasionally. Carefully spoon batter over pecan mixture.

3   Bake 35 to 45 minutes or until cake springs back when touched lightly in center. Cool 5 minutes; remove from pans. Cool completely, about 1 hour.

4   In small bowl, beat 1¾ cups whipping cream until soft peaks form. Add powdered sugar and vanilla; beat on high speed until stiff peaks form.

5   To assemble cake, place 1 cake layer on serving plate, praline side up. Spread with half of whipped cream. Top with second cake layer, praline side up; spread top with remaining whipped cream. Garnish with pecan halves and chocolate curls. Store cake in refrigerator.

High Altitude (3500–6500 ft): Do not use 8-inch pans. Bake 40 to 45 minutes.

1 Serving: Calories 450; Total Fat 29g (Saturated Fat 12g; Trans Fat 1g); Cholesterol 90mg; Sodium 320mg; Total Carbohydrate 43g (Dietary Fiber 1g) Exchanges: 1 Starch, 2 Other Carbohydrate, 5 ½ Fat; Carbohydrate Choices: 3

Cake can be made in 13 × 9-inch pan. Bake at 325°F 50 to 60 minutes. Cool 5 minutes; turn upside down onto serving platter, and cool completely. Frost cake or pipe with whipped cream; garnish. Serve with any remaining whipped cream.

2 | SOUPS AND SANDWICHES

White Chili with Salsa Verde (page 50)

Mexican Vegetable Soup

Nancy Hindenach   Dearborn Heights, MI
Bake-Off® Contest 33, 1988
$2,000 Winner

Prep Time: 45 Minutes
Start to Finish: 45 Minutes
11 servings (1 cup each)

1 lb ground beef
1 package (1.25 oz) taco seasoning mix
1 can (46 oz) tomato juice (6 cups)
1 can (12 oz) tomato paste
1 bag (1 lb) frozen mixed vegetables
1 can (15 oz) spicy chili beans
2 cups crushed corn chips
2 cups shredded Cheddar cheese (8 oz)

1   In 5-quart Dutch oven, cook beef over medium-high heat 5 to 7 minutes, stirring frequently, until thoroughly cooked; drain.

2   Stir in remaining ingredients except chips and cheese. Heat just to boiling. Reduce heat; simmer uncovered 20 to 25 minutes, stirring occasionally, until vegetables are tender.

3   Top each serving with chips and cheese.

High Altitude (3500–6500 ft): No change.

1 Cup: Calories 370; Total Fat 18g (Saturated Fat 7g; Trans Fat 0.5g); Cholesterol 45mg; Sodium 1440mg; Total Carbohydrate 34g (Dietary Fiber 5g) Exchanges: ½ Starch, 1 Other Carbohydrate, 2 Vegetable, 2 Medium-Fat Meat, 1½ Fat; Carbohydrate Choices: 2

Creamy Broccoli and Wild Rice Soup

Pat Bradley   Rohnert Park, CA
Bake-Off® Contest 35, 1992
$10,000 Winner

Prep Time: 25 Minutes
Start to Finish: 25 Minutes
4 servings (1½ cups each)

1 box (10 oz) frozen cut broccoli in a cheese flavored sauce
1 box (10 oz) frozen white and wild rice
2 tablespoons butter or margarine
½ cup chopped onion (1 medium)
½ cup chopped celery
½ cup sliced almonds
¼ lb cooked ham, cubed (¾ cup)
½ teaspoon dried thyme leaves
½ teaspoon dried marjoram leaves
¼ teaspoon salt
⅛ teaspoon pepper
3 cups whole milk or half-and-half
Paprika

1   Cook broccoli with cheese sauce and rice as directed on boxes. Set aside.

2   Meanwhile, in 4-quart saucepan, melt butter over medium-high heat. Cook onion, celery and almonds in butter, stirring frequently, until vegetables are crisp-tender and almonds are lightly browned.

3   Stir in cooked broccoli with cheese sauce, cooked rice, ham, thyme, marjoram, salt and pepper. Stir in milk. Cook, stirring frequently, until hot. DO NOT BOIL. Sprinkle individual servings with paprika.

High Altitude (3500–6500 ft): No change.

1 Serving: Calories 400; Total Fat 23g (Saturated Fat 9g; Trans Fat 0.5g); Cholesterol 50mg; Sodium 1310mg; Total Carbohydrate 30g (Dietary Fiber 4g) Exchanges: ½ Starch, ½ Other Carbohydrate, ½ Milk, 1 Vegetable, 1½ Lean Meat, 3 Fat; Carbohydrate Choices: 2

Harvest Fresh Spinach Soup

Olga Jason   New Bedford, MA
Bake-Off® Contest 33, 1988

Prep Time: 40 Minutes
Start to Finish: 40 Minutes
5 servings (1 cup each)

¼ cup butter or margarine
¼ cup chopped onion
¼ cup Pillsbury BEST® all-purpose flour
1 teaspoon salt, if desired
½ teaspoon ground mustard
¼ teaspoon ground nutmeg
1 can (10½ oz) condensed chicken broth
½ cup shredded carrot
1 box (9 oz) frozen spinach
2½ cups milk

1   In 2-quart saucepan, melt butter over medium heat. Cook and stir onion in butter until tender. Reduce heat to low. Stir in flour, salt, ground mustard and nutmeg; cook and stir until mixture is smooth and bubbly. Gradually stir in broth. Heat to

All I Want for Christmas

How can you stack the deck to end up with a child who becomes a talented home cook? Several Bake-Off® contestants reported stories similar to the one Nancy Hindenach shared. "One Christmas, when I was nine years old, Santa brought me a baking kit full of little boxes of cake mixes, frostings and little pans to bake them in. I had so much fun making cakes for my family that I asked for the kit for my next two Christmases." Years, later, Nancy's family still reaps the benefit of those tasty gifts.

boiling, stirring constantly. Add carrot and spinach. Reduce heat to medium; simmer about 10 minutes, stirring occasionally, until carrot is tender and spinach is thawed.*

2 In blender or food processor, place spinach mixture. Cover; blend until smooth. Return mixture to saucepan; stir in milk. Cook over low heat, stirring frequently, until hot.

Microwave Directions: In 8-cup microwavable measuring cup or large bowl, microwave butter and onion uncovered on High 45 to 60 seconds or until onion is tender. Stir in flour, salt, ground mustard and nutmeg; gradually stir in broth. Microwave on High 4 to 5 minutes or until mixture comes to a boil, stirring once halfway through cooking. Add carrot and spinach. Microwave on High 8 to 9 minutes or until carrot is tender and spinach is thawed, stirring twice during cooking.* In blender or food processor, place spinach mixture. Cover; blend until smooth. Return mixture to measuring cup; stir in milk. Microwave on High 4 to 6 minutes or until hot, stirring twice during cooking.

To serve soup cold, at this point cool spinach mixture to lukewarm; puree in blender or food processor until smooth. Stir in milk. Cover; refrigerate until thoroughly chilled. Garnish each serving with lemon slice, if desired.

High Altitude (3500–6500 ft): No change.

1 Serving: Calories 210; Total Fat 13g (Saturated Fat 8g; Trans Fat 0g); Cholesterol 35mg; Sodium 530mg; Total Carbohydrate 15g (Dietary Fiber 2g) Exchanges: ½ Starch, ½ Low-Fat Milk, 1 Vegetable, 2 Fat; Carbohydrate Choices: 1

Corn and Pumpkin Soup with Jalapeño Pesto

Marilou Robinson Portland, OR
Bake-Off® Contest 35, 1992
$2,000 Winner

> Prep Time: 30 Minutes
> Start to Finish: 1 Hour 5 Minutes
> 11 servings (1 cup each)

JALAPEÑO PESTO
1 cup fresh cilantro
1 cup fresh parsley
½ cup pine nuts, lightly toasted*
½ cup grated Parmesan cheese
5 cloves garlic, finely chopped
4 jalapeño chiles, seeded, chopped
1 teaspoon lime juice
½ teaspoon grated lime peel
¾ cup olive oil

SOUP
4 cans (14 oz each) chicken broth
2 cans (11 oz each) vacuum-packed whole kernel corn, drained
¼ cup finely chopped onion
2 tablespoons finely chopped jalapeño chiles
1 can (15 oz) pumpkin (not pumpkin pie mix)
1 cup half-and-half
½ teaspoon salt
¼ teaspoon pepper
11 corn tortillas (8 or 6 inch) or flour tortillas (8 inch), warmed

1 In food processor or blender, place cilantro, parsley, pine nuts, cheese and garlic. Cover; process 10 to 15 seconds to chop mixture. Add 4 chopped jalapeño chiles, lime juice and lime peel; process 5 to 10 seconds to blend. With machine running, add oil through feed tube or opening in blender lid in slow, steady stream just until well blended. Set aside.

2 In 4-quart saucepan, heat broth, corn, onion and 2 tablespoons jalapeño chiles to boiling. Reduce heat; cover and simmer 20 to 25 minutes or until onion and jalapeño chiles are tender. Stir in pumpkin; blend well. Cover; simmer 5 to 10 minutes or until hot. Add half-and-half, salt and pepper; cook and stir just until hot. DO NOT BOIL.

3 To serve, line 11 soup bowls with warmed tortillas; ladle hot soup into tortilla-lined bowls. Spoon slightly less than 2 tablespoons jalapeño pesto onto each serving.

To toast pine nuts, spread on cookie sheet; bake at 350°F 3 to 6 minutes, stirring occasionally, until light golden brown.

High Altitude (3500–6500 ft): No change.

1 Cup: Calories 370; Total Fat 25g (Saturated Fat 5g; Trans Fat 0g); Cholesterol 10mg; Sodium 930mg; Total Carbohydrate 28g (Dietary Fiber 4g) Exchanges: 2 Starch, ½ High-Fat Meat, 4 Fat; Carbohydrate Choices: 2

Spicy Cajun Corn Soup

Hilda Theriot   Mandeville, LA
Bake-Off® Contest 34, 1990

Prep Time: 35 Minutes
Start to Finish: 1 Hour 35 Minutes
10 servings (1½ cups each)

½ cup vegetable oil
½ cup Pillsbury BEST® all-purpose
   or unbleached flour
1 cup finely chopped onions
1 cup finely chopped green bell pepper
6 green onions, finely chopped, reserving
   ⅓ cup chopped green tops for garnish
2 cups coarsely chopped fresh tomatoes
1 can (14.5 oz) diced tomatoes,
   undrained
1 can (6 oz) tomato paste
3 cups water
2 bags (1 lb each) frozen whole kernel
   corn
3 cups cubed cooked ham (1 lb)
1½ lb smoked sausage, cut into ½-inch
   slices
¾ to 1½ teaspoons salt
¼ to ½ teaspoon crushed red pepper
   flakes
¼ to ½ teaspoon ground red pepper
   (cayenne)
¼ to ½ teaspoon red pepper sauce

1   In 5- to 6-quart Dutch oven, heat oil over medium heat until hot. Gradually add flour, blending well with wire whisk. Cook flour 4 to 7 minutes or until golden brown.

2   Add onions, bell pepper and green onions; cook 5 minutes, stirring frequently, until vegetables are tender. Add fresh and canned tomatoes, tomato paste and water; mix well. Add all remaining ingredients except reserved green onion tops. Heat to boiling, stirring frequently.

3   Reduce heat to low; partially cover and simmer 1 hour, stirring occasionally. Garnish each serving with green onion tops.

High Altitude (3500–6500 ft): No change.

1 Serving: Calories 530; Total Fat 34g (Saturated Fat 10g; Trans Fat 0.5g); Cholesterol 65mg; Sodium 1610mg; Total Carbohydrate 33g (Dietary Fiber 4g) Exchanges: 1 Starch, ½ Other Carbohydrate, 2 Vegetable, 2 High-Fat Meat, 3 ½ Fat; Carbohydrate Choices: 2

Spicy Meatball Soup

Debra Freeman   Jefferson, MD
Bake-Off® Contest 36, 1994
$10,000 Winner

Prep Time: 45 Minutes
Start to Finish: 1 Hour 45 Minutes
6 servings (1½ cups each)

MEATBALLS
1 lb extra-lean (at least 90%) ground beef
1 can (11 oz) vacuum-packed whole
   kernel corn, drained
⅓ cup hot picante or salsa
½ cup thinly sliced green onions with tops
2 tablespoons chopped fresh cilantro
½ to 1 teaspoon salt
1 teaspoon ground cumin
1 teaspoon finely chopped garlic
1 egg white

SOUP
1 can (28 oz) whole tomatoes,
   undrained, cut up
1 can (15.5 oz) dark or light red kidney
   beans, drained
1 cup chopped green bell pepper
1 cup beef broth
⅔ cup hot picante or salsa
2 tablespoons chopped fresh cilantro
1 teaspoon ground cumin
1 teaspoon chili powder
½ teaspoon finely chopped garlic

meet hilda theriot

AFTER YEARS OF THINKING about entering the Bake-Off® Contest, Hilda Theriot finally gave it a try with this soup, a long-time favorite of her husband Gerald. But it's Christmas cookies that are her true passion; each year she and her daughter bake more than 360 cookies to give away as gifts. Hilda, who works as a receptionist, said her interest in cooking didn't blossom until 10 years into her marriage, and then only after she gained confidence from watching Julia Child's television show.

TOPPINGS, IF DESIRED

¼ cup chopped fresh cilantro

¼ cup chopped green onions with
  tops

¼ cup sour cream

1 In large bowl, mix beef,
½ cup of the corn and remaining
meatball ingredients. Shape into
1-inch balls; place on cookie sheet.
Refrigerate about 30 minutes or
until set.

2 In 5-quart Dutch oven or
stockpot, mix remaining corn
and all soup ingredients. Heat to
boiling over high heat. Reduce
heat to low; carefully add uncooked
meatballs. Simmer uncovered 45 to
60 minutes or until flavors blend
and meatballs are no longer pink
in center.

3 Garnish individual servings with
toppings.

High Altitude (3500–6500 ft):
No change.

1 Serving: Calories 300; Total Fat 7g (Saturated Fat
2.5g; Trans Fat 0g); Cholesterol 45mg; Sodium 1110mg;
Total Carbohydrate 33g (Dietary Fiber 7g) Exchanges:
2 Starch, 1 Vegetable, 2 Lean Meat; Carbohydrate
Choices: 2

It's All About Teamwork

Marilou Robinson didn't need a big, daring family to be a recipe-inventing success. When selected as a finalist, she shared the credit: "My biggest encouragement is my husband Bud—he is not an adventurous eater, preferring meat and potatoes, but he will run all over the city to find a particular ingredient. He loves to invite people over to try my new recipes, even though he may not participate!"

Jamaican Ham and Bean Soup

Marilou Robinson   Portland, OR
Bake-Off® Contest 40, 2002

Prep Time: 30 Minutes
Start to Finish: 30 Minutes
6 servings (1⅓ cups each)

SOUP

1 tablespoon vegetable oil

⅓ cup frozen chopped onion

2 cans (16 oz each) vegetarian refried
  beans

1 can (11 oz) vacuum-packed whole
  kernel corn with red and green
  peppers, undrained

1 can (11 oz) vacuum-packed white
  shoepeg corn, undrained

1 can (4.5 oz) chopped green chiles

½ cup chunky-style salsa

1 can (14½ oz) chicken broth

1 teaspoon Jamaican jerk seasoning

1 lb lean cooked ham, cut into ½-inch
  pieces

1 can (2¼ oz) sliced ripe olives, drained

⅓ cup lime juice

GARNISH

6 tablespoons sour cream

6 lime slices

1 In 4-quart saucepan, heat oil
over medium heat until hot. Cook
onion in oil 3 to 4 minutes, stirring
frequently, until tender.

2 Stir in refried beans, corn,
chiles, salsa, broth and jerk seasoning. Heat to boiling. Reduce heat
to low; simmer 5 minutes, stirring
occasionally.

3 Stir in ham, olives and lime
juice. Cook 3 to 4 minutes, stirring
occasionally, until hot. Ladle soup
into individual bowls. Top each
serving with 1 tablespoon sour
cream and lime slice.

High Altitude (3500–6500 ft):
No change.

1 Serving: Calories 460; Total Fat 16g (Saturated Fat
5g; Trans Fat 0g); Cholesterol 65mg; Sodium 2750mg;
Total Carbohydrate 49g (Dietary Fiber 11g) Exchanges:
2 Starch, 1 Other Carbohydrate, 3 ½ Very Lean Meat,
2½ Fat; Carbohydrate Choices: 3

Black Bean–Chorizo Soup in Tortilla Bowls

Sita Lepczyk Williams   Blacksburg, VA
Bake-Off® Contest 42, 2006

Prep Time: 25 Minutes
Start to Finish: 25 Minutes
2 servings (1½ cups soup in 1 tortilla
bowl each)

2 flour tortillas (8 to 10 inch)
**5 oz smoked chorizo sausage links,
   coarsely chopped**
1 large clove garlic, finely chopped
⅓ cup dry sherry or chicken broth
½ teaspoon chili powder
**1 can (19 oz) ready-to-serve hearty
   black bean soup**
1 can (4.5 oz) chopped green chiles
**⅓ cup shredded Mexican cheese
   blend**
2 tablespoons sour cream
2 tablespoons chopped fresh cilantro

1   Move oven rack to lowest position. Heat oven to 350°F. Spray 2 (10-ounce) ovenproof custard cups with cooking spray; place on cookie sheet.

2   Place tortillas on microwavable plate; cover with microwavable plastic wrap. Microwave on High 45 to 60 seconds, turning after 30 seconds, until very soft. Center tortillas over cups, press into cups so top edges are even. Press tortilla folds against side of each cup to make bowl as large as possible.

3   Place on lowest oven rack; bake 8 to 10 minutes or until tortillas are stiff enough to hold their shape. Remove tortilla bowls from cups; place on cookie sheet. Place on middle oven rack; bake 5 to 7 minutes longer or until browned and stiff. Remove tortilla bowls from cookie sheet; place on cooling rack.

4   Meanwhile, heat 10-inch regular or cast-iron skillet over high heat. Add sausage; cook and stir about 30 seconds or until browned. Add garlic; cook and stir 30 to 60 seconds longer. Remove skillet from heat; stir in sherry. Return skillet to high heat; cook and stir 2 to 3 minutes or until liquid has almost evaporated. Stir in chili powder, soup and green chiles. Reduce heat to medium-low; cook, stirring occasionally, until hot.

5   Place tortilla bowls on individual plates. Divide soup evenly among bowls. Top each with cheese, sour cream and cilantro. Serve immediately.

High Altitude (3500–6500 ft): No change.

1 Serving: Calories 770; Total Fat 40g (Saturated Fat 17g; Trans Fat 1g); Cholesterol 85mg; Sodium 3070mg; Total Carbohydrate 63g (Dietary Fiber 11g) Exchanges: 3 Starch, 1 Other Carbohydrate, 3½ Very Lean Meat, 7½ Fat; Carbohydrate Choices: 4

Pursue Your Dreams

Sometimes, the time is now. "Getting the call from Pillsbury made me realize that you have to go for things when the time is right," says Sita Lepczyk Williams. "My dream for several years was to be a jewelry designer, and going to the contest motivated me to get my business cards made and get my Web site going . . . ." Just as she sees the rewards from her artistic creativity, Sita's creativity in the kitchen

brings her rewards, too. "It is an indescribable feeling knowing that you have invented a dish that others enjoy," she says. "It's easy to let fear eat you up and never go for it. But you only live once, so you should take advantage of every opportunity."

Black Bean–Chorizo Soup in Tortilla Bowls

Zesty Chicken Vegetable Bisque

Taylor Arnold   Kemah, TX
Bake-Off® Contest 33, 1988

Prep Time: 45 Minutes
Start to Finish: 1 Hour 10 Minutes
6 servings

6 boneless skinless chicken breasts
3 tablespoons butter or margarine
1 cup sliced onions
3 cloves garlic, finely chopped
2 tablespoons Pillsbury BEST®
   all-purpose flour
2 cans (14½ oz each) chicken broth
1 can (16 oz) whole tomatoes,
   undrained, cut up
1 tablespoon chopped fresh parsley
1 teaspoon dried thyme leaves
½ to 1½ teaspoons salt
1 teaspoon red pepper sauce
2 dried bay leaves
1 cup uncooked regular rice
2 cups water
2 cups chopped green bell peppers
1 cup frozen whole kernel corn (from
   1-lb bag)
1 cup frozen sweet peas (from 1-lb bag)
1 jar (4.5 oz) sliced mushrooms,
   undrained

1   In deep 10- to 12-inch skillet, brown chicken breasts in butter over medium heat. Remove chicken breasts from skillet. Add onions and garlic; cook about 3 minutes or until onions are tender. Remove from heat. Stir in flour. Stir in broth, tomatoes, parsley, thyme, salt, pepper sauce and bay leaves. Cook rice in water as directed on package.

2   Add chicken breasts to skillet; cook over low heat 30 minutes, stirring occasionally. Add bell peppers; cook 10 minutes longer. Add corn, peas and mushrooms; cook 10 to 15 minutes longer or until chicken is tender. Remove bay leaves.

3   To serve, place ½ cup rice in each individual serving bowl. Top with chicken breast and generous 1 cup of bisque.

High Altitude (3500–6500 ft): No change.

1 Serving: Calories 410; Total Fat 11g (Saturated Fat 5g; Trans Fat 0g); Cholesterol 90mg; Sodium 1390mg; Total Carbohydrate 42g (Dietary Fiber 4g) Exchanges: 2 Starch, ½ Other Carbohydrate, 1½ Vegetable, 3½ Very Lean Meat, 1½ Fat; Carbohydrate Choices: 3

Southwest Tortellini Chowder

Loanne Chiu   Fort Worth, TX
Bake-Off® Contest 37, 1996
$2,000 Winner

Prep Time: 25 Minutes
Start to Finish: 25 Minutes
6 servings (1½ cups each)

3 cans (10½ oz each) condensed
   chicken broth
1½ cups mild chunky-style salsa
   or picante
½ teaspoon grated orange peel
2 packages (9 oz each) refrigerated
   meat-filled or cheese-filled tortellini*
2 cups frozen cut broccoli
   (from 1-lb bag)
1 cup frozen whole kernel corn
   (from 1-lb bag)
½ cup coarsely chopped red bell pepper
1 can (5 oz) evaporated milk
Dash salt
¼ cup chopped fresh cilantro

1   In Dutch oven or 4-quart saucepan, heat broth, salsa and orange peel to boiling. Reduce heat to low; simmer 3 minutes.

2   Stir in tortellini and vegetables; cook over medium heat 6 to 8 minutes or until tortellini and vegetables are tender.

3   Stir in milk and salt; cook 1 to 2 minutes or just until hot, stirring occasionally. DO NOT BOIL. Top each serving of chowder with cilantro. Serve immediately.

One 16-ounce package frozen tortellini can be substituted for both packages of refrigerated tortellini. Add frozen tortellini to simmered broth mixture; cook 4 minutes. Add vegetables; cook an additional 6 to 8 minutes or until tortellini and vegetables are tender.

High Altitude (3500–6500 ft):
No change.

1½ Cups: Calories 400; Total Fat 10g (Saturated Fat 4.5g; Trans Fat 0g); Cholesterol 40mg; Sodium 1670mg; Total Carbohydrate 56g (Dietary Fiber 5g) Exchanges: 2 Starch, 1 Other Carbohydrate, 1 Vegetable, 2 Medium-Fat Meat; Carbohydrate Choices: 4

Southwest Tortellini Chowder

Creamy Chicken-Vegetable Chowder

Mary Lou Cook   Welches, OR
Bake-Off® Contest 34, 1990
$2,000 Winner

Prep Time: 25 Minutes
Start to Finish: 25 Minutes
6 servings

CHOWDER

1½ cups milk or half-and-half
1 cup chicken broth
1 can (10 ¾ oz) condensed cream
  of potato soup
1 can (10 ¾ oz) condensed cream
  of chicken soup
2 cups cubed cooked chicken or turkey
⅓ cup chopped green onions
1 can (11 oz) vacuum-packed whole kernel
  corn with red and green peppers, drained
1 jar (4.5 oz) sliced mushrooms, drained
1 can (4.5 oz) chopped green chiles
1½ cups shredded Cheddar cheese (6 oz)

CRESCENT ROLLS

1 can (8 oz) Pillsbury® refrigerated
  crescent dinner rolls
¼ cup crushed nacho-flavored tortilla chips

1   In 4-quart saucepan or Dutch oven, mix milk, broth, potato soup and chicken soup. Stir in remaining chowder ingredients except cheese. Cook over medium heat 5 to 8 minutes, stirring occasionally, until onions are tender. Remove from heat. Add cheese; stir until melted.

2   While chowder is heating, heat oven to 375°F. Shape crescent dough as directed on can. Gently press top of each roll in crushed chips. Place on ungreased cookie sheet. Bake 11 to 13 minutes or until golden brown.

3   Serve chowder with crescent rolls.

High Altitude (3500–6500 ft): No change.

1 Serving: Calories 540; Total Fat 28g (Saturated Fat 12g; Trans Fat 2.5g); Cholesterol 80mg; Sodium 2020mg; Total Carbohydrate 43g (Dietary Fiber 3g) Exchanges: 2 Starch, 1 Other Carbohydrate, 3½ Lean Meat, 3 Fat; Carbohydrate Choices: 3

White Chili with Salsa Verde

Reta M. Smith   Libertyville, IL
Bake-Off® Contest 35, 1992
$10,000 Winner

Prep Time: 45 Minutes
Start to Finish: 1 Hour 15 Minutes
8 servings (1¼ cups each)

SALSA VERDE*

2 cups coarsely chopped fresh
  tomatillos or 2 cans (11 oz each)
  tomatillos, chopped, well drained**
½ cup chopped onion
½ cup chopped fresh cilantro
2 to 3 tablespoons lime juice
½ teaspoon lemon-pepper seasoning
½ teaspoon dried oregano leaves
½ teaspoon adobo seasoning***
  or garlic powder
1 pickled jalapeño chile, chopped
1 clove garlic, finely chopped

CHILI

2½ cups water
1 teaspoon lemon-pepper seasoning
1 teaspoon cumin seed
4 bone-in chicken breasts (about 1½ lb),
  skin removed
1 clove garlic, finely chopped
1 cup chopped onions
2 boxes (9 oz each) frozen shoepeg
  white corn, thawed
2 cans (4.5 oz each) chopped green
  chiles, undrained
1 teaspoon ground cumin
2 to 3 tablespoons lime juice
2 cans (15.5 oz each) great northern
  beans, undrained
⅔ cup crushed tortilla chips
½ cup shredded reduced-fat Monterey
  Jack cheese (2 oz)

1   In medium bowl, mix salsa verde ingredients. Refrigerate 30 minutes to blend flavors.

2   Meanwhile, in 4-quart saucepan, heat water, 1 teaspoon lemon-pepper seasoning and cumin seed to boiling.

Necessity Is the Mother of Invention

"After my husband received his doctorate in 1960," recalls Reta Smith, "we moved to a very small community in northwest Missouri and lived on a farm. He began a very busy large-animal veterinary practice. We raised three children and also had a cow and calf operation. Our home was run like a restaurant and small hotel, since we lived in a very remote area. I went to a grocery warehouse every three months to do our shopping. . . . With this in mind, my cooking was very creative, and as the time grew closer to my next three-month trip, it became even more so." With training like this, it's not surprising Reta could come up with her creative Bake-Off® Contest recipe!

White Chili with Salsa Verde

Add chicken. Reduce heat to low; cover and simmer 20 to 28 minutes or until chicken is fork-tender and juices run clear. Remove chicken from bones; cut into 1-inch pieces. Return chicken to saucepan.

3 Spray 8-inch skillet with cooking spray. Heat over medium heat until hot. Add 1 clove garlic; cook and stir 1 minute. Remove from skillet; add to chicken mixture.

4 Add 1 cup onions to skillet; cook and stir until tender. Add cooked onions, corn, chiles, cumin and 2 to 3 tablespoons lime juice to chicken mixture. Heat to boiling. Add beans; cook until hot.

5 To serve, place about 1 table-spoon each of tortilla chips and cheese in each of 8 individual soup bowls; ladle soup over cheese. Serve with salsa verde.

If desired, substitute one 16-oz jar salsa verde (green salsa).
**If fresh or canned tomatillos are not available, 2 cups coarsely chopped green tomatoes can be substituted.*

***Adobo is a specialty seasoning available in Hispanic grocery stores.*

High Altitude (3500–6500 ft): Add up to ¼ cup water if chili is too thick.

1¼ Cups: Calories 360; Total Fat 7g (Saturated Fat 2g; Trans Fat 0g); Cholesterol 40mg; Sodium 1030mg; Total Carbohydrate 47g (Dietary Fiber 10g) Exchanges: 2 Starch, 1 Other Carbohydrate, 3 Very Lean Meat, 1 Fat; Carbohydrate Choices: 3

Creole Gumbo

Elaine Thornton   Long Beach, MS
Bake-Off® Contest 6, 1954

Prep Time: 45 minutes
Start to Finish: 1 Hour
4 servings (1¼ cups each)

GUMBO
3 tablespoons olive oil
¾ cup chopped celery
⅓ cup chopped green bell pepper
⅓ cup chopped onion
2 cloves garlic, finely chopped
¼ cup Pillsbury BEST® all-purpose flour
3 cups water
1 can (16 oz) whole tomatoes, undrained, cut up
1 tablespoon chopped fresh parsley
1 teaspoon salt
⅛ teaspoon pepper
1 cup diced canned, frozen or fresh okra
1 can (6 oz) crabmeat, drained

CROUTONS
1 can (12 oz) Pillsbury® Golden Layers® refrigerated flaky biscuits
1 tablespoon butter or margarine, melted
2 tablespoons grated Parmesan cheese
Paprika

1 In 4-quart saucepan, heat oil over medium heat until hot. Cook celery, bell pepper, onion and garlic in oil 5 minutes. Stir in flour; cook about 10 minutes, stirring constantly, until mixture browns. Gradually add water and tomatoes, stirring constantly. Stir in remaining gumbo ingredients. Heat to boiling. Reduce heat; cover and simmer 1 hour.

2 Meanwhile, heat oven to 400°F. Separate dough into 10 biscuits; cut each into 4 pieces. Place on ungreased cookie sheet. Brush with butter; sprinkle with Parmesan cheese and paprika. Bake 6 to 9 minutes or until golden brown. Remove from cookie sheet immediately; cool on cooling racks. Pour gumbo into individual serving bowls; top each serving with croutons.

High Altitude (3500–6500 ft): No change.

1 Serving: Calories 510; Total Fat 26g (Saturated Fat 6g; Trans Fat 4g); Cholesterol 40mg; Sodium 1840mg; Total Carbohydrate 51g (Dietary Fiber 3g) Exchanges: 2 Starch, 1 Other Carbohydrate, 1 Vegetable, 1 Very Lean Meat, 5 Fat; Carbohydrate Choices: 3½

Calabacita Chicken Stew

Calabacita Chicken Stew

Linda S. Brown   Dallas, TX
Bake-Off® Contest 42, 2006

Prep Time: 50 Minutes
Start to Finish: 50 Minutes
6 servings (1⅔ cups each)

1 tablespoon extra-virgin olive oil
1½ lb uncooked chicken breast tenders
   (not breaded)
8 to 10 small to medium zucchini
   (2½ lb), peeled, thinly sliced (8 cups)
1 medium white onion, chopped (½ cup)
1 can (15.25 oz) vacuum-packed whole
   kernel corn, undrained
1 can (14.5 oz) diced tomatoes with
   green pepper and onion, undrained
1 can (4.5 oz) chopped green chiles,
   undrained
1½ teaspoons garlic powder
½ teaspoon ground cumin
Salt and pepper, if desired
½ cup chopped fresh cilantro

1   In 5- to 6-quart saucepan or
Dutch oven, heat oil over medium
heat. Add chicken; cover and cook
4 to 6 minutes, stirring occasionally,
until no longer pink in center.

2   Stir in remaining ingredients
except cilantro. Heat to boiling.
Reduce heat to medium-low; cover
and simmer about 20 minutes,
stirring occasionally, until zucchini
is tender.

3   Stir in cilantro; cook 3 minutes
longer, stirring occasionally.

High Altitude (3500–6500 ft): No change.

1 Serving: Calories 250; Total Fat 4g (Saturated Fat 0.5g;
Trans Fat 0g); Cholesterol 50mg; Sodium 800mg;
Total Carbohydrate 25g (Dietary Fiber 4g) Exchanges:
½ Starch, ½ Other Carbohydrate, 2 Vegetable, 3 Very
Lean Meat, ½ Fat; Carbohydrate Choices: 1½

Italian Spinach Dumpling Stew

Joan Schweger   Elburn, IL
Bake-Off® Contest 34, 1990
$2,000 Winner

Prep Time: 25 Minutes
Start to Finish: 40 Minutes
6 servings

1 lb ground beef
2 tablespoons vegetable oil,
   if desired
1 jar (32 oz) tomato pasta sauce
1 jar (4.5 oz) sliced mushrooms,
   undrained
2 tablespoons creamy garlic or creamy
   Italian dressing
¼ cup water

DUMPLINGS
1 cup Pillsbury BEST® all-purpose
   flour
2 teaspoons baking powder
¼ teaspoon salt
1 box (9 oz) frozen spinach, thawed,
   squeezed to drain
½ cup grated Romano or Parmesan
   cheese
2 tablespoons vegetable oil
1 egg
¼ to ⅓ cup milk

1   In 10-inch skillet, cook beef in
2 tablespoons oil over medium-
high heat 5 to 7 minutes, stirring
frequently, until thoroughly cooked;
drain. Stir in sauce, mushrooms,
dressing and water. Heat to boiling. Reduce heat; simmer while
preparing dumplings, stirring
occasionally.

2   In medium bowl, mix flour,
baking powder and salt. In small
bowl, mix spinach, cheese, 2 tablespoons oil, egg and ¼ cup milk.

Add to dry ingredients; stir until
dry ingredients are just moistened,
adding additional milk if necessary
to make a soft dough. Drop dough
by rounded tablespoonfuls onto
hot stew mixture. Cover tightly.
Simmer 12 to 15 minutes or until
dumplings are fluffy and no longer
doughy on bottom.

High Altitude (3500–6500 ft): Simmer
dumplings 17 to 22 minutes.

1 Serving: Calories 490; Total Fat 23g (Saturated Fat 7g;
Trans Fat 0.5g); Cholesterol 90mg; Sodium 1330mg;
Total Carbohydrate 48g (Dietary Fiber 4g) Exchanges:
1 Starch, 1½ Other Carbohydrate, 1 Vegetable,
2½ Medium-Fat Meat, 2 Fat; Carbohydrate Choices: 3

Spicy Curried Lentil Stew

Dawn Cadwallader   Unico, TN
Bake-Off® Contest 41, 2004

Prep Time: 30 Minutes
Start to Finish: 30 Minutes
8 servings (1¼ cups each)

1 lb ready-to-eat baby-cut carrots
1 large onion, quartered
4 cloves garlic
⅛ to ¼ teaspoon finely chopped seeded habanero chile, if desired
1 tablespoon extra-virgin olive oil
2 tablespoons curry powder
1 teaspoon ground ginger
1 teaspoon salt
2 dried bay leaves
1 box (9 oz) frozen spinach, thawed, squeezed to drain*
2 cans (19 oz each) ready-to-serve lentil soup
1 can (28 oz) tomato puree
½ cup fresh cilantro leaves
1 can (14 oz) coconut milk (not cream of coconut)
2 cups plain fat-free yogurt, if desired

1   In food processor, place carrots, onion, garlic and chile. Cover; process with 20 on/off pulses until chopped. In 4-quart saucepan or Dutch oven, heat oil over medium heat until hot. Stir in chopped vegetables, curry powder, ginger, salt and bay leaves. Cook 10 minutes, stirring occasionally.

2   Meanwhile, in food processor, place thawed spinach. Cover; process with 10 on/off pulses until finely chopped. Add spinach to vegetable mixture. Stir in both cans of soup and the tomato puree. Cover; cook over medium heat 5 to 7 minutes, stirring frequently, until carrots are crisp-tender.

3   Meanwhile, in food processor, place cilantro. Cover; process with several on/off pulses just until finely chopped.

4   Remove saucepan from heat. Stir in cilantro and coconut milk. Remove bay leaves. Top individual servings with yogurt.

* To quickly thaw frozen spinach, cut small slit in center of pouch; microwave on High 2 to 3 minutes or until thawed. Remove spinach from pouch; squeeze dry with paper towels.

High Altitude (3500–6500 ft):
No change.

1 Serving: Calories 300; Total Fat 12g (Saturated Fat 8g; Trans Fat 0g); Cholesterol 0mg; Sodium 1250mg; Total Carbohydrate 38g (Dietary Fiber 9g) Exchanges: 1 Starch, 1 Other Carbohydrate, 2 Vegetable, ½ Very Lean Meat, 2 Fat; Carbohydrate Choices: 2½

Savory Crescent Chicken Squares

Doris Castle   River Forest, IL
Bake-Off® Contest 25, 1974
$25,000 One of Two Grand Prize Winners

Prep Time: 20 Minutes
Start to Finish: 50 Minutes
4 sandwiches

1 package (3 oz) cream cheese, softened
1 tablespoon butter or margarine, softened
2 cups cubed cooked chicken
1 tablespoon chopped fresh chives
¼ teaspoon salt
⅛ teaspoon pepper
2 tablespoons milk
1 tablespoon chopped pimientos, if desired
1 can (8 oz) Pillsbury® refrigerated crescent dinner rolls
1 tablespoon butter or margarine, melted
¾ cup seasoned croutons, crushed

1   Heat oven to 350°F. In medium bowl, beat cream cheese and 1 tablespoon softened butter until smooth. Stir in chicken, chives, salt, pepper, milk and pimientos.

2   Separate dough into 4 rectangles. Firmly press perforations to seal. Spoon ½ cup chicken mixture onto center of each rectangle. Pull 4 corners of dough to center of chicken mixture; twist firmly. Pinch edges to seal. Place on ungreased cookie sheet.

3   Brush tops of sandwiches with 1 tablespoon melted butter. Sprinkle with crushed croutons.

4   Bake 25 to 30 minutes or until golden brown.

High Altitude (3500–6500 ft): No change.

1 Sandwich: Calories 500; Total Fat 32g (Saturated Fat 14g; Trans Fat 4g); Cholesterol 100mg; Sodium 850mg; Total Carbohydrate 28g (Dietary Fiber 1g) Exchanges: 1½ Starch, ½ Other Carbohydrate, 3 Medium-Fat Meat, 3 Fat; Carbohydrate Choices: 2

Savory Chicken Crescent Squares

Chicken Salad Focaccia Sandwiches

Westy Gabany Olney, MD
Bake-Off® Contest 38, 1998
$2,000 Winner

Prep Time: 30 Minutes
Start to Finish: 30 Minutes
4 sandwiches

FOCACCIA

1 can (13.8 oz) Pillsbury® refrigerated
  classic pizza crust
2 to 3 tablespoons olive oil
2 cloves garlic, finely chopped
½ to 1½ teaspoons kosher (coarse) salt
1½ teaspoons dried rosemary leaves

SALAD

1 can (10 oz) chunk chicken in water,
  drained, or 1⅓ cups chopped cooked
  chicken
½ cup chopped celery
½ cup mayonnaise or salad dressing
2 green onions, chopped
1 teaspoon dried tarragon leaves
½ teaspoon yellow mustard
Dash garlic powder
Dash onion powder

1 Heat oven to 350°F. Lightly spray cookie sheet with cooking spray. Unroll dough onto cookie sheet to make 12 × 10-inch rectangle. Starting with short end, fold dough in half; press lightly.

2 In small bowl, mix oil and chopped garlic. Spread over dough. Sprinkle with salt and rosemary. Bake 20 to 25 minutes or until edges are golden brown.

3 Meanwhile, in medium bowl, mix salad ingredients. Refrigerate 15 minutes.

4 To serve, cut warm focaccia into 4 pieces. Split each piece to make 2 layers. Spoon and spread salad on bottom halves of focaccia pieces; cover with top halves to make sandwiches.

High Altitude (3500–6500 ft): No change.

1 Sandwich: Calories 560; Total Fat 32g (Saturated Fat 5g; Trans Fat 0g); Cholesterol 35mg; Sodium 1380mg; Total Carbohydrate 50g (Dietary Fiber 0g) Exchanges: 2½ Starch, 1 Other Carbohydrate, 1½ Medium-Fat Meat, 4½ Fat; Carbohydrate Choices: 3

Cashew Chicken Crescent Sandwiches

Vicki Burgess Houston, TX
Bake-Off® Contest 38, 1998

Prep Time: 10 Minutes
Start to Finish: 30 Minutes
8 sandwiches

2 cans (4.25 oz each) chicken spread
1 jar (4.5 oz) sliced mushrooms,
  drained, chopped
¼ cup chopped cashews
¼ cup chopped fresh chives
⅛ teaspoon pepper
2 cans (8 oz each) Pillsbury®
  refrigerated crescent dinner rolls
4 slices (¾ oz each) American cheese,
  cut in half
Red grape clusters, if desired

1 Heat oven to 350°F. In medium bowl, mix chicken spread, mushrooms, cashews, chives and pepper.

2 Separate dough into 8 rectangles. Firmly press perforations to seal. Place cheese slice half in center of each rectangle. Spoon chicken mixture evenly over cheese. Fold short ends of dough over filling; pinch edges to seal. Place dough packets on ungreased large cookie sheet or 2 small cookie sheets.

3 Bake 18 to 20 minutes or until golden brown. Serve warm or cool. Garnish with grape clusters.

High Altitude (3500–6500 ft): Heat oven to 375°F.

1 Sandwich: Calories 340; Total Fat 21g (Saturated Fat 8g; Trans Fat 3.5g); Cholesterol 25mg; Sodium 880mg; Total Carbohydrate 26g (Dietary Fiber 1g) Exchanges: 1½ Starch, 1 High-Fat Meat, 2½ Fat; Carbohydrate Choices: 2

Chicken to Go Biscuits

Regina Rouh Long Beach, CA
Bake-Off® Contest 21, 1970

Prep Time: 20 Minutes
Start to Finish: 45 Minutes
8 servings

2 tablespoons butter or margarine
2 tablespoons Pillsbury BEST®
  all-purpose or unbleached flour
¼ teaspoon salt
Dash pepper
½ cup milk
2 cups cubed cooked chicken
1¼ cups shredded Cheddar cheese (5 oz)
½ cup chopped or sliced drained
  mushrooms (4 oz)
1 can (16.3 oz) Pillsbury® Grands!®
  refrigerated buttermilk biscuits
1 egg, slightly beaten
3 cups cornflakes, crushed, or 1 cup
  cornflake crumbs

1 Heat oven to 350°F. In 2-quart saucepan over medium heat, melt butter; stir in flour, salt and pepper until well blended. Add milk all at once. Cook about 1 minute, stirring occasionally, until thickened. Stir

in chicken, cheese and mushrooms; set aside.

2   Separate biscuit dough into 8 biscuits. Roll or pat each into 5-inch round. Place about ⅓ cup chicken mixture on half of each biscuit round to within ½ inch of edge. Fold dough over filling, pressing edges firmly with fork to seal.

3   Dip rolls into egg, then coat with crushed cornflakes. Place on ungreased cookie sheet. Bake 20 to 25 minutes or until golden brown.

High Altitude (3500–6500 ft): No change.

1 Serving: Calories 820; Total Fat 41g (Saturated Fat 19g; Trans Fat 7g); Cholesterol 170mg; Sodium 1850mg; Total Carbohydrate 72g (Dietary Fiber 1g) Exchanges: 3½ Starch, 1½ Other Carbohydrate, 4 Medium-Fat Meat, 3½ Fat; Carbohydrate Choices: 5

Ham and Cheese Biscuit Sandwiches

Carol J. Gross   Grand Junction, CO
Bake-Off® Contest 31, 1984
$2,000 Winner

Prep Time: 25 Minutes
Start to Finish: 45 Minutes
5 sandwiches

1 cup diced cooked ham
1 cup shredded Swiss cheese (4 oz)
½ cup finely chopped peeled apple
1 can (12 oz) Pillsbury® Golden Layers® refrigerated flaky biscuits
1 egg
1 teaspoon water
Chopped tomato, if desired

1   Heat oven to 375°F. Lightly spray large cookie sheet with cooking spray. In small bowl, mix ham, cheese and apple.

2   Separate dough into 10 biscuits. Press or roll 5 biscuits to form 4-inch rounds. Place on cookie sheet. Place about ½ cup ham mixture on center of each biscuit round. Press or roll remaining 5 biscuits into 5-inch rounds; place over ham mixture. Press edges with fork to seal. In small bowl, beat egg and water. Brush over filled biscuits.

3   Bake 13 to 18 minutes or until golden brown. To serve, cut each biscuit sandwich in half. Garnish with tomato. Serve warm.

High Altitude (3500–6500 ft): No change.

1 Sandwich: Calories 360; Total Fat 19g (Saturated Fat 7g; Trans Fat 3g); Cholesterol 80mg; Sodium 1180mg; Total Carbohydrate 31g (Dietary Fiber 0g) Exchanges: 2 Starch, 1½ Medium-Fat Meat, 2 Fat; Carbohydrate Choices: 2

Grands!® Roast Beef Sandwiches

Candace Barnhart   Hollywood, CA
Bake-Off® Contest 39, 2000

Prep Time: 15 Minutes
Start to Finish: 40 Minutes
8 sandwiches

SANDWICHES
1 can (16.3 oz) Pillsbury® Grands!® refrigerated buttermilk biscuits
2 tablespoons butter or margarine, melted
¼ cup garlic herb dry bread crumbs
⅓ cup mayonnaise or salad dressing
1 can (4.5 oz) chopped green chiles
8 slices (1 oz each) cooked roast beef (from deli)
1 cup finely shredded Monterey Jack cheese (4 oz)

SAUCE, IF DESIRED
½ cup mayonnaise or salad dressing
¼ cup Dijon mustard

1   Heat oven to 375°F. Separate dough into 8 biscuits. Brush tops and sides of biscuits with melted butter; coat with bread crumbs. Place 2 inches apart, crumb side up, on ungreased cookie sheet. Sprinkle any remaining bread crumbs over biscuits.

2   Bake 14 to 16 minutes or until golden brown. Cool 5 minutes. Set oven control to broil.

3   Meanwhile, in small bowl, stir together ⅓ cup mayonnaise and the green chiles. Split biscuits; place tops and bottoms, cut sides up, on same cookie sheet. Spread mayonnaise mixture evenly on top halves of biscuits. Arrange roast beef slices on bottom halves, folding to fit. Top with cheese.

4   Broil 4 to 6 inches from heat 2 to 3 minutes or until cheese is melted and mayonnaise mixture is bubbly. Place top halves of biscuits over bottom halves. In small bowl, stir together sauce ingredients. Serve with sandwiches.

High Altitude (3500–6500 ft): No change.

1 Sandwich: Calories 400; Total Fat 26g (Saturated Fat 10g; Trans Fat 3.5g); Cholesterol 40mg; Sodium 1070mg; Total Carbohydrate 28g (Dietary Fiber 0g) Exchanges: 1½ Starch, ½ Other Carbohydrate, 1½ Medium-Fat Meat, 3 Fat; Carbohydrate Choices: 2

Crispy Deli Wraps

Crispy Deli Wraps

Bobbie Keefer   Byers, CO
Bake-Off® Contest 42, 2006

Prep Time: 15 Minutes
Start to Finish: 45 Minutes
4 wraps

WRAPS

1 box (9 oz) frozen spinach
2 cups baked horn-shaped corn snacks
¼ cup butter or margarine, melted
1 can (8 oz) Pillsbury® refrigerated crescent dinner rolls
16 thin slices cooked ham or turkey (about ½ lb)
4 sticks (1 oz each) mozzarella string cheese

DIPPING SAUCE, IF DESIRED

⅓ cup mayonnaise or salad dressing
⅓ cup Dijon mustard
⅓ cup honey

1   Heat oven to 375°F. Line large cookie sheet with cooking parchment paper. Remove frozen spinach from pouch; place in colander. Rinse with warm water until thawed; drain well. Squeeze spinach dry with paper towel; divide evenly into 4 portions. Set aside.

2   Meanwhile, place corn snacks in resealable food-storage plastic bag; seal bag. With rolling pin, finely crush snacks; pour into shallow dish or pie plate. In another shallow dish or pie plate, place melted butter; set aside. Unroll dough; separate into 4 rectangles. Press each into 6 × 4-inch rectangle, firmly pressing perforations to seal.

3   Arrange ham in 4 stacks with 4 slices each. Top each stack with 1 portion of spinach, spreading spinach evenly over ham. Place 1 stick of cheese on one short side of spinach-topped ham. Roll up each stack.

4   Place 1 filled ham roll on one long side of each dough rectangle. Fold sides of dough up over ham roll and roll to opposite long side; press edge and ends to seal and completely cover ham roll. Roll each in butter, then in crushed corn snacks to coat; place seam side down on cookie sheet.

5   Bake 20 to 28 minutes or until deep golden brown. Meanwhile, in small bowl, mix sauce ingredients with wire whisk. Serve warm wraps with sauce for dipping.

High Altitude (3500–6500 ft): Bake 24 to 28 minutes.

1 Wrap: Calories 560; Total Fat 36g (Saturated Fat 17g; Trans Fat 3.5g); Cholesterol 80mg; Sodium 1690mg; Total Carbohydrate 33g (Dietary Fiber 2g) Exchanges: 2 Starch, 3 Medium-Fat Meat, 4 Fat; Carbohydrate Choices: 2

Reuben in the Round Crescents

Irene Dunn   Cuyahoga Falls, OH
Bake-Off® Contest 27, 1976

Prep Time: 25 Minutes
Start to Finish: 50 Minutes
8 servings

2 cans (8 oz each) Pillsbury® refrigerated crescent dinner rolls
1 package (8 oz) thinly sliced pastrami or corned beef
1 package (6 oz) Swiss or mozzarella cheese (4 slices)
1 can (8 oz) sauerkraut (1 cup), drained
½ teaspoon caraway seed
½ teaspoon sesame seed

1   Heat oven to 400°F. Separate 1 can of dough into 4 rectangles; place in ungreased 12-inch pizza pan or 13 × 9-inch pan. Press over bottom and ½ inch up sides to form crust, firmly pressing perforations to seal.

2   Layer pastrami, cheese and sauerkraut over dough; sprinkle with caraway seed. Separate second can of dough into 8 triangles; with points toward center, arrange spoke-fashion over filling (do not seal outer edges of triangles to bottom crust). Sprinkle with sesame seed.

3   Bake 15 to 25 minutes or until golden brown. Cut into wedges or squares.

High Altitude (3500–6500 ft): No change.

1 Serving: Calories 340; Total Fat 20g (Saturated Fat 8g; Trans Fat 3g); Cholesterol 30mg; Sodium 1050mg; Total Carbohydrate 25g (Dietary Fiber 1g) Exchanges: 1½ Starch, 1½ High-Fat Meat, 1½ Fat; Carbohydrate Choices: 1½

Smoked Turkey Quesadillas

Dean Philipp Portland, OR
Bake-Off® Contest 40, 2002

Prep Time: 30 Minutes
Start to Finish: 30 Minutes
4 servings

1 ripe avocado, pitted, peeled
4 oz cream cheese or ⅓-less-fat cream cheese (Neufchâtel), softened
½ teaspoon ground cumin
¼ teaspoon garlic powder
¼ teaspoon salt
⅛ teaspoon pepper
½ cup julienne-cut oil-packed sun-dried tomatoes, drained
1 can (4.5 oz) chopped green chiles, drained
1 cup shredded hot pepper Monterey Jack or Monterey Jack cheese (4 oz)
1 package (11.5 oz) flour tortillas for burritos (8 tortillas)
8 slices (1½ oz each) smoked turkey breast
1 cup shredded Cheddar cheese (4 oz)
2 tablespoons butter or margarine
4 ripe olive slices, if desired

1   In medium bowl, mash avocado. Add cream cheese, cumin, garlic powder, salt and pepper; blend well. Stir in tomatoes and chiles.

2   Sprinkle ¼ cup of the Monterey Jack cheese on 4 of the tortillas. Top each with turkey slice. Spread avocado mixture over turkey. Top with remaining turkey slices. Sprinkle with ¼ cup of the Cheddar cheese. Top with remaining tortillas.

3   In 12-inch skillet, melt ½ tablespoon of the butter over medium heat. Add 1 quesadilla; cook 2 to 4 minutes or until golden brown, turning once. Repeat with remaining butter and quesadillas. Garnish with remaining Monterey Jack and Cheddar cheese. Top each quesadilla with olive slice.

High Altitude (3500–6500 ft): No change.

1 Serving: Calories 820; Total Fat 52g (Saturated Fat 24g, Trans Fat 3g); Cholesterol 140mg; Sodium 2780mg; Total Carbohydrate 52g (Dietary Fiber 4g) Exchanges: 2½ Starch, 1 Other Carbohydrate, 4 Medium-Fat Meat, 6 Fat; Carbohydrate Choices: 3½

Crunchy Crescent Hamwiches

Ann Van Dorin Webster, NY
Bake-Off® Contest 27, 1976

Prep Time: 20 Minutes
Start to Finish: 40 Minutes
8 sandwiches

1 package (3 oz) cream cheese, softened
2 tablespoons mayonnaise or salad dressing
½ teaspoon ground mustard
¼ teaspoon celery salt
1 cup diced cooked ham
½ cup frozen whole kernel corn (from 1-lb bag), thawed
¼ cup shredded Swiss or Monterey Jack cheese (1 oz)
2 teaspoons chopped onion or ½ teaspoon dried minced onion
1 can (8 oz) Pillsbury® refrigerated crescent dinner rolls
1 tablespoon butter or margarine, melted
¼ to ½ cup finely crushed corn or potato chips

1   Heat oven to 375°F. In medium bowl, mix cream cheese, mayonnaise, mustard and celery salt until smooth; stir in ham, corn, cheese and onion. Separate crescent dough into 4 rectangles; firmly press perforations to seal. Cut each rectangle in half crosswise; press to 4-inch squares. Spoon about ¼ cup ham mixture onto center of each square. Pull 4 corners of dough to top center of filling; twist firmly and pinch corners to seal. Brush each with butter; sprinkle with chips. Place on ungreased large cookie sheet.

2   Bake 15 to 20 minutes or until golden brown. Serve immediately. Cover and refrigerate any remaining hamwiches.

High Altitude (3500–6500 ft): No change.

1 Sandwich: Calories 250; Total Fat 17g (Saturated Fat 7g; Trans Fat 1.5g); Cholesterol 30mg; Sodium 600mg; Total Carbohydrate 15g (Dietary Fiber 0g) Exchanges: 1 Starch, 1 High-Fat Meat, 1½ Fat; Carbohydrate Choices: 1

Smoked Turkey Quesadillas

Swiss Ham Ring-Around

Swiss Ham Ring-Around

Mrs. Lyman Francis   Cheshire, CT
Bake-Off® Contest 20, 1969

Prep Time: 20 Minutes
Start to Finish: 50 Minutes
8 servings

1 tablespoon butter or margarine, softened
¼ cup chopped fresh parsley or
    2 tablespoons dried parsley flakes
2 tablespoons finely chopped onion or
    1½ teaspoons dried minced onion
2 tablespoons yellow mustard
1 teaspoon lemon juice
1½ cups shredded Swiss cheese (6 oz)
1 cup chopped fresh broccoli or frozen
    chopped broccoli, cooked, drained
1 cup diced cooked ham
1 can (8 oz) Pillsbury® refrigerated
    crescent dinner rolls

1   Heat oven to 350°F. Grease large cookie sheet. In large bowl, mix butter, parsley, onion, mustard and lemon juice. Add cheese, cooked broccoli and ham; mix lightly. Set aside.

2   Unroll dough into 8 triangles. Arrange triangles on cookie sheet with shortest sides toward center, overlapping in wreath shape and leaving a 3-inch round opening in center.

3   Spoon ham filling on widest part of dough. Pull end points of triangles over filling and tuck under dough to form a ring.

4   Bake 25 to 30 minutes or until golden brown.

High Altitude (3500–6500 ft): In step 1, stir 2 tablespoons Pillsbury BEST® all-purpose flour into ham and cheese mixture.

1 Serving: Calories 240; Total Fat 15g (Saturated Fat 7g; Trans Fat 1.5g); Cholesterol 35mg; Sodium 570mg; Total Carbohydrate 14g (Dietary Fiber 0g) Exchanges: 1 Starch, 1½ Medium-Fat Meat, 1 Fat; Carbohydrate Choices: 1

Ham and Swiss Crescent Braid

Lorraine Maggio   Manlius, NY
Bake-Off® Contest 39, 2000
$10,000 Winner

Prep Time: 15 Minutes
Start to Finish: 55 Minutes
8 servings

¾ lb cooked ham, chopped (2¼ cups)
1 cup frozen broccoli florets, thawed
1 cup shredded Swiss cheese (4 oz)
1 jar (4.5 oz) sliced mushrooms, drained
½ cup mayonnaise or salad dressing
1 tablespoon honey mustard
2 cans (8 oz each) Pillsbury®
    refrigerated crescent dinner rolls
1 egg white, beaten
2 tablespoons slivered almonds

1   Heat oven to 375°F. Spray cookie sheet with cooking spray. In large bowl, mix ham, broccoli, cheese, mushrooms, mayonnaise and mustard.

2   Unroll both cans of dough. Place dough with long sides together on cookie sheet, forming 15 × 12-inch rectangle. Press edges and perforations to seal.

3   Spoon and spread ham mixture in 6-inch strip lengthwise down center of dough. With scissors or sharp knife, make cuts 1½ inches apart on long sides of dough to within ½ inch of filling. Twisting each strip once, alternately cross strips over filling. Tuck short ends under; press to seal. Brush dough with beaten egg white; sprinkle with almonds.

4   Bake 28 to 33 minutes or until deep golden brown. Cool 5 minutes. Cut into crosswise slices.

High Altitude (over 3500 ft): Not recommended.

1 Serving: Calories 460; Total Fat 32g (Saturated Fat 10g; Trans Fat 3g); Cholesterol 45mg; Sodium 1270mg; Total Carbohydrate 25g (Dietary Fiber 1g) Exchanges: 1½ Starch, 2 Medium-Fat Meat, 4 Fat; Carbohydrate Choices: 1½

Italian Sausage Crescent Sandwiches

Cecilia V. Lagerak   Westminster, CO
Bake-Off® Contest 26, 1975

Prep Time: 25 Minutes
Start to Finish: 45 Minutes
8 sandwiches

1 lb bulk Italian sausage, crumbled
½ cup chopped green bell pepper
⅓ cup chopped onion
1 can (16 oz) pizza sauce
2 cans (8 oz each) Pillsbury®
    refrigerated crescent dinner rolls
1 package (6 oz) mozzarella cheese
    slices, halved, folded

1   Heat oven to 375°F. In 10-inch skillet, cook sausage, bell pepper and onion over medium-high heat, stirring frequently, until sausage is no longer pink and vegetables are tender; drain. Add 3 tablespoons of the pizza sauce; mix well.

2   Separate dough into 8 rectangles. Firmly press perforations to seal. Place about ¼ cup sausage mixture and ½ slice of cheese, folded, on one end of each rectangle. Fold dough in half over filling; press edges with fork to seal. Place on ungreased cookie sheet.

3   Bake 15 to 18 minutes or until golden brown. Meanwhile, in 1-quart saucepan, heat remaining pizza sauce over low heat until hot. Serve sandwiches with warm pizza sauce.

High Altitude (3500–6500 ft): No change.

1 Sandwich: Calories 440; Total Fat 28g (Saturated Fat 11g; Trans Fat 3g); Cholesterol 35mg; Sodium 1300mg; Total Carbohydrate 30g (Dietary Fiber 2g) Exchanges: 1½ Starch, ½ Other Carbohydrate, 2 High-Fat Meat, 2 Fat; Carbohydrate Choices: 2

Italian Meatball Hoagie Braids

Italian Meatball Hoagie Braids

Beverley Rossell Morgantown, IN
Bake-Off® Contest 39, 2000

Prep Time: 15 Minutes
Start to Finish: 35 Minutes
8 sandwiches

**2 cans (8 oz each) Pillsbury®
  refrigerated crescent dinner rolls**
**16 (1½-inch) frozen fully cooked Italian
  meatballs (about 1 lb), thawed,
  halved**
1 cup tomato-basil pasta sauce
1 cup shredded mozzarella cheese (4 oz)
1 egg, slightly beaten
¼ cup grated Parmesan cheese

1 Heat oven to 375°F. Spray
2 cookie sheets with cooking spray.
Separate dough into 8 rectangles.
Place rectangles on cookie sheets.
Firmly press perforations to seal.

2 Place 4 meatball halves lengthwise down center of each rectangle.
Top each with 2 tablespoons sauce
and 2 tablespoons mozzarella
cheese. With scissors or sharp knife,
make cuts 1 inch apart on each side
of filling. Alternately cross strips
over filling. Brush dough with
beaten egg; sprinkle with Parmesan
cheese.

3 Bake 15 to 20 minutes or until
golden brown.

High Altitude (3500–6500 ft): No change.

1 Sandwich: Calories 450; Total Fat 25g (Saturated
Fat 10g; Trans Fat 3.5g); Cholesterol 95mg; Sodium
1040mg; Total Carbohydrate 35g (Dietary Fiber 1g)
Exchanges: 2 Starch, ½ Other Carbohydrate, 2 High-Fat
Meat, 1½ Fat; Carbohydrate Choices: 2

An "Electrifying" Situation

Just hours before Pillsbury's first Bake-Off® Contest in 1949, known
then as the Grand National Recipe and Baking Contest, organizers were
dismayed to find that baking in the world's largest kitchen would be
impossible. The 100 electric ranges set up in the Waldorf-Astoria Hotel
ballroom in New York City needed alternating current to run, but
the generator that supplied the hotel was for direct current
only! During the middle of the night, Pillsbury had electricians
break a hole in the wall and drop a cable down into the city
subway system to tap into the alternating current cable there.
The contest went on the next day without a hitch!

Spinach, Prosciutto and Roasted Pepper Calzone

Jen Riley West Roxbury, MA
Bake-Off® Contest 40, 2002
$2,000 Winner

Prep Time: 15 Minutes
Start to Finish: 50 Minutes
6 servings

**2 cans (8 oz each) Pillsbury®
  refrigerated crescent dinner rolls**
**1 box (9 oz) frozen spinach, thawed,
  squeezed to drain***
8 oz thinly sliced provolone cheese
**2 large red bell peppers, roasted,
  quartered, or 1 jar (12 oz) roasted
  red bell peppers, drained, quartered**
4 oz thinly sliced prosciutto
2 tablespoons pesto
1 egg yolk
1 tablespoon water

1 Heat oven to 350°F. Grease large
cookie sheet. Unroll both cans of
dough into 2 long rectangles. Place
dough rectangles with long sides
together on cookie sheet, forming
15 × 10-inch rectangle. Press edges
and perforations to seal.

2 Place spinach lengthwise in
4-inch-wide strip down center of
dough to within ½ inch of each
end. Top with half of the cheese,
the roasted peppers and prosciutto.
Spread pesto over prosciutto. Top
with remaining cheese. Bring long
sides of dough up over filling, overlapping 1 inch; press edges and
ends to seal.

3 In small bowl, beat egg yolk and
water. Brush over top of dough. Bake
25 to 35 minutes or until golden
brown. Cut into crosswise slices.

*To quickly thaw spinach, cut small
slit in center of pouch; microwave on
High 2 to 3 minutes or until thawed.
Remove spinach from pouch; squeeze dry
with paper towels.*

High Altitude (3500–6500 ft): Bake 28 to
33 minutes.

1 Serving: Calories 510; Total Fat 31g (Saturated
Fat 13g; Trans Fat 4.5g); Cholesterol 70mg; Sodium
1270mg; Total Carbohydrate 35g (Dietary Fiber 2g)
Exchanges: 1½ Starch, ½ Other Carbohydrate,
1 Vegetable, 2 Medium-Fat Meat, 4 Fat; Carbohydrate
Choices: 2

Neat-to-Eat Sloppy Joe Crescents

Neat-to-Eat Sloppy Joe Crescents

Rhoda Schrag   Ritzville, WA
Bake-Off® Contest 24, 1973

Prep Time: 15 Minutes
Start to Finish: 35 Minutes
4 sandwiches

¾ lb ground beef
½ cup ketchup
¼ cup chopped onion
1 tablespoon yellow mustard
2 teaspoons Worcestershire sauce
⅛ teaspoon pepper
½ cup shredded Cheddar cheese (2 oz)
1 can (8 oz) Pillsbury® refrigerated
    crescent dinner rolls
Sesame seed, if desired

1   Heat oven to 375°F. In 10-inch skillet, cook beef over medium-high heat 5 to 7 minutes, stirring frequently, until thoroughly cooked; drain well. Stir in ketchup, onion, mustard, Worcestershire sauce, pepper and cheese.

2   Separate dough into 4 rectangles; firmly press perforations to seal. Press each rectangle into a 5-inch square. Spoon about ½ cup of meat mixture onto center of each square. Fold dough over to make triangle; seal edges with fork. Place triangles on ungreased cookie sheet. Cut 1 to 2 slits in top of each triangle. Sprinkle with sesame seed.

3   Bake 14 to 20 minutes or until golden brown.

High Altitude (3500–6500 ft): No change.

1 Sandwich: Calories 460; Total Fat 26g (Saturated Fat 11g; Trans Fat 4g); Cholesterol 70mg; Sodium 970mg; Total Carbohydrate 32g (Dietary Fiber 1g) Exchanges: 1 Starch, 1 Other Carbohydrate, 3 Medium-Fat Meat, 2 Fat; Carbohydrate Choices: 2

Double Cheeseburger Pizza Rounds

Debra Kelly   Wheeling, IL
Bake-Off® Contest 39, 2000
$2,000 Winner

Prep Time: 15 Minutes
Start to Finish: 35 Minutes
8 pizzas

½ lb lean (at least 80%) ground beef
    or turkey
1 can (16.3 oz) Pillsbury® Grands!®
    refrigerated buttermilk biscuits
1 egg yolk
¼ teaspoon water
1 tablespoon sesame seed
1 jar (14 oz) pizza sauce
1 cup crumbled feta cheese (4 oz)
2 tablespoons chopped ripe olives
Dash Worcestershire sauce
Dash red pepper sauce
Dash salt
Dash pepper
1 cup shredded pizza cheese blend
    or mozzarella cheese (4 oz)

1   Heat oven to 375°F. Spray large cookie sheet with cooking spray. In 10-inch skillet, cook beef over medium-high heat 8 to 10 minutes, stirring frequently, until thoroughly cooked; drain.

2   Meanwhile, separate dough into 8 biscuits. Place 2½ inches apart on cookie sheet. With bottom of flat 2-inch diameter glass or fingers, press out each biscuit to form 3½-inch round with ¼-inch rim around outside edge. In small bowl, beat egg yolk and water. Brush over tops and sides of biscuits. Sprinkle each with sesame seed.

3   Add remaining ingredients except cheese to beef; cook about 1 minute, stirring constantly.

4   Spoon about ¼ cup beef mixture into indentation in each biscuit. Sprinkle each with cheese.

5   Bake 12 to 17 minutes or until biscuits are golden brown and cheese is bubbly. Carefully remove from cookie sheet.

High Altitude (3500–6500 ft): No change.

1 Pizza: Calories 350; Total Fat 19g (Saturated Fat 9g; Trans Fat 3.5g); Cholesterol 65mg; Sodium 1150mg; Total Carbohydrate 29g (Dietary Fiber 1g) Exchanges: 1½ Starch, ½ Other Carbohydrate, 1½ Medium-Fat Meat, 2 Fat; Carbohydrate Choices: 2

Crescent Samosa Sandwiches

Elisabeth Crawford   San Francisco, CA
Bake-Off® Contest 36, 1994
$2,000 Winner

Prep Time: 45 Minutes
Start to Finish: 45 Minutes
16 sandwiches

FILLING
1 tablespoon vegetable oil
½ cup finely chopped onion
2 cloves garlic, finely chopped
¼ lb lean (at least 80%) ground beef
1 cup diced cooked potato
½ cup diced cooked carrot
½ cup frozen sweet peas (from 1-lb bag), thawed
5 teaspoons soy sauce
1 teaspoon curry powder
½ teaspoon ground cumin
¼ teaspoon ground coriander
¼ teaspoon ground ginger
¼ teaspoon ground turmeric
Dash crushed red pepper flakes

CRESCENTS
2 cans (8 oz each) Pillsbury® refrigerated crescent dinner rolls

HONEY DIPPING SAUCE
⅓ cup honey
1 tablespoon lime juice
1 tablespoon soy sauce
¼ teaspoon crushed red pepper flakes
2 cloves garlic, finely chopped

1   Heat oven to 375°F. In 10-inch skillet, heat oil over medium heat until hot. Cook and stir onion and 2 cloves garlic in oil about 5 minutes or until onion is tender. Remove from skillet. Add beef; cook and stir 3 to 5 minutes or until browned. Drain. Stir in onion mixture and remaining filling ingredients. Season to taste with salt, if desired.

2   Separate 1 can of dough into 4 rectangles; firmly press perforations to seal. (Keep remaining can refrigerated until ready to use.) Cut rectangles in half crosswise to make 8 squares. Spoon 1 heaping tablespoonful filling onto center of each square. Fold dough over to make triangle; firmly press edges to seal. Repeat with remaining can of dough and filling. Place on ungreased cookie sheets. If desired, sprinkle with additional cumin.

3   Bake 10 to 15 minutes or until golden brown, switching positions of cookie sheets halfway through bake time. Meanwhile, in small bowl, mix sauce ingredients. Serve warm sandwiches with sauce.

High Altitude (3500–6500 ft): Bake 12 to 15 minutes.

1 Sandwich and 1½ teaspoons Sauce: Calories 170; Total Fat 8g (Saturated Fat 2.5g; Trans Fat 1.5g); Cholesterol 0mg; Sodium 380mg; Total Carbohydrate 21g (Dietary Fiber 1g) Exchanges: 1 Starch, ½ Other Carbohydrate, 1½ Fat; Carbohydrate Choices: 1½

Fish 'n Crescent Roll-Ups

Louise K. Ross   Sonora, CA
Bake-Off® Contest 26, 1975

Prep Time: 10 Minutes
Start to Finish: 25 Minutes
8 sandwiches

3 tablespoons tartar sauce
2 teaspoons finely chopped onion
1 can (8 oz) Pillsbury® refrigerated crescent dinner rolls
8 frozen breaded fish sticks
1 tablespoon butter or margarine, melted
Sesame seed

1   Heat oven to 375°F. In small bowl, mix tartar sauce and onion.

2   Separate dough into 8 triangles. Place 1 fish stick on shortest side of each triangle. Spoon 1 teaspoon tartar sauce mixture onto each fish stick.

3   Roll up each, starting at shortest side of triangle and rolling to opposite point. (Fish sticks will not be completely covered.) Place roll-ups, point side down, on ungreased cookie sheet. Brush each with butter. Sprinkle with sesame seed.

4   Bake 11 to 13 minutes or until golden brown.

High Altitude (3500–6500 ft): Thaw breaded fish sticks before using.

1 Sandwich: Calories 190; Total Fat 13g (Saturated Fat 3.5g; Trans Fat 2g); Cholesterol 10mg; Sodium 330mg; Total Carbohydrate 16g (Dietary Fiber 0g) Exchanges: 1 Starch, 2½ Fat; Carbohydrate Choices: 1

Tuna Cheese Flips

Marilyn Belschner Amherst, NE
Bake-Off® Contest 27, 1976

Prep Time: 20 Minutes
Start to Finish: 45 Minutes
10 sandwiches

2 cans (6 oz each) tuna, drained, flaked
⅛ teaspoon lemon-pepper seasoning
⅓ cup sliced ripe or green olives, drained
⅓ cup mayonnaise or salad dressing
½ cup shredded Monterey Jack or Cheddar cheese (2 oz)
1 can (12 oz) Pillsbury® Golden Layers® refrigerated flaky biscuits
1 egg, beaten, or 2 tablespoons milk
1 cup crushed potato chips

1 Heat oven to 375°F.

2 In small bowl, mix tuna, lemon-pepper seasoning, olives, mayonnaise and cheese. Separate dough into 10 biscuits. Press or roll each to form 5-inch circle. Spoon about ¼ cup tuna mixture onto center of each circle. Fold dough in half over filling; press edges with fork to seal. Brush both sides of each sandwich with egg; press both sides in chips. Place on ungreased cookie sheet. With sharp knife, make two or three ½-inch slits in top of each sandwich.

3 Bake 18 to 24 minutes or until deep golden brown.

High Altitude (3500–6500 ft): Heat oven to 350°F. Bake 18 to 22 minutes.

1 Sandwich: Calories 250; Total Fat 15g (Saturated Fat 3.5g; Trans Fat 1.5g); Cholesterol 40mg; Sodium 610mg; Total Carbohydrate 18g (Dietary Fiber 0g) Exchanges: 1 Starch, 1½ Very Lean Meat, 2½ Fat; Carbohydrate Choices: 1

Quality Family Time

Many Bake-Off® Contest finalists agree that the feelings that come out of preparing and sharing a meal are as significant as the ingredients that go into it: "I feel meal time is a very important together time for the family," Marilyn Belschner says. "A time when family members can communicate with each other under pleasant circumstances, while enjoying food that will nourish their bodies. Of all the ills that threaten mankind today, few can penetrate a happy family at a well-appointed table."

Fiesta Shrimp Tacos with Cucumber Salsa

Kristine Snyder Kihei, HI
Bake-Off® Contest 39, 2000
$2,000 Winner

Prep Time: 20 Minutes
Start to Finish: 20 Minutes
6 servings

1 package (4.6 oz) taco shells (12 shells)
1½ cups fat-free sour cream
½ cup chopped seeded peeled cucumber
1 package (1.25 oz) taco seasoning mix
2 avocados, pitted, peeled and coarsely chopped
1 tablespoon lime juice
1 lb uncooked deveined peeled medium shrimp, tails removed
1 tablespoon olive oil
1 cup salsa
½ cup chopped fresh cilantro

1 Heat taco shells as directed on package. Meanwhile, in medium bowl, mix sour cream, cucumber and 2 tablespoons of the taco seasoning mix. In small bowl, mix avocados and lime juice; toss to coat. Set aside.

2 In another medium bowl, mix shrimp and remaining taco seasoning mix; toss to coat.

3 In 10-inch skillet, heat oil over medium-high heat until hot. Add shrimp; cook 3 to 5 minutes, stirring frequently, until shrimp turn pink.

4 Spoon shrimp into warm taco shells. Top each with sour cream mixture, avocados, salsa and cilantro.

High Altitude (3500–6500 ft): No change.

1 Serving (2 Tacos): Calories 350; Total Fat 17g (Saturated Fat 2.5g; Trans Fat 1.5g); Cholesterol 115mg; Sodium 1120mg; Total Carbohydrate 35g (Dietary Fiber 5g) Exchanges: 1 Starch, 1 Other Carbohydrate, 2 Very Lean Meat, 3 Fat; Carbohydrate Choices: 2

Spicy Asian Lettuce Wraps

Maria Baldwin Mesa, AZ
Bake-Off® Contest 40, 2002

Prep Time: 50 Minutes
Start to Finish: 50 Minutes
8 wraps

1 lb boneless skinless chicken breast halves
1 bag (1 lb 5 oz) frozen stir-fry lo mein meal starter
2 tablespoons chili-garlic sauce
2 tablespoons soy sauce
3 tablespoons vegetable oil
2 cloves garlic, finely chopped
1 tablespoon sugar
2 tablespoons peanut butter
2 tablespoons water

8 large leaves Bibb lettuce
1½ cups grated carrots
⅓ cup chopped peanuts
¼ cup finely chopped green onions
2 tablespoons finely chopped fresh cilantro, if desired

1   To flatten each chicken breast half, place boned side up between 2 pieces of plastic wrap or waxed paper. Working from center, gently pound chicken with flat side of meat mallet or rolling pin until about ¼ inch thick; remove wrap.

2   In small microwavable bowl, microwave frozen sauce from meal starter on High 15 to 30 seconds or until thawed. Add chili-garlic sauce and soy sauce; mix well. In medium bowl, mix chicken, ¼ cup of the soy sauce mixture and 2 tablespoons of the oil.

3   Heat 12-inch nonstick skillet over medium-high heat until hot. Add chicken mixture; cook 5 to 6 minutes, turning occasionally, until chicken is no longer pink in center. Remove chicken from skillet; cut into 1-inch pieces. Cover to keep warm. In same skillet, heat remaining 1 tablespoon oil over medium-high heat until hot. Add 3 tablespoons of the soy sauce mixture, the garlic and frozen

meet maria baldwin

MARIA BALDWIN'S FAMILY are big fans of her cooking, and they knew she had what it took to be a finalist in the Bake-Off® Contest. "My husband kept bugging me and bugging me," Maria says.

But the day before the contest deadline she had no recipe to submit. Maria and her daughter, Kathryn, went for lunch that day at a nearby restaurant, where they ordered the lettuce wraps.

When she returned home, there was her husband, still urging her to enter the contest. So to put an end to his nagging, she says, the next night she took a Green Giant®

Create a Meal!® meal starter, added several of her own ingredients, and served her family her tasty new Spicy Asian Lettuce Wraps. At that point, the kids chimed in: "You've got to send this recipe to Pillsbury—in a hurry!"

Maria submitted her recipe on the contest Web site about three minutes before the deadline. The results went well beyond what she had ever imagined. "I was shocked," Maria says of being chosen as a finalist. But the excitement continued when her lettuce wraps won the GE Innovation Award and $5,000 worth of kitchen appliances.

Maria offers this advice for contest hopefuls: "If you try, you can eventually come up with something." Or, if you're like Maria, your family will nag you until you do.

noodles and vegetables from meal starter; cook and stir 6 to 8 minutes or until vegetables are crisp-tender.

4 To remaining soy sauce mixture in small bowl, add sugar, peanut butter and water; mix well. Pat lettuce dry with paper towel; arrange on part of large serving platter. Spoon carrots onto platter next to lettuce. Arrange cooked vegetables and noodles on platter. Place chicken over vegetables and noodles. Sprinkle chicken with peanuts, onions and cilantro.

5 To serve, spread peanut sauce in center of each lettuce leaf. Top with chicken-vegetable mixture and carrots. Wrap lettuce around filling.

High Altitude (3500–6500 ft): Cook chicken mixture over medium-high heat 6 to 8 minutes.

1 Wrap: Calories 260; Total Fat 13g (Saturated Fat 2g; Trans Fat 0g); Cholesterol 35mg; Sodium 680mg; Total Carbohydrate 19g (Dietary Fiber 3g) Exchanges: ½ Starch, ½ Other Carbohydrate, 1 Vegetable, 2 Very Lean Meat, 2 Fat; Carbohydrate Choices: 1

Crescent Burritos

Jeanne Holt Mendota Heights, MN
Bake-Off® Contest 31, 1984

Prep Time: 35 Minutes
Start to Finish: 1 Hour
8 servings

½ lb lean (at least 80%) ground beef
2 tablespoons chopped onion
2 tablespoons taco seasoning mix
   (from 1.25-oz package)
½ cup water
½ cup refried beans (from 16-oz can)
2 cans (8 oz each) Pillsbury®
   refrigerated crescent dinner rolls
½ cup chunky-style salsa
4 slices (¾ oz each) American cheese,
   cut diagonally in half
1 cup sour cream
¼ cup sliced ripe olives

1 Heat oven to 350°F. Spray cookie sheet with cooking spray. In 10-inch nonstick skillet, cook beef and onion over medium-high heat, stirring frequently, until beef is thoroughly cooked; drain.

2 Stir in taco seasoning mix and water. Reduce heat to medium; cook about 5 minutes, stirring frequently, until water has evaporated. Remove from heat; stir in beans.

3 Separate dough into 8 rectangles; firmly press perforations to seal. Spoon about 2 tablespoons beef mixture and 1 tablespoon of the salsa onto each rectangle; spread to within ½ inch of one short side. Starting with other short side, roll up each rectangle; pinch edges to seal. Place seam side down on cookie sheet.

4 Bake 18 to 23 minutes or until golden brown. Top each burrito with cheese; bake 2 to 3 minutes longer or until cheese is melted. Serve with sour cream and olives.

High Altitude (3500–6500 ft): No change.

1 Serving: Calories 390; Total Fat 25g (Saturated Fat 11g; Trans Fat 3.5g); Cholesterol 50mg; Sodium 1030mg; Total Carbohydrate 29g (Dietary Fiber 1g) Exchanges: 2 Starch, 1 High-Fat Meat, 3 Fat; Carbohydrate Choices: 2

Cowboy Tacos

Joan Schweger Elburn, IL
Bake-Off® Contest 37, 1996

Prep Time: 30 Minutes
Start to Finish: 30 Minutes
12 tacos

TACOS
1 lb boneless pork loin, cut into
   1 × 1 × ¼-inch strips
1 package (1.25 oz) taco seasoning mix
1 to 2 tablespoons vegetable oil
1 cup chunky style salsa
1 cup canned spicy chili beans,
   undrained
¼ cup apricot preserves
1 package (4.6 oz) taco shells
   (12 shells)

GARNISH
⅓ cup sliced ripe olives
5 or 6 green onions, chopped

1 In shallow bowl, toss pork and taco seasoning mix to coat.

2 In 10-inch skillet, heat oil over medium-high heat until hot. Add pork; cook and stir 3 to 5 minutes or until no longer pink in center.

3 Stir in salsa, beans and preserves. Reduce heat to low; simmer 10 to 12 minutes, stirring occasionally, until hot.

4 Meanwhile, heat taco shells as directed on package.

5 To serve, spoon ⅓ cup pork mixture into each taco shell. Top each with olives and onions.

High Altitude (3500–6500 ft): No change.

1 Taco: Calories 180; Total Fat 7g (Saturated Fat 2g; Trans Fat 1g); Cholesterol 25mg; Sodium 680mg; Total Carbohydrate 20g (Dietary Fiber 1g) Exchanges: ½ Starch, 1 Other Carbohydrate, 1 Very Lean Meat, 1 Fat; Carbohydrate Choices: 1

Cowboy Tacos

3 | MAIN DISHES

Chuck Wagon Cheeseburger Skillet (page 99)

Deluxe Turkey Club Pizza

Teresa Hannan Smith   Sacramento, CA
Bake-Off® Contest 35, 1992
$2,000 Winner

> **Prep Time:** 25 Minutes
> **Start to Finish:** 35 Minutes
> 6 servings

1 can (13.8 oz) Pillsbury® refrigerated
   classic pizza crust
2 teaspoons sesame seed
6 slices bacon, cut into 1-inch pieces
¼ cup light or regular mayonnaise
½ to 1 teaspoon grated lemon peel
1 cup shredded Monterey Jack cheese
   (4 oz)
1 tablespoon thinly sliced fresh basil
   or 1 teaspoon dried basil leaves
¼ lb cooked turkey breast slices,
   cut into 1-inch strips
2 small plum (Roma) tomatoes
   or 1 small tomato, thinly sliced
½ cup shredded Swiss cheese (2 oz)
Fresh basil leaves, if desired

1   Heat oven to 425°F. Lightly spray 12-inch pizza pan or 13 × 9-inch pan with cooking spray. Unroll dough; place in pan. Starting at center, press out dough to edge of pan to form crust. Sprinkle sesame seed evenly over dough. Bake 10 to 12 minutes or until crust is light golden brown.

2   Meanwhile, in 10-inch skillet, cook bacon over medium heat until crisp. Remove bacon from skillet; drain on paper towels. In small bowl, mix mayonnaise and lemon peel until well blended.

3   Spread mayonnaise mixture over crust. Top with Monterey Jack cheese, sliced basil, turkey, cooked bacon and tomatoes; sprinkle with Swiss cheese.

4   Bake 7 to 9 minutes longer or until crust is golden brown and cheese is melted. Garnish with fresh basil leaves.

High Altitude (3500–6500 ft): In step 1, bake 10 to 13 minutes.

1 Serving: Calories 380; Total Fat 18g (Saturated Fat 8g; Trans Fat 0g); Cholesterol 55mg; Sodium 850mg; Total Carbohydrate 33g (Dietary Fiber 0g) Exchanges: 1½ Starch, ½ Other Carbohydrate, 2½ Medium-Fat Meat, 1 Fat; Carbohydrate Choices: 2

Caesar Chicken Salad Squares

Lisa Huff   Birmingham, AL
Bake-Off® Contest 41, 2004

> **Prep Time:** 15 Minutes
> **Start to Finish:** 40 Minutes
> 4 servings

FILLING
2 cups cubed (⅛ to ¼ inch) cooked
   chicken breast or 1 can (12.5 oz)
   chunk chicken breast in water, drained
½ cup shredded mozzarella cheese
   or Italian cheese blend (2 oz)
1 tablespoon grated Parmesan cheese
1 tablespoon bacon flavor bits
2 tablespoons regular or reduced-fat
   Caesar dressing
1 tablespoon regular or light
   mayonnaise
1 teaspoon finely chopped garlic
1 teaspoon lemon juice

CRUST
1 can (8 oz) Pillsbury® refrigerated
   regular or reduced fat crescent
   dinner rolls

GARNISH, IF DESIRED
¼ cup Caesar dressing
1 cup shredded romaine lettuce

1   Heat oven to 375°F. In medium bowl, mix filling ingredients.

2   Unroll dough; separate into 4 rectangles. Place on ungreased cookie sheet; press each into 6 × 4-inch rectangle, firmly pressing perforations to seal. Spoon about ½ cup chicken mixture onto center of each dough rectangle. With knife, cut each corner of each rectangle from edge to within ½ inch of filling. Bring the 8 points of each rectangle up over filling; firmly pinch to seal, forming a square.

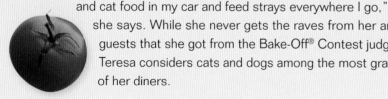

Furry Friends

Cooks tend to be a generous lot, and Teresa Hannan Smith makes a point of sharing the bounty of her life not just with guests at her table but with four-legged folk wherever she is. "I carry three kinds of dog and cat food in my car and feed strays everywhere I go," she says. While she never gets the raves from her animal guests that she got from the Bake-Off® Contest judges, Teresa considers cats and dogs among the most gratifying of her diners.

3 Bake 16 to 21 minutes or until deep golden brown. Remove from cookie sheet. Garnish each with 1 tablespoon Caesar dressing and ¼ cup shredded lettuce.

High Altitude (3500–6500 ft): No change.

1 Serving: Calories 440; Total Fat 26g (Saturated Fat 8g; Trans Fat 3g); Cholesterol 70mg; Sodium 710mg; Total Carbohydrate 24g (Dietary Fiber 0g) Exchanges: 1 Starch, ½ Other Carbohydrate, 4 Lean Meat, 2½ Fat; Carbohydrate Choices: 1½

Chicken Waldorf Pizza

Ernie Crow   Rockville, MD
Bake-Off® Contest 39, 2000

Prep Time: 20 Minutes
Start to Finish: 30 Minutes
6 servings

1 can (13.8 oz) Pillsbury® refrigerated classic pizza crust
1 cup chopped cooked chicken
1 cup chopped apple
½ cup sliced almonds, toasted*
½ cup mayonnaise or salad dressing
1 teaspoon dried tarragon leaves
⅛ teaspoon salt
⅛ teaspoon pepper
2 cups shredded Swiss cheese (8 oz)
2 teaspoons chopped green onions

1 Heat oven to 425°F. Lightly spray 14-inch pizza pan with cooking spray.** Unroll dough in pan. Starting at center, press out dough to edge of pan.

2 Bake 6 to 8 minutes or until crust begins to brown.

3 Meanwhile, in medium bowl, mix chicken, apple, almonds, mayonnaise, tarragon, salt and pepper. Spread mixture evenly over crust. Sprinkle with cheese.

4 Bake 10 to 12 minutes longer or until cheese is melted and crust is deep golden brown. Sprinkle with green onions. Cut into 12 wedges.

To toast almonds, spread in a single layer on a cookie sheet and bake at 350°F 5 to 7 minutes or until aromatic and golden, shaking pan occasionally.

**A large cookie sheet can be used in place of the 14-inch pizza pan. Spray the cookie sheet with cooking spray; press and shape the dough on the sheet into a 14-inch circle or square.*

High Altitude (3500–6500 ft): No change.

1 Serving (2 wedges): Calories 540; Total Fat 32g (Saturated Fat 10g; Trans Fat 0g); Cholesterol 60mg; Sodium 720mg; Total Carbohydrate 38g (Dietary Fiber 1g) Exchanges: 2 Starch, ½ Other Carbohydrate, 2½ Lean Meat, 4½ Fat; Carbohydrate Choices: 2½

Orange-Chicken-Chipotle Pizza

April Carty-Sipp   Collingswood, NJ
Bake-Off® Contest 41, 2004

Prep Time: 15 Minutes
Start to Finish: 30 Minutes
6 servings

1 can (13.8 oz) Pillsbury® refrigerated classic pizza crust
2 tablespoons extra-virgin olive oil
1 large onion, quartered, sliced
3 boneless skinless chicken breasts, cut into ½-inch pieces
⅓ cup orange marmalade
1 teaspoon seasoned salt
1 teaspoon ground cumin
1 to 3 chipotle chiles in adobo sauce (from 7-oz can), finely chopped
1 can (11 oz) mandarin orange segments, well drained on paper towels
1 cup shredded Monterey Jack cheese (4 oz)
1 cup shredded sharp Cheddar cheese (4 oz)

1 Heat oven to 425°F. Lightly spray 14-inch pizza pan with cooking spray. Unroll dough; place on pan. Starting at center, press out dough to edge of pan. Bake 6 to 8 minutes or just until crust begins to brown.

2 Meanwhile, in 10-inch skillet, heat oil over medium heat until hot. Cook onion in oil 6 to 8 minutes, stirring frequently, until caramelized.

3 Remove partially baked crust from oven; reduce oven temperature to 375°F. Add chicken to skillet; cook 5 to 6 minutes, stirring frequently, until chicken is no longer pink in center. Stir in marmalade, salt, cumin, chipotle chiles and mandarin orange segments. Remove from heat; cool 1 minute.

4 Spread chicken mixture evenly over crust. Sprinkle both cheeses over top.

5 Bake at 375°F 10 to 13 minutes or until cheese is melted and crust is deep golden brown. Cut into wedges.

High Altitude (3500–6500 ft): In step 1, bake 8 to 10 minutes. In step 5, bake 12 to 15 minutes.

1 Serving: Calories 500; Total Fat 21g (Saturated Fat 9g; Trans Fat 0g); Cholesterol 75mg; Sodium 990mg; Total Carbohydrate 51g (Dietary Fiber 1g) Exchanges: 2 Starch, ½ Fruit, 1 Other Carbohydrate, 3 Lean Meat, 2 Fat; Carbohydrate Choices: 3½

Chicken Fajita Pizza

Elizabeth Daniels   Kula, Maui, HI
Bake-Off® Contest 34, 1990

Prep Time: 20 Minutes
Start to Finish: 40 Minutes
8 servings

1 can (13.8 oz) Pillsbury® refrigerated
   classic pizza crust
1 tablespoon olive or vegetable oil
4 boneless skinless chicken breasts
   (about 1¼ lb), cut into thin bite-size
   strips
1 to 2 teaspoons chili powder
½ to 1 teaspoon salt
½ teaspoon garlic powder
1 cup thinly sliced onions
1 cup green or red bell pepper strips
   (2 × ¼ inch)
½ cup chunky-style salsa
2 cups shredded Monterey Jack cheese
   (8 oz)

1   Heat oven to 425°F. Spray 12-inch pizza pan or 13 × 9-inch pan with cooking spray. Unroll dough; place in pan. Starting at center, press out dough to edge of pan to form crust.

2   Bake 7 to 9 minutes or until very light golden brown.

3   Meanwhile, in 10-inch skillet, heat oil over medium-high heat. Add chicken; sprinkle with chili powder, salt and garlic powder. Cook and stir 3 to 5 minutes or until lightly browned. Add onions and bell pepper strips; cook and stir 2 to 3 minutes longer or until chicken is no longer pink in center

and vegetables are crisp-tender. Spoon chicken mixture evenly over crust. Spoon salsa over chicken; sprinkle with cheese.

4   Bake 14 to 18 minutes longer or until crust is golden brown. Cut into wedges or squares to serve.

High Altitude (3500–6500 ft): After adding onions and bell pepper strips, cook and stir 3 to 5 minutes longer.

1 Serving: Calories 340; Total Fat 14g (Saturated Fat 7g; Trans Fat 0g); Cholesterol 70mg; Sodium 810mg; Total Carbohydrate 27g (Dietary Fiber 0g) Exchanges: 1½ Starch, ½ Other Carbohydrate, 3 Very Lean Meat, 2 Fat; Carbohydrate Choices: 2

Mojo Black Bean–Chicken Pizza

Ginny Solomon   Brooksville, FL
Bake-Off® Contest 42, 2006

Prep Time: 20 Minutes
Start to Finish: 30 Minutes
8 servings

¼ cup chopped fresh cilantro or parsley
¼ cup mojo criollo marinade (Spanish
   marinating sauce) or zesty Italian
   dressing
½ small red onion, cut into very thin
   strips
¼ teaspoon kosher (coarse) salt
⅛ teaspoon cracked black pepper
1 can (15 oz) black beans, drained,
   rinsed
1 package (6 oz) refrigerated grilled
   chicken strips*
1 can (13.8 oz) Pillsbury® refrigerated
   classic pizza crust
¾ cup shredded Monterey Jack cheese
   (3 oz)
¾ cup shredded mozzarella cheese
   (3 oz)

1   Heat oven to 400°F. In medium bowl, mix cilantro, marinade, onion, salt, pepper, beans and chicken. Let stand 10 to 15 minutes to marinate.

2   Meanwhile, lightly spray large cookie sheet with cooking spray. Unroll dough on cookie sheet; starting in center, press into 15 × 11-inch rectangle.

3   Bake 8 to 12 minutes or until light golden brown. Spread chicken mixture over partially baked crust to within ½ inch of edges. Sprinkle both cheeses over top.

4   Bake 8 minutes longer or until cheese is melted and crust is golden brown around edges. Cut into 8 rectangles.

High Altitude (3500–6500 ft): No change.

1 Serving: Calories 290; Total Fat 8g (Saturated Fat 4g; Trans Fat 0g); Cholesterol 30mg; Sodium 820mg; Total Carbohydrate 37g (Dietary Fiber 5g) Exchanges: 2 Starch, ½ Other Carbohydrate, 1½ Very Lean Meat, 1 Fat; Carbohydrate Choices: 2½

One large boneless skinless chicken breast, cooked on the grill and cut into thin strips, can be used in place of the refrigerated grilled chicken strips.

Chicken Fajita Pizza

Chicken Pizza Primavera

Janet Burns Virginia Beach, VA
Bake-Off® Contest 41, 2004

Prep Time: 15 Minutes
Start to Finish: 40 Minutes
4 servings

1 can (13.8 oz) Pillsbury® refrigerated classic pizza crust
Olive oil cooking spray
2 tablespoons shredded Asiago cheese
¼ to ½ teaspoon garlic salt
2 tablespoons light ranch dressing
1 package (6 oz) refrigerated cooked Italian-style chicken breast strips, chopped
⅓ cup finely chopped red bell pepper
⅓ cup thinly sliced red onion
½ cup torn baby spinach
1 ½ cups shredded Italian cheese blend (6 oz)
1 teaspoon dried pizza seasoning

1 Heat oven to 400°F. Lightly grease 12-inch pizza pan or pizza stone with shortening, or spray with cooking spray. Unroll dough on pan. Starting at center, press out dough to edge of pan.

2 Lightly spray dough with olive oil cooking spray. Sprinkle Asiago cheese and garlic salt over dough. Bake 8 to 10 minutes or until lightly browned.

3 Spread ranch dressing over crust. Top with chicken, bell pepper, onion and spinach. Sprinkle Italian cheese blend and pizza seasoning over top.

4 Bake 9 to 12 minutes longer or until cheese is melted and pizza is hot. Cut into wedges.

High Altitude (3500–6500 ft): No change.

1 Serving: Calories 480; Total Fat 18g (Saturated Fat 9g; Trans Fat 0g); Cholesterol 70mg; Sodium 1570mg; Total Carbohydrate 51g (Dietary Fiber 0g) Exchanges: 2½ Starch, 1 Other Carbohydrate, 3 Lean Meat, 1½ Fat; Carbohydrate Choices: 3½

Pizza-Quiche

Marilyn Erickson   San Jose, CA
Bake-Off® Contest 33, 1988
$10,000 Winner

Prep Time: 25 Minutes
Start to Finish: 1 Hour 25 Minutes
8 to 10 servings

1 Pillsbury® refrigerated pie crust
   (from 15-oz box), softened as
   directed on box
1 teaspoon Pillsbury BEST® all-purpose
   flour

FILLING
3 cups shredded mozzarella cheese
   (12 oz)
2 cups shredded Cheddar cheese (8 oz)
½ cup sliced pepperoni (2 oz), if desired
1 jar (4.5 oz) sliced mushrooms, drained
¾ cup milk
2 eggs
1 teaspoon Italian seasoning
1 small clove garlic, finely chopped
1 jar (16 oz) tomato pasta sauce

1   Heat oven to 400°F. Make pie
crust as directed on box for One-
Crust Filled Pie, using 9-inch pie
plate or 9-inch quiche pan.

2   Layer mozzarella and Cheddar
cheese in pie crust-lined pan. Top
with pepperoni and mushrooms.
In medium bowl, beat milk, eggs,
Italian seasoning and garlic. Pour
mixture over mushrooms.

3   Bake 40 to 45 minutes or until
knife inserted near center comes out
clean. Let stand 15 minutes before
serving.

4   Meanwhile, in 1-quart saucepan,
simmer pasta sauce 2 to 3 minutes
or until hot. To serve, cut quiche
into wedges; spoon sauce over each
wedge.

High Altitude (3500–6500 ft): No change.

1 Serving: Calories 460; Total Fat 29g (Saturated Fat 15g;
Trans Fat 0g); Cholesterol 110mg; Sodium 870mg;
Total Carbohydrate 28g (Dietary Fiber 1g) Exchanges:
1½ Starch, ½ Other Carbohydrate, 2½ High-Fat Meat,
1½ Fat; Carbohydrate Choices: 2

Mushroom-Crab-Asparagus Tart

Linda Miranda   Wakefield, RI
Bake-Off® Contest 41, 2004

Prep Time: 20 Minutes
Start to Finish: 1 Hour 5 Minutes
8 servings

1 box (9 oz) frozen asparagus cuts
¼ cup butter or margarine
1 lb fresh mushrooms, coarsely
   chopped
½ cup Parmesan bread crumbs
¼ teaspoon pepper
2 cups shredded sharp Cheddar
   or Swiss cheese (8 oz)
½ lb lump crabmeat or 1 can (6 oz)
   lump crabmeat, drained
1 container (8 oz) garlic-and-herb
   spreadable cheese
4 eggs
2 tablespoons chopped fresh parsley

1   Heat oven to 375°F. Spray
bottom and side of 12-inch tart pan
with removable bottom or 13 × 9-
inch (3-quart) glass baking dish
with cooking spray. Cook asparagus
as directed on box; drain and cool.

2   Meanwhile, in 12-inch skillet,
melt butter over medium heat.
Cook mushrooms in butter about
5 minutes, stirring frequently, just
until tender. Stir in bread crumbs
and pepper. Press mushroom
mixture evenly in bottom and up
side of tart pan or in bottom of
baking dish. Sprinkle shredded
cheese over mushrooms. Top with
asparagus and crabmeat.

3   In medium bowl or blender,
place spreadable cheese, eggs and
1 tablespoon of the parsley. Beat with
electric mixer on medium speed, or
cover and blend on low speed until
smooth. Pour evenly over crabmeat.

4   Bake 30 to 35 minutes or until
set in center and edges are golden
brown. Sprinkle remaining tablespoon parsley on top. Let stand
10 minutes before serving. Carefully
remove side of pan. Cut into wedges
or squares.

High Altitude (3500–6500 ft): No change.

1 Serving: Calories 380; Total Fat 29g (Saturated Fat 17g;
Trans Fat 1g); Cholesterol 210mg; Sodium 630mg;
Total Carbohydrate 9g (Dietary Fiber 1g) Exchanges:
1 Vegetable, 3 Medium-Fat Meat, 3 Fat; Carbohydrate
Choices: ½

She Went Thataway

Notifying the 100 finalists of their
selection for the contest can sometimes pose a challenge. Before
cell phones became common, one
finalist was traveling around the
country in a travel trailer with no
itinerary or plans to contact her
family. The highway patrols from
several states, plus for-
est rangers and park
officials, joined in the
quest to locate the
finalist.

Wild Rice and Ham Country Tart

Robert Holt   Mendota Heights, MN
Bake-Off® Contest 34, 1990
$2,000 Winner

> **Prep Time:** 30 Minutes
> **Start to Finish:** 1 Hour 15 Minutes
> 8 servings

1 Pillsbury® refrigerated pie crust
   (from 15-oz box), softened as
   directed on box

FILLING

1 cup cubed cooked ham
½ cup cooked wild rice (from 15-oz can)
⅓ cup finely chopped red bell pepper
¼ cup thinly sliced green onion tops
1 jar (4.5 oz) sliced mushrooms,
   well drained

CUSTARD

3 eggs
1 cup sour cream
1 tablespoon country-style Dijon mustard
½ teaspoon salt
⅛ teaspoon pepper

TOPPING

2 cups shredded Swiss cheese (8 oz)
11 pecan halves

1   Heat oven to 425°F. Make pie crust as directed on box for One-Crust Baked Shell, using 10-inch tart pan with removable bottom or 9-inch pie plate. Place crust in pan; press in bottom and up sides of pan. Trim edges if necessary. Do not prick crust. Bake 10 to 12 minutes or until crust is very light golden brown. Remove from oven. Reduce heat to 400°F.

2   In medium bowl, stir together filling ingredients; set aside. In small bowl, beat eggs until blended. Stir in remaining custard ingredients.

3   Sprinkle 1 cup of the cheese over bottom of baked shell. Spread filling mixture over cheese. Pour custard mixture over filling; sprinkle with remaining 1 cup cheese. Arrange pecan halves on top.

4   Bake at 400°F 30 to 35 minutes or until knife inserted in center comes out clean. Let stand 10 minutes before serving.

High Altitude (3500–6500 ft): Add 1 tablespoon Pillsbury BEST® all-purpose flour to ham mixture.

1 Serving: Calories 370; Total Fat 26g (Saturated Fat 12g; Trans Fat 0g); Cholesterol 140mg; Sodium 740mg; Total Carbohydrate 20g (Dietary Fiber 0g) Exchanges: 1 Starch, 2 Lean Meat, 4 Fat; Carbohydrate Choices: 1

Philly Cheese Steak Crescent Pizza

Jackie Medley   Covington, KY
Bake-Off® Contest 38, 1998

> **Prep Time:** 30 Minutes
> **Start to Finish:** 30 Minutes
> 8 servings

1 can (8 oz) Pillsbury® refrigerated
   crescent dinner rolls
½ lb thinly sliced cooked roast beef
   (from deli)
1 tablespoon Italian dressing (not
   creamy)
1 to 1½ cups shredded mozzarella
   cheese (4 to 6 oz)
2 tablespoons olive or vegetable oil
1 cup coarsely chopped green bell
   pepper
1 cup coarsely chopped onions
½ teaspoon beef-flavor instant bouillon

1   Heat oven to 375°F. Unroll dough into 2 long rectangles. Place in ungreased 13 × 9-inch pan; press over bottom and ½ inch up sides to form crust. Wrap beef tightly in foil. Place crescent dough and beef in oven. Bake about 10 minutes or until crust is light golden brown.

2   Arrange warm beef over crust. Brush with dressing. Sprinkle with cheese.

3   Bake 8 to 10 minutes longer or until edges of crust are golden brown and cheese is melted.

4   Meanwhile, in 8-inch skillet, heat oil over medium heat until hot. Add bell pepper, onions and bouillon; cook 3 to 5 minutes, stirring frequently, until vegetables are tender.

5   To serve, spoon cooked vegetables over melted cheese. Cut into squares.

High Altitude (3500–6500 ft): No change.

1 Serving: Calories 260; Total Fat 17g (Saturated Fat 6g; Trans Fat 2g); Cholesterol 30mg; Sodium 440mg; Total Carbohydrate 15g (Dietary Fiber 1g) Exchanges: 1 Starch, 1½ Very Lean Meat, 3 Fat; Carbohydrate Choices: 1

Philly Cheese Steak Crescent Pizza

Southwestern Chicken Pie

Harriet Mathis   Orlando, FL
Bake-Off® Contest 39, 2000

Prep Time: 15 Minutes
Start to Finish: 1 Hour 10 Minutes
6 servings

1 box (15 oz) Pillsbury® refrigerated pie crusts, softened as directed on box
1 package (9 oz) frozen cooked southwestern-seasoned chicken breast strips, thawed, cut into bite-size pieces
½ cup uncooked instant white rice
1 can (15 oz) black beans, drained, rinsed
1 can (11 oz) whole kernel corn with red and green peppers, drained
1 can (2¼ oz) sliced ripe olives, drained
1 teaspoon garlic powder
1 teaspoon ground cumin
½ teaspoon salt
½ teaspoon pepper
1 cup sour cream
1 cup chunky-style salsa
2 cups shredded Colby–Monterey Jack cheese blend (8 oz)
1 egg, beaten
1 to 2 teaspoons chopped fresh parsley

1   Heat oven to 400°F. Make pie crusts as directed on box for Two-Crust Pie, using 9-inch glass pie plate.

2   In large bowl, mix all remaining ingredients except egg and parsley. Pour into crust-lined pie plate. Top with second crust; seal edge and flute. Cut slits in several places in top crust. Brush top with beaten egg; sprinkle with parsley.

3   Bake 38 to 48 minutes or until golden brown. After 15 to 20 minutes of baking, cover crust edge with strips of foil to prevent excessive browning. Let stand 5 minutes before serving. Cover and refrigerate any remaining pie.

High Altitude (3500–6500 ft): Bake 50 to 55 minutes

1 Serving: Calories 790; Total Fat 42g (Saturated Fat 20g; Trans Fat 0.5g); Cholesterol 125mg; Sodium 1440mg; Total Carbohydrate 75g (Dietary Fiber 8g) Exchanges: 4 Starch, 1 Other Carbohydrate, 2 Very Lean Meat, 7½ Fat Carbohydrate Choices: 5

Italian Cheese Rustica Pie

Gloria T. Bove   Bethlehem, PA
Bake-Off® Contest 32, 1986
$2,000 Winner

Prep Time: 45 Minutes
Start to Finish: 1 Hour 55 Minutes
8 servings

1 box (15 oz) Pillsbury® refrigerated pie crusts, softened as directed on box
3 eggs
1 cup cubed cooked ham
1 cup ricotta or small curd cottage cheese
1 cup shredded mozzarella cheese (4 oz)
1 cup cubed provolone or Swiss cheese (4 oz)
4 tablespoons grated Parmesan cheese
1 tablespoon finely chopped fresh parsley or ½ teaspoon dried parsley flakes
¼ teaspoon dried oregano leaves
Dash pepper
Beaten egg, if desired

1   Make pie crust as directed on box for Two-Crust pie, using 9-inch pie plate. Move oven rack to lowest position. Heat oven to 375°F.

2   In large bowl, slightly beat 3 eggs. Stir in ham, ricotta cheese, mozzarella cheese, provolone cheese, 3 tablespoons of the Parmesan cheese, the parsley, oregano and pepper. Spoon mixture into pie crust-lined pan. Top with second crust; seal edges and flute. Cut slits in crust in several places. Brush beaten egg over crust. Sprinkle with remaining 1 tablespoon Parmesan cheese.

3   Place pan on lowest oven rack. Bake 50 to 60 minutes or until golden brown. Cover edge of crust with strips of foil after 15 to 20 minutes of baking if necessary to prevent excessive browning. Let stand 10 minutes before serving.

High Altitude (3500–6500 ft): No change.

1 Serving: Calories 440; Total Fat 27g (Saturated Fat 12g; Trans Fat 0g); Cholesterol 125mg; Sodium 780mg; Total Carbohydrate 29g (Dietary Fiber 0g) Exchanges: 2 Starch, 1½ Medium-Fat Meat, 3½ Fat; Carbohydrate Choices: 2

Layered Italian Beef Pie

Ruth Boudreaux   Broussard, LA
Bake-Off® Contest 32, 1986

Prep Time: 30 Minutes
Start to Finish: 1 Hour 15 Minutes
8 servings

1 Pillsbury® refrigerated pie crust (from 15-oz box), softened as directed on box
1 lb lean (at least 80%) ground beef
1 cup tomato pasta sauce with mushrooms and onions
2 eggs
¼ cup grated Parmesan cheese
1 box (9 oz) frozen spinach, thawed, squeezed to drain*
2 cups shredded mozzarella cheese (8 oz)
½ cup sliced ripe olives

1 Heat oven to 450°F. Make pie crust as directed on box for One-Crust Baked Shell, using 9-inch glass pie plate. Bake 9 to 11 minutes or until light golden brown. Reduce oven temperature to 350°F.

2 Meanwhile, in 10-inch skillet, cook beef over medium-high heat 5 to 7 minutes, stirring frequently, until thoroughly cooked. Drain well. Add pasta sauce; mix well. Heat to boiling. Reduce heat; simmer about 10 minutes or until hot.

3 In medium bowl, beat eggs until well blended. Add Parmesan cheese and spinach; mix well. Spoon half of beef mixture into baked shell. Sprinkle with 1 cup of the mozzarella cheese and ¼ cup of the olives. Spoon spinach mixture evenly over cheese. Top with remaining beef mixture.

4 Bake at 350°F 25 to 35 minutes or until filling is hot. If necessary, cover edge of crust with strips of foil after 15 to 20 minutes of baking to prevent excessive browning. Sprinkle pie with remaining 1 cup mozzarella cheese and ¼ cup olives. Bake 4 to 5 minutes longer or until cheese is melted. Let stand 5 minutes before serving.

To quickly thaw spinach, cut small slit in center of pouch; microwave on High 2 to 3 minutes or until thawed. Remove spinach from pouch; squeeze dry with paper towels.

High Altitude (3500–6500 ft): After topping pie with cheese and olives, bake 5 to 7 minutes longer.

1 Serving: Calories 380; Total Fat 23g (Saturated Fat 10g; Trans Fat 0.5g); Cholesterol 110mg; Sodium 600mg; Total Carbohydrate 22g (Dietary Fiber 1g) Exchanges: 1 Starch, ½ Other Carbohydrate, 2½ Medium-Fat Meat, 2 Fat; Carbohydrate Choices: 1½

meet ruth boudreaux

LOCATION, LOCATION, LOCATION. That phrase doesn't apply only to choice real estate purchases. Sometimes it's the location that brings people to the Bake-Off® Contest.

Ruth Boudreaux has been focused on the location of the contest since 1986. That's the year she first went to the Pillsbury Bake-Off® Contest and to Disney World, where the 32nd Bake-Off® Contest was held. Ruth's hearty Italian pie filled with layers of ground beef, cheese, spinach and olives captured a place for her among the finalists who traveled from 32 states to compete at Disney World's Contemporary Hotel.

Then a freelance draftsman and mother of two young sons, Ruth says the treatment she received at the Bake-Off® Contest made her feel like the Magic Kingdom was made magical just for her. "Mr. and Mrs. Pillsbury had the room right across from us," she says in awe. "And it was the first time I ate lobster."

Since then, Ruth has traveled from her home in Louisiana to Disney World 10 times in 13 years. But she admits that none of her personal Disney trips has come close to the magic of her first Bake-Off® Contest experience. "For a small-town hick like me," she says, "the whole experience was all-around amazing."

Chick-n-Broccoli Pot Pies

Linda Mowery Worthington, IN
Bake-Off® Contest 28, 1978
$25,000 One of Two Grand Prize Winners

Prep Time: 20 Minutes
Start to Finish: 45 Minutes
10 servings

1 can (12 oz) Pillsbury® Golden Layers®
  refrigerated flaky biscuits
⅔ cup shredded Cheddar or American
  cheese
⅔ cup crisp rice cereal
1 box (9 oz) frozen cut broccoli, thawed
1 cup cubed cooked chicken or turkey
1 can (10¾ oz) reduced-sodium
  condensed cream of chicken or
  mushroom soup
⅓ cup slivered or sliced almonds

1 Heat oven to 375°F. Separate dough into 10 biscuits. Place 1 biscuit in each of 10 ungreased muffin cups; firmly press in bottom and up sides, forming ½-inch rim over edge of each muffin cup. Spoon about 1 tablespoon each of cheese and cereal into each biscuit-lined cup. Press mixture into bottom of each cup.

2 Cut large pieces of broccoli in half. In large bowl, mix broccoli, chicken and soup. Spoon about ⅓ cup of chicken mixture over cereal in each cup. Cups will be full.* Sprinkle with almonds.

3 Bake 20 to 25 minutes or until edges of biscuits are deep golden brown.

* To make ahead, chicken mixture can be prepared to this point. Cover and refrigerate up to 2 hours. Sprinkle with almonds; bake as directed.

High Altitude (3500–6500 ft): No change.

1 Serving: Calories 220; Total Fat 10g (Saturated Fat 3g; Trans Fat 1.5g); Cholesterol 20mg; Sodium 560mg; Total Carbohydrate 20g (Dietary Fiber 1g) Exchanges: 1 Starch, ½ Other Carbohydrate, 1 Medium-Fat Meat, 1 Fat; Carbohydrate Choices: 1

Turkey–Sweet Potato Pot Pies

Dolly Craig Denver, CO
Bake-Off® Contest 41, 2004

Prep Time: 15 Minutes
Start to Finish: 55 Minutes
4 servings

1 can (15 oz) sweet potatoes, drained,
  cut into bite-size pieces (2 cups)
1½ cups cubed cooked turkey or
  chicken
1 cup frozen sweet peas (from 1-lb bag),
  thawed, drained*
3 tablespoons chopped sweet yellow
  onion
3 teaspoons curry powder
Salt and pepper to taste, if desired
1 can (18.6 oz) ready-to-serve chicken
  pot pie style soup
1 Pillsbury® refrigerated pie crust
  (from 15-oz box), softened as
  directed on box

1 Heat oven to 400°F. In large bowl, mix all ingredients except pie crust. Divide mixture evenly among 4 (1¼- to 2-cup) ungreased individual ramekins.**

2 Remove pie crust from pouch; place crust flat on cutting board. Cut crust into 4 quarters. Top each filled ramekin with 1 quarter crust. With kitchen scissors or knife, trim crust edges. Pinch and flute edge, filling in areas with trimmed pie crust pieces where needed. With knife, cut several small slits in crusts for steam to escape. Place ramekins on cookie sheet.

3 Bake 25 to 33 minutes or until filling is bubbly and crust is deep golden brown, covering crust edge with foil during last 10 to 15 minutes of baking to prevent excessive browning. Cool 5 minutes before serving.

* To quickly thaw frozen peas, place in colander or strainer; rinse with warm water until thawed. Drain well.

** A 1¼- to 1½-quart casserole can be substituted for ramekins. Place whole crust over filled casserole. Do not place casserole on cookie sheet.

High Altitude (3500–6500 ft): No change.

1 Serving: Calories 490; Total Fat 18g (Saturated Fat 6g; Trans Fat 0g); Cholesterol 60mg; Sodium 800mg; Total Carbohydrate 61g (Dietary Fiber 5g) Exchanges: 2½ Starch, 1½ Other Carbohydrate, 2 Lean Meat, 2 Fat; Carbohydrate Choices: 4

Turkey–Sweet Potato Pot Pies

Crafty Crescent Lasagna

Crafty Crescent Lasagna

Betty Taylor   Dallas, TX
Bake-Off® Contest 19, 1968
$5,000 Winner

> **Prep Time:** 30 Minutes
> **Start to Finish:** 1 Hour
> 8 servings

MEAT FILLING
½ lb pork sausage
½ lb ground beef
¾ cup chopped onions
1 tablespoon dried parsley flakes
½ teaspoon dried basil leaves
½ teaspoon dried oregano leaves
1 small clove garlic, finely chopped
Dash pepper
1 can (6 oz) tomato paste

CHEESE FILLING
¼ cup grated Parmesan cheese
1 cup creamed cottage cheese
1 egg

CRUST
2 cans (8 oz each) Pillsbury®
    refrigerated crescent dinner rolls
2 (7 × 4-inch) slices mozzarella cheese
1 tablespoon milk
1 tablespoon sesame seed

1   Heat oven to 375°F. In 10-inch skillet, cook sausage and beef until beef is brown; drain. Stir in remaining meat filling ingredients; simmer uncovered 5 minutes, stirring occasionally.

2   In small bowl, mix cheese filling ingredients. Unroll dough into 4 long rectangles. Place on ungreased cookie sheet with long sides overlapping ½ inch; firmly press edges and perforations to seal. Press or roll out to form 15 × 13-inch rectangle. Spoon half of meat filling mixture in 6-inch strip lengthwise down center of dough to within 1 inch of each end. Spoon cheese filling mixture over meat mixture; top with remaining meat mixture. Arrange mozzarella cheese slices over meat mixture. Fold shortest sides of dough 1 inch over filling. Fold long sides of dough tightly over filling, overlapping edges in center ¼ inch; firmly pinch center seam and ends to seal. Brush with milk; sprinkle with sesame seed.

3   Bake 23 to 27 minutes or until deep golden brown.

High Altitude (3500–6500 ft): Bake 26 to 30 minutes.

1 Serving: Calories 440; Total Fat 25g (Saturated Fat 10g; Trans Fat 3.5g); Cholesterol 70mg; Sodium 980mg; Total Carbohydrate 30g (Dietary Fiber 2g) Exchanges: 1½ Starch, ½ Other Carbohydrate, 2½ Medium-Fat Meat, 2½ Fat; Carbohydrate Choices: 2

Cheesy Biscuit Burger Ring

Carla Garnto   Byron, GA
Bake-Off® Contest 40, 2002

> **Prep Time:** 35 Minutes
> **Start to Finish:** 1 Hour 30 Minutes
> 16 servings

1 lb lean (at least 80%) ground beef
1 package (1.25 oz) taco seasoning mix
1 can (4.5 oz) chopped green chiles
½ cup water
¼ cup fat-free egg product or 1 egg, beaten
2 cups finely shredded Mexican cheese blend (8 oz)
2 cans (16.3 oz each) Pillsbury® Grands!® refrigerated buttermilk biscuits
1 cup chunky-style salsa

1   Heat oven to 375°F. Spray 12-cup fluted tube cake pan with cooking spray. In 10-inch skillet, cook beef over medium heat, stirring frequently, until thoroughly cooked; drain well. Stir in taco seasoning mix, chiles, water and egg product. Cook and stir 1 to 2 minutes or until mixture thickens. Stir in 1 cup of the cheese. Cool while shaping biscuits.

2   Separate dough into 16 biscuits. Split each biscuit to make 32 rounds. Press out each biscuit half to form 4-inch round. Place 1 rounded tablespoon beef mixture in center of each round. Bring up sides of dough over filling; pinch edges to seal. Place, seam side down, randomly in pan.

3   Bake 33 to 43 minutes or until dark golden brown. Cool in pan 5 minutes. If desired, line serving platter with leaf lettuce. Turn biscuit ring upside down over lettuce. Immediately sprinkle with remaining 1 cup cheese. Let stand 5 minutes to melt cheese. Cut into slices. Serve with salsa. If desired, garnish with pimiento-stuffed green olives, chopped green onions or fresh parsley.

High Altitude (3500–6500 ft): Bake 38 to 43 minutes.

1 Serving: Calories 300; Total Fat 16g (Saturated Fat 7g; Trans Fat 3.5g); Cholesterol 30mg; Sodium 1130mg; Total Carbohydrate 27g (Dietary Fiber 0g) Exchanges: 1½ Starch, ½ Other Carbohydrate, 1 Medium-Fat Meat, 2 Fat; Carbohydrate Choices: 2

Biscuit-Topped Italian Casserole

Robert Wick Altamonte Sprints, FL
Bake-Off® Contest 33, 1988

Prep Time: 50 Minutes
Start to Finish: 1 Hour 20 Minutes
10 servings

1 tablespoon vegetable oil, if desired
1 lb ground beef
½ cup chopped onion
¾ cup water
½ teaspoon salt, if desired
¼ teaspoon pepper
1 can (8 oz) tomato sauce
1 can (6 oz) tomato paste
2 cups shredded mozzarella cheese (8 oz)
1½ cups frozen mixed vegetables
    (from 1-lb bag), thawed
2 cans (12 oz each) Pillsbury® Golden
    Layers® refrigerated flaky biscuits
1 tablespoon butter or margarine, melted
½ teaspoon dried oregano leaves, crushed

1 Heat oven to 375°F. Grease 13 × 9-inch (3-quart) baking dish. In 10-inch skillet, heat oil until hot. Cook beef and onion in oil until beef is thoroughly cooked; drain. Stir in water, salt, pepper, tomato sauce and tomato paste; simmer 15 minutes, stirring occasionally. Place half of hot meat mixture in baking dish; sprinkle with ⅔ cup of the cheese. Spoon mixed vegetables evenly over cheese; sprinkle an additional ⅔ cup cheese over vegetables. Spoon remaining hot meat mixture evenly over cheese and vegetables; sprinkle with remaining ⅔ cup cheese.

2 Separate dough into 20 biscuits. Separate each biscuit into 3 layers. Arrange layers over hot meat mixture, overlapping, in 3 rows of 20 layers each. Gently brush biscuits with butter; sprinkle with oregano.

3 Bake 22 to 27 minutes or until biscuit topping is golden brown.

High Altitude (3500–6500 ft): Bake 27 to 32 minutes.

1 Serving: Calories 410; Total Fat 20g (Saturated Fat 8g; Trans Fat 3.5g); Cholesterol 45mg; Sodium 1130mg; Total Carbohydrate 38g (Dietary Fiber 3g) Exchanges: 2 Starch, ½ Other Carbohydrate, 2 Medium-Fat Meat, 1½ Fat; Carbohydrate Choices: 2½

Hungry Boys' Casserole

Mira Walilko Detroit, MI
Bake-Off® Contest 15, 1963
$25,000 Grand Prize Winner

Prep Time: 40 Minutes
Start to Finish: 1 Hour 5 Minutes
8 servings

CASSEROLE
1½ lb ground beef
1 cup chopped celery
½ cup chopped onion
½ cup chopped green bell pepper
1 clove garlic, finely chopped
1 can (6 oz) tomato paste
¾ cup water
1 teaspoon paprika
½ teaspoon salt
1 can (16 oz) baked beans, undrained
2 cups garbanzo beans, drained
    (from 19-oz can)

BISCUITS
1½ cups Pillsbury BEST® all-purpose
    or unbleached flour
2 teaspoons baking powder
½ teaspoon salt
¼ cup butter or margarine
½ to ¾ cup milk
2 tablespoons sliced stuffed green olives
1 tablespoon slivered almonds

1 In 12-inch skillet, cook beef, celery, onion, bell pepper and garlic over medium-high heat, stirring frequently, until beef is browned and thoroughly cooked and vegetables are crisp-tender. Drain. Reduce heat to low. Stir in tomato paste, water, paprika and ½ teaspoon salt. Add baked beans and garbanzo beans; simmer while preparing biscuits, stirring occasionally.

2 Heat oven to 425°F. Lightly spoon flour into measuring cup; level off. In large bowl, mix flour, baking powder and ½ teaspoon salt. With pastry blender or fork, cut in butter until mixture looks like coarse crumbs. Gradually stir in enough milk until mixture leaves sides of bowl and forms a soft, moist dough.

3 On floured surface, gently knead dough 8 times. Roll dough to ¼-inch thickness. Cut with floured 2½-inch doughnut cutter. Reserve dough centers. Reroll dough to cut additional biscuits.

4 Reserve ½ cup of hot beef mixture. Pour remaining beef mixture into ungreased 13 × 9-inch (3-quart) glass baking dish. Arrange biscuits without centers over beef mixture. Stir olives and almonds into reserved ½ cup beef mixture; spoon into center of each biscuit. Top each with biscuit centers.

5 Bake 15 to 25 minutes or until biscuits are golden brown.

High Altitude (3500–6500 ft): No change.

1 Serving: Calories 460; Total Fat 18g (Saturated Fat 8g; Trans Fat 1g); Cholesterol 75mg; Sodium 1020mg; Total Carbohydrate 47g (Dietary Fiber 8g) Exchanges: 2½ Starch, ½ Other Carbohydrate, 2½ Medium-Fat Meat, 1 Fat; Carbohydrate Choices: 3

California Casserole

Margaret Hatheway
Santa Barbara, CA
Bake-Off® Contest 8, 1956
$25,000 Grand Prize Winner

Prep Time: 1 Hour
Start to Finish: 1 Hour 25 Minutes
10 servings

CASSEROLE

⅓ cup Pillsbury BEST® all-purpose flour
1 teaspoon paprika
2 lb boneless veal, cut into 1-inch pieces
¼ cup vegetable oil
½ teaspoon salt
⅛ teaspoon pepper
1 cup water
1 can (10 ¾ oz) condensed cream of chicken soup
1½ cups water
1 jar (16 oz) small onions (1½ cups), drained

DUMPLINGS

2 cups Pillsbury BEST® all-purpose flour
4 teaspoons baking powder
1 tablespoon poppy seed, if desired
1 teaspoon instant minced onion
1 teaspoon celery seed
1 teaspoon poultry seasoning
¼ teaspoon salt
¼ cup vegetable oil
¾ to 1 cup milk
2 tablespoons butter or margarine, melted
½ cup dry bread crumbs

SAUCE

1 can (10¾ oz) condensed cream of chicken soup
1 cup sour cream
¼ cup milk

International Culinary Diplomacy

Part of Margaret Hatheway's Grand Prize in the 8th Bake-Off® Contest was a Cook's Tour of Europe, with stops in Rome, Paris and London. She learned how to make steak and kidney pie in England, crepes in France and pasta in Italy. In return Margaret taught all the chefs she met how to make her prize-winning California Casserole. They inquired about the casseroles of the remaining states, but Margaret replied that that was the work of future generations.

1 In small bowl or plastic bag, mix ⅓ cup all-purpose flour and the paprika. Add veal; coat well with flour mixture. In 10-inch skillet, heat ¼ cup oil over medium-high heat. Cook veal in oil until browned. Add ½ teaspoon salt, the pepper and 1 cup water. Heat to boiling. Reduce heat; simmer uncovered about 30 minutes or until veal is tender. Transfer veal mixture to ungreased 13 × 9-inch (3-quart) baking dish or 3-quart casserole.

2 In same skillet, heat 1 can cream of chicken soup and 1½ cups water to boiling, stirring constantly. Pour over veal mixture in baking dish. Add onions; mix well.

3 Heat oven to 425°F. In large bowl, mix 2 cups flour, the baking powder, poppy seed, minced onion, celery seed, poultry seasoning and

¼ teaspoon salt. Add ¼ cup oil and enough milk so that, when stirred, dry ingredients are just moistened.

4 In small bowl, combine butter and bread crumbs. Drop rounded tablespoons of dough into crumb mixture; roll to coat well. Arrange dumplings over warm veal mixture. Bake 20 to 25 minutes or until dumplings are deep golden brown.

5 Meanwhile, in 2-quart saucepan, mix sauce ingredients. Heat just to boiling. Reduce heat; simmer 2 to 3 minutes, stirring frequently, until hot. Serve sauce with casserole and dumplings.

High Altitude (3500–6500 ft): No change.

1 Serving: Calories 500; Total Fat 27g (Saturated Fat 9g; Trans Fat 0g); Cholesterol 105mg; Sodium 960mg; Total Carbohydrate 37g (Dietary Fiber 2g) Exchanges: 2 Starch, ½ Other Carbohydrate, 3 Lean Meat, 3 Fat; Carbohydrate Choices: 2½

Pineapple–Black Bean Enchiladas

Pineapple–Black Bean Enchiladas

Mary Iovinelli Buescher Bloomington, MN
Bake-Off® Contest 42, 2006
$10,000 America's Favorite Recipe
Winner and $10,000 3-A-Day™ Dairy
Award Winner

Prep Time: 30 Minutes
Start to Finish: 1 Hour 10 Minutes
8 servings

2 teaspoons vegetable oil
1 large yellow onion, chopped
    (about 1 cup)
1 medium red bell pepper, chopped
    (about 1 cup)
1 can (20 oz) pineapple tidbits in juice,
    drained, ⅓ cup juice reserved
1 can (15 oz) black beans, drained,
    rinsed
1 can (4.5 oz) chopped green chiles
1 teaspoon salt
½ cup chopped fresh cilantro
3 cups shredded reduced-fat Cheddar
    cheese (12 oz)
1 can (10 oz) mild enchilada sauce
8 whole wheat flour tortillas (8 or 9 inch)
½ cup reduced-fat sour cream
8 teaspoons chopped fresh cilantro

1 Heat oven to 350°F. Spray
13 × 9-inch (3-quart) glass baking
dish with cooking spray. In 12-
inch nonstick skillet, heat oil over
medium heat. Cook onion and bell
pepper in oil 4 to 5 minutes or
until softened. Stir in pineapple,
beans, green chiles and salt. Cook
and stir until hot. Remove skillet
from heat. Stir in ½ cup cilantro
and 2 cups of the cheese.

2 Spoon and spread 1 tablespoon
enchilada sauce onto each tortilla.
Spoon about ¾ cup vegetable
mixture over sauce on each. Roll up
tortillas; place seam side down in
baking dish.

3 In small bowl, mix reserved
⅓ cup pineapple juice and remaining enchilada sauce; pour over
entire surface of enchiladas in dish.
Sprinkle with remaining 1 cup
cheese. Spray sheet of foil large
enough to cover baking dish with
cooking spray; place sprayed side
down over baking dish, and seal
tightly.

4 Bake 35 to 40 minutes, removing foil last 5 to 10 minutes of bake
time, until cheese is melted and
sauce is bubbly. Top each baked
enchilada with 1 tablespoon sour
cream and 1 teaspoon cilantro.

High Altitude (3500–6500 ft): Bake
40 to 45 minutes, removing foil last
5 to 10 minutes of bake time.

1 Serving: Calories 340; Total Fat 7g (Saturated Fat 3g;
Trans Fat 0g); Cholesterol 15mg; Sodium 1120mg;
Total Carbohydrate 49g (Dietary Fiber 9g) Exchanges:
2 Starch, 1 Other Carbohydrate, 2 Lean Meat;
Carbohydrate Choices: 3

Healthy…and Delicious!

Who says healthy food can't taste good? Mary Iovinelli Buescher
developed her enchilada recipe for her best friend's bridal shower. A
clinical dietitian, Mary wanted to please her friend—a vegetarian—and
satisfy guests accustomed to eating meat. Her recipe, which offers both
sweet and spicy flavors, was a big hit. Mary describes it as "an easy-
to-make recipe with so much flavor you forget it is healthy."
The contest judges agreed, awarding her recipe $10,000
category winner, plus Mary earned a second $10,000
prize when consumers voting online ranked it as their
favorite recipe of the 42nd contest.

Chicken Cheese Enchiladas

Barbie Lee Tavernier, FL
Bake-Off® Contest 40, 2002
$2,000 Winner

Prep Time: 15 Minutes
Start to Finish: 40 Minutes
6 servings

1 package (1.25 oz) taco seasoning mix
1 tablespoon olive or vegetable oil
½ cup water
1 lb boneless skinless chicken breasts, cut into bite-size pieces or strips
3 cups shredded Monterey Jack cheese (12 oz)
⅓ cup chopped fresh cilantro
½ teaspoon salt
1 container (15 oz) ricotta cheese
1 can (4.5 oz) chopped green chiles
1 egg
1 jar (16 oz) chunky style salsa
1 package (10.5 oz) flour tortillas for soft tacos & fajitas (6 inch)

1 Heat oven to 350°F. In resealable food-storage plastic bag, mix taco seasoning mix, oil and ¼ cup of the water. Add chicken pieces; turn to mix. Refrigerate 5 minutes or up to 12 hours.

2 In medium bowl, mix 2½ cups of the Monterey Jack cheese, the cilantro, salt, ricotta cheese, chiles and egg.

3 Heat 10-inch nonstick skillet over medium-high heat until hot. Add chicken with marinade; cook and stir 5 to 10 minutes or until chicken is no longer pink in center.

4 In ungreased 13 × 9-inch (3-quart) glass baking dish, mix ½ cup of the salsa and remaining ¼ cup water. Spread evenly in bottom of baking dish. Spoon ⅓ cup cheese mixture down center of each tortilla. Top with chicken; roll up. Place filled tortillas, seam side down, over salsa mixture in baking dish. Drizzle enchiladas with remaining salsa. Sprinkle with remaining ½ cup Monterey Jack cheese.

5 Bake 20 to 25 minutes or until cheese is melted.

High Altitude (3500–6500 ft): Heat oven to 375°F. Bake 25 to 30 minutes. Cover with foil during last 10 to 15 minutes of baking if tortillas begin to dry out.

1 Serving: Calories 640; Total Fat 33g (Saturated Fat 17g; Trans Fat 2g); Cholesterol 155mg; Sodium 2340mg; Total Carbohydrate 40g (Dietary Fiber 2g) Exchanges: 1½ Starch, 1 Other Carbohydrate, 5½ Medium-Fat Meat, 1 Fat; Carbohydrate Choices: 2½

Cajun Red Beans and Rice

Del Tinsley Nashville, TN
Bake-Off® Contest 35, 1992

Prep Time: 40 Minutes
Start to Finish: 40 Minutes
6 servings

¾ lb chopped cooked hickory-smoked andouille sausage, skinned, or hot Italian sausage
1 cup chopped onions
1 cup uncooked regular rice
2 cups water
2 cans (15.5 oz each) red beans, drained
1 can (8 oz) tomato sauce
½ cup diced green bell pepper
½ cup diced yellow bell pepper
2 cloves garlic, finely chopped
1 teaspoon dried oregano leaves
1 teaspoon dried thyme leaves
1 tablespoon dry sherry, if desired
⅓ cup sliced green onions
Red pepper sauce

From the Kitchen, With Love

Jazz great Louis Armstrong signed his letters "red beans and ricely yours," because the dish was so close to his heart. Red beans and rice is a fiercely adored comfort food for those that grew up eating it. Del Tinsley has long known the value of simple recipes in a busy kitchen. "From the time I started walking," she says, "I followed Nana (my grandmother) around the kitchen like a little puppy dog. I never thought I couldn't cook, I just imitated her." From underfoot Del learned how to make dinner, with love.

1 In 10-inch skillet, brown sausage and onions over medium-high heat 3 minutes, stirring frequently; drain. Cook rice in water as directed on package.

2 Stir into sausage mixture the beans, tomato sauce, bell peppers, garlic, oregano and thyme. Reduce heat to low; simmer 15 minutes, stirring occasionally. Stir in sherry. Serve over rice; garnish with green onions. Serve with red pepper sauce.

High Altitude (3500–6500 ft): In step 2, cover the skillet while simmering.

1 Serving (1 cup meat mixture and ⅔ cup rice): Calories 460 (Calories from Fat 110); Total Fat 12g; Cholesterol 25mg; Sodium 1350mg; Total Carbohydrate 64g (Dietary Fiber 10g) Exchanges: 3 Starch, 1 Other Carbohydrate, 1 Vegetable, 1½ Lean Meat, 1 Fat; Carbohydrate Choices: 4

Chicken with Black Bean and Corn Salsa

Carol Blake   El Dorado Hills, CA
Bake-Off® Contest 41, 2004

Prep Time: 40 Minutes
Start to Finish: 40 Minutes
6 servings

GARNISH
2 (6-inch) corn tortillas
Cooking spray
Reserved orange juice mixture
2 tablespoons chopped fresh cilantro

SALSA
½ cup orange juice
2 tablespoons olive oil
1 tablespoon Dijon mustard
1 tablespoon honey
¼ teaspoon ground red pepper (cayenne)
⅛ teaspoon ground cumin
1 can (15 oz) black beans, drained
1 can (11 oz) white shoepeg corn, drained
1 medium tomato, finely chopped (¾ cup)

CHICKEN
1 teaspoon salt
6 boneless skinless chicken breasts
2 tablespoons olive oil
1 medium red bell pepper, cut into strips
1 medium green bell pepper, cut into strips
2 medium green onions, sliced (2 tablespoons)
3 cloves garlic, finely chopped
¼ cup dry white wine
1 tablespoon chopped fresh thyme or ¼ teaspoon dried thyme leaves

1 Heat oven to 400°F. Cut each tortilla in half; cut each half crosswise into ¼-inch strips. Place on ungreased cookie sheet; spray strips with cooking spray. Bake 8 to 10 minutes until lightly toasted, stirring once halfway through baking. Set aside.

2 In medium bowl, mix orange juice, 2 tablespoons oil, the mustard, honey, ground red pepper and cumin.

In small bowl, reserve 6 tablespoons orange juice mixture for garnish. To remaining mixture, stir in beans, corn and tomato.

3 Sprinkle salt on both sides of each chicken breast. In 12-inch nonstick skillet, heat 1 tablespoon of the oil over medium-high heat. Cook chicken in oil 5 to 8 minutes on each side or until chicken is fork-tender and juice is clear when center of thickest part is cut (170°F). Remove chicken from skillet; place on plate, and cover to keep warm.

4 To same skillet, add remaining 1 tablespoon oil. Add both bell peppers, onions and garlic; cook and stir 1 minute. Add wine and thyme; cook and stir 1 minute longer.

5 To serve, spread 1 tablespoon reserved orange juice mixture on each serving plate. Cut each chicken breast diagonally into slices; place over mixture on plates. Spoon bell pepper mixture over chicken. Top each with ½ cup salsa. Sprinkle each with 1 teaspoon cilantro. Top each with tortilla strips.

High Altitude (3500–6500 ft): No change.

1 Serving: Calories 420; Total Fat 15g (Saturated Fat 2.5g; Trans Fat 0g); Cholesterol 75mg; Sodium 870mg; Total Carbohydrate 38g (Dietary Fiber 9g) Exchanges: 1 Starch, 1 Other Carbohydrate, 1 Vegetable, 4 Very Lean Meat, 2½ Fat; Carbohydrate Choices: 2½

Baked Sonoran Chicken

Tori Johnson   Gilbert, AZ
Bake-Off® Contest 42, 2006

> **Prep Time:** 1 Hour
> **Start to Finish:** 1 Hour
> 4 servings

4 large boneless skinless chicken
  breasts (5 to 6 oz each)*
2 cups crispy horn-shaped corn snacks,
  crushed**
1 can (4.5 oz) chopped green chiles,
  drained
6 oz queso fresco (Mexican cheese),
  cut into 4 equal slices
Salt and pepper, if desired
1 cup frozen whole kernel corn
  (from 1-lb bag), thawed
1 tablespoon olive oil
⅓ cup roasted red bell peppers (from a jar)
1 cup whipping cream
½ cup water
2 tablespoons unsalted or regular butter
  or margarine
2 teaspoons finely chopped fresh garlic
1 chicken-flavored bouillon cube
⅔ cup uncooked regular rice
1⅓ cups water
4 flour tortillas (10 to 12 inch)
2 tablespoons chopped fresh cilantro

1   Heat oven to 425°F. Line cookie
sheet with foil. Place each chicken
breast, smooth side down, between
pieces of plastic wrap or waxed
paper; gently pound with flat side
of meat mallet or rolling pin until
about ¼ inch thick.

2   Over each chicken breast,
sprinkle ¼ cup crushed corn snacks
and ¼ of the green chiles; place
1 slice cheese in center. Fold ends of
chicken over and tuck in sides; secure
with toothpicks. Sprinkle with salt

and pepper. Place seam side down
on one side of cookie sheet. In small
bowl, toss thawed corn with oil.
Place corn on other side of cookie
sheet. Bake 20 minutes until
chicken is no longer pink in center.

3   Meanwhile, in blender, place
roasted peppers, whipping cream
and ½ cup water. Cover; blend on
high speed 15 seconds or until
smooth. In 2-quart saucepan, melt
butter over medium heat. Add
garlic; cook and stir 1 minute. Add
pepper mixture and bouillon cube;
heat to boiling. Cook about 15 minutes, stirring constantly, until sauce
is reduced and thickened.

4   Cook rice in 1⅓ cups water as
directed on package. Remove chicken
from cookie sheet; place on cutting
board. Let stand 5 minutes. Cut
chicken into ¼-inch-thick slices.

5   In 12-inch skillet, heat each tortilla over high heat until blistered on
each side; place on individual dinner
plates. Place ½ cup rice on one half
of each tortilla; fan slices of 1 chicken
breast leaning on rice. Top chicken
on each evenly with roasted pepper
sauce, roasted corn and cilantro.

*Each chicken breast must weigh at least
5 ounces for success of recipe.*
**To crush corn snacks, place in
resealable food-storage plastic bag; seal
bag and crush with rolling pin.*

High Altitude (3500–6500 ft): No change.

1 Serving: Calories 920; Total Fat 45g (Saturated Fat
24g; Trans Fat 2g); Cholesterol 180mg; Sodium 1790mg;
Total Carbohydrate 80g (Dietary Fiber 4g) Exchanges:
4 Starch, 1 Other Carbohydrate, 5 Very Lean Meat,
8 Fat; Carbohydrate Choices: 5

Chicken Curry Stir-Fry

P.S. Kenney   Denver, CO
Bake-Off® Contest 36, 1994
$10,000 Winner

> **Prep Time:** 25 Minutes
> **Start to Finish:** 25 Minutes
> 6 servings

2 cups uncooked regular long-grain
  white rice
4 cups water
¼ cup olive or vegetable oil
1 medium onion, chopped (½ cup)
4 boneless skinless chicken breasts,
  cut into 1-inch cubes
2 tablespoons water
2 teaspoons curry powder
¼ teaspoon salt
⅛ teaspoon pepper
⅓ cup peanuts, if desired
⅓ cup chutney
2 tablespoons coconut
2 tablespoons dried currants
2 cups frozen mixed vegetables
1 to 2 red bell peppers, cut into strips

1   Cook rice in water as directed
on package.

2   Meanwhile, in 10-inch skillet,
heat oil over medium-high heat
until hot. Cook and stir onion in
oil stir 2 minutes. Add chicken,
2 tablespoons water, the curry
powder, salt and pepper; cook and
stir 6 to 8 minutes or until chicken
is no longer pink in center.

3   Add peanuts, chutney, coconut,
currants and frozen mixed vegetables; cook and stir 7 to 8 minutes or
until vegetables are crisp-tender.

4   To serve, spoon rice onto serving
platter. Top with chicken mixture.
Garnish with bell pepper strips.

High Altitude (3500–6500 ft): No change.

1 Serving: Calories 510; Total Fat 13g (Saturated Fat 3g;
Trans Fat 0g); Cholesterol 50mg; Sodium 180mg;
Total Carbohydrate 72g (Dietary Fiber 4g) Exchanges:
3 Starch, 1½ Other Carbohydrate, 1 Vegetable, 2 Very
Lean Meat, 2 Fat; Carbohydrate Choices: 5

Chicken Curry Stir-Fry

Orange-Cumin Chicken and Vegetables

Thai Curry Chicken and Vegetables

Manika Misra   North Miami Beach, FL
Bake-Off® Contest 35, 1992
$2,000 Winner

Prep Time: 1 Hour
Start to Finish: 1 Hour
5 servings

1¾ cups uncooked regular long-grain white rice
3¼ cups water
2 tablespoons vegetable oil
1 teaspoon five-spice powder
½ to 1½ teaspoons salt
½ teaspoon monosodium glutamate, if desired
½ teaspoon garlic powder
½ teaspoon ground ginger
½ teaspoon pepper
½ teaspoon ground red pepper (cayenne)
1 tablespoon soy sauce
1½ lb boneless skinless chicken breasts, cut into 1-inch pieces
1 cup chicken broth
3 teaspoons curry powder
2 tablespoons rice vinegar or vinegar
1 can (14 oz) coconut milk (not cream of coconut)
1 cup ready-to-eat baby-cut carrots
2 cups frozen broccoli florets
1 can (8 oz) sliced water chestnuts, drained

1   Cook rice in water as directed on package. Cover to keep warm.

2   In 10-inch skillet or wok, heat oil over medium-high heat until hot. Stir in five-spice powder, salt, monosodium glutamate, garlic powder, ginger, pepper, ground red pepper and soy sauce. Add chicken; cook and stir 5 to 8 minutes or until coated with seasonings, lightly browned and no longer pink in center. Stir in broth, curry powder, vinegar, coconut milk and carrots. Heat to boiling. Reduce heat; simmer uncovered 20 to 25 minutes, stirring occasionally, until carrots are tender.

3   Stir in broccoli and water chestnuts. Heat to boiling; cook 3 to 5 minutes or until vegetables are crisp-tender. Serve over rice.

High Altitude (3500–6500 ft): No change.

1 Serving (2 cups chicken and vegetables, 1 cup rice): Calories 690; Total Fat 25g (Saturated Fat 15g; Trans Fat 0g); Cholesterol 80mg; Sodium 1530mg; Total Carbohydrate 75g (Dietary Fiber 5g) Exchanges: 3½ Starch, 1 Other Carbohydrate, 1 Vegetable, 4 Very Lean Meat, 4 Fat; Carbohydrate Choices: 5

Orange-Cumin Chicken and Vegetables

Arnold Shulman   Sedona, AZ
Bake-Off® Contest 39, 2000

Prep Time: 30 Minutes
Start to Finish: 30 Minutes
4 servings

2 cups uncooked instant white rice, if desired
2 cups water, if desired
1 teaspoon coriander
¼ teaspoon salt
¼ teaspoon coarse ground black pepper
4 boneless skinless chicken breasts
¼ cup salsa
1 teaspoon cornstarch
½ teaspoon cumin
1 tablespoon vegetable oil
1 red bell pepper, cut into thin strips
1 box (9 oz) frozen sugar snap peas
¾ cup orange juice

1   Cook rice in water as directed on package. Cover to keep warm. Meanwhile, in small bowl, mix coriander, salt and pepper. Rub mixture on all sides of chicken breasts. Discard any remaining seasoning mixture. In another small bowl, mix salsa, cornstarch and cumin.

2   In 10-inch skillet, heat oil over medium-high heat until hot. Add chicken; cook about 2 minutes on each side or until browned. Add bell pepper and sugar snap peas; cook and stir 4 minutes. Reduce heat to medium-low. Add 2 tablespoons of the orange juice; cover and cook about 6 minutes or until chicken is fork-tender and juice is clear when thickest part is cut (170°F), and vegetables are crisp-tender. Remove chicken from skillet; cover to keep warm.

3   Add salsa mixture and remaining orange juice to skillet; mix well. Heat to boiling. Cook until slightly thickened, stirring occasionally. Cut chicken crosswise into ½-inch slices. Arrange chicken on individual plates. Spoon vegetable mixture over chicken. Serve with rice.

High Altitude (3500–6500 ft): In step 2, reduce heat to medium. After adding orange juice, cover and cook about 8 minutes.

1 Serving: Calories 240; Total Fat 8g (Saturated Fat 1.5g; Trans Fat 0g); Cholesterol 75mg; Sodium 320mg; Total Carbohydrate 14g (Dietary Fiber 3g) Exchanges: ½ Other Carbohydrate, 1 Vegetable, 4 Very Lean Meat, 1 Fat; Carbohydrate Choices: 1

Chicken and Broccoli Cavatappi

Joni Busch Rogers, MN
Bake-Off® Contest 41, 2004

Prep Time: 30 Minutes
Start to Finish: 30 Minutes
6 servings (1½ cups each)

8 oz (2⅔ cups) uncooked cavatappi
  pasta
1 tablespoon oil (from jar of sun-dried
  tomatoes)
1 lb chicken tenderloins, cut in half
  crosswise
2 tablespoons finely chopped green
  onions (2 medium)
3 teaspoons ground mustard
2 teaspoons finely chopped garlic
¼ cup chopped drained oil-packed
  sun-dried tomatoes (from 7-oz jar)
1 bag (24 oz) frozen broccoli in a three
  cheese sauce
1 container (6.5 oz) garlic-and-herb
  cream cheese spread
¼ cup milk
Salt and pepper to taste, if desired

1 In 4½- or 5-quart Dutch oven, cook pasta as directed on package. Drain; rinse well. Return to Dutch oven; cover to keep warm.

2 Meanwhile, in 12-inch skillet, heat oil over medium-high heat until hot. Add chicken; cook and stir 2 to 4 minutes or until chicken begins to brown. Stir in onions, mustard and garlic. Cook until garlic is softened. Stir in tomatoes until blended. Cook 2 to 3 minutes, stirring occasionally, until chicken is no longer pink in center. If necessary, drain off any liquid.

3 Add frozen broccoli with sauce chips; cook about 4 minutes, stirring occasionally, until sauce chips have melted. Stir in cream cheese spread. Add milk; cook about 2 minutes, stirring constantly, until well blended and hot.

4 Gently stir broccoli mixture into cooked pasta to coat. Salt and pepper to taste. Pour into serving bowl.

High Altitude (3500–6500 ft): If after stirring in cream cheese spread, mixture is too thick, increase milk up to ½ cup; cook 4 to 5 minutes, stirring constantly.

1 Serving: Calories 520; Total Fat 19g (Saturated Fat 9g; Trans Fat 0g); Cholesterol 80mg; Sodium 770mg; Total Carbohydrate 54g (Dietary Fiber 5g) Exchanges: 2 Starch, 1 Other Carbohydrate, 2 Vegetable, 3 Very Lean Meat, 3 Fat; Carbohydrate Choices: 3½

Chicken Broccoli Stroganoff

Patricia Kiewiet La Grange, IL
Bake-Off® Contest 33, 1988

Prep Time: 30 Minutes
Start to Finish: 30 Minutes
6 servings

2 cups frozen cut broccoli
  (from 1-lb bag)
1 tablespoon butter or margarine
¼ cup chopped onion
3 tablespoons Pillsbury BEST®
  all-purpose flour
1 can (10½ oz) condensed chicken
  broth
2 cups cubed cooked chicken*
1 jar (2.5 oz) sliced mushrooms, drained
1 container (8 oz) sour cream (1 cup)
Hot cooked noodles
Chopped fresh parsley

1 Cook broccoli in microwave as directed on bag until crisp-tender. Drain; set aside.

2 In 2-quart microwavable casserole, microwave butter on High about 20 seconds or until melted. Add onion; toss to coat. Cover with microwavable plastic wrap. Microwave on High about 2 minutes or until crisp-tender. Add flour; blend well. Using wire whisk, stir broth into onion mixture; blend well.

3 Microwave on High 4 to 6 minutes or until mixture thickens and bubbles, stirring once halfway through cooking.** Stir in chicken, cooked broccoli, mushrooms and sour cream. Microwave uncovered on High 3 to 5 minutes or until mixture is hot and bubbles around edges, stirring once halfway through cooking. Serve over noodles; garnish with parsley.

Cooked turkey or ham can be substituted for chicken.
**For compact microwave ovens under 600 watts, microwave broth-onion mixture on High 7 to 8 minutes or until mixture thickens and bubbles, stirring once halfway through cooking. Continue as directed above.*

High Altitude (3500–6500 ft): In step 2, add ¼ cup water with broth. In step 3, increase second microwave time to 5 to 7 minutes.

1 Serving: Calories 250; Total Fat 16g (Saturated Fat 8g; Trans Fat 0.5g); Cholesterol 70mg; Sodium 430mg; Total Carbohydrate 8g (Dietary Fiber 2g) Exchanges: 1 Vegetable, 2½ Lean Meat, 1½ Fat; Carbohydrate Choices: ½

Chuck Wagon Cheeseburger Skillet

Rosemary Warmuth   Wheeling, WV
Bake-Off® Contest 40, 2002

Prep Time: 15 Minutes
Start to Finish: 40 Minutes
5 servings

4 slices bacon
1 lb lean (at least 80%) ground beef
3 tablespoons chopped onion
3 tablespoons vegetable oil
2½ cups frozen hash-brown potatoes, thawed
1 can (11 oz) vacuum-packed whole kernel corn with red and green peppers, drained
1 can (4.5 oz) chopped green chiles, drained
½ cup barbecue sauce
2 cups shredded Cheddar cheese (8 oz)
¼ teaspoon salt, if desired
¼ teaspoon pepper, if desired
1 can (16.3 oz) Pillsbury® Grands!® refrigerated buttermilk biscuits or reduced-fat buttermilk biscuits

1   Heat oven to 400°F. Cook bacon until crisp. Drain on paper towel; crumble. Set aside. In 12-inch cast-iron or ovenproof skillet, cook beef and onion over medium heat, stirring frequently, until beef is thoroughly cooked; drain. Place beef mixture in medium bowl; cover to keep warm.

2   In same skillet, heat oil over medium-high heat until hot. Add potatoes; cook 3 to 5 minutes, stirring constantly, until browned. Stir in cooked beef, corn, chiles, barbecue sauce, cheese, salt and pepper. Cook until hot, stirring occasionally. Sprinkle with bacon.

3   Separate dough into 8 biscuits. Arrange biscuits over hot mixture. Bake 16 to 24 minutes or until biscuits are deep golden brown and bottoms are no longer doughy.

High Altitude (3500–6500 ft): No change.

1 Serving: Calories 940; Total Fat 50g (Saturated Fat 20g; Trans Fat 6g); Cholesterol 110mg; Sodium 2280mg; Total Carbohydrate 83g (Dietary Fiber 4g) Exchanges: 3 ½ Starch, 2 Other Carbohydrate, 4 Medium-Fat Meat, 5½ Fat; Carbohydrate Choices: 5½

Weeknight Beef Burgundy

Susan O'Connor   Tequestas, FL
Bake-Off® Contest 41, 2004

Prep Time: 30 Minutes
Start to Finish: 30 Minutes
6 servings (1¾ cups each)

RICE
3 cups uncooked instant white rice
3 cups water

BEEF BURGUNDY
6 tablespoons butter or margarine
1½ cups sliced fresh mushrooms (4 oz)
½ cup chopped onion (1 medium)
⅓ cup finely chopped fresh parsley
2 cans (18.8 oz each) ready-to-serve sirloin steak & vegetables soup
⅔ cup dry red wine
2½ tablespoons cornstarch
⅛ teaspoon pepper
1 can (14.5 oz) sliced carrots, drained

1   Cook rice in water as directed on package.

2   Meanwhile, in 12-inch nonstick skillet, melt butter over medium-high heat. Cook mushrooms, onion and parsley in butter 7 to 10 minutes, stirring frequently, until vegetables are tender.

3   Stir in both cans of soup. Reduce heat to low; cook, stirring occasionally, until hot.

4   In small bowl, mix wine, cornstarch and pepper until smooth. Increase heat to high; stir wine mixture into vegetables, cooking and stirring until mixture boils. Reduce heat to medium; cook about 1 minute, stirring constantly, until mixture thickens slightly. Add carrots; cook 1 to 2 minutes, stirring frequently, until mixture is well blended and hot. Serve over rice.

High Altitude (3500–6500 ft): Add 2 tablespoons water to wine mixture. Over high heat, stir wine mixture into vegetables, cooking and stirring until mixture boils. Reduce heat to medium; cook 2 to 3 minutes, stirring constantly, until mixture thickens slightly.

1 Serving: Calories 460; Total Fat 13g (Saturated Fat 8g; Trans Fat 0g); Cholesterol 45mg; Sodium 920mg; Total Carbohydrate 70g (Dietary Fiber 3g) Exchanges: 3 Starch, 1 Other Carbohydrate, 2 Vegetable, 2½ Fat; Carbohydrate Choices: 4½

Taco Steak Pasta

Taco Steak Pasta

Kathi Manzagol   Monterey, CA
Bake-Off® Contest 42, 2006

Prep Time: 30 Minutes
Start to Finish: 30 Minutes
4 servings (1¼ cups each)

1 tablespoon vegetable oil
1 lb boneless lean beef sirloin steak,
   cut into bite-size strips
2¾ cups hot water
½ cup milk
1 box (7.1 oz) cheesy beef taco
   skillet-meal mix for hamburger
½ cup finely chopped red bell pepper
½ teaspoon ground chipotle chiles
¼ cup whipping cream
1 can (11 oz) vacuum-packed super
   sweet yellow and white corn,
   drained
½ cup sliced almonds

1   In 10- or 12-inch skillet, heat oil
over medium-high heat. Cook and
stir beef strips in oil until browned;
drain. Stir in hot water, milk, sauce
mix and uncooked pasta. Increase
heat to high; heat to boiling, stirring occasionally. Reduce heat to
medium-low; cover and simmer
about 11 minutes, stirring occasionally, until pasta is tender (sauce
will thicken as it stands).

2   Stir bell pepper, ground chipotle
chiles, whipping cream and corn into
pasta mixture. Cook about 2 minutes, stirring occasionally, until hot.
Remove from heat. Sprinkle with
almonds.

High Altitude (3500–6500 ft): No change.

1 Serving: Calories 530; Total Fat 20g (Saturated Fat 5g;
Trans Fat 0g); Cholesterol 80mg; Sodium 1240mg;
Total Carbohydrate 53g (Dietary Fiber 4g) Exchanges:
3 Starch, ½ Other Carbohydrate, 4 Lean Meat, 1 Fat;
Carbohydrate Choices: 3 ½

Pork Chop Skillet and Confetti Salsa

Conchita Smith   Lomita, CA
Bake-Off® Contest 38, 1998

Prep Time: 20 Minutes
Start to Finish: 30 Minutes
5 servings

PORK CHOPS
5 boneless pork loin chops (1¼ lb)
½ teaspoon salt
1 cup water
1 can (14 oz) chicken broth
1½ cups uncooked regular long-grain
   white rice
1 cup chunky style salsa

CONFETTI SALSA
1 can (11 oz) vacuum-packed whole
   kernel corn with red and green
   peppers, drained
1 avocado, pitted, peeled and chopped
1 papaya, peeled, seeded and chopped
1 tablespoon olive or vegetable oil
4 teaspoons fresh lime juice

1   Heat 12-inch nonstick skillet or
4-quart Dutch oven over medium-
high heat. Sprinkle pork chops with
salt; place in skillet. Cook 1 to 2
minutes, turning once, just until
they begin to brown.

2   Add water and broth; heat
to boiling. Stir in rice. Reduce
heat to medium-low; cover and
simmer about 20 minutes or until
pork is no longer pink and meat
thermometer inserted in center
reads 160°F, rice is tender and
liquid is absorbed. Meanwhile, in
medium bowl, mix confetti salsa
ingredients.

3   Stir the 1 cup salsa into rice mixture in skillet; cook about 1 minute
or until hot. Serve confetti salsa over
chops and rice. If desired, sprinkle
with chopped fresh cilantro.

High Altitude (3500–6500 ft): Increase
water to 1¼ cups; cover and simmer pork
chops and rice about 22 minutes.

1 Serving: Calories 590; Total Fat 18g (Saturated Fat 4.5g;
Trans Fat 0g); Cholesterol 70mg; Sodium 1190mg;
Total Carbohydrate 73g (Dietary Fiber 5g) Exchanges:
4 Starch, 1 Other Carbohydrate, 3 Lean Meat, 1 Fat;
Carbohydrate Choices: 5

This Soup Is Earth-Shattering!

Some cooks may joke about having a "disaster" in the kitchen when a
recipe doesn't go as planned. Kathi Manzagol had just deemed her pot
of homemade soup ready to serve when an earthquake shook her home.
Later, emerging from the closet, Kathi headed to the kitchen to find five
quarts of black bean soup splattered on the floor. "I have never made
soup from scratch again!" she says. Kathi has often lent a hand
with real disasters. She and her husband are trained disaster
volunteers for the Red Cross, called on to travel on very little
notice to help at the site of natural catastrophes.

Orange Pork and Sweet Potatoes

Sharee Roberts Paducah, KY
Bake-Off® Contest 41, 2004

Prep Time: 15 Minutes
Start to Finish: 1 Hour 5 Minutes
4 servings

3 tablespoons butter or margarine
4 boneless pork loin chops (about 1 lb)
1 teaspoon salt
½ to 1 teaspoon pepper
2 medium dark-orange sweet potatoes, peeled, cut into ½-inch-thick slices (about 1 lb)
¼ cup orange juice
3 tablespoons packed brown sugar
1 container (6 oz) orange crème fat-free yogurt

1 Heat oven to 375°F. In 10-inch skillet, melt butter over medium-high heat. Add pork chops; sprinkle with salt and pepper. Cook 2 to 4 minutes, turning once, until browned on both sides.

2 In ungreased 8-inch square (2-quart) glass baking dish, layer sweet potato slices. Place pork chops over potatoes.

3 In same skillet, cook orange juice and brown sugar over medium heat until brown sugar is melted; pour over pork and potatoes. Cover dish tightly with foil.

4 Bake 35 to 50 minutes or until pork is no longer pink and meat thermometer inserted in center reads 160°F.

5 Remove pork chops and potatoes from dish; place on serving platter. Pour remaining liquid from dish into 1-quart saucepan; stir in yogurt. Cook over medium heat, stirring occasionally, until sauce is hot. Pour sauce over pork chops and sweet potatoes.

High Altitude (3500–6500 ft): No change.

1 Serving: Calories 410; Total Fat 17g (Saturated Fat 8g; Trans Fat 0g); Cholesterol 95mg; Sodium 750mg; Total Carbohydrate 35g (Dietary Fiber 3g) Exchanges: 1 Starch, 1½ Other Carbohydrate, 3½ Lean Meat, 1 Fat; Carbohydrate Choices: 2

Piñata Pork Roast

Mary Edwards Long Beach, CA
Bake-Off® Contest 42, 2006

Prep Time: 30 Minutes
Start to Finish: 2 Hours 10 Minutes
12 servings

6 taco shells (from 4.6-oz box), crushed to ½-inch pieces (about 1¼ cups)
2 cups frozen gold & white corn (from 1-lb bag)
1½ cups shredded Mexican cheese blend (6 oz)
2 tablespoons chopped fresh cilantro
2 tablespoons chopped green onions (2 medium)
1 boneless pork loin roast (about 4 lb), trimmed of fat, butterflied by butcher to be flattened and rolled*
Salt and freshly cracked black pepper, if desired
1 package (1.25 oz) taco seasoning mix
½ teaspoon garlic salt
½ teaspoon ground cumin
½ cup chicken broth
1½ teaspoons grated lime peel
1 tablespoon fresh lime juice
½ cup grape tomatoes or cherry tomatoes, cut in half
1 ripe avocado, pitted, peeled and cut into bite-size pieces
Lime slices, if desired
Additional fresh cilantro, if desired

1 Heat oven to 350°F. In medium bowl, mix crushed taco shells, 1 cup of the frozen corn, the cheese, chopped cilantro and onions.

2 Open pork roast to lay flat; sprinkle with salt and pepper. Press taco shell mixture evenly onto pork to within about ¾ inch of edge.

3 Starting with one long side, tightly roll up pork jelly-roll fashion; tie with kitchen string at 1½-inch intervals. Rub taco seasoning mix evenly over rolled pork. Place seam side down on rack in ungreased large heavy ovenproof roasting pan. Insert ovenproof meat thermometer so tip is in center of thickest part of pork.

4 Roast uncovered 1 hour 15 minutes to 1 hour 30 minutes or until meat thermometer inserted into center of pork reads 155°F. Remove pork from pan; place on cutting board or serving platter. Cover with foil; let stand about 10 minutes or until thermometer reads 160°F.

5 If necessary, drain off any excess fat from roasting pan; place pan over medium-high heat. Stir in garlic salt, cumin, broth and remaining 1 cup corn. Cook 2 to 3 minutes, stirring occasionally, just until corn is tender. Stir in lime peel, lime juice, tomatoes and avocado. Cook just until hot. Remove string from pork; cut across grain into slices. Serve pork with corn-avocado salsa; garnish with lime and cilantro.

*You can butterfly the pork roast if a butcher isn't available. Cut pork roast horizontally down length of pork, about 1/2 inch from top of pork, to within 1/2 inch of opposite side; open flat. Turn pork so you can cut other side. Repeat with other side of pork, cutting from the inside edge to within 1/2 inch of outer edge; open flat. Sprinkle with salt and pepper. Fill and roll as directed in steps 2 and 3.

High Altitude (3500–6500 ft): No change.

1 Serving: Calories 380; Total Fat 20g (Saturated Fat 7g; Trans Fat 0.5g); Cholesterol 110mg; Sodium 540mg; Total Carbohydrate 12g (Dietary Fiber 2g) Exchanges: 1 Starch, 5 Very Lean Meat, 3 Fat; Carbohydrate Choices: 1

Piñata Pork Roast

Spicy Pork Chops Caribbean

Susan Carroll   Rochester, NY
Bake-Off® Contest 40, 2002

Prep Time: 15 Minutes
Start to Finish: 35 Minutes
4 servings

1 package (8 oz) uncooked yellow rice
2½ cups water
4 boneless pork chops, ½ inch thick
1 package (3 oz) seasoned coating mix
   for pork
1¼ cups frozen small sweet peas
   (from 1-lb bag)
2 tablespoons vegetable oil
1¼ cups frozen chopped onions
1 cup fresh cilantro leaves
2 firm ripe bananas, peeled, thinly
   sliced
2 cans (4.5 oz each) chopped green
   chiles
1 jar (7 oz) roasted red bell peppers,
   drained, coarsely chopped
½ teaspoon curry powder
½ teaspoon pumpkin pie spice

¼ to 1 teaspoon crushed red pepper flakes
¼ teaspoon dried shredded orange peel
   or freshly grated orange peel
⅓ cup orange juice

1   Heat oven to 425°F. Line 15 × 10 × 1-inch pan with foil. Cook rice in water as directed on package. Cover to keep warm.

2   Meanwhile, coat pork chops with coating mix as directed on package. Place in pan. Bake 15 to 20 minutes or until pork is no longer pink in center. Cook peas as directed on package; drain. Stir peas into rice.

3   In 10-inch skillet, heat oil over medium heat until hot. Add onions, cilantro and bananas; cook 3 minutes, stirring frequently, until bananas are just tender. Stir in remaining ingredients. Heat to boiling. Reduce heat to low; cook about 5 minutes, stirring occasionally, until thickened.

4   Spoon rice mixture onto individual serving plates. Top each with pork chop and banana mixture. If desired, garnish with avocado and additional cilantro.

High Altitude (3500–6500 ft): No change.

1 Serving: Calories 620; Total Fat 16g (Saturated Fat 4g; Trans Fat 0g); Cholesterol 65mg; Sodium 1890mg; Total Carbohydrate 85g (Dietary Fiber 7g) Exchanges: 4 Starch, 1 Fruit, ½ Other Carbohydrate, 1 Vegetable, 2½ Lean Meat, 1 Fat; Carbohydrate Choices: 5½

Creamy Seafood Pasta

Angela Buchanan   Boulder, CO
Bake-Off® Contest 41, 2004

Prep Time: 30 Minutes
Start to Finish: 30 Minutes
8 servings (1¼ cups each)

16 oz uncooked linguine
1 can (18.5 oz) ready-to-serve
   New England clam chowder
1 cup milk
½ cup shredded Parmesan cheese
2 cloves garlic, finely chopped
2 tablespoons olive oil
1½ lb uncooked deveined peeled
   large shrimp, tail shells removed
1 package (8 oz) sliced fresh
   mushrooms (3 cups)
4 medium green onions, chopped
   (¼ cup)
¼ to ½ teaspoon crushed red pepper
   flakes
½ cup chopped fresh parsley
Salt and pepper to taste, if desired
½ cup shredded Parmesan cheese,
   if desired

Bake-Off® Contest Fun Never Ends

Kathryn Chute had three small children when she was selected as a finalist in 1958. Her middle son went on to become a writer for a major daily newspaper. When the Bake-Off® Contest was held in the newspaper's home city in 1994, he was asked about growing up with a Pillsbury Bake-Off® participant. Chute says, "For a Bake-Off® Contest winner, the contest never ends."

1 In 5- to 6-quart Dutch oven, cook linguine as directed on package. Drain well; return to Dutch oven and cover to keep warm.

2 Meanwhile, in blender, place clam chowder, milk, ½ cup Parmesan cheese and the garlic. Cover; blend on medium speed until mixture is smooth. Set aside.

3 In 12-inch nonstick skillet or wok, heat oil over medium-high heat until hot. Cook shrimp, mushrooms and onions in oil about 5 minutes, stirring frequently, until shrimp turn pink.

4 Stir in pepper flakes and soup mixture; cook until hot. Stir in parsley. Salt and pepper to taste.

5 Pour over cooked linguine in Dutch oven; toss gently to coat. Top individual servings with shredded Parmesan cheese.

High Altitude (3500–6500 ft): No change.

1 Serving: Calories 440; Total Fat 11g (Saturated Fat 3g; Trans Fat 0g); Cholesterol 130mg; Sodium 710mg; Total Carbohydrate 59g (Dietary Fiber 4g) Exchanges: 3 Starch, 1 Other Carbohydrate, 2½ Very Lean Meat, 1½ Fat; Carbohydrate Choices: 4

Creamy Seafood Pasta

Easy Seafood Dinner

Nancy Signorelli Miami, FL
Bake-Off® Contest 33, 1988

Prep Time: 50 Minutes
Start to Finish: 50 Minutes
6 servings

1 can (8 oz) Pillsbury® refrigerated
    crescent dinner rolls
1 can (4 ¼ oz) tiny shrimp, drained,
    liquid reserved
1 lb frozen cod or haddock, thawed,
    cut into ½-inch cubes
4 medium green onions, sliced (¼ cup)
⅓ cup Pillsbury BEST® all-purpose flour
1 cup milk
1 tablespoon dried parsley flakes
½ to 1 teaspoon garlic powder
1 cup sour cream
3 tablespoons dry sherry, if desired
1½ cups frozen sweet peas (from 1-lb
    bag), thawed, drained
1 can (8 oz) sliced water chestnuts,
    drained
1 jar (2.5 oz) sliced mushrooms, drained

1 Heat oven to 350°F. Remove dough from can in rolled sections; do not unroll. Cut each section into 6 slices. Place on ungreased cookie sheet; slightly flatten each slice. Bake 13 to 16 minutes or until golden brown. Set aside.

2 In 10-inch skillet, heat reserved shrimp liquid, cod and green onions to boiling. Reduce heat; cover and simmer 3 to 5 minutes or until fish flakes easily with fork. Remove from heat; do not drain.

3 In 2-quart saucepan stir flour into milk with wire whisk. Cook over medium heat about 2 minutes, stirring constantly, until mixture thickens and boils. Stir in parsley flakes, garlic powder, sour cream and sherry. Add shrimp, peas, water chestnuts and mushrooms; mix well. Gently blend sour cream mixture into fish mixture in skillet.* Heat over low heat about 5 minutes, stirring occasionally. To serve, place 2 baked crescent pinwheels on plate; spoon about 1 cup of fish mixture over pinwheels.

* To make ahead, fish mixture can be prepared to this point. Cover and refrigerate. Just before serving, prepare crescent pinwheels as directed. Heat seafood mixture, covered, over low heat, stirring occasionally. Serve as directed above.

High Altitude (3500–6500 ft): In step 3, after adding sour cream mixture, heat over medium-low heat about 5 minutes.

1 Serving: Calories 390; Total Fat 18g (Saturated Fat 8g; Trans Fat 2.5g); Cholesterol 115mg; Sodium 490mg; Total Carbohydrate 33g (Dietary Fiber 3g) Exchanges: 1 Starch, 1 Other Carbohydrate, 1 Vegetable, 3 Very Lean Meat, 3 Fat; Carbohydrate Choices: 2

4 | SIDE DISHES AND SALADS

You Won't Know It's Not Potato Salad (page 118)

Asparagus with Sweet Pepper–Walnut Sauce

Elizabeth Nichols   Baton Rouge, LA
Bake-Off® Contest 38, 1998

Prep Time: 10 Minutes
Start to Finish: 10 Minutes
4 servings

2 tablespoons walnut or vegetable oil
½ cup chopped roasted red bell peppers
  (from a jar)
¼ cup chopped walnuts
1 small clove garlic, finely chopped
1 can (15 oz) asparagus spears
Dash salt
Dash pepper

1   In 8-inch skillet, heat oil over medium-high heat until hot. Cook and stir roasted peppers, walnuts and garlic in oil 1½ to 2 minutes or until hot.

2   Carefully drain asparagus; place on paper towels and pat dry. Arrange in serving dish. Spoon warm roasted pepper mixture over asparagus. Sprinkle with salt and pepper.

High Altitude (3500–6500 ft): No change.

1 Serving: Calories 140; Total Fat 12g (Saturated Fat 1g; Trans Fat 0g); Cholesterol 0mg; Sodium 230mg; Total Carbohydrate 4g (Dietary Fiber 2g) Exchanges: 1 Vegetable, 2½ Fat; Carbohydrate Choices: 0

Broccoli Bonanza

Libby LaDuca   North Potomac, MD
Bake-Off® Contest 39, 2000

Prep Time: 15 Minutes
Start to Finish: 15 Minutes
6 servings (1 cup each)

6 oz (¾ cup) uncooked acini de pepe,
  rosamarina or orzo pasta
3 tablespoons olive oil
2 cloves garlic, finely chopped
2 boxes (9 oz each) frozen cut broccoli,
  thawed*
½ cup unseasoned dry bread crumbs
½ teaspoon coarse or regular salt
2 cups coarsely chopped tomatoes
2 tablespoons balsamic vinegar

1   Cook and drain pasta as directed on package. Cover to keep warm.

2   Meanwhile, in 10-inch skillet, heat oil over medium heat until hot. Cook and stir garlic and broccoli in oil 3 minutes. Stir in bread crumbs and salt; cook 1 minute.

3   Stir in tomatoes and vinegar. Cook 1 to 2 minutes, stirring occasionally, until tomatoes are warm. Stir in cooked pasta. Serve warm.

To quickly thaw broccoli, cut small slit in center of each pouch; microwave on High 2 to 3 minutes or until thawed. Remove broccoli from pouches; drain well.

High Altitude (3500–6500 ft): No change.

1 Serving: Calories 260; Total Fat 8g (Saturated Fat 1.5g; Trans Fat 0g); Cholesterol 0mg; Sodium 390mg; Total Carbohydrate 38g (Dietary Fiber 5g) Exchanges: 1½ Starch, ½ Other Carbohydrate, 2 Vegetable, 1½ Fat; Carbohydrate Choices: 2½

Creamy Parmesan Broccoli

Mildred D'Elia   Islip, NY
Bake-Off® Contest 39, 2000

Prep Time: 15 Minutes
Start to Finish: 35 Minutes
5 servings

1 lb frozen broccoli spears or 4 cups
  frozen broccoli florets
2 tablespoons olive oil
¾ cup grated Parmesan cheese
8 medium green onions, chopped (½ cup)
½ cup sour cream
¼ cup mayonnaise or salad dressing
2 tablespoons milk
⅛ teaspoon pepper
¼ cup pine nuts or chopped walnuts,
  toasted*

1   Heat oven to 350°F. Cook broccoli as directed on package; drain. Place in ungreased 12 × 8-inch (2-quart) baking dish or 2-quart casserole. Drizzle with oil. Sprinkle with ¼ cup of the cheese; toss to coat.

2   In medium bowl, mix remaining ½ cup cheese and remaining ingredients except pine nuts. Spoon over broccoli.

3   Bake 18 to 20 minutes or until sauce begins to bubble and brown. Sprinkle with pine nuts.

To toast pine nuts, spread on cookie sheet; bake at 350°F 3 to 6 minutes, stirring occasionally, until light golden brown.

High Altitude (3500–6500 ft): Bake 21 to 23 minutes.

1 Serving: Calories 320; Total Fat 27g (Saturated Fat 8g; Trans Fat 0g); Cholesterol 35mg; Sodium 320mg; Total Carbohydrate 9g (Dietary Fiber 3g) Exchanges: 1 Vegetable, 1 High-Fat Meat, 4 Fat; Carbohydrate Choices: ½

Creamy Parmesan Broccoli

Broccoli and Corn in Gingered Curry Cream

Ellen Maria Anders Big Bend, WI
Bake-Off® Contest 38, 1998
$2,000 Winner

Prep Time: 20 Minutes
Start to Finish: 20 Minutes
8 servings (½ cup each)

2 tablespoons butter or margarine
1 bag (1 lb) frozen broccoli florets
2 boxes (10 oz each) frozen corn in a
    butter sauce, thawed
¼ cup water
½ cup whipping cream or half-and-half
1 teaspoon curry powder
1 teaspoon minced garlic in water
    (from 4.5-oz jar)
1 teaspoon grated gingerroot
½ teaspoon salt
½ teaspoon white pepper
1 lemon, cut into 8 wedges

GARNISH, IF DESIRED
2 teaspoons grated lemon peel
8 green onion fans
8 red bell pepper rings

1   In 12-inch skillet, melt butter over medium heat. Add broccoli and corn; stir to coat. Increase heat to high; add water. Cook 3 to 5 minutes, stirring occasionally, until broccoli is thawed.

2   In small bowl, mix whipping cream, curry powder, garlic, gingerroot, salt and pepper. Stir into cooked vegetables; cook 2 to 4 minutes, stirring occasionally, until vegetables are crisp-tender. Serve with lemon wedges. Garnish as desired.

High Altitude (3500–6500 ft): No change.

1 Serving: Calories 160; Total Fat 9g (Saturated Fat 5g; Trans Fat 0g); Cholesterol 25mg; Sodium 390mg; Total Carbohydrate 16g (Dietary Fiber 3g) Exchanges: ½ Starch, ½ Other Carbohydrate, 1 Vegetable, 1½ Fat; Carbohydrate Choices: 1

Corn and Cheese-Stuffed Peppers

Gloria Rendon Murray, UT
Bake-Off® Contest 41, 2004

Prep Time: 15 Minutes
Start to Finish: 1 Hour 10 Minutes
4 servings

4 large red, green and/or yellow bell
    peppers, tops cut off, seeds and
    membranes removed
12 oz refrigerated polenta (from 1-lb
    roll), cut into ¼-inch pieces (2 cups)
1 can (11 oz) vacuum-packed whole
    kernel corn with red and green
    peppers, drained
¾ cup shredded Monterey Jack cheese
    (3 oz)
¾ cup shredded provolone cheese (3 oz)
Salt and pepper to taste, if desired
1 cup reduced-fat sour cream, if desired

1   Heat oven to 350°F. If necessary, cut thin slice off bottom of each bell pepper so peppers stand upright.

2   In medium bowl, mix polenta pieces, corn and half of each of the cheeses. Salt and pepper to taste. Spoon polenta mixture into bell peppers; sprinkle with remaining cheese. Place filled peppers in ungreased 8-inch square (2-quart) glass baking dish. Fill dish halfway with water. Spray 12-inch square piece of foil with cooking spray; cover dish tightly. Bake 30 minutes.

3   Remove foil; bake 15 to 20 minutes or until bell peppers are crisp-tender and filling is hot. Cool 5 minutes. Carefully remove bell peppers from dish. Garnish with sour cream.

High Altitude (3500–6500 ft): No change.

1 Serving: Calories 330; Total Fat 13g (Saturated Fat 8g; Trans Fat 0g); Cholesterol 35mg; Sodium 820mg; Total Carbohydrate 37g (Dietary Fiber 5g) Exchanges: 2 Starch, 2 Vegetable, 1 High-Fat Meat, ½ Fat; Carbohydrate Choices: 2½

Cauliflower Crunch

Rosemary Leicht Bethel, OH
Bake-Off® Contest 39, 2000
$2,000 Winner

Prep Time: 15 Minutes
Start to Finish: 40 Minutes
4 servings (¾ cup each)

3 tablespoons olive or vegetable oil
8 sun-dried tomatoes, cut into strips
2 cloves garlic, finely chopped
1 can (4.5 oz) chopped green chiles,
    drained
2 boxes (10 oz each) frozen cauliflower
    in a cheese flavored sauce, thawed*
¼ cup unseasoned dry bread crumbs
¼ cup grated Parmesan cheese

1   Heat oven to 400°F. In 8-inch skillet, heat 1 tablespoon of the oil over medium heat until hot. Cook tomatoes, garlic and green chiles in skillet 1 to 2 minutes, stirring occasionally, until hot. Spread in bottom of ungreased 9- or 10-inch quiche dish or glass pie plate. Top with cauliflower in cheese sauce.

2   In small bowl, mix bread crumbs, Parmesan cheese and remaining 2 tablespoons oil. Sprinkle over cauliflower mixture.

3   Bake 20 to 22 minutes or until edges are bubbly and bread crumbs are golden brown.

To quickly thaw cauliflower, cut small slit in center of each pouch; microwave on High 2 to 3 minutes or until thawed.

High Altitude (3500–6500 ft): No change.

1 Serving: Calories 240; Total Fat 16g (Saturated Fat 4g; Trans Fat 0g); Cholesterol 5mg; Sodium 1270mg; Total Carbohydrate 17g (Dietary Fiber 3g) Exchanges: 1 Starch, 1 Vegetable, 3 Fat; Carbohydrate Choices: 1

Corn and Cheese-Stuffed Peppers

Cheesy Potato Corn Cakes

Mary Jones Cumberland, ME
Bake-Off® Contest 39, 2000
$2,000 Winner

Prep Time: 35 Minutes
Start to Finish: 35 Minutes
8 servings

2 cups mashed potato flakes
1 can (11 oz) vacuum-packed whole
  kernel corn with red and green
  peppers, drained
¾ cup shredded Cheddar cheese (3 oz)
2 tablespoons Pillsbury BEST®
  all-purpose or unbleached flour
2 tablespoons cornmeal
1½ teaspoons seasoned salt
1 teaspoon dried basil leaves
½ teaspoon garlic powder
¼ teaspoon pepper
2 cups milk
1 egg, beaten
¼ cup butter or margarine
Grated Parmesan cheese, if desired

1   In large bowl, mix potato flakes, corn, Cheddar cheese, flour, cornmeal, seasoned salt, basil, garlic powder and pepper. Add milk and egg; mix well. Let stand 2 to 3 minutes or until liquid is absorbed.

2   In 12-inch nonstick skillet, melt 1 to 2 tablespoons of the butter over medium heat. Drop potato mixture by ¼ cupfuls into skillet. Carefully press each to form 3-inch round. Cook 6 to 8 minutes or until golden brown, turning once. Sprinkle with Parmesan cheese. Repeat with remaining butter and potato mixture as necessary.

High Altitude (3500–6500 ft): Cook 8 to 10 minutes.

1 Serving (2 Corn Cakes): Calories 250; Total Fat 11g (Saturated Fat 7g; Trans Fat 0g); Cholesterol 60mg; Sodium 540mg; Total Carbohydrate 27g (Dietary Fiber 1g) Exchanges: 2 Starch, 2 Fat; Carbohydrate Choices: 2

Hot 'n Spicy Sautéed Mushrooms

Gladys Randall Houston, TX
Bake-Off® Contest 33, 1988

Prep Time: 15 Minutes
Start to Finish: 15 Minutes
6 servings (½ cup each)

½ cup butter or margarine
½ cup chopped green bell pepper
½ cup chopped red bell pepper
4 medium green onions, sliced (¼ cup)
2 cloves garlic, finely chopped
3 jars (6 oz each) sliced mushrooms,
  drained*
¼ cup sherry
½ teaspoon Creole or Cajun seasoning
¼ teaspoon ground red pepper (cayenne)
¼ teaspoon pepper

1   In 10-inch skillet, melt butter over medium heat. Cook and stir bell peppers, onions and garlic in butter until tender. Stir in remaining ingredients.

2   Simmer 2 to 3 minutes, stirring occasionally, until hot.

* Four jars (4.5 oz each) sliced mushrooms, drained, can be substituted for 3 jars (6 oz each).

High Altitude (3500–6500 ft): No change.

1 Serving: Calories 170; Total Fat 16g (Saturated Fat 10g; Trans Fat 0.5g); Cholesterol 40mg; Sodium 460mg; Total Carbohydrate 6g (Dietary Fiber 2g) Exchanges: 1 Vegetable, 3 Fat; Carbohydrate Choices: ½

Practice Makes Perfect

Cooking is very much a chicken-and-egg sort of endeavor. If you've never had a good meat loaf, how can you know if yours is any good? Gladys Randall figured out this principle when she was a young child, the hard way. "I would see a baked pie on top of the stove. I tried to bake a lemon pie by putting it on top of the burner. I thought that was the way it's done." Gladys kept trying, her adventurous spirit intact. "It took me two years to learn how to make a traditional Italian stuffing. One day a guest at Christmas, who was ninety-two years old, said 'Very good—but too loose. You make it together, like a meatball.' Then I knew what I was doing wrong!'" Gladys listened, learned and became master of her kitchen.

Honey-Nut Snap Peas

Susan Trueblood Rolla, MO
Bake-Off® Contest 39, 2000

Prep Time: 10 Minutes
Start to Finish: 10 Minutes
4 servings (¾ cup each)

1 bag (1 lb) frozen sugar snap peas
2 tablespoons water
½ cup pine nuts or peanuts
1 tablespoon butter or margarine
1 tablespoon honey
1 teaspoon yellow mustard

1 In 1½-quart microwavable casserole, place sugar snap peas and water; cover. Microwave on High 6 to 9 minutes, stirring once halfway through cooking, until crisp-tender; drain.

2 Add remaining ingredients; toss gently to mix. Serve warm.

High Altitude (3500–6500 ft): No change.

1 Serving: Calories 220; Total Fat 13g (Saturated Fat 3.5g; Trans Fat 0g); Cholesterol 10mg; Sodium 100mg; Total Carbohydrate 16g (Dietary Fiber 5g) Exchanges: 1 Other Carbohydrate, 1 Vegetable, 1 High-Fat Meat, 1 Fat; Carbohydrate Choices: 1

Potato Corn Bake

Marion Bedient   Cameron, WI
Bake-Off® Contest 34, 1990

Prep Time: 25 Minutes
Start to Finish: 55 Minutes
6 servings

½ lb bacon, cut into ¾-inch pieces
½ cup finely chopped green bell pepper
⅓ cup finely chopped onion
1 can (14.75 oz) cream-style corn
2 cups milk
3 tablespoons butter or margarine
¾ teaspoon salt, if desired
⅛ teaspoon pepper
2 cups mashed potato flakes
½ cup sour cream
¼ cup grated Parmesan cheese
2 tablespoons finely chopped green
    onion tops, if desired

1   Heat oven to 375°F. Grease
8-inch square or 11 × 7-inch
(2-quart) glass baking dish. In
3-quart saucepan, cook bacon
until crisp. Drain, reserving
1 tablespoon bacon drippings.

Set bacon aside. Return 1 tablespoon bacon drippings to saucepan.
Add bell pepper and onion to
drippings. Cook over medium heat
until tender.

2   Stir in corn, milk, butter, salt
and pepper; cook until hot and
bubbly. Remove from heat; stir
in potato flakes and sour cream
until well blended. Spoon mixture
into baking dish. Top with bacon,
Parmesan cheese and onions.* Bake
25 to 30 minutes or until hot.

** To make ahead, prepare, cover and
refrigerate up to 4 hours before baking.
Bake at 375°F 25 to 30 minutes or
until hot.*

High Altitude (3500–6500 ft): No change.

1 Serving: Calories 380; Total Fat 20g (Saturated Fat 10g;
Trans Fat 0.5g); Cholesterol 50mg; Sodium 570mg;
Total Carbohydrate 38g (Dietary Fiber 3g) Exchanges:
2 Starch, ½ Other Carbohydrate, 1 High-Fat Meat,
2 Fat; Carbohydrate Choices: 2½

Easy Cheesy Salsa Potatoes

Shannon Fountain   Winooski, VT
Bake-Off® Contest 39, 2000

Prep Time: 10 Minutes
Start to Finish: 1 Hour 10 Minutes
8 servings (1 cup each)

2 cups shredded Cheddar cheese (8 oz)
1 cup chunky style salsa
½ cup finely chopped onion
½ cup sour cream
1 can (10¾ oz) condensed Cheddar
    cheese soup
½ teaspoon pepper
1 bag (24 oz) frozen hash-brown
    potatoes (about 8 cups), thawed
½ cup unseasoned dry bread crumbs
¼ cup butter or margarine, melted

1   Heat oven to 350°F. Grease
13 × 9-inch (3-quart) baking dish
or pan. In large bowl, mix cheese,
salsa, onion, sour cream, soup and
pepper. Add potatoes; mix well.
Spread in baking dish.

2   In small bowl, mix bread crumbs
and melted butter. Sprinkle over
potatoes.

3   Bake 45 to 60 minutes or until
cheese is melted and potatoes are
tender.

High Altitude (3500–6500 ft): Bake 50 to
65 minutes.

1 Serving: Calories 390; Total Fat 22g (Saturated Fat 13g;
Trans Fat 1g); Cholesterol 60mg; Sodium 850mg;
Total Carbohydrate 36g (Dietary Fiber 3g) Exchanges:
2 Starch, ½ Other Carbohydrate, 1 High-Fat Meat,
2½ Fat; Carbohydrate Choices: 2½

From Humble Beginnings

When Shannon Fountain became a finalist, she described her kitchen
as "old," saying she'd never had a new set of pots and pans. But
not to worry. "My mother always says the best foods come from the
worst-looking pans because they're so well used," she notes.

Shannon's Bake-Off® Contest recipe—her only entry—was
adapted from a local church cookbook. She introduced it at
a family meal, "and my husband Chris loved the zip of the
salsa." Now it's a mainstay at family gatherings, potlucks
and regular dinners.

Mexicorn® Topped Tomatoes

Roxanne Chan Albany, CA
Bake-Off® Contest 42, 2006

Prep Time: 20 Minutes
Start to Finish: 20 Minutes
6 servings

1 can (11 oz) vacuum-packed whole kernel corn with red and green peppers, drained

1 can (4.5 oz) chopped green chiles, drained

½ cup finely chopped fresh or refrigerated mango

2 tablespoons finely chopped green onions (2 medium)

2 tablespoons sliced ripe olives

1 tablespoon finely chopped fresh cilantro

1 tablespoon chopped chipotle chile in adobo sauce (from 7-oz can)

1 tablespoon lime juice (½ medium)

1 teaspoon olive oil

4 large firm ripe tomatoes, cut crosswise into ¼-inch slices

Pumpkin seeds*

1 In medium bowl, mix all ingredients except tomatoes and pumpkin seeds.

2 On serving platter, arrange tomatoes, overlapping slices. Spoon corn mixture down center of tomatoes. Sprinkle with pumpkin seeds.

Roasted hulled pumpkin seeds (pepitas) can be used as garnish.

High Altitude (3500–6500 ft): No change.

1 Serving: Calories 100; Total Fat 2g (Saturated Fat 0g; Trans Fat 0g); Cholesterol 0mg; Sodium 530mg; Total Carbohydrate 18g (Dietary Fiber 3g) Exchanges: 1 Other Carbohydrate, 1 Vegetable, ½ Fat; Carbohydrate Choices: 1

Cheesy Broccoli-Stuffed Zucchini

Dar Godschalx Prescott, AZ
Bake-Off® Contest 40, 2002

Prep Time: 30 Minutes
Start to Finish: 1 hour
4 servings

1 tablespoon vegetable oil
½ cup chopped onion
¼ cup roasted red bell peppers
    (from a jar), drained, chopped
2 boxes (10 oz each) frozen broccoli in
    a cheese flavored sauce, thawed
1 jar (4.5 oz) sliced mushrooms, drained
2 zucchini (9 inches each)*
½ cup unseasoned dry bread crumbs
2 tablespoons butter or margarine, melted

1   Heat oven to 350°F. In 10-inch skillet, heat oil over medium heat until hot. Cook and stir onion in oil about 3 minutes or until tender. Add roasted peppers, broccoli in sauce, and mushrooms; cook 2 to 3 minutes, stirring occasionally, until broccoli is crisp-tender.

2   Cut each zucchini in half lengthwise. Scoop out center, leaving ¼-inch shell. Spoon broccoli mixture into each zucchini half. Place in ungreased 12 × 8-inch (2-quart) glass baking dish.

3   In small bowl, mix bread crumbs and melted butter. Sprinkle over stuffed zucchini. Cover with foil.

4   Bake 20 minutes. Uncover; bake 8 to 12 minutes longer or until topping is golden brown and vegetables are tender.

*Three 7-inch zucchini can be substituted for the 9-inch size. Fill and bake as directed in recipe.

High Altitude (3500–6500 ft): Heat oven to 375°F. Increase first bake time to 25 minutes.

1 Serving: Calories 250; Total Fat 13g (Saturated Fat 6g; Trans Fat 0g); Cholesterol 15mg; Sodium 870mg; Total Carbohydrate 27g (Dietary Fiber 5g) Exchanges: 1 Starch, 2 Vegetable, 2½ Fat; Carbohydrate Choices: 2

Carolina Brunch-Style Grits

Inez Duke Mars Hill, NC
Bake-Off® Contest 39, 2000
$2,000 Winner

Prep Time: 15 Minutes
Start to Finish: 45 Minutes
8 servings

1 cup uncooked quick-cooking grits
4 cups water
1 can (11 oz) vacuum-packed whole
    kernel corn with red and green
    peppers, drained
1 box (9 oz) frozen spinach, thawed*
1 package (1.25 oz) taco seasoning mix
2 tablespoons chopped onion
2 tablespoons butter or margarine
2 cups shredded Cheddar cheese (8 oz)

1   Heat oven to 350°F. Cook grits in water as directed on package.

2   In ungreased 13 × 9-inch (3-quart) glass baking dish, mix cooked grits and remaining ingredients except 1 cup of the cheese. Sprinkle with remaining 1 cup cheese.

3   Bake 22 to 27 minutes or until edges are bubbly and cheese is melted.

*To quickly thaw spinach, cut small slit in center of pouch; microwave on High 2 to 3 minutes or until thawed. Remove spinach from pouch; squeeze dry with paper towels.

High Altitude (3500–6500 ft): Heat oven to 375°F.

1 Serving: Calories 270; Total Fat 13g (Saturated Fat 8g; Trans Fat 0g); Cholesterol 35mg; Sodium 770mg; Total Carbohydrate 27g (Dietary Fiber 2g) Exchanges: 1½ Starch, 1 High-Fat Meat, 1 Fat; Carbohydrate Choices: 2

African-Style Skillet Slaw

Anita Price Richmond, VA
Bake-Off® Contest 39, 2000

Prep Time: 20 Minutes
Start to Finish: 20 Minutes
6 servings (⅔ cup each)

SLAW
2 tablespoons vegetable oil
3 cups finely shredded cabbage
½ cup grated carrot
½ cup grated peeled sweet potato
8 medium green onions, sliced (½ cup)
1 can (11 oz) vacuum-packed super
    sweet yellow and white corn, drained
2 tablespoons honey
2 tablespoons cider vinegar
¼ cup coconut, toasted*
¼ cup dry-roasted peanuts
Red pepper sauce
Salt
Pepper

GARNISH
Paprika
Cabbage leaves
Chow mein noodles
Golden raisins

1   In 10-inch skillet, heat oil over medium-high heat until hot. Cook cabbage, carrot, sweet potato, onions and corn in oil 5 to 8 minutes, stirring occasionally, until vegetables are crisp-tender.

2   Add honey and vinegar; mix well. Stir in coconut and peanuts. Season to taste with pepper sauce, salt and pepper.

3 Sprinkle serving platter with paprika. Arrange cabbage leaves on platter. Spoon slaw onto platter. Top with chow mein noodles and golden raisins.

* To toast coconut, spread on cookie sheet; bake at 350°F 7 to 8 minutes, stirring occasionally, or until light golden brown. Or spread coconut in 6-inch skillet; cook over medium heat about 7 minutes, stirring frequently, until light golden brown.

High Altitude (3500–6500 ft): No change.

1 Serving: Calories 190; Total Fat 9g (Saturated Fat 2g; Trans Fat 0g); Cholesterol 0mg; Sodium 200mg; Total Carbohydrate 23g (Dietary Fiber 3g) Exchanges: 1 Other Carbohydrate, 1½ Vegetable, 2 Fat; Carbohydrate Choices: 1½

Cabbage Salad Vinaigrette with Crunchy Noodles

Birdie Casement Denver, CO
Bake-Off® Contest 34, 1990
$2,000 Winner

    Prep Time: 25 Minutes
    Start to Finish: 2 Hours 25 Minutes
    16 servings (½ cup each)

SALAD
4½ cups (1 medium head) shredded red or green cabbage
5 green onions, thinly sliced (including tops)
1 can (11 oz) vacuum-packed whole kernel corn, drained
1½ cups frozen sweet peas (from 1-lb bag), cooked, drained
1 jar (4.5 oz) sliced mushrooms, undrained

DRESSING
1 package (3 oz) instant Oriental noodles with chicken-flavor seasoning packet
¼ cup tarragon vinegar
¼ cup vegetable oil
3 tablespoons sugar
½ teaspoon pepper
½ cup slivered almonds, toasted*
2 tablespoons sesame seed, toasted**

1 In large bowl, mix salad ingredients. In small bowl, mix contents of seasoning packet from noodles, vinegar, oil, sugar and pepper. Pour dressing over salad ingredients; toss to coat. Refrigerate at least 2 hours to chill.

2 Break noodles into ¾-inch pieces. Before serving, stir noodles, almonds and sesame seed into salad mixture. Store in refrigerator.

* To toast almonds, spread on cookie sheet; bake at 375°F 5 to 6 minutes or until light golden brown, stirring occasionally. Or spread in thin layer in microwavable pie pan, and microwave on High 6 to 7 minutes, stirring frequently, until light golden brown.

** To toast sesame seed, spread in baking pan; bake at 375°F 5 to 7 minutes or until light golden brown. Or spread in medium skillet and stir over medium heat 8 to 10 minutes or until light golden brown.

High Altitude (3500–6500 ft): No change.

1 Serving: Calories 130; Total Fat 7g (Saturated Fat 1g; Trans Fat 0g); Cholesterol 0mg; Sodium 170mg; Total Carbohydrate 13g (Dietary Fiber 2g) Exchanges: ½ Starch, 1 Vegetable, 1½ Fat; Carbohydrate Choices: 1

A Home-Cooked Heritage

If anyone ever asks you what it was like to live richly through the twentieth century, direct them to the story of Birdie Casement. "I married Russ," Birdie said, "then World War II changed our lives. We found ourselves wrestling with gas rationing, sugar stamps, tire shortages, among other shortages, and two wee tots. . . . The following years were a merry-go-round of PTA, fund-raising, cake bakes, Brownies, Cub Scouts, car pooling, measles, trips to the zoo, picnics and all the fun, tears, brawls and challenges that go hand in hand with parenthood. Time flies and soon no one was hurrying home for that noon-time sandwich." Birdie became a kindergarten teacher and was nominated for Colorado teacher of the year. At the Bake-Off® Contest, she wowed everybody with her ebullience, her wisdom and, of course, her salad.

You Won't Know It's Not Potato Salad

Lori Holtsclaw   Rochester Hills, MI
Bake-Off® Contest 42, 2006

Prep Time: 40 Minutes
Start to Finish: 2 Hours 10 Minutes
16 servings (½ cup each)

4 eggs
8 cups frozen cauliflower florets (2 lb)
1 bag (10 oz) frozen organic peas
   and carrots
1¾ cups reduced-fat mayonnaise
   or salad dressing
1 teaspoon granulated sugar
1 teaspoon salt
¼ teaspoon pepper
¼ teaspoon paprika
1 tablespoon cider vinegar
1 teaspoon yellow mustard
1 cup chopped celery
⅔ cup chopped onion

1   In 2-quart saucepan, place eggs in single layer; add enough cold water to cover eggs by 1 inch. Cover; heat to boiling. Remove from heat; let stand covered 15 minutes. Drain eggs. Immediately run cold water over eggs until completely cooled. Peel and chop eggs.

2   Meanwhile, in large (4-quart) microwavable bowl, place frozen cauliflower and frozen peas and carrots; cover with microwavable waxed paper. Microwave on High 20 to 25 minutes, stirring once halfway through microwaving. Drain vegetables in colander; rinse with cold water to cool. Place colander of vegetables over same large bowl; refrigerate at least 30 minutes until cooled.

3   In small bowl, mix mayonnaise, sugar, salt, pepper, ⅛ teaspoon of the paprika, the vinegar and mustard; set aside.

4   Remove vegetables from refrigerator; discard any liquid in bowl. Pat drained vegetables dry with paper towels; chop any large cauliflower pieces into ¾-inch chunks to look like chopped potatoes. Place cauliflower, peas and carrots in same bowl. Add celery, onion and chopped eggs.

5   Pour mayonnaise mixture over salad; stir until vegetables and eggs are well coated. Sprinkle remaining ⅛ teaspoon paprika over salad. If desired, cover and refrigerate at least 1 hour until well chilled before serving.

High Altitude (3500–6500 ft): In step 1, after heating water with eggs to boiling, boil gently 5 minutes. Remove from heat; cover and let stand 15 minutes.

1 Serving: Calories 130; Total Fat 10g (Saturated Fat 2g; Trans Fat 0g); Cholesterol 60mg; Sodium 370mg; Total Carbohydrate 7g (Dietary Fiber 2g) Exchanges: 1½ Vegetable, 2 Fat; Carbohydrate Choices: ½

Texas Two-Step Slaw

Betty Schroedl   Jefferson, WI
Bake-Off® Contest 38, 1998
$10,000 Winner

> **Prep Time:** 15 Minutes
> **Start to Finish:** 15 Minutes
> 8 servings (1 cup each)

SALAD
4 cups shredded green cabbage
1 cup shredded red cabbage
¼ cup chopped red onion
2 medium jalapeño chiles, seeded,
    finely chopped*
2 tablespoons chopped fresh cilantro
1 can (11 oz) vacuum-packed whole
    kernel corn with red and green
    peppers, drained
1 cup shredded Cheddar cheese (4 oz)
Fresh cilantro sprigs

DRESSING
¾ cup ranch dressing
1 tablespoon fresh lime juice
1 teaspoon ground cumin

1   In large bowl, mix all salad ingredients except cilantro sprigs.

2   In small bowl, mix dressing ingredients. Pour over salad; toss to coat. Serve immediately or refrigerate until serving time. Garnish with cilantro sprigs.

* When handling jalapeño chiles, wear plastic or rubber gloves to protect hands. Do not touch face or eyes.

High Altitude (3500–6500 ft): No change.

1 Serving: Calories 220; Total Fat 16g (Saturated Fat 5g; Trans Fat 0g); Cholesterol 20mg; Sodium 400mg; Total Carbohydrate 12g (Dietary Fiber 2g) Exchanges: ½ Other Carbohydrate, 1 Vegetable, ½ High-Fat Meat, 2½ Fat; Carbohydrate Choices: 1

Inspired by Your Surroundings

If the world hands you lemons, make lemonade. Too many cucumbers in the garden? Create a Bake-Off® recipe! Vivian Levine found a solution to the question of what to do with an abundance of cukes in her home garden. She harvested some cucumbers, chopped them and added Mexican flavors to make a salad for dinner. Her salad was a hit. "My husband, Alan, and daughter and I loved it," she reports. And Vivian was on her way to the Bake-Off® Contest, thanks to those prolific cucumber plants.

Crunchy Mexicorn® Salad

Vivian Levine   Oak Ridge, TN
Bake-Off® Contest 39, 2000

> **Prep Time:** 15 Minutes
> **Start to Finish:** 15 Minutes
> 6 servings

2 large cucumbers, peeled, seeded
    and cut into ½-inch cubes
    (3 cups)
3 medium green onions, thinly sliced
    (3 tablespoons)
1 can (15 oz) pinto beans, drained,
    rinsed
1 can (11 oz) vacuum-packed whole
    kernel corn with red and green
    peppers, drained
1 can (3.8 oz) sliced ripe olives,
    drained
1½ cups chunky-style salsa
3 to 4 cups corn chips
Sour cream, if desired
Additional green onions, thinly sliced,
    if desired

1   In large bowl, toss cucumbers, 3 green onions, beans, corn, olives and salsa.

2   Arrange about ½ to ⅔ cup corn chips on each individual serving plate. Top each with about 1¼ cups cucumber mixture. Top each salad with sour cream and additional sliced green onions. Serve immediately.

High Altitude (3500–6500 ft): No change.

1 Serving: Calories 310; Total Fat 11g (Saturated Fat 1.5g; Trans Fat 0g); Cholesterol 0mg; Sodium 830mg; Total Carbohydrate 43g (Dietary Fiber 9g) Exchanges: 2 Starch, ½ Other Carbohydrate, 1 Vegetable, 2 Fat; Carbohydrate Choices: 3

Mediterranean Corn Salad

Ellen Nishimura   Fair Oaks, CA
Bake-Off® Contest 34, 1990
$2,000 Winner

> **Prep Time:** 20 Minutes
> **Start to Finish:** 2 Hours 20 Minutes
> 8 servings (½ cup each)

SALAD
1 can (15.25 oz) vacuum-packed whole
   kernel corn, drained
8 oz mozzarella cheese, cut into ¼-inch
   cubes
1 can (2¼ oz) sliced ripe olives, drained
1 large tomato, seeded, cut into ½-inch
   pieces
¼ cup chopped fresh basil leaves
¼ cup chopped fresh parsley

DRESSING
¼ cup olive oil
3 tablespoons cider vinegar
1 teaspoon grated lemon peel
1 large clove garlic, finely chopped
Salt
Pepper
Fresh spinach leaves, if desired
Toasted pine nuts, if desired*

1 In large bowl, mix salad
ingredients.

2 In small bowl, beat olive oil,
vinegar, lemon peel and garlic with
wire whisk. Pour over salad; toss
gently. Salt and pepper to taste.
Refrigerate 1 to 2 hours to blend
flavors. Serve on spinach-lined
plates. Sprinkle each serving with
pine nuts.

** To toast pine nuts, spread evenly in
shallow pan; bake at 375°F 3 to 5
minutes, stirring occasionally, until
light golden brown.*

High Altitude (3500–6500 ft): No change.

1 Serving: Calories 200; Total Fat 13g (Saturated Fat
4.5g; Trans Fat 0g); Cholesterol 15mg; Sodium 380mg;
Total Carbohydrate 12g (Dietary Fiber 1g) Exchanges:
½ Other Carbohydrate, 1 Vegetable, 1 Medium-Fat
Meat, 1½ Fat; Carbohydrate Choices: 1

Pilgrim Corn Salad

Margo Scofield   Fair Oaks, CA
Bake-Off® Contest 39, 2000

> **Prep Time:** 20 Minutes
> **Start to Finish:** 20 Minutes
> 8 servings (½ cup each)

2 cans (11 oz each) vacuum-packed
   white shoepeg corn, drained
¾ cup sweetened dried cranberries
¼ cup chopped pecans
2 tablespoons balsamic vinegar
2 tablespoons olive oil
1 tablespoon apricot preserves
1 teaspoon Dijon mustard
1 teaspoon Worcestershire sauce
2 tablespoons finely chopped fresh basil
   leaves
Fresh basil sprigs
8 pecan halves

1 In medium bowl, toss corn,
cranberries and chopped pecans.

2 In small bowl, beat vinegar,
oil, preserves, mustard and
Worcestershire sauce with wire
whisk until smooth. Add vinegar
mixture and chopped basil to corn
mixture; toss to coat well. Let stand
10 minutes.

3 To serve, stir gently to mix.
Garnish with basil sprigs and pecan
halves.

High Altitude (3500–6500 ft): No change.

1 Serving: Calories 180; Total Fat 8g (Saturated Fat
1g; Trans Fat 0g); Cholesterol 0mg; Sodium 180mg;
Total Carbohydrate 25g (Dietary Fiber 2g) Exchanges:
½ Starch, 1 Other Carbohydrate, 1½ Fat; Carbohydrate
Choices: 1½

It Was a Dark and Stormy Night

Asked about a memorable cooking experience, Ellen Nishimura shared
this story when she became a finalist: "Three years ago my husband
trained for a marathon. The day before the race, it started to rain. He was
determined to run no matter what. That night the rain developed into one
of the worst storms all winter. I was so worried I couldn't sleep, and at
three in the morning, I got up and started to bake cookies to try to relax.

My husband slept through the storm—and my baking—and at
six o'clock in the morning, he found me in the kitchen—with
over nine dozen cookies. I took them to work. Lou ran the
marathon in the storm and hasn't run another since—but my
coworkers keep encouraging him to try again."

Pilgrim Corn Salad

Spicy Broccoli-Mango Salad

Spicy Broccoli-Mango Salad

Deborah Phinney   Lakewood, OH
Bake-Off® Contest 41, 2004

Prep Time: 25 Minutes
Start to Finish: 25 Minutes
6 servings (1 cup each)

SWEET-HOT PECANS

4 teaspoons sugar

¼ to ½ teaspoon ground red pepper (cayenne)

½ cup pecan halves, broken into coarse pieces

DRESSING

2 containers (6 oz each) orange crème fat-free yogurt

⅓ cup light mayonnaise

1 tablespoon cider vinegar

⅛ teaspoon salt

SALAD

5 cups fresh broccoli florets and cut-up stems (1 small bunch)

1½ cups diced peeled seeded mango (2 medium)

¼ cup finely chopped red onion

1   Lightly spray 8-inch skillet with cooking spray. Add sugar and ground red pepper; mix well. Stir in pecans. Cook over low heat, stirring occasionally, until sugar mixture is melted and pecans are coated. Remove from heat; set aside to cool.

2   In small bowl, mix dressing ingredients with wire whisk until smooth. In large bowl, mix salad ingredients.

3   Add dressing to salad; toss gently to mix. Just before serving, stir in cooled pecans. Cover and refrigerate any remaining salad.

High Altitude (3500–6500 ft): No change.

1 Serving: Calories 240; Total Fat 11g (Saturated Fat 1.5g; Trans Fat 0g); Cholesterol 10mg; Sodium 190mg; Total Carbohydrate 29g (Dietary Fiber 3g) Exchanges: ½ Fruit, 1 Other Carbohydrate, 1 Vegetable, ½ High-Fat Meat, 1½ Fat; Carbohydrate Choices: 2

Spicy Corn and Black Bean Salad

Marlys Ward   Mankato, MN
Bake-Off® Contest 34, 1990

Prep Time: 15 Minutes
Start to Finish: 2 Hours 15 Minutes
11 servings (½ cup each)

SALAD

½ cup peeled, thinly sliced cucumber

2 tablespoons finely chopped fresh jalapeño chile

8 medium green onions, sliced (½ cup)

2 cans (11 oz each) vacuum-packed whole kernel corn with red and green peppers, drained

1 can (15 oz) black beans, drained, rinsed

1 jar (4.5 oz) sliced mushrooms, drained

DRESSING

⅓ cup vegetable oil

¼ cup rice wine vinegar or white vinegar

¼ cup orange juice

½ teaspoon salt

2 cloves garlic, finely chopped

¼ cup chopped fresh cilantro

1 tablespoon grated orange peel

1 to 2 teaspoons cumin seed

Lettuce leaves

1   In large bowl, mix salad ingredients. In small bowl, mix oil, vinegar, orange juice, salt and garlic with wire whisk. Pour over salad; toss gently. Cover; refrigerate 1 to 2 hours to blend flavors.

2   Just before serving, drain salad. Stir in cilantro, orange peel and cumin seed. Serve in lettuce-lined bowl or on lettuce-lined plates. Store in refrigerator.

High Altitude (3500–6500 ft): No change.

1 Serving: Calories 170; Total Fat 7g (Saturated Fat 1g; Trans Fat 0g); Cholesterol 0mg; Sodium 330mg; Total Carbohydrate 21g (Dietary Fiber 5g) Exchanges: 1½ Starch, 1 Fat; Carbohydrate Choices: 1½

Roosevelt Gives Winning Vote

Former first lady Eleanor Roosevelt was a prominent advocate of women's achievements during her husband's political career and beyond. She attended the first Bake-Off® Contest and wrote about it in her newspaper column, "My Day." "This is a healthy contest and a highly American one. It may sell Pillsbury® flour, but it also reaches far down into the lives of the housewives of America. These were the women who ran their homes and cooked at home," she told readers, "they were not professional cooks."

Southwestern Couscous Salad

Rocky Brown   Carmichaels, PA
Bake-Off® Contest 35, 1992

Prep Time: 35 Minutes
Start to Finish: 1 Hour 35 Minutes
12 servings (½ cup each)

SALAD
1½ cups water
1 cup uncooked couscous
1½ cups frozen whole kernel corn (from 1-lb bag), cooked, cooled
1 can (15 oz) black beans, drained, rinsed
¼ cup chopped seeded tomato
¼ cup chopped green bell pepper
¼ cup chopped red bell pepper
2 medium green onions, sliced (2 tablespoons)
2 tablespoons chopped fresh cilantro or parsley

DRESSING
⅓ cup olive oil or vegetable oil
¼ to ⅓ cup lime juice
¼ teaspoon salt, if desired
¼ teaspoon garlic powder
¼ teaspoon ground cumin
⅛ teaspoon ground red pepper (cayenne)

GARNISH, IF DESIRED
Lettuce leaves
Fresh cilantro
Lime slices

1   In 1-quart saucepan, heat water to boiling; remove from heat. Stir in couscous. Cover; let stand 5 minutes. Cool completely.

2   In large bowl, toss salad ingredients. In small jar with tight-fitting lid, shake dressing ingredients.

Pour over salad; toss to coat. Cover; refrigerate 1 hour to blend flavors.

3   Line serving platter with lettuce leaves; spoon salad over lettuce leaves. Garnish with cilantro and lime slices.

High Altitude (3500–6500 ft): No change.

1 Serving: Calories 170; Total Fat 6g (Saturated Fat 1g; Trans Fat 0g); Cholesterol 0mg; Sodium 0mg; Total Carbohydrate 24g (Dietary Fiber 4g) Exchanges: 1½ Starch, 1 Fat; Carbohydrate Choices: 1½

Island Paradise Salad

Judith Mettlin   Snyder, NY
Bake-Off® Contest 39, 2000
$10,000 Winner

Prep Time: 20 Minutes
Start to Finish: 20 Minutes
8 servings (1¼ cups each)

DRESSING
1 teaspoon grated lime peel
3 tablespoons honey
2 tablespoons fresh lime juice
1 tablespoon canola or vegetable oil

SALAD
2 cups frozen sugar snap peas (from 1-lb bag)
3 cups torn romaine lettuce
3 cups torn Bibb lettuce
1 avocado, peeled, pitted and cut into ½-inch cubes
1 large ripe mango, peeled, seed removed and cut into ½-inch cubes
1 small red onion, thinly sliced, separated into rings
½ cup unsweetened or regular shredded coconut

1   In small bowl, mix dressing ingredients.

2   Cook sugar snap peas as directed on bag; drain. Rinse with cold water to cool; drain well.

3   In large bowl, mix cooked sugar snap peas and all remaining salad ingredients except coconut. Add dressing; toss to coat. Sprinkle with coconut.

High Altitude (3500–6500 ft): No change.

1 Serving: Calories 150; Total Fat 9g (Saturated Fat 3.5g; Trans Fat 0g); Cholesterol 0mg; Sodium 10mg; Total Carbohydrate 15g (Dietary Fiber 4g) Exchanges: ½ Other Carbohydrate, 1 Vegetable, 2 Fat; Carbohydrate Choices: 1

Mexican Macaroni Salad

Cheryl Amato   South Amboy, NJ
Bake-Off® Contest 42, 2006

Prep Time: 30 Minutes
Start to Finish: 1 Hour 30 Minutes
8 servings (1¼ cups each)

6 cups uncooked rotini pasta (1 lb)
1 to 2 tablespoons grated lime peel (from 2 medium limes)
3 to 4 tablespoons lime juice (from 2 medium limes)
1 cup ranch dressing
1 package (1.25 oz) taco seasoning mix
1 large avocado, pitted, peeled and finely chopped
1 pint (2 cups) cherry or grape tomatoes, cut in half
1 cup shredded Cheddar cheese (4 oz)
2 tablespoons finely chopped fresh cilantro
2 medium green onions, sliced (including tops)
1 can (19 oz) red kidney beans, drained, rinsed
1 can (6 oz) pitted large ripe olives, drained, cut in half
1 can (4.5 oz) chopped green chiles, drained

1 Cook and drain pasta as directed on package. Rinse with cold water to cool; drain well.

2 Meanwhile, grate peel from limes; place in small bowl. Squeeze juice from limes; add to peel in bowl. Stir in dressing and taco seasoning mix. Stir avocado into dressing mixture.

3 In large serving bowl, toss pasta with remaining ingredients. Pour dressing mixture over salad; toss gently to mix. Cover; refrigerate at least 1 hour before serving to blend flavors.

High Altitude (3500–6500 ft): No change.

1 Serving: Calories 610; Total Fat 27g (Saturated Fat 6g; Trans Fat 0g); Cholesterol 25mg; Sodium 1190mg; Total Carbohydrate 72g (Dietary Fiber 9g) Exchanges: 4 Starch, 1 Other Carbohydrate, 1 Lean Meat, 4 Fat; Carbohydrate Choices: 5

Mexican Macaroni Salad

Shrimp and Rice Salad

Nina Hutchison   Windsor, CA
Bake-Off® Contest 42, 2006

Prep Time: 25 Minutes
Start to Finish: 4 Hours 45 Minutes
6 servings (1⅔ cups each)

1½ cups water
1 box (6.4 oz) chicken fried rice skillet-meal mix for chicken
½ cup frozen sweet peas (from 1-lb bag)
¾ cup chopped fresh cilantro
¾ cup sliced pimiento-stuffed green olives
½ cup chopped red onion
5 tablespoons balsamic vinegar
2 tablespoons vegetable oil
2 medium tomatoes, chopped (1½ cups)
1 large Anaheim chile, finely chopped (3 tablespoons)
1 can (15 oz) black beans, drained, rinsed
1 bag (12 oz) frozen cooked cocktail shrimp (60 to 80 count per pound), thawed
1 can (11 oz) vacuum-packed white shoepeg corn, drained

1   In 10-inch skillet, heat water, uncooked rice and seasoning mix to boiling over high heat, stirring occasionally. Reduce heat to low; cover and simmer 7 minutes.

2   Stir in frozen peas. Cover; cook 3 to 5 minutes longer or until water is completely absorbed. Pour rice mixture into large bowl. Cool about 15 minutes.

3   Stir in remaining ingredients. Cover; refrigerate 3 to 4 hours before serving.

High Altitude (3500–6500 ft): Follow High Altitude directions on skillet-meal box.

1 Serving: Calories 400; Total Fat 9g (Saturated Fat 1.5g; Trans Fat 0g); Cholesterol 110mg; Sodium 1190mg; Total Carbohydrate 56g (Dietary Fiber 9g) Exchanges: 3 Starch, ½ Other Carbohydrate, 2 Very Lean Meat, 1½ Fat; Carbohydrate Choices: 4

Sesame Stir-Fry Shrimp Salad

Kathryn Keeler   Ashland, MA
Bake-Off® Contest 41, 2004

Prep Time: 30 Minutes
Start to Finish: 30 Minutes
4 servings

2 oz uncooked cellophane noodles (bean threads)
1 bag (1 lb 5 oz) frozen stir-fry vegetables and sesame stir-fry sauce meal starter
3 tablespoons chopped fresh cilantro
2 tablespoons rice vinegar or white vinegar
1 tablespoon lime juice
Dash ground red pepper (cayenne) or to taste
3 cups three-color (green and red cabbage and carrots) coleslaw mix (from 16-oz bag)
1½ cups cooked deveined peeled medium shrimp (about ½ lb), tail shells removed
Chopped peanuts, if desired

1   With kitchen scissors or sharp knife, cut loops of dried noodles into 3- to 5-inch-long pieces; place in 1-quart bowl. Pour boiling water over noodles; let soak 5 to 7 minutes or until flexible but still slightly firm. Drain in colander; rinse and set aside.

2   Meanwhile, in large bowl, reserve 3 tablespoons sesame sauce from meal starter. Spray 12-inch skillet or wok with cooking spray;

Starstruck

Award-winning actresses Greer Garson (1942, *Mrs. Miniver*) and Helen Hayes (1931, *The Sin of Madelon Claudet*) watched as other women were recognized for their creative talents in 1958 and 1959. Movie stars Irene Dunne, of the classic *My Favorite Wife* (with heartthrob Cary Grant), and Jeanette MacDonald, best known for her musical films with Nelson Eddy (*Love Me Tonight*), mingled through the crowds in the 1950s too, happy to pose with the finalists who were stars in their own kitchens. Television or celebrity hosts have always played an important role in the Bake-Off® Contest. Art Linkletter's antics provided thousands of wonderful moments.

Later, Bob Barker hosted eleven ceremonies. Recent years have seen celebrities including Gary Collins, Willard Scott, Alex Trebek, Marie Osmond and Joy Behar leading the festivities. But the stars that shine the brightest have always been the Bake-Off® finalists themselves.

heat over medium-high heat. Add remaining sesame sauce and frozen vegetables from meal starter. Cover; cook 5 to 7 minutes, stirring frequently, just until vegetables are crisp-tender. Remove from heat; cover to keep warm.

3 To reserved sauce in bowl, stir in cilantro, vinegar, lime juice and ground red pepper. Add drained noodles, coleslaw blend and shrimp; toss to coat. Add cooked vegetables and sauce from skillet; toss. Top with peanuts.

High Altitude (3500–6500 ft): No change.

1 Serving: Calories 210; Total Fat 4.5g (Saturated Fat 1g; Trans Fat 0g); Cholesterol 105mg; Sodium 910mg; Total Carbohydrate 27g (Dietary Fiber 5g) Exchanges: ½ Starch, 1 Other Carbohydrate, 1 Vegetable, 1½ Very Lean Meat, ½ Fat; Carbohydrate Choices: 2

Sesame Stir-Fry Shrimp Salad

Antipasto Tortellini Salad

Vickie Cox   Sacramento, CA
Bake-Off® Contest 35, 1992
$2,000 Winner

> Prep Time: 30 Minutes
> Start to Finish: 2 Hour 30 Minutes
> 12 servings (1 cup each)

1 package (16 oz) fresh or frozen
  uncooked cheese-filled tortellini
4 oz (1 cup) chopped salami
4 oz provolone cheese, cut into
  2 × ¼ × ¼-inch strips
1 can (11 oz) vacuum-packed whole
  kernel corn, drained
1 box (9 oz) frozen spinach, thawed,
  squeezed to drain
1 jar (6 oz) marinated artichoke hearts,
  drained, chopped
1 can (6 oz) pitted ripe olives, drained,
  sliced (1½ cups)
1½ cups creamy Italian dressing
1 teaspoon Dijon mustard
½ cup grated Parmesan cheese
1 jar (2 oz) diced pimiento, drained,
  if desired

1   Cook tortellini to desired
doneness as directed on package.
Drain; rinse with cold water.

2   In very large bowl, mix tortellini, salami, provolone cheese,
corn, spinach, artichoke hearts and
1 cup of the olives. In small bowl,
mix dressing, mustard and ¼ cup of
the Parmesan cheese. Pour dressing
over salad; toss gently. Top with
remaining olives and Parmesan
cheese. Cover; refrigerate 1 to 2
hours to blend flavors. Just before
serving, garnish with pimiento.

High Altitude (3500–6500 ft): No change.

1 Serving: Calories 320 (Calories from Fat 150); Total
Fat 17g (Saturated Fat 5g; Trans Fat 0g); Cholesterol 35mg;
Sodium 1020mg; Total Carbohydrate 29g (Dietary
Fiber 3g) Exchanges: 1½ Starch, ½ Other Carbohydrate,
1 High-Fat Meat, 1½ Fat; Carbohydrate Choices: 2

Black Bean Cake Salad with Cilantro-Lime Cream

Lisa Silcox   Abingdon, VA
Bake-Off® Contest 42, 2006

> Prep Time: 35 Minutes
> Start to Finish: 35 Minutes
> 6 servings

BEAN CAKES
1 can (15 oz) black beans, drained
1 egg, slightly beaten
1 cup unseasoned dry bread crumbs
2 tablespoons finely chopped red onion
1 teaspoon garlic powder
1 teaspoon ground cumin
¼ teaspoon salt, if desired
1 teaspoon lime juice
1 can (4.5 oz) chopped green chiles

CILANTRO-LIME SOUR CREAM
½ cup reduced-fat sour cream
1 tablespoon chopped fresh cilantro
¼ teaspoon sugar
⅛ teaspoon salt
2 teaspoons lime juice

SALAD
1 tablespoon sugar
⅛ teaspoon salt
¼ cup extra-virgin olive oil
2 tablespoons red wine vinegar
2 teaspoons finely chopped jalapeño
  chile (from a jar)
1 teaspoon jalapeño liquid (from jar)
1 bag (5 oz) spring or baby salad greens

GARNISH
Fresh sprigs of cilantro, if desired

1   Heat oven to 400°F. Spray
cookie sheet with cooking spray.
In medium bowl, mash beans with
fork or pastry blender. Stir in egg,
¾ cup of the bread crumbs and
remaining bean cake ingredients.
Shape mixture into 6 patties,
3 inches in diameter and ½ inch
thick. Sprinkle both sides of bean
patties with remaining ¼ cup bread
crumbs; place on cookie sheet.

2   Bake 10 minutes. Turn bean
cakes over; bake 10 to 13 minutes
longer or until bread crumbs begin
to turn golden brown.

3   Meanwhile, in small bowl, mix
cilantro-lime sour cream ingredients; set aside. In large bowl, beat
all salad ingredients except salad
greens with wire whisk until well
blended. Add salad greens; toss
until coated.

4   To serve, arrange salad evenly
on individual plates. Top each with
bean cake and dollop of cilantro-
lime sour cream. Garnish with
cilantro sprigs.

High Altitude (3500–6500 ft): No change.

1 Serving: Calories 300; Total Fat 14g (Saturated Fat 3.5g;
Trans Fat 0g); Cholesterol 45mg; Sodium 600mg;
Total Carbohydrate 35g (Dietary Fiber 8g) Exchanges:
1½ Starch, 1 Other Carbohydrate, ½ Very Lean Meat,
2½ Fat; Carbohydrate Choices: 2

Fiesta Chicken Salad

Greta Eberhardt   San Pedro, CA
Bake-Off® Contest 37, 1996
$2,000 Winner

> Prep Time: 30 Minutes
> Start to Finish: 50 Minutes
> 8 servings

¼ cup butter or margarine, cut into
    4 pieces
6 boneless skinless chicken breasts
2 eggs
1¼ cups picante or salsa
1⅓ cups unseasoned dry bread crumbs
1 teaspoon salt
1 teaspoon ground cumin
1 teaspoon chili powder
½ teaspoon ground oregano
4 medium green onions, sliced (¼ cup)
8 cups mixed salad greens
3 medium tomatoes, chopped
1 bottle (8 oz) red wine vinegar and oil
    dressing
1 cup sour cream
1 avocado, peeled, sliced

1   Heat oven to 400°F. In ungreased 15 × 10 × 1-inch baking pan, melt butter in oven. Remove from oven. Tilt pan to coat with butter.

2   Meanwhile, cut chicken breasts in half lengthwise. Cut crosswise into ½-inch slices. In large bowl, beat eggs; stir in chicken and ¼ cup of the picante.

3   In shallow bowl, mix bread crumbs, salt, cumin, chili powder and oregano. Add chicken pieces to bread crumb mixture, a few at a time; turn to coat. Place coated chicken in butter-coated pan. Bake 15 to 20 minutes or until chicken is no longer pink in center.

4   Reserve 1 tablespoon of the green onions for garnish. In large bowl, gently toss remaining onions, salad greens and tomatoes. Pour half of the dressing over salad; toss to coat. Arrange evenly on 8 individual plates.

5   Spoon chicken onto center of each salad. Top each with 1 tablespoon sour cream and about ½ teaspoon reserved green onions. Garnish each plate with avocado slices. Serve salads with remaining half of salad dressing, ½ cup sour cream and 1 cup picante.

High Altitude (3500–6500 ft): No change.

1 Serving: Calories 410; Total Fat 25g (Saturated Fat 9g; Trans Fat 0.5g); Cholesterol 140mg; Sodium 1090mg; Total Carbohydrate 21g (Dietary Fiber 4g) Exchanges: 1 Other Carbohydrate, 1 Vegetable, 3½ Very Lean Meat, 4½ Fat; Carbohydrate Choices: 1½

Margarita Chicken Pasta Salad

Michelle Gregovic   Houston, TX
Bake-Off® Contest 38, 1998

> Prep Time: 30 Minutes
> Start to Finish: 30 Minutes
> 6 servings (1½ cups each)

SALAD
4 cups uncooked rainbow rotini pasta
    (10 oz)
1 lb chicken breast strips for stir-frying
1 package (1.25 oz) taco seasoning
    mix
1 tablespoon olive or vegetable oil
1 can (11 oz) vacuum-packed whole
    kernel corn with red and green
    peppers, drained
1 can (15 oz) black beans, drained,
    rinsed

DRESSING
½ cup fresh orange juice
¼ cup olive or vegetable oil
¼ cup sour cream
3 tablespoons fresh lime juice
1 teaspoon sugar
¼ teaspoon ground cumin
⅛ teaspoon salt
4 teaspoons tequila, if desired
1 cup loosely packed fresh cilantro leaves
1 can (4.5 oz) chopped green chiles

GARNISH, IF DESIRED
Lime wedges
Cilantro leaves

1   Cook and drain pasta as directed on package. Rinse with cold water to cool; drain well.

2   Meanwhile, in resealable food-storage plastic bag, place chicken and taco seasoning mix; shake to coat. In 10-inch nonstick skillet, heat 1 tablespoon oil over medium heat until hot. Cook chicken in oil 8 to 10 minutes, stirring frequently, until golden brown and no longer pink in center. Remove from heat; set aside.

3   In blender or food processor, place dressing ingredients. Cover; blend about 30 seconds or until well blended.

4   In large serving bowl, toss cooked rotini, corn, beans and dressing. Fold in cooked chicken. Serve warm or cold. Garnish with lime wedges and cilantro leaves.

High Altitude (3500–6500 ft): No change.

1 Serving: Calories 580; Total Fat 18g (Saturated Fat 3.5g; Trans Fat 0g); Cholesterol 50mg; Sodium 1320mg; Total Carbohydrate 74g (Dietary Fiber 10g) Exchanges: 4 Starch, 1 Other Carbohydrate, 2½ Very Lean Meat, 2½ Fat; Carbohydrate Choices: 5

Layered Caribbean Chicken Salad

Barbara Jansky   Estero, FL
Bake-Off® Contest 41, 2004
$5,000 Dinner Made Easy Runner-Up
Winner

Prep Time: 30 Minutes
Start to Finish: 30 Minutes
6 servings (1½ cups each)

DRESSING
1 container (6 oz) piña colada fat-free
   yogurt
1½ to 2 tablespoons lime juice
1 teaspoon Caribbean jerk seasoning

SALAD
3 cups shredded romaine lettuce
2 cups cubed cooked chicken
1 cup shredded Monterey Jack cheese
   (4 oz)
1 can (15 oz) black beans, drained,
   rinsed
1½ cups diced peeled ripe fresh mango
½ cup chopped seeded plum (Roma)
   tomatoes (1 to 2 medium)
1 cup shredded Cheddar cheese (4 oz)
½ cup thinly sliced green onions
   (8 medium)
½ cup cashews
Fresh edible flowers, if desired

1 In small bowl, mix dressing
ingredients until well blended.

2 In 3- or 4-quart clear glass
serving bowl, layer salad ingredients
in order listed, except cashews and
flowers. Spoon dressing evenly over
salad; sprinkle cashews over top.
Garnish with flowers.

High Altitude (3500–6500 ft): No change.

1 Serving: Calories 450; Total Fat 21g (Saturated Fat 10g;
Trans Fat 0g); Cholesterol 80mg; Sodium 320mg;
Total Carbohydrate 34g (Dietary Fiber 8g) Exchanges:
1 Starch, 1 Other Carbohydrate, 1 Vegetable, 3½ Lean
Meat, 2 Fat; Carbohydrate Choices: 2

Seven-Layer Chinese Chicken Salad

Ellen Nishimura   Fair Oaks, CA
Bake-Off® Contest 38, 1998
$2,000 Winner

Prep Time: 15 Minutes
Start to Finish: 15 Minutes
5 servings (2 cups each)

SALAD
5 cups shredded romaine lettuce
1 package (3 oz) Oriental-flavor ramen
   noodle soup mix
2 cups diced cooked chicken
1 can (11 oz) vacuum-packed white
   shoepeg corn, drained
1 large tomato, diced
2 medium green onions, sliced
   (2 tablespoons)
½ cup coarsely chopped unsalted
   dry-roasted peanuts

DRESSING
2 tablespoons sugar
1 teaspoon salt
¾ teaspoon grated gingerroot
½ teaspoon pepper
¼ cup vegetable oil
3 tablespoons vinegar

1   In bottom of large (3-quart) clear glass serving bowl, arrange romaine. Discard seasoning packet from soup mix; coarsely crush noodles. Layer noodles and remaining salad ingredients, in order listed, over romaine.

2   In small jar with tight-fitting lid, shake dressing ingredients until well blended. Pour over salad. Serve immediately.

High Altitude (3500–6500 ft): No change.

1 Serving: Calories 460; Total Fat 26g (Saturated Fat 5g; Trans Fat 1g); Cholesterol 50mg; Sodium 930mg; Total Carbohydrate 33g (Dietary Fiber 4g) Exchanges: 1 Starch, 1 Other Carbohydrate, 1 Vegetable, 2½ Lean Meat, 3½ Fat; Carbohydrate Choices: 2

Tuscan Roasted Potato–Chicken Salad

Karen Tedesco   Webster Groves, MO
Bake-Off® Contest 42, 2006

Prep Time: 30 Minutes
Start to Finish: 30 Minutes
4 servings (1½ cups each)

1 bag (19 oz) frozen roasted potatoes
   with garlic & herb sauce
1 cup diced fresh mozzarella cheese
   (6 oz)
⅓ cup oil-packed sun-dried tomatoes
   (from a jar), drained, cut into strips
2 to 3 teaspoons chopped fresh
   rosemary
1 can (15 oz) cannellini beans, drained,
   rinsed
1 package (6 oz) refrigerated grilled
   chicken breast strips, heated in
   microwave as directed on package,
   coarsely chopped
⅓ cup basil pesto
2 teaspoons fresh lemon juice
Salt and pepper, if desired
3 cups mixed baby salad greens
¼ cup pine nuts, toasted*

1   In 2-quart microwavable bowl or casserole, microwave frozen potatoes and sauce chips, covered, on High 9 to 13 minutes, stirring once halfway through microwaving, until potatoes are tender. Stir potatoes to mix with sauce. Pour potato mixture into large bowl.

2   Stir in cheese, tomatoes, rosemary, beans and warm chicken. Add pesto and lemon juice; gently toss to coat. Season to taste with salt and pepper.

3   Arrange salad greens on large serving platter. Spoon potato salad over lettuce; sprinkle with pine nuts. Serve warm or at room temperature.

* To toast pine nuts, place in single layer on cookie sheet; bake at 350°F 8 minutes, stirring once, until golden brown.

High Altitude (3500–6500 ft): No change.

1 Serving: Calories 610; Total Fat 30g (Saturated Fat 10g; Trans Fat 1g); Cholesterol 55mg; Sodium 1290mg; Total Carbohydrate 48g (Dietary Fiber 9g) Exchanges: 3 Starch, 1 Vegetable, 3½ Very Lean Meat, 5 Fat; Carbohydrate Choices: 3

Baja Chicken Salad with Taco Vinaigrette

Pat Harmon Baden, PA
Bake-Off® Contest 40, 2002

Prep Time: 30 Minutes
Start to Finish: 30 Minutes
6 servings

1 package (1.25 oz) taco seasoning mix
1 tablespoon packed brown sugar
½ cup vegetable oil
½ cup cider vinegar
4 boneless skinless chicken breasts, cut into 1-inch pieces
1 to 2 tablespoons vegetable oil
1 bag (10 oz) mixed salad greens or baby greens
1 cup grape tomatoes, halved
½ cup sliced red onion
⅔ cup shredded Cheddar-Monterey Jack cheese blend
⅓ cup sour cream
1 avocado, pitted, peeled and sliced
3 tablespoons sliced ripe olives
Blue tortilla chips

1 In medium bowl, mix taco seasoning mix, brown sugar, ½ cup oil and the vinegar. Place chicken in shallow medium bowl. Pour ½ cup seasoning mixture over chicken. Reserve remaining mixture for dressing.

2 In 8-inch nonstick skillet, heat 1 to 2 tablespoons oil over medium-high heat until hot. With slotted spoon, remove chicken from seasoning mixture; add to skillet. Cook about 5 minutes, stirring frequently, until no longer pink in center. Discard remaining used seasoning mixture.

3 In large bowl, toss mixed greens, tomatoes and onion. Add reserved seasoning mixture; toss to coat. Arrange salad mixture on serving platter. Top with chicken, cheese, sour cream, avocado and olives. Arrange tortilla chips around salad.

High Altitude (3500–6500 ft): No change.

1 Serving: Calories 410; Total Fat 30g (Saturated Fat 8g; Trans Fat 0g); Cholesterol 70mg; Sodium 550mg; Total Carbohydrate 12g (Dietary Fiber 3g) Exchanges: ½ Other Carbohydrate, 1 Vegetable, 3 Very Lean Meat, 5½ Fat; Carbohydrate Choices: 1

Nutty Chicken Dinner Salad

Holly Young Bountiful UT
Bake-Off® Contest 42, 2006

Prep Time: 40 Minutes
Start to Finish: 40 Minutes
4 servings

1 bag (10 oz) organic frozen raspberries
½ cup oil and vinegar dressing
¼ cup chopped pecans
1 tablespoon packed brown sugar
2 tablespoons mayonnaise or salad dressing
2 tablespoons maple-flavored syrup or real maple syrup
4 cinnamon crunchy granola bars (2 pouches from 8.9-oz box), finely crushed (¾ cup)*
1 egg

1 lb uncooked chicken breast tenders (not breaded)
½ teaspoon salt
⅛ teaspoon pepper
3 tablespoon vegetable oil
1 bag (10 oz) mixed baby salad greens
½ cup thinly sliced red onion
2 slices (¾ to 1 oz each) Swiss cheese, cut into thin julienne strips
¼ cup pecan halves, toasted ** or glazed

1 Spread frozen raspberries on paper towel; let stand to thaw while making dressing and salad. In small bowl, mix dressing, chopped pecans, brown sugar, mayonnaise and syrup with wire whisk until well blended. Refrigerate until serving time.

2 Place finely crushed granola bars on paper plate or in pie plate. In shallow bowl or another pie plate, beat egg with fork. Sprinkle chicken with salt and pepper.

3 In 12-inch nonstick skillet, heat oil over medium heat. Add chicken to beaten egg; stir to coat. Dip each chicken strip lightly into crushed granola bars; add to skillet. Cook 6 to 8 minutes, turning once, until chicken is no longer pink in center and browned on all sides. Remove from skillet; drain on paper towels.

4 In large serving bowl, mix salad greens, onion, cheese and thawed raspberries. Toss, adding only enough dressing to evenly coat ingredients. Arrange greens mixture on individual plates. Place chicken evenly over greens. Arrange pecan halves on top. Drizzle with remaining dressing.

* To crush granola bars, unwrap and place in small resealable food-storage plastic bag; use rolling pin to finely crush bars.

** To toast pecans, bake uncovered in ungreased shallow pan in 350°F oven about 10 minutes, stirring occasionally, until golden brown.

High Altitude (3500–6500 ft): In step 3, cook over medium-high heat.

1 Serving: Calories 680; Total Fat 41g (Saturated Fat 7g; Trans Fat 0g); Cholesterol 135mg; Sodium 840mg; Total Carbohydrate 42g (Dietary Fiber 8g) Exchanges: 1½ Starch, 1 Other Carbohydrate, 1 Vegetable, 4 Very Lean Meat, 7 ½ Fat; Carbohydrate Choices: 3

Nutty Chicken Dinner Salad

If at First You Don't Succeed...

Life is not easy for any of us. "We must have perseverance and, above all, confidence in ourselves," said the scientist Marie Curie. Karen Casillas certainly took this adage to heart after an early disaster. "I made an orange cake with orange frosting when I was six, from a mix." The cake did not turn out well. "My mom gave it to our dog! And six years later we dug up a complete piece—whole!—when putting in a garden. No kidding!" Karen persevered, however, mastered cooking and got herself into the Bake-Off® Contest. Marie Curie surely would have been impressed.

Chicken 'n Corn Tostada Salad

Karen S. Casillas Corona Hills, CA
Bake-Off® Contest 35, 1992

> **Prep Time:** 40 Minutes
> **Start to Finish:** 1 Hour 10 Minutes
> 10 servings (1½ cups each)

DRESSING
¼ cup cider vinegar or vinegar
3 tablespoons honey
1½ teaspoons ground cumin
¼ teaspoon salt
⅛ teaspoon pepper

SALAD
1 tablespoon olive oil or vegetable oil
4 boneless skinless chicken breasts, cut into 2 × ½-inch strips
½ teaspoon garlic salt
1 bag (1 lb) frozen extra sweet whole kernel corn
1 cup chopped seeded plum (Roma) tomatoes or tomatoes
1 can (15 oz) black beans, drained, rinsed
5 green onions, thinly sliced, including tops
2 medium avocados, peeled, chopped
1 head butterhead, Boston or Bibb lettuce, torn into bite-size pieces
1 small red bell pepper, chopped
2 cups shredded Monterey Jack cheese (8 oz)
3 cups slightly crushed blue corn tortilla chips or tortilla chips

GARNISH, IF DESIRED
1¼ cups picante or salsa
1¼ cups sour cream

1 In small jar with tight-fitting lid, shake dressing ingredients; set aside.

2 In 10-inch skillet, heat oil over medium-high heat until hot. Add chicken; cook about 5 minutes or until no longer pink. Transfer chicken to very large bowl; sprinkle with garlic salt. Make corn as directed on bag; drain. Stir into chicken. Cover; refrigerate about 30 minutes.

3 Add tomatoes, black beans, onions, avocados, lettuce and bell pepper to chicken mixture; toss. Shake dressing and pour over salad mixture; toss lightly.* Just before serving, add cheese and tortilla chips; toss gently. Garnish with salsa and sour cream. Serve immediately.

* To make ahead, recipe can be prepared to this point. Cover; store in refrigerator.

High Altitude (3500–6500 ft): In step 2, cook chicken 5 to 7 minutes.

1 Serving: Calories 420; Total Fat 21g (Saturated Fat 6g; Trans Fat 0g); Cholesterol 50mg; Sodium 340mg; Total Carbohydrate 35g (Dietary Fiber 8g) Exchanges: 1 Starch, 1 Other Carbohydrate, 1 Vegetable, 2½ Lean Meat, 2½ Fat; Carbohydrate Choices: 2

Chicken and Black Bean Tostizzas (page 147)

Easy Cheesy Crescent Sandwich

Laura Quigley   New York, NY
Bake-Off® Contest 23, 1972
$1,000 Winner

> Prep Time: 15 Minutes
> Start to Finish: 35 Minutes
> 4 to 6 servings

1½ cups shredded Cheddar cheese (6 oz)
3 tablespoons milk
1 teaspoon ground mustard
Pinch ground red pepper (cayenne)
1 can (8 oz) Pillsbury® refrigerated
   crescent dinner rolls
½ teaspoon poppy seed

1   Heat oven to 400°F.

2   Mix first 4 ingredients. Separate crescent dough into 4 rectangles. Press 2 rectangles over bottom of ungreased 8- or 9-inch square pan. Spread half of cheese mixture over dough. Place remaining 2 rectangles over cheese; gently stretch to cover. Spread with remaining cheese mixture; sprinkle with poppy seed.

3   Bake 15 to 20 minutes or until golden brown. Cut in squares; serve warm.

High Altitude (3500–6500 ft): Do not use 8-inch pan.

1 Serving: Calories 390; Total Fat 27g (Saturated Fat 13g; Trans Fat 3.5g); Cholesterol 45mg; Sodium 710mg; Total Carbohydrate 23g (Dietary Fiber 0g) Exchanges: 1½ Starch, 1½ High-Fat Meat, 3 Fat; Carbohydrate Choices: 1½

Flaky Deli Slices

Arlene Glaser   Parma, OH
Bake-Off® Contest 39, 2000

> Prep Time: 15 Minutes
> Start to Finish: 35 Minutes
> 32 appetizers

1 box (15 oz) Pillsbury® refrigerated pie
   crusts, softened as directed on box
¼ cup grated Parmesan cheese
¾ lb very thinly sliced cooked ham
¼ lb thinly sliced pepperoni
1 cup shredded Cheddar cheese (4 oz)

1   Heat oven to 450°F. Unroll crusts. Sprinkle each crust evenly with Parmesan cheese.

2   Top each crust with ham, pepperoni and Cheddar cheese to within 1 inch of edges. Loosely roll up each crust. Place rolls, seam side down, on ungreased cookie sheet. Fold ends under.

3   Bake 12 to 17 minutes or until golden brown. Cool 5 minutes. Cut each roll into 16 slices. Serve warm.

High Altitude (over 3500 ft): Not recommended.

1 Appetizer: Calories 110; Total Fat 7g (Saturated Fat 3g; Trans Fat 0g); Cholesterol 15mg; Sodium 280mg; Total Carbohydrate 7g (Dietary Fiber 0g) Exchanges: ½ Starch, ½ High-Fat Meat, ½ Fat; Carbohydrate Choices: ½

Ham-it-Up Crescent Snacks

Marsha Kramer   Columbus, OH
Bake-Off® Contest 22, 1971
$2,000 Winner

> Prep Time: 10 Minutes
> Start to Finish: 30 Minutes
> 20 snacks

1 can (8 oz) Pillsbury® refrigerated
   crescent dinner rolls
4 thin slices cooked ham
4 teaspoons yellow mustard
1 cup shredded Cheddar or American
   cheese (4 oz)
Sesame seed

1   Heat oven to 375°F. Unroll dough and separate into 4 rectangles; firmly press perforations to seal. Place ham slices on rectangles, trimming to fit. Spread mustard over ham. Sprinkle with cheese.

2   Starting with one short side, tightly roll up each rectangle; press edge to seal. Coat rolls with sesame seed. With serrated knife, cut each roll into 5 slices; place cut side down on ungreased cookie sheet.

3   Bake 15 to 20 minutes or until golden brown. Immediately remove from cookie sheet. Serve warm.

High Altitude (3500–6500 ft): Bake 13 to 18 minutes.

1 Snack: Calories 70; Total Fat 4.5g (Saturated Fat 2g; Trans Fat 0.5g); Cholesterol 5mg; Sodium 170mg; Total Carbohydrate 5g (Dietary Fiber 0g) Exchanges: ½ Starch, 1 Fat; Carbohydrate Choices: ½

Ham-it-Up Crescent Snacks

Mozzarella and Pesto Crescent Tarts

Tracie Ojakangas   Springfield, MO
Bake-Off® Contest 39, 2000
$2,000 Winner

Prep Time: 20 Minutes
Start to Finish: 35 Minutes
16 servings

1 can (8 oz) Pillsbury® refrigerated
   crescent dinner rolls
2 tablespoons basil pesto
2 medium tomatoes, seeded, sliced*
1 small red onion, thinly sliced
1 to 2 teaspoons chopped fresh
   rosemary or ½ teaspoon dried
   rosemary leaves
½ cup diced fresh mozzarella cheese or
   shredded mozzarella cheese (2 oz)
¼ cup shredded fresh Parmesan cheese

1   Heat oven to 425°F. Unroll dough into 2 long rectangles. Place 3 inches apart on ungreased cookie sheet. Firmly press perforations to seal. Press to form two 10 × 3-inch strips, forming rim around edge of dough.

2   Spread each strip with 1 tablespoon pesto. Top each with tomatoes, onion and rosemary. Sprinkle each with mozzarella and Parmesan cheese.

3   Bake 10 to 14 minutes or until edges are golden brown and cheese is melted. Cut each into crosswise slices. Serve warm or cool.

Four medium plum (Roma) tomatoes can be substituted for the regular tomatoes.

High Altitude (3500–6500 ft): No change.

1 Serving: Calories 90; Total Fat 5g (Saturated Fat 2g; Trans Fat 1g); Cholesterol 0mg; Sodium 170mg; Total Carbohydrate 7g (Dietary Fiber 0g) Exchanges: ½ Starch, 1 Fat; Carbohydrate Choices: ½

Mother-in-Law Knows Best

The challenge of cooking as good as a mother-in-law provides lots of fodder for jokes about life in a marriage. Tracie Ojakangas had an especially tough challenge. Her mother-in-law, Beatrice Ojakangas, had been a Bake-Off® finalist in the '50s, and Beatrice's mother-in-law, Grace Wold, made it to the finals in the '70s. Tracie continued to keep the standard high for any future daughter-in-laws in the family. Not only did she become a finalist in 2000 with her pesto-topped appetizer tarts, she also won a $2,000 prize.

Tex-Mex Appetizer Tart

Richard McHargue   Richmond, KY
Bake-Off® Contest 38, 1998
$10,000 Winner

Prep Time: 15 Minutes
Start to Finish: 1 Hour
16 servings

CRUST
1 Pillsbury® refrigerated pie crust
   (from 15-oz box), softened as
   directed on box

FILLING
1½ cups shredded Colby–Monterey
   Jack cheese blend (6 oz)
½ cup roasted red bell peppers
   (from a jar), drained, chopped
½ cup mayonnaise or salad dressing
1 can (4.5 oz) chopped green chiles

TOPPING
¼ cup chopped fresh cilantro or parsley

1   Heat oven to 375°F. On ungreased cookie sheet, unroll pie crust.

2   In medium bowl, mix filling ingredients. Spread over crust to within 1 inch of edge. Fold crust edge over filling to form 1-inch border to prevent filling from leaking; flute.

3   Bake 25 to 35 minutes or until crust is golden brown. Sprinkle with cilantro. Let stand 10 minutes before serving. Cut into wedges. Serve warm.

High Altitude (3500–6500 ft): No change.

1 Serving: Calories 150; Total Fat 12g (Saturated Fat 4g; Trans Fat 0g); Cholesterol 15mg; Sodium 290mg; Total Carbohydrate 8g (Dietary Fiber 0g) Exchanges: ½ Starch, 2½ Fat; Carbohydrate Choices: ½

Chiles Rellenos Puffs

Sue Tyner   Tustin, CA
Bake-Off® Contest 41, 2004
$5,000 America's Greatest Cheese
Recipe Award Winner

Prep Time: 25 Minutes
Start to Finish: 55 Minutes
24 appetizers

1½ cups water
½ cup butter or margarine
1 cup Pillsbury BEST® all-purpose flour
½ cup cornmeal
1 teaspoon salt
6 eggs, beaten
¾ cup shredded Monterey Jack cheese
   (3 oz)
¾ cup shredded sharp Cheddar cheese
   (3 oz)
2 cans (4.5 oz each) chopped green
   chiles, drained

1   Heat oven to 400°F. Spray
24 regular-size muffin cups
with cooking spray.* In 3-quart
saucepan, heat water and butter to
a full rolling boil over high heat.
Remove from heat.

2   Stir in flour, cornmeal and salt
until mixture forms a dough and all
lumps have disappeared. Gradually
stir in beaten eggs until well
blended. Stir in both cheeses and
the chiles. Spoon dough evenly into
muffin cups, filling each ¾ full.

3   Bake 25 to 29 minutes or until
golden brown. Cool 2 minutes;
remove from muffin cups. Serve
warm.

*If you have only one 12-cup muffin
pan, spoon half of dough into pan;*
*refrigerate remaining dough while
baking first puffs. When first puffs are
done, remove them and spoon refrigerated
dough into pan; bake 28 to 35 minutes.*

High Altitude (3500–6500 ft): No change.

1 Appetizer: Calories 110; Total Fat 8g (Saturated
Fat 4.5g; Trans Fat 0g); Cholesterol 70mg; Sodium
360mg; Total Carbohydrate 7g (Dietary Fiber 0g)
Exchanges: ½ Starch, ½ High-Fat Meat, ½ Fat;
Carbohydrate Choices: ½

Sicilian Mushroom Flatbread

Patricia Schroedl   Jefferson, WI
Bake-Off® Contest 36, 1994
$2,000 Winner

Prep Time: 15 Minutes
Start to Finish: 30 Minutes
8 servings

2 teaspoons olive oil or vegetable oil
⅓ cup finely chopped onion
2 tablespoons finely chopped oil-packed
   sun-dried tomatoes
1 tablespoon finely chopped fresh
   oregano or 1 teaspoon dried oregano
   leaves
2 to 3 teaspoons finely chopped fresh
   rosemary or 1 teaspoon dried
   rosemary leaves
1 teaspoon finely chopped garlic
1 jar (4.5 oz) sliced mushrooms, drained
1 can (13.8 oz) Pillsbury® refrigerated
   classic pizza crust
¼ cup grated Parmesan cheese

1   Heat oven to 425°F. Grease
15 × 10 × 1-inch pan or large
cookie sheet. In 6-inch skillet, heat
oil over medium heat. Cook and stir
onion, tomatoes, oregano, rosemary
and garlic in oil about 4 minutes
or until onion is tender. Stir in
mushrooms. Remove from heat.

Range Savers

Skilled technicians wait in the
wings to troubleshoot any
problems that might arise with the
electric ranges during the contest.
To practice, the technicians run
through drills identifying potential
problems and speedy solutions.

Just in case there's trouble, two
extra work stations are created
on the contest floor, and additional extra ranges are kept
nearby. Should a range mal-
function, a new one
can be hooked up
at a finalist's station
in less than five
minutes.

2   Unroll dough in pan; starting
at center, press out to 12 × 9-inch
rectangle. Spread onion mixture
evenly over dough. Sprinkle with
cheese.

3   Bake 12 to 14 minutes or until
edges of crust are golden brown.
Cut into 16 rectangles.

High Altitude (3500–6500 ft): No change.

1 Serving (2 Appetizers): Calories 160; Total Fat 4g
(Saturated Fat 1g; Trans Fat 0g); Cholesterol 0mg;
Sodium 470mg; Total Carbohydrate 25g (Dietary
Fiber 0g) Exchanges: 1½ Starch, 1 Fat; Carbohydrate
Choices: 1½

Pizza Bubble Ring

Pizza Bubble Ring

Patty Ankney Somerset, PA
Bake-Off® Contest 41, 2004
$5,000 America's Greatest Cheese
Recipe Award Winner

> Prep Time: 20 Minutes
> Start to Finish: 1 Hour 5 Minutes
> 20 servings

6 to 8 tablespoons butter or margarine, melted
1 teaspoon Italian seasoning
½ teaspoon garlic powder
2 cans (12 oz each) Pillsbury® Golden Layers® refrigerated flaky biscuits
40 small slices pepperoni (about 3 oz)
8 oz mozzarella cheese, cut into 20 pieces
¼ cup grated Parmesan cheese
1¼ cups pizza sauce, heated

1 Heat oven to 350°F. Spray 12-cup fluted tube cake pan with cooking spray. In small bowl, mix melted butter, Italian seasoning and garlic powder.

2 Separate 1 can of dough into 10 biscuits; press or roll each into 3-inch round. Place 2 pepperoni slices in center of each biscuit round. Top each with piece of mozzarella cheese. Bring dough up around filling; press edge to seal and shape each into ball. Roll in butter mixture; place 10 balls in pan.

3 Sprinkle dough balls with Parmesan cheese. Repeat with remaining can biscuit rounds, placing balls over balls in pan. Pour remaining butter mixture over top.

4 Bake 33 to 38 minutes or until deep golden brown. Cool 5 minutes. Gently loosen bread from sides of pan. Place large heatproof plate upside down over pan; turn plate and pan over. Remove pan. Serve warm with warm pizza sauce for dipping.

High Altitude (3500–6500 ft): Bake 35 to 40 minutes.

1 Serving: Calories 200; Total Fat 12g (Saturated Fat 6g; Trans Fat 1.5g); Cholesterol 20mg; Sodium 610mg; Total Carbohydrate 16g (Dietary Fiber 0g) Exchanges: 1 Starch, ½ High-Fat Meat, 1½ Fat; Carbohydrate Choices: 1

Creamy Spinach-Artichoke Mini Pizzas

Heather Halonie Webster, WI
Bake-Off® Contest 41, 2004
$5,000 Fast Snacks & Appetizers
Runner-Up Winner

> Prep Time: 15 Minutes
> Start to Finish: 40 Minutes
> 10 pizzas

4 oz cream cheese (from 8-oz package), softened
2 tablespoons sour cream
¾ cup frozen spinach (from 1-lb bag), thawed, squeezed to drain*
½ cup artichoke hearts (from 14-oz can), drained, patted dry with paper towels
1 box (10.6 oz) Pillsbury® refrigerated Italian garlic breadsticks with herbs
¼ cup shredded Parmesan cheese

1 Heat oven to 350°F. In medium bowl, mix cream cheese, sour cream, thawed spinach and artichoke hearts until well blended, breaking up artichokes during stirring.

2 Unroll dough into 1 large rectangle. Spread garlic mixture from box evenly over dough. Separate dough into 10 breadsticks. Reroll each breadstick, coiling dough into spiral shape with garlic mixture inside; place 2 inches apart on ungreased cookie sheet. Starting at center, press out each coil into 3½-inch round (edges will curl up slightly). Spoon and spread cream cheese mixture on top of each round. Sprinkle with cheese.

3 Bake 17 to 22 minutes or until cheese is melted and edges are golden brown. Immediately remove from cookie sheet. Serve warm.

To quickly thaw frozen spinach, place in colander; rinse with cool water until thawed. Drain well; squeeze dry with paper towels.

High Altitude (3500–6500 ft): No change.

1 Pizza: Calories 150; Total Fat 8g (Saturated Fat 4g; Trans Fat 1g); Cholesterol 15mg; Sodium 390mg; Total Carbohydrate 14g (Dietary Fiber 0g) Exchanges: 1 Starch, 1½ Fat; Carbohydrate Choices: 1

Spicy Provolone Cheese Pizza

Gilda Lester   Chadds Ford, PA
Bake-Off® Contest 34, 1990

Prep Time: 20 Minutes
Start to Finish: 35 Minutes
24 servings

1 can (13.8 oz) Pillsbury® refrigerated classic pizza crust
2 to 4 tablespoons olive oil
1 cup finely chopped onion (1 large)
3 cloves garlic, finely chopped
½ teaspoon dried oregano leaves
½ teaspoon dried basil leaves
½ teaspoon dried parsley flakes
½ teaspoon dried thyme leaves
¼ to ½ teaspoon crushed red pepper flakes
8 oz sliced provolone cheese
¼ cup sliced ripe olives, drained

1   Heat oven to 425°F. Lightly grease large cookie sheet or 15 × 10 × 1-inch pan. Unroll dough on cookie sheet. Starting at center, press out dough to form 15 × 10-inch rectangle. Form ¼-inch rim around edges.

2   In 8-inch skillet, heat oil over medium-high heat until hot. Cook onion and garlic in oil about 5 minutes, stirring frequently, until lightly browned. Stir in oregano, basil, parsley, thyme and pepper flakes.

3   Spoon onion mixture evenly over dough. Arrange cheese slices over onions. Sprinkle with olives.

4   Bake 9 to 13 minutes or until cheese is melted and crust is golden brown. Cut into squares. Serve warm.

High Altitude (3500–6500 ft): No change.

1 Serving: Calories 90; Total Fat 4.5g (Saturated Fat 2g; Trans Fat 0g); Cholesterol 5mg; Sodium 210mg; Total Carbohydrate 9g (Dietary Fiber 0g) Exchanges: ½ Starch, 1 Fat; Carbohydrate Choices: ½

Pepperoni 'n Cheese Crescents

Susan Barbour   Wilmington, DE
Bake-Off® Contest 30, 1982

Prep Time: 15 Minutes
Start to Finish: 30 Minutes
8 servings

1 can (8 oz) Pillsbury® refrigerated crescent dinner rolls
24 slices pepperoni
½ cup shredded mozzarella cheese (2 oz)
1 cup tomato pasta or pizza sauce, heated

1   Heat oven to 375°F. Unroll and separate dough into 8 triangles; press out each triangle slightly.

2   Place 3 pepperoni slices, slightly overlapping, on center of each triangle. Top each with about 1 tablespoon cheese. Roll up, starting at shortest side of triangle and rolling to opposite point. On ungreased cookie sheet, place rolls point side down.

3   Bake 10 to 14 minutes or until golden brown. Serve warm crescents with warm pasta sauce for dipping.

High Altitude (3500–6500 ft): No change.

1 Serving (1 crescent and 2 tablespoons sauce each): Calories 240; Total Fat 15g (Saturated Fat 6g; Trans Fat 1.5g); Cholesterol 25mg; Sodium 700mg; Total Carbohydrate 18g (Dietary Fiber 1g) Exchanges: ½ Starch, ½ Other Carbohydrate, 1 High-Fat Meat, 1½ Fat; Carbohydrate Choices: 1

Fireside Memories with Grandma

Gilda Lester's first experiences with pizza created fond memories. "My grandmother had a hearth oven, which she used to bake bread for the week, Gilda recalled. "I helped her, and she always saved a small piece of dough for a pizza for me. I wouldn't give up those days with my grandmother for anything. I helped start the fire, then when the embers had smoldered for just the right amount of time, we cleared the oven for the loaves of bread. Most of my recipes are in my head. They are things that my grandmother, and then my mother, passed on to me."

Spicy Provolone Cheese Pizza

Pizza Pizzazz Snacks

Alice C. Cory   King of Prussia, PA
Bake-Off® Contest 31, 1984

> Prep Time: 15 Minutes
> Start to Finish: 30 Minutes
> 10 snacks

1 can (12 oz) Pillsbury® Golden Layers® refrigerated flaky biscuits
¼ cup tomato pasta sauce
¼ cup chopped pepperoni
2 tablespoons grated Parmesan cheese
1 to 2 tablespoons butter or margarine, melted
¼ teaspoon dried oregano leaves
⅛ teaspoon garlic powder

1   Heat oven to 400°F. Separate dough into 10 biscuits. Separate each biscuit into 2 layers. Place 10 biscuit layers on ungreased cookie sheet; press or roll each to form 2½-inch round. Spoon about 1 teaspoon pasta sauce onto center of each biscuit round. Top each with about 1 teaspoon pepperoni and about ½ teaspoon cheese.

2   Press or roll remaining biscuit layers into 2½-inch rounds. Place over topped biscuit rounds, stretching slightly to fit. Press edges with fork to seal. Brush melted butter over tops. Sprinkle with oregano and garlic powder.

3   Bake 10 to 15 minutes or until deep golden brown. Serve warm.

High Altitude (3500–6500 ft): Use 1 tablespoon melted butter.

1 Snack: Calories 140; Total Fat 7g (Saturated Fat 2.5g; Trans Fat 1.5g); Cholesterol 10mg; Sodium 470mg; Total Carbohydrate 15g (Dietary Fiber 0g) Exchanges: 1 Starch, 1½ Fat; Carbohydrate Choices: 1

Stuffed-Crust Pizza Snacks

Ellen Hyde   Culpeper, VA
Bake-Off® Contest 39, 2000

> Prep Time: 30 Minutes
> Start to Finish: 55 Minutes
> 24 servings

2 cans (13.8 oz each) Pillsbury® classic refrigerated pizza crust
8 oz mozzarella cheese, cut into 48 cubes
48 slices pepperoni (3 oz)
¼ cup olive or vegetable oil
1½ teaspoons Italian seasoning
2 tablespoons grated Parmesan cheese
1 jar (14 oz) pizza sauce, heated

1   Heat oven to 400°F. Grease 13 × 9-inch pan or 2 (9-inch) metal pie pans with shortening or cooking spray. Remove dough from both cans. Unroll dough; starting at center, press out dough into 2 (12 × 8-inch) rectangles. Cut each into 24 squares.

2   Top each square with cheese cube and pepperoni slice. Wrap dough around filling to completely cover, firmly pressing edges to seal. Place seam side down with sides touching in pan(s).

3   In small bowl, mix oil and Italian seasoning; drizzle over dough in pan(s). Sprinkle with Parmesan cheese.

4   Bake 16 to 22 minutes or until golden brown. Serve warm with warm pizza sauce for dipping.

High Altitude (3500–6500 ft): Bake 18 to 24 minutes.

1 Serving (2 snacks and 1 tablespoon sauce): Calories 150; Total Fat 7g (Saturated Fat 2.5g; Trans Fat 0g); Cholesterol 10mg; Sodium 430mg; Total Carbohydrate 17g (Dietary Fiber 0g) Exchanges: 1 Starch, ½ High-Fat Meat, ½ Fat; Carbohydrate Choices: 1

Greek Quesadillas

Jennifer McCusker-Orth   Kingsport, TN
Bake-Off® Contest 41, 2004

> Prep Time: 30 Minutes
> Start to Finish: 30 Minutes
> 8 servings

DIPPING SAUCE
1 container (6 oz) plain fat-free yogurt
1 tablespoon chopped fresh dill
1 teaspoon extra-virgin olive oil
1 teaspoon lemon juice
1 clove garlic, finely chopped

QUESADILLAS
1 cup crumbled feta cheese (4 oz)
1 cup shredded mozzarella cheese (4 oz)
1 cup diced peeled cucumber (1 small)
1 cup finely chopped tomato (1 large)
½ cup chopped pitted kalamata olives
⅛ teaspoon salt
⅛ teaspoon pepper
1 package (11.5 oz) flour tortillas (8 inch)

1   In small bowl, mix dipping sauce ingredients; set aside. In large bowl, mix feta cheese, mozzarella cheese, cucumber, tomato, olives, salt and pepper.

2   Heat 12-inch nonstick skillet over medium heat until hot. Sprinkle ½ cup cheese mixture onto half of each tortilla. Fold untopped half of each tortilla over cheese mixture; gently press down with pancake turner.

3   Cook quesadillas, 3 at a time, in hot skillet about 2 minutes on each side, gently pressing down with pancake turner, until tortillas are lightly browned and crisp and cheese is melted. Remove from skillet; place on cutting board. Cut each quesadilla in half. Serve warm with dipping sauce.

High Altitude (3500–6500 ft): No change.

1 Serving (1 quesadilla and 1½ tablespoons sauce): Calories 240; Total Fat 11g (Saturated Fat 5g; Trans Fat 1g); Cholesterol 20mg; Sodium 660mg; Total Carbohydrate 25g (Dietary Fiber 0g) Exchanges: 1½ Starch, 1 High-Fat Meat, ½ Fat; Carbohydrate Choices: 1½

Greek Quesadillas

Inspiration Through Books

Judy Wood doesn't simply remember eating her mother's cooking as a child: "I remember going through my mother's cookbooks on Sunday afternoons to find something I could make," recalls Judy, who has been cooking since she was a child. Her elegant appetizer created some new memories—of a $10,000 prize at the 2000 Bake-Off® Contest. "I love pesto and feta cheese, so I included both," Judy says. "And the walnuts give it a nice crunch." She serves the appetizer before special dinners and at parties. "And sometimes I serve the twists alone as the bread for a meal," Judy notes.

1 Appetizer: Calories 210; Total Fat 15g (Saturated Fat 6g; Trans Fat 1.5g); Cholesterol 15mg; Sodium 380mg; Total Carbohydrate 12g (Dietary Fiber 0g) Exchanges: 1 Starch, 3 Fat; Carbohydrate Choices: 1

Italian Ham Appetizer Squares

Kelly Roos   Pottsville, PA
Bake-Off® Contest 39, 2000
$2,000 Winner

Prep Time: 30 Minutes
Start to Finish: 30 Minutes
18 servings

1 package (10.6 oz) Pillsbury® refrigerated Italian garlic breadsticks with herbs
6 thin slices cooked ham (about 3 oz)
6 thin slices provolone cheese (about 4 oz)
1 medium tomato, chopped (¾ cup)
6 or 7 pitted large ripe olives, sliced
½ cup chopped fresh basil leaves
2 tablespoons Italian vinaigrette dressing

1   Heat oven to 375°F. Unroll dough; separate into 2 equal sections along center perforation. Place 1 inch apart in ungreased 15 × 10 × 1-inch pan or 13 × 9-inch (3-quart) glass baking dish. Press perforations to seal. Spread garlic spread from container evenly over each dough section.

2   Bake 9 to 11 minutes or until light golden brown. Top each crust with ham, cheese, tomato and olives.

3   Bake about 5 minutes longer or until cheese is melted and edges are golden brown. Cut each into 9 squares. Sprinkle with basil. Drizzle with dressing. Serve warm.

High Altitude (3500–6500 ft): No change.

1 Serving: Calories 80; Total Fat 4g (Saturated Fat 1.5g; Trans Fat 0g); Cholesterol 5mg; Sodium 300mg; Total Carbohydrate 7g (Dietary Fiber 0g) Exchanges: ½ Starch, 1 Fat; Carbohydrate Choices: ½

Pesto Crescent Twists with Feta Spread

Judy Wood   Birmingham, AL
Bake-Off® Contest 39, 2000
$10,000 Winner

Prep Time: 20 Minutes
Start to Finish: 40 Minutes
16 appetizers

2 cans (8 oz each) Pillsbury® refrigerated crescent dinner rolls
½ cup basil pesto
2 tablespoons finely chopped walnuts
¼ cup sour cream
1 cup crumbled feta cheese (4 oz)
1 package (3 oz) cream cheese, softened
2 teaspoons olive oil
1 teaspoon basil pesto

1   Heat oven to 375°F. Grease cookie sheets. Unroll 1 can of dough onto cutting board or sheet of waxed paper. Firmly press perforations to seal. Press or roll to form 13 × 7-inch rectangle. In small bowl, mix ½ cup pesto and the walnuts. Spread mixture over dough.

2   Unroll remaining can of dough. Firmly press perforations to seal. Press or roll to form 13 × 7-inch rectangle. Carefully place dough rectangle over pesto and walnut filling. Cut filled dough in half crosswise to make two 7 × 6½-inch pieces. Cut each half into 8 strips. Twist each strip 4 or 5 times; place on cookie sheets.

3   Bake 14 to 19 minutes or until golden brown.

4   Meanwhile, in medium bowl, mix sour cream, feta cheese and cream cheese until well blended. Place in small serving bowl. In small bowl, mix oil and 1 teaspoon pesto. Drizzle over cheese mixture. With tip of knife, stir to marble. Serve warm twists with spread. Cover and refrigerate any remaining spread.

High Altitude (3500–6500 ft): Bake 12 to 17 minutes.

Chicken and Black Bean Tostizzas

Karen Durrett   Portland, OR
Bake-Off® Contest 36, 1994

Prep Time: 15 Minutes
Start to Finish: 40 Minutes
8 servings

PIZZA

1 can (16.3 oz) Pillsbury® Grands!® refrigerated flaky biscuits
1 cup diced cooked chicken
1 cup black beans (from 15-oz can), drained
½ cup chunky-style salsa
¼ cup chopped fresh cilantro
¼ teaspoon ground cumin
2 medium green onions, chopped (2 tablespoons)
½ cup green or red bell pepper strips (1 inch long)
1½ cups shredded Cheddar cheese (6 oz)

GARNISH, IF DESIRED

½ cup sour cream
½ cup guacamole

1   Heat oven to 350°F. Separate dough into 8 biscuits. On ungreased cookie sheets, press or roll each biscuit into 5½-inch circle.

2   In medium bowl, mix chicken, black beans, salsa, cilantro and cumin. Spread evenly over biscuits to within ¼ inch of edges. Top evenly with onions, bell pepper strips and cheese.

3   Bake 20 to 24 minutes or until biscuits are golden brown and cheese is melted. Garnish with sour cream and guacamole.

High Altitude (3500–6500 ft): No change.

1 Serving: Calories 350; Total Fat 17g (Saturated Fat 7g; Trans Fat 3.5g); Cholesterol 35mg; Sodium 890mg; Total Carbohydrate 32g (Dietary Fiber 2g) Exchanges: 1½ Starch, ½ Other Carbohydrate, 1½ Lean Meat, 2½ Fat; Carbohydrate Choices: 2

Jalapeño-Chicken Crescent Pinwheels

Lupe Cortés Forest, VA
Bake-Off® Contest 41, 2004

Prep Time: 20 Minutes
Start to Finish: 40 Minutes
32 appetizers

4 oz (half 8-oz package) cream cheese, softened
½ cup chopped cooked chicken
¼ cup chopped fresh cilantro
2 to 3 tablespoons finely chopped sliced jalapeño chiles (from 12-oz jar)
2 medium green onions, finely chopped (2 tablespoons)
⅛ teaspoon salt
1 can (8 oz) Pillsbury® refrigerated crescent dinner rolls

1 Heat oven to 375°F. In small bowl, mix all ingredients except dough; set aside.

2 Unroll dough; separate into 2 long rectangles. Place 1 rectangle on cutting board; press perforations to seal. Spread half of cream cheese mixture on dough rectangle to within ½ inch of edges.

3 Starting with one long side, roll up rectangle; press seam to seal. With serrated knife, cut roll into 16 slices; place cut side down on ungreased cookie sheet. Repeat with remaining dough rectangle.

4 Bake 14 to 16 minutes or until light golden brown. Immediately remove from cookie sheet. Serve warm.

High Altitude (3500–6500 ft): No change.

1 Appetizer: Calories 45; Total Fat 3g (Saturated Fat 1.5g; Trans Fat 0g); Cholesterol 5mg; Sodium 85mg; Total Carbohydrate 3g (Dietary Fiber 0g) Exchanges: 1 Fat; Carbohydrate Choices: 0

meet pat murphy

PAT MURPHY simply ran out of oil.

"I had my son for the weekend," Pat says, "and usually we cook whatever he wants to eat." Pat's son, Charles, who was ten at the time, wanted chicken wings. When Pat realized he didn't have enough oil to fry wings, his usual method for cooking them, he decided to rummage through what he had. "It was somewhat of an accident," he says, that he combined Old El Paso® taco seasoning, flour and just enough oil to coat the wings before he baked them.

They were a hit. "My son ate a whole bunch of them. They went down so fast I don't even think he tasted them."

The "accident" turned into a recipe called Mexican Party Wings, which won the $10,000 category prize for Casual Snacks and Appetizers at the 2002 Bake-Off® Contest, plus a bit of notoriety for Pat, a postal service employee. Pat had kept quiet about his Bake-Off® Contest trip, but an article in the *Modesto Bee* and an interview with Marie Osmond on the televised contest awards program got him lots of local attention.

But none of the attention matched the kid-flavored praise that Pat's son doled out. Says Pat, "The first time I saw my son after the Bake-Off® Contest he said, 'Wow, Dad! I guess you really can cook!'"

Mexican Party Wings

Pat Murphy   Modesto, CA
Bake-Off® Contest 40, 2002
$10,000 Winner

Prep Time: 20 Minutes
Start to Finish: 55 Minutes
24 servings

1 cup ranch dressing
1 can (4.5 oz) chopped green chiles
½ cup Pillsbury BEST® all-purpose flour
1 package (1.25 oz) taco seasoning mix
2 teaspoons vegetable oil
**24 chicken wing drummettes
  (about 2 lb)**
Dried parsley flakes
Fresh chervil leaves, if desired

1   Heat oven to 350°F. Spray large cookie sheet with cooking spray. In blender, place dressing and chiles. Cover; blend until smooth. Spoon into small serving bowl. Refrigerate while making drummettes.

2   In shallow dish, mix flour and taco seasoning mix. Stir in oil with fork. Coat drummettes with flour mixture. Coat drummettes again to use up flour mixture. Place on cookie sheet.

3   Bake 15 minutes. Turn drummettes; bake 14 to 17 minutes longer or until chicken is fork-tender and juice of chicken is clear when thickest part is cut to bone (180°F). Sprinkle parsley flakes on dressing mixture; serve as dip with warm drummettes. Garnish with chervil.

High Altitude (3500–6500 ft): Bake 20 minutes. Turn drummettes; bake 18 to 23 minutes longer.

1 Serving: Calories 100; Total Fat 7g (Saturated Fat 1.5g; Trans Fat 0g); Cholesterol 20mg; Sodium 320mg; Total Carbohydrate 4g (Dietary Fiber 0g) Exchanges: 1 High-Fat Meat; Carbohydrate Choices: 0

Cinco de Mayo Glazed Chicken Wings

Cinco de Mayo Glazed Chicken Wings

Linda Drumm   Victor, ID
Bake-Off® Contest 42, 2006

Prep Time: 50 Minutes
Start to Finish: 50 Minutes
5 servings

1 tablespoon canola or vegetable oil
2½ lb chicken wings, cut apart at joints, wing tips discarded
2 medium green onions with tops, thinly sliced
1 teaspoon crushed red pepper flakes
2 cans (12 oz each) lemon-lime carbonated beverage
1 can (4.5 oz) chopped green chiles, drained
1 package (1.25 oz) taco seasoning mix
10 lettuce leaves, if desired

1   In 12-inch nonstick skillet, heat oil over medium-high heat. Add chicken wings and onions; sprinkle with pepper flakes. Cook uncovered 5 to 8 minutes, stirring occasionally, until brown; drain.

2   Stir in carbonated beverage, green chiles and taco seasoning mix. Increase heat to high; cook uncovered 15 minutes, stirring occasionally. Reduce heat to medium-high; cook 5 to 10 minutes, stirring frequently, until chicken wings are completely glazed, small amount of glaze remains in skillet, and juice of chicken is clear when thickest part is cut to bone (180°F).

3   To serve, line serving plate with lettuce; arrange chicken wings over lettuce. Serve immediately.

High Altitude (3500–6500 ft): In step 1, cook 8 to 11 minutes.

1 Serving (4 wings): Calories 360; Total Fat 20g (Saturated Fat 5g; Trans Fat 0g); Cholesterol 70mg; Sodium 1180mg; Total Carbohydrate 22g (Dietary Fiber 0g) Exchanges: 1½ Other Carbohydrate, 3 Medium-Fat Meat, 1 Fat; Carbohydrate Choices: 1½

Crescent "Chick-Be-Quicks"

Rosemarie Berger   Jamestown, NC
Bake-Off® Contest 33, 1988
$2,000 Winner

Prep Time: 15 Minutes
Start to Finish: 30 Minutes
16 servings

¾ cup crushed canned French-fried onions
1 tablespoon Pillsbury BEST® all-purpose flour
¼ teaspoon seasoned salt
1 can (8 oz) Pillsbury® refrigerated crescent dinner rolls
1 whole chicken breast, skinned, boned and cut into 16 pieces (½ lb)
1 egg, beaten
Sesame or poppy seed

1   Heat oven to 375°F. Lightly grease cookie sheet.

2   In small bowl, mix French-fried onions, flour and seasoned salt; set aside. Separate dough into 8 triangles. Cut each in half lengthwise to make 16 long triangles. Dip chicken pieces in beaten egg; coat with onion mixture. Place 1 coated piece on wide end of each triangle; roll to opposite point. Place point side down on greased cookie sheet. Brush tops with remaining beaten egg; sprinkle with sesame seed.

3   Bake 12 to 15 minutes or until golden brown. Serve warm or cold.

High Altitude (3500–6500 ft): Bake 15 to 18 minutes.

1 Serving: Calories 90; Total Fat 5g (Saturated Fat 1.5g; Trans Fat 1g); Cholesterol 20mg; Sodium 160mg; Total Carbohydrate 7g (Dietary Fiber 0g) Exchanges: ½ Starch, ½ Very Lean Meat, 1 Fat; Carbohydrate Choices: ½

Signed Keepsakes

While the spotlight at the contest is on the 100 finalists, these recipe creators enjoy the chance to mingle with celebrities famous for their endeavors outside the kitchen and may even get a memento of their meeting.

- In 1960, Ivy Baker Priest, then the treasurer of the United States, was the Bake-Off® Contest's guest of honor. She signed dollar bills for the finalists—the only person legally allowed this privilege.

- Television host Art Linkletter appeared as a Bake-Off® emcee 19 times, making him one of the most frequent attendees. Linkletter got a big kick out of walking on the Bake-Off® Contest floor, and was seen signing autographs on everything from program books to flour bags, even the occasional egg!

Spicy Mexican Quiche Cups

Nikki Cadotte   Webster, WI
Bake-Off® Contest 40, 2002

Prep Time: 30 Minutes
Start to Finish: 50 Minutes
22 appetizers

½ lb bulk hot Italian sausage

6 eggs

6 tablespoons chunky-style salsa

½ cup shredded Cheddar cheese (2 oz)

½ cup shredded mozzarella cheese (2 oz)

½ cup chopped jalapeño chiles, seeds removed

1 box (15 oz) Pillsbury® refrigerated pie crusts, softened as directed on box

1   Heat oven to 425°F. In 8-inch skillet, cook sausage over medium heat, stirring frequently, until no longer pink; drain. Cool 10 minutes.

2   In medium bowl, beat eggs thoroughly. Stir in salsa; set aside. In another medium bowl, mix cheeses and chiles. Stir in cooled cooked sausage; set aside.

3   Unroll pie crusts on work surface. With rolling pin, roll each crust lightly into 12-inch round. With 3½-inch round cutter, cut 22 rounds from crusts, rerolling scraps as necessary. In 22 ungreased regular-size muffin cups or fluted tartlet pans, press rounds in bottoms and up sides.

4   Spoon 1 heaping tablespoon cheese mixture into each cup. Top each with about 1 tablespoon egg mixture; divide any remaining egg mixture among cups.

5   Bake 14 to 18 minutes or until filling is set. Serve warm.

High Altitude (3500–6500 ft): No change.

1 Appetizer: Calories 150; Total Fat 10g (Saturated Fat 4g; Trans Fat 0g); Cholesterol 70mg; Sodium 250mg; Total Carbohydrate 11g (Dietary Fiber 0g) Exchanges: ½ Starch, ½ Medium-Fat Meat, 1½ Fat; Carbohydrate Choices: 1

Party Spinach Cups

Beverly Ann Crummey   Brooksville, FL
Bake-Off® Contest 33, 1988
$10,000 Winner

Prep Time: 30 Minutes
Start to Finish: 50 Minutes
20 appetizers

1 tablespoon olive or vegetable oil

⅔ cup chopped onion

1 small clove garlic, finely chopped

1 box (9 oz) frozen spinach, thawed, well drained

1 can (4 oz) mushroom pieces and stems, drained, chopped

½ cup Italian-style bread crumbs

½ cup shredded Cheddar cheese (2 oz)

½ cup plain yogurt

⅛ teaspoon salt

⅛ teaspoon pepper

1 can (12 oz) Pillsbury® Golden Layers® refrigerated flaky biscuits

Sour cream, if desired

1   Heat oven to 375°F. Lightly grease 20 miniature muffin cups.

2   In 10-inch skillet, heat oil over medium heat until hot. Cook and stir onion and garlic in oil until tender. Stir in spinach, mushrooms, bread crumbs, cheese, yogurt, salt and pepper. Separate dough into 10 biscuits; separate each into 2 layers. Place each layer in muffin cup; firmly press in bottom and up side. Spoon generous tablespoonful spinach mixture into each cup.

3   Bake 15 to 20 minutes or until golden brown. Garnish each with sour cream. Serve warm.

High Altitude (3500–6500 ft): No change.

1 Appetizer: Calories 90; Total Fat 4g (Saturated Fat 1.5g; Trans Fat 1g); Cholesterol 0mg; Sodium 300mg; Total Carbohydrate 11g (Dietary Fiber 0g) Exchanges: ½ Starch, ½ Other Carbohydrate, ½ Fat; Carbohydrate Choices: 1

Puffy Chiles Rellenos

Helen Novak   Fontana, CA
Bake-Off® Contest 29, 1980
$2,000 Winner

Prep Time: 35 Minutes
Start to Finish: 50 Minutes
10 servings

2 cans (4 oz each) peeled whole green chiles

2 cups Monterey Jack or Cheddar cheese (8 oz)

1 can (12 oz) Pillsbury® Golden Layers® refrigerated flaky biscuits

TOPPING

3 eggs, separated

¼ teaspoon salt

1 jar (8 oz) taco sauce

1   Heat oven to 375°F. Grease cookie sheet.

2   Cut chiles lengthwise to make 10 pieces. Remove seeds and ribs; rinse and drain. Cut cheese into ten 3 × ½ × ½-inch pieces. Wrap each

piece of cheese with piece of chile. Separate dough into 10 biscuits. Press or roll out each to 4-inch circle. Place 1 chile-wrapped cheese piece onto each circle; fold dough over to cover completely. Firmly pinch edges to seal. Form each into finger-shaped roll; place seam side up on cookie sheet.*

3 Bake 10 to 12 minutes or until light golden brown. Meanwhile, make topping. In small bowl, beat egg whites until stiff peaks form. In second small bowl, beat egg yolks and salt. Gently fold egg yolk mixture into beaten egg whites until just blended. Spoon mounds of egg mixture over each partially baked roll, covering each completely.

4 Bake 12 to 15 minutes longer or until golden brown. In 1-quart saucepan, heat taco sauce. Spoon hot taco sauce over chiles rellenos.

To make ahead, rellenos can be prepared to this point. Cover and refrigerate up to 2 hours. Continue as directed above.

High Altitude (3500–6500 ft): Use cookie sheet with sides.

1 Serving: Calories 230; Total Fat 13g (Saturated Fat 6g; Trans Fat 1.5g); Cholesterol 85mg; Sodium 1070mg; Total Carbohydrate 17g (Dietary Fiber 0g) Exchanges: 1 Starch, 1 High-Fat Meat, 1 Fat; Carbohydrate Choices: 1

Easy Bruschetta Snacks

Darlene Godschalx Prescott Valley, AZ
Bake-Off® Contest 38, 1998

> Prep Time: 20 Minutes
> Start to Finish: 40 Minutes
> 15 appetizers

6 teaspoons olive oil
4½ teaspoons sesame seed
1 can (8 oz) Pillsbury® refrigerated crescent dinner rolls
1 can (6 oz) pitted ripe olives, drained
1 cup finely chopped tomato
¾ cup grated Parmesan and Romano cheese blend

1 Heat oven to 375°F. Brush large cookie sheet with 1 teaspoon of the oil; sprinkle evenly with 2 teaspoons of the sesame seed. Unroll dough; place over sesame seed, firmly pressing perforations to seal. Press to form 15x12-inch rectangle. Brush dough with 2 teaspoons of the oil; sprinkle evenly with remaining sesame seed.

2 Bake 10 minutes.

3 Meanwhile, in food processor or blender, place olives and remaining 3 teaspoons olive oil. Cover; process until olives are finely chopped. Spread olive mixture over crust. Top with tomato and cheese blend.

4 Bake 5 to 7 minutes longer or until edges are golden brown. Cut into rectangles.

High Altitude (3500–6500 ft): No change.

1 Appetizer: Calories 110; Total Fat 8g (Saturated Fat 2.5g; Trans Fat 1g); Cholesterol 0mg; Sodium 280mg; Total Carbohydrate 7g (Dietary Fiber 0g) Exchanges: ½ Starch, 1½ Fat; Carbohydrate Choices: ½

Mushroom Piroshki Appetizers

Marcia L. Gallner Omaha, NE
Bake-Off® Contest 29, 1980
$2,000 Winner

> Start to Finish: 1 Hour 5 Minutes
> Prep Time: 50 Minutes
> 30 appetizers

¼ cup butter or margarine
½ cup finely chopped onion (1 medium)
1 package (8 oz) fresh mushrooms, finely chopped
1 hard-cooked egg yolk, chopped
½ to ¾ teaspoon salt
¼ teaspoon pepper
3 Pillsbury® refrigerated pie crusts (from two 15-oz boxes), softened as directed on box
1 egg, beaten, if desired

1 In 10-inch skillet, melt butter over medium heat. Cook and stir onion in butter just until tender. Add mushrooms; cook 3 minutes, stirring frequently. Stir in egg yolk, salt and pepper. Cool 10 minutes.

2 Meanwhile, heat oven to 400°F. Unroll 3 pie crusts. With 2¾-inch round cutter, cut 10 rounds from each crust.

3 Spoon rounded teaspoon cooled mushroom mixture onto half of each pie-crust round. Fold dough over filling; press edges with fork to seal. Place on ungreased large cookie sheet. Brush with beaten egg.

4 Bake 12 to 15 minutes or until light golden brown. Serve warm.

High Altitude (3500–6500 ft): No change.

1 Appetizer: Calories 80; Total Fat 5g (Saturated Fat 2.5g; Trans Fat 0g); Cholesterol 15mg; Sodium 110mg; Total Carbohydrate 7g (Dietary Fiber 0g) Exchanges: ½ Starch, 1 Fat; Carbohydrate Choices: ½

Cheesy Crescent Apple Snacks

Mrs. Floyd W. Graefe   Council, ID
Bake-Off® Contest 25, 1974

> Prep Time: 25 Minutes
> Start to Finish: 45 Minutes
> 8 snacks

1 medium apple, peeled, chopped (1 cup)
½ cup shredded Cheddar cheese (2 oz)
2 to 4 tablespoons sugar
¼ cup chopped nuts
1 tablespoon Pillsbury BEST® all-purpose flour
1 teaspoon ground cinnamon
1 can (8 oz) Pillsbury® refrigerated crescent dinner rolls

GLAZE
⅓ cup powdered sugar
1 tablespoon milk
½ teaspoon vanilla

1 Heat oven to 375°F.

2 In small bowl, mix first 6 ingredients. Separate crescent dough into 4 rectangles; firmly press perforations to seal. Cut each rectangle in half crosswise to form 8 squares. Spoon 2 heaping tablespoons apple mixture onto center of each square. Pull 4 corners of dough to top center of apple mixture, twist slightly and seal edges. Place on ungreased cookie sheet.

3 Bake 12 to 18 minutes until golden brown. In small bowl, mix glaze ingredients; drizzle over snacks. Remove from pan immediately. Serve warm.

High Altitude (3500–6500 ft): No change.

1 Snack: Calories 210; Total Fat 11g (Saturated Fat 4g; Trans Fat 1.5g); Cholesterol 10mg; Sodium 270mg; Total Carbohydrate 23g (Dietary Fiber 0g) Exchanges: 1 Starch, ½ Other Carbohydrate, 2 Fat; Carbohydrate Choices: 1½

Not for Ladies Only

T. O. Davis of Waynesboro, Mississippi, was among three men who competed in the first Pillsbury Bake-Off® Contest in 1949 in New York City. Throughout the years, many men have been finalists and won cash prizes, including the Grand Prize.

Swaddled Peppers

Barb Walters   Pottstown, PA
Bake-Off® Contest 41, 2004

> Prep Time: 35 Minutes
> Start to Finish: 50 Minutes
> 16 appetizers

4 oz cream cheese (from 8-oz package), softened
1 teaspoon grated lime peel
1 tablespoon chopped fresh cilantro
1 tablespoon lime juice
8 fresh whole jalapeño chiles
1 can (8 oz) Pillsbury® refrigerated crescent dinner rolls
¼ cup butter or margarine, melted
4 oz fresh Parmesan cheese, grated (1 cup)

1 Heat oven to 375°F. Spray cookie sheet with cooking spray. Stir together cream cheese, lime peel, cilantro and lime juice until well blended; set aside. Carefully remove stems from chiles; cut each in half lengthwise.* Remove and discard seeds.

2 Unroll dough on cutting board; separate into 8 triangles. From center of longest side to opposite point, cut each triangle in half, making 16 triangles.

3 For each appetizer, spoon 1 teaspoon cream cheese mixture into chile half; place chile, cream cheese side down, on dough triangle with point of chile near top point of triangle. Wrap sides of triangle up over chile; pinch to seal. Bring point of triangle down over end of chile to cover; pinch to seal. In separate shallow dishes, place melted butter and Parmesan cheese. Dip each dough-wrapped chile into butter; roll in cheese to coat. Place on cookie sheet.

4 Bake 10 to 15 minutes or until golden brown. Immediately remove from cookie sheet. Serve warm.

Handle jalapeño chiles carefully, as their oil can cause burning. If possible, use food-safe plastic gloves when working with the chiles.

High Altitude (3500–6500 ft): No change.

1 Appetizer: Calories 130; Total Fat 10g (Saturated Fat 6g; Trans Fat 1g); Cholesterol 20mg; Sodium 270mg; Total Carbohydrate 6g (Dietary Fiber 0g) Exchanges: ½ Starch, 2 Fat; Carbohydrate Choices: ½

Swaddled Peppers

Sun-Dried Tomato and Goat Cheese Appetizers

Sun-Dried Tomato and Goat Cheese Appetizers

Tracy Schuhmacher   Penfield, NY
Bake-Off® Contest 41, 2004
$10,000 and a GE Profile™ Oven with Trivection Technology—Fast Snacks & Appetizers Category Winner

> **Prep Time:** 15 Minutes
> **Start to Finish:** 40 Minutes
> 20 appetizers

1 can (12 oz) Pillsbury® Golden Layers® refrigerated buttermilk flaky biscuits
½ cup mayonnaise or salad dressing
2 oz chèvre (goat) cheese, crumbled (½ cup)
¼ cup chopped drained oil-packed sun-dried tomatoes
1 teaspoon dried minced onion
1 teaspoon dried pesto seasoning
1 tablespoon grated Parmesan cheese

1   Heat oven to 375°F. Separate dough into 10 biscuits; separate each evenly into 2 layers, making 20 dough rounds. Press each in ungreased miniature muffin cup.

2   In small bowl, mix mayonnaise, chèvre cheese, tomatoes, onion and pesto seasoning. Spoon about 1½ teaspoons mayonnaise mixture into each cup. Sprinkle each with Parmesan cheese.

3   Bake 10 to 16 minutes or until golden brown. Remove from muffin cups. Cool 5 minutes before serving.

High Altitude (3500–6500 ft): Bake 12 to 16 minutes.

1 Appetizer: Calories 110 (Calories from Fat 70); Total Fat 8g (Saturated Fat 2g; Trans Fat 1g); Cholesterol 0mg; Sodium 230mg; Total Carbohydrate 8g (Dietary Fiber 0g) Exchanges: ½ Starch, 1½ Fat Carbohydrate Choices: ½

Easy Crescent Spinach Pies

Ruth B. Jones   Edmund, OK
Bake-Off® Contest 30, 1982

> **Prep Time:** 30 Minutes
> **Start to Finish:** 45 Minutes
> 24 turnovers

2 tablespoons olive oil or vegetable oil
½ cup chopped onion or 2 tablespoons dried minced onion
1 box (10 oz) frozen chopped spinach, thawed, squeezed to drain
⅓ cup feta or ricotta cheese, crumbled
⅛ teaspoon pepper
1 egg, slightly beaten
2 cans (8 oz each) Pillsbury® refrigerated crescent dinner rolls
2 to 4 tablespoons butter or margarine, melted

1   Heat oven to 375°F.

2   In 8-inch skillet, heat oil until hot. Cook onion in oil until tender. Remove from heat. Stir in spinach, cheese, pepper and egg. Separate dough into 8 rectangles; firmly press perforations to seal. Roll each to 12 × 4-inch rectangle.* Cut each rectangle into three 4-inch squares. Place 1 rounded tablespoonful spinach mixture on center of each square; fold dough over filling, forming a triangle. Press edges with fork to seal; place on ungreased cookie sheets. Brush with butter.

3   Bake 10 to 15 minutes or until golden brown.

For larger turnovers, press or roll each dough rectangle to 8 × 4-inch rectangle. Cut each in half to form two 4-inch squares. Fill each turnover with 2 tablespoonfuls spinach mixture. Bake as directed. 16 turnovers.

High Altitude (3500–6500 ft): No change.

1 Turnover: Calories 100; Total Fat 7g (Saturated Fat 2.5g; Trans Fat 1g); Cholesterol 15mg; Sodium 190mg; Total Carbohydrate 8g (Dietary Fiber 0g) Exchanges: ½ Starch, 1½ Fat; Carbohydrate Choices: ½

Olive Cheese Nuggets

Johnnie H. Williamson   Collins, MS
Bake-Off® Contest 8, 1956

> **Prep Time:** 30 Minutes
> **Start to Finish:** 45 Minutes
> 24 snacks

1 cup shredded sharp Cheddar cheese (4 oz)
¼ cup butter or margarine, softened
¾ cup Pillsbury BEST® all-purpose flour
⅛ teaspoon salt
½ teaspoon paprika
24 small stuffed green olives

1   Heat oven to 400°F.

2   In medium bowl, mix Cheddar cheese and butter. In small bowl, mix flour, salt and paprika. Add to cheese mixture in medium bowl; mix with hands to form dough (mixture will be stiff). Shape dough around olives, using about a teaspoonful of dough for each olive. Place on ungreased cookie sheet.* Bake 12 to 15 minutes or until firm. Serve hot or cold.

If desired, at this point cover and refrigerate 4 to 5 hours or overnight before baking.

High Altitude (3500–6500 ft): Add 1 to 2 tablespoons water to make a dough.

1 Snack: Calories 60; Total Fat 4g (Saturated Fat 2.5g; Trans Fat 0g); Cholesterol 10mg; Sodium 120mg; Total Carbohydrate 3g (Dietary Fiber 0g) Exchanges: ½ High-Fat Meat; Carbohydrate Choices: 0

Southwestern Black Bean Salsa

Barbara Hayse   Dallas, TX
Bake-Off® Contest 37, 1996

> Prep Time: 5 Minutes
> Start to Finish: 1 Hour 5 Minutes
> 20 servings

2 jars (16 oz each) chunky-style picante
½ teaspoon sugar
1 tablespoon fresh lime juice
⅓ cup finely chopped fresh cilantro
⅓ cup chopped green onions, including tops
⅓ cup chopped red onion
⅓ cup canned whole kernel sweet corn, drained
1 can (15 oz) black beans, drained, rinsed

1   In large bowl, mix picante, sugar and lime juice. Add remaining ingredients; stir gently. Cover; refrigerate at least 1 hour to blend flavors.

2   Serve salsa as appetizer with tortilla chips for dipping. If desired, serve as a side dish topped with sour cream.

High Altitude (3500–6500 ft): No change.

1 Serving (¼ Cup): Calories 45; Total Fat 0g (Saturated Fat 0g; Trans Fat 0g); Cholesterol 0mg; Sodium 280mg; Total Carbohydrate 9g (Dietary Fiber 3g) Exchanges: ½ Starch; Carbohydrate Choices: ½

Crab Cakes Italiano

Robert Gadsby   Brunswick, GA
Bake-Off® Contest 38, 1998

> Prep Time: 35 Minutes
> Start to Finish: 35 Minutes
> 8 servings

SAUCE
½ cup mayonnaise or reduced-fat mayonnaise
2 tablespoons basil pesto

CRAB CAKES
1 lb fresh lump crabmeat,* cleaned and rinsed, or imitation crabmeat, shredded
½ cup Italian-style bread crumbs
⅓ cup mayonnaise or reduced-fat mayonnaise
2 tablespoons basil pesto
1 egg, beaten
2 tablespoons olive oil

GARNISH, IF DESIRED
Plum (Roma) tomato slices
Fresh basil sprigs
Julienne-cut sun-dried tomatoes

1   In small bowl, mix sauce ingredients. Cover and refrigerate until serving.

2   In large bowl, mix all crab cake ingredients except oil. Shape into eight 3-inch patties, using about ⅓ cup mixture for each.

3   In 10-inch nonstick skillet, heat oil over medium heat. Cook patties in oil 4 to 5 minutes on each side, turning once, until golden brown and thoroughly cooked. Drain on paper towels. Serve topped with sauce. Garnish as desired.

Canned crabmeat (drained) or frozen crabmeat (thawed and drained) can be substituted for the fresh crabmeat.

High Altitude (3500–6500 ft): No change.

1 Serving: Calories 330; Total Fat 27g (Saturated Fat 4.5g; Trans Fat 0g); Cholesterol 90mg; Sodium 470mg; Total Carbohydrate 6g (Dietary Fiber 0g) Exchanges: ½ Starch, 1½ Very Lean Meat, 5 Fat; Carbohydrate Choices: ½

Shrimp Cocktail Crescent Snacks

Carole Ann Flieller   Floresville, TX
Bake-Off® Contest 26, 1975

> Prep Time: 15 Minutes
> Start to Finish: 35 Minutes
> 16 snacks

1 can (4 ½ oz) broken shrimp, drained (¾ cup)
2 tablespoons butter or margarine, melted (reserve 1 tablespoon)
1 tablespoon lemon juice
1 tablespoon prepared horseradish
1 tablespoon ketchup
1 can (8 oz) Pillsbury® refrigerated crescent dinner rolls
1 tablespoon grated Parmesan cheese
Sesame seed

1   Heat oven to 375°F.

2   Mix first 5 ingredients. Separate crescent dough into 8 triangles; cut each in half diagonally to make 16 triangles. Place rounded teaspoonful shrimp mixture on center of each triangle; fold long end over all. Place on ungreased cookie sheet. Brush with remaining butter; sprinkle with Parmesan cheese and sesame seed.

3   Bake 15 to 18 minutes or until golden brown. Serve warm. Cover and refrigerate any remaining snacks.

High Altitude (3500–6500 ft): No change.

1 Snack: Calories 80; Total Fat 5g (Saturated Fat 2g; Trans Fat 1g); Cholesterol 20mg; Sodium 150mg; Total Carbohydrate 6g (Dietary Fiber 0g) Exchanges: ½ Starch, 1 Fat; Carbohydrate Choices: ½

Spicy Shrimp Pot Stickers

Wendy P. Osborne   Syracuse, NY
Bake-Off® Contest 41, 2004

Prep Time: 30 Minutes
Start to Finish: 45 Minutes
10 servings

POT STICKERS
1 egg white
1 tablespoon water
¼ lb (½ cup) cooked cocktail shrimp, tail
   shells removed
¼ cup sliced peeled carrot
1 medium green onion, cut into pieces
2 tablespoons teriyaki sauce
1 teaspoon ground ginger
¼ teaspoon crushed red pepper flakes
1 can (12 oz) Pillsbury® Golden Layers®
   refrigerated buttermilk flaky biscuits

DIPPING SAUCE
⅓ cup orange marmalade
3 tablespoons teriyaki sauce

1   Heat oven to 400°F. Line large cookie sheet with parchment paper. In small bowl, beat egg white and water with wire whisk or fork until foamy; set aside.

2   In food processor, place shrimp, carrot and onion. Cover; process until finely chopped. In medium bowl, mix shrimp mixture, teriyaki sauce, ginger and red pepper flakes with fork until well blended.

3   Separate dough into 10 biscuits; separate each evenly into 2 layers, making 20 biscuit rounds. Press or roll each into 3½-inch dough round. Place 1 rounded teaspoon shrimp filling in a line about ½ inch up from bottom of each dough round.

4   For each pot sticker, bring sides of dough round up slightly over filling; bring bottom edge of dough up over filling. Brush top edge with egg white mixture; continue rolling up to seal. Place sealed side down on paper-lined cookie sheet. Brush rolls with remaining egg mixture.

5   Bake 10 to 14 minutes or until golden brown. Meanwhile, in small bowl, mix dipping sauce ingredients with wire whisk or fork. Serve warm pot stickers with dipping sauce.

High Altitude (3500–6500 ft): No change.

1 Serving (2 pot stickers and 2 teaspoons sauce): Calories 160; Total Fat 4.5g (Saturated Fat 1g; Trans Fat 1.5g); Cholesterol 20mg; Sodium 740mg; Total Carbohydrate 23g (Dietary Fiber 0g) Exchanges: 1 Starch, ½ Other Carbohydrate, 1 Fat; Carbohydrate Choices: 1½

Chai Crunch

Carol Thoreson   Rockford, IL
Bake-Off® Contest 41, 2004

Prep Time: 10 Minutes
Start to Finish: 1 Hour 25 Minutes
22 servings

3 cups bite-size squares oven-toasted
   corn cereal
3 cups bite-size squares 100%
   whole-grain wheat cereal
3 cups O-shaped honey-nut cereal
1½ cups sliced almonds
1 cup dried banana chips
½ cup butter or margarine
½ cup honey
1 teaspoon instant nonfat dry milk
   or original-flavor nondairy creamer,
   if desired*
½ teaspoon ground cardamom
½ teaspoon ground ginger
½ teaspoon ground cinnamon
½ teaspoon ground nutmeg
½ teaspoon ground cloves
½ teaspoon dried orange peel
1 teaspoon vanilla

1   Heat oven to 300°F. In ungreased large roasting pan, mix cereals, almonds and banana chips.

2   In 1-quart saucepan, melt butter over medium heat. Remove from heat. Stir in honey, dry milk, cardamom, ginger, cinnamon, nutmeg, cloves, orange peel and vanilla until well mixed. Pour over cereal mixture, stirring until evenly coated.

3   Bake 45 to 60 minutes or until golden brown, stirring every 15 minutes. Spread on waxed paper or paper towels to cool, about 15 minutes. Store in airtight container.

*If dried milk or creamer is used, flavor will be less spicy and a little sweeter.

High Altitude (3500–6500 ft): No change.

1 Serving (½ Cup): Calories 190; Total Fat 9g (Saturated Fat 4g; Trans Fat 0g); Cholesterol 10mg; Sodium 170mg; Total Carbohydrate 24g (Dietary Fiber 3g) Exchanges: 1 Starch, ½ Other Carbohydrate, 1½ Fat; Carbohydrate Choices: 1½

Cinnamon-Fruit Snack Mix

Rebecca Nurse   Waterford, PA
Bake-Off® Contest 42, 2006

Prep Time: 20 Minutes
Start to Finish: 1 Hour 50 Minutes
32 servings

2 cups cinnamon toast flavor cereal
1 cup bran cereal shreds
1½ cups flaked coconut
1 cup pecan halves
1 cup blanched whole almonds
½ cup sunflower nuts
½ cup wheat germ
½ cup ground flax seed
1 teaspoon salt
1 teaspoon ground cinnamon
¼ cup vegetable oil
1 can (14 oz) fat-free sweetened
   condensed milk (not evaporated)
1 cup chopped dried apricots
1 cup banana chips
1 cup sweetened dried cranberries
½ cup dried cherries
½ cup golden raisins

1   Heat oven to 300°F. Spray 15 × 10 × 1-inch pan with cooking spray. In large bowl, mix both cereals, coconut, pecans, almonds, sunflower nuts, wheat germ, flax seed, salt and cinnamon. In small bowl, mix oil and condensed milk. Pour over cereal mixture; toss until well coated. Spread evenly in pan.

2   Bake 50 to 60 minutes, stirring every 15 minutes to break up any large clumps, until light golden brown. Cool 30 minutes.

3   In large bowl, mix cereal mixture, apricots, banana chips, cranberries, cherries and raisins. Store in tightly covered container.

High Altitude (3500–6500 ft): No change.

1 Serving (½ cup): Calories 230; Total Fat 11g (Saturated Fat 2.5g; Trans Fat 0g); Cholesterol 0mg; Sodium 120mg; Total Carbohydrate 28g (Dietary Fiber 3g) Exchanges: 1 Starch, 1 Other Carbohydrate, 2 Fat; Carbohydrate Choices: 2

Chai Crunch

Biscuit Mini Focaccia (page 185)

Cappuccino Crunch Muffins

Janet Barton   Sandy, UT
Bake-Off® Contest 39, 2000

Prep Time: 10 Minutes
Start to Finish: 35 Minutes
14 muffins

1 box (15.4 oz) Pillsbury® nut quick
   bread & muffin mix
½ cup unsweetened baking cocoa
1 tablespoon instant coffee granules or
   crystals, or instant espresso coffee
   granules
1 cup toffee bits
½ cup semisweet chocolate chips
1 cup buttermilk*
⅓ cup vegetable oil
2 eggs

1   Heat oven to 400°F. Place paper
baking cup in each of 14 regular-
size muffin cups.

2   In large bowl, mix quick bread
mix, contents of nut packet, cocoa
and coffee granules. Stir in toffee
bits and chocolate chips. Add
buttermilk, oil and eggs; stir just
until moistened. Divide batter
evenly among muffin cups.

3   Bake 19 to 23 minutes or until
toothpick inserted in center comes
out clean. Cool 5 minutes; remove
from pan. Serve warm or cool.

** To substitute for buttermilk, use
1 tablespoon vinegar or lemon juice
plus milk to make 1 cup.*

High Altitude (3500–6500 ft): Use
16 paper baking cups. Add 2 tablespoons
Pillsbury BEST® all-purpose flour to dry
bread mix.

1 Muffin: Calories 320; Total Fat 16g (Saturated Fat 6g;
Trans Fat 0g); Cholesterol 40mg; Sodium 290mg;
Total Carbohydrate 39g (Dietary Fiber 1g) Exchanges:
1½ Starch, 1 Other Carbohydrate, 3 Fat; Carbohydrate
Choices: 2½

Chocolate Chunk Pistachio Muffins

Sally Vog   Springfield, OR
Bake-Off® Contest 34, 1990

Prep Time: 20 Minutes
Start to Finish: 50 Minutes
10 muffins

2 cups Pillsbury BEST® all-purpose flour
¾ cup sugar
2 teaspoons baking powder
½ teaspoon ground cinnamon
¼ teaspoon baking soda
¼ teaspoon salt
6 oz sweet baking chocolate, coarsely
   chopped
½ cup coarsely chopped pistachio nuts
1 cup milk
½ cup butter or margarine, melted
1 teaspoon grated lemon peel
1 teaspoon vanilla
1 egg, slightly beaten
⅓ cup seedless raspberry jam

1   Heat oven to 375°F. Place paper
baking cup in each of 10 jumbo
muffin cups, or grease bottoms only
of muffin cups.* In large bowl,
mix flour, sugar, baking powder,
cinnamon, baking soda and salt.
Reserve ⅓ cup of the largest pieces
of chopped chocolate; reserve

2 tablespoons of the pistachio
nuts. Stir remaining chopped
chocolate and pistachio nuts into
dry ingredients. In small bowl,
mix milk, melted butter, lemon
peel, vanilla and egg. Add to dry
ingredients all at once; stir just
until dry ingredients are moistened.

2   Fill each muffin cup with
2 heaping tablespoons batter.
Spoon rounded teaspoon jam on
center of batter in each cup. Spoon
about 1 heaping tablespoon of the
remaining batter over jam in each
cup, covering jam. Top each with
reserved chopped chocolate and
pistachio nuts.

3   Bake 20 to 25 minutes or until
toothpick inserted in center comes
out clean. Cool 5 minutes; remove
from pan. Serve warm or cool.

** To make 20 regular-size muffins,
fill each regular-size muffin cup with
1 tablespoon batter. Spoon rounded
½ teaspoon jam on center of batter in
each cup. Spoon remaining batter evenly
over each filled cup, covering jam. Top
each with reserved chopped chocolate and
pistachio nuts. Bake 15 to 20 minutes.
Cool 5 minutes; remove from pan.*

High Altitude (3500–6500 ft): Increase
Pillsbury BEST® all-purpose flour to
2¼ cups.

1 Muffin: Calories 410; Total Fat 18g (Saturated Fat 10g;
Trans Fat 0g); Cholesterol 50mg; Sodium 280mg; Total
Carbohydrate 56g (Dietary Fiber 2g) Exchanges: 1½
Starch, 2 Other Carbohydrate, 3½ Fat; Carbohydrate
Choices: 4

Crunchy Banana Muffins

Lorraine Maggio Manlius, NY
Bake-Off® Contest 40, 2002

Prep Time: 15 Minutes
Start to Finish: 1 Hour
8 muffins

1 box (14 oz) Pillsbury® banana quick
    bread & muffin mix
1 cup milk
½ cup butter or unsalted butter, melted,
    cooled
2 teaspoons vanilla
2 eggs
½ cup finely chopped walnuts
½ cup low-fat granola cereal
½ cup coconut
¼ cup quick-cooking oats
2 tablespoons wheat germ, if desired
1 small banana, diced (about ½ cup)
2 tablespoons coarse sugar

1 Heat oven to 375°F. Place paper baking cup in each of 8 jumbo muffin cups, or spray with cooking spray. In large bowl, mix quick bread mix, milk, melted butter, vanilla and eggs 50 to 75 strokes with spoon until mix is moistened.

2 Add remaining ingredients except coarse sugar; mix well. Divide batter evenly among muffin cups. Sprinkle batter in each cup with coarse sugar.

3 Bake 22 to 32 minutes or until toothpick inserted in center comes out clean. Cool 2 minutes; remove from muffin cups. Cool 10 minutes. Serve warm or cool.

High Altitude (3500–6500 ft): Add 2 table-spoons Pillsbury BEST® all-purpose flour to dry bread mix.

1 Muffin: Calories 460; Total Fat 22g (Saturated Fat 10g; Trans Fat 0.5g); Cholesterol 85mg; Sodium 420mg; Total Carbohydrate 57g (Dietary Fiber 1g) Exchanges: 2 Starch, 2 Other Carbohydrate, 4 Fat; Carbohydrate Choices: 4

Lemon Raspberry Muffins

Lemon Raspberry Muffins

Stephanie Luetkehans   Chicago, IL
Bake-Off® Contest 33, 1988

Prep Time: 15 Minutes
Start to Finish: 45 Minutes
12 muffins

2 cups Pillsbury BEST® all-purpose flour
1 cup sugar
3 teaspoons baking powder
½ teaspoon salt
1 cup half-and-half
½ cup vegetable oil
1 teaspoon lemon extract
2 eggs
1 cup fresh or frozen raspberries
   without syrup (do not thaw)

1   Heat oven to 425°F. Place paper baking cup in each of 12 regular-size muffin cups.

2   In large bowl, mix flour, sugar, baking powder and salt. In small bowl, mix half-and-half, oil, lemon extract and eggs. Add to dry ingredients; stir just until ingredients are moistened. Carefully fold in raspberries. Divide batter evenly among muffin cups.

3   Bake 18 to 23 minutes or until golden brown. Cool 5 minutes; remove from pans.

High Altitude (3500–6500 ft): Use 16 paper baking cups. Decrease baking powder to 2 teaspoons.

1 Muffin: Calories 270; Total Fat 13g (Saturated Fat 3g; Trans Fat 0g); Cholesterol 45mg; Sodium 240mg; Total Carbohydrate 35g (Dietary Fiber 1g) Exchanges: ½ Starch, 2 Other Carbohydrate, 2½ Fat; Carbohydrate Choices: 2

Cheesy Herb Muffins

Alice Lehnhoff   St. Louis, MO
Bake-Off® Contest 34, 1990

Prep Time: 20 Minutes
Start to Finish: 45 Minutes
12 muffins

TOPPING
¼ cup finely chopped onion
¼ cup finely chopped fresh parsley
1½ to 3 teaspoons dill seed
1 teaspoon chopped fresh cilantro

MUFFINS
2 cups Pillsbury BEST® all-purpose,
   unbleached or self-rising flour*
1 tablespoon sugar
3 teaspoons baking powder
½ teaspoon salt
¼ cup butter or margarine
4 oz Muenster cheese, cut into ¼-inch
   cubes
2 tablespoons grated Romano cheese
1 cup milk
1 egg

1   In small bowl, mix topping ingredients; set aside.

2   Heat oven to 400°F. Grease 12 regular-size muffin cups. In large bowl, mix flour, sugar, baking powder and salt. Using pastry blender or fork, cut in butter until mixture looks like coarse crumbs. Stir in cheeses. In small bowl, mix milk and egg. Add to dry ingredients all at once; stir until dry ingredients are just moistened. Diving batter evenly among muffin cups, filling each cup ¾ full. Sprinkle topping evenly over batter in each cup; lightly press into batter.

3   Bake 19 to 21 minutes or until light golden brown. Cool 1 minute. Using knife or small spatula, loosen sides of muffins. Remove from pan. Serve hot or warm.

If using self-rising flour, omit baking powder and salt.

High Altitude (3500–6500 ft): No change.

1 Muffin: Calories 170; Total Fat 8g (Saturated Fat 5g; Trans Fat 0g); Cholesterol 40mg; Sodium 340mg; Total Carbohydrate 19g (Dietary Fiber 0g) Exchanges: 1 Starch, ½ High-Fat Meat, 1 Fat; Carbohydrate Choices: 1

Power Up

It takes a lot of power to run 100 ranges. The first step in setting up the mini kitchens on the Bake-Off® Contest floor is bringing in specialized equipment to accommodate the electrical demands. Four 100,000-watt transformers are used to convert the 480-volt power (typical in hotels and commercial buildings) to residential 120/240 voltage. Nine 400-ampere circuit breaker panel boards help control the ranges. In comparison, the average American home has just one 100-ampere circuit board. And more than one mile of electrical cable is used to install the appliances. After all the equipment is connected, a full-scale power check is done to make sure the electrical system can handle

Savory Cheese and Scallion Scones

Susan Brinkley Eminence, MO
Bake-Off® Contest 37, 1996

> Prep Time: 20 Minutes
> Start to Finish: 55 Minutes
> 8 scones

SCONES

2¾ cups Pillsbury BEST® all-purpose
    flour
5 teaspoons baking powder
½ teaspoon salt, if desired
1 cup crumbled feta cheese (4 oz)
4 oz cream cheese or ⅓-less-fat cream
    cheese (Neufchâtel), cut into 1-inch
    cubes
4 medium scallions or green onions,
    chopped
1 cup half-and-half or milk
1 egg

GLAZE, IF DESIRED

1 egg
2 tablespoons milk

1 Heat oven to 400°F. Grease large cookie sheet. In large bowl, mix flour, baking powder and salt. With pastry blender or fork, cut in feta cheese and cream cheese until mixture is crumbly. Gently toss in scallions. In small bowl, mix half-and-half and 1 egg. Add half-and-half mixture to flour mixture; stir lightly, just until soft dough forms.

2 Place dough on well-floured surface; knead lightly 5 or 6 times. Pat or press dough into 1-inch-thick round. With floured knife, cut into 8 wedges. Place wedges 2 inches apart on cookie sheet. In small bowl, mix glaze ingredients. Brush over tops of wedges.

3 Bake 25 to 30 minutes or until golden brown. Remove scones from cookie sheet. Cool 5 minutes. Serve warm or cool. Cover and refrigerate any remaining scones.

High Altitude (3500–6500 ft): No change.

1 Scone: Calories 300; Total Fat 13g (Saturated Fat 8g; Trans Fat 0g); Cholesterol 65mg; Sodium 530mg; Total Carbohydrate 36g (Dietary Fiber 1g) Exchanges: 2 Starch, ½ Other Carbohydrate, ½ High-Fat Meat, 1½ Fat; Carbohydrate Choices: 2½

Cranberry-Walnut Scones

Michelle DeCoy Pittsburg, CA
Bake-Off® Contest 37, 1996

> Prep Time: 20 Minutes
> Start to Finish: 50 Minutes
> 12 scones

2 cups Pillsbury BEST® all-purpose flour
2 tablespoons sugar
2 teaspoons baking powder
1 teaspoon freshly grated nutmeg
    or ground nutmeg
½ teaspoon baking soda
½ teaspoon salt
½ cup unsalted butter, butter or
    margarine
1 package (3.53 oz) sweetened
    dried cranberries (½ cup)
½ cup chopped walnuts
¾ cup buttermilk*
1 egg, separated
2 teaspoons sugar

1 Heat oven to 375°F. Lightly grease cookie sheet or line with parchment paper. In large bowl, mix flour, 2 tablespoons sugar, the baking powder, nutmeg, baking soda and salt. With pastry blender or fork, cut in butter until mixture looks like coarse crumbs. Stir in cranberries and walnuts.

2 In small bowl, mix buttermilk and egg yolk. Add to flour mixture; stir just until dry ingredients are moistened.

3 Place dough on lightly floured surface; gently knead 12 times. Divide dough in half; place on cookie sheet. Pat each half into 6-inch round. Cut each into 6 wedges; do not separate.

4 In small bowl, beat egg white slightly. Brush over tops of scones. Sprinkle with 2 teaspoons sugar.

5 Bake 15 to 20 minutes or until golden brown. Remove from cookie sheet. Cool 10 minutes. Cut into wedges. Serve warm.

* To substitute for buttermilk, use 2 teaspoons vinegar or lemon juice plus milk to make ¾ cup.

High Altitude (3500–6500 ft): No change.

1 Scone: Calories 220; Total Fat 12g (Saturated Fat 5g; Trans Fat 0g); Cholesterol 40mg; Sodium 250mg; Total Carbohydrate 25g (Dietary Fiber 1g) Exchanges: 1 Starch, ½ Other Carbohydrate, 2½ Fat; Carbohydrate Choices: 1½

Cranberry-Walnut Scones

Lemon Nutmeg Scones

Anita Atoulikian   Parma, OH
Bake-Off® Contest 34, 1990
$2,000 Winner

Prep Time: 25 Minutes
Start to Finish: 40 Minutes
8 scones

1¾ cups Pillsbury BEST® all-purpose
   flour
¼ cup cornstarch
½ teaspoon baking soda
¼ teaspoon ground nutmeg
6 tablespoons butter or margarine
1 container (6 oz) lemon fat-free yogurt
⅓ cup golden raisins
2 eggs
3 teaspoons sugar
⅛ teaspoon ground nutmeg
1 package (3 oz) cream cheese,
   softened

1   Heat oven to 400°F. Grease cookie sheet. In large bowl, mix flour, cornstarch, baking soda and ¼ teaspoon nutmeg. With pastry blender or fork, cut in butter until mixture looks like coarse crumbs.

2   In small bowl, mix ½ cup of the yogurt, the raisins and eggs. Add to dry ingredients all at once; stir until dry ingredients are just moistened. (Dough will be sticky.) On floured surface, shape dough into ball. On greased cookie sheet, press dough into 8-inch circle, about ¾ inch thick.

3   In small bowl, mix sugar and ⅛ teaspoon nutmeg; sprinkle over top of dough. Cut into 8 wedges; separate so wedges are 1 inch apart. Bake 9 to 11 minutes or until very light golden brown.

4   Meanwhile, in small bowl mix remaining yogurt and cream cheese; beat until well blended. Serve with warm scones.

High Altitude (3500–6500 ft): Increase Pillsbury BEST® all-purpose flour to 2¼ cups.

1 Scones: Calories 290; Total Fat 14g (Saturated Fat 8g; Trans Fat 0g); Cholesterol 90mg; Sodium 280mg; Total Carbohydrate 35g (Dietary Fiber 1g) Exchanges: 1½ Starch, 1 Other Carbohydrate, 2½ Fat; Carbohydrate Choices: 2

Middleberry Scones

Lisa Keys   Middlebury, CT
Bake-Off® Contest 36, 1994
$2,000 Winner

Prep Time: 15 Minutes
Start to Finish: 35 Minutes
8 scones

SCONES
1½ cups Pillsbury BEST® all-purpose
   flour
½ cup Pillsbury BEST® whole wheat
   flour
2 tablespoons sugar
1 tablespoon baking powder
½ teaspoon salt
½ teaspoon ground cinnamon
1 teaspoon grated orange peel
¼ cup butter or margarine
⅔ cup half-and-half
1 egg
⅓ cup raspberry or strawberry
   preserves
1 teaspoon sugar

SPREAD AND GARNISH
1 package (3 oz) cream cheese,
   softened
16 fresh raspberries or strawberries,
   if desired
1 teaspoon grated orange peel,
   if desired

1   Heat oven to 425°F. Lightly grease cookie sheet. In large bowl, mix flours, 2 tablespoons sugar, the baking powder, salt, cinnamon and 1 teaspoon orange peel. With fork or pastry blender, cut in butter until mixture looks like coarse crumbs.

Scones: Deliciously Simple

Scones were first popular in the last half of the nineteenth century, when baking powder became readily available. Perhaps that is why we associate them most with Victorian teatime. However, scones are almost exactly like biscuits—a simple quick bread that can be dressed up with spices and additions until they are quite extravagant. "Cinnamon and orange flavors are my favorite," Lisa Keys says. "I love the smell of my kitchen when these scones are baking. They are fragrant and special indeed, yet simple and quick." Cooks everywhere are thankful for the indispensable combination of sodium bicarbonate and acid salt—otherwise known as baking powder.

2 In small bowl, mix half-and-half and egg. Add to flour mixture; stir just until dry ingredients are moistened. Place dough on well-floured surface; knead lightly 4 times. Divide in half; pat each half into 8-inch circle. Place 1 circle on cookie sheet; spread preserves to within 1 inch of edge. Place remaining circle over preserves; pinch edges to seal. Sprinkle top with 1 teaspoon sugar. Cut into 8 wedges; do not separate.

3 Bake 15 to 18 minutes or until edges are golden brown. Cut through scones. Serve warm with cream cheese; garnish with remaining ingredients.

High Altitude (3500–6500 ft): No change.

1 Scone: Calories 290; Total Fat 13g (Saturated Fat 8g; Trans Fat 0g); Cholesterol 60mg; Sodium 420mg; Total Carbohydrate 38g (Dietary Fiber 2g) Exchanges: 1½ Starch, 1 Other Carbohydrate, 2½ Fat; Carbohydrate Choices: 2½

Orange-Glazed Tropical Fruit Scones

Fran Neavoll Salem, OR
Bake-Off® Contest 37, 1996
$10,000 Winner

> Prep Time: 20 Minutes
> Start to Finish: 35 Minutes
> 8 scones

SCONES
2 cups Pillsbury BEST® all-purpose flour
2 tablespoons sugar
3 teaspoons baking powder
1 teaspoon salt
1½ teaspoons grated orange peel
¼ cup butter or margarine
⅓ cup milk
2 eggs, beaten
1 cup tropical three-fruit mix or dried mixed fruit
½ cup white vanilla baking chips

GLAZE
1 cup powdered sugar
2 to 3 tablespoons orange juice

SPREAD
⅓ cup apricot-pineapple or apricot preserves

1 Heat oven to 400°F. In large bowl, mix flour, sugar, baking powder, salt and orange peel. With pastry blender or fork, cut in butter until mixture looks like coarse crumbs. Stir in milk and eggs. Stir in dried fruit and white vanilla baking chips until well mixed.

2 Place dough on lightly floured surface; knead 6 or 7 times until smooth. Divide dough in half. Pat each half into 6-inch circle. With floured knife, cut each circle into 4 wedges. Place wedges 2 inches apart on ungreased cookie sheet.

3 Bake 12 to 16 minutes or until golden brown. Cool 1 minute.

4 Meanwhile, in small bowl, mix powdered sugar and enough orange juice for desired drizzling consistency until smooth. Drizzle mixture over top and sides of each scone. Cool 5 minutes. If desired, split each scone and spread with 2 teaspoons preserves, or serve preserves with scones. Serve warm.

High Altitude (3500–6500 ft): Increase Pillsbury BEST® all-purpose flour to 2 cups plus 2 tablespoons. Bake 14 to 19 minutes.

1 Scone: Calories 420; Total Fat 12g (Saturated Fat 7g; Trans Fat 0g); Cholesterol 70mg; Sodium 580mg; Total Carbohydrate 73g (Dietary Fiber 2g) Exchanges: 2 Starch, ½ Fruit, 2½ Other Carbohydrate, 2 Fat; Carbohydrate Choices: 5

Banana-Wheat Quick Bread

Barbara Goldstein New York, NY
Bake-Off® Contest 24, 1973

> Prep Time: 15 Minutes
> Start to Finish: 1 Hour 30 Minutes
> 1 loaf (16 slices)

1¼ cups Pillsbury BEST® all-purpose flour
½ cup Pillsbury BEST® whole wheat flour
1 cup sugar
1 teaspoon baking soda
1 teaspoon salt
1½ cups mashed ripe bananas (3 medium)
¼ cup butter or margarine, softened
2 tablespoons orange juice
1 egg
¼ teaspoon lemon juice, if desired
¼ to ½ cup raisins

1 Heat oven to 350°F. Grease and flour bottom only of 9 × 5- or 8 × 4-inch loaf pan.

2 In large bowl, beat all ingredients except raisins with electric mixer on medium speed 3 minutes. Fold in raisins. Pour batter into pan.

3 Bake 55 to 65 minutes or until toothpick inserted in center comes out clean. Cool 10 minutes; remove from pan to cooling rack. Cool completely. Wrap tightly and store in refrigerator.

High Altitude (3500–6500 ft): Increase Pillsbury BEST® all-purpose flour to 1½ cups.

1 Slice: Calories 160; Total Fat 3.5g (Saturated Fat 2g; Trans Fat 0g); Cholesterol 20mg; Sodium 250mg; Total Carbohydrate 30g (Dietary Fiber 1g) Exchanges: 1 Starch, 1 Other Carbohydrate, ½ Fat; Carbohydrate Choices: 2

Crunchy Banana-Colada Bread

Crunchy Banana-Colada Bread

Susan Adams   Naperville, IL
Bake-Off® Contest 41, 2004
$5,000—Breakfast Favorites Runner-Up Winner

> Prep Time: 15 Minutes
> Start to Finish: 3 Hours 40 Minutes
> 1 loaf (16 slices)

¾ cup sugar

½ cup unsalted or regular butter, softened

2 eggs

1 cup mashed very ripe bananas (2 medium)

1 container (6 oz) piña colada fat-free yogurt

1½ cups Pillsbury BEST® all-purpose flour

1 teaspoon baking soda

1 teaspoon salt

4 banana nut crunchy granola bars (2 pouches from 8.9-oz box), coarsely crushed*

¼ cup flaked coconut

1   Heat oven to 350°F (325°F for dark pan). Generously grease 9 × 5-inch loaf pan with shortening, or spray with cooking spray. In large bowl, beat sugar and butter with electric mixer on medium speed until well blended. Beat in eggs, bananas and yogurt.

2   Add flour, baking soda and salt; beat well. Stir in ½ cup of the crushed granola bars. Pour batter into pan.

3   In small bowl, mix remaining ¼ cup crushed granola bars and the coconut. Sprinkle evenly over batter in pan; press in lightly.

4   Bake 60 to 70 minutes or until toothpick inserted in center comes out clean, covering with foil during last 15 to 20 minutes of baking to prevent excessive browning. Cool in pan on cooling rack 15 minutes. Remove from pan to cooling rack. Cool completely, about 2 hours. Wrap tightly and store in refrigerator.

* To easily crush granola bars, do not unwrap. Use rolling pin to crush bars.

High Altitude (3500–6500 ft): Bake 65 to 70 minutes.

1 Slice: Calories 190; Total Fat 8g (Saturated Fat 4.5g; Trans Fat 0g); Cholesterol 40mg; Sodium 260mg; Total Carbohydrate 28g (Dietary Fiber 1g) Exchanges: ½ Starch, 1½ Other Carbohydrate, 1½ Fat; Carbohydrate Choices: 2

Aloha Banana Bread

Sharron Kollmeyer   Honolulu, HI
Bake-Off® Contest 12, 1960

> Prep Time: 15 Minutes
> Start to Finish: 2 Hours 25 Minutes
> 1 loaf (16 slices)

2 cups Pillsbury BEST® all-purpose flour*

1 teaspoon soda

½ teaspoon salt

½ cup butter or margarine

1 cup sugar

2 eggs

1 cup mashed very ripe bananas (2 medium)

1 tablespoon grated orange peel

¼ cup milk

1 teaspoon vanilla

½ teaspoon almond extract

1 cup flaked coconut

½ cup chopped nuts

1   Heat oven to 350°F. Grease and flour bottom only of 9 × 5-inch loaf pan.

2   In small bowl, mix flour, soda and salt. In large bowl, beat butter and sugar with electric mixer on medium speed. Beat in eggs, bananas and orange peel. In another small bowl, mix milk, vanilla and almond extract. Beat milk mixture alternately with flour mixture into butter mixture, beating thoroughly on low speed after each addition. Stir in coconut and nuts.

3   Pour batter into pan. Bake 60 to 70 minutes or until toothpick inserted in center comes out clean. Cool in pan 10 minutes on cooling rack; remove from pan. Cool completely, about 1 hour.

* If using self-rising flour, omit soda and salt.

High Altitude (3500–6500 ft): Heat oven to 375°F. Increase milk to ⅓ cup. Bake 65 to 75 minutes.

1 Slice: Calories 230; Total Fat 11g (Saturated Fat 6g; Trans Fat 0g); Cholesterol 40mg; Sodium 220mg; Total Carbohydrate 31g (Dietary Fiber 1g) Exchanges: 1 Starch, 1 Other Carbohydrate, 2 Fat; Carbohydrate Choices: 2

Playing with Tradition

Some cooks pass down old family recipes and never change a thing. And then there's Susan Adams. A professional portrait photographer, Susan took the family's long-time favorite banana bread and decided to liven it up. "I first served my recipe at a family gathering. . ." says Susan, "and everyone loved it." The Bake-Off® Contest judges loved it, too, awarding the bread a $5,000 prize.

Lickity Quick Lemonade Bread

Mrs. Joseph Pellecchia   East Boston, MA
Bake-Off® Contest 18, 1967

Prep Time: 15 Minutes
Start to Finish: 1 Hour 30 Minutes
1 loaf (12 slices)

1 cup sugar
½ cup shortening
½ cup milk
1½ cups Pillsbury BEST® all-purpose
   flour*
2 teaspoons baking powder
2 eggs
1 tablespoon plus ⅓ cup frozen
   lemonade concentrate, thawed

1   Heat oven to 350°F. Grease
9 × 5-inch loaf pan.

2   In large bowl, beat all ingredients except the ⅓ cup lemonade concentrate with electric mixer on low speed 30 seconds; beat 3 minutes at medium speed. Pour into pan.

3   Bake 50 to 60 minutes or until toothpick inserted in center comes out clean. Loosen bread from edges of pan. Pour ⅓ cup concentrate over bread. Cool in pan on cooling rack 15 minutes; remove from pan.

If using self-rising flour, omit baking powder.

High Altitude (3500–6500 ft): Heat oven to 375°F. Decrease sugar to ¾ cup. Increase milk to ⅔ cup.

1 Slice: Calories 240; Total Fat 10g (Saturated Fat 2.5g; Trans Fat 1.5g); Cholesterol 35mg; Sodium 95mg; Total Carbohydrate 34g (Dietary Fiber 0g) Exchanges: 1 Starch, 1 Other Carbohydrate, 2 Fat; Carbohydrate Choices: 2

Graham Cracker Brown Bread

Grace M. Kain   West Boothbay Harbor, ME
Bake-Off® Contest 10, 1958

Prep Time: 20 Minutes
Start to Finish: 2 Hours 10 Minutes
2 loaves (16 slices each)

2 cups graham cracker crumbs or
   finely crushed graham crackers
   (30 squares)
½ cup shortening
1¾ cups buttermilk*
¾ cup molasses
2 eggs, slightly beaten
1¾ cups Pillsbury BEST® all-purpose
   flour
2 teaspoons baking soda
1 teaspoon salt
¼ to ½ teaspoon ground nutmeg
1 cup raisins

1   Heat oven to 375°F. Grease and flour bottoms only of two 8 × 4-inch loaf pans. In large bowl, beat graham cracker crumbs and shortening with electric mixer on medium speed until well blended. Add buttermilk, molasses and eggs; beat well.

2   In small bowl, mix flour, baking soda, salt and nutmeg. Add to graham cracker mixture; beat at low speed until well blended. Fold in raisins. Pour batter into pans.

3   Bake 35 to 40 minutes or until toothpick inserted in center comes out clean. Cool 10 minutes. Remove from pans to cooling rack. Cool completely, about 1 hour.

To substitute for buttermilk, use 5 teaspoons vinegar or lemon juice plus milk to make 1¾ cups.

High Altitude (3500–6500 ft): Decrease buttermilk to 1½ cups, increase Pillsbury BEST® all-purpose flour to 2 cups. Add ¼ cup water with buttermilk, molasses and eggs. Bake 40 to 45 minutes.

1 Slice: Calories 120; Total Fat 4.5g (Saturated Fat 1g; Trans Fat 0.5g); Cholesterol 15mg; Sodium 200mg; Total Carbohydrate 19g (Dietary Fiber 0g) Exchanges: 1 Starch, 1 Fat; Carbohydrate Choices: 1

Crunchy Bran Cornbread

Ella Qupper   Davenport, IA
Bake-Off® Contest 24, 1973

Prep Time: 15 Minutes
Start to Finish: 50 Minutes
9 to 12 servings

1½ cups whole bran cereal
1 cup Pillsbury BEST® all-purpose
   or unbleached flour*
½ cup cornmeal
½ cup sugar
3 teaspoons baking powder
½ teaspoon salt
1 cup milk
½ cup shortening
2 eggs

1   Heat oven to 400°F. Grease 8- or 9-inch square or 11 × 17-inch pan.

2   In large bowl, beat all ingredients with electric mixer on medium speed 2 minutes. Pour into pan.

3   Bake 25 to 35 minutes or until toothpick inserted in center comes out clean.

If using self-rising flour, omit baking powder and salt.

High Altitude (3500–6500 ft): No change.

1 Serving: Calories 300 (Calories from Fat 120); Total Fat 14g (Saturated Fat 3.5g; Trans Fat 2g); Cholesterol 50mg; Sodium 340mg; Total Carbohydrate 37g (Dietary Fiber 4g) Exchanges: 2 Starch, ½ Other Carbohydrate, 2½ Fat Carbohydrate Choices: 2½

Graham Cracker Brown Bread

Easy Cheese Batter Bread

Mrs. Frances Sisinni   Milwaukee, WI
Bake-Off® Contest 23, 1972

Prep Time: 15 Minutes
Start to Finish: 2 Hours 55 Minutes
1 loaf (18 slices)

2½ cups Pillsbury BEST® all-purpose
   flour
2 teaspoons sugar
1½ teaspoons salt
1 package regular active dry yeast
1 cup shredded Cheddar cheese
   (4 oz)
¾ cup milk
½ cup butter or margarine
3 eggs

1   In large bowl, mix 1½ cups of the flour, the sugar, salt and yeast. Stir in cheese.

2   In 1-quart saucepan, heat milk and butter until very warm (120°F to 130°F). Add warm liquid and eggs to flour mixture; beat with electric mixer on low speed until moistened, scraping bowl frequently. Beat on medium speed 3 minutes, scraping bowl frequently. With spoon, stir in remaining 1 cup flour. Cover loosely with plastic wrap and cloth towel; let rise in warm place (80°F to 85°F) 45 to 60 minutes or until light and doubled in size.

3   Generously grease 1½- or 2-quart casserole or 9 × 5-inch loaf pan with shortening or cooking spray. Gently push fist into dough to deflate. Place dough in casserole. Cover; let rise in warm place 20 to 25 minutes or until light and doubled in size.

4   Heat oven to 350°F. Uncover dough; bake 40 to 45 minutes or until deep golden brown. Immediately remove from casserole to cooling rack. Cool at least 30 minutes before serving.

High Altitude (3500–6500 ft): Heat oven to 375°F.

1 Slice: Calories 150; Total Fat 8g (Saturated Fat 5g; Trans Fat 0g); Cholesterol 55mg; Sodium 290mg; Total Carbohydrate 15g (Dietary Fiber 0g) Exchanges: 1 Starch, 1½ Fat; Carbohydrate Choices: 1

Mexican Cilantro Batter Bread

Frances Sheppard   Corsicana, TX
Bake-Off® Contest 35, 1992

Prep Time: 25 Minutes
Start to Finish: 2 Hours 30 Minutes
1 loaf (16 slices)

4½ cups Pillsbury BEST® all-purpose
   flour
2 tablespoons sugar
1 teaspoon salt
1 teaspoon garlic powder
1 package regular active dry yeast
1 cup water
1 cup milk
2 tablespoons butter or margarine
½ cup chopped fresh cilantro
3 teaspoons freeze-dried chopped
   chives
1 can (4.5 oz) chopped green chiles,
   drained
1 tablespoon poppy seed

1   In large bowl, mix 2 cups flour, the sugar, salt, garlic powder and yeast. In 1-quart saucepan, heat water, milk and butter until very warm (120°F to 130°F). Add warm liquid to flour mixture; beat with electric mixer on medium speed 2 minutes. By hand, stir in remaining 2½ cups flour, the cilantro, chives and green chiles to make stiff batter. Cover; let rise in warm place (80°F to 85°F) 45 to 60 minutes or until light and doubled in size.

2   Generously grease 12-cup fluted tube cake pan or 10-inch angel food (tube) cake pan. Sprinkle bottom and sides of pan with poppy seed. Stir down dough to remove all air bubbles. Carefully spoon into pan. Cover loosely with greased plastic wrap and cloth towel. Let rise in warm place 30 to 45 minutes or until light and doubled in size.

3   Heat oven to 375°F. Uncover dough. Bake 35 to 40 minutes or until deep golden brown. Cool 5 minutes; remove from pan. Serve warm or cool.

High Altitude (3500–6500 ft): No change.

1 Slice: Calories 160; Total Fat 2.5g (Saturated Fat 1g; Trans Fat 0g); Cholesterol 5mg; Sodium 280mg; Total Carbohydrate 30g (Dietary Fiber 1g) Exchanges: 1½ Starch, ½ Other Carbohydrate, ½ Fat; Carbohydrate Choices: 2

Mexican Cilantro Batter Bread

Applesauce Rye Bread

Wendy Ruffini Provo, UT
Bake-Off® Contest 30, 1982

Prep Time: 50 Minutes
Start to Finish: 3 Hours 50 Minutes
2 loaves (12 slices each)

2½ to 3 cups Pillsbury BEST®
   all-purpose or unbleached flour
3 teaspoons caraway seed
1 teaspoon salt
1 teaspoon anise seed
2 teaspoons grated orange peel
2 packages regular active dry yeast
¼ cup firmly packed brown sugar
¼ cup butter or margarine
2 cups applesauce
2 cups medium rye flour

1 Generously grease two 8 × 4- or 9 × 5-inch loaf pans. In large bowl, mix 2 cups all-purpose flour, the caraway seed, salt, anise seed, orange peel and yeast. In 1-quart saucepan, heat brown sugar, butter and apple-sauce until very warm (120°F to 130°F). Add warm mixture to flour mixture. Beat with electric mixer on low speed until moistened; beat at medium speed 3 minutes. By hand, stir in rye flour to form a stiff dough.

2 Place dough on floured surface; knead in up to 1 cup all-purpose flour about 10 minutes or until dough is smooth and elastic. Place dough in greased bowl; cover loosely with plastic wrap and cloth towel. Let rise in warm place (80°F to 85°F) about 1 hour or until light and doubled in size.

3 Push down dough with fist. Divide dough into 2 parts; shape into loaves. Place in pans. Cover; let rise in warm place about 1 hour or until light and doubled in size.

4 Heat oven to 350°F. Bake 50 to 60 minutes or until loaves sound hollow when lightly tapped. (Cover with foil after 30 minutes to prevent overbrowning.) Remove from pans immediately. If desired, brush with melted butter.

High Altitude (3500–6500 ft): Rising times may be shorter.

1 Slice: Calories 120; Total Fat 2.5g (Saturated Fat 1.5g; Trans Fat 0g); Cholesterol 5mg; Sodium 115mg; Total Carbohydrate 23g (Dietary Fiber 2g) Exchanges: 1 Starch, ½ Other Carbohydrate, ½ Fat; Carbohydrate Choices: 1½

Honey Granola Bread

Gloria Kirchman Mankato, MN
Bake-Off® Contest 30, 1982

Prep Time: 45 Minutes
Start to Finish: 2 Hours 25 Minutes
2 loaves (17 slices each)

5 to 5½ cups Pillsbury BEST®
   all-purpose flour
1 cup granola cereal
2 teaspoons salt
2 packages regular active dry yeast
1½ cups water
1 cup plain low-fat yogurt
½ cup honey
¼ cup oil or shortening
2 eggs
2 cups Pillsbury BEST® whole wheat flour

1 In large bowl, mix 3 cups all-purpose flour, the granola cereal, salt and yeast. In 2-quart saucepan, heat water, yogurt, honey and oil until very warm (120°F to 130°F). Add warm liquid and eggs to flour mixture; beat with electric mixer at low speed until moistened. Beat 3 minutes at medium speed. By hand, stir in whole wheat flour and an additional 1 cup all-purpose flour to form a stiff dough.

2 Place dough on floured surface; knead in remaining 1 to 1½ cups all-purpose flour about 10 minutes or until dough is smooth and elastic. Place dough in greased bowl; cover loosely with plastic wrap and cloth towel. Let rise in warm place (80°F to 85°F) about 1 hour or until light and doubled in size.

3 Generously grease two 9 × 5- or 8 × 4-inch loaf pans. Push down dough with fist several times to remove all air bubbles. Divide dough in half; shape into 2 loaves. Place in pans. Cover; let rise in warm place 30 to 45 minutes or until light and doubled in size.

4 Heat oven to 350°F. Uncover dough. Bake 30 to 40 minutes or until loaves sound hollow when lightly tapped. Immediately remove from pans to cooling racks. If desired, brush loaves with melted butter.

High Altitude (3500–6500 ft): Bake 40 to 50 minutes.

1 Slice: Calories 150; Total Fat 3g (Saturated Fat 0.5g; Trans Fat 0g); Cholesterol 15mg; Sodium 150mg; Total Carbohydrate 26g (Dietary Fiber 1g) Exchanges: 1½ Starch, ½ Fat; Carbohydrate Choices: 2

Quick-Start Sourdough Bread

Elisa Adine Henderson
Yucca Valley, CA
Bake-Off® Contest 30, 1982

Prep Time: 50 Minutes
Start to Finish: 3 Hours 20 Minutes
2 loaves (12 slices each)

Cornmeal, if desired
2 packages regular active dry yeast
1½ cups warm water (105°F to 115°F)
1 cup plain yogurt
3 teaspoons salt
5 to 6 cups Pillsbury BEST® all-purpose
or unbleached flour*

1 Grease cookie sheet; sprinkle with cornmeal. In large bowl, dissolve yeast in warm water; stir in yogurt and salt. Add 2½ cups flour. Beat with electric mixer on low speed until moistened; beat 3 minutes on medium speed. By hand, stir in 2 to 2½ cups flour to form a stiff dough.

2 Place dough on floured surface; knead in up to 1 cup flour 5 to 8 minutes or until dough is smooth and elastic. Place dough in greased bowl; cover loosely with plastic wrap and cloth towel. Let rise in warm place (80°F to 85°F) about 1 hour or until light and doubled in size.

3 Push down dough with fist. Divide dough into 2 parts; shape into balls. Place on cookie sheet. Cover; let rise in warm place about 1 hour or until light and doubled in size.

4 Heat oven to 400°F. With sharp knife, cut 3 slashes in top of each loaf. Brush loaves with water. Bake 35 to 45 minutes, brushing loaves with water every 15 minutes, until loaves sound hollow when lightly tapped. Immediately remove loaves from pan to cooling rack.

High Altitude (3500–6500 ft): Rising times may be shorter. Bake 20 to 25 minutes.

1 Slice: Calories 100; Total Fat 0g (Saturated Fat 0g; Trans Fat 0g); Cholesterol 0mg; Sodium 300mg; Total Carbohydrate 21g (Dietary Fiber 0g) Exchanges: 1½ Starch; Carbohydrate Choices: 1½

Bread Flour may be substituted for all-purpose or unbleached flour. Increase kneading time to 10 minutes. Increase rising time to 1 to 1½ hours and allow dough to rest 5 minutes before shaping. Self-rising flour is not recommended.

Savory Wheat French Bread

Carol A. Bishop Monroeville, NJ
Bake-Off® Contest 29, 1980

Prep Time: 45 Minutes
Start to Finish: 3 Hours 20 Minutes
2 loaves (16 slices each)

Cornmeal
3 cups Pillsbury BEST® whole wheat flour
1 cup grated Parmesan cheese
3 teaspoons salt
3 teaspoons dried oregano leaves
1½ teaspoons garlic powder
2 packages regular active dry yeast
3¼ cups water
2 tablespoons honey
5½ cups Pillsbury BEST® all-purpose or
unbleached flour*
1 egg, beaten

1 Grease 2 cookie sheets; sprinkle with cornmeal. In large bowl, mix whole wheat flour, cheese, salt, oregano, garlic powder and yeast. In 2-quart saucepan, heat water and honey until very warm (120°F to 130°F). Add warm liquid to flour mixture. Beat with electric mixer on low speed until moistened; beat 3 minutes on medium speed. By hand, stir in 4 cups all-purpose flour to form a stiff dough.

2 Place dough on floured surface. Knead in ½ to 1½ cups all-purpose flour about 8 minutes or until dough is smooth and elastic. Place in greased bowl; cover loosely with plastic wrap and cloth towel. Let rise in warm place (80°F to 85°F) about 1 hour or until light and doubled in size.

3 Push down dough with fist. Divide dough in half; form into two 14-inch long loaves, tapering ends. Place on cookie sheets. Cut diagonal slashes in loaves, about ¼ inch deep. Cover; let rise in warm place 45 to 60 minutes or until light and doubled in size. Lightly brush loaves with beaten egg. Heat oven to 400°F. Bake 20 minutes; brush with cold water. Bake 10 to 15 minutes longer or until loaves sound hollow when lightly tapped.

High Altitude (3500–6500 ft): No change.

1 Slice: Calories 140; Total Fat 1.5g (Saturated Fat 0.5g; Trans Fat 0g); Cholesterol 10mg; Sodium 270mg; Total Carbohydrate 26g (Dietary Fiber 2g) Exchanges: 1½ Starch, ½ Other Carbohydrate; Carbohydrate Choices: 2

Self-rising flour is not recommended.

Mexican Fiesta Biscuit Bake

Crescent Onion Bread

Betty Engles   Midland, MI
Bake-Off® Contest 25, 1974

Prep Time: 20 Minutes
Start to Finish: 40 Minutes
1 loaf (12 slices)

2 cans (8 oz each) Pillsbury®
   refrigerated crescent dinner rolls
3 tablespoons dried minced onion
2 tablespoons grated Parmesan cheese
2 tablespoons French dressing
2 tablespoons butter or margarine,
   melted
2 teaspoons grated Parmesan cheese

1   Heat oven to 375°F. Generously grease 8- or 9-inch round cake or pie pan.

2   Separate crescent dough into four large rectangles; firmly press perforations to seal. In small bowl, mix onion, 2 tablespoons cheese and the dressing. Spread filling over each rectangle. Starting at longer side, roll up; press edges to seal. Beginning at outer edge of pan, place 1 dough roll; add each additional roll, coiling toward center and forming a spiral. Seal ends of dough together as they are added.

3   Bake 15 to 20 minutes until golden brown. Brush with melted butter; sprinkle with 2 teaspoons cheese.

High Altitude (3500–6500 ft): No change.

1 Slice: Calories 180; Total Fat 11g (Saturated Fat 4g; Trans Fat 2g); Cholesterol 5mg; Sodium 360mg; Total Carbohydrate 17g (Dietary Fiber 0g) Exchanges: 1 Starch, 2 Fat; Carbohydrate Choices: 1

Mexican Fiesta Biscuit Bake

Madge Savage   Howard, OH
Bake-Off® Contest 36, 1994
$10,000 Winner

Prep Time: 15 Minutes
Start to Finish: 1 Hour 15 Minutes
12 to 15 servings

2 tablespoons butter or margarine
1 can (16.3 oz) AND 1 can (10.2 oz)
   Pillsbury® Grands!® refrigerated
   buttermilk homestyle biscuits
1 jar (16 oz) chunky-style salsa
   (1¾ cups)
3 cups shredded Monterey Jack cheese
   (12 oz)
½ cup chopped green bell pepper
8 medium green onions, sliced (½ cup)
1 can (2¼ oz) sliced ripe olives, drained
1 cup chunky-style salsa, if desired

1   Heat oven to 375°F. In 13 × 9-inch glass baking dish or non-aluminum pan, melt butter in oven. Tilt to evenly coat dish.

2   Separate dough into 13 biscuits (8 from one can, 5 from the other); cut each biscuit into eighths. In large bowl, place biscuit pieces; toss with 1¾ cups salsa. Spoon evenly into butter-coated dish. Sprinkle with cheese, bell pepper, onions and olives.

3   Bake 35 to 45 minutes or until edges are deep golden brown and center is set. Let stand 15 minutes. Cut into squares; serve with 1 cup salsa.

High Altitude (3500–6500 ft): No change.

1 Serving: Calories 350; Total Fat 20g (Saturated Fat 10g; Trans Fat 3.5g); Cholesterol 30mg; Sodium 1150mg; Total Carbohydrate 31g (Dietary Fiber 0g) Exchanges: 1½ Starch, ½ Other Carbohydrate, 1 High-Fat Meat, 2 Fat; Carbohydrate Choices: 2

Zesty Cheese Biscuit Loaf

Willa Fulbright   Dardanelle, AR
Bake-Off® Contest 30, 1982

Prep Time: 20 Minutes
Start to Finish: 1 Hour 5 Minutes
1 loaf (10 slices)

¼ cup butter or margarine
1 cup chopped green onions with tops
1 teaspoon chili powder
2 cans (12 oz each) Pillsbury® Golden
   Layers® refrigerated flaky biscuits
½ cup shredded Monterey Jack or
   mozzarella cheese (2 oz)

1   Heat oven to 350°F. Grease 9 × 5- or 8 × 4-inch loaf pan.

2   In 1-quart saucepan, melt butter. Cook and stir onions in butter; stir in chili powder. Remove from heat; cool. Separate dough into 20 biscuits. Dip both sides of each biscuit into onion mixture. Place biscuits in pan, forming 4 rows of 5 biscuits each. Spoon 1 teaspoon cheese between each pair of biscuits. Spread any remaining onion mixture or cheese over biscuits.

3   Bake 35 to 40 minutes or until deep golden brown. Cool 5 minutes. Loosen edges; remove from pan. Serve warm.

High Altitude (3500–6500 ft): No change.

1 Slice: Calories 280; Total Fat 15g (Saturated Fat 6g; Trans Fat 3g); Cholesterol 15mg; Sodium 790mg; Total Carbohydrate 29g (Dietary Fiber 0g) Exchanges: 1½ Starch, ½ Other Carbohydrate, 3 Fat; Carbohydrate Choices: 2

Whole Wheat Raisin Loaf

Lenora H. Smith   Baton Rouge, LA
Bake-Off® Contest 27, 1976
$25,000 One of Two Grand Prize Winners

Prep Time: 30 Minutes
Start to Finish: 4 Hours 5 Minutes
2 loaves (16 slices each)

2 to 3 cups Pillsbury BEST® all-purpose
   flour
½ cup sugar
3 teaspoons salt
1 teaspoon ground cinnamon
½ teaspoon ground nutmeg
2 packages regular active dry yeast
2 cups milk
¾ cup water
¼ cup vegetable oil
4 cups Pillsbury BEST® whole wheat
   flour
1 cup quick-cooking or old-fashioned
   oats
1 cup raisins
1 tablespoon butter or margarine,
   melted
1 teaspoon sugar, if desired

1   In large bowl, mix 1½ cups all-purpose flour, ½ cup sugar, the salt, cinnamon, nutmeg and yeast. In 2-quart saucepan, heat milk, water and oil until very warm (120°F to 130°F). Add warm liquid to flour mixture; beat with electric mixer on low speed until moistened. Beat 3 minutes on medium speed. By hand, stir in whole wheat flour, oats, raisins and an additional ¼ to ¾ cup all-purpose flour until dough pulls cleanly away from sides of bowl.

2   Place dough on floured surface; knead in remaining ¼ to ¾ cup all-purpose flour about 5 minutes or until dough is smooth and elastic. Place dough in greased bowl; cover loosely with greased plastic wrap and cloth towel. Let rise in warm place (80°F to 85°F) 20 to 30 minutes or until light and doubled in size.

3   Grease two 9 × 5- or 8 × 4-inch loaf pans. Push down dough with fist several times to remove all air bubbles. Divide dough in half; shape into two loaves. Place in pans. Cover; let rise in warm place 30 to 45 minutes or until light and doubled in size.

4   Heat oven to 375°F. Uncover dough. Bake 40 to 50 minutes or until deep golden brown and loaves sound hollow when lightly tapped. If loaves become too brown, cover loosely with foil during last 10 minutes of baking. Immediately remove from pans to cooling racks. Cool completely, about 1 hour 30 minutes. Brush tops of loaves with melted butter; sprinkle with 1 teaspoon sugar.

High Altitude (3500–6500 ft): No change.

1 Slice: Calories 150; Total Fat 3g (Saturated Fat 1g; Trans Fat 0g); Cholesterol 0mg; Sodium 230mg; Total Carbohydrate 26g (Dietary Fiber 2g) Exchanges: 1½ Starch, ½ Fat; Carbohydrate Choices: 2

Onion Lover's Twist

Nan Robb   Huachucha City, AZ
Bake-Off® Contest 21, 1970
$25,000 Grand Prize Winner

Prep Time: 40 Minutes
Start to Finish: 2 Hours 45 Minutes
1 loaf (32 slices)

BREAD
3½ to 4½ cups Pillsbury BEST®
   all-purpose flour
¼ cup sugar
1½ teaspoons salt
1 package regular active dry yeast
¾ cup water
½ cup milk
¼ cup butter or margarine
1 egg

FILLING
¼ cup butter or margarine
1 cup finely chopped onions or ¼ cup
   dried minced onion
1 tablespoon grated Parmesan cheese
1 tablespoon sesame or poppy seed
1 teaspoon paprika
½ to 1 teaspoon garlic salt

1   In large bowl, mix 2 cups of the flour, the sugar, salt and yeast. In 1-quart saucepan, heat water, milk and ¼ cup butter until very warm (120°F to 130°F). Add warm liquid and egg to flour mixture. Beat with electric mixer on low speed until moistened; beat 3 minutes at medium speed. By hand, stir in remaining 1½ to 2½ cups flour to form a soft dough. Cover loosely with greased plastic wrap and cloth towel. Let rise in warm place (80°F to 95°F) 45 to 60 minutes or until light and doubled in size.

2 Grease large cookie sheet. In 1-quart saucepan, melt ¼ cup butter; stir in remaining filling ingredients. Set aside. Stir down dough to remove all air bubbles. Place dough on floured surface; toss until no longer sticky. Roll dough into 18 × 12-inch rectangle. Cut rectangle in half crosswise to make two 12 × 9-inch rectangles; cut each rectangle into three 9 × 4-inch strips. Spread about 2 tablespoons onion mixture over each strip to ½ inch of edges. Bring lengthwise edges of each strip together to enclose filling; pinch edges and ends to seal.

3 On cookie sheet, braid 3 rolls together; pinch ends to seal. Repeat with remaining 3 rolls for second loaf. Cover; let rise in warm place 25 to 30 minutes or until light and doubled in size.

4 Heat oven to 350°F. Uncover dough. Bake 27 to 35 minutes or until golden brown and loaves sound hollow when lightly tapped. Immediately remove from cookie sheet to cooling racks.

High Altitude (3500–6500 ft): No change.

1 Slice: Calories 90; Total Fat 3.5g (Saturated Fat 2g; Trans Fat 0g); Cholesterol 15mg; Sodium 150mg; Total Carbohydrate 13g (Dietary Fiber 0g) Exchanges: 1 Starch, ½ Fat; Carbohydrate Choices: 1

Onion Lover's Twist

meet karen kwan

Karen Kwan's kitchen experiences started at an early age, thanks to her mother. "She had us in the kitchen from age three on, helping her roll out pie crusts. She had a philosophy about kids doing the pie crusts—because we had really tiny hands and a light touch, she thought the crusts worked out better than those made with adult-sized hands."

As an adult, Karen continued to share her love of cooking with her mother. Together, they created an annual tradition, hosting extended family in a Christmas-season tea. They invited about 30 women: "It's sort of like *The Joy Luck Club*," Karen said, "where I call most of the women 'Auntie,' even though we're not blood related." Karen and her mother split the cooking, creating an elaborate array of miniature pastries and sandwiches, scones and tartlets.

Her youthful cooking experience also paid off when she earned a trip to the Bake-Off® Contest at age 25, with a grilled chicken salad. Her savory Cheddar Twisters captured her a coveted second contest visit four years later in 1998. Karen credits her ethnic background with giving her a special perspective. "Because I'm Chinese-American, I'm a unique combination of traditional Asian values and American free-thinking," Karen says.

Cheddar Twisters

Karen Kwan   Belmont, CA
Bake-Off® Contest 38, 1998

Prep Time: 10 Minutes
Start to Finish: 35 Minutes
8 rolls

2 cans (8 oz each) Pillsbury®
   refrigerated crescent dinner rolls
1½ cups finely shredded sharp Cheddar
   cheese (6 oz)
4 medium green onions, chopped (¼ cup)
1 egg
1 teaspoon water
2 teaspoons sesame seed
½ teaspoon garlic salt with parsley
   blend (from 4.8-oz jar)*

1   Heat oven to 375°F. Lightly grease large cookie sheet with shortening or cooking spray. Unroll both cans of dough. Separate into 8 rectangles; firmly press perforations to seal.

2   In small bowl, mix cheese and onions. Spoon slightly less than ¼ cup cheese mixture in 1-inch-wide strip lengthwise down center of each rectangle to within ¼ inch of each end. Fold dough in half lengthwise to form long strip; firmly press edges to seal. Twist each strip 4 or 5 times; bring ends together to form ring and pinch to seal. Place on cookie sheet.

3   In another small bowl, beat egg and water until well blended; brush over dough. Sprinkle with sesame seed and garlic salt blend.

4   Bake 15 to 20 minutes or until golden brown. Immediately remove from cookie sheet; cool 5 minutes. Serve warm.

One-half teaspoon garlic salt and a dash of parsley flakes can be substituted for the garlic salt with parsley blend.

High Altitude (3500–6500 ft): No change.

1 Roll: Calories 310; Total Fat 20g (Saturated Fat 9g; Trans Fat 3g); Cholesterol 50mg; Sodium 640mg; Total Carbohydrate 23g (Dietary Fiber 0g) Exchanges: 1 Starch, ½ Other Carbohydrate, 1 High-Fat Meat, 2 Fat; Carbohydrate Choices: 1½

Italian Biscuit Flatbread

Edith L. Shulman   Sedona, AZ
Bake-Off® Contest 32, 1986
$2,000 Winner

Prep Time: 25 Minutes
Start to Finish: 40 Minutes
10 flatbreads

⅓ cup mayonnaise or salad dressing
⅓ cup grated Parmesan cheese
¼ teaspoon dried basil leaves
¼ teaspoon dried oregano leaves
3 medium green onions, sliced
   (3 tablespoons)
1 clove garlic, finely chopped,
   or ⅛ teaspoon garlic powder
1 can (12 oz) Pillsbury® Golden Layers®
   refrigerated flaky biscuits

1 Heat oven to 400°F. In small bowl, mix mayonnaise and cheese. Stir in basil, oregano, onions and garlic.

2 Separate dough into 10 biscuits. On ungreased cookie sheets, press each biscuit to form 4-inch round. Spread about 1 tablespoon cheese mixture onto each round to within ¼ inch of edge.

3 Bake 10 to 13 minutes or until golden brown. Serve warm.

High Altitude (3500–6500 ft): No change.

1 Flatbread: Calories 170; Total Fat 11g (Saturated Fat 2.5g; Trans Fat 1.5g); Cholesterol 5mg; Sodium 450mg; Total Carbohydrate 15g (Dietary Fiber 0g) Exchanges: 1 Starch, 2 Fat; Carbohydrate Choices: 1

Cheese-Crusted Flatbread

Lois Mattson Duluth, MN
Bake-Off® Contest 16, 1964

> **Prep Time:** 30 Minutes
> **Start to Finish:** 2 Hours 40 Minutes
> 16 servings

2½ to 3 cups Pillsbury BEST®
   all-purpose flour
1 tablespoon sugar
1 teaspoon salt
1 package regular active dry yeast
¾ cup milk
¼ cup water
2 tablespoons butter or margarine
2 tablespoons chopped onion
¼ cup butter or margarine, melted
½ teaspoon dried oregano leaves
½ teaspoon paprika
¼ teaspoon garlic salt
¼ teaspoon celery seed
1 cup shredded Cheddar cheese (4 oz)

1 In large bowl, mix 2 cups flour, the sugar, salt and yeast. In 1-quart saucepan, heat milk, water and 2 tablespoons butter until very warm (120°F to 130°F). Add warm liquid to flour mixture; mix well.

Stir in remaining ½ to 1 cup flour to form a stiff dough.

2 Place dough on lightly floured surface; knead about 5 minutes or until smooth. Place dough in greased bowl. Cover loosely with greased plastic wrap and cloth towel. Let rise in warm place (80°F to 85°F) 45 to 60 minutes or until light and doubled in size.

3 Grease two 9-inch round cake or pie pans. Divide dough in half; press each half in pan. In small bowl, mix onion, ¼ cup butter, the oregano, paprika, garlic salt and celery seed. Spread mixture over dough. Prick tops generously with fork. Sprinkle evenly with cheese. Cover; let rise in warm place 30 to 45 minutes or until light and doubled in size.

4 Heat oven to 375°F. Uncover dough. Bake 20 to 25 minutes or until golden brown. Serve warm.

High Altitude (3500–6500 ft): No change.

1 Serving: Calories 150; Total Fat 7g (Saturated Fat 4.5g; Trans Fat 0g); Cholesterol 20mg; Sodium 240mg; Total Carbohydrate 17g (Dietary Fiber 0g) Exchanges: 1 Starch, 1½ Fat; Carbohydrate Choices: 1

Country French Herb Flatbread

Leslie DiFiglio St. Charles, IL
Bake-Off® Contest 38, 1998

> **Prep Time:** 15 Minutes
> **Start to Finish:** 35 Minutes
> 20 appetizers

1 can (13.8 oz) Pillsbury® refrigerated
   classic pizza crust
4½ teaspoons olive oil
2 teaspoons herbes de Provence*
5 to 6 oil-packed sun-dried tomatoes,
   drained, chopped

⅓ cup chèvre (goat) cheese,
   softened
2 eggs
Dash pepper
Fresh thyme or rosemary sprigs,
   if desired
Red and/or yellow cherry tomatoes,
   if desired

1 Heat oven to 400°F. Spray 13 × 9-inch pan with cooking spray. Unroll dough in pan. Starting at center, press out dough to edges of pan. Make indentations over surface of dough. Brush with 3 teaspoons of the oil. Sprinkle with 1 teaspoon of the herbes de Provence. Top with sun-dried tomatoes.

2 In medium bowl, mix cheese, eggs, remaining 1½ teaspoons oil and remaining 1 teaspoon herbes de Provence, using wire whisk. Pour evenly over tomatoes; spread carefully.

3 Bake 15 to 20 minutes or until edges are golden brown. Sprinkle with pepper. If necessary, loosen sides of bread from pan. Cut into squares. Arrange on serving platter. Garnish with thyme sprigs and cherry tomatoes.

To substitute for herbes de Provence, mix ½ teaspoon each dried thyme, marjoram, rosemary and basil leaves.

High Altitude (3500–6500 ft): Bake 20 to 25 minutes.

1 Appetizer: Calories 70; Total Fat 3g (Saturated Fat 1g; Trans Fat 0g); Cholesterol 20mg; Sodium 160mg; Total Carbohydrate 10g (Dietary Fiber 0g) Exchanges: ½ Starch, ½ Fat; Carbohydrate Choices: ½

Quick 'n Easy Herb Flatbread

Quick 'n Easy Herb Flatbread

Cathy Olafson   Colorado Springs, CO
Bake-Off® Contest 39, 2000

Prep Time: 10 Minutes
Start to Finish: 25 Minutes
9 servings

1 can (13.8 oz) Pillsbury® refrigerated
   classic pizza crust
1 tablespoon olive or vegetable oil
½ to 1 teaspoon dried basil leaves
½ to 1 teaspoon dried rosemary leaves,
   crushed
½ teaspoon finely chopped garlic
⅛ teaspoon salt
1 small tomato
¼ cup shredded fresh Parmesan cheese

1   Heat oven to 425°F. Spray cookie sheet with cooking spray. Unroll dough on cookie sheet. Starting at center, press out dough to form 12 × 8-inch rectangle.

2   In small bowl, mix oil, basil, rosemary and garlic. Brush over dough; sprinkle with salt. Chop tomato; place in shallow bowl. With back of spoon, crush tomato. Spread tomato over dough.

3   Bake 5 to 9 minutes or until edges are light golden brown. Sprinkle with cheese. Bake 2 to 3 minutes longer or until cheese is melted and edges are golden brown. Cut into squares. Serve warm.

High Altitude (3500–6500 ft): In step 3, increase first bake time to 7 to 11 minutes.

1 Serving: Calories 140; Total Fat 3.5g (Saturated Fat 1g; Trans Fat 0g); Cholesterol 0mg; Sodium 400mg; Total Carbohydrate 21g (Dietary Fiber 0g) Exchanges: 1½ Starch, ½ Fat; Carbohydrate Choices: 1½

Biscuit Mini Focaccia

Linda J. Greeson   Spring Valley, CA
Bake-Off® Contest 37, 1996
$2,000 Winner

Prep Time: 30 Minutes
Start to Finish: 40 Minutes
10 servings

½ cup fresh basil leaves
¼ cup fresh thyme sprigs
2 cloves garlic, chopped
¼ teaspoon salt, if desired
Dash pepper
¼ cup olive oil or vegetable oil
1 can (12 oz) Pillsbury® Golden Layers®
   refrigerated flaky biscuits
¼ cup pine nuts
⅓ cup grated Parmesan cheese

1   Heat oven to 400°F. In blender or food processor, place basil, thyme, garlic, salt, pepper and oil. Cover; blend until finely chopped, scraping down sides of container if necessary.

2   Separate dough into 10 biscuits. On ungreased cookie sheets, press or roll each biscuit to 3-inch round. Make several indentations in tops of biscuits. Spread about 1 teaspoon basil mixture evenly over each biscuit. Sprinkle each biscuit evenly with 1 teaspoon pine nuts; press gently. Sprinkle with cheese.

3   Bake 10 to 12 minutes or until biscuits are golden brown. Serve warm.

High Altitude (3500–6500 ft): No change.

1 Serving: Calories 190; Total Fat 13g (Saturated Fat 2.5g; Trans Fat 1.5g); Cholesterol 0mg; Sodium 410mg; Total Carbohydrate 15g (Dietary Fiber 0g) Exchanges: 1 Starch, 2½ Fat; Carbohydrate Choices: 1

Inspiration from an Unlikely Source

Cathy Olafson got interested in cooking at age 13, and one reason is . . . the Oakland Raiders. "My parents were big football fans and attended every Raiders home game," Cathy explains, "so I was in charge of dinner those nights." Surprises are a part of cooking as well as football. Take, for instance, her Bake-Off® herb flatbread. "I was trying to duplicate my grandmother's focaccia," says Cathy. "It actually came out totally different, but I liked what I ended up with." So did her husband, Jack, who encouraged her to enter the contest.

Seeded Crescent Wedges

Barbara Lento Aliquippa, PA
Bake-Off® Contest 39, 2000

> Prep Time: 10 Minutes
> Start to Finish: 30 Minutes
> 32 appetizers

2 tablespoons sunflower nuts
1 tablespoon caraway seed
1 tablespoon sesame seed
1 can (8 oz) Pillsbury® refrigerated crescent dinner rolls
2 tablespoons Dijon mustard
1 tablespoon bourbon whiskey or apple juice
1 tablespoon honey

1 Heat oven to 375°F. Spray large cookie sheet with cooking spray. In small bowl, mix sunflower nuts, caraway seed and sesame seed.

2 Separate dough into 4 rectangles. Place on cookie sheet. Firmly press perforations to seal. Cut each rectangle into 8 wedges.

3 In small bowl, mix mustard, bourbon whiskey and honey; brush over wedges. Separate wedges slightly. Sprinkle each wedge with seed mixture.

4 Bake 9 to 14 minutes or until golden brown. Remove from cookie sheet. Cool 5 minutes. Serve warm or cool.

High Altitude (3500–6500 ft): No change.

1 Appetizer: Calories 35; Total Fat 2g (Saturated Fat 0.5g; Trans Fat 0g); Cholesterol 0mg; Sodium 80mg; Total Carbohydrate 4g (Dietary Fiber 0g) Exchanges: ½ Fat; Carbohydrate Choices: 0

Pepper Biscuit Pull-Apart

Julie Ann Halverson Big Lake, MN
Bake-Off® Contest 34, 1990

> Prep Time: 20 Minutes
> Start to Finish: 35 Minutes
> 10 servings

¼ teaspoon garlic powder
¼ teaspoon salt, if desired
¼ teaspoon dried basil leaves, crushed
¼ teaspoon dried oregano leaves, crushed
1 can (12 oz) Pillsbury® Golden Layers® refrigerated flaky biscuits
4½ teaspoons olive oil
¼ cup chopped green bell pepper
¼ cup chopped red bell pepper
¼ cup shredded mozzarella cheese (1 oz)
2 tablespoons grated Romano or Parmesan cheese

1 Heat oven to 400°F. In small bowl, mix garlic powder, salt, basil and oregano.

2 Separate dough into 10 biscuits. Place 1 biscuit in center of ungreased cookie sheet. Arrange remaining biscuits in circle, edges slightly over-lapping, around center biscuit. Gently press out to form 10-inch round. Brush biscuits with oil. Top with bell peppers and cheeses. Sprinkle garlic powder mixture over top.

3 Bake 12 to 15 minutes or until golden brown. To serve, pull apart warm biscuits.

High Altitude (3500–6500 ft): No change.

1 Serving: Calories 140; Total Fat 7g (Saturated Fat 2g; Trans Fat 1.5g); Cholesterol 0mg; Sodium 390mg; Total Carbohydrate 15g (Dietary Fiber 0g) Exchanges: 1 Starch, 1½ Fat; Carbohydrate Choices: 1

Easy English Muffins

Julia Hauber Winfield, KS
Bake-Off® Contest 19, 1968

> Prep Time: 1 Hour
> Start to Finish: 1 Hour 45 Minutes
> 26 muffins

2 packages regular active dry yeast
2 cups warm water (105°F to 115°F)
5 to 6 cups Pillsbury BEST® all-purpose flour
1 tablespoon sugar
3 teaspoons salt
½ cup shortening
Cornmeal
Butter or margarine

1 In large bowl, dissolve yeast in warm water. Add 3 cups flour, the sugar, salt and shortening to yeast mixture, stirring with spoon until moistened. Stir vigorously until smooth. Using wire whisk or electric mixer on low speed,

An Idea Is Born

Where do original recipe ideas come from? Barbara Lento's Bake-Off® Contest recipe "was born on a sleepless summer night," she reports. "I took it to work to be tested by my quality assurance team, and it didn't last long." In Barbara's job as an airline systems scheduler, one of her special challenges was putting the operation back together after severe weather. Luckily, the forecast was only bright for her crescent wedges.

gradually add remaining 2 to 3 cups flour to form a stiff dough, beating well after each addition. On floured surface, gently knead dough 5 to 6 times or until no longer sticky. Roll dough ¼ to ⅜ inch thick; cut with 3- to 4-inch floured round cutter.

2 Sprinkle cornmeal evenly over 2 ungreased cookie sheets. Place dough cutouts on cornmeal; sprinkle with additional cornmeal. Cover loosely with plastic wrap and cloth towel. Let rise in warm place until light, 30 to 45 minutes.

3 Heat griddle to 350°F. With wide spatula, turn dough cutouts upside down onto ungreased griddle. Bake 5 to 6 minutes on each side or until light golden brown; cool. Split, toast and butter.

High Altitude (3500–6500 ft): No change.

1 Muffin: Calories 130; Total Fat 4g (Saturated Fat 1g; Trans Fat 0.5g); Cholesterol 0mg; Sodium 270mg; Total Carbohydrate 19g (Dietary Fiber 0g) Exchanges: 1 Starch, 1 Fat; Carbohydrate Choices: 1

Old Plantation Rolls

Mrs. William Edwin Baker
Colorado Springs, CO
Bake-Off® Contest 1, 1949

> Prep Time: 30 Minutes
> Start to Finish: 2 Hours 30 Minutes
> 24 rolls

5 to 6 cups Pillsbury BEST® all-purpose flour
¼ cup sugar
1 teaspoon baking powder
1 teaspoon salt
½ teaspoon baking soda
1 package regular active dry yeast
1 cup water
1 cup milk
½ cup shortening
1 egg

Just Stay Calm

Grace under pressure—one of a cook's most necessary gifts. That's where the saying "If you can't take the heat, get out of the kitchen" comes from. "A tornado alert once sent us to the basement for an hour," Julia Hauber remembers. "Everyone else worried about being killed. I just worried about my rare roast beef and kept running upstairs to check it." Despite the approaching storm, Julia's guests arrived. "We had our first course, hors d'oeuvres and drinks, in the southwest (safest) corner of the basement . . . which unfortunately was the powder room." Amazingly, the roast turned out perfect, and grace was triumphant.

1 Grease 24 regular-size muffin cups. In large bowl, mix 3 cups flour, the sugar, baking powder, salt, baking soda and yeast. In 1-quart saucepan, heat water, milk and shortening until very warm (120°F to 130°F). Add warm liquid and egg to flour mixture. Beat with electric mixer on low speed until moistened; beat 3 minutes on medium speed. By hand, stir in remaining 2 to 3 cups flour to form a stiff dough. Cover loosely with greased plastic wrap and cloth towel. Let rise in warm place (80°F to 85°F) about 1 hour or until light and doubled in size.

2 Push down dough several times with fist to remove all air bubbles.* Place dough on well-floured surface; toss until no longer sticky. Divide dough into 24 equal pieces; shape into balls.** Place 1 ball in each muffin cup. With scissors or sharp

knife, cut X-shape in each ball, forming 4 equal pieces. Cover; let rise in warm place 35 to 45 minutes or until light and doubled in size.

3 Heat oven to 400°F. Uncover dough. Bake 13 to 15 minutes or until golden brown. Immediately remove from pans.

Rolls can be prepared to this point, covered and refrigerated overnight. Increase second rise time to 1 hour 15 minutes.
**For cloverleaf shape, divide dough into 72 pieces; shape into balls. Place 3 balls in each muffin cup. Cover; let rise in warm place 35 to 45 minutes or until light and doubled in size. Bake as directed above.*

High Altitude (3500–6500 ft): No change.

1 Roll: Calories 150; Total Fat 5g (Saturated Fat 1.5g; Trans Fat 0.5g); Cholesterol 10mg; Sodium 150mg; Total Carbohydrate 23g (Dietary Fiber 0g) Exchanges: 1 Starch, ½ Other Carbohydrate, 1 Fat; Carbohydrate Choices: 1½

Speedy Brioche

Mrs. Darrell L. Henderson   Chesapeake, VA
Bake-Off® Contest 19, 1968

Prep Time: 30 Minutes
Start to Finish: 1 Hour 40 Minutes
24 rolls

2 packages regular active dry yeast
¼ cup warm water
1¼ cups buttermilk, room temperature
2 eggs
¾ cup butter or margarine, softened
⅓ cup sugar
2 teaspoons baking powder
1 tablespoon salt
5 to 5½ cups Pillsbury BEST®
**   all-purpose flour***
Additional butter or margarine

1   Heat oven to 350°F. In large bowl, soften yeast in warm water. Add buttermilk, eggs, butter, sugar, baking powder, salt and 2½ cups flour. Beat with electric mixer on low speed. Beat 2 minutes on medium speed. By hand, stir in remaining flour. Place on lightly floured surface; knead 3 to 5 minutes or until smooth.

2   Grease 24 brioche or regular-size muffin cups. Divide dough into 24 equal parts. Remove about ⅓ of dough from each part; shape all parts into smooth balls. Place larger balls in pans. Make a deep indentation in center of each large ball; place smaller ball in each indentation. Cover; let rise in warm place about 45 minutes or until light.

3   Bake 20 to 25 minutes or until golden brown. Remove from pans immediately and brush tops with additional butter. Serve warm.

* If using self-rising flour, omit baking powder and salt.

High Altitude (3500–6500 ft): No change.

1 Roll: Calories 170; Total Fat 7g (Saturated Fat 4g; Trans Fat 0g); Cholesterol 35mg; Sodium 400mg; Total Carbohydrate 24g (Dietary Fiber 0g) Exchanges: 1 Starch, ½ Other Carbohydrate, 1½ Fat; Carbohydrate Choices: 1½

The Judges: A Look Behind the Scenes

The task of choosing a million-dollar winner and the other category prizes is one the Bake-Off® Contest judges take very seriously. The judging panel at the finals is chosen for their food expertise and unbiased viewpoint and is made up of food professionals like food editors of newspapers and magazines, consumer affairs representatives from the supermarket industry and radio personalities. Here's a little glimpse of what happens behind the closed doors of the judges' room.

- Judges score entries without any knowledge of who created the dish or where the finalist lives.

They are asked to avoid contact with the finalists at the event or in advance.

- To cleanse their palates between tasting recipes, judges sip water or nibble on unsalted breadsticks or raw carrot and celery sticks.

- The judges work in jury room secrecy, behind closed doors. In fact, a guard is posted at the door of the judging room to prevent unauthorized people from entering.

- Judges adhere carefully to the contest judging criteria of taste, appearance, creativity and consumer appeal in evaluating the recipes.

Maple Cream Coffee Treat (page 209)

Crème Caramel Chai Smoothies

Pamela Ivbuls   Omaha, NE
Bake-Off® Contest 41, 2004

Prep Time: 10 Minutes
Start to Finish: 10 Minutes
4 servings (¾ cup each)

SMOOTHIES

2 containers (6 oz each) crème caramel
   thick & creamy low-fat yogurt
1 package (1.1 oz) chai tea latte mix
1 ripe medium banana, cut into ½-inch
   slices
½ cup milk
1 tablespoon caramel-flavored sundae
   syrup
1½ cups crushed ice

GARNISH

4 tablespoons whipped cream topping
4 teaspoons caramel-flavored sundae
   syrup

1   In 5-cup blender, place smoothie ingredients. Cover; blend on low speed 10 seconds. Scrape down sides of blender. Blend on medium speed 20 to 30 seconds longer or until smooth.

2   Divide mixture evenly among 4 (8-ounce) glasses. Garnish each serving with 1 tablespoon whipped cream topping; drizzle each with 1 teaspoon sundae syrup. Serve immediately.

High Altitude (3500–6500 ft): No change.

1 Serving (¾ Cup): Calories 210; Total Fat 4g (Saturated Fat 2g; Trans Fat 0g); Cholesterol 10mg; Sodium 150mg; Total Carbohydrate 39g (Dietary Fiber 0g) Exchanges: 2½ Other Carbohydrate, ½ Low-Fat Milk; Carbohydrate Choices: 2½

Breakfast Banana Sundaes

Erin Mylroie   St. George, UT
Bake-Off® Contest 41, 2004

Prep Time: 15 Minutes
Start to Finish: 15 Minutes
4 servings

1 teaspoon butter or margarine
¼ cup chopped walnuts
2 tablespoons packed brown sugar
2 firm, ripe large bananas, sliced
¼ cup orange juice
¼ teaspoon rum extract, if desired
4 oats 'n honey crunchy granola bars
   (2 pouches from 8.9-oz box), crushed*
4 containers (6 oz each) vanilla nonfat
   yogurt
4 teaspoons chopped walnuts

1   In 8-inch skillet, melt butter over medium heat. Add ¼ cup walnuts and the brown sugar; stir until sugar is melted. Add bananas; cook 1 to 2 minutes, stirring gently, until bananas are coated.

2   Stir in orange juice and rum extract. Cook about 1 minute longer or until liquid is thick and syrupy. Remove from heat. Reserve 4 banana slices for garnish.

3   Spoon about ⅓ cup remaining banana mixture into each of 4 (10-ounce) dessert bowls. Sprinkle crushed granola bars over banana mixture in each bowl, reserving some for topping. Spoon 1 container yogurt over granola in each bowl.

4   Garnish each serving with 1 teaspoon walnuts, reserved crushed granola bars and 1 reserved banana slice. Serve immediately.

To easily crush granola bars, do not unwrap; use rolling pin to crush bars.

High Altitude (3500–6500 ft): No change.

1 Serving: Calories 420; Total Fat 11g (Saturated Fat 2g; Trans Fat 0g); Cholesterol 5mg; Sodium 180mg; Total Carbohydrate 68g (Dietary Fiber 6g) Exchanges: 1 Starch, 1 Fruit, 1½ Other Carbohydrate, 1 Skim Milk, 2 Fat; Carbohydrate Choices: 4½

Kiwi-Pineapple Yogurt Parfaits

Sherri King-Rodrigues   Warren, RI
Bake-Off® Contest 41, 2004

Prep Time: 15 Minutes
Start to Finish: 15 Minutes
2 servings (1½ cups each)

GRANOLA MIXTURE

4 oats 'n honey crunchy granola bars
   (2 pouches from 8.9-oz box), broken
   into pieces
12 to 14 whole macadamia nuts

YOGURT MIXTURE

1 container (6 oz) vanilla nonfat yogurt
½ cup frozen (thawed) reduced-fat
   whipped topping
1 tablespoon shredded coconut
1 tablespoon finely grated white
   chocolate baking bar

FRUIT MIXTURE

½ cup coarsely chopped peeled kiwifruit
   (1½ medium)
½ cup drained coarsely chopped fresh
   pineapple or well-drained canned
   pineapple tidbits
1½ teaspoons honey

GARNISH, IF DESIRED

White chocolate baking bar curls or
   shavings
2 kiwifruit slices

1   In food processor or gallon-size resealable food-storage plastic bag, place granola bars and nuts; process or crush with meat mallet until chopped.

2   In small bowl, mix yogurt mixture ingredients; set aside. In another small bowl, gently toss

fruit mixture ingredients until coated; set aside.

3 In each of 2 (12- to 14-ounce) tulip-shaped parfait glasses,* alternately spoon about 3 table-spoons granola mixture, ¼ cup yogurt mixture and ¼ cup fruit mixture; repeat layers. Top each parfait with a sprinkle of remaining granola mixture. Garnish each with white chocolate curls and kiwifruit slice. Serve immediately.

Any 12- to 14-ounce tall parfait, dessert or wine glasses can be used.

High Altitude (3500–6500 ft): No change.

1 Serving: Calories 550; Total Fat 24g (Saturated Fat 7g; Trans Fat 0g); Cholesterol 0mg; Sodium 230mg; Total Carbohydrate 72g (Dietary Fiber 6g) Exchanges: 3 Starch, 1 Fruit, 1 Other Carbohydrate, 4 Fat; Carbohydrate Choices: 5

Kiwi-Pineapple Yogurt Parfaits

Blueberry Burrito Blintzes

Blueberry Burrito Blintzes

Kathy Anne Sepich Gresham, OR
Bake-Off® Contest 42, 2006

Prep Time: 30 Minutes
Start to Finish: 30 Minutes
8 servings

1 bag (10 oz) organic frozen blueberries
½ cup small-curd 2% reduced-fat
   cottage cheese
2 tablespoons granulated sugar
½ teaspoon grated lemon peel
¼ to ½ teaspoon ground nutmeg
¼ to ½ teaspoon ground cinnamon
4 oz reduced-fat cream cheese
   (Neufchâtel), softened
1 container (6 oz) blueberry patch
   nonfat yogurt
1 package (11.5 oz) flour tortillas, 8 inch
   (8 tortillas)
1 tablespoon butter or margarine
¼ cup blueberry syrup
Powdered sugar, if desired
Lemon slices, if desired

1 Thaw blueberries as directed
on bag; drain, reserving liquid.
In medium bowl, mix cottage
cheese, sugar, lemon peel, nutmeg,
cinnamon, cream cheese and yogurt
until well blended. Gently stir in
drained blueberries.

2 Place large sheet of waxed paper
on work surface. For each blintz,
place 1 flour tortilla on waxed paper.
Spoon about ⅓ cup yogurt mixture
in center. With pastry brush, moisten
outer edge of tortilla with reserved
blueberry liquid. Fold opposite sides
of tortilla over filling, ends meeting
in center; fold remaining 2 sides of
tortilla over each other.

3 In 12-inch nonstick skillet, melt
½ tablespoon of the butter over
medium heat. Cook 4 blintzes at
a time, seam side down, about

2 minutes on each side until golden
brown. Place blintzes, seam side
down, on serving platter; drizzle
with syrup. Sprinkle with powdered
sugar; garnish with lemon slices.

High Altitude (3500–6500 ft): Cook
blintzes about 5 minutes on each side.

1 Serving: Calories 270; Total Fat 10g (Saturated Fat 4.5g;
Trans Fat 1g); Cholesterol 15mg; Sodium 440mg; Total
Carbohydrate 40g (Dietary Fiber 1g) Exchanges: 1½ Starch,
1 Other Carbohydrate, 2 Fat; Carbohydrate Choices: 2½

Honey Puff Pancake

Kathryn K. Yardumian
Oceanside, CA
Bake-Off® Contest 29, 1980

Prep Time: 15 Minutes
Start to Finish: 40 Minutes
6 servings

1 cup milk
6 eggs
3 tablespoons honey
1 package (3 oz) cream cheese, softened
1 cup Pillsbury BEST® all-purpose
   or unbleached flour*
½ teaspoon salt
½ teaspoon baking powder
3 tablespoons butter or margarine
Powdered sugar
Jelly
Lemon wedges

1 Heat oven to 400°F. In blender,
place milk, eggs, honey, cream
cheese, flour, salt and baking
powder; let stand while preparing
skillet.** Grease 10-inch ovenproof
skillet with 1 tablespoon butter.
Add remaining 2 tablespoons butter
to skillet; heat in oven about 2 minutes or just until butter sizzles.

2 While skillet is in oven, cover
and blend ingredients on high
speed 1 minute; scrape sides. Blend
about 1 minute longer or until
smooth. Immediately pour batter
into hot skillet.

3 Bake 20 to 25 minutes or until
puffed and dark golden brown.
Serve immediately topped with a
sprinkling of powdered sugar, a
spoonful of jelly and a lemon wedge.

Self-rising flour not recommended.
**If using electric mixer, beat on high
speed 2 minutes.*

High Altitude (3500–6500 ft): No change.

1 Serving: Calories 320; Total Fat 17g (Saturated Fat 9g;
Trans Fat 0g); Cholesterol 245mg; Sodium 400mg;
Total Carbohydrate 32g (Dietary Fiber 0g) Exchanges:
1 Starch, 1 Other Carbohydrate, 1 Medium-Fat Meat,
2½ Fat; Carbohydrate Choices: 2

Just a Pinch of Tradition

Who says they don't like hand-me-downs? Kathryn Yardumian's recipe
for a baked pancake was handed down from her mother, who originally
learned the recipe from her mother. Kathryn turned the hand-me-
down recipe into a winner that earned her a trip to the
Bake-Off® Contest. Kathryn's version had a few changes
from the original, including Kathryn said, more precise
measurements than the "pinch of this and handful of flour"
her mother had used.

Quick 'n Delicious

"If a meal's not quick and easy, it's not made in my home," says Sandy Bradley. Sandy learned how to cook "by reading cookbooks and trial and error," she says. Her recipe for Ham 'n Eggs Frittata Biscuits was inspired by a restaurant dish she modified to reflect her own tastes. But hers wasn't the only palate pleased: "I served this to my husband and toddler for Father's Day. Wow!" Now she makes the recipe often after coming home from work or for a Sunday breakfast. "It fits well with a busy lifestyle," she says.

Bacon Quiche Biscuit Cups

Doris Geist Bethlehem, PA
Bake-Off® Contest 34, 1990

Prep Time: 30 Minutes
Start to Finish: 1 Hour
10 servings

1 package (8 oz) cream cheese, softened
2 tablespoons milk
2 eggs
½ cup shredded Swiss cheese (2 oz)
2 medium green onions, chopped (2 tablespoons)
1 can (12 oz) Pillsbury® Golden Layers® refrigerated flaky biscuits
5 slices bacon, crisply cooked, finely crumbled

1 Heat oven to 375°F. Grease 10 regular-size muffin cups. In small bowl, beat cream cheese, milk and eggs with electric mixer on low speed until smooth. Stir in cheese and onions; set aside.

2 Separate dough into 10 biscuits. Place 1 biscuit in each muffin cup; firmly press in bottom and up sides, forming ¼-inch rim. Place half of bacon in bottom of dough-lined muffin cups. Spoon about 2 tablespoonfuls cheese mixture over bacon in cups.

3 Bake 21 to 26 minutes or until filling is set and edges of biscuits are golden brown. Sprinkle each with remaining bacon; lightly press into filling. Remove from pan.

High Altitude (3500–6500 ft): No change.

1 Serving: Calories 240; Total Fat 17g (Saturated Fat 8g; Trans Fat 2g); Cholesterol 75mg; Sodium 540mg; Total Carbohydrate 15g (Dietary Fiber 0g) Exchanges: 1 Starch, ½ High-Fat Meat, 2½ Fat; Carbohydrate Choices: 1

Ham 'n Eggs Frittata Biscuits

Sandy Bradley Bolingbrook, IL
Bake-Off® Contest 40, 2002

Prep Time: 15 Minutes
Start to Finish: 35 Minutes
8 servings

1 can (16.3 oz) Pillsbury® Grands!® refrigerated buttermilk biscuits
3 eggs
1¼ to 1½ teaspoons Italian seasoning
½ cup diced cooked ham
1 cup shredded Italian cheese blend (4 oz)
¼ cup roasted red bell peppers (from a jar), drained, chopped
½ cup diced seeded plum (Roma) tomatoes
2 tablespoons thinly sliced fresh basil leaves
Fresh basil sprigs
Cherry tomatoes

1 Heat oven to 375°F. Spray large cookie sheet with cooking spray. Separate dough into 8 biscuits. Place 3 inches apart on cookie sheet. Press out each biscuit to form 4-inch round with ¼-inch rim around outside edge.

2 In small bowl, beat 1 of the eggs. Brush egg over tops and sides of biscuits. Sprinkle with 1 teaspoon of the Italian seasoning.

3 In another small bowl, beat remaining 2 eggs and remaining ¼ to ½ teaspoon Italian seasoning. Spoon evenly into indentations in each biscuit. Top with ham, ½ cup of the cheese, the roasted peppers, tomatoes, sliced basil and remaining ½ cup cheese.

4 Bake 15 to 20 minutes or until biscuits are golden brown and eggs are set. Garnish with basil sprigs and cherry tomatoes.

High Altitude (3500–6500 ft): Bake 14 to 17 minutes.

1 Serving: Calories 280; Total Fat 15g (Saturated Fat 5g; Trans Fat 3.5g); Cholesterol 95mg; Sodium 800mg; Total Carbohydrate 25g (Dietary Fiber 0g) Exchanges: 1½ Starch, 1 High-Fat Meat, 1½ Fat; Carbohydrate Choices: 1½

Grands!® Breakfast Brûlées

Gail Singer Calabasas, CA
Bake-Off® Contest 41, 2004

Prep Time: 15 Minutes
Start to Finish: 1 Hour
8 servings

2 eggs
¼ cup whipping cream
⅛ teaspoon ground nutmeg
2 containers (6 oz each) French vanilla
  fat-free yogurt
1 can (16.3 oz) Pillsbury® Grands!® Flaky
  Layers refrigerated original biscuits
⅓ cup sugar
3 tablespoons butter or margarine,
  melted

1 Heat oven to 375°F. Spray 8 (6-ounce) ramekins or custard cups with cooking spray; place on cookie sheet with sides. In medium bowl, beat eggs, cream, nutmeg and yogurt with electric mixer on medium speed until well blended.

2 Separate dough into 8 biscuits; separate each evenly into 2 layers, making 16 dough rounds. Place sugar in shallow dish. Brush both sides of each dough round with melted butter; coat both sides with sugar. Place 1 dough round in bottom of each ramekin. Spoon ¼ cup yogurt mixture over dough round in each ramekin. Top with remaining dough rounds.

3 Bake 20 to 26 minutes or until tops are deep golden brown. Cool 15 minutes before serving.

High Altitude (3500–6500 ft): Bake 26 to 32 minutes.

1 Serving: Calories 350; Total Fat 17g (Saturated Fat 7g; Trans Fat 4g); Cholesterol 75mg; Sodium 620mg; Total Carbohydrate 41g (Dietary Fiber 0g) Exchanges: 2 Starch, 1 Other Carbohydrate, 3 Fat; Carbohydrate Choices: 3

Easy Breakfast Pizza

Ernest Crow Rockville, MD
Bake-Off® Contest 38, 1998

Prep Time: 15 Minutes
Start to Finish: 30 Minutes
8 servings

1 can (13.8 oz) Pillsbury® refrigerated classic pizza crust
8 eggs
¼ cup half-and-half or milk
⅛ teaspoon salt
⅛ teaspoon pepper
2 tablespoons butter or margarine
1 container (8 oz) chives-and-onion, garden vegetable or regular cream cheese spread
8 slices crisply cooked bacon
Green onions, if desired

1 Heat oven to 425°F. Grease 12-inch pizza pan with shortening. Unroll dough in pan. Starting at center, press out dough to edge of pan. Bake 6 to 7 minutes or until crust begins to brown.

2 Meanwhile, in medium bowl, beat eggs, half-and-half, salt and pepper with wire whisk until well blended. In 10-inch skillet, melt butter over medium heat. Add egg mixture; cook, stirring occasionally, until thoroughly cooked but still moist. Remove from heat.

3 Spoon cooked egg mixture over crust. Drop cream cheese spread by teaspoonfuls over eggs. Arrange bacon in spoke fashion on top of pizza.

4 Bake 8 to 12 minutes longer or until toppings are hot and crust is deep golden brown. Garnish with onions.

High Altitude (3500–6500 ft): No change.

1 Serving: Calories 360; Total Fat 22g (Saturated Fat 11g; Trans Fat 0g); Cholesterol 255mg; Sodium 850mg; Total Carbohydrate 25g (Dietary Fiber 0g) Exchanges: 1½ Starch, 1½ High-Fat Meat, 2 Fat; Carbohydrate Choices: 1½

Rise 'n Shine Lattice Pizza

Maria Baldwin Mesa, AZ
Bake-Off® Contest 42, 2006
$10,000 Category Winner

Prep Time: 35 Minutes
Start to Finish: 1 Hour 15 Minutes
8 servings

1 box (9 oz) frozen roasted potatoes with garlic & herbs
½ cup chives-and-onion cream cheese spread (from 8-oz container)
1 teaspoon Italian seasoning
2 eggs
¾ to 1 cup basil pesto (6 to 8 oz)
1 can (13.8 oz) Pillsbury® refrigerated classic pizza crust
2 cups grated Asiago or Parmesan cheese (8 oz)
1 package or jar (3 oz) cooked real bacon bits
1 box (10.6 oz) Pillsbury® refrigerated Italian garlic with herbs breadsticks

1 Heat oven to 350°F. Cut small slit in center of pouch of potatoes. Microwave on High 2 to 3 minutes or just until warm; set aside. In small bowl, beat cream cheese, Italian seasoning and eggs with electric mixer on medium speed until well blended; set aside.

2 Line large cookie sheet with cooking parchment paper. Place pesto in small strainer over bowl to drain off excess oil. Lightly brush oil from pesto onto parchment paper. Unroll pizza crust dough on paper-lined cookie sheet; starting at center, press out dough into 14-inch square.

3 Spread pesto over dough to within 1 inch of edges; sprinkle cheese over pesto. Roll up edges of dough to make 11-inch square. Spoon potatoes evenly over cheese. Pour egg mixture around potatoes. Sprinkle with bacon bits.

4 Separate breadstick dough into 10 strips; set garlic butter aside. Twist and stretch each strip of dough over potatoes in lattice pattern, tucking ends of strips under pizza dough. Remove cover from garlic butter; microwave on High 10 seconds to soften. Brush garlic butter over edges and strips of dough.

5 Bake 30 to 40 minutes or until edges are browned and center is set, covering with foil during last 10 minutes of bake time if necessary to prevent excessive browning. Immediately remove from cookie sheet. Cut into rectangles to serve.

High Altitude (3500–6500 ft): Heat oven to 375°F.

1 Serving: Calories 620; Total Fat 37g (Saturated Fat 14g; Trans Fat 1.5g); Cholesterol 125mg; Sodium 1710mg; Total Carbohydrate 47g (Dietary Fiber 2g) Exchanges: 2 Starch, 1 Other Carbohydrate, 2½ High-Fat Meat, 3 Fat; Carbohydrate Choices: 3

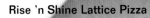

Rise 'n Shine Lattice Pizza

Bacon and Potato Breakfast Pizza

Richard McHargue   Richmond, KY
Bake-Off® Contest 41, 2004

Prep Time: 15 Minutes
Start to Finish: 40 Minutes
8 servings

1 can (8 oz) Pillsbury® refrigerated
   crescent dinner rolls
1 box (9 oz) frozen roasted potatoes
   with garlic & herbs
4 eggs
⅓ cup milk
8 slices packaged precooked bacon,
   cut into 1-inch pieces
1½ cups shredded Cheddar cheese
   (6 oz)
Salt and pepper, if desired
2 tablespoons chopped fresh parsley

1   Heat oven to 350°F. Spray
13 × 9-inch pan with cooking
spray. Unroll dough in pan; press
in bottom and ½ inch up sides to
form crust; press perforations to seal.

2   Bake 5 minutes. Meanwhile,
cut small slit in center of roasted
potatoes pouch; microwave on High
2 to 3 minutes or until thawed.
Remove potatoes from pouch; cut
larger pieces in half.

3   In medium bowl, beat eggs.
Stir in milk, bacon, 1 cup of
the cheese, the thawed potatoes,
salt and pepper. Spoon potato
mixture evenly over crust. Sprinkle
remaining ½ cup cheese and the
parsley over top.

4   Bake 20 to 25 minutes longer
or until set and edges are golden
brown. Cut into squares.

High Altitude (3500–6500 ft): In step 2,
bake crust 7 minutes. In step 4, bake
pizza 25 to 30 minutes.

1 Serving: Calories 320; Total Fat 21g (Saturated Fat 9g;
Trans Fat 2g); Cholesterol 140mg; Sodium 660mg;
Total Carbohydrate 19g (Dietary Fiber 0g) Exchanges:
1 Starch, ½ Other Carbohydrate, 1½ High-Fat Meat,
1½ Fat; Carbohydrate Choices: 1

Care to Dance?

If Richard McHargue gets excited enough about a new recipe idea
to dance a jig, he certainly has the skills. In addition to being a great
cook, Richard, a real estate agent, is an expert at clogging, a lively
American folk dance in which clogs are worn to beat out the rhythm.
Richard teaches clogging and performs with his dance group for
charitable organizations. Choreographing his Bake-Off® recipe
was simple for Richard: "Breakfast is my favorite meal, so I
put breakfast foods together," creating a savory breakfast
pizza topped with bacon, potatoes and egg.

Ham 'n Eggs Crescent Brunch Pizza

Bobby Braun   Marietta, GA
Bake-Off® Contest 32, 1986
$2,000 Winner

Prep Time: 30 Minutes
Start to Finish: 1 Hour 10 Minutes
8 servings

1 can (8 oz) Pillsbury® refrigerated
   crescent dinner rolls
4 eggs
½ teaspoon Italian seasoning
½ teaspoon salt, if desired
1 to 1¼ cups cubed, cooked ham
1 to 1¼ cups shredded mozzarella
   cheese (4 to 5 oz)
1 box (9 oz) frozen cut broccoli, thawed,
   drained
1 jar (4.5 oz) sliced mushrooms, drained
2 tablespoons chopped green bell
   pepper
1 large tomato, peeled, seeded, diced
   (about 1 cup)
2 tablespoons grated Parmesan cheese

1   Heat oven to 350°F.

2   Separate dough into 8 triangles.
Place triangles in ungreased 12-inch
pizza pan or 13 × 9-inch pan; press
over bottom and ½ inch up sides
to form crust. Seal perforations.
Beat eggs, Italian seasoning and
salt with fork or wire whisk; pour
into dough-lined pan. Top with
ham, mozzarella cheese, broccoli,
mushrooms, bell pepper and
tomato; sprinkle with Parmesan
cheese.

3   Bake 30 to 40 minutes or until
eggs are set and crust is golden
brown.

1 Serving: Calories 240; Total Fat 14g (Saturated Fat 5g; Trans Fat 1.5g); Cholesterol 125mg; Sodium 670mg; Total Carbohydrate 15g (Dietary Fiber 2g) Exchanges: 1 Starch, 1½ Medium-Fat Meat, 1 Fat; Carbohydrate Choices: 1

Quick Corn and Mushroom Brunch Squares

Helen Huber   Conroe, TX
Bake-Off® Contest 33, 1988

Prep Time: 15 Minutes
Start to Finish: 1 Hour
12 to 15 servings

2 cans (8 oz each) Pillsbury® refrigerated crescent dinner rolls
2 cups chopped cooked ham
1½ cups shredded Monterey Jack cheese (6 oz)
1½ cups shredded Swiss cheese (6 oz)
1 can (11 oz) vacuum-packed whole kernel corn with red and green peppers, drained
1 jar (4.5 oz) sliced mushrooms, drained
6 eggs
1 cup milk
½ teaspoon salt, if desired
¼ to ½ teaspoon pepper

1   Heat oven to 375°F.

2   Unroll dough into 4 long rectangles; place in ungreased 15 × 10 × 1-inch pan. Press over bottom and ¾ inch up sides to form crust. Seal perforations. Sprinkle ham, cheeses, corn and mushrooms evenly over crust. In medium bowl, beat eggs, milk, salt and pepper until well blended. Pour evenly over ham, cheeses and vegetables.

3   Bake 35 to 40 minutes or until crust is deep golden brown, egg

mixture is set and knife inserted in center comes out clean. Cool 5 minutes; cut into squares.

High Altitude (3500–6500 ft): No change.

1 Serving: Calories 360; Total Fat 22g (Saturated Fat 10g; Trans Fat 2g); Cholesterol 145mg; Sodium 890mg; Total Carbohydrate 22g (Dietary Fiber 1g) Exchanges: 1 Starch, ½ Other Carbohydrate, 2½ High-Fat Meat; Carbohydrate Choices: 1½

Quesadilla Quiche

Laurie Keane   Escondido, CA
Bake-Off® Contest 33, 1988
$2,000 Winner

Prep Time: 25 Minutes
Start to Finish: 1 Hour 25 Minutes
6 servings

CRUST
1 box (15 oz) Pillsbury® refrigerated pie crusts, softened as directed on box

FILLING
1 tablespoon butter or margarine
1 cup coarsely chopped onions
1 cup coarsely chopped tomato, drained
1 can (3.8 oz) sliced ripe olives, drained
¼ teaspoon garlic powder or garlic salt
¼ teaspoon ground cumin
⅛ teaspoon pepper
1 can (4.5 oz) chopped green chiles, drained
2 eggs, beaten
2 to 3 drops red pepper sauce
1 cup shredded Monterey Jack cheese (4 oz)
1 cup shredded Cheddar cheese (4 oz)
Sour cream, if desired
Chunky-style salsa or picante, if desired

1   Make pie crust as directed on box for Two-Crust Pie, using 10-inch tart pan with removable bottom or 9-inch glass pie plate.

Place 1 crust in pan; press in bottom and up side. Trim edges if necessary.

2   Move oven rack to lowest position; heat oven to 375°F. In 8-inch skillet, melt butter over medium heat. Cook and stir onions in butter until tender. Reserve 1 tablespoon each chopped tomato and ripe olives; stir remaining tomato and olives, the garlic powder, cumin, pepper and chiles into cooked onion.

3   In small bowl, beat eggs and red pepper sauce with fork; reserve 2 teaspoons mixture. Stir in ½ cup of the Monterey Jack cheese and ½ cup of the Cheddar cheese. Sprinkle remaining cheeses in bottom of pie crust-lined pan. Spoon onion mixture evenly over cheese. Carefully pour egg mixture over onion mixture; spread to cover.

4   Top with second crust; seal edges. Cut slits in crust in decorative design in several places. Brush with reserved egg mixture.

5   Place pan on lowest oven rack; bake 45 to 55 minutes or until golden brown. Let stand 5 minutes; remove sides of pan. Serve warm with sour cream, salsa and reserved chopped tomatoes and olives.

High Altitude (3500–6500 ft): Bake 50 to 55 minutes.

1 Serving: Calories 540; Total Fat 36g (Saturated Fat 16g; Trans Fat 0g); Cholesterol 120mg; Sodium 1010mg; Total Carbohydrate 41g (Dietary Fiber 2g) Exchanges: 2½ Starch, ½ Other Carbohydrate, ½ High-Fat Meat, 6 Fat; Carbohydrate Choices: 3

Dotted Swiss and Spinach Quiche

Ellen Burr   Truro, MA
Bake-Off® Contest 34, 1990

Prep Time: 30 Minutes
Start to Finish: 1 Hour 10 Minutes
8 servings

CRUST
1 Pillsbury® refrigerated pie crust (from 15-oz box), softened as directed on box
2 teaspoons honey mustard or sweet hot mustard

FILLING
1 tablespoon butter or margarine
4 medium green onions, chopped (¼ cup)

1 box (9 oz) frozen spinach, thawed, squeezed to drain*
½ cup finely chopped cooked ham (2 oz)
½ teaspoon dried thyme leaves
¼ cup Pillsbury BEST® all-purpose flour
⅛ teaspoon pepper
⅛ teaspoon ground nutmeg
1 cup whipping cream
3 eggs
1 cup shredded Swiss cheese (4 oz)
2 tablespoons sesame seed, toasted* *

1   Place pie crust in 9-inch glass pie plate as directed on box for One-Crust Filled Pie. Brush mustard over bottom of crust.

2   Move oven rack to lowest position. Heat oven to 375°F. In 8-inch skillet, melt butter over medium heat. Cook and stir onions in butter until crisp-tender. Stir in spinach, ham and thyme. Reduce heat to low; cook until spinach is hot. Spread spinach mixture over mustard in crust.

3   In small bowl, beat flour, pepper, nutmeg, whipping cream and eggs with wire whisk until well blended. Pour egg mixture over spinach layer; sprinkle with cheese. Sprinkle toasted sesame seed over crust and filling surface.

4   Place pie plate on oven rack. Bake 30 to 35 minutes or until knife inserted in center comes out clean and crust edge is deep golden brown. After 15 to 20 minutes of baking, cover crust edge with strips of foil to prevent excessive browning. Cool 5 minutes before serving.

*To quickly thaw frozen spinach, place in colander or strainer; rinse with warm water until thawed. Squeeze spinach to drain well.

* * To toast sesame seed, spread on cookie sheet; bake at 400°F 3 to 5 minutes or until light golden brown.

High Altitude (3500–6500 ft): Bake 33 to 38 minutes.

1 Serving: Calories 350; Total Fat 26g (Saturated Fat 13g; Trans Fat 0g); Cholesterol 135mg; Sodium 310mg; Total Carbohydrate 20g (Dietary Fiber 1g) Exchanges: 1½ Starch, 1 High-Fat Meat, 3 Fat; Carbohydrate Choices: 1

Broccoli, Potato and Bacon Quiche

Tanya Nicole Margala   Newport Beach, CA
Bake-Off® Contest 42, 2006

Prep Time: 20 Minutes
Start to Finish: 1 Hour 5 Minutes
8 servings

1 bag (19 oz) frozen roasted potatoes
  with broccoli & cheese sauce
1 Pillsbury® refrigerated pie crust
  (from 15-oz box), softened as
  directed on box
4 eggs
⅔ cup whipping cream
7 slices bacon, cooked, crumbled
  (about ⅓ cup)
1 cup finely shredded Parmesan cheese
  (4 oz)
1 cup finely shredded Cheddar cheese
  (4 oz)
½ teaspoon dried basil leaves
½ teaspoon pepper
¼ teaspoon parsley flakes
⅛ teaspoon salt, if desired
1 teaspoon finely chopped fresh chives

1   Heat oven to 350°F. Microwave frozen potatoes with broccoli & cheese sauce as directed on bag.

2   Meanwhile, place pie crust in 9-inch glass pie plate as directed on box for One-Crust Filled Pie.

3   In large bowl, beat eggs and whipping cream with wire whisk until well blended. Stir in cooked potato mixture and remaining ingredients except chives. Pour filling into crust-lined plate; spread evenly. Sprinkle chives over filling.

4   Bake 30 to 40 minutes or until edge of filling is light golden brown and knife inserted in center comes out clean. Let stand 5 minutes before serving.

High Altitude (3500–6500 ft): Heat oven to 375°F. Bake 33 to 43 minutes.

1 Serving: Calories 420; Total Fat 28g (Saturated Fat 14g; Trans Fat 0g); Cholesterol 170mg; Sodium 910mg; Total Carbohydrate 24g (Dietary Fiber 1g) Exchanges: 1½ Starch, 2 High-Fat Meat, 2 Fat; Carbohydrate Choices: 1½

Ham 'n Cheese Omelet Bake

Julie Amberson Browns Point, WA
Bake-Off® Contest 41, 2004
$10,000 and a GE Profile™ Oven
with Trivection Technology—
Breakfast Favorites Category Winner

Prep Time: 15 Minutes
Start to Finish: 1 Hour 15 Minutes
8 servings

1 box (10 oz) frozen cut broccoli in a
   cheese flavored sauce
1 can (10.2 oz) Pillsbury® Grands!®
   Flaky Layers refrigerated original
   biscuits
10 eggs
1½ cups milk
1 teaspoon ground mustard
Salt and pepper, if desired
2 cups diced cooked ham
⅓ cup chopped onion
1 cup shredded Cheddar cheese (4 oz)
1 cup shredded Swiss cheese (4 oz)
1 jar (4.5 oz) sliced mushrooms, drained

1   Heat oven to 350°F. Cut small
slit in center of broccoli and cheese
sauce pouch. Microwave on High
3 to 4 minutes, rotating pouch
¼ turn once halfway through
microwaving. Set aside to cool
slightly.

2   Meanwhile, spray bottom only
of 13 × 9-inch (3-quart) glass
baking dish with cooking spray.
Separate dough into 5 biscuits. Cut
each biscuit into 8 pieces; arrange
evenly in dish.

3   In large bowl, beat eggs, milk,
mustard, salt and pepper with wire
whisk until well blended. Stir in
ham, onion, cheeses, mushrooms
and cooked broccoli and cheese
sauce. Pour mixture over biscuit
pieces in dish. Press down with back
of spoon, making sure all biscuit
pieces are covered with egg mixture.

4   Bake 40 to 50 minutes or until
edges are deep golden brown and
center is set. Let stand 10 minutes
before serving. Cut into squares.

High Altitude (3500–6500 ft): Heat oven
to 375°F.

1 Serving: Calories 430; Total Fat 26g (Saturated Fat
11g; Trans Fat 2.5g); Cholesterol 315mg; Sodium
1270mg; Total Carbohydrate 22g (Dietary Fiber 1g)
Exchanges: 1½ Starch, 3 Medium-Fat Meat, 2 Fat;
Carbohydrate Choices: 1½

Tex-Mex Breakfast Bake

Lynne Milliron Austin, TX
Bake-Off® Contest 41, 2004

Prep Time: 20 Minutes
Start to Finish: 1 Hour 10 Minutes
6 servings

¼ lb bulk lean breakfast sausage
1 can (10 oz) red enchilada sauce
2½ oz crumbled queso fresco (Mexican
   cheese) or farmer cheese
⅓ cup sour cream
4 medium green onions, chopped
   (¼ cup)
1 can (16.3 oz) Pillsbury® Grands!®
   refrigerated flaky biscuits
1¼ cups shredded Colby–Monterey
   Jack cheese blend (5 oz)
¼ cup chopped fresh cilantro

1   Heat oven to 350°F. Spray
8 × 8- or 11 × 7-inch (2-quart)
glass baking dish with cooking
spray. In 10-inch skillet, cook
sausage over medium-high heat,
stirring frequently, until no longer
pink. Drain sausage on paper towels.

2   Meanwhile, in small bowl, mix
¼ cup of the enchilada sauce, the
queso fresco, sour cream and onions;
set aside. Pour remaining enchilada
sauce into medium bowl. Separate
dough into 8 biscuits; cut each into
8 pieces. Gently stir dough pieces
into enchilada sauce to coat. Spoon
mixture into baking dish; spread
evenly. Sprinkle sausage evenly on
top of biscuit pieces. Spread sour
cream mixture evenly over top.

Family Roots Often Run Deep

Lynn Milliron is a fifth generation Texan, giving her a lifetime of
experience cooking Tex-Mex flavored dishes. Her preference for
savory—instead of sweet—dishes for breakfast means her
family gets to enjoy hearty creations like Tex-Mex Breakfast
Bake with grits for Saturday breakfasts. Among the
ingredients giving her breakfast bake its Tex-Mex appeal
are queso fresco, enchilada sauce and cilantro.

3 Bake 30 to 35 minutes or until center is set and edges are deep golden brown. Sprinkle Colby–Monterey Jack cheese over top.

4 Bake about 10 minutes longer or until cheese is bubbly. Sprinkle with cilantro. Let stand 5 minutes before serving. Cut into squares.

High Altitude (3500–6500 ft): Heat oven to 375°F. Use 11 × 7-inch (2-quart) glass baking dish. Bake 45 to 50 minutes. Sprinkle Colby–Monterey Jack cheese over top; bake about 5 minutes longer.

1 Serving: Calories 440; Total Fat 26g (Saturated Fat 10g; Trans Fat 5g); Cholesterol 40mg; Sodium 1170mg; Total Carbohydrate 36g (Dietary Fiber 0g) Exchanges: 1½ Starch, 1 Other Carbohydrate, 1½ High-Fat Meat, 2½ Fat; Carbohydrate Choices: 2½

Banana Pecan Pancake Bake

Pam Ivbuls Omaha, NE
Bake-Off® Contest 42, 2006

> **Prep Time:** 20 Minutes
> **Start to Finish:** 1 Hour 25 Minutes
> 12 servings

PANCAKES

2 boxes (16.4 oz each) frozen original pancakes (24 pancakes)

2 tablespoons butter or margarine, softened

3 eggs

1 cup half-and-half

¼ cup maple-flavored syrup with butter

½ teaspoon ground cinnamon

2 containers (6 oz each) banana cream pie nonfat yogurt

4 medium bananas, cut diagonally into ¼-inch slices

½ cup chopped pecans

GARNISHES

¾ cup extra-creamy whipped topping with real cream

12 diagonal slices bananas (¼ inch thick)

¾ cup maple-flavored syrup with butter

½ teaspoon ground cinnamon

2 tablespoons chopped pecans, if desired

Additional ground cinnamon, if desired

1 Heat oven to 350°F. Remove frozen pancakes from boxes; unwrap and carefully separate. Set aside to partially thaw. With small pastry brush, coat bottom and sides of 15 × 10 × 1-inch pan with softened butter.

2 In 5-cup blender or large food processor, place eggs, half-and-half, ¼ cup syrup, ½ teaspoon cinnamon and the yogurt; cover and blend on low speed about 10 seconds or until smooth. If necessary, scrape down sides with rubber spatula, and blend 5 to 10 seconds longer. Set aside.

3 In pan, place 12 of the pancakes in 4 rows of 3 pancakes each, overlapping slightly if necessary. Pour 1½ cups yogurt mixture evenly over pancakes (if necessary, use small spoon to coat surface of each pancake with yogurt mixture).

4 Place banana slices in single layer over pancakes. Place remaining 12 pancakes over banana-topped pancakes. Pour remaining yogurt mixture evenly over all pancakes. With large turkey baster, coat pancakes evenly with yogurt mixture from pan. Let stand 10 minutes to allow yogurt mixture to soak into pancakes. With baster, coat pancakes again with yogurt mixture from pan. Let stand 5 minutes longer. Sprinkle ½ cup pecans evenly over top.

5 Bake 30 to 40 minutes or until edges are set and light golden brown. Let stand 10 minutes before serving.

6 Cut into 12 servings; place on individual plates. Top each with 1 tablespoon whipped topping, 1 banana slice and 1 tablespoon syrup; sprinkle each with dash cinnamon and ½ teaspoon pecans. Sprinkle edge of each plate with additional cinnamon.

High Altitude (3500–6500 ft): No change.

1 Serving: Calories 430; Total Fat 13g (Saturated Fat 5g; Trans Fat 0g); Cholesterol 80mg; Sodium 370mg; Total Carbohydrate 71g (Dietary Fiber 3g) Exchanges: 2 Starch, 2½ Other Carbohydrate, 2½ Fat; Carbohydrate Choices: 5

Cinnamon French Toast Bake

Cinnamon French Toast Bake

Will Sperry   Bunker Hill, WV
Bake-Off® Contest 41, 2004

Prep Time: 15 Minutes
Start to Finish: 1 Hour
12 servings

¼ cup butter or margarine, melted
2 cans (12.4 oz each) Pillsbury®
   refrigerated cinnamon rolls
   with icing
6 eggs
½ cup whipping cream
2 teaspoons ground cinnamon
2 teaspoons vanilla
1 cup chopped pecans
1 cup maple syrup
Powdered sugar
½ cup maple syrup, if desired

1   Heat oven to 375°F. Pour melted butter into ungreased 13 × 9-inch (3-quart) glass baking dish. Separate both cans of dough into 16 rolls; set icing aside. Cut each roll into 8 pieces; place pieces over butter in dish.

2   In medium bowl, beat eggs. Beat in cream, cinnamon and vanilla until well blended; gently pour over roll pieces. Sprinkle with pecans; drizzle with 1 cup syrup.

3   Bake 20 to 28 minutes or until golden brown. Cool 15 minutes. Meanwhile, remove covers from icing; microwave on Medium (50%) 10 to 15 seconds or until thin enough to drizzle.

4   Drizzle icing over top; sprinkle with powdered sugar. If desired, spoon syrup from dish over individual servings. Serve with the additional ½ cup maple syrup.

High Altitude (3500–6500 ft): Bake 25 to 30 minutes.

1 Serving: Calories 440; Total Fat 23g (Saturated Fat 8g; Trans Fat 3g); Cholesterol 125mg; Sodium 520mg; Total Carbohydrate 51g (Dietary Fiber 1g) Exchanges: 1½ Starch, 2 Other Carbohydrate, 4½ Fat; Carbohydrate Choices: 3½

Blueberry-Banana-Granola French Toast

Carolyn Roberts   Los Angeles, CA
Bake-Off® Contest 42, 2006

Prep Time: 10 Minutes
Start to Finish: 1 Hour 10 Minutes
8 servings

1 can (12.4 oz) Pillsbury® refrigerated
   cinnamon rolls with icing
8 oats 'n honey crunchy granola bars
   (4 pouches from 8.9-oz box),
   crushed (1½ cups)*
4 eggs
¾ cup fat-free (skim) milk
1 can (14 oz) fat-free sweetened
   condensed milk (not evaporated)
3 medium bananas, cut into 1-inch
   pieces
1 bag (10 oz) organic frozen
   blueberries, thawed
1 aerosol can (7 oz) fat-free whipped
   cream topping

1   Heat oven to 350°F (325°F for dark pan). Spray 13 × 9-inch pan or 12 × 2-inch round cake pan with butter-flavor or regular cooking spray. Separate dough into 8 rolls; set icing aside. Cut each roll into quarters; arrange evenly in pan. Sprinkle ¾ cup of the crushed granola bars evenly over dough pieces.

2   In large food processor or 5-cup blender, place eggs, milk and condensed milk. Cover; process 1 minute. Add bananas; process 1 minute longer. Pour egg mixture over dough in pan. Sprinkle with remaining ¾ cup crushed granola bars.

3   Bake 35 to 45 minutes or until golden brown and set in center. Spoon and spread reserved icing over warm rolls. Cool 15 minutes before serving.

4   To serve, spoon baked French toast into shallow bowls or cut into 8 servings. Top each serving with 3 tablespoons blueberries; garnish with 2 tablespoons whipped cream topping.

To easily crush granola bars, do not unwrap; use rolling pin to crush bars.

High Altitude (3500–6500 ft): Heat oven to 375°F. Add 2 tablespoons Pillsbury BEST® all-purpose flour to ingredients in blender. Bake 30 to 40 minutes.

1 Serving: Calories 520; Total Fat 12g (Saturated Fat 3.5g; Trans Fat 2g); Cholesterol 115mg; Sodium 530mg; Total Carbohydrate 90g (Dietary Fiber 3g) Exchanges: 2 Starch, 1 Fruit, 3 Other Carbohydrate, 1 Medium-Fat Meat, 1 Fat; Carbohydrate Choices: 6

Banana-Walnut Brunch Squares

Debbie Bracker   Carl Junction, MO
Bake-Off® Contest 41, 2004

Prep Time: 15 Minutes
Start to Finish: 1 Hour 5 Minutes
9 servings

3 eggs
1 cup mashed ripe bananas
    (2 to 3 medium)
3 tablespoons granulated sugar
1 can (17.5 oz) Pillsbury® Grands!®
    refrigerated cinnamon rolls with
    cream cheese icing
½ cup Pillsbury BEST® all-purpose flour
⅓ cup packed light brown sugar
¼ cup butter or margarine, softened
¾ cup coarsely chopped walnuts
¼ cup maple syrup
Banana slices, if desired

1   Heat oven to 350°F. Spray 8-inch square (2-quart) glass baking dish with cooking spray. In large bowl, beat eggs, bananas and granulated sugar with wire whisk until well blended.

2   Separate dough into 5 rolls; set icing aside. Cut each roll into 8 equal pie-shaped wedges. Gently stir dough pieces into egg mixture until well coated. Spoon mixture into baking dish; spread evenly.

3   In medium bowl, mix flour and brown sugar. With fork, cut in butter until mixture looks like coarse crumbs. Stir in walnuts. Sprinkle mixture over dough mixture.

4   Bake 35 to 40 minutes or until center is puffed and set and edges are deep golden brown. Cool 10 minutes. Meanwhile, in small bowl, mix icing and syrup until blended. To serve, cut into squares; place on individual serving plates. Drizzle icing mixture over each serving; garnish with banana slices.

High Altitude (3500–6500 ft): Heat oven to 375°F.

1 Serving: Calories 440; Total Fat 18g (Saturated Fat 6g; Trans Fat 1.5g); Cholesterol 85mg; Sodium 430mg; Total Carbohydrate 61g (Dietary Fiber 2g) Exchanges: 2 Starch, 2 Other Carbohydrate, 3½ Fat; Carbohydrate Choices: 4

Tropical Waffle Bake

Diane Toomey   Allentown, PA
Bake-Off® Contest 42, 2006

Prep Time: 25 Minutes
Start to Finish: 1 Hour 10 Minutes
6 servings

5 frozen buttermilk waffles
    (from 12-oz bag), thawed
1½ cups finely chopped bananas
    (2 medium)
2 cans (8 oz each) crushed pineapple
    in juice, drained and juice reserved
4 eggs
⅔ cup granulated sugar
5 tablespoons packed brown sugar
6 oats 'n honey crunchy granola bars
    (3 pouches from 8.9-oz box),
    crushed (heaping 1 cup)*
½ cup chopped macadamia nuts
3 tablespoons Pillsbury BEST®
    all-purpose flour
¼ cup butter or margarine, softened
1 jar (10 oz) strawberry spreadable fruit
Whipped cream, if desired

1   Heat oven to 350°F. Spray 8-inch square (2-quart) glass baking dish with cooking spray. Break waffles into 1- to 2-inch pieces; place in bottom of baking dish. Gently stir bananas into reserved pineapple juice to coat. With slotted spoon, place bananas evenly over waffles; discard any remaining juice.

2   In medium bowl, beat eggs, granulated sugar and 2 tablespoons of the brown sugar with wire whisk until blended. Stir in drained pineapple. Pour mixture over waffles and bananas in dish. In another medium bowl, mix crushed granola bars, nuts, flour, remaining 3 tablespoons brown sugar and the butter until crumbly; sprinkle over top.

3   Bake 30 to 35 minutes or until knife inserted in center comes out clean. Cool 10 minutes.

4   In small microwavable bowl, microwave spreadable fruit on High 1 minute. Stir; if necessary, continue to microwave on High in 15-second increments until melted and smooth. Cut waffle bake into 6 servings. Top each serving with about 2 tablespoons warm fruit spread and 1 to 2 tablespoons whipped cream.

To easily crush granola bars, do not unwrap; use rolling pin to crush bars.

High Altitude (3500–6500 ft): Heat oven to 375°F.

1 Serving: Calories 710; Total Fat 24g (Saturated Fat 8g; Trans Fat 1g); Cholesterol 160mg; Sodium 390mg; Total Carbohydrate 114g (Dietary Fiber 7g) Exchanges: 3 Starch, 1 Fruit, 3 ½ Other Carbohydrate, 4½ Fat; Carbohydrate Choices: 7½

Banana-Walnut Brunch Squares

Ring-a-Lings

Bertha Jorgensen   Portland, OR
Bake-Off® Contest 7, 1955
$25,000 Grand Prize Winner

Prep Time: 40 Minutes
Start to Finish: 2 Hours 25 Minutes
22 rolls

DOUGH
4 to 4½ cups Pillsbury BEST®
   all-purpose or unbleached flour
⅓ cup granulated sugar
2 teaspoons salt
2 teaspoons grated orange peel
2 packages regular active dry yeast
1 cup milk
⅓ cup butter or margarine
2 eggs

FILLING
1 cup powdered sugar
⅓ cup butter or margarine, softened
1 cup hazelnuts (filberts), pecans
   or walnuts, ground

GLAZE
3 tablespoons granulated sugar
¼ cup orange juice

1   In large bowl, stir together
2 cups of the flour, ⅓ cup sugar, the
salt, orange peel and yeast.

2   In 1½-quart saucepan, heat milk
and ⅓ cup butter until very warm
(120°F to 130°F). Add warm liquid
and eggs to flour mixture; beat at
low speed until moistened. Beat
3 minutes at medium speed. Stir
in remaining 2 to 2½ cups flour to
make a stiff dough. Place dough in
greased bowl; cover loosely with
plastic wrap and cloth towel. Let
rise in warm place (80°F to 85°F)

35 to 50 minutes or until light and
doubled in size.

3   In small bowl, stir powdered
sugar and ⅓ cup soft butter until
smooth. Stir in hazelnuts; set aside.
In second small bowl, stir together
glaze ingredients; cover and set aside.

4   Grease 2 large cookie sheets
with shortening or spray with
cooking spray. Stir down dough to
remove all air bubbles. On floured
surface, roll dough to 22 × 12-inch
rectangle. Spread filling mixture
lengthwise over half of dough. Fold
dough over filling. Cut crosswise
into 1-inch strips; twist each strip
4 to 5 times. To shape rolls, hold
folded end of strip down on cookie
sheet to form center; coil strip
around center. Tuck loose end
under. Repeat with remaining
twisted strips. Cover; let rise in
warm place 30 to 45 minutes or
until light and doubled in size.

5   Heat oven to 375°F. Uncover
dough. Bake 9 to 12 minutes or
until light golden brown. Brush
tops of rolls with glaze. Bake 3 to
5 minutes longer or until golden
brown. Immediately remove from
cookie sheets; cool on cooling racks.
Serve warm.

High Altitude (3500–6500 ft): No change.

1 Roll: Calories 210; Total Fat 9g (Saturated Fat 4g;
Trans Fat 0g); Cholesterol 35mg; Sodium 270mg;
Total Carbohydrate 29g (Dietary Fiber 1g) Exchanges:
1 Starch, 1 Other Carbohydrate, 1½ Fat; Carbohydrate
Choices: 2

Easy Crescent Danish Rolls

Barbara S. Gibson   Ft. Wayne, IN
Bake-Off® Contest 26, 1975
$25,000 One of Two Grand Prize Winners

Prep Time: 20 Minutes
Start to Finish: 45 Minutes
8 rolls

ROLLS
1 package (8 oz) cream cheese,
   softened
½ cup granulated sugar
1 tablespoon lemon juice
2 cans (8 oz each) Pillsbury®
   refrigerated crescent dinner rolls
4 teaspoons preserves or jam

GLAZE
½ cup powdered sugar
1 teaspoon vanilla
2 to 3 teaspoons milk

1   Heat oven to 350°F. In small
bowl, beat cream cheese, granulated
sugar and lemon juice until smooth.

2   Separate dough into 8 rectangles;
firmly press perforations to seal.
Spread each rectangle with about
2 tablespoons cream cheese mixture.
Starting at longer side, roll up each
rectangle, firmly pinching edges
and ends to seal. Gently stretch
each roll to about 10 inches. Coil
each roll into a spiral with seam on
the inside, tucking end under. Make
deep indentation in center of each
roll; fill with ½ teaspoon preserves.
Place on ungreased large cookie sheet.

3   Bake 20 to 25 minutes or until
deep golden brown. In small bowl,
blend glaze ingredients, adding
enough milk for desired drizzling
consistency. Drizzle over warm rolls.

High Altitude (3500–6500 ft): Bake 23 to 26 minutes.

1 Roll: Calories 400; Total Fat 22g (Saturated Fat 10g; Trans Fat 3.5g); Cholesterol 30mg; Sodium 530mg; Total Carbohydrate 45g (Dietary Fiber 0g) Exchanges: 2 Starch, 1 Other Carbohydrate, 4 Fat; Carbohydrate Choices: 3

Maple Cream Coffee Treat

Reta Ebbinnk Torrance, CA
Bake-Off® Contest 28, 1978
$5,000 Winner

Prep Time: 15 Minutes
Start to Finish: 50 Minutes
20 sweet rolls

1 cup packed brown sugar
½ cup chopped nuts
⅓ cup maple-flavored syrup or dark corn syrup
¼ cup butter or margarine, melted
1 package (8 oz) cream cheese, softened
¼ cup powdered sugar
2 tablespoons butter or margarine, softened
½ cup coconut
2 cans (12 oz each) Pillsbury® Golden Layers® refrigerated buttermilk flaky biscuits

1 Heat oven to 350°F. In ungreased 13 × 9-inch pan, mix brown sugar, nuts, syrup and ¼ cup butter; spread evenly in bottom of pan. In small bowl, beat cream cheese, powdered sugar and 2 tablespoons butter with spoon until smooth. Stir in coconut.

2 Separate dough into 20 biscuits; press or roll each into 4-inch round. Spoon 1 tablespoon cream

cheese mixture down center of each biscuit round to within ¼ inch of edge. Overlap sides of dough over filling, forming finger-shaped rolls; arrange seam side down in 2 rows of 10 rolls each over brown sugar mixture in pan.

3 Bake 25 to 30 minutes or until deep golden brown. Cool 5 minutes. Turn pan upside down onto sheet of foil or waxed paper, or onto serving platter; remove pan. Serve warm. Store in refrigerator.

High Altitude (3500–6500 ft): Bake 30 to 35 minutes.

1 Sweet Roll: Calories 270; Total Fat 14g (Saturated Fat 6g; Trans Fat 2g); Cholesterol 20mg; Sodium 430mg; Total Carbohydrate 32g (Dietary Fiber 0g) Exchanges: 1 Starch, 1 Other Carbohydrate, 3 Fat; Carbohydrate Choices: 2

Poppin' Fresh® Citrus-Glazed Crullers

Erika Couch Ballston Spa, NY
Bake-Off® Contest 39, 2000

Prep Time: 15 Minutes
Start to Finish: 40 Minutes
12 rolls

ROLLS
¼ cup butter or margarine, melted
½ cup granulated sugar
1 can (11 oz) Pillsbury® refrigerated original breadsticks

GLAZE
⅔ cup powdered sugar
¼ teaspoon grated orange peel
¼ teaspoon grated lemon peel
1 tablespoon orange juice
1 teaspoon lemon juice

1 Heat oven to 375°F. Line cookie sheet with parchment paper, or spray with cooking spray. In shallow dish, place melted butter; in another shallow dish, place granulated sugar.

2 Unroll dough; separate into breadsticks. Dip both sides of each breadstick in butter; coat with sugar. Twist each breadstick; place on cookie sheet, pressing ends down firmly.

3 Bake 13 to 17 minutes or until golden brown. Meanwhile, in small bowl, blend all glaze ingredients until smooth.

4 Immediately drizzle glaze over hot rolls. Remove from cookie sheet; cool 5 minutes before serving.

High Altitude (3500–6500 ft): No change.

1 Roll: Calories 160; Total Fat 5g (Saturated Fat 3g; Trans Fat 0g); Cholesterol 10mg; Sodium 210mg; Total Carbohydrate 28g (Dietary Fiber 0g) Exchanges: 1 Starch, ½ Other Carbohydrate, 1 Fat; Carbohydrate Choices: 2

Cherry-Almond Swirls

Jenny Riegsecker   Delta, OH
Bake-Off® Contest 41, 2004

Prep Time: 20 Minutes
Start to Finish: 40 Minutes
12 rolls

¼ cup granulated sugar
½ cup slivered almonds
1 package (3 oz) cream cheese,
    softened, cut into pieces
¼ teaspoon vanilla
⅛ teaspoon almond extract
1 egg yolk
1 can (8 oz) Pillsbury® refrigerated
    crescent dinner rolls
¼ cup cherry preserves
½ cup powdered sugar
2 teaspoons water

1   Heat oven to 375°F. Spray
12 regular-size muffin cups with
cooking spray. In food processor,
place granulated sugar and almonds.
Cover; process about 30 seconds or
until almonds are finely ground.
Add cream cheese, vanilla, almond
extract and egg yolk; process about
10 seconds or until well blended.

2   On lightly floured surface,
unroll dough into 1 large rectangle.
With floured rolling pin or fingers,
roll or press dough into 12 × 9-
inch rectangle, firmly pressing
perforations to seal.

3   Spread cream cheese mixture
evenly over dough rectangle. Starting
with one long side, roll up dough
into log (filling will be soft). With
serrated knife, cut log into 12 slices;
place cut side up in muffin cups.

4   Bake 11 to 15 minutes or until
light golden brown. With handle of
wooden spoon, make indentation in
center of each roll; spoon 1 teaspoon
preserves into each.

5   Bake 2 to 4 minutes longer or
until golden brown. Run knife
around edge of each muffin cup to
loosen. Remove rolls from cups;
place on cooling racks.

6   In small bowl, blend powdered
sugar and water until smooth;
drizzle over warm rolls. Serve warm
or cool. Cover and refrigerate any
remaining rolls.

High Altitude (3500–6500 ft): In step 4,
bake 13 to 17 minutes.

1 Roll: Calories 180; Total Fat 9g (Saturated Fat 3g;
Trans Fat 1g); Cholesterol 25mg; Sodium 170mg;
Total Carbohydrate 22g (Dietary Fiber 0g); Exchanges:
½ Starch, 1 Other Carbohydrate, 2 Fat; Carbohydrate
Choices: 1½

Crescent Bear Claws

Maureen McBride   San Jose, CA
Bake-Off® Contest 42, 2006

Prep Time: 20 Minutes
Start to Finish: 45 Minutes
6 bear claws

FILLING
1 egg
2 tablespoons milk
1 cup unseasoned dry bread crumbs
2 tablespoons granulated sugar
2 tablespoons butter or margarine, melted
¼ cup water
2 teaspoons almond extract

GLAZE
½ cup granulated sugar
¼ cup water
1 tablespoon light corn syrup

ROLLS
1 can (8 oz) Pillsbury® refrigerated
    crescent dinner rolls
⅓ to ½ cup sliced almonds

ICING
1 cup powdered sugar
2 tablespoons water

1   Heat oven to 375°F. Line cookie
sheet with cooking parchment
paper. In medium bowl, beat egg
lightly with wire whisk. Place half
of egg (about 1½ tablespoons) in
custard cup; beat in milk until
blended and set aside. To remaining
egg in bowl, stir in remaining
filling ingredients until well
blended.

2   Meanwhile, in 1-quart heavy
saucepan, mix glaze ingredients.
Heat to boiling. Remove from heat;
cool while making rolls.

3   On lightly floured work surface,
unroll dough; press into 12 × 8-
inch rectangle, firmly pressing
perforations to seal. Spoon filling
into 12 × 2-inch strip lengthwise
down center ⅓ of dough. Fold ⅓ of
dough over filling. Fold filling-
topped section over last ⅓ of dough
so seam is on bottom of folded
dough. With hand, gently flatten
1-inch-wide strip of dough along
one long side of folded dough.
Cut folded dough crosswise into
6 (2-inch) pastries. Along flattened
edge of each pastry, cut 1-inch-long
cuts about ½ inch apart.

4   Lightly brush egg-milk mixture
over each pastry. Place almonds on
plate; turn each pastry upside down
onto almonds and press gently

so almonds stick to dough. Place almond side up on cookie sheet, spreading each cut slightly to form claw shape. Sprinkle remaining almonds over tops of pastries.

5 Bake 15 to 18 minutes or until golden brown. Remove to cooling rack; cool 5 minutes. Drizzle cooled glaze over each pastry. In another small bowl, mix icing ingredients until smooth (if icing is too thick, add ½ teaspoon water at a time until thin enough to drizzle). Drizzle icing over cooled pastries.

High Altitude (3500–6500 ft): Bake 14 to 17 minutes.

1 Bear Claw: Calories 470; Total Fat 16g (Saturated Fat 6g; Trans Fat 2g); Cholesterol 45mg; Sodium 470mg; Total Carbohydrate 73g (Dietary Fiber 2g) Exchanges: 2 Starch, 3 Other Carbohydrate, 3 Fat; Carbohydrate Choices: 5

Crescent Bear Claws

Granola Sweet Rolls on a Stick

Robin Ross St. Petersburg, FL
Bake-Off® Contest 42, 2006

> Prep Time: 15 Minutes
> Start to Finish: 40 Minutes
> 5 servings

1 can (7.3 oz) Pillsbury® refrigerated cinnamon rolls with icing
1 container (6 oz) French vanilla fat-free yogurt
4 cinnamon crunchy granola bars (2 pouches from 8.9-oz box), finely crushed (¾ cup)*
1 large banana
5 round wooden sticks with 1 pointed end (10 inch)

1 Heat oven to 375°F. Grease large cookie sheet with shortening or cooking spray. Separate dough into 5 rolls; set icing aside. Place rolls on cookie sheet. With sharp knife or 1- to 1¼-inch cookie cutter, cut hole in center of each roll; set roll cutouts aside.

2 Place yogurt in shallow bowl. Place crushed granola bars in another shallow bowl. Peel banana; cut off small slice from each end and cut remaining banana into 5 equal pieces. Place banana pieces in yogurt; stir with spoon until coated. Roll banana pieces in crushed granola bars to coat well. Place 1 coated banana piece in hole in each roll, making hole larger if necessary. Set remaining yogurt aside.

3 Thread stick through side of each roll, through banana and out other side of roll. Slide roll down stick about ⅓ of length. Thread 1 reserved roll cutout onto stick.

4 Bake 12 to 17 minutes or until golden brown and dough around center of roll is no longer doughy. Cool 5 minutes. Meanwhile, stir icing into remaining yogurt for sauce. If desired, cut off sharp ends from sticks with kitchen scissors. Loosen rolls and remove from cookie sheet. Serve with yogurt sauce for dipping.

* To easily crush granola bars, do not unwrap; use rolling pin to crush bars.

High Altitude (3500–6500 ft): No change.

1 Serving (1 roll and 1½ tablespoons sauce): Calories 280; Total Fat 8g (Saturated Fat 2g; Trans Fat 2g); Cholesterol 0mg; Sodium 420mg; Total Carbohydrate 47g (Dietary Fiber 1g) Exchanges: 1½ Starch, 1½ Other Carbohydrate, 1½ Fat; Carbohydrate Choices: 3

Sticky Chewy Chocolate Pecan Rolls

Steve Grieger El Cajon, CA
Bake-Off® Contest 40, 2002

> Prep Time: 20 Minutes
> Start to Finish: 50 Minutes
> 8 rolls

¼ cup packed brown sugar
1 teaspoon ground cinnamon
¼ cup butter or unsalted butter, softened
½ cup chopped pecans
2 tablespoons granulated sugar
1 can (8 oz) Pillsbury® refrigerated crescent dinner rolls
1 tablespoon butter or unsalted butter, melted
½ cup milk chocolate chips

1 Heat oven to 375°F. In small bowl, mix brown sugar, ½ teaspoon of the cinnamon and ¼ cup butter. Spread mixture in bottom and up sides of 8 (2 ¾ × 1¼-inch) nonstick muffin cups. Sprinkle each cup with 1 tablespoon pecans.

2 In another small bowl, mix granulated sugar and remaining ½ teaspoon cinnamon; set aside. Unroll dough on work surface. Firmly press perforations to seal. Press to form 12 × 8-inch rectangle. Brush dough with 1 tablespoon melted butter. Sprinkle with sugar mixture and chocolate chips.

3 Starting with one short side, roll up tightly; pinch edge to seal. With serrated knife, cut into 8 (1-inch) slices. Place each slice, cut side down, over pecans in muffin cup.

4 Bake 15 to 20 minutes or until deep golden brown. Immediately turn rolls upside down onto serving platter. Cool 10 minutes. Serve warm.

High Altitude (3500–6500 ft): No change.

1 Roll: Calories 320; Total Fat 21g (Saturated Fat 8g; Trans Fat 2g); Cholesterol 20mg; Sodium 280mg; Total Carbohydrate 28g (Dietary Fiber 1g) Exchanges: 1 Starch, 1 Other Carbohydrate, 4 Fat; Carbohydrate Choices: 2

Sticky Chewy Chocolate Pecan Rolls

Country Apple Coffee Cake

Susan F. Porubcan Jefferson, WI
Bake-Off® Contest 31, 1984
$40,000 Grand Prize Winner

Prep Time: 20 Minutes
Start to Finish: 1 Hour 10 Minutes
8 servings

COFFEE CAKE
2 tablespoons butter or margarine, softened
1½ cups chopped peeled apples
1 can (12 oz) Pillsbury® Golden Layers®
    refrigerated flaky biscuits
⅓ cup packed brown sugar
¼ teaspoon ground cinnamon
⅓ cup light corn syrup
1½ teaspoons whiskey, if desired
1 egg
½ cup pecan halves or pieces

GLAZE
⅓ cup powdered sugar
¼ teaspoon vanilla
1 to 2 teaspoons milk

1 Heat oven to 350°F. Using 1 tablespoon of the butter, generously grease 9-inch round cake pan or 8-inch square pan. Spread 1 cup of the apples in pan. Separate dough into 10 biscuits. Cut each into quarters. Arrange biscuit pieces, points up, over apples. Top with remaining ½ cup apples.

2 In small bowl, mix remaining 1 tablespoon butter, the brown sugar, cinnamon, corn syrup, whiskey and egg; beat 2 to 3 minutes or until sugar is partially dissolved. Stir in pecans. Spoon over biscuit pieces and apples.

3 Bake 35 to 45 minutes or until deep golden brown. Cool 5 minutes. If desired, remove from pan.

4 In small bowl, mix glaze ingredients, adding enough milk for desired drizzling consistency. Drizzle over warm cake. Serve warm or cool. Store in refrigerator.

High Altitude (3500–6500 ft): No change.

1 Serving: Calories 330; Total Fat 14g (Saturated Fat 3.5g; Trans Fat 2g); Cholesterol 35mg; Sodium 490mg; Total Carbohydrate 46g (Dietary Fiber 1g) Exchanges: 1½ Starch, 1½ Other Carbohydrate, 2½ Fat; Carbohydrate Choices: 3

meet susan porubcan

SUSAN PORUBCAN almost didn't make it to the 1984 Bake-Off® Contest. After her father passed away a week before the competition and she became very ill, Susan called contest officials to say she might not make the trip. But in her heart she knew she couldn't miss it. After a trip to the doctor, she managed to catch a plane to the contest in San Diego.

It was a trip worth making: Susan's apple-laced coffee cake took that year's $40,000 Grand Prize. And it created enough friendships and memories to last a lifetime.

The prize money paid off her mortgage, helping the mother of young twins at a critical time. However, a more intangible prize came along with her win: the friends she made and has kept for more than 20 years.

The contest finalists she befriended came from all over the country. "For years we kept in touch with a round-robin letter, and we still send each other cards," she says. "We all shared a real commonality."

Susan's win also touched lives back home where she lived then, Whitewater, Wisconsin. "There were some wonderful older people in town who were so proud . . . that someone they knew had won," Susan says. "They would share so much of their lives with me because they wanted to connect themselves to this piece of American life. It was almost like they won part of the contest, too."

Raspberry Ripple Crescent Coffee Cake

Priscilla Yee   Concord, CA
Bake-Off® Contest 32, 1986

> Prep Time: 20 Minutes
> Start to Finish: 1 Hour
> 8 servings

COFFEE CAKE

¾ cup granulated sugar

¼ cup butter or margarine, softened

2 eggs

¾ cup ground almonds

¼ cup Pillsbury BEST® all-purpose flour

1 teaspoon grated lemon peel

1 can (8 oz) Pillsbury® refrigerated crescent dinner rolls

8 teaspoons raspberry preserves

¼ cup sliced almonds

GLAZE

⅓ cup powdered sugar

1 to 2 teaspoons milk

1   Heat oven to 375°F. Grease 9-inch round cake pan or 9-inch pie pan. In large bowl, beat granulated sugar, butter and eggs until smooth. Add ground almonds, flour and lemon peel; mix well. Set aside.

2   Separate dough into 8 triangles. Spread 1 teaspoon preserves on each triangle. Roll up, starting at shortest side of triangle and rolling to opposite point. Place rolls in pan in 2 circles, arranging 5 rolls around outside edge and 3 in center. Pour and carefully spread almond mixture evenly over rolls. Sprinkle with almonds.

3   Bake 27 to 37 minutes or until coffee cake is deep golden brown and center is set. If necessary, cover coffee cake with foil during last 5 to 10 minutes of bake time to prevent excessive browning.

4   In small bowl, mix glaze ingredients, adding enough milk for desired drizzling consistency. Drizzle over warm cake. Serve warm.

High Altitude (3500–6500 ft): Bake 32 to 37 minutes.

1 Serving: Calories 380; Total Fat 19g (Saturated Fat 7g; Trans Fat 1.5g); Cholesterol 70mg; Sodium 280mg; Total Carbohydrate 45g (Dietary Fiber 2g) Exchanges: 2 Starch, 1 Other Carbohydrate, 3 ½ Fat; Carbohydrate Choices: 3

Lemon-Pecan Sunburst Coffee Cake

Jennifer Peterson   Lincoln City, OR
Bake-Off® Contest 38, 1998

> Prep Time: 15 Minutes
> Start to Finish: 50 Minutes
> 8 servings

COFFEE CAKE

1 can (16.3 oz) Pillsbury® Grands!® refrigerated flaky biscuits

¼ cup finely chopped pecans

¼ cup granulated sugar

2 teaspoons grated lemon peel

2 tablespoons butter or margarine, melted

GLAZE

½ cup powdered sugar

1½ oz cream cheese (from 3-oz package), softened

2½ to 3 teaspoons lemon juice

1   Heat oven to 375°F. Grease 9- or 8-inch round cake pan. Separate dough into 8 biscuits. Place 1 biscuit in center of pan. Cut remaining biscuits in half, forming 14 half rounds. Arrange pieces around center biscuit in sunburst pattern with cut sides facing same direction.

2   In small bowl, mix pecans, granulated sugar and lemon peel. Brush butter over tops of biscuits; sprinkle with pecan mixture.

3   Bake 20 to 25 minutes or until golden brown.

4   Meanwhile, in small bowl, mix glaze ingredients, adding enough lemon juice for desired drizzling consistency; blend until smooth. Drizzle over warm coffee cake. Cool 10 minutes. Serve warm.

High Altitude (3500–6500 ft): Bake 23 to 28 minutes.

1 Serving: Calories 320; Total Fat 16g (Saturated Fat 5g; Trans Fat 3.5g); Cholesterol 15mg; Sodium 590mg; Total Carbohydrate 39g (Dietary Fiber 0g) Exchanges: 1½ Starch, 1 Other Carbohydrate, 3 Fat; Carbohydrate Choices: 2½

One Hot Entry

One finalist's entry arrived at the Bake-Off® Contest judging agency badly burned around the edges, attached to a letter from the U.S. Postal Service saying: "Our sincere apologies for the present condition of the enclosed mail. The damage resulted from an accident and fire while the mail was being transported by a commercial carrier." The charred entry made it all the way through the selection process and saw its creator all the way to the contest. Today, all entries are received online.

Country Blueberry Coffee Cake

Wendy Hart   Ray City, GA
Bake-Off® Contest 38, 1998
$2,000 Winner

Prep Time: 15 Minutes
Start to Finish: 1 Hour 10 Minutes
9 servings

½ cup packed brown sugar
½ teaspoon ground cinnamon
1 can (12 oz) Pillsbury® Golden Layers®
    refrigerated buttermilk flaky biscuits
¼ cup butter or margarine, melted
1 cup quick-cooking oats
1½ cups fresh or frozen blueberries
¼ cup granulated sugar
2 tablespoons butter or margarine,
    cut into small pieces

1   Heat oven to 375°F. Generously grease 8- or 9-inch square (2-quart) glass baking dish. In small bowl, mix brown sugar and cinnamon with fork.

2   Separate dough into 10 biscuits. Cut each biscuit into quarters. Dip each piece into melted butter; coat with brown sugar mixture. Arrange in single layer in baking dish. Sprinkle with ½ cup of the oats.

3   In medium bowl, toss blueberries and granulated sugar. Spoon over oats and biscuits; sprinkle with remaining ½ cup oats. Top with butter pieces.

4   Bake 30 to 35 minutes or until coffee cake is golden brown and center is done. Cool 20 minutes. Serve warm.

High Altitude (3500–6500 ft): Bake 35 to 40 minutes.

1 Serving: Calories 310; Total Fat 13g (Saturated Fat 6g; Trans Fat 2g); Cholesterol 20mg; Sodium 460mg; Total Carbohydrate 43g (Dietary Fiber 1g) Exchanges: 1 Starch, 2 Other Carbohydrate, 2½ Fat; Carbohydrate Choices: 3

Chocolate Crescent Twist

Steve Grieger Oceanside, CA
Bake-Off® Contest 38, 1998

Prep Time: 15 Minutes
Start to Finish: 1 Hour 15 Minutes
6 servings

STREUSEL
3 tablespoons Pillsbury BEST®
    all-purpose flour
3 tablespoons sugar
1 tablespoon butter or margarine

TWIST
1 can (8 oz) Pillsbury® refrigerated
    crescent dinner rolls
⅔ cup semisweet chocolate chips
1 tablespoon sugar
1 to 3 teaspoons ground cinnamon
1 tablespoon butter or margarine,
    melted
1 tablespoon semisweet chocolate
    chips

1   Heat oven to 375°F. Grease and flour 8 × 4- or 7 × 3-inch loaf pan. In small bowl, mix flour and 3 tablespoons sugar. With fork, cut in 1 tablespoon butter until crumbly.

2   Unroll dough to form 12 × 8-inch rectangle; firmly press perforations to seal. Sprinkle with ⅔ cup chocolate chips, 1 tablespoon sugar, the cinnamon and half of the streusel mixture.

3   Starting at long side of rectangle, roll up; pinch edge to seal. Join ends to form ring; pinch to seal. Gently twist ring to form figure 8; place in pan. Brush with melted butter; sprinkle with remaining half of streusel. Sprinkle with 1 tablespoon chocolate chips; press lightly into dough.

4   Bake 30 to 40 minutes or until deep golden brown. Cool on cooling rack 20 minutes. Remove from pan. Serve warm.

High Altitude (3500–6500 ft): Bake 35 to 45 minutes.

1 Serving: Calories 330; Total Fat 18g (Saturated Fat 9g; Trans Fat 2g); Cholesterol 10mg; Sodium 320mg; Total Carbohydrate 39g (Dietary Fiber 2g) Exchanges: 1 Starch, 1½ Other Carbohydrate, 3½ Fat; Carbohydrate Choices: 2½

Crescent Poppy Seed Coffee Cake

Susan H. Cox Unionville, PA
Bake-Off® Contest 29, 1980

Prep Time: 25 Minutes
Start to Finish: 55 Minutes
2 coffee cakes (24 servings)

COFFEE CAKE
¼ cup chopped almonds
¼ cup golden or seedless raisins
1 jar (10 oz) or 1 can (12 oz) poppy seed
    cake and pastry filling*
2 tablespoons honey
¼ teaspoon rum extract
2 cans (8 oz each) Pillsbury®
    refrigerated crescent dinner rolls

GLAZE
¾ cup powdered sugar
4 to 5 teaspoons lemon juice
Poppy seed, if desired

1   Heat oven to 350°F.

2   In medium bowl, mix almonds, raisins, poppy seed filling, honey and rum extract. Separate 1 can of dough into 4 rectangles. Overlap edges, firmly pressing edges and perforations to seal; press or roll to form 12 × 9-inch rectangle. Spread half of filling over dough. Starting at longest side, roll up; seal. Place seam-side-down on one side of ungreased cookie sheet or double French bread baking pan. Using kitchen scissors or sharp knife, make cuts at 1-inch intervals half way through coffee cake. Repeat with second can of dough and remainder of filling.

3   Bake 25 to 30 minutes or until deep golden brown. Remove from pan to cool. Mix powdered sugar and lemon juice until smooth; drizzle over warm coffee cakes. Sprinkle lightly with poppy seed. Serve warm. Cut into slices to serve.

High Altitude (3500–6500 ft): No change.

1 Serving: Calories 160; Total Fat 6g (Saturated Fat 1.5g; Trans Fat 1g); Cholesterol 0mg; Sodium 160mg; Total Carbohydrate 24g (Dietary Fiber 1g) Exchanges: ½ Starch, 1 Other Carbohydrate, 1 Fat; Carbohydrate Choices: 1½

To substitute for canned filling, grind ¼ cup poppy seed in blender 1 minute. In 2-quart saucepan, mix ground poppy seed, ½ cup sugar and ¼ cup milk. Cook over medium heat 20 to 25 minutes or until thick and milk is absorbed. Cool to lukewarm; add ½ teaspoon each vanilla and almond extract and 1 slightly beaten egg white.

Crescent Walnut-Raisin Potica

Crescent Walnut-Raisin Potica

Mikki Gottwalt New Brighton, MN
Bake-Off® Contest 41, 2004

Prep Time: 15 Minutes
Start to Finish: 55 Minutes
16 servings

BREAD
1 cup chopped walnuts
½ cup raisins
2 tablespoons packed brown sugar
½ teaspoon ground cinnamon
1 tablespoon butter or margarine, melted
1 tablespoon half-and-half
1 tablespoon honey
1 egg
1 can (8 oz) Pillsbury® refrigerated crescent dinner rolls

ICING
½ cup powdered sugar
⅛ teaspoon almond extract
1½ to 2 teaspoons milk or half-and-half

1 Heat oven to 375°F. Grease cookie sheet with shortening or spray with cooking spray. In food processor, place all bread ingredients except dough. Cover; process until finely chopped. Set aside.

2 On lightly floured surface, unroll dough into 1 large rectangle; press or roll into 14 × 10-inch rectangle, firmly pressing perforations to seal. Spread nut mixture evenly over dough to within ½ inch of long sides.

3 Starting with one long side of rectangle, tightly roll up dough, carefully stretching roll until 17

inches long; press edge and ends to seal. Place on cookie sheet; loosely coil into spiral shape.

4 Bake 28 to 33 minutes or until deep golden brown. Cover loosely with foil if bread is browning too quickly. Cool 10 minutes. Meanwhile, in small bowl, mix powdered sugar, almond extract and enough milk for desired drizzling consistency until smooth. Drizzle icing over warm bread. Cut into wedges. Serve warm.

High Altitude (3500–6500 ft): No change.

1 Serving: Calories 160; Total Fat 9g (Saturated Fat 2g; Trans Fat 1g); Cholesterol 15mg; Sodium 120mg; Total Carbohydrate 17g (Dietary Fiber 0g) Exchanges: ½ Starch, ½ Other Carbohydrate, 2 Fat; Carbohydrate Choices: 1

Gooey Caramel Apple Pull-Aparts

Lisa McDaniel Highland, IL
Bake-Off® Contest 42, 2006

Prep Time: 10 Minutes
Start to Finish: 1 Hour 20 Minutes
12 servings

4 pecan crunch crunchy granola bars (2 pouches from 8.9-oz box), crushed (¾ cup)*
¼ cup chopped pecans
1 teaspoon ground cinnamon
1 cup whipping cream
½ cup packed light brown sugar
2 cans (17.5 oz each) Pillsbury® Grands!® refrigerated cinnamon rolls with icing
1 medium Granny Smith apple, peeled, coarsely chopped (about 1¼ cups)

1 Heat oven to 350°F. Spray 12-cup fluted tube cake pan with cooking spray. In small bowl, mix crushed granola bars, pecans and ½ teaspoon of the cinnamon. Sprinkle mixture evenly in bottom of pan.

2 In large bowl, mix whipping cream, brown sugar and remaining ½ teaspoon cinnamon. Separate both cans of dough into 10 rolls; set icing aside. Cut each roll into quarters. Stir roll pieces and apples into whipping cream mixture to coat. Spoon mixture into pan; spread evenly.

3 Bake 50 to 60 minutes or until deep golden brown. Immediately place heatproof serving plate or platter upside down over pan; turn plate and pan over (do not remove pan). Cool 5 minutes. Remove pan; scrape any remaining topping in pan onto coffee cake. Cool 5 minutes longer. Drizzle icing over top. Serve warm.

* To easily crush granola bars, do not unwrap; use rolling pin to crush bars.

High Altitude (3500–6500 ft): Heat oven to 375°F. Bake 40 to 50 minutes.

1 Serving: Calories 420; Total Fat 16g (Saturated Fat 6g; Trans Fat 2.5g); Cholesterol 20mg; Sodium 590mg; Total Carbohydrate 61g (Dietary Fiber 1g) Exchanges: 2 Starch, 2 Other Carbohydrate, 3 Fat; Carbohydrate Choices: 4

Lemon Almond Breakfast Pastry

Sharon Richardson   Dallas, TX
Bake-Off® Contest 33, 1988
$2,000 Winner

Prep Time: 15 Minutes
Start to Finish: 1 Hour 15 Minutes
16 servings

FILLING

½ cup butter or margarine, softened
1 package (7 oz) almond paste, broken
   into small pieces
2 eggs
5 teaspoons Pillsbury BEST®
   all-purpose flour
1 to 2 teaspoons grated lemon peel

CRUST

1 box (15 oz) Pillsbury® refrigerated pie
   crusts, softened as directed on box
1 teaspoon Pillsbury BEST® all-purpose
   flour
1 egg, beaten
1 tablespoon milk
2 tablespoons sugar

1   In small bowl, beat butter and almond paste with electric mixer until smooth, or process in food processor. Add 2 eggs; mix well. By hand, stir in 5 teaspoons flour and the lemon peel until just blended. Cover; place in freezer 20 to 30 minutes or until thick.

2   Heat oven to 400°F. Sprinkle 1 pie crust with 1 teaspoon flour. Place floured side down on ungreased 12-inch pizza pan or cookie sheet. Spread cold filling over crust to within 2 inches of edge. Brush edge with beaten egg. Refrigerate while preparing top crust.

3   Cut 1-inch circle from center of second pie crust. Using very sharp knife and curving motions, decoratively score crust in pinwheel design. (Do not cut through crust or filling will leak out.) Carefully place over filled bottom crust. Press edges to seal; flute. In small bowl, mix remaining beaten egg and milk. Brush over pastry; sprinkle with sugar.

4   Bake 22 to 27 minutes or until golden brown. Serve warm.

High Altitude (3500–6500 ft): Bake 25 to 30 minutes.

1 Serving: Calories 250; Total Fat 17g (Saturated Fat 7g; Trans Fat 0g); Cholesterol 60mg; Sodium 160mg; Total Carbohydrate 22g (Dietary Fiber 0g) Exchanges: 1 Starch, ½ Other Carbohydrate, 3 Fat; Carbohydrate Choices: 1½

Easy Danish Kringle

Dean Philipp   New York, NY
Bake-Off® Contest 38, 1998

Prep Time: 15 Minutes
Start to Finish: 1 Hour 15 Minutes
8 servings

1 Pillsbury® refrigerated pie crust
   (from 15-oz box), softened as
   directed on box
⅔ cup chopped pecans
⅓ cup packed brown sugar
3 tablespoons butter or margarine,
   softened
½ cup powdered sugar
¼ teaspoon vanilla
2 to 3 teaspoons milk
3 tablespoons chopped pecans,
   if desired

1   Heat oven to 375°F. On ungreased large cookie sheet, unroll pie crust.

2   In medium bowl, mix ⅔ cup pecans, the brown sugar and butter. Sprinkle over half of pie crust to within ¾ inch of edge. Brush edge with water; fold crust over pecan mixture. Move to center of cookie sheet. Press edges with fork to seal; prick top with fork.

3   Bake 17 to 22 minutes or until golden brown. Cool 5 minutes.

4   In small bowl, mix powdered sugar, vanilla and enough milk for desired drizzling consistency until smooth. Drizzle over kringle; sprinkle with 3 tablespoons pecans. Cool 30 minutes before serving.

High Altitude (3500–6500 ft): No change.

1 Serving: Calories 290; Total Fat 18g (Saturated Fat 6g; Trans Fat 0g); Cholesterol 15mg; Sodium 140mg; Total Carbohydrate 31g (Dietary Fiber 0g) Exchanges: ½ Starch, 1½ Other Carbohydrate, 3½ Fat; Carbohydrate Choices: 2

Guess-Again Candy Crunch (page 252)

Moonbeam Cookies

Janice Oeffler   Danbury, WI
Bake-Off® Contest 39, 2000

Prep Time: 1 Hour
Start to Finish: 1 Hour
About 3 dozen cookies

1 roll (16.5 oz) Pillsbury® Create 'n
   Bake® refrigerated sugar cookies
1 cup coconut
½ cup lemon curd (from 10-oz jar)
2 oz vanilla-flavored candy coating
   (almond bark), chopped, or ⅓ cup
   white vanilla baking chips

1   Heat oven to 350°F. In large
bowl, break up cookie dough. Stir or
knead in coconut. Shape dough into
1-inch balls. On ungreased cookie
sheets, place balls 2 inches apart.

2   With handle of wooden spoon,
make indentation in center of each
cookie. Spoon about ½ teaspoon
lemon curd into each indentation.

3   Bake 10 to 13 minutes or
until edges are light golden brown.
Remove from cookie sheets to cooling rack. Cool 5 minutes.

4   In small microwavable bowl,
microwave candy coating on
Medium (50%) 2 minutes; stir well.
Drizzle over cookies.

High Altitude (3500–6500 ft): No change.

1 Cookie: Calories 90; Total Fat 4g (Saturated Fat 1.5g;
Trans Fat 0.5g); Cholesterol 10mg; Sodium 45mg; Total
Carbohydrate 13g (Dietary Fiber 0g) Exchanges: 1 Other
Carbohydrate, ½ Fat; Carbohydrate Choices: 1

Hawaiian Cookie Tarts

Elizabeth Zemelko   Knox, IN
Bake-Off® Contest 34, 1990

Prep Time: 35 Minutes
Start to Finish: 1 Hour 45 Minutes
36 cookie tarts

COOKIES
1¾ cups Pillsbury BEST® all-purpose
   flour
½ cup powdered sugar
2 tablespoons cornstarch
1 cup butter or margarine, softened
1 teaspoon vanilla

FILLING
1 cup pineapple preserves*
½ cup granulated sugar
1 egg
1½ cups coconut
Additional powdered sugar
   (about 2 tablespoons)

1   Heat oven to 350°F. In large
bowl, stir together flour, ½ cup
powdered sugar and the cornstarch.
With spoon, beat in butter and
vanilla until soft dough forms.

2   Shape dough into 1-inch balls.
Place 1 ball in each of 36 ungreased
mini muffin cups; press in bottom
and up side of each cup. Spoon
1 teaspoon pineapple preserves into
each dough-lined cup.

3   In small bowl, beat granulated
sugar and egg with fork until well
blended. Stir in coconut until well
coated with egg mixture. Spoon
1 teaspoon coconut mixture over
preserves in each cup.

4   Bake 23 to 33 minutes or until
cookie crusts are very light golden
brown. Cool in pans on cooling
racks 20 minutes.

5   To release cookies from cups,
hold muffin pan upside down at
an angle over cooling rack. With
handle of table knife, firmly tap
bottom of each cup until cookie
releases. Cool completely, about
15 minutes. Just before serving,
sprinkle with additional powdered
sugar. Store in refrigerator.

*One-half cup apricot preserves mixed
with ½ cup drained crushed pineapple can
be substituted for the pineapple preserves.*

High Altitude (3500–6500 ft): No change.

1 Cookie Tart: Calories 140; Total Fat 7g (Saturated
Fat 4.5g; Trans Fat 0g); Cholesterol 20mg; Sodium 50mg;
Total Carbohydrate 18g (Dietary Fiber 0g) Exchanges:
1 Other Carbohydrate, 1½ Fat; Carbohydrate Choices: 1

Cooking 'Round the Clock

Cooking for a large family is one of the most absorbing and challeng-
ing kinds of work, and Elizabeth Zemelko has been involved with
food and cooking from an early age. "I grew up in a Slovak-speaking
home, with Ma, Pa, ten kids, and three boarders. We ate in three
shifts: those who worked, those who went to school, and then us
little ones, with Ma, had the leftovers. What a beautiful survival,
now that I look back on everything. Once Ma said to me,
'I can't believe how much these hands have done in work.'"
When the work is raising and feeding a family, it is a labor
of love and the rewards are profound.

Hawaiian Cookie Tarts

Chocolate Buttersweets

Vance Fletcher   Indianapolis, IN
Bake-Off® Contest 16, 1964

Prep Time: 1 Hour 35 Minutes
Start to Finish: 2 Hours 15 Minutes
About 3 dozen cookies

COOKIES
½ cup butter or margarine, softened
½ cup powdered sugar
¼ teaspoon salt
1 teaspoon vanilla
1 to 1¼ cups Pillsbury BEST®
  all-purpose flour

FILLING
1 package (3 oz) cream cheese,
  softened
1 cup powdered sugar
2 tablespoons Pillsbury BEST®
  all-purpose flour
1 teaspoon vanilla
½ cup chopped walnuts
½ cup flaked coconut

FROSTING
½ cup semisweet chocolate chips
2 tablespoons butter or margarine
2 tablespoons water
½ cup powdered sugar

1   Heat oven to 350°F. In large bowl, beat ½ cup butter, ½ cup powdered sugar, the salt and 1 teaspoon vanilla with electric mixer on medium speed, scraping bowl occasionally, until blended. Gradually beat in 1 to 1¼ cups flour until soft dough forms.

2   Shape teaspoonfuls of dough into balls. On ungreased cookie sheets, place balls 2 inches apart. With thumb or handle of wooden spoon, make indentation in center of each cookie.

3   Bake 12 to 15 minutes or until edges are lightly browned. Meanwhile, in small bowl, beat cream cheese, 1 cup powdered sugar, 2 tablespoons flour and 1 teaspoon vanilla on medium speed until well blended. Stir in walnuts and coconut.

4   Immediately remove cookies from cookie sheets to cooling racks. Spoon about ½ teaspoon filling into each cookie. Cool completely, about 30 minutes.

5   In 1-quart saucepan, heat chocolate chips, 2 tablespoons butter and the water over low heat, stirring occasionally, until chips are melted. Remove from heat. With spoon, beat in ½ cup powdered sugar until smooth. Frost cooled cookies.

High Altitude (3500–6500 ft): Bake 9 to 12 minutes.

1 Cookie: Calories 110; Total Fat 6g (Saturated Fat 3.5g; Trans Fat 0g); Cholesterol 10mg; Sodium 50mg; Total Carbohydrate 12g (Dietary Fiber 0g) Exchanges: 1 Other Carbohydrate, 1 Fat; Carbohydrate Choices: 1

Nutmeg Cookie Logs

Julia Woods
South Charleston, WV
Bake-Off® Contest 8, 1956

Prep Time: 50 Minutes
Start to Finish: 2 Hours 5 Minutes
5 dozen cookies

COOKIES

¾ cup granulated sugar
1 cup butter or margarine, softened
2 teaspoons vanilla
2 teaspoons rum extract
1 egg
3 cups Pillsbury BEST® all-purpose flour
1 teaspoon ground nutmeg

FROSTING

2 cups powdered sugar
3 tablespoons butter or margarine, softened
¾ teaspoon rum extract
¼ teaspoon vanilla
2 to 3 tablespoons half-and-half or milk
Additional ground nutmeg

1　In large bowl, beat granulated sugar, 1 cup butter, 2 teaspoons vanilla, 2 teaspoons rum extract and egg with electric mixer on medium speed until light and fluffy. With spoon, stir in flour and 1 teaspoon nutmeg. Cover with plastic wrap; refrigerate about 45 minutes for easier handling.

2　Heat oven to 350°F. Divide dough into 12 pieces. On floured surface, shape each piece of dough into long rope, ½ inch in diameter and about 15 inches long. Cut into 3-inch logs. On ungreased cookie sheets, place logs 1 inch apart.

3　Bake 12 to 15 minutes or until edges are light golden brown. Immediately remove from cookie sheets to cooling racks. Cool completely, about 20 minutes.

4　In small bowl, mix all frosting ingredients except nutmeg, adding enough half-and-half for desired spreading consistency. Spread on tops and sides of cookies. If desired, mark frosting with tines of fork to look like bark. Sprinkle lightly with additional nutmeg. Let stand until frosting is set before storing.

High Altitude (3500–6500 ft): No change.

1 Cookie: Calories 80; Total Fat 4g (Saturated Fat 2.5g; Trans Fat 0g); Cholesterol 15mg; Sodium 25mg; Total Carbohydrate 11g (Dietary Fiber 0g) Exchanges: ½ Other Carbohydrate, 1 Fat; Carbohydrate Choices: 1

Brazilian Jubilee Cookies

Mrs. F. H. Speers　Midland, TX
Bake-Off® Contest 4, 1952

Prep Time: 1 Hour 15 Minutes
Start to Finish: 1 Hour 15 Minutes
About 3 dozen cookies

¾ cup granulated sugar
¼ cup packed brown sugar
½ cup shortening
2 teaspoons vanilla
1 egg
1½ cups Pillsbury BEST® all-purpose flour
1 to 2 tablespoons instant coffee granules or crystals
1 teaspoon baking powder
½ teaspoon salt
½ teaspoon ground cinnamon
1 cup chopped Brazil nuts
36 milk chocolate stars (from 14-oz bag)
Additional chopped Brazil nuts, if desired

1　Heat oven to 350°F. Grease cookie sheets with shortening or cooking spray. In large bowl, beat sugars and shortening with electric mixer on medium speed, scraping bowl occasionally, until well blended. Beat in vanilla and egg. On low speed, beat in flour, instant coffee, baking powder, salt, cinnamon and 1 cup nuts until dough forms.

2　Shape dough by tablespoonfuls into balls. Place 2 inches apart on cookie sheets.

3　Bake 12 to 15 minutes or until golden brown. Immediately top each cookie with 1 chocolate star. Remove from cookie sheets to cooling rack; cool 5 minutes (chocolate will soften). Spread chocolate over cookies to frost. Sprinkle with additional chopped nuts.

High Altitude (3500–6500 ft): No change.

1 Cookie: Calories 120; Total Fat 7g (Saturated Fat 2g; Trans Fat 0g); Cholesterol 5mg; Sodium 85mg; Total Carbohydrate 13g (Dietary Fiber 0g) Exchanges: 1 Other Carbohydrate, 1½ Fat; Carbohydrate Choices: 1

Starlight Mint Surprise Cookies

Starlight Mint Surprise Cookies

Laura Rott   Naperville, IL
Bake-Off® Contest 1, 1949
$10,000 Winner

Prep Time: 1 Hour
Start to Finish: 3 Hours
5 dozen cookies

1 cup granulated sugar
½ cup packed brown sugar
¾ cup butter or margarine, softened
2 tablespoons water
1 teaspoon vanilla
2 eggs
3 cups Pillsbury BEST® all-purpose flour
1 teaspoon baking soda
½ teaspoon salt
60 thin rectangular crème de menthe
    chocolate candies (from three
    4.67-oz packages), unwrapped
60 walnut halves or pieces

1 In large bowl, beat sugars, butter, water, vanilla and eggs with electric mixer on medium speed, scraping bowl occasionally, until blended. On low speed, beat in flour, baking soda and salt until well blended. Cover with plastic wrap; refrigerate at least 2 hours for easier handling.

2 Heat oven to 375°F. Using about 1 tablespoon dough, press dough around each chocolate candy to cover completely. Place 2 inches apart on ungreased cookie sheets. Top each with walnut half.

3 Bake 7 to 9 minutes or until light golden brown. Immediately remove from cookie sheets to cooling rack.

High Altitude (3500–6500 ft): No change.

1 Cookie: Calories 110; Total Fat 5g (Saturated Fat 2.5g; Trans Fat 0g); Cholesterol 15mg; Sodium 65mg; Total Carbohydrate 13g (Dietary Fiber 0g) Exchanges: 1 Other Carbohydrate, 1 Fat; Carbohydrate Choices: 1

Caramel-Filled Chocolate Cookies

Jean Olson   Wallingford, IA
Bake-Off® Contest 34, 1990
$2,000 Winner

Prep Time: 1 Hour
Start to Finish: 1 Hour 30 Minutes
4 dozen cookies

2½ cups Pillsbury BEST® all-purpose flour
¾ cup unsweetened baking cocoa
1 teaspoon baking soda
1 cup granulated sugar
1 cup packed brown sugar
1 cup butter or margarine, softened
2 teaspoons vanilla
2 eggs
1 cup chopped pecans
1 tablespoon granulated sugar
48 round milk chocolate-covered
    caramels (from 12-oz bag), unwrapped
4 oz vanilla-flavored candy coating
    (almond bark), if desired

1 In small bowl, stir together flour, cocoa and baking soda; set aside. In large bowl, beat 1 cup granulated sugar, the brown sugar and butter with electric mixer on medium speed, scraping bowl occasionally, until light and fluffy. Beat in vanilla and eggs. On low speed, beat in flour mixture until well blended. Stir in ½ cup of the pecans. If necessary, cover with plastic wrap and refrigerate 30 minutes for easier handling.

2 Heat oven to 375°F. In small bowl, mix remaining ½ cup pecans and 1 tablespoon sugar. With floured hands, shape about 1 tablespoon dough around each caramel, covering completely. Press 1 side of each ball into pecan mixture. Place nut side up 2 inches apart on ungreased cookie sheets.

3 Bake 7 to 10 minutes or until set and slightly cracked. Cool 2 minutes; remove from cookie sheets to cooling rack. Cool completely, about 15 minutes.

4 In 1-quart saucepan, melt candy coating over low heat, stirring constantly until smooth. Drizzle over cookies.

High Altitude (3500–6500 ft): Increase Pillsbury BEST® all-purpose flour to 2¾ cups.

1 Cookie: Calories 150; Total Fat 7g (Saturated Fat 3.5g; Trans Fat 0g); Cholesterol 20mg; Sodium 70mg; Total Carbohydrate 19g (Dietary Fiber 0g) Exchanges: 1½ Other Carbohydrate, 1½ Fat; Carbohydrate Choices: 1

Officer, That Man Stole My Bake-Off® Prize!

At the first-ever Bake-Off® Contest awards ceremony, an excited Laura Rott received a $10,000 second prize for her cookies with the surprise of a chocolate mint hidden inside. With some time to spare before her trip back home, Laura tucked the check into her purse and set out to see more of the sights of New York City. Unfortunately, she had another surprise: An enterprising pickpocket managed to purloin her prize check! No harm, though because Bake-Off® Contest officials canceled her original check and re-issued a new one. What's no surprise is that Laura's cookies have become a classic.

Peanut Butter Brownie Cookies

Deb McGowan Louisville, OH
Bake-Off® Contest 41, 2004
$5,000 Winner—Weekends Made Special
Runner-Up Winner

> **Prep Time:** 1 Hour
> **Start to Finish:** 1 Hour 30 Minutes
> 24 cookies

1 box (19.5 oz) Pillsbury® Brownie Classics® traditional fudge brownie mix
¼ cup butter or margarine, melted
4 oz cream cheese (from 8-oz package), softened
1 egg
1 cup powdered sugar
1 cup creamy peanut butter
½ container (1-lb size) Pillsbury® Creamy Supreme® chocolate fudge frosting (about ¾ cup)

1 Heat oven to 350°F. In medium bowl, beat brownie mix, melted butter, cream cheese and egg 50 strokes with spoon until well blended (dough will be sticky).

2 Onto ungreased cookie sheets, drop dough by rounded tablespoonfuls 2 inches apart to make 24 cookies; smooth edge of each to form round cookie.

3 In small bowl, mix powdered sugar and peanut butter with spoon until mixture forms a ball. With hands, roll rounded teaspoonfuls into 24 balls. Lightly press 1 ball into center of each ball of dough.

4 Bake 10 to 14 minutes or until edges are set. Cool cookies on cookie sheets at least 30 minutes.

5 Remove cooled cookies from cookie sheets. Spread thin layer of frosting over peanut butter portion of each cooled cookie.

High Altitude (3500–6500 ft): Before baking, flatten cookies slightly. Bake 11 to 15 minutes.

1 Cookie: Calories 260; Total Fat 13g (Saturated Fat 4g; Trans Fat 0.5g); Cholesterol 20mg; Sodium 160mg; Total Carbohydrate 32g (Dietary Fiber 1g) Exchanges: 1 Starch, 1 Other Carbohydrate, 2½ Fat; Carbohydrate Choices: 2

Candy Bar Cookies

Alice Reese Minneapolis, MN
Bake-Off® Contest 13, 1961
$25,000 Winner

> **Prep Time:** 1 Hour 15 Minutes
> **Start to Finish:** 1 Hour 15 Minutes
> 40 cookies

BASE
¾ cup powdered sugar
¾ cup butter or margarine, softened
2 tablespoons whipping cream
1 teaspoon vanilla
2 cups Pillsbury BEST® all-purpose flour

FILLING
21 caramels, unwrapped
3 tablespoons whipping cream
3 tablespoons butter or margarine
¾ cup powdered sugar
¾ cup chopped pecans

GLAZE
⅓ cup semisweet chocolate chips
1 tablespoon whipping cream
2 teaspoons butter or margarine
3 tablespoons powdered sugar
1 teaspoon vanilla
40 pecan halves (½ cup), if desired

1 In large bowl, mix all base ingredients except flour with spoon until well blended. Stir in flour until dough forms. If necessary, cover dough with plastic wrap, and refrigerate 1 hour for easier handling.

2 Heat oven to 325°F. On well-floured surface, roll out half of dough at a time into 10 × 8-inch rectangle. With pastry wheel or knife, cut into 2-inch squares. Place ½ inch apart on ungreased cookie sheets.

3 Bake 10 to 13 minutes or until set. Immediately remove from cookie sheets to cooling racks. Cool completely, about 15 minutes.

4 In 2-quart saucepan, heat caramels, 3 tablespoons whipping cream and 3 tablespoons butter over low heat, stirring frequently, until caramels are melted and mixture is smooth. Remove from heat. Stir in ¾ cup powdered sugar and the chopped pecans (add additional whipping cream a few drops at a time if needed for desired spreading consistency). Spread 1 teaspoon warm filling on each cookie square.

5 In 1-quart saucepan, heat chocolate chips, 1 tablespoon whipping cream and 2 teaspoons butter over low heat, stirring frequently, until chips are melted and mixture is smooth. REMOVE FROM HEAT. Stir in 3 tablespoons powdered sugar and 1 teaspoon vanilla. Spread glaze evenly over caramel filling on each cookie. Top each with pecan half.

High Altitude (3500–6500 ft): No change.

1 Cookie: Calories 130; Total Fat 8g (Saturated Fat 4g; Trans Fat 0g); Cholesterol 15mg; Sodium 45mg; Total Carbohydrate 15g (Dietary Fiber 0g) Exchanges: 1 Other Carbohydrate, 1½ Fat; Carbohydrate Choices: 1

Peanut Butter Brownie Cookies

Choconut Chippers

Deborah Anderson Fairborn, OH
Bake-Off® Contest 32, 1986
$2,000 Winner

Prep Time: 1 Hour 25 Minutes
Start to Finish: 1 Hour 25 Minutes
About 6 dozen cookies

¾ **cup granulated sugar**
¾ **cup packed brown sugar**
¼ **cup vegetable oil**
1 **teaspoon vanilla**
2 **egg whites or 1 whole egg**
1 **box (6-serving size) chocolate fudge**
   pudding and pie filling mix (not instant)
1 **container (8 oz) sour cream (1 cup)**
2 **cups Pillsbury BEST® all-purpose flour**
1½ **cups quick-cooking or old-fashioned**
   oats
1 **teaspoon baking soda**
½ **teaspoon salt**
2 **cups chopped pecans**
1 **bag (12 oz) semisweet chocolate**
   chips (2 cups)

1 Heat oven to 375°F. Grease
cookie sheets with shortening or
cooking spray. In large bowl, beat
sugars, oil, vanilla, egg whites,
pudding mix and sour cream
with electric mixer on low speed
until moistened; beat on medium
speed 2 minutes, scraping bowl
occasionally.

2 On low speed, beat in flour, oats,
baking soda and salt until blended.
Stir in pecans and chocolate chips.
If necessary, cover with plastic wrap
and refrigerate 1 hour for easier
handling.

3 Onto cookie sheets, drop dough
by rounded tablespoonfuls 2 inches
apart.

4 Bake 6 to 7 minutes or until set.
Cool 1 minute; remove from cookie
sheets to cooling rack.

High Altitude (3500–6500 ft): No change.

1 Cookie: Calories 110; Total Fat 5g (Saturated Fat 1.5g;
Trans Fat 0g); Cholesterol 0mg; Sodium 50mg; Total
Carbohydrate 13g (Dietary Fiber 0g) Exchanges:
1 Other Carbohydrate, 1 Fat; Carbohydrate Choices: 1

White Chocolate Chunk Cookies

Dottie Due Edgewood, KY
Bake-Off® Contest 33, 1988
$2,000 Winner

Prep Time: 1 Hour 15 Minutes
Start to Finish: 1 Hour 15 Minutes
About 5 dozen cookies

¾ **cup granulated sugar**
¾ **cup packed brown sugar**
1 **cup shortening**
3 **eggs**
1 **teaspoon vanilla**
2½ **cups Pillsbury BEST® all-purpose flour**
1 **teaspoon baking powder**
1 **teaspoon baking soda**
½ **teaspoon salt**
1 **cup coconut**
½ **cup old-fashioned or quick-cooking oats**
½ **cup chopped walnuts**
2 **packages (6 oz each) white chocolate**
   baking bars, cut into ¼- to ½-inch chunks

1 Heat oven to 350°F. In large
bowl, beat sugars and shortening
with electric mixer on medium
speed, scraping bowl occasionally,
until light and fluffy. Add eggs, one
at a time, beating well after each
addition. Beat in vanilla. On low
speed, beat in flour, baking powder,
baking soda and salt until well blended.
Stir in remaining ingredients.

2 Onto ungreased cookie sheets,
drop dough by rounded tablespoonfuls 2 inches apart.

3 Bake 10 to 15 minutes or until
light golden brown. Cool 1 minute;
remove from cookie sheets to cooling
rack.

High Altitude (3500–6500 ft): Heat oven to
375°F. Decrease baking powder and baking
soda to ½ teaspoon each. Bake 8 to 12
minutes.

1 Cookie: Calories 120; Total Fat 7g (Saturated Fat 2.5g;
Trans Fat 0.5g); Cholesterol 10mg; Sodium 60mg; Total
Carbohydrate 14g (Dietary Fiber 0g) Exchanges: 1 Other
Carbohydrate, 1½ Fat; Carbohydrate Choices: 1

The Collector

A self-described white chocolate fanatic, Robin Wilson started
experimenting with different flavor combinations to come up with her
special Bake-Off® Contest recipe. "I sometimes had five or six new
recipes to take to work for co-workers to sample," says Robin, an
office manager. She has lots of resources for inspiration at home:
Robin has a collection of more than 1,800 cookbooks. "I'm
constantly buying new and used cookbooks," she says.
"Most people come back from vacation with various
souvenirs. I return with a multitude of cookbooks."

White Chocolate–Ginger Cookies

Robin Wilson   Altamonte Springs, FL
Bake-Off® Contest 41, 2004

Prep Time: 1 Hour 20 Minutes
Start to Finish: 1 Hour 20 Minutes
About 12 cookies

COOKIES
1 roll (16.5 oz) Pillsbury® Create 'n
   Bake® refrigerated sugar cookies
¼ cup packed dark brown sugar
1¼ teaspoons ground cinnamon
¼ teaspoon ground ginger
¼ teaspoon ground nutmeg
2 teaspoons grated orange peel
1 package (6 oz) white chocolate baking
   bars, coarsely chopped
¾ cup chopped pecans
⅓ cup finely chopped crystallized
   ginger*

GLAZE
½ **cup powdered sugar**
⅛ **teaspoon ground cinnamon**
3 to 3½ **teaspoons orange juice**

1   Heat oven to 350°F. In large bowl, break up cookie dough. Stir in brown sugar, 1¼ teaspoons cinnamon, the ginger, nutmeg and orange peel until well combined. Stir in white chocolate baking bars, pecans and crystallized ginger. On ungreased cookie sheets, drop dough by ¼ cupfuls 3 inches apart.

2   Bake 13 to 17 minutes or until edges are golden brown. Cool 2 minutes. Remove from cookie sheets to cooling rack. Cool completely, about 15 minutes.

3   In small bowl, blend powdered sugar, ⅛ teaspoon cinnamon and enough orange juice for desired drizzling consistency. Drizzle glaze over cooled cookies. Let stand until glaze is set.

* To easily chop crystallized ginger, cut with kitchen scissors into small pieces.

High Altitude (3500–6500 ft): No change.

1 Cookie: Calories 350; Total Fat 17g (Saturated Fat 5g; Trans Fat 2g); Cholesterol 15mg; Sodium 120mg; Total Carbohydrate 44g (Dietary Fiber 0g) Exchanges: ½ Starch, 2½ Other Carbohydrate, 3½ Fat; Carbohydrate Choices: 3

Texan-Sized Almond Crunch Cookies

Texan-Sized Almond Crunch Cookies

Barbara Hodgson   Elkhart, IN
Bake-Off® Contest 30, 1982
$2,000 Winner

> **Prep Time:** 1 Hour 55 Minutes
> **Start to Finish:** 1 Hour 55 Minutes
> About 4 dozen large cookies

1 cup granulated sugar
1 cup powdered sugar
1 cup butter or margarine, softened
1 cup vegetable oil
1 teaspoon almond extract
2 eggs
3½ cups Pillsbury BEST® all-purpose flour
1 cup Pillsbury BEST® whole wheat flour
1 teaspoon baking soda
1 teaspoon salt
1 teaspoon cream of tartar
2 cups coarsely chopped almonds
1¼ cups toffee bits (from 10-oz bag)
Additional granulated sugar (about ¼ cup)

1   Heat oven to 350°F. In large bowl, beat sugars, butter and oil with electric mixer on medium speed, scraping bowl occasionally, until well blended. Beat in almond extract and eggs. On low speed, gradually beat in flours, baking soda, salt and cream of tartar. Stir in almonds and toffee bits. If necessary, cover with plastic wrap and refrigerate 1 hour for easier handling.

2   Shape large tablespoonfuls of dough into balls; roll in additional granulated sugar. Place 5 inches apart on ungreased cookie sheets. With fork dipped in sugar, flatten balls in crisscross pattern.

3   Bake 12 to 18 minutes or until light golden brown around edges. Cool 1 minute; remove from cookie sheets to cooling rack.

High Altitude (3500–6500 ft): No change.

1 Cookie: Calories 220; Total Fat 13g (Saturated Fat 4.5g; Trans Fat 0g); Cholesterol 25mg; Sodium 130mg; Total Carbohydrate 21g (Dietary Fiber 1g) Exchanges: ½ Starch, 1 Other Carbohydrate, 2½ Fat; Carbohydrate Choices: 1½

Funfetti Cookies

Molly Taylor   Maryville, TN
Bake-Off® Contest 34, 1990

> **Prep Time:** 40 Minutes
> **Start to Finish:** 40 Minutes
> About 3 dozen cookies

1 box (18.9 oz) Pillsbury® Moist
  Supreme® Funfetti® cake mix
⅓ cup vegetable oil
2 eggs
½ container (15.6 oz-size) Pillsbury®
  Creamy Supreme® Funfetti® pink
  frosting

1   Heat oven to 375°F. In large bowl, mix cake mix, oil and eggs with spoon until thoroughly moistened. Shape dough into 1-inch balls. Place 2 inches apart on ungreased cookie sheets. With bottom of glass dipped in flour, flatten balls to ¼-inch thickness.

2   Bake 6 to 8 minutes or until edges are light golden brown. Cool 1 minute; remove from cookie sheets to cooling rack.

3   Spread frosting over warm cookies. Immediately sprinkle each with candy bits from frosting. Let frosting set before storing in tightly covered container.

High Altitude (3500–6500 ft): Add ½ cup Pillsbury BEST® all-purpose flour to dry cake mix.

1 Cookie: Calories 110; Total Fat 4.5g (Saturated Fat 1.5g; Trans Fat 0g); Cholesterol 10mg; Sodium 105mg; Total Carbohydrate 16g (Dietary Fiber 0g) Exchanges: 1 Other Carbohydrate, 1 Fat; Carbohydrate Choices: 1

Cinnamon-Toffee-Pecan Cookies

Jennifer Meyer   Elmwood Park, IL
Bake-Off® Contest 39, 2000

> **Prep Time:** 50 Minutes
> **Start to Finish:** 50 Minutes
> About 2 dozen cookies

1 roll (16.5 oz) Pillsbury® Create 'n
  Bake® refrigerated sugar cookies
2 teaspoons ground cinnamon
½ teaspoon ground nutmeg
2 teaspoons vanilla
¾ cup chopped pecans
½ cup toffee bits (from 10-oz bag)

1   Heat oven to 350°F. Spray cookie sheets with cooking spray. In large bowl, break up cookie dough. Stir in cinnamon, nutmeg and vanilla until well mixed. Stir in pecans and toffee bits until well mixed.

2   Onto cookie sheets, drop dough by heaping teaspoonfuls 3 inches apart.

3   Bake 11 to 14 minutes or until edges are golden brown. Cool 3 minutes; remove from cookie sheets to cooling rack.

High Altitude (3500–6500 ft): Bake 12 to 15 minutes.

1 Cookie: Calories 140; Total Fat 8g (Saturated Fat 2g; Trans Fat 1g); Cholesterol 10mg; Sodium 75mg; Total Carbohydrate 15g (Dietary Fiber 0g) Exchanges: 1 Other Carbohydrate, 1½ Fat; Carbohydrate Choices: 1

Milk Chocolate–Butterscotch Café Cookies

Cindy Schmuelling   Fort Mitchell, KY
Bake-Off® Contest 40, 2002

> **Prep Time:** 40 Minutes
> **Start to Finish:** 40 Minutes
> About 9 large cookies

1 roll (16.5 oz) Pillsbury® Create 'n Bake® refrigerated sugar cookies
⅓ cup packed brown sugar
1 teaspoon vanilla
¾ cup old-fashioned oats
½ cup butterscotch chips
2 bars (1.55 oz each) milk chocolate candy, unwrapped, chopped

1   Heat oven to 350°F. Spray 1 large or 2 small cookie sheets with cooking spray. In large bowl, break up cookie dough. Stir in brown sugar and vanilla. Stir in oats, butterscotch chips and chocolate. (Dough will be stiff.)

2   Onto cookie sheets, drop dough by rounded ¼ cupfuls 2 inches apart. Flatten each to ½-inch thickness.

3   Bake 13 to 18 minutes or until cookies are slightly puffed and edges are golden brown. Cool 1 minute; remove from cookie sheets to cooling rack.

High Altitude (3500–6500 ft): No change.

1 Cookie: Calories 390; Total Fat 17g (Saturated Fat 6g; Trans Fat 2.5g); Cholesterol 20mg; Sodium 160mg; Total Carbohydrate 57g (Dietary Fiber 0g) Exchanges: 1 Starch, 3 Other Carbohydrate, 3 Fat; Carbohydrate Choices: 4

So-Easy Sugar Cookies

Kathryn Blackburn   National Park, NJ
Bake-Off® Contest 30, 1982

> **Prep Time:** 15 Minutes
> **Start to Finish:** 35 Minutes
> 4 dozen cookies

¾ cup sugar
⅓ cup butter or margarine, softened, or shortening
⅓ cup vegetable oil
1 tablespoon milk
1 to 2 teaspoons almond extract
1 egg
1½ cups Pillsbury BEST® all-purpose flour
1½ teaspoons baking powder
¼ teaspoon salt
1 tablespoon sugar or colored sugar

1   Heat oven to 375°F. In large bowl, beat ¾ cup sugar, the butter, oil, milk, almond extract and egg with electric mixer on medium speed, scraping bowl occasionally, until light and fluffy. On low speed, beat in flour, baking powder and salt until well blended. Spread evenly in ungreased 15 × 10 × 1-inch pan. Sprinkle with 1 tablespoon sugar.

2   Bake 10 to 12 minutes or until light golden brown. Cool 5 minutes. Cut diagonally into diamond-shaped cookies or into 8 rows by 6 rows to make 48 square cookies.

Food Processor Directions: In food processor, place ¾ cup sugar, the butter, oil, milk, almond extract and egg. Cover; process until light

The Three Little Helpers

Time. You can save it, savor it, spend it or even waste it. With three young children, Kathryn Blackburn found herself baking every day. "To save time, I developed a sugar cookie recipe that could be made as a bar cookie." She entered her one recipe, and several months later found herself a Bake-Off® Contest finalist. Once at the contest, Kathryn wasn't fazed by the bustle. "Actually, it was a lot easier cooking at the Bake-Off® than in my own kitchen with my three little helpers constantly underfoot." But she acknowledges that without the little helpers, she might never have created her winning cookie recipe.

and fluffy. Add flour, baking powder and salt. Cover; process with on/off pulses just until flour is well blended (do not overprocess or cookies will be tough).

High Altitude (3500–6500 ft): Decrease baking powder to 1 teaspoon.

1 Cookie: Calories 50; Total Fat 3g (Saturated Fat 1g; Trans Fat 0g); Cholesterol 10mg; Sodium 40mg; Total Carbohydrate 6g (Dietary Fiber 0g); Exchanges: ½ Other Carbohydrate, ½ Fat; Carbohydrate Choices: ½

Cherry Winks

Ruth Derousseau   Rice Lake, WI
Bake-Off® Contest 2, 1950
$5,000 Winner

> **Prep Time:** 1 Hour 20 Minutes
> **Start to Finish:** 1 Hour 20 Minutes
> 5 dozen cookies

1 cup sugar
¾ cup shortening
2 tablespoons milk
1 teaspoon vanilla
2 eggs
2¼ cups Pillsbury BEST® all-purpose flour
1 teaspoon baking powder
½ teaspoon baking soda
½ teaspoon salt
1 cup chopped pecans
1 cup chopped dates
⅓ cup chopped maraschino cherries, patted dry with paper towels
1½ cups coarsely crushed corn flakes cereal
15 maraschino cherries, quartered

1   In large bowl, beat sugar and shortening with electric mixer on medium speed, scraping bowl occasionally, until well blended. Beat in milk, vanilla and eggs. On low speed, beat in flour, baking powder, baking soda and salt, scraping bowl occasionally, until dough forms. Stir

in pecans, dates and ⅓ cup chopped cherries. If necessary, cover with plastic wrap and refrigerate 15 minutes for easier handling.

2   Heat oven to 375°F. Grease cookie sheets with shortening or cooking spray. Drop dough by rounded teaspoonfuls into cereal; coat thoroughly. Shape into balls. Place 2 inches apart on cookie sheets. Lightly press maraschino cherry quarter into top of each ball.

3   Bake 10 to 15 minutes or until light golden brown. Cool 1 minute; remove from cookie sheets to cooling rack.

High Altitude (3500–6500 ft): No change.

1 Cookie: Calories 80; Total Fat 4g (Saturated Fat 1g; Trans Fat 0g); Cholesterol 5mg; Sodium 45mg; Total Carbohydrate 11g (Dietary Fiber 0g) Exchanges: ½ Other Carbohydrate, 1 Fat; Carbohydrate Choices: 1

Apricot Snowcaps

Virginia Johnson   Blanchardville, WI
Bake-Off® Contest 35, 1992

> **Prep Time:** 1 Hour
> **Start to Finish:** 1 Hour
> About 3 dozen cookies

COOKIES
½ cup sugar
½ cup firmly packed brown sugar
¼ cup butter or margarine, softened
¼ cup shortening
½ teaspoon vanilla
1 egg
1 cup Pillsbury BEST® all-purpose or unbleached flour
½ teaspoon baking powder
½ teaspoon baking soda
½ teaspoon salt
1 cup quick-cooking oats
½ cup apricot filling (from 12-oz can)

GLAZE
1 package (6 oz) white chocolate baking bars, chopped
2 tablespoons shortening

1   Heat oven to 350°F.

2   In large bowl, beat sugar, brown sugar, butter and ¼ cup shortening with electric mixer on medium speed until light and fluffy. Add vanilla and egg; blend well. Add flour, baking powder, baking soda and salt; mix well. Stir in oats. Shape dough into 1-inch balls; place 2 inches apart on ungreased cookie sheets. Make a small indentation in each cookie; fill with ½ teaspoon apricot filling.

3   Bake 9 to 13 minutes or until light golden brown. Cool 1 minute; remove from cookie sheets to cooling rack. Meanwhile, in 1-quart saucepan over very low heat, melt glaze ingredients. Spoon or drizzle over warm cookies. Cool completely.

High Altitude (3500–6500 ft): Decrease sugar to ⅓ cup; increase Pillsbury BEST® flour to 1⅓ cups.

1 Cookie: Calories 120; Total Fat 5g (Saturated Fat 2.5g; Trans Fat 0g); Cholesterol 10mg; Sodium 75mg; Total Carbohydrate 16g (Dietary Fiber 0g) Exchanges: ½ Starch, ½ Other Carbohydrate, 1 Fat; Carbohydrate Choices: 1

Fudgy Bonbons

Mary Anne Tyndall   Whiteville, NC
Bake-Off® Contest 36, 1994
$50,000 Grand Prize Winner

Prep Time: 1 Hour 10 Minutes
Start to Finish: 1 Hour 10 Minutes
5 dozen cookies

1 bag (12 oz) semisweet chocolate
   chips (2 cups)
¼ cup butter or margarine
1 can (14 oz) sweetened condensed
   milk (not evaporated)
2 cups Pillsbury BEST® all-purpose flour
½ cup finely chopped nuts, if desired
1 teaspoon vanilla
60 Hershey®'s Kisses® milk chocolates,
   unwrapped
2 oz white chocolate baking bar or
   vanilla-flavored candy coating
   (almond bark)
1 teaspoon shortening or vegetable oil

1 Heat oven to 350°F. In 2-quart saucepan, heat chocolate chips and butter over very low heat, stirring frequently, until chips are melted and smooth. Stir in sweetened condensed milk (mixture will be stiff).

2 In medium bowl, mix flour, nuts, chocolate mixture and vanilla with spoon until dough forms. Shape 1 measuring tablespoon dough around each milk chocolate candy, covering completely. Place 1 inch apart on ungreased cookie sheets.

3 Bake 6 to 8 minutes (do not overbake). Cookies will be soft and appear shiny but will become firm as they cool. Immediately remove from cookie sheets to cooling rack. Cool completely, about 15 minutes.

4 In 1-quart saucepan, heat white chocolate baking bar and shortening over low heat, stirring occasionally, until melted and smooth. Drizzle over cookies. Allow to set before storing in tightly covered container.

High Altitude (3500–6500 ft): Increase Pillsbury BEST® all-purpose flour to 2¼ cups.

1 Cookie: Calories 100; Total Fat 5g (Saturated Fat 2.5g; Trans Fat 0g); Cholesterol 5mg; Sodium 20mg; Total Carbohydrate 14g (Dietary Fiber 0g) Exchanges: 1 Other Carbohydrate, 1 Fat; Carbohydrate Choices: 1

Hershey's and Kisses trademarks and associated trade dress are registered trademarks of The Hershey Company used under license.

meet mary anne tyndall

"The first Bake-Off® Contest that I remember was in 1969 when the winning recipe was Magic Marshmallow Crescent Puffs," says Mary Anne Tyndall. "I thought, 'My goodness, that is so simple and delicious. I want to do that.'"

Twenty-five years later, she succeeded. Mary Anne won the $50,000 Grand Prize in 1994 with her decadent Fudgy Bonbons. Mary Anne's love of chocolate—and her appreciation for the "Puffs"—inspired her to tuck a chocolate candy into chocolate dough.

"I was looking at a recipe for a drop cookie, and I started to add some ingredients to it," she explains.

"When I added flour, it became the consistency of modeling clay, and I had the idea to wrap the dough around a piece of chocolate and bake it. When I bit into it, it was so soft and yummy."

Although Mary Anne dreamed about entering the contest for years, she didn't expect all the attention she received when she returned home to Whiteville, North Carolina.

Perhaps most memorable was hearing from people she hadn't seen in years. A former high school teacher, Mary Anne received congratulations from her students, now living all over the country, who heard about her win on the TV news. "I think I was in a fog because it all happened so fast," she explains. "But it was so fun."

Chocolate-Cherry Bars

Francis I. Jerzak   Porter, MN
Bake-Off® Contest 25, 1974
$25,000 Winner

> **Prep Time:** 15 Minutes
> **Start to Finish:** 2 Hours
> 48 bars

BARS
1 box (18.25 oz) Pillsbury® Moist
   Supreme® devil's food cake mix
1 can (21 oz) cherry pie filling
1 teaspoon almond extract
2 eggs, beaten

FROSTING
1 cup sugar
⅓ cup milk
5 tablespoons butter or margarine
1 cup semisweet chocolate chips (6 oz)

1   Heat oven to 350°F (325°F for dark or nonstick pan). Grease 15 × 10 × 1-inch or 13 × 9-inch pan with shortening or cooking spray; lightly flour. In large bowl, mix bar ingredients with spoon until well blended. Spread in pan.

2   Bake 15 × 10 × 1-inch pan 20 to 30 minutes, 13 × 9-inch pan 25 to 30 minutes or until toothpick inserted in center comes out clean.

3   In 1-quart saucepan, mix sugar, milk and butter. Heat to boiling. Boil 1 minute, stirring constantly. Remove from heat. Stir in chocolate chips until smooth. Pour and spread over warm bars. Cool completely in pan on cooling rack, about 1 hour 15 minutes. For bars, cut into 8 rows by 6 rows.

High Altitude (3500–6500 ft): Bake 15 × 10 × 1-inch pan 25 to 35 minutes, 13×9-inch pan 30 to 35 minutes.

1 Bar: Calories 110; Total Fat 3.5g (Saturated Fat 2g; Trans Fat 0g); Cholesterol 10mg; Sodium 95mg; Total Carbohydrate 19g (Dietary Fiber 0g) Exchanges: 1½ Other Carbohydrate, ½ Fat; Carbohydrate Choices: 1

Rocky Road Fudge Bars

Mary Wilson   Leesburg, GA
Bake-Off® Contest 23, 1972
$5,000 Winner

> **Prep Time:** 25 Minutes
> **Start to Finish:** 2 Hours
> 48 bars

BASE
½ cup butter or margarine
1 oz unsweetened baking chocolate,
   cut into pieces
1 cup Pillsbury BEST® all-purpose flour
1 cup granulated sugar
1 teaspoon baking powder
1 teaspoon vanilla
2 eggs
¾ cup chopped nuts

FILLING
6 oz cream cheese (from 8-oz package),
   softened
¼ cup butter or margarine, softened
½ cup granulated sugar
2 tablespoons Pillsbury BEST®
   all-purpose flour
½ teaspoon vanilla
1 egg
¼ cup chopped nuts
1 cup semisweet chocolate chips (6 oz)
2 cups miniature marshmallows

FROSTING
Remaining 2 oz cream cheese
   (from 8-oz package)
¼ cup butter or margarine
¼ cup milk
1 oz unsweetened baking chocolate,
   cut into pieces
3 cups powdered sugar
1 teaspoon vanilla

1   Heat oven to 350°F. Grease 13 × 9-inch pan with shortening or cooking spray; lightly flour.

In 2-quart saucepan, melt ½ cup butter and 1 ounce baking chocolate over low heat, stirring until smooth. Remove from heat. Stir in 1 cup flour and remaining base ingredients until well mixed. Spread in pan.

2   In small bowl, beat 6 ounces cream cheese, ¼ cup butter, ½ cup granulated sugar, 2 tablespoons flour, ½ teaspoon vanilla and 1 egg with electric mixer on medium speed 1 minute, scraping bowl occasionally, until smooth and fluffy. Stir in ¼ cup nuts. Spread over chocolate mixture; sprinkle evenly with chocolate chips.

3   Bake 25 to 35 minutes or until toothpick inserted in center comes out clean. Immediately sprinkle with marshmallows.

4   Bake 2 minutes longer. Meanwhile, in 3-quart saucepan, heat remaining 2 ounces cream cheese, ¼ cup butter, the milk and 1 ounce baking chocolate over low heat, stirring until well blended. Remove from heat. Stir in powdered sugar and 1 teaspoon vanilla until smooth. Immediately pour frosting over puffed marshmallows. Refrigerate until firm, about 1 hour. For bars, cut into 8 rows by 6 rows. Cover and refrigerate any remaining bars.

High Altitude (3500–6500 ft): No change.

1 Bar: Calories 170; Total Fat 9g (Saturated Fat 5g; Trans Fat 0g); Cholesterol 30mg; Sodium 60mg; Total Carbohydrate 21g (Dietary Fiber 0g) Exchanges: ½ Starch, 1 Other Carbohydrate, 1½ Fat; Carbohydrate Choices: 1½

The Big Easy Inspiration

Inspiration can be right under your nose—or across the country. Oregonian Joanna Crumley says her recipe was inspired by a trip to New Orleans, where she discovered pralines. Joanna then paired the sweet goodness of pralines' brown sugar and pecans with her longtime favorites, chocolate chip cookies and brownies. The result: Praline Brookies.

Praline Brookies

Joanna Crumley   Hubbard, OR
Bake-Off® Contest 42, 2006

> **Prep Time:** 20 Minutes
> **Start to Finish:** 3 Hours 30 Minutes
> 24 brownies

1 box (19.5 oz) Pillsbury® Brownie Classics traditional fudge brownie mix
Vegetable oil, water and eggs called for on brownie mix box
¼ cup butter or margarine
¼ cup milk
½ cup granulated sugar
½ cup packed brown sugar
½ cup coarsely chopped pecans
½ teaspoon vanilla
1 roll (16.5 oz) Pillsbury® Create 'n Bake® refrigerated chocolate chip cookies

1   Heat oven to 350°F (325°F for dark pan). Grease 13 × 9-inch pan with shortening or cooking spray. Make brownie batter as directed on box. Spread batter evenly in pan.

2   Bake 25 minutes. Meanwhile, in 2-quart saucepan, heat butter, milk, sugars, pecans and vanilla to boiling over medium heat, stirring constantly. Reduce heat to medium-low; simmer 3 minutes, stirring occasionally. Remove from heat; set aside until brownies are baked.

3   Immediately pour praline mixture evenly over partially baked brownies. Cut cookie dough crosswise into 4 equal pieces; cut each piece into 4 slices. Carefully place slices in 3 rows of 5 slices each, using last slice to fill in spaces. (Spaces between cookie dough pieces will spread during baking to cover top.)

4   Bake 23 to 28 minutes longer or until cookie topping is deep golden brown. Cool 2 hours. For brownies, cut into 6 rows by 4 rows.

High Altitude (3500–6500 ft): Follow High Altitude brownie mix directions for 13 × 9-inch pan. Bake 26 to 31 minutes.

1 Brownie: Calories 300; Total Fat 14g (Saturated Fat 3.5g; Trans Fat 1g); Cholesterol 25mg; Sodium 140mg; Total Carbohydrate 40g (Dietary Fiber 1g) Exchanges: ½ Starch, 2 Other Carbohydrate, 3 Fat; Carbohydrate Choices: 2½

Amaretto Coffee Brownies

Ken Halverson   Big Lake, MN
Bake-Off® Contest 38, 1998

> **Prep Time:** 25 Minutes
> **Start to Finish:** 2 Hours 40 Minutes
> 24 brownies

12 oz cream cheese, softened
1 jar (7 oz) marshmallow creme (1½ cups)
2 tablespoons instant coffee granules or crystals
1 tablespoon amaretto or 1 teaspoon almond extract
1 box (19.5 oz) Pillsbury® Brownie Classics traditional fudge brownie mix
½ cup butter or margarine, softened
⅓ cup milk
2 eggs
¾ cup chopped walnuts

1   Heat oven to 350°F. Grease 13 × 9-inch pan with shortening or cooking spray. In large bowl, beat cream cheese, marshmallow creme, coffee granules and amaretto with electric mixer on medium speed until smooth; set aside.

2   In another large bowl, beat brownie mix and butter with electric mixer on low speed 45 to 60 seconds or until crumbly. Reserve 1 cup brownie mixture in small bowl for topping. Add milk and eggs to remaining brownie mixture; beat until smooth. Spread batter evenly in pan.

3   Spread cream cheese mixture evenly over brownie mixture. Stir walnuts into reserved 1 cup brownie mixture; sprinkle evenly over cream cheese mixture.

4 Bake 40 to 45 minutes or until edges are firm to the touch. Cool completely, about 1 hour 30 minutes. For brownies, cut into 6 rows by 4 rows. Store in refrigerator.

High Altitude (3500–6500 ft): Add ½ cup Pillsbury BEST® all-purpose flour to dry brownie mix. Bake 45 to 50 minutes.

1 Brownie: Calories 250; Total Fat 14g (Saturated Fat 6g; Trans Fat 0g); Cholesterol 45mg; Sodium 150mg; Total Carbohydrate 27g (Dietary Fiber 1g) Exchanges: 1 Starch, 1 Other Carbohydrate, 2½ Fat; Carbohydrate Choices: 2

Triple Espresso Brownies

Sheryl Hakko Eugene, OR
Bake-Off® Contest 34, 1990

> **Prep Time:** 20 Minutes
> **Start to Finish:** 1 Hour 45 Minutes
> 48 brownies

BROWNIES
1 box (19.5 oz) Pillsbury® Brownie
  Classics traditional fudge
  brownie mix
Vegetable oil, water and eggs called
  for on brownie mix box
2 teaspoons instant espresso coffee
  granules
1 teaspoon vanilla

FILLING
¼ cup butter or margarine, softened
½ cup packed brown sugar
1 egg
2 teaspoons instant espresso coffee
  granules
1 teaspoon vanilla
1 cup coarsely chopped walnuts
2 bars (5 oz each) sweet dark baking
  chocolate or 1 bar (9.7 oz)
  semisweet dark baking chocolate

GLAZE
½ cup semisweet chocolate chips
1 tablespoon butter or margarine
⅛ teaspoon instant espresso coffee
  granules
1 to 2 teaspoons milk or whipping cream

1 Heat oven to 350°F. Grease bottom only of 13 × 9-inch pan with shortening or cooking spray. In large bowl, beat brownie ingredients 50 strokes with spoon. Spread in pan.

2 Bake 28 minutes. Meanwhile, in small bowl, beat ¼ cup butter and the brown sugar with electric mixer on medium speed until light and fluffy. Add 1 egg, 2 teaspoons coffee granules and 1 teaspoon vanilla; beat until well blended. In medium bowl, mix walnuts and chopped chocolate. With spoon, stir in brown sugar mixture until well blended. Spoon and carefully spread filling over baked brownies.

3 Bake 17 to 20 minutes longer or until light brown.

4 In 1-quart saucepan, melt chocolate chips and 1 tablespoon butter over low heat, stirring constantly, until smooth. Remove from heat. With wire whisk, stir in ⅛ teaspoon coffee granules and enough milk for desired drizzling consistency. Drizzle over warm brownies. Cool completely, about 45 minutes. For brownies, cut into 8 rows by 6 rows.

High Altitude (3500–6500 ft): Add ½ cup Pillsbury BEST® all-purpose flour to dry brownie mix. Increase water to ⅓ cup.

1 Brownie: Calories 150; Total Fat 9g (Saturated Fat 3g; Trans Fat 0g); Cholesterol 15mg; Sodium 45mg; Total Carbohydrate 17g (Dietary Fiber 1g) Exchanges: 1 Other Carbohydrate, 2 Fat; Carbohydrate Choices: 1

Reading the News and Eating it Too

Many Bake-Off® Contest recipes have been inspired by trends and world events in the news. Split Levels and Steady Daters (both cookies) popped up in the 1950s; Jam Session Coffee Cake, Cheese-Niks (inspired by the Russian-launched Sputnik) and Meat Balls a Go-Go followed in the 1960s. Edelweiss Fudge Pie trailed on the heels of the movie *The Sound of Music,* and Cheesy Moon Bread and Hawaiian Moon Drops celebrated the achievement of the imperiled journey of Apollo 13.

Caramel Swirl Cheesecake Brownies

Rebecca Moe   Carmichael, CA
Bake-Off® Contest 36, 1994
$2,000 Winner

Prep Time: 30 Minutes
Start to Finish: 2 Hours 45 Minutes
24 brownies

BASE

1 box (19.5 oz) Pillsbury® Brownie
    Classics traditional fudge
    brownie mix
½ cup butter or margarine, softened
¼ cup creamy peanut butter
1 egg

FILLING

2 packages (8 oz each) cream cheese,
    softened
⅓ cup creamy peanut butter
1 cup granulated sugar
3 tablespoons Pillsbury BEST®
    all-purpose flour
¼ cup sour cream
2 teaspoons vanilla
2 eggs

CARAMEL SAUCE

12 caramels, unwrapped
3 tablespoons whipping cream

1   Heat oven to 325°F. Grease bottom only of 13 × 9-inch pan with shortening or cooking spray. In large bowl, beat base ingredients with spoon until dough forms. Press lightly in bottom of pan.

2   In large bowl, beat cream cheese and ⅓ cup peanut butter with electric mixer on low speed until smooth. Add granulated sugar, flour, sour cream and vanilla; beat until blended. Add 2 eggs, 1 at a time, beating just until blended. Pour filling over base.

3   In 1-quart heavy saucepan, cook caramels and whipping cream over low heat, stirring constantly, until caramels are melted and mixture is smooth. Drop spoonfuls of caramel sauce randomly over filling. For swirl design, pull knife through batter in wide curves; turn pan and repeat.

4   Bake 35 to 45 minutes or until center is set and edges are light golden brown. Cool in pan on cooling rack 30 minutes. Refrigerate 1 hour before serving. For brownies, cut into 6 rows by 4 rows. Cover and refrigerate any remaining brownies.

High Altitude (3500–6500 ft): Add 2 tablespoons Pillsbury BEST® all-purpose flour to dry brownie mix.

1 Brownie: Calories 320; Total Fat 18g (Saturated Fat 9g; Trans Fat 0g); Cholesterol 60mg; Sodium 200mg; Total Carbohydrate 34g (Dietary Fiber 1g) Exchanges: 1 Starch, 1½ Other Carbohydrate, 3 ½ Fat; Carbohydrate Choices: 2

Oatmeal Carmelitas

Erlyce Larson   Kennedy, MN
Bake-Off® Contest 18, 1967

Prep Time: 30 Minutes
Start to Finish: 2 Hours 55 Minutes
36 bars

BASE

2 cups Pillsbury BEST® all-purpose flour
2 cups quick-cooking oats
1½ cups packed brown sugar
1 teaspoon baking soda
½ teaspoon salt
1¼ cups butter or margarine, softened

FILLING

1 jar (12.5 oz) caramel topping (1 cup)
3 tablespoons Pillsbury BEST®
    all-purpose flour
1 cup semisweet chocolate chips (6 oz)
½ cup chopped nuts

1   Heat oven to 350°F. Grease 13 × 9-inch pan with shortening or cooking spray. In large bowl, beat base ingredients with electric mixer on low speed until crumbly. Reserve half of crumb mixture (about 3 cups) for topping. Press remaining crumb mixture in bottom of pan.

2   Bake 10 minutes. Meanwhile, in small bowl, mix caramel topping and 3 tablespoons flour. Sprinkle chocolate chips and nuts over partially baked base. Drizzle evenly with caramel mixture; sprinkle with reserved crumb mixture.

3   Bake 18 to 22 minutes longer or until golden brown. Cool completely in pan on cooling rack, about 1 hour. Refrigerate until filling is set, 1 to 2 hours. For bars, cut into 6 rows by 6 rows. Store tightly covered.

High Altitude (3500–6500 ft): No change.

1 Bar: Calories 200; Total Fat 9g (Saturated Fat 5g; Trans Fat 0g); Cholesterol 15mg; Sodium 150mg; Total Carbohydrate 27g (Dietary Fiber 1g) Exchanges: ½ Starch, 1½ Other Carbohydrate, 1½ Fat; Carbohydrate Choices: 2

Oatmeal Carmelitas

Chewy Chocolate–Peanut Butter Bars

Chewy Chocolate–Peanut Butter Bars

Marjorie Bergemann Greenbelt, MD
Bake-Off® Contest 39, 2000
$2,000 Winner

> **Prep Time:** 15 Minutes
> **Start to Finish:** 2 Hours 45 Minutes
> 36 bars

1 roll (16.5 oz) Pillsbury® Create 'n Bake® refrigerated sugar cookies
1 can (14 oz) sweetened condensed milk (not evaporated)
1 cup crunchy peanut butter
1 teaspoon vanilla
3 egg yolks
1 bag (12 oz) semisweet chocolate chips (2 cups)

1 Heat oven to 350°F. Spray 13 × 9-inch pan with cooking spray. Cut cookie dough in half crosswise. Cut each section in half lengthwise. Press dough evenly in bottom of pan to form crust.

2 Bake 10 minutes. Meanwhile, in medium bowl, mix condensed milk, peanut butter, vanilla and egg yolks until smooth. Spoon milk mixture evenly over partially baked crust; carefully spread.

3 Bake 20 to 25 minutes longer or until set. Sprinkle with chocolate chips; let stand 3 minutes to soften. Spread chocolate evenly over top. Cool completely, about 1 hour 30 minutes. Refrigerate until chocolate is set, about 30 minutes. For bars, cut into 6 rows by 6 rows.

High Altitude (3500–6500 ft): Bake crust 12 to 15 minutes.

1 Bar: Calories 190; Total Fat 10g (Saturated Fat 4g; Trans Fat 0.5g); Cholesterol 25mg; Sodium 85mg; Total Carbohydrate 21g (Dietary Fiber 0g) Exchanges: ½ Starch, 1 Other Carbohydrate, 2 Fat; Carbohydrate Choices: 1½

Raspberry-Filled White Chocolate Bars

Mark Bocianski Wheaton, IL
Bake-Off® Contest 34, 1990

> **Prep Time:** 25 Minutes
> **Start to Finish:** 2 Hours 20 Minutes
> 24 bars

½ cup butter or margarine
1 bag (12 oz) white vanilla baking chips (2 cups) or 12 oz white chocolate baking bars, chopped
2 eggs
½ cup sugar
1 cup Pillsbury BEST® all-purpose flour
½ teaspoon salt
1 teaspoon amaretto or almond extract
½ cup raspberry spreadable fruit or jam
¼ cup sliced almonds, toasted*

1 Heat oven to 325°F. Grease 9-inch square pan or 8-inch square (1½-quart) glass baking dish with shortening or cooking spray; lightly flour. In 1-quart saucepan, melt butter over low heat. Remove from heat. Add 1 cup of the baking chips (or 6 ounces chopped baking bar). LET STAND; DO NOT STIR.

2 Meanwhile, in large bowl, beat eggs with electric mixer on high speed until frothy. Gradually beat in sugar until lemon colored. On medium speed, beat in baking chip mixture. On low speed, beat in flour, salt and amaretto just until combined. Spread half of batter (about 1 cup) in pan. Set remaining batter aside.

3 Bake 15 to 20 minutes or until light golden brown.

4 Stir remaining 1 cup baking chips (or 6 ounces chopped baking bar) into remaining half of batter; set aside. In 1-quart saucepan, melt spreadable fruit over low heat. Spread evenly over warm, partially baked crust. Gently spoon teaspoonfuls of remaining batter over spreadable fruit. (Some fruit may show through batter.) Sprinkle with almonds.

5 Bake 25 to 35 minutes longer or until toothpick inserted in center comes out clean. Cool completely, about 1 hour. For bars, cut into 6 rows by 4 rows.

* To toast almonds, spread in ungreased shallow pan and bake at 350°F 6 to 10 minutes, stirring occasionally, until light brown.

High Altitude (3500–6500 ft): No change.

1 Bar: Calories 170; Total Fat 9g (Saturated Fat 5g; Trans Fat 0g); Cholesterol 30mg; Sodium 110mg; Total Carbohydrate 21g (Dietary Fiber 0g) Exchanges: 1½ Other Carbohydrate, 2 Fat; Carbohydrate Choices: 1½

Cherry Truffle Squares

Catherine Stovern Veteran, WY
Bake-Off® Contest 39, 2000

> **Prep Time:** 15 Minutes
> **Start to Finish:** 1 Hour 40 Minutes
> 48 squares

CRUST
1 roll (16.5 oz) Pillsbury® Create 'n
   Bake® refrigerated sugar cookies

FILLING
⅓ cup semisweet chocolate chips
¼ cup butter or margarine
¼ cup unsweetened baking cocoa
3 tablespoons light corn syrup
1 tablespoon milk
2 cups powdered sugar
1 jar (10 oz) maraschino cherries (about
   30 cherries), drained, chopped

TOPPING
1 cup white vanilla baking chips (6 oz)
2 tablespoons shortening

GARNISH, IF DESIRED
Chocolate shavings or curls

1 Heat oven to 350°F. Cut cookie dough in half crosswise. Cut each section in half lengthwise. Press dough in bottom of ungreased 13 × 9-inch pan to form base.

2 Bake 12 to 16 minutes or until light golden brown. Cool completely, about 45 minutes.

3 In medium microwavable bowl, microwave chocolate chips and butter uncovered on High 1 to 2 minutes, stirring every 30 seconds, until melted and smooth. Stir in cocoa, corn syrup and milk until well blended. Stir in powdered sugar until smooth. Press mixture over cooled crust. Top with cherries; gently press into filling.

4 In small microwavable bowl, microwave baking chips and shortening uncovered on High 30 seconds. Stir; continue microwaving, stirring every 10 seconds, until chips are melted and can be stirred smooth. Spoon and spread over filling. Refrigerate about 20 minutes or until set. For squares, cut into 8 rows by 6 rows. Garnish each square with chocolate shavings.

High Altitude (3500–6500 ft): No change.

1 Square: Calories 110; Total Fat 5g (Saturated Fat 2g; Trans Fat 0.5g); Cholesterol 5mg; Sodium 40mg; Total Carbohydrate 16g (Dietary Fiber 0g) Exchanges: 1 Other Carbohydrate, 1 Fat; Carbohydrate Choices: 1

Mock Lemon Meringue Bars

Robin Janine Peterson Peoria, AZ
Bake-Off® Contest 42, 2006

> **Prep Time:** 15 Minutes
> **Start to Finish:** 2 Hours 5 Minutes
> 24 bars

1 roll (16.5 oz) Pillsbury® Create 'n
   Bake® refrigerated sugar cookies
1 cup lemon curd (from 11¼- to 12-oz jar)
1 package (3 oz) cream cheese,
   softened
½ cup marshmallow creme
1 container (6 oz) French vanilla fat-free
   yogurt
1 cup frozen (thawed) whipped topping

1 Heat oven to 350°F. Grease 13 × 9-inch pan with shortening or cooking spray. In pan, break up cookie dough. Press dough evenly in bottom of pan to form crust.

2 Bake 15 to 20 minutes or until edges are golden brown and center is set. Cool 30 minutes.

3 Spread lemon curd over cooled crust. In large bowl, beat cream cheese, marshmallow creme and yogurt with wooden spoon until well blended. Fold in whipped topping. Spread over lemon curd, swirling to look like meringue topping. Refrigerate at least 1 hour until serving time. For bars, cut into 6 rows by 4 rows. Cover and refrigerate any remaining bars.

High Altitude (3500–6500 ft): No change.

1 Bar: Calories 160; Total Fat 7g (Saturated Fat 2.5g; Trans Fat 1g); Cholesterol 20mg; Sodium 80mg; Total Carbohydrate 25g (Dietary Fiber 0g) Exchanges: 1½ Other Carbohydrate, 1½ Fat; Carbohydrate Choices: 1½

Mock Lemon Meringue Bars

White Chocolate–Key Lime Calypso Bars

Didi Fraioli Huntington, NY
Bake-Off® Contest 40, 2002

Prep Time: 20 Minutes
Start to Finish: 3 Hours 5 Minutes
36 bars

1 roll (16.5 oz) Pillsbury® Create 'n Bake® refrigerated sugar cookies
1 cup chopped pistachio nuts
1 cup coconut
1½ cups white vanilla baking chips (9 oz)
1 can (14 oz) sweetened condensed milk (not evaporated)
½ cup Key lime juice, fresh lime juice or frozen (thawed) limeade concentrate
3 egg yolks
1 teaspoon vegetable oil

1 Heat oven to 350°F. Grease 13 × 9-inch pan with shortening or cooking spray. In large bowl, break up cookie dough. Stir or knead in nuts and coconut until well blended. Press dough mixture evenly in bottom of pan to form crust. Sprinkle 1 cup of the vanilla baking chips over dough; press lightly into dough.

2 Bake 14 to 16 minutes or until light golden brown. Meanwhile, in medium bowl, beat condensed milk, lime juice and egg yolks with spoon until well blended. Pour milk mixture evenly over crust.

3 Bake 20 to 25 minutes longer or until filling is set.

4 In small microwavable bowl, microwave remaining ½ cup vanilla baking chips and the oil uncovered on High 45 seconds. Stir until smooth; if necessary, microwave 15 seconds longer. Drizzle over warm bars. Cool at room temperature 1 hour. Refrigerate until chilled, about 1 hour. For bars, cut into 6 rows by 6 rows. Cover and refrigerate any remaining bars.

High Altitude (3500–6500 ft): Bake crust 16 to 18 minutes.

1 Bar: Calories 170; Total Fat 8g (Saturated Fat 3.5g; Trans Fat 0.5g); Cholesterol 25mg; Sodium 70mg; Total Carbohydrate 20g (Dietary Fiber 0g) Exchanges: ½ Starch, 1 Other Carbohydrate, 1½ Fat; Carbohydrate Choices: 1

Chocolate Chip, Oats 'n Caramel Cookie Squares

Niela Frantellizzi Boca Raton, FL
Bake-Off® Contest 37, 1996

Prep Time: 35 Minutes
Start to Finish: 2 Hours 40 Minutes
16 bars

1 roll (16.5 oz) Pillsbury® Create 'n Bake® refrigerated chocolate chip cookies
1 cup quick-cooking oats
Dash salt, if desired
⅔ cup caramel topping
5 tablespoons Pillsbury BEST® all-purpose flour
1 teaspoon vanilla
¾ cup chopped walnuts
1 bag (6 oz) semisweet chocolate chips (1 cup)

1 Heat oven to 350°F. In large bowl, break up cookie dough. Stir or knead in oats and salt. Reserve ½ cup dough for topping. In ungreased 9-inch square pan, press remaining dough mixture evenly in bottom to form crust.

2 Bake 10 to 12 minutes or until dough puffs and appears dry.

3 In small bowl, mix caramel topping, flour and vanilla until well blended. Sprinkle walnuts and chocolate chips evenly over crust. Drizzle evenly with caramel mixture. Crumble reserved ½ cup dough mixture over caramel.

4 Bake 20 to 25 minutes longer or until golden brown. Cool 10 minutes. Run knife around sides of pan to loosen bars. Cool completely, about 1 hour 30 minutes. For bars, cut into 4 rows by 4 rows. Store tightly covered.

High Altitude (3500–6500 ft): Bake crust 12 to 14 minutes. After topping crust, bake 22 to 27 minutes longer.

1 Bar: Calories 280; Total Fat 12g (Saturated Fat 4g; Trans Fat 1g); Cholesterol 5mg; Sodium 140mg; Total Carbohydrate 40g (Dietary Fiber 1g) Exchanges: 1 Starch, 1½ Other Carbohydrate, 2½ Fat; Carbohydrate Choices: 2½

Chocolate Chip, Oats 'n Caramel Cookie Squares

Caramel Cashew Bars

Kathleen Kildsig Kiel, WI
Bake-Off® Contest 40, 2002
$2,000 Winner

> **Prep Time:** 20 Minutes
> **Start to Finish:** 1 Hour 20 Minutes
> 36 bars

1 roll (16.5 oz) Pillsbury® Create 'n Bake® refrigerated chocolate chip cookies
1 bag (11.5 oz) milk chocolate chips (2 cups)
1 container (18 oz) caramel apple dip (1½ cups)
3 cups crisp rice cereal
1¼ cups chopped cashews

1 Heat oven to 350°F. In ungreased 13 × 9-inch pan, break up cookie dough. Press dough evenly in bottom of pan to form crust.

2 Bake 15 to 18 minutes or until light golden brown. Cool 15 minutes.

3 Meanwhile, in 3- to 4-quart saucepan, heat 1 cup of the chocolate chips and 1 cup of the dip over medium heat, stirring constantly, until melted and smooth. Remove from heat. Stir in cereal and cashews.

4 Spread cereal mixture over crust. In 1-quart saucepan, heat remaining chocolate chips and dip over medium heat, stirring constantly, until melted and smooth. Spread over cereal mixture. Refrigerate until chocolate mixture is set, about 30 minutes. For bars, cut into 6 by 6 rows.

High Altitude (3500–6500 ft): Bake crust 16 to 19 minutes.

1 Bar: Calories 180; Total Fat 7g (Saturated Fat 2.5g; Trans Fat 0g); Cholesterol 0mg; Sodium 120mg; Total Carbohydrate 26g (Dietary Fiber 0g) Exchanges: 1 Starch, 1 Other Carbohydrate, 1 Fat; Carbohydrate Choices: 2

Peanut Butter Custard Bars

Norita Solt Bettendorf, IA
Bake-Off® Contest 42, 2006

> **Prep Time:** 20 Minutes
> **Start to Finish:** 2 Hours 40 Minutes
> 36 bars

1 roll (16.5 oz) Pillsbury® Create 'n Bake® refrigerated peanut butter cookies
1 bag (10 oz) peanut butter chips
3 eggs
½ cup packed light brown sugar
3 tablespoons peanut butter
2 containers (6 oz each) crème caramel thick & creamy low-fat yogurt
4 peanut butter crunchy granola bars (2 pouches from 8.9-oz box), crushed (¾ cup)*

1 Heat oven to 350°F. Grease 13 × 9-inch pan with shortening or cooking spray. Press cookie dough evenly in bottom of pan. Sprinkle with peanut butter chips; press lightly into dough. Set aside.

2 In medium bowl, beat eggs, brown sugar, peanut butter and yogurt with wire whisk until thoroughly blended. Pour mixture over dough. Sprinkle crushed granola bars evenly over top of egg mixture.

3 Bake 40 to 50 minutes or until bars pull away from edges of pan and are set in center. Cool completely in pan, about 1 hour 30 minutes. Cut into 9 rows by 4 rows. Cover and refrigerate any remaining bars.

To easily crush granola bars, do not unwrap; use rolling pin to crush bars.

High Altitude (3500–6500 ft): Break up cookie dough into bowl; knead or stir 3 tablespoons Pillsbury BEST® all-purpose flour into dough. Press dough in pan.

1 Bar: Calories 150; Total Fat 7g (Saturated Fat 1.5g; Trans Fat 0g); Cholesterol 20mg; Sodium 110mg; Total Carbohydrate 18g (Dietary Fiber 0g) Exchanges: 1 Starch, 1½ Fat; Carbohydrate Choices: 1

Sugar-Crusted Almond Pastries

Karla Kunoff Bloomington, IN
Bake-Off® Contest 37, 1996
$2,000 Winner

> **Prep Time:** 15 Minutes
> **Start to Finish:** 1 Hour
> 36 bars

2 cans (8 oz each) Pillsbury® refrigerated crescent dinner rolls
½ cup butter (do not use margarine)
2 cups slivered almonds
1⅓ cups sugar

1 Heat oven to 375°F. Unroll both cans of dough into 2 large rectangles. Place in ungreased 15 × 10 × 1-inch pan; press over bottom to form crust, firmly pressing perforations to seal.

2 In 2-quart saucepan, melt butter over medium heat. Add almonds and sugar; cook 5 to 8 minutes, stirring frequently, until almonds just begin to brown. Spoon and spread mixture evenly over dough.

3 Bake 11 to 16 minutes or until crust is deep golden brown. Cool 30 minutes. For bars, cut into 6 rows by 6 rows. Serve warm or cool.

High Altitude (3500–6500 ft): In step 1, prebake crust 5 minutes. In step 3, bake 13 to 18 minutes.

1 Bar: Calories 140; Total Fat 8g (Saturated Fat 2.5g; Trans Fat 1g); Cholesterol 5mg; Sodium 115mg; Total Carbohydrate 13g (Dietary Fiber 0g) Exchanges: ½ Starch, ½ Other Carbohydrate, 1½ Fat; Carbohydrate Choices: 1

Sugar-Crusted Almond Pastries

meet isabelle collins

SHARING HER EXPERIENCES with earning the $25,000 Grand Prize at the 1972 Bake-Off® Contest, Isabelle Collins says, "We were in the process of a little do-it-yourself project at the time I won." In reality, Isabelle and her family were building a new home, and she was so busy, "I couldn't even remember the recipe I submitted," she admits.

She's still amazed her easy-to-make Quick 'n Chewy Crescent Bars won the top prize. "You just press out the crescent rolls," she says. "It's so simple!"

For Isabelle, winning couldn't have come at a better time. "There were a lot of hidden expenses on the house that we weren't expecting, and we were about $1,000 behind on our bills." When a contest photographer came to take her picture, the family was living in the basement of the unfinished home, with no kitchen. Isabelle had to run over to a neighbor's house to bake her bars for the photo.

Winning the Bake-Off® Contest changed that whole picture. The money allowed Isabelle to finish the house, put in a garage, sidewalks and draperies, and purchase a pickup truck. It also enabled her to be a stay-at-home mom. "It was really a godsend," Isabelle said. "It landed in our laps at a time when we really needed it."

Quick 'n Chewy Crescent Bars

Isabelle Collins   Ramona, CA
Bake-Off® Contest 23, 1972
$25,000 One of Two Grand Prize Winners

Prep Time: 15 Minutes
Start to Finish: 1 Hour 30 Minutes
48 bars

1 cup coconut
¾ cup packed brown sugar
½ cup Pillsbury BEST® all-purpose flour
½ cup chopped pecans
¼ cup butter or margarine
1 can (8 oz) Pillsbury® refrigerated crescent dinner rolls
1 can (14 oz) sweetened condensed milk (not evaporated)

1 Heat oven to 400°F. In medium bowl, mix coconut, brown sugar, flour and pecans. With pastry blender or fork, cut in butter until mixture looks like coarse crumbs. Set aside.

2 Unroll dough into 2 long rectangles. Place rectangles in ungreased 15 × 10 × 1-inch pan; press in bottom of pan, firmly pressing perforations to seal.

3 Pour condensed milk evenly over dough; spread to within ½ inch of edges. Sprinkle coconut mixture over condensed milk; press in lightly.

4 Bake 12 to 15 minutes or until deep golden brown. Cool completely in pan on cooling rack, about 1 hour. For bars, cut into 8 rows by 6 rows.

High Altitude (3500–6500 ft): After pressing dough in bottom of pan and sealing perforations, bake 3 minutes.

1 Bar: Calories 90; Total Fat 4g (Saturated Fat 2g; Trans Fat 0g); Cholesterol 5mg; Sodium 60mg; Total Carbohydrate 12g (Dietary Fiber 0g) Exchanges: 1 Other Carbohydrate, 1 Fat; Carbohydrate Choices: 1

Pecan Pie Surprise Bars

Pearl Hall   Snohomish, WA
Bake-Off® Contest 22, 1971
$25,000 Grand Prize Winner

Prep Time: 15 Minutes
Start to Finish: 1 Hour 55 Minutes
36 bars

BASE
1 box (18.25 oz) Pillsbury® Moist
  Supreme® classic yellow or golden
  butter recipe cake mix
⅓ cup butter or margarine, softened
1 egg

FILLING
Reserved ⅔ cup dry cake mix
½ cup packed brown sugar
1½ cups dark corn syrup
1 teaspoon vanilla
3 eggs
1 cup chopped pecans

1   Heat oven to 350°F. Grease
13 × 9-inch pan with shortening
or cooking spray. Reserve ⅔ cup of
the dry cake mix for filling. In large
bowl, beat remaining dry cake mix,
the butter and 1 egg with electric
mixer on low speed until well
blended. Press in bottom of pan.

2   Bake 15 to 20 minutes or until
light golden brown. Meanwhile,
in large bowl, beat reserved ⅔ cup
dry cake mix, the brown sugar,
corn syrup, vanilla and 3 eggs on
low speed until moistened. Beat

on medium speed about 1 minute
or until well blended. Pour filling
mixture over warm base; sprinkle
with pecans.

3   Bake 30 to 35 minutes longer or
until filling is set. Cool completely
in pan on cooling rack, about 45 minutes. For bars, cut into 6 rows by
6 rows. Cover and refrigerate any
remaining bars.

High Altitude (3500–6500 ft): Heat oven
to 375°F. Stir ⅓ cup Pillsbury BEST®
all-purpose flour into dry cake mix before
removing ⅔ cup for filling. Decrease dark
corn syrup to 1¼ cups.

1 Bar: Calories 160; Total Fat 5g (Saturated Fat 2g;
Trans Fat 0g); Cholesterol 30mg; Sodium 120mg;
Total Carbohydrate 26g (Dietary Fiber 0g) Exchanges:
½ Starch, 1½ Other Carbohydrate, 1 Fat; Carbohydrate
Choices: 2

Cereal S'more Bars

Barbara Styles   St. Cloud, MN
Bake-Off® Contest 41, 2004

Prep Time: 15 Minutes
Start to Finish: 45 Minutes
24 bars

3 cups frosted cocoa corn puff cereal
3 cups honey graham cereal squares
1 cup peanuts
½ cup peanut butter
1 bag (10.5 oz) miniature marshmallows
2 tablespoons milk

1   Spray bottom and sides of
13 × 9-inch pan with cooking spray
or grease with shortening. In large
bowl, mix cereals and peanuts.

2   In 3-quart saucepan, heat peanut
butter, marshmallows and milk over
low heat, stirring occasionally, until
peanut butter and marshmallows
are melted and mixture is smooth.

3   Pour peanut butter mixture over
cereal mixture, stirring to coat well.
Press mixture in pan. Cool at least
30 minutes before serving. For bars,
cut into 6 rows by 4 rows.

High Altitude (3500–6500 ft): No change.

1 Bar: Calories 150; Total Fat 6g (Saturated Fat 1g;
Trans Fat 0g); Cholesterol 0mg; Sodium 125mg;
Total Carbohydrate 20g (Dietary Fiber 1g) Exchanges:
1 Starch, ½ Other Carbohydrate, 1 Fat; Carbohydrate
Choices: 1

Awaiting the Stork

One finalist was not able to
participate in the 42nd Bake-Off®
Contest. She had a good reason.
She was expecting the birth of
a baby—born, in fact, the day
after the contest. The contest
has been conducted with 99
finalists several times in the
past. The most common
reason for finalist
absence? Awaiting
a baby's birth.

Guess-Again Candy Crunch

Pat Parsons Bakersfield, CA
Bake-Off® Contest 39, 2000
GE Innovation Award

Prep Time: 30 Minutes
Start to Finish: 30 Minutes
50 pieces

½ **cup white chocolate candy melts**
    or coating wafers*
½ **cup peanut butter**
1 **cup unseasoned dry bread crumbs**
1 **cup light or dark chocolate candy**
    melts for candy making*
¼ **cup dry-roasted peanuts,**
    finely chopped

1 Line cookie sheet with waxed paper. In small microwavable bowl, mix white chocolate candy melts and peanut butter; microwave uncovered on Medium (50%) 2 minutes. Stir until smooth; stir in bread crumbs. Place mixture on cookie sheet. Top with another sheet of waxed paper; pat or roll into ¼-inch-thick rectangle. Remove top waxed paper.

2 In small microwavable bowl, microwave ½ cup of the light chocolate candy melts uncovered on Medium (50%) 2 minutes. Stir until smooth; spread evenly over peanut butter layer. Sprinkle with 2 tablespoons of the peanuts. Freeze 5 minutes or refrigerate 15 minutes to set chocolate.

3 In same small microwavable bowl, microwave remaining ½ cup light chocolate candy melts uncovered on Medium (50%) 2 minutes. Stir until smooth.

4 Remove candy from freezer. Turn candy over; remove waxed paper. Spread light chocolate over peanut butter layer. Immediately sprinkle with remaining 2 tablespoons peanuts; press in lightly. Refrigerate until firm, about 10 minutes. Break or cut into small pieces. Store in refrigerator; serve cold.

* Chopped vanilla-flavored and chocolate-flavored candy coating, or white vanilla baking chips and semisweet chocolate chips can be substituted for the white and light or dark chocolate candy melts.

High Altitude (3500–6500 ft): No change.

1 Piece: Calories 60; Total Fat 3.5g (Saturated Fat 1.5g; Trans Fat 0g); Cholesterol 0mg; Sodium 40mg; Total Carbohydrate 6g (Dietary Fiber 0g) Exchanges: ½ Other Carbohydrate, 1 Fat; Carbohydrate Choices: ½

9 | CAKES AND TORTES

Tuxedo Brownie Torte (page 284)

Lemon Platinum Cake

Elizabeth Penney San Diego, CA
Bake-Off® Contest 33, 1988

Prep Time: 55 Minutes
Start to Finish: 3 Hours 10 Minutes
16 servings

CAKE
8 egg whites
1 teaspoon cream of tartar
½ teaspoon salt
1 cup sugar
7 egg yolks
1 cup Pillsbury BEST® all-purpose flour
2 teaspoons grated lemon peel
⅓ cup lemon juice

FILLING
1 cup sugar
¼ cup cornstarch
Dash salt
1¼ cups water
2 egg yolks
1 tablespoon butter or margarine
2 teaspoons grated lemon peel
3 tablespoons lemon juice

TOPPING
2 cups whipping cream
3 to 4 drops yellow food color, if desired
2 kiwifruit, peeled, sliced and cut in half crosswise, if desired

1 Heat oven to 325°F. In large bowl, beat egg whites with electric mixer on high speed until foamy.

Add cream of tartar and ½ teaspoon salt; beat until soft peaks form. Gradually add ½ cup of the sugar, beating until stiff peaks form. Set aside.

2 In small bowl, beat 7 egg yolks on medium speed about 2 minutes or until lemon colored. Gradually add remaining ½ cup sugar, beating until thick and light lemon colored. Add flour, 2 teaspoons lemon peel and ⅓ cup lemon juice; beat on low speed 1 minute.

3 With spoon, gently fold egg yolk mixture into egg white mixture. Pour batter into ungreased 10-inch angel food (tube) cake pan.

4 Bake 40 to 55 minutes or until top springs back when touched lightly in center. Immediately turn cake upside down onto funnel or narrow-necked glass bottle. Cool completely, about 1 hour 15 minutes. Remove from pan.

5 While cake is cooling, in 1-quart saucepan, mix 1 cup sugar, the cornstarch and dash salt. Gradually stir in water. Cook over medium heat until mixture boils and thickens, stirring constantly; remove from heat. In small bowl,

beat 2 egg yolks; gradually blend small amount of hot mixture into egg yolks. Add egg yolk mixture to saucepan; cook over low heat 2 to 3 minutes, stirring constantly, until thickened. Remove from heat; stir in remaining filling ingredients. Cool 1 hour. Reserve ½ cup filling for topping.

6 In small bowl, beat whipping cream until slightly thickened. Add reserved ½ cup filling and food color; beat until thickened, about 30 seconds. DO NOT OVERBEAT.

7 To assemble cake, slice cake horizontally to make 3 layers. Place bottom layer on serving plate; spread with half of filling (about ½ cup). Place middle layer on top; spread with remaining filling. Top with third layer. Spread side, center and top of cake with topping. Refrigerate at least 1 hour before serving. Just before serving, arrange kiwifruit slices on cake. Cover and refrigerate any remaining cake.

High Altitude (3500–6500 ft): No change.

1 Serving: Calories 270; Total Fat 13g (Saturated Fat 7g; Trans Fat 0g); Cholesterol 150mg; Sodium 135mg; Total Carbohydrate 35g (Dietary Fiber 0g) Exchanges: ½ Starch, 2 Other Carbohydrate, ½ High-Fat Meat, 1½ Fat; Carbohydrate Choices: 2

Lemon Platinum Cake

Very Berry Lemon Cake

Alice Wyman   Pembina, ND
Bake-Off® Contest 20, 1969
$10,000 Winner

> Prep Time: 15 Minutes
> Start to Finish: 1 Hour 15 Minutes
> 16 servings

CAKE
1 can (17 oz) blueberries, drained,
   liquid reserved*
1 box (18.25 oz) Pillsbury® Moist
   Supreme® lemon cake mix
1 cup plain yogurt or sour cream
4 eggs
Powdered sugar

SAUCE
¼ cup sugar
1 tablespoon cornstarch
1 cup reserved blueberry liquid

1   Heat oven to 350°F. Grease and flour 10-inch angel food (tube) cake pan. Rinse blueberries with cold water; drain on paper towel. In large bowl, mix cake mix, yogurt and eggs. Beat with electric mixer at medium speed 2 minutes, scraping bowl occasionally. Carefully fold in blueberries. Pour batter into pan.

2   Bake 35 to 45 minutes or until toothpick inserted in center comes out clean. Cool in pan 15 minutes; remove from pan. Cool completely.

3   In 1-quart saucepan, mix sugar and cornstarch. If necessary, add enough water to blueberry liquid to make 1 cup. Gradually stir in blueberry liquid. Heat to boiling; cook and stir until thickened. To serve, sprinkle with powdered sugar and serve with blueberry sauce.

One cup fresh or frozen blueberries, unthawed, can be substituted for the canned blueberries. If using fresh or frozen blueberries, make sauce by mixing ¼ cup sugar, 1 tablespoon cornstarch, ½ cup water and 1 cup blueberries. Cook as directed above.

High Altitude (3500–6500 ft): Heat oven to 375°F. Add ¼ cup water and 3 tablespoons Pillsbury BEST® all-purpose flour with the eggs.

1 Serving: Calories 200; Total Fat 4g (Saturated Fat 1.5g; Trans Fat 1g); Cholesterol 55mg; Sodium 240mg; Total Carbohydrate 38g (Dietary Fiber 0g) Exchanges: ½ Starch, 2 Other Carbohydrate, 1 Fat; Carbohydrate Choices: 2½

Banana Crunch Cake

Bonnie Brooks   Salisbury, MD
Bake-Off® Contest 24, 1973
$25,000 One of Two Grand Prize Winners

> Prep Time: 15 Minutes
> Start to Finish: 3 Hours 30 Minutes
> 16 servings

1 cup coconut
1 cup quick-cooking or old-fashioned
   oats
¾ cup packed brown sugar
½ cup Pillsbury BEST® all-purpose flour
½ cup chopped pecans
½ cup butter or margarine
1½ cups sliced very ripe bananas
   (2 large)
½ cup sour cream
4 eggs
1 box (18.25 oz) Pillsbury® Moist
   Supreme® classic yellow cake mix

1   Heat oven to 350°F. Grease 10-inch tube cake pan with shortening; lightly flour. In medium bowl, mix coconut, oats, brown sugar, flour and pecans. With fork or pastry blender, cut in butter until mixture is crumbly; set aside.

2   In large bowl, beat bananas, sour cream and eggs with electric mixer on low speed about 30 seconds or until blended. Add cake mix; beat on medium speed 2 minutes, scraping bowl occasionally.

3   Spread ⅓ of batter in pan; sprinkle with ⅓ of coconut mixture. Repeat layers 2 more times using remaining batter and coconut mixture, ending with coconut mixture.

4   Bake 50 to 60 minutes or until toothpick inserted near center comes out clean. Cool in pan 15 minutes. Remove from pan; place on heatproof serving plate, coconut side up. Cool completely, about 2 hours, before serving.

High Altitude (3500–6500 ft): Decrease butter to 6 tablespoons. Bake 60 to 65 minutes.

1 Serving: Calories 350; Total Fat 16g (Saturated Fat 8g; Trans Fat 1g); Cholesterol 75mg; Sodium 290mg; Total Carbohydrate 49g (Dietary Fiber 1g) Exchanges: 1 Starch, 2 Other Carbohydrate, 3 Fat; Carbohydrate Choices: 3

Nutty Graham Picnic Cake

Esther Tomich   San Pedro, CA
Bake-Off® Contest 28, 1978
$25,000 One of Two Grand Prize Winners

> Prep Time: 30 Minutes
> Start to Finish: 2 Hours 30 Minutes
> 16 servings

CAKE
2 cups Pillsbury BEST® all-purpose flour
1 cup finely crushed graham crackers
  (16 squares)
1 cup packed brown sugar
½ cup granulated sugar
1 teaspoon baking powder
1 teaspoon baking soda
1 teaspoon salt
½ teaspoon ground cinnamon
1 cup butter or margarine, softened
1 cup orange juice
1 tablespoon grated orange peel
3 eggs
1 cup chopped nuts

GLAZE
2 tablespoons packed brown sugar
5 teaspoons milk
1 tablespoon butter or margarine
¾ cup powdered sugar
¼ cup chopped nuts

1   Heat oven to 350°F. Generously grease 12-cup fluted tube cake pan or 10-inch angel food (tube) cake pan; lightly flour. In large bowl, beat all cake ingredients except nuts with electric mixer on medium speed 3 minutes. With spoon, stir in 1 cup nuts. Pour batter into pan.

2   Bake 40 to 60 minutes or until toothpick inserted in center comes out clean. Cool in pan 15 minutes. Turn upside down onto heatproof serving plate; remove pan. Cool completely, about 1 hour.

3   In 1-quart saucepan, cook 2 tablespoons brown sugar, the milk and 1 tablespoon butter over low heat, stirring constantly, just until sugar is dissolved. Remove from heat. Stir in powdered sugar until smooth. Drizzle glaze over cake; sprinkle with ¼ cup nuts.

High Altitude (3500–6500 ft): No change.

1 Serving: Calories 380; Total Fat 20g (Saturated Fat 9g; Trans Fat 0.5g); Cholesterol 70mg; Sodium 390mg; Total Carbohydrate 46g (Dietary Fiber 1g) Exchanges: ½ Starch, 2½ Other Carbohydrate, ½ High-Fat Meat, 3 Fat; Carbohydrate Choices: 3

Caramel Apple Cake

Josephine DeMarco   Chicago, IL
Bake-Off® Contest 27, 1976
$5,000 Winner

> Prep Time: 20 Minutes
> Start to Finish: 1 Hour 50 Minutes
> 15 servings

CAKE
1¾ cups Pillsbury BEST® all-purpose
  flour
1½ cups packed brown sugar
½ teaspoon salt
½ teaspoon baking powder
½ teaspoon baking soda
1½ teaspoons ground cinnamon
1 teaspoon vanilla
¾ cup butter or margarine, softened
3 eggs
1½ cups (2 to 3 medium) finely chopped
  peeled apples
½ to 1 cup chopped nuts
½ cup raisins, if desired

FROSTING
2 cups powdered sugar
¼ teaspoon ground cinnamon
¼ cup butter or margarine, melted
½ teaspoon vanilla
4 to 5 teaspoons milk

1   Heat oven to 350°F. Grease and flour 13 × 9-inch pan. In large bowl, mix flour, brown sugar, salt, baking powder, baking soda, 1½ teaspoons cinnamon, 1 teaspoon vanilla, ¾ cup butter and the eggs; beat 3 minutes at medium speed. Stir in apples, nuts and raisins. Pour into pan.

2   Bake 30 to 40 minutes or until toothpick inserted in center comes out clean. Cool completely.

3   In small bowl, beat frosting ingredients, adding enough milk for desired spreading consistency. Spread over cooled cake.

High Altitude (3500–6500 ft): Heat oven to 375°F. Decrease brown sugar to 1 cup. Bake 25 to 35 minutes.

1 Serving: Calories 360; Total Fat 16g (Saturated Fat 8g; Trans Fat 0.5g); Cholesterol 75mg; Sodium 250mg; Total Carbohydrate 51g (Dietary Fiber 1g) Exchanges: 1 Starch, 2½ Other Carbohydrate, 3 Fat; Carbohydrate Choices: 3½

Country Apple Cake with Caramel Sauce

Country Apple Cake with Caramel Sauce

Beverly Healy   Nampa, ID
Bake-Off® Contest 38, 1998

Prep Time: 15 Minutes
Start to Finish: 1 Hour 35 Minutes
12 servings

CAKE

2 tablespoons vegetable oil
2 eggs
1 box (15.4 oz) Pillsbury® nut quick
    bread and muffin mix
3 cups apple pie filling (from two
    21-oz cans)
2 teaspoons ground cinnamon
½ teaspoon ground nutmeg
½ cup chopped walnuts

SAUCE AND TOPPING

½ cup granulated sugar
½ cup packed brown sugar
½ cup butter or margarine
½ cup whipping cream
1 teaspoon vanilla
Vanilla ice cream or whipped cream,
    if desired

1   Heat oven to 350°F. Spray
13 × 9-inch pan with cooking
spray. In large bowl, beat oil and
eggs until well blended. Add
quick bread mix, apple pie filling,
cinnamon and nutmeg; stir 50 to
75 strokes with spoon until mix is
moistened. Stir in nuts from foil
packet and ½ cup chopped walnuts.
Spoon into pan; spread evenly.

2   Bake 43 to 50 minutes or until
cake is deep golden brown and
toothpick inserted in center comes
out clean. Cool 30 minutes.

3   Meanwhile, in 2-quart saucepan,
heat granulated sugar, brown
sugar, butter and whipping cream
to boiling, stirring occasionally.
Remove from heat; stir in vanilla.

4   To serve, cut warm cake into
squares; place on individual dessert
plates. Top each serving with warm
sauce and ice cream.

High Altitude (3500–6500 ft): Add ¼ cup
Pillsbury BEST® all-purpose flour to dry
quick bread mix.

1 Serving: Calories 610; Total Fat 21g (Saturated Fat 9g;
Trans Fat 0.5g); Cholesterol 65mg; Sodium 330mg;
Total Carbohydrate 101g (Dietary Fiber 1g) Exchanges:
1½ Starch, 5 Other Carbohydrate, 4 Fat; Carbohydrate
Choices: 7

Maple-Applesauce Cobbler Cake

Kimberly A. Cordas   Chesterland, OH
Bake-Off® Contest 37, 1996

Prep Time: 10 Minutes
Start to Finish: 1 Hour 5 Minutes
8 servings

CAKE

1 tablespoon butter or margarine,
    softened
2 tablespoons packed brown sugar
¼ teaspoon ground cinnamon
½ cup applesauce
2 tablespoons maple-flavored syrup
1 can (16.3 oz) Pillsbury® Grands!®
    refrigerated buttermilk or original
    flaky biscuits
¼ cup golden raisins
¼ cup chopped pecans

TOPPING

1½ cups applesauce
½ cup maple-flavored syrup
2 cups frozen (thawed) whipped
    topping

1   Heat oven to 350°F. Grease
9-inch round cake or square pan
with 1 tablespoon butter. In small
bowl, mix brown sugar, cinnamon,
½ cup applesauce and 2 tablespoons
syrup until well blended.

2   Separate dough into 8 biscuits.
Cut each biscuit into 8 pieces;
place in pan. Sprinkle raisins and
pecans over biscuit pieces. Spoon
applesauce mixture over raisins and
pecans.

3   Bake 35 to 45 minutes or until
deep golden brown. Cool 10 minutes.

4   Meanwhile, in 2-quart saucepan, cook 1½ cups applesauce and
½ cup syrup over low heat, stirring constantly, until hot.

5   To serve, spoon warm cake into
individual serving dishes. Spoon
¼ cup applesauce mixture over each
serving; top each with whipped
topping. Cover and refrigerate any
remaining cake.

High Altitude (3500–6500 ft): No change.

1 Serving: Calories 430; Total Fat 16g (Saturated Fat 6g;
Trans Fat 3.5g); Cholesterol 0mg; Sodium 580mg;
Total Carbohydrate 67g (Dietary Fiber 2g) Exchanges:
1 Starch, ½ Fruit, 3 Other Carbohydrate, 3 Fat;
Carbohydrate Choices: 4½

Orange Kiss-Me Cake

Orange Kiss-Me Cake

Lily Wuebel   Redwood City, CA
Bake-Off® Contest 2, 1950
$25,000 Grand Prize Winner

> Prep Time: 30 Minutes
> Start to Finish: 2 Hours 15 Minutes
> 16 servings

CAKE
1 orange
1 cup raisins
⅓ cup walnuts
2 cups Pillsbury BEST® all-purpose flour
1 cup sugar
1 teaspoon baking soda
1 teaspoon salt
1 cup milk
½ cup butter or margarine, softened, or shortening
2 eggs

TOPPING
Reserved ⅓ cup orange juice
⅓ cup sugar
1 teaspoon ground cinnamon
¼ cup finely chopped walnuts

1 Heat oven to 350°F. Grease 13 × 9-inch pan with shortening; lightly flour. Squeeze juice from orange, reserving ⅓ cup juice for topping; remove seeds. In blender, food processor or food mill, grind orange peel and pulp, raisins and ⅓ cup walnuts; set aside.

2 In large bowl, beat cake ingredients with electric mixer on low speed until moistened; beat on medium speed 3 minutes. Stir in orange-raisin mixture. Pour batter into pan.

3 Bake 35 to 45 minutes or until toothpick inserted in center comes out clean. Drizzle reserved ⅓ cup orange juice over warm cake in pan.

4 In small bowl, mix ⅓ cup sugar and the cinnamon. Stir in ¼ cup walnuts; sprinkle over cake. Cool completely, about 1 hour.

High Altitude (3500–6500 ft): Heat oven to 375°F. Increase Pillsbury BEST® all-purpose flour to 2 cups plus 2 tablespoons. Bake 35 to 40 minutes.

1 Serving: Calories 260; Total Fat 10g (Saturated Fat 4.5g; Trans Fat 0g); Cholesterol 45mg; Sodium 280mg; Total Carbohydrate 38g (Dietary Fiber 1g) Exchanges: 1 Starch, 1½ Other Carbohydrate, 2 Fat; Carbohydrate Choices: 2½

Caramel Pear Upside-Down Cake

Margaret Faxon   Palmyra, MO
Bake-Off® Contest 5, 1953

> Prep Time: 15 Minutes
> Start to Finish: 1 Hour 10 Minutes
> 12 servings

1 can (29 oz) pear halves, drained, ½ cup liquid reserved
28 caramels (half of 14-oz bag), unwrapped
2 tablespoons butter or margarine
1 box (18.25 oz) Pillsbury® Moist Supreme® classic yellow cake mix
1 cup water
⅓ cup vegetable oil
3 eggs
¼ cup chopped nuts
Whipped cream, if desired

1 Heat oven to 350°F. Generously grease 13 × 9-inch pan.

2 Slice pear halves; arrange over bottom of greased pan. In 1-quart saucepan over medium heat, melt caramels in reserved pear liquid, stirring frequently until smooth. Stir in butter; blend well. Pour mixture evenly over pears. In large bowl, beat cake mix, water, oil and eggs with electric mixer on low speed until moistened; beat 2 minutes on high speed. Spoon batter evenly over pear mixture.

3 Bake 40 to 50 minutes or until toothpick inserted in center comes out clean. Cool 5 minutes. Turn upside down onto heatproof serving plate; remove pan. Sprinkle with nuts. Serve warm or cool with whipped cream.

High Altitude (3500–6500 ft): Heat oven to 375°F. Add 3 tablespoons Pillsbury BEST® all-purpose flour to dry cake mix. Bake 35 to 45 minutes.

1 Serving: Calories 430; Total Fat 16g (Saturated Fat 4.5g; Trans Fat 1g); Cholesterol 60mg; Sodium 370mg; Total Carbohydrate 68g (Dietary Fiber 1g) Exchanges: 1 Starch, 3½ Other Carbohydrate, 3 Fat; Carbohydrate Choices: 4½

Here's to the Heroes of the Kitchen

Part of Pillsbury's reason for starting the Bake-Off® Contest was to celebrate the many unsung heroes of America's kitchens, who hadn't received public credit for the trays of cookies, the platters of cakes and the baskets of bread that issued from their kitchens. Of course, for every Bake-Off® winner, there is still an unpublicized kitchen hero for whom the appreciation of her family is reward enough. Lily Wuebel was lucky enough to have both. When asked what he thought of his wife's $25,000 cake, Peter Wuebel said he'd always loved the cake, and "it's worth a million to me."

Raspberry-Filled Apricot Cake

Kristina Vannie Libertyville, IL
Bake-Off® Contest 35, 1992
$2,000 Winner

Prep Time: 20 Minutes
Start to Finish: 3 Hours 10 Minutes
16 servings

CAKE
1 box (18.25 oz) Pillsbury® Moist
   Supreme® classic yellow cake mix
1⅓ cups apricot nectar
2 eggs

FILLING
1 cup raspberry spreadable fruit or jam

FROSTING
1 box (4-serving size) vanilla sugar-free
   instant pudding and pie filling mix
½ cup fat-free (skim) milk
2 tablespoons apricot nectar
1 container (8 oz) frozen reduced-fat
   whipped topping, thawed
3 tablespoons coconut, toasted *

1   Heat oven to 350°F. Lightly grease and flour two 9- or 8-inch round cake pans. In large bowl, mix cake mix, 1⅓ cups apricot nectar and eggs with electric mixer on low speed until moistened; beat 2 minutes on high speed. Pour into pans.

2   Bake 25 to 35 minutes or until toothpick inserted in center comes out clean. Cool 15 minutes. Remove from pans to cooling racks; cool completely.

3   To assemble cake, cut each cake layer in half horizontally to make 4 layers. Place 1 cake layer, cut side up, on serving plate; spread with ⅓ cup spreadable fruit. Repeat with second and third cake layers and spreadable fruit. Top with remaining cake layer.

4   In small bowl, mix pudding mix, milk and 2 tablespoons apricot

meet kristina vanni

THERE ARE TWO KINDS of cooks: those who master cooking as adults and those who learn the skill from the cradle, peeking out from their bassinets or playpens, wondering what smells so good and what all the excitement is about.

"I'm from a cooking family," says Kristina Vanni. "My great-grandma taught my grandma, and my grandma taught my mom, my mom taught, well—it's just gone on and on. When I was little, my mom would be cooking in the kitchen, and even before I was in school, I would just sit there and watch. So I think

I absorbed a whole lot just by watching—I always liked to play with the flour; it was my little indoor sandbox."

This chain of cooks resulted in something truly extraordinary: Both Kristina and her grandmother, Pat Bradley, won trips to the 35th Bake-Off® Contest. Young Kristina certainly proved herself a great up-and-coming cook that year, capturing a cash prize (just like Grandma) for her Raspberry-Filled Apricot Cake—a crowd pleasing, lower-calorie dessert.

"Cooking is definitely a family thing," says Kristina. "The kitchen is the center of the house, the place everyone passes through. It's where a lot of things go on—it's always a nice warm place." But it's not just the heat from the range. It's the warmth of nurturing when a family shares its love of creative cooking.

nectar. Add thawed whipped topping; beat with electric mixer on low speed 2 minutes. Frost side and top of cake. Sprinkle top with toasted coconut. Refrigerate at least 2 hours before serving. Cover and refrigerate any remaining cake.

To toast coconut, spread on cookie sheet; bake at 350°F 7 to 8 minutes, stirring occasionally, until light golden brown. Or spread in thin layer in microwavable pie plate. Microwave on Low (10%) 4½ to 8 minutes or until light golden brown, tossing with fork after each minute.

High Altitude (3500–6500 ft): Add ⅓ cup Pillsbury BEST® all-purpose flour to dry cake mix. Bake 8-inch pans 30 to 40 minutes.

1 Serving: Calories 250; Total Fat 6g (Saturated Fat 3g; Trans Fat 1g); Cholesterol 25mg; Sodium 260mg; Total Carbohydrate 47g (Dietary Fiber 1g) Exchanges: 1 Starch, 2 Other Carbohydrate, 1 Fat; Carbohydrate Choices: 3

Starlight Double-Delight Cake

Helen Weston   La Jolla, CA
Bake-Off® Contest 3, 1951
$25,000 Grand Prize Winner

> Prep Time: 25 Minutes
> Start to Finish: 2 Hours 15 Minutes
> 12 servings

FROSTING

2 packages (3 oz each) cream cheese, softened
½ cup butter or margarine, softened
½ teaspoon vanilla
½ teaspoon peppermint extract
6 cups powdered sugar
¼ cup hot water
4 oz semisweet baking chocolate, melted

Making a List and Checking It Twice (Or More)

Bake-Off® Contest staff believe in the motto, "Be prepared." That's why a checklist of ingredients and equipment is created for each of the 100 finalists. It's used to pack nonperishable food and equipment for each work station in a box that's shipped from Minneapolis to the event, and then rechecked when the items are unpacked into the mini-kitchens at the finals. From the list, individual bags with each finalist's refrigerated and frozen ingredients are filled at the contest site and stored in specially marked refrigerators on the competition floor. With $1 million at stake, the list gets checked again and again to be sure each finalist has what is needed.

CAKE

¼ cup butter or margarine, softened
3 eggs
2 cups Pillsbury BEST® all-purpose flour
1½ teaspoons baking soda
1 teaspoon salt
¾ cup milk

1   Heat oven to 350°F. Grease two 9-inch round cake pans with shortening; lightly flour. In large bowl, beat cream cheese, ½ cup butter, the vanilla and peppermint extract with electric mixer on medium speed for 1 minute or until smooth. Alternately add powdered sugar and hot water, beating until smooth. Beat in slightly cooled chocolate until well blended, about 2 minutes.

2   In another large bowl, beat 2 cups of the frosting mixture and ¼ cup butter on medium speed until well blended. Cover remaining frosting; set aside. Add 1 egg at a time to frosting and butter mixture, beating

well after each addition. On low speed, beat in flour, baking soda, salt and milk until smooth. Pour batter into pans.

3   Bake 25 to 35 minutes or until toothpick inserted in center comes out clean. Cool 15 minutes on cooling rack; run knife around edge of pan and remove cakes to cooling racks. Cool completely, about 1 hour.

4   To assemble cake, place 1 cake layer, top side down, on serving plate; spread with about ¼ of frosting. Top with second layer, top side up; spread side and top of cake with remaining frosting. Cover and refrigerate any remaining cake.

High Altitude (3500–6500 ft): Increase Pillsbury BEST® all-purpose flour to 2½ cups; use 1½ cups of frosting mixture in cake.

1 Serving: Calories 550; Total Fat 21g (Saturated Fat 13g; Trans Fat 0.5g); Cholesterol 100mg; Sodium 500mg; Total Carbohydrate 83g (Dietary Fiber 1g) Exchanges: ½ Starch, 5 Other Carbohydrate, ½ High-Fat Meat, 3½ Fat; Carbohydrate Choices: 5½

Costa Rican Cream Cake

Costa Rican Cream Cake

Janice Weinrick LaMesa, CA
Bake-Off® Contest 34, 1990
$2,000 Winner

Prep Time: 30 Minutes
Start to Finish: 4 Hours 15 Minutes
15 servings

CAKE
1 box (18.25 oz) Pillsbury® Moist
   Supreme® classic yellow cake mix
1 cup water
⅓ cup vegetable oil
3 eggs

SAUCE
1 cup whipping cream
⅓ cup rum, or 1 teaspoon rum extract
   plus ⅓ cup water
1 can (14 oz) sweetened condensed
   milk (not evaporated)
1 can (12 oz) evaporated milk

TOPPING
1 cup whipping cream
⅓ cup coconut, toasted*
⅓ cup chopped macadamia nuts

1 Heat oven to 350°F. Grease
13 × 9-inch (3-quart) baking
dish. In large bowl, beat cake
ingredients with electric mixer
on low speed until moistened;
beat 2 minutes on high speed.
Pour into baking dish.

2 Bake 25 to 35 minutes or until
toothpick inserted in center comes
out clean. Meanwhile, in large
bowl, mix sauce ingredients. Cool
cake 5 minutes. Using long-tined
fork, pierce hot cake in pan every
1 to 2 inches. Slowly pour sauce
mixture over cake. Do not cover
cake; refrigerate at least 3 hours
to chill. (Cake will absorb most of
sauce mixture.)

3 Just, before serving, in small
bowl, beat 1 cup whipping cream
until stiff peaks form. Spread over
cold cake. Sprinkle with coconut
and macadamia nuts. Cover and
refrigerate any remaining cake.

Mergers and Acquisitions

Bake-Off® winners' creativity is not confined to their cooking. Janice Weinrick was equally innovative when deciding what name to use after she was married. "In keeping with merger mania," Janice related, "we took half of my husband Michael's name (Weintraub) and half of mine (Myrick) and created the name 'Weinrick,' which became our legally married name." With her mind again on mergers, Janice adapted a traditional Costa Rican Cream Cake for the contemporary American kitchen, proving that doing things by half measures is sometimes a brilliant solution.

To toast coconut, spread on cookie sheet; bake at 350°F 7 to 8 minutes, stirring occasionally, until light golden brown. Or spread in thin layer in microwavable pie plate. Microwave on Low (10%) 4½ to 8 minutes or until light golden brown, tossing with fork after each minute.

High Altitude (3500–6500 ft): Add ⅓ cup Pillsbury BEST® all-purpose flour to dry cake mix; increase water to 1 cup plus 2 tablespoons.

1 Serving: Calories 440; Total Fat 25g (Saturated Fat 12g; Trans Fat 1.5g); Cholesterol 95mg; Sodium 310mg; Total Carbohydrate 47g (Dietary Fiber 0g) Exchanges: 1 Starch, 2 Other Carbohydrate, ½ High-Fat Meat, 4 Fat; Carbohydrate Choices: 3

Cake 'n Cheese Cake

Imogene Noar Paramount, CA
Bake-Off® Contest 14, 1962
$1,500 Winner

> **Prep Time:** 20 Minutes
> **Start to Finish:** 4 Hours 10 Minutes
> 10 servings

FILLING
1 package (8 oz) cream cheese, softened
⅔ cup sugar
½ cup sour cream
1 teaspoon vanilla
2 eggs

CAKE
1 cup Pillsbury BEST® all-purpose flour
1 teaspoon baking powder
Dash salt
½ cup butter or margarine, softened
⅔ cup sugar
2 eggs
1 tablespoon milk
1 teaspoon vanilla

TOPPING
1 cup sour cream
2 tablespoons sugar
1 teaspoon vanilla

1 Heat oven to 325°F. Grease and flour bottom only of 10-inch deep dish pie pan or 9-inch square pan. In small bowl, beat cream cheese and ⅔ cup sugar until light and fluffy. Add ½ cup sour cream and 1 teaspoon vanilla; blend well. Add eggs 1 at a time, beating at low speed. Set aside.

2 In medium bowl, mix flour, baking powder and salt. In large bowl, beat butter and ⅔ cup sugar until light and fluffy. Add eggs 1 at a time, beating well after each addition. Stir in milk and 1 teaspoon vanilla. Beat in dry ingredients on low speed until moistened. Beat 1 minute on medium speed. Spread batter in bottom and up side of pie pan, spreading thinner on side. Pour cream cheese mixture over batter.

3 Bake 40 to 45 minutes or until cheesecake is almost set in center and cake is golden brown.

4 Meanwhile, in small bowl, mix topping ingredients; spread evenly over cake. Bake 5 minutes longer. Cool; refrigerate 3 to 4 hours before serving. Cover and refrigerate any remaining cake.

High Altitude (3500–6500 ft): Decrease sugar in filling to ½ cup; decrease sugar in cake to ½ cup.

1 Serving: Calories 430; Total Fat 26g (Saturated Fat 16g; Trans Fat 1g); Cholesterol 155mg; Sodium 240mg; Total Carbohydrate 41g (Dietary Fiber 0g) Exchanges: 1 Starch, 2 Other Carbohydrate, ½ High-Fat Meat, 4 Fat; Carbohydrate Choices: 3

Butterscotch-Rum Ripple Cake

Claranne M. Schirle San Jose, CA
Bake-Off® Contest 23, 1972

> **Prep Time:** 30 Minutes
> **Start to Finish:** 3 Hours 15 Minutes
> 16 servings

CAKE
3 cups Pillsbury BEST® all-purpose flour
2 cups granulated sugar
1 teaspoon baking soda
1 teaspoon salt
1 cup butter or margarine, softened
1 cup sour cream
1 tablespoon rum extract
1 teaspoon vanilla
5 eggs (1 cup)

RIPPLE
1 box (4-serving size) butterscotch instant pudding and pie filling mix
¾ cup butterscotch topping (from a jar)
1 egg

GLAZE AND GARNISH
¼ cup butter or margarine
¼ cup packed brown sugar
1 cup powdered sugar
1 teaspoon rum extract
1 to 3 tablespoons hot water
2 tablespoons chopped nuts

1 Heat oven to 325°F (300°F for pan with colored outer surface). Grease 12-cup fluted tube cake pan or 10-inch angel food (tube) cake pan with shortening; lightly flour (if fluted pan has opening in center tube, cover with foil).

2 In large bowl, beat cake ingredients with electric mixer on medium speed 3 minutes. Place 2 cups batter in small bowl; beat in ripple ingredients on medium speed 1 minute. Spoon half of cake batter into pan, then half of ripple batter. Marble layers with knife in a folding motion, turning pan while folding. Repeat with remaining batters; marble with knife.

3 Bake 1 hour 20 minutes to 1 hour 30 minutes or until toothpick inserted near center comes out clean. Cool in pan 15 minutes. Turn upside down onto heatproof serving plate; remove pan. Cool completely, about 1 hour.

4 In 1-quart saucepan, heat ¼ cup butter and the brown sugar to boiling over medium-high heat, stirring constantly; cook until thickened. Remove from heat. Stir in powdered sugar and 1 teaspoon rum extract. Stir in water until drizzling consistency. Drizzle glaze over cake. Sprinkle with nuts. Serve warm or cool.

High Altitude (3500–6500 ft): Heat oven to 350°F. Decrease butterscotch topping to ½ cup. Bake 1 hour 10 minutes to 1 hour 15 minutes.

1 Serving: Calories 490; Total Fat 20g (Saturated Fat 12g; Trans Fat 0.5g); Cholesterol 125mg; Sodium 500mg;Total Carbohydrate 71g (Dietary Fiber 0g) Exchanges: 1½ Starch, 3 Other Carbohydrate, 4 Fat; Carbohydrate Choices: 5

Almond-Filled Cookie Cake

Elizabeth Meijer Tucson, AZ
Bake-Off® Contest 30, 1982
$40,000 Grand Prize Winner

> Prep Time: 20 Minutes
> Start to Finish: 3 Hours 20 Minutes
> 24 servings

CRUST
2⅔ cups Pillsbury BEST® all-purpose flour
1⅓ cups sugar
1⅓ cups butter, softened (do not use margarine)
½ teaspoon salt
1 egg

FILLING
1 cup finely chopped almonds
½ cup sugar
1 teaspoon grated lemon peel
1 egg, slightly beaten

GARNISH
4 whole blanched almonds

1 Heat oven to 325°F. Place cookie sheet in oven to preheat. Grease 10- or 9-inch springform pan. In large bowl, beat crust ingredients with electric mixer on low speed until dough forms. If desired, refrigerate for easier handling. Divide dough in half; spread half in bottom of pan.

2 In small bowl, mix filling ingredients. Spread over crust to within ½ inch of side of pan. Between 2 sheets of waxed paper, press

remaining dough to 10- or 9-inch round. Remove top sheet of waxed paper; place dough over filling. Remove waxed paper; press dough into place. Top with whole almonds.

3 Place cake on preheated cookie sheet; bake 1 hour 5 minutes to 1 hour 15 minutes or until top is light golden brown. Cool 15 minutes; remove side of pan. Cool completely, about 1 hour 30 minutes, before serving.

High Altitude (3500–6500 ft): No change.

1 Serving: Calories 240; Total Fat 14g (Saturated Fat 7g; Trans Fat 0g); Cholesterol 45mg; Sodium 125mg; Total Carbohydrate 27g (Dietary Fiber 1g) Exchanges: ½ Starch, 1½ Other Carbohydrate, 2½ Fat; Carbohydrate Choices: 2

Streusel Spice Cake

Rose DeDominicis Verona, PA
Bake-Off® Contest 23, 1972
$25,000 One of Two Grand Prize Winners

> Prep Time: 30 Minutes
> Start to Finish: 3 Hours 10 Minutes
> 16 servings

CAKE
1 box (18.25 oz) Pillsbury® Moist Supreme® classic yellow cake mix
¾ cup milk
½ cup butter or margarine, softened
5 eggs
¼ cup coconut
¼ cup chopped nuts
1 oz unsweetened baking chocolate, melted

FILLING
½ cup coconut
½ cup chopped nuts
½ cup packed brown sugar
2 tablespoons Pillsbury BEST® all-purpose flour
2 teaspoons ground cinnamon

GLAZE
1 cup powdered sugar
1 tablespoon butter or margarine, softened
2 to 3 tablespoons milk

1 Heat oven to 350°F. Grease 10-inch angel food (tube) cake pan or 12-cup fluted tube cake pan; lightly flour. In large bowl, beat cake mix, ¾ cup milk, ½ cup butter and the eggs with electric mixer on low speed until moistened; beat on high speed 2 minutes. Stir in ¼ cup coconut and ¼ cup nuts. With spoon, marble chocolate through batter. Pour half of batter (about 2 cups) into pan.

2 In small bowl, mix filling ingredients. Reserve ½ cup filling; sprinkle remaining filling over batter in pan. Cover with remaining batter; sprinkle with reserved ½ cup filling.

3 Bake 55 to 70 minutes or until toothpick inserted near center comes out clean. Cool in pan 30 minutes. Turn upside down onto heatproof serving plate; remove pan. Cool completely, about 1 hour.

4 In small bowl, mix glaze ingredients until smooth, adding enough milk for desired drizzling consistency. Drizzle glaze over cake.

High Altitude (3500–6500 ft): Heat oven to 375°F. Add ⅓ cup Pillsbury BEST® all-purpose flour to dry cake mix. Bake 45 to 55 minutes.

1 Serving: Calories 350; Total Fat 17g (Saturated Fat 8g; Trans Fat 1g); Cholesterol 85mg; Sodium 290mg; Total Carbohydrate 45g (Dietary Fiber 1g) Exchanges: ½ Starch, 2½ Other Carbohydrate, ½ High-Fat Meat, 2½ Fat; Carbohydrate Choices: 3

Buttercream Pound Cake

Phyllis Lidert   Fort Lauderdale, FL
Bake-Off® Contest 19, 1968
$25,000 Grand Prize Winner

Prep Time: 30 Minutes
Start to Finish: 3 Hours 5 Minutes
16 servings

CAKE
2 cups (1 lb) butter, softened (do not
   use margarine)
2½ cups powdered sugar
6 eggs
2 teaspoons grated lemon peel
3 tablespoons lemon juice
4 cups Pillsbury BEST® all-purpose flour
1 tablespoon baking powder
1 can (12½ oz) poppy seed filling

GLAZE
1 cup powdered sugar
1 to 2 tablespoons lemon juice or milk

1   Heat oven to 350°F. In large bowl, beat butter with electric mixer on medium speed until light and fluffy. On low speed, gradually beat in 2½ cups powdered sugar. On medium speed, add 1 egg at a time, beating well after each addition. Beat in lemon peel and 3 tablespoons lemon juice. On low speed, gradually beat in flour and baking powder until well blended.

2   Place 3 cups batter in medium bowl; stir in poppy seed filling. Spread half of plain batter in bottom of ungreased 10-inch angel food (tube) cake pan. Alternately add spoonfuls of poppy seed batter and remaining plain batter.

3   Bake 1 hour 15 minutes to 1 hour 25 minutes or until toothpick inserted near center comes out clean. Cool 15 minutes; remove from pan. Cool completely, about 1 hour.

4   In small bowl, mix glaze ingredients, adding enough lemon juice for desired drizzling consistency; drizzle over cake.

High Altitude (3500–6500 ft): Increase Pillsbury BEST® all-purpose flour to 4½ cups.

1 Serving: Calories 540; Total Fat 28g (Saturated Fat 15g; Trans Fat 1g); Cholesterol 140mg; Sodium 300mg; Total Carbohydrate 65g (Dietary Fiber 3g) Exchanges: 1 Starch, 3½ Other Carbohydrate, ½ Medium-Fat Meat, 5 Fat; Carbohydrate Choices: 4

Innovation Creates Demand

America's home cooks enjoy stirring up new ideas, and the Bake-Off® Contest has fueled that passion and helped start new food trends.

- In 1966, the wildly popular Tunnel of Fudge Cake called for the little-known Bundt® cake pan. Pillsbury got thousands of requests for help in finding the unique ring-shaped, fluted pan, which then became a standard item in kitchens across the country.

- Buttercream Pound Cake, the lemon-flavored grand prize-winning recipe in 1968, featured a real novelty—a swirl of poppy seed. After the recipe was published, poppy seed and lemon cake became a classic combination just like apples and cinnamon.

- In 1954, Open Sesame Pie featured an inventive sesame seed crust. At the time, the seed was a regional specialty of a small area of the South, but after the contest, there was instant national demand for the little nutty-tasting seed. Since then, sesame seed became a regularly stocked grocery-store item.

Kentucky Butter Cake

Albert G. Lewis, Jr.   Platte City, MO
Bake-Off® Contest 15, 1963

Prep Time: 30 Minutes
Start to Finish: 3 Hours 20 Minutes
12 servings

CAKE
2 cups granulated sugar
1 cup butter, softened
2 teaspoons vanilla or rum extract
4 eggs
3 cups Pillsbury BEST® all-purpose flour
1 teaspoon salt
1 teaspoon baking powder
½ teaspoon baking soda
1 cup buttermilk*

BUTTER SAUCE
¾ cup granulated sugar
⅓ cup butter
3 tablespoons water
1 to 2 teaspoons vanilla or rum extract

GARNISH

2 to 3 teaspoons powdered sugar

1 Heat oven to 325°F. Generously grease 12-cup fluted tube cake pan or 10-inch angel food (tube) cake pan with shortening; lightly flour. In large bowl, beat 2 cups granulated sugar and 1 cup butter with electric mixer on medium speed until well blended. Beat in vanilla and eggs. Add remaining cake ingredients; beat on low speed until moistened. Beat on medium speed 3 minutes. Pour batter into pan.

2 Bake 55 to 70 minutes or until toothpick inserted in center comes out clean.

3 In 1-quart saucepan, cook sauce ingredients over low heat, stirring occasionally, until butter melts. DO NOT BOIL. With long-tined fork, pierce cake 10 to 12 times. Slowly pour hot sauce over warm cake. Let stand until sauce is absorbed, 5 to 10 minutes.

4 Turn cake upside down onto heatproof serving plate; remove pan. Cool completely, about 1 hour 30 minutes. Just before serving, sprinkle with powdered sugar.

* To substitute for buttermilk, use 1 tablespoon vinegar or lemon juice plus milk to make 1 cup.

High Altitude (3500–6500 ft): Heat oven to 350°F.

1 Serving: Calories 520; Total Fat 23g (Saturated Fat 14g; Trans Fat 1g); Cholesterol 125mg; Sodium 480mg;Total Carbohydrate 72g (Dietary Fiber 0g) Exchanges: 2 Starch, 3 Other Carbohydrate, 4 Fat; Carbohydrate Choices: 5

Chocolate Fudge Snack Cake

Nancy Woodside   Sonora, CA
Bake-Off® Contest 34, 1990
$10,000 Winner

Prep Time: 15 Minutes
Start to Finish: 1 Hour
16 servings

CAKE

½ cup butter or margarine
1 jar (11.75 oz) hot fudge topping
1½ cups Pillsbury BEST® all-purpose flour
1½ cups sugar
1 cup mashed potato flakes
1 teaspoon baking soda
¾ cup buttermilk*
1 teaspoon vanilla
2 eggs
1 cup finely chopped walnuts
1 cup semisweet chocolate chips (6 oz)

GLAZE

½ cup sugar
¼ cup buttermilk**
¼ cup butter or margarine
1½ teaspoons light corn syrup or water
¼ teaspoon baking soda
½ teaspoon vanilla
2 tablespoons chopped walnuts

1 Heat oven to 350°F. Grease and flour 13 × 9-inch pan. In 1-quart saucepan, melt ½ cup butter and the fudge topping over low heat, stirring constantly, until smooth. In large bowl, beat remaining cake ingredients except 1 cup walnuts and the chocolate chips with electric mixer on low speed until well blended. Add fudge mixture; beat 2 minutes on medium speed. By hand, stir in 1 cup walnuts and the chocolate chips. Pour batter into pan.

2 Bake 40 to 45 minutes or until toothpick inserted in center comes out clean.

3 In 1-quart saucepan, heat all glaze ingredients except vanilla and 2 tablespoons walnuts to boiling over medium heat. Reduce heat; simmer about 5 minutes, stirring constantly, until light golden brown. Remove from heat; stir in vanilla. Pour warm glaze over warm cake, spreading to cover. Sprinkle with 2 tablespoons walnuts. Serve warm or cool.

* To substitute for buttermilk in cake, use 2¼ teaspoons vinegar or lemon juice plus milk to make ¾ cup.

** To substitute for buttermilk in glaze, use ¾ teaspoon vinegar or lemon juice plus milk to make ¼ cup.

High Altitude (3500–6500 ft): Increase Pillsbury BEST® all-purpose flour to 1¾ cups; decrease sugar in cake to 1 cup. Increase simmer time for glaze to 8 minutes.

1 Serving: Calories 440; Total Fat 20g (Saturated Fat 9g; Trans Fat 0g); Cholesterol 50mg; Sodium 260mg; Total Carbohydrate 60g (Dietary Fiber 2g) Exchanges: 1 Starch, 3 Other Carbohydrate, ½ High-Fat Meat, 3 Fat; Carbohydrate Choices: 4

Caramel In-Between Fudge Cake

Judee Disco Norwich, CT
Bake-Off® Contest 21, 1970

Prep Time: 35 Minutes
Start to Finish: 2 Hours 20 Minutes
18 servings

FILLING
28 caramels (half of 14-oz bag),
   unwrapped
1 tablespoon butter or margarine
1 can (14 oz) sweetened condensed milk
   (not evaporated)

CAKE
1 box (19.5 oz) Pillsbury® Moist
   Supreme® dark chocolate cake mix
1 cup water
1 tablespoon shortening, if desired
3 eggs

FROSTING AND GARNISH
½ cup butter or margarine,
   softened
2 envelopes (1 oz each) premelted
   unsweetened baking chocolate
   or 2 oz unsweetened baking
   chocolate, melted
3 tablespoons half-and-half or milk
1 teaspoon vanilla
2 cups powdered sugar
⅓ cup sliced almonds, toasted*

1 Heat oven to 350°F. Generously grease bottom only of 13 × 9-inch pan with shortening; lightly flour. In 2-quart saucepan, cook filling ingredients over medium-low heat about 8 minutes, stirring constantly, until caramels are melted.

2 In large bowl, beat cake ingredients with electric mixer on low speed 30 seconds. Beat on medium speed 2 minutes, scraping bowl occasionally. Spread half of batter (about 2 cups) evenly in pan. Bake 20 minutes.

3 Spread filling evenly over partially baked cake; cover with remaining batter. Bake 20 to 25 minutes longer or until toothpick inserted in center comes out clean. Cool completely, about 1 hour.

4 In small bowl, beat ½ cup butter, the chocolate, half-and-half and vanilla with electric mixer on medium speed until well blended. Gradually add powdered sugar, beating 2 to 3 minutes or until light and fluffy. Frost cooled cake. Sprinkle almonds over top.

* To toast almonds, bake uncovered in ungreased shallow pan in 350°F oven about 10 minutes, stirring occasionally, until golden brown.

High Altitude (3500–6500 ft): In step 1, cook filling about 13 minutes. In step 3, bake 28 to 33 minutes.

1 Serving: Calories 410; Total Fat 15g (Saturated Fat 8g; Trans Fat 0.5g); Cholesterol 60mg; Sodium 370mg; Total Carbohydrate 64g (Dietary Fiber 1g) Exchanges: 1 Starch, 3 Other Carbohydrate, ½ High-Fat Meat, 2 Fat; Carbohydrate Choices: 4

Ring-of-Coconut Fudge Cake

Charles Glomb Whitehall, PA
Bake-Off® Contest 22, 1971
$10,000 Winner

Prep Time: 25 Minutes
Start to Finish: 3 Hours 50 Minutes
16 servings

FILLING
1 package (8 oz) cream cheese, softened
¼ cup granulated sugar
1 teaspoon vanilla
1 egg
½ cup flaked coconut
1 cup semisweet or milk chocolate chips

CAKE
2 cups granulated sugar
1 cup vegetable oil
2 eggs
3 cups Pillsbury BEST® all-purpose flour
¾ cup unsweetened baking cocoa
2 teaspoons baking soda
2 teaspoons baking powder
1½ teaspoons salt
1 cup hot brewed coffee or water
1 cup buttermilk*
1 teaspoon vanilla
½ cup chopped nuts

GLAZE
1 cup powdered sugar
3 tablespoons unsweetened baking cocoa
2 tablespoons butter or margarine
2 teaspoons vanilla
1 to 3 tablespoons hot water

1 Heat oven to 350°F. Generously grease 10-inch angel food (tube) cake pan or 12-cup fluted tube cake pan; lightly flour. In medium bowl, mix filling ingredients until well blended; set aside.

2 In large bowl, beat 2 cups granulated sugar, the oil and eggs with electric mixer on high speed 1 minute. Add remaining cake ingredients except nuts; beat on medium speed 3 minutes, scraping bowl occasionally. Stir in nuts. Pour ⅔ of batter evenly into pan. Carefully spoon filling over batter; top with remaining batter.

3 Bake 1 hour 10 minutes to 1 hour 15 minutes or until top springs back when touched lightly in center. Cool in pan 15 minutes. Turn upside down onto heatproof serving plate; remove pan. Cool completely, about 2 hours.

4 In medium bowl, mix glaze ingredients, adding enough hot water for desired glaze consistency. Spoon glaze over cake, allowing some to run down side. Cover and refrigerate any remaining cake.

* To substitute for buttermilk, use 1 tablespoon vinegar or lemon juice plus milk to make 1 cup.

High Altitude (3500–6500 ft): No change.

1 Serving: Calories 550; Total Fat 28g (Saturated Fat 10g; Trans Fat 0g); Cholesterol 60mg; Sodium 530mg; Total Carbohydrate 66g (Dietary Fiber 3g) Exchanges: 1 Starch, 3 ½ Other Carbohydrate, ½ High-Fat Meat, 4½ Fat; Carbohydrate Choices: 4½

Almond Mocha Cake

Debbie Russell   Colorado Springs, CO
Bake-Off® Contest 33, 1988

Prep Time: 15 Minutes
Start to Finish: 2 Hours 35 Minutes
16 servings

1¼ cups strong coffee*
½ cup butter or margarine
1 bag (12 oz) semisweet chocolate
    chips (2 cups)
1 cup granulated sugar
¼ cup amaretto or 2 teaspoons almond
    extract* *
2 cups Pillsbury BEST® all-purpose flour
1 teaspoon baking soda
½ teaspoon salt
1 teaspoon vanilla
2 eggs
½ cup chopped almonds
Powdered sugar

1   Heat oven to 325°F. Generously grease and flour 12-cup fluted tube cake pan or 10-inch angel food (tube) cake pan. In 2-quart saucepan over low heat, warm coffee. Add butter and chocolate chips; cook until mixture is smooth, stirring constantly. Remove from heat; stir in sugar and amaretto. Place in large bowl; cool 5 minutes.

2   With electric mixer on low speed, gradually blend flour, baking soda and salt into chocolate mixture until moistened. Add vanilla and eggs; beat on medium speed about 30 seconds or just until well blended. Stir in nuts; pour into pan.

3   Bake 60 to 75 minutes or until toothpick inserted in center comes out clean. Cool in pan 15 minutes. Turn upside down onto heatproof serving plate; remove pan. Cool completely; sprinkle with powdered sugar.

*To make strong coffee, add 3 rounded teaspoons instant espresso coffee granules to 1¼ cups boiling water.

* *If using almond extract for amaretto, increase coffee to 1½ cups.

High Altitude (3500–6500 ft): No change.

1 Serving: Calories 310; Total Fat 15g (Saturated Fat 8g; Trans Fat 0g); Cholesterol 40mg; Sodium 130mg; Total Carbohydrate 40g (Dietary Fiber 2g) Exchanges: 1 Starch, 1½ Other Carbohydrate, 3 Fat; Carbohydrate Choices: 2½

Praline Ice Cream Cake

Mrs. Thomas Griffin   El Paso, TX
Bake-Off® Contest 18, 1967
$1,000 Winner

Prep Time: 20 Minutes
Start to Finish: 1 Hour 25 Minutes
12 servings

½ cup butter or margarine
1 pint (2 cups) vanilla ice cream,
    softened
2 eggs
1½ cups Pillsbury BEST® all-purpose
    flour*
⅔ cup sugar
1 tablespoon baking powder
½ teaspoon salt
1 cup finely crushed graham crackers
    (16 squares)
½ cup sour cream
1 cup caramel topping
½ cup chopped pecans or pecan halves
Sweetened whipped cream or additional
    ice cream, if desired

1   Heat oven to 350°F. Grease 13 × 9-inch pan.

2   In 3-quart saucepan, melt butter. Remove from heat. Stir in 1 pint ice cream. Stir in eggs, flour, sugar, baking powder, salt

Always Looking for the Next Big Adventure

Setting out after new recipes takes a certain amount of bravery and self-confidence—the confidence that your ideas are good ones, and the bravery to accept failures without too much embarrassment. Both Bake-Off® finalist Debbie Russell and her husband certainly don't lack bravery. "I met him in a canoe, we became engaged in a hot air balloon and we spent our honeymoon sailing and scuba diving," Debbie recalls. "My husband and I are both adventurous, daring and eat anything. I enjoy experimenting with foods on him." When those experiments result in Almond Mocha Cake, it's a good guess that Debbie's husband enjoys the taste testing.

and crushed graham crackers until smooth. Pour into pan.

3 Bake 30 to 35 minutes. Mix sour cream and topping. Pour over warm cake. Top with pecans. Cool; cut into squares. Serve with ice cream or sweetened whipped cream.

* If using self-rising flour, omit baking powder and salt.

High Altitude (3500–6500 ft): Heat oven to 375°F. Add 2 tablespoons milk with the eggs. Decrease sugar to ½ cup.

1 Serving: Calories 390; Total Fat 17g (Saturated Fat 8g; Trans Fat 0.5g); Cholesterol 75mg; Sodium 440mg; Total Carbohydrate 53g (Dietary Fiber 1g) Exchanges: ½ Starch, 3 Other Carbohydrate, ½ High-Fat Meat, 2½ Fat; Carbohydrate Choices: 3 ½

Mardi Gras Party Cake

Eunice G. Surles Lake Charles, LA
Bake-Off® Contest 11, 1959
$25,000 Grand Prize Winner

Prep Time: 30 Minutes
Start to Finish: 2 Hours 20 Minutes
16 servings

CAKE
⅔ cup butterscotch chips
¼ cup water
2¼ cups Pillsbury BEST® all-purpose flour
1¼ cups granulated sugar
1 teaspoon baking soda
1 teaspoon salt
½ teaspoon baking powder
1 cup buttermilk*
½ cup shortening
3 eggs

FILLING
½ cup granulated sugar
1 tablespoon cornstarch
½ cup half-and-half or evaporated milk
⅓ cup water
⅓ cup butterscotch chips
1 egg, slightly beaten
2 tablespoons butter or margarine
1 cup coconut
1 cup chopped nuts

SEAFOAM CREAM
1 cup whipping cream
¼ cup packed brown sugar
½ teaspoon vanilla

1 Heat oven to 350°F. Generously grease and flour two 9-inch round cake pans.** In 1-quart saucepan, melt ⅔ cup butterscotch chips in ¼ cup water over low heat, stirring until smooth. Cool slightly. In large bowl, beat remaining cake ingredients and cooled butterscotch mixture with electric mixer on low speed until moistened; beat 3 minutes on medium speed. Pour batter into pans.

2 Bake 20 to 30 minutes or until toothpick inserted in center comes out clean. Cool 10 minutes. Remove from pans to cooling racks. Cool completely.

3 In 2-quart saucepan, mix ½ cup granulated sugar and the cornstarch; stir in half-and-half, ⅓ cup water, ⅓ cup butterscotch chips and 1 egg. Cook over medium heat, stirring constantly, until mixture thickens.

Remove from heat. Stir in butter, coconut and nuts; cool slightly.

4 In small bowl, beat whipping cream until soft peaks form. Gradually add brown sugar and vanilla, beating until stiff peaks form.

5 To assemble cake, place 1 cake layer top side down on serving plate. Spread with half of filling mixture. Top with second layer, top side up; spread remaining filling on top to within ½ inch of edge. Frost sides and top edge of cake with seafoam cream. Refrigerate at least 1 hour before serving. Cover and refrigerate any remaining cake.

* To substitute for buttermilk, use 1 teaspoon vinegar or lemon juice plus milk to make 1 cup.

** Cake can be baked in 13 × 9-inch pan. Grease bottom only of pan. Bake at 350°F 30 to 35 minutes or until toothpick inserted in center comes out clean. Cool completely. Spread top of cooled cake with filling mixture. Serve topped with seafoam cream.

High Altitude (3500–6500 ft): Bake 30 to 35 minutes. Cool 7 minutes; remove from pans. Cool completely.

1 Serving: Calories 450; Total Fat 24g (Saturated Fat 11g; Trans Fat 1.5g); Cholesterol 75mg; Sodium 310mg; Total Carbohydrate 51g (Dietary Fiber 1g) Exchanges: ½ Starch, 3 Other Carbohydrate, ½ High-Fat Meat, 4 Fat; Carbohydrate Choices: 3½

"My Inspiration" Cake

Lois Kanago   Denver, CO
Bake-Off® Contest 5, 1953
$25,000 Grand Prize Winner

> **Prep Time:** 25 Minutes
> **Start to Finish:** 2 Hours 10 Minutes
> 16 servings

CAKE
1 cup chopped pecans
2¼ cups Pillsbury BEST® all-purpose
   or unbleached flour
1½ cups granulated sugar
4 teaspoons baking powder
½ teaspoon salt
⅔ cup shortening
1¼ cups milk
1 teaspoon vanilla
4 egg whites
2 oz semisweet baking chocolate, grated

FROSTING
½ cup granulated sugar
2 oz unsweetened baking chocolate
¼ cup water
½ cup shortening
1 teaspoon vanilla
2¼ cups powdered sugar
1 to 2 tablespoons water

1   Heat oven to 350°F. Grease and flour two 9-inch round cake pans. Sprinkle pecans evenly in pans.

2   In large bowl, beat remaining cake ingredients except egg whites and grated chocolate 1½ minutes with electric mixer at medium speed. Add egg whites; beat 1½ minutes. Carefully spoon ¼ of batter into each pan. Sprinkle with grated chocolate. Spoon remaining batter over grated chocolate; spread carefully.

3   Bake 30 to 40 minutes or until cake is golden brown and top springs back when touched lightly in center. Cool 10 minutes; remove from pans to cooling racks. Cool completely, about 1 hour.

4 Meanwhile, in 1-quart saucepan, heat ½ cup sugar, the unsweetened baking chocolate and ¼ cup water over low heat until melted, stirring constantly until smooth. Remove from heat; cool.

5 In small bowl, mix ½ cup shortening and 1 teaspoon vanilla. Gradually beat in 2 cups of the powdered sugar until well blended. Reserve ⅓ cup white frosting. To remaining frosting, add cooled chocolate, remaining ¼ cup powdered sugar and enough water for desired spreading consistency.

6 To assemble cake, place 1 layer, pecan side up, on serving plate. Spread with about ½ cup chocolate frosting. Top with second layer, pecan side up. Frost side and ½ inch around top edge of cake with remaining chocolate frosting. If necessary, thin reserved white frosting with enough water for desired piping consistency; pipe around edge of nuts on top of cake.

High Altitude (3500–6500 ft): In cake, increase Pillsbury BEST® flour to 2½ cups; decrease baking powder to 3 teaspoons.

1 Serving: Calories 470; Total Fat 23g (Saturated Fat 6g; Trans Fat 2.5g); Cholesterol 0mg; Sodium 220mg; Total Carbohydrate 61g (Dietary Fiber 2g) Exchanges: ½ Starch, 3½ Other Carbohydrate, ½ High-Fat Meat, 3½ Fat; Carbohydrate Choices: 4

Key Lime Cream Torte

Joan Wittan North Potomac, MD
Bake-Off® Contest 35, 1992

Prep Time: 35 Minutes
Start to Finish: 4 Hours 15 Minutes
12 servings

CAKE
1 box (18.25 oz) Pillsbury® Moist Supreme® golden butter recipe cake mix
2 tablespoons lime juice plus water to equal 1 cup
½ cup butter or margarine, softened
3 eggs

FILLING
1 can (14 oz) sweetened condensed milk (not evaporated)
½ cup lime juice
2 cups whipping cream

GARNISH, IF DESIRED
Lime slices

1 Heat oven to 350°F. Grease two 9- or 8-inch round cake pans with shortening; lightly flour. In large bowl, beat cake ingredients with electric mixer on low speed about 30 seconds or until moistened. Beat on medium speed 2 minutes, scraping bowl occasionally. Pour batter evenly into pans.

2 Bake 9-inch pans 27 to 32 minutes, 8-inch pans 32 to 37 minutes or until toothpick inserted in center comes out clean. Cool 15 minutes. Remove from pans to cooling racks. Cool completely, about 1 hour.

3 In small bowl, mix condensed milk and ½ cup lime juice until well blended. In large bowl, beat whipping cream with electric mixer on high speed until stiff peaks form. Reserve 1 cup of the whipped cream. Fold condensed milk mixture into remaining whipped cream just until blended.

4 To assemble torte, cut each layer in half horizontally to make 4 layers. Place 1 cake layer, cut side up, on serving plate. Spread with ⅓ of the whipped cream filling. Repeat with second and third cake layers. Top with remaining cake layer. Pipe in decorative pattern or spread reserved whipped cream over top of torte. Refrigerate at least 2 hours before serving. Garnish with lime slices. Cover and refrigerate any remaining torte.

High Altitude (3500–6500 ft): Increase water to 1¼ cups.

1 Serving: Calories 490; Total Fat 27g (Saturated Fat 16g; Trans Fat 1.5g); Cholesterol 130mg; Sodium 410mg; Total Carbohydrate 55g (Dietary Fiber 0g) Exchanges: 1 Starch, 2½ Other Carbohydrate, ½ High-Fat Meat, 4½ Fat; Carbohydrate Choices: 3½

Tiramisu Toffee Torte

Tiramisu Toffee Torte

Christie Henson   Conway, AR
Bake-Off® Contest 35, 1992
$2,000 Winner

Prep Time: 35 Minutes
Start to Finish: 2 Hours 5 Minutes
12 servings

CAKE
1 box (18.25 oz) Pillsbury® Moist
  Supreme® classic white cake mix
1 cup strong brewed coffee, room
  temperature
4 egg whites
4 toffee candy bars (1.4 oz each),
  very finely chopped

FROSTING
⅔ cup sugar
⅓ cup chocolate-flavor syrup
4 oz cream cheese, softened
2 cups whipping cream
2 teaspoons vanilla
1 cup strong brewed coffee,
  room temperature

GARNISH, IF DESIRED
Chopped toffee candy bars or
  chocolate curls

1   Heat oven to 350°F. Grease two 9- or 8-inch round cake pans; lightly flour. In large bowl, beat cake mix, 1 cup coffee and the egg whites with electric mixer on low speed about 30 seconds or until moistened. Beat on medium speed 2 minutes, scraping bowl occasionally. Fold in chopped toffee bars. Spread batter evenly in pans.

2   Bake 9-inch pans 20 to 30 minutes, 8-inch pans 30 to 40 minutes or until toothpick inserted in center comes out clean. Cool 10 minutes. Remove from pans to cooling racks. Cool completely, about 1 hour.

3   In medium bowl, beat sugar, chocolate syrup and cream cheese with electric mixer on medium speed until smooth. Add whipping cream and vanilla; beat until light and fluffy. Refrigerate until ready to use.

4   To assemble cake, cut each cake layer in half horizontally to make 4 layers. Drizzle each cut side with ¼ cup coffee. Place 1 cake layer, coffee side up, on serving plate; spread with ¾ cup frosting. Repeat with second and third cake layers. Top with remaining cake layer. Frost side and top of cake with remaining frosting. Garnish with chopped toffee bars. Cover and refrigerate torte.

High Altitude (3500–6500 ft): Do not use 8-inch pans. Bake 9-inch pans 25 to 30 minutes.

1 Serving: Calories 480; Total Fat 24g (Saturated Fat 13g; Trans Fat 1.5g); Cholesterol 60mg; Sodium 400mg; Total Carbohydrate 60g (Dietary Fiber 0g) Exchanges: ½ Starch, 3½ Other Carbohydrate, ½ High-Fat Meat, 4 Fat; Carbohydrate Choices: 4

Early Experiments Lead to Success

If at first you don't succeed, try, try, again . . . Christie Henson volunteered an early disaster story: "One time I made cream pie and added the eggs too late. I ended up with scrambled eggs in my chocolate pie." Christie never gave up, thanks to the unwavering support of her family. "My poor father ate whatever I made, no matter how it turned out." Christie ultimately mastered the tricky arts of éclair making and converting European classics for busy American cooks—and then she captured a cash prize at the Bake-Off® Contest for her efforts.

Thick 'n Fudgy Triple-Chocolate Pudding Cake

Janice Kollar   Woodbridge, NJ
Bake-Off® Contest 39, 2000
$2,000 Winner

Prep Time: 15 Minutes
Start to Finish: 1 Hour 30 Minutes
9 servings

1 box (15.8 oz) Pillsbury® double chocolate brownie mix with chocolate syrup
½ teaspoon baking powder
½ cup milk
¼ cup butter or margarine, melted
1 teaspoon vanilla
1½ cups water
1½ teaspoons instant espresso coffee granules
1 cup Pillsbury® Creamy Supreme® chocolate fudge frosting (from 1-lb container)
Whipped cream or vanilla ice cream

1   Heat oven to 350°F. Spray 9- or 8-inch square pan with cooking spray. In large bowl, mix brownie mix and baking powder. Stir in milk, butter, vanilla and chocolate syrup from packet in brownie mix. Spread batter in pan.

2   In 2-quart saucepan, heat water to boiling. Add espresso granules; stir to dissolve. Add frosting; cook over low heat, stirring frequently, until melted and smooth. Slowly pour over batter in pan. DO NOT STIR.

3   Bake 40 to 45 minutes or until edges are bubbly and cake begins to pull away from sides of pan (top may appear shiny in spots). Cool 30 minutes before serving. Serve warm or cold with whipped cream.

Cover and refrigerate any remaining cake.

High Altitude (3500–6500 ft): Add ⅓ cup Pillsbury BEST® all-purpose flour to dry brownie mix; decrease water to 1 cup.

1 Serving: Calories 410; Total Fat 18g (Saturated Fat 11g; Trans Fat 1g); Cholesterol 15mg; Sodium 200mg; Total Carbohydrate 59g (Dietary Fiber 2g) Exchanges: 1 Starch, 3 Other Carbohydrate, 3½ Fat; Carbohydrate Choices: 4

Praline Torte with Chocolate Truffle Filling

Merrie Wimmer   Flower Mound, TX
Bake-Off® Contest 35, 1992
$2,000 Winner

Prep Time: 45 Minutes
Start to Finish: 4 Hours 5 Minutes
12 servings

TORTE
1⅔ cups Pillsbury BEST® all-purpose flour
2 teaspoons baking powder
¼ teaspoon salt
4 eggs, separated
1½ cups sugar
1½ cups butter or margarine, softened
¾ cup milk

CHOCOLATE TRUFFLE CREAM FILLING
6 oz dark chocolate candy bar or semisweet baking chocolate, chopped
1 tablespoon butter or margarine
⅓ cup whipping cream

MOCHA PRALINE CREAM
½ cup sliced almonds
¼ cup sugar
1½ cups whipping cream
1 tablespoon sugar
1 teaspoon instant coffee granules or crystals
¼ teaspoon almond extract

1   Heat oven to 375°F. Grease and flour three 8- or 9-inch round cake pans.* In medium bowl, mix flour, baking powder and salt. In small bowl, beat egg whites with electric mixer on high speed until soft peaks form.

2   In large bowl, beat 1½ cups sugar, 1½ cups butter and the egg yolks until light and fluffy. Add flour mixture alternately with milk, beating well after each addition. Fold in beaten egg whites. Pour batter into pans.

3   Bake 15 to 20 minutes or until toothpick inserted in center comes out clean. Cool 5 minutes. Remove from pans to cooling racks. Cool completely, about 1 hour.

4   In 1-quart saucepan, melt chocolate over very low heat, stirring constantly until smooth. Remove from heat; stir in 1 tablespoon butter and ⅓ cup whipping cream. If necessary, refrigerate 15 to 30 minutes or until thickened and of desired spreading consistency.

5   Line cookie sheet with foil. In 6-inch skillet over low heat, cook almonds and ¼ cup sugar, stirring constantly, until sugar is melted and almonds are coated. Place on foil-lined cookie sheet; cool. Place coated almonds in plastic bag; coarsely crush with wooden mallet or rolling pin. Set aside.

6   Place 1 cake layer on serving plate; spread with half of filling. Repeat with second cake layer and remaining filling. Top with remaining cake layer.

7   In small bowl, beat 1½ cups whipping cream, 1 tablespoon

sugar, the instant coffee granules and almond extract just until stiff peaks form. DO NOT OVERBEAT. Reserve 2 tablespoons crushed almonds for garnish. Fold in remaining crushed almonds. Frost top and side of cake. Refrigerate 2 to 3 hours before serving. Just before serving, garnish with reserved crushed almonds. Cover and refrigerate any remaining cake.

Layers can be baked 1 at a time if 3 pans are not available. Cover and refrigerate remaining batter until pan is available.

High Altitude (3500–6500 ft): In torte, increase Pillsbury BEST® all-purpose flour to 2 cups; decrease baking powder to 1½ teaspoons; decrease sugar to 1¼ cups; decrease butter to 1 cup. Bake 18 to 23 minutes.

1 Serving: Calories 640; Total Fat 44g (Saturated Fat 26g; Trans Fat 1.5g); Cholesterol 175mg; Sodium 340mg; Total Carbohydrate 55g (Dietary Fiber 2g) Exchanges: ½ Starch, 3 Other Carbohydrate, ½ High-Fat Meat, 8 Fat; Carbohydrate Choices: 3½

Dark Chocolate Sacher Torte

Phyllis Trier Grand View, NY
Bake-Off® Contest 31, 1984

> **Prep Time:** 30 Minutes
> **Start to Finish:** 3 Hours 45 Minutes
> 16 servings

CAKE
½ cup finely chopped dried apricots
½ cup rum*
1 box (18.25 oz) Pillsbury® Moist
   Supreme® devil's food or dark
   chocolate cake mix
¾ cup water
⅓ cup vegetable oil
3 eggs

GLAZE
2 jars (10 oz each) apricot preserves
2 tablespoons rum**

FROSTING
1 cup semisweet chocolate chips (6 oz)
¾ cup butter or margarine
½ to 1 cup sliced almonds

A Memorable Mother's Day Treat

Many mothers deserve sainthood for their willingness to sample the special "treats" concocted for them by their offspring on Mother's Day. Merrie Wimmer's mother should be among them. At age seven, Merrie and her brother baked cookies for their mom for Mother's Day. Unfortunately, they used just three ingredients: flour, sugar and water. Former childhood bakers wishing to redeem themselves would do well to bake Merrie's recipe for this Mother's Day. The luscious three layer cake with a fudge truffle filling and praline whipped cream frosting will do much to erase any memories of earlier fiascos.

1 Heat oven to 350°F. Grease and flour two 9- or 8-inch round cake pans. In small bowl, mix apricots and ½ cup rum; let stand 10 minutes. In large bowl, beat apricot-rum mixture and remaining cake ingredients with electric mixer on low speed until moistened; beat 2 minutes at high speed. Pour into pans.

2 Bake 9-inch pans 25 to 35 minutes, 8-inch pans 35 to 45 minutes, or until toothpick inserted in center comes out clean. Cool 15 minutes. Remove from pans to cooling racks. Cool completely.

3 In 1-quart saucepan over low heat, melt glaze ingredients; strain to remove large apricot pieces. To assemble torte, carefully slice each layer in half horizontally to make 4 layers. Place 1 layer on serving plate; spread with ¼ cup glaze. Repeat with remaining layers and glaze, ending with cake layer. Spread remaining ¼ cup glaze

over top of torte, allowing some to run down sides. Refrigerate about 1 hour or until glaze is set.

4 In 1-quart saucepan, melt chocolate chips and butter over low heat, stirring constantly, until smooth. Refrigerate about 30 minutes, stirring occasionally, until slightly thickened. Spread frosting over side and top of torte. Arrange almond slices around side. Refrigerate at least 1 hour before serving. Garnish as desired. Cover and refrigerate any remaining torte.

Substitute 2 teaspoons rum extract plus water to make ½ cup.
**Substitute 1 teaspoon rum extract plus water to make 2 tablespoons.*

High Altitude (3500–6500 ft): Heat oven to 375°F. Add 3 tablespoons Pillsbury BEST® all-purpose flour to dry cake mix. Bake 30 to 40 minutes.

1 Serving: Calories 450; Total Fat 21g (Saturated Fat 10g; Trans Fat 0.5g); Cholesterol 65mg; Sodium 340mg; Total Carbohydrate 61g (Dietary Fiber 2g) Exchanges: 1 Starch, 3 Other Carbohydrate, 4 Fat; Carbohydrate Choices: 4

Fudge-Strawberry Cream Torte

Rebecca Kremer Hudson, WI
Bake-Off® Contest 42, 2006

Prep Time: 1 Hour 15 Minutes
Start to Finish: 3 Hours 35 Minutes
12 servings

BROWNIE LAYERS
1 box (19.5 oz) Pillsbury® Brownie
 Classics traditional fudge
 brownie mix
½ cup vegetable oil
¼ cup water
3 eggs

STRAWBERRY CREAM
3 tablespoons granulated sugar
1 package (8 oz) cream cheese,
 softened
1 container (6 oz) strawberry thick
 & creamy low-fat yogurt
1½ cups finely chopped fresh
 strawberries

CHOCOLATE FUDGE
½ cup whipping cream
1½ cups semisweet chocolate chips
 (9 oz)

GARNISH
1 teaspoon powdered sugar
6 small to medium fresh whole
 strawberries, halved

1 Heat oven to 350°F. Spray bottoms of two 9-inch round cake pans with cooking spray and line with waxed paper; spray waxed paper with cooking spray. Make brownie batter as directed on box for cake-like brownies using oil, water and eggs. Spread half of batter in each pan. Bake 18 to 23 minutes. Cool in pans on cooling racks 10 minutes. Run knife around

brownie layers to loosen. Place racks upside down over pans; turn racks and pans over. Remove pans. Cool completely, about 35 minutes.

2 Meanwhile, in small bowl, beat granulated sugar and cream cheese with electric mixer on medium speed until well blended. Beat in strawberry yogurt until smooth and creamy. Fold in chopped strawberries. Refrigerate while brownie layers cool.

3 In 1-quart saucepan, heat whipping cream over medium heat, stirring constantly, just until cream begins to boil. Remove from heat. Add chocolate chips; press into cream. Cover; let stand 3 minutes. Vigorously beat with wire whisk until smooth. Cool completely, about 30 minutes.

4 To assemble torte, place 1 brownie layer on serving plate. Spread half of strawberry cream evenly over brownie to within 1 inch of edge. Carefully spoon and spread half of chocolate fudge almost to edge of strawberry cream. Repeat layers, ending with chocolate fudge. Arrange halved strawberries in spoke fashion on top of torte. Refrigerate at least 1 hour before serving.

5 To serve,* sprinkle powdered sugar over top of torte and around plate. Carefully cut torte with hot knife into wedges to avoid cracking of chocolate fudge on top. Loosely cover and refrigerate any remaining torte.

If torte has been stored for more than 3 hours before serving, let stand at room temperature 10 minutes before cutting.

High Altitude (3500–6500 ft): Stir ½ cup Pillsbury BEST® all-purpose flour into dry brownie mix. Increase water to ⅓ cup. Bake 21 to 25 minutes.

1 Serving: Calories 550; Total Fat 31g (Saturated Fat 13g; Trans Fat 0g); Cholesterol 85mg; Sodium 210mg; Total Carbohydrate 61g (Dietary Fiber 3g) Exchanges: 1 Starch, 3 Other Carbohydrate, ½ High-Fat Meat, 5 Fat; Carbohydrate Choices: 4

Brownie Ganache Torte

Barbara Estabrook Rhinelander, WI
Bake-Off® Contest 41, 2004

Prep Time: 40 Minutes
Start to Finish: 4 Hours 50 Minutes
16 servings

CRUST
1¼ cups graham cracker crumbs
¼ cup almond toffee bits
1 tablespoon packed brown sugar
¼ cup butter or margarine, melted

CHOCOLATE LAYER
½ cup whipping cream
1 tablespoon coffee-flavored liqueur
 or strong brewed coffee
1 cup semisweet chocolate chips

FILLING
1 box (19.5 oz) Pillsbury® Brownie
 Classics fudge toffee or traditional
 fudge brownie mix
6 tablespoons butter or margarine, melted
3 tablespoons water
3 egg whites
½ cup chopped slivered almonds,
 toasted*

TOPPING, IF DESIRED
Whipped cream

1 Lightly butter bottom only of 10-inch springform pan or spray with cooking spray. In medium bowl, mix crust ingredients with fork until crumbs are coated. Press in bottom of pan.

2 In 1-quart saucepan, heat whipping cream over medium-low heat until hot. Stir in liqueur. With wire whisk, stir in chocolate chips until smooth. Remove from heat. Place ¼ cup chocolate mixture in small microwavable bowl; set aside for drizzle. Pour and carefully spread remaining chocolate mixture over crust. Freeze 20 minutes.

3 Meanwhile, heat oven to 325°F. In large bowl, beat brownie mix, 6 tablespoons melted butter and the water 50 strokes with spoon (mixture will be thick). In small bowl, beat egg whites with electric mixer on high speed 1 to 2 minutes or until soft peaks form. Add to brownie mixture; beat on low speed just until blended, about 30 seconds (batter will appear lumpy). Spread batter over chocolate layer. Sprinkle almonds evenly over top.

4 Bake 45 to 60 minutes or until center is puffed and set and edges are firm (middle will be soft). DO NOT OVERBAKE. Cool on cooling rack 2 hours.

5 Run knife around side of pan; remove side. Microwave reserved chocolate mixture on High 10 to 15 seconds or until desired drizzling consistency; drizzle over torte. To serve at room temperature, cool 1 hour longer, or refrigerate until serving time. Top individual servings with whipped cream.

* To toast chopped almonds, bake uncovered in ungreased shallow pan in 350°F oven about 10 minutes, stirring occasionally, until golden brown. Or cook in ungreased heavy skillet over medium-low heat 5 to 7 minutes, stirring frequently until browning begins, then stirring constantly until golden brown.

High Altitude (3500–6500 ft): When making crust, decrease melted butter to 3 tablespoons. When making filling, add ¼ cup Pillsbury BEST® all-purpose flour to dry brownie mix, increase water to ¼ cup and use 2 whole eggs (mix eggs in bowl with brownie mix, melted butter and water). Heat oven to 350°F. Bake 1 hour 5 minutes to 1 hour 10 minutes.

1 Serving: Calories 360; Total Fat 19g (Saturated Fat 9g; Trans Fat 0.5g); Cholesterol 30mg; Sodium 210mg; Total Carbohydrate 44g (Dietary Fiber 2g) Exchanges: 1 Starch, 2 Other Carbohydrate, 3½ Fat; Carbohydrate Choices: 3

Brownie Ganache Torte

Heavenly Chocolate-Raspberry Torte

Pat Freymuth   Colorado Springs, CO
Bake-Off® Contest 42, 2006

Prep Time: 20 Minutes
Start to Finish: 2 Hours 35 Minutes
12 servings

1 bag (12 oz) dark chocolate chips
   (2 cups)
1 container (6 oz) raspberry fat-free
   yogurt
6 roasted almond crunchy granola bars
   (3 pouches from 8.9-oz box), finely
   crushed (heaping 1 cup)*
1 cup egg whites (about 7)
2 tablespoons plus 1 teaspoon fat-free
   half-and-half
2 teaspoons raspberry-flavored syrup
   (for coffee drinks) or red raspberry
   syrup (for pancakes)
¼ cup powdered sugar
Fresh raspberries, if desired
Fresh mint leaves, if desired

1 Heat oven to 350°F. Lightly spray bottom of 9-inch round cake pan with cooking spray; line bottom with parchment paper. Spray paper and side of pan with cooking spray.

2 Reserve ½ cup of the chocolate chips for glaze; place remaining chips in medium microwavable bowl (or place in top of double boiler). Stir in yogurt until chips are coated. Microwave uncovered on High in 1-minute increments, stirring after each minute, until chips are completely melted (or heat in double boiler over simmering water, stirring frequently, until melted). Stir in crushed granola bars and egg whites until well blended. Pour batter into pan.

3 Bake 20 to 30 minutes or until side of torte has risen and center is shiny but firm when touched (if center rises, torte has been overbaked). Cool in pan on cooling rack, about 30 minutes (as torte cools, side will pull away from pan and torte will slightly sink). Refrigerate until chilled, about 1 hour.

4 In small microwavable bowl, microwave reserved ½ cup chocolate chips and the half-and-half uncovered on High in 30-second increments, stirring after each, until chips are melted. Cool slightly, about 2 minutes.

5 Place rack upside down over pan; turn rack and pan over. Remove pan and parchment paper. Pour chocolate mixture over torte; spread over top and side. Slide torte onto serving plate.

6 In small bowl, mix syrup and powdered sugar. Place in small resealable food-storage plastic bag; seal bag and cut tiny hole in one bottom corner. Drizzle over top of torte in spiral pattern; gently run toothpick back and forth through spiral pattern to feather. Refrigerate until glaze is set and firm to the touch, about 20 minutes.

7 Before serving, garnish tray and/or individual dessert plates with raspberries and mint. Cut torte into wedges with warm, dry knife, cleaning knife between cuts. Cover and refrigerate any remaining torte.

To easily crush granola bars, do not unwrap; use rolling pin to crush bars.

High Altitude (3500–6500 ft): Bake 25 to 30 minutes.

1 Serving: Calories 240; Total Fat 10g (Saturated Fat 5g;
Trans Fat 0g); Cholesterol 0mg; Sodium 95mg;
Total Carbohydrate 31g (Dietary Fiber 2g) Exchanges:
½ Starch, 1½ Other Carbohydrate, ½ High-Fat Meat,
1 Fat; Carbohydrate Choices: 2

Shhhh! This Cake is Actually Good for You

Pat Freymuth became known as the "Cake Walk Queen" for the dozen cakes she regularly baked for the school carnival's cakewalk. So it's not surprising that she created a luxurious dessert torte for her Bake-Off® Contest entry. To make this better-for-you dessert,

Pat adapted her torte recipe from a fat-laden version that was her husband's favorite. The result, Pat says, is a "rich, dark, creamy chocolate heaven. You don't even need to let them know they're eating cholesterol-fighting oats."

Heavenly Chocolate Raspberry Torte

"Milleniyum" Chocolate Torte

Steven Mandell   Stevenson, MD
Bake-Off® Contest 40, 2002
$2,000 Winner

Prep Time: 20 Minutes
Start to Finish: 3 Hours 30 Minutes
16 servings

1 cup whipping cream
1 bag (12 oz) semisweet chocolate
   chips (2 cups)
1 tablespoon instant coffee granules
   or crystals
¼ cup butter or margarine
3 tablespoons water
1 box (15.5 oz) Pillsbury® Fudge
   Supreme chocolate chunk
   premium brownie mix
2 eggs
1 package (8 oz) cream cheese, softened
Whipped cream or vanilla ice cream,
   if desired

1   Heat oven to 350°F. Grease 10- or 9-inch springform pan. In 2-quart saucepan, heat whipping cream over medium heat until very hot. DO NOT BOIL. Stir in chocolate chips until melted and smooth. Set aside. (Mixture will thicken.)

2   In 1-quart saucepan, heat coffee granules, butter and water over medium heat, stirring occasionally, until butter is melted. In large bowl, mix coffee mixture, brownie mix and 1 of the eggs. Spread batter in pan.

3   In small bowl, beat cream cheese with electric mixer on medium speed until light and fluffy. Add remaining egg; beat until smooth.

Add ½ cup of the chocolate mixture; blend well. Spread evenly over brownie mixture in pan.

4   Bake 10-inch pan 35 to 45 minutes, 9-inch pan 45 to 55 minutes or until top springs back when touched lightly in center and surface appears dry. Cool 10 minutes. Run knife around side of pan to loosen; remove side of pan. Cool completely, about 1 hour 15 minutes.

5   Place torte on serving platter. Spread remaining chocolate mixture over top of torte, letting mixture run down side. Refrigerate at least 1 hour until chilled. Serve with whipped cream. Cover and refrigerate any remaining torte.

High Altitude (3500–6500 ft): Add 3 tablespoons Pillsbury BEST® all-purpose flour to dry brownie mix.

1 Serving: Calories 360; Total Fat 22g (Saturated Fat 13g; Trans Fat 1g); Cholesterol 65mg; Sodium 150mg; Total Carbohydrate 36g (Dietary Fiber 2g) Exchanges: 1 Starch, 1½ Other Carbohydrate, 4 Fat; Carbohydrate Choices: 2½

Tuxedo Brownie Torte

Patricia Lapiezo   LaMesa, CA
Bake-Off® Contest 35, 1992

Prep Time: 45 Minutes
Start to Finish: 4 Hours 15 Minutes
16 servings

BROWNIE
1 box (19.5 oz) Pillsbury® Brownie
   Classics traditional fudge
   brownie mix
½ cup vegetable oil
¼ cup water
2 eggs

FILLING
1 package (10 oz) frozen raspberries
   in syrup, thawed
1 tablespoon granulated sugar
1 tablespoon cornstarch
1 cup fresh raspberries or frozen whole
   raspberries without syrup, thawed,
   drained on paper towel, reserving
   3 for garnish

TOPPING
1 package (8 oz) cream cheese, softened
⅓ cup powdered sugar
2 tablespoons white crème de cacao,
   if desired
1 cup white vanilla baking chips, melted
1 cup whipping cream, whipped

GARNISH
1 tablespoon grated semisweet baking
   chocolate
3 whole fresh or frozen raspberries,
   if desired
3 fresh mint leaves, if desired

1   Heat oven to 350°F. Grease bottom and side of 9- or 10-inch springform pan with shortening. In large bowl, beat brownie ingredients 50 strokes with spoon. Spread batter in pan.

2   Bake 40 to 45 minutes or until center is set. Cool 30 minutes. Run knife around side of pan to loosen; remove side. Cool completely, about 30 minutes.

3   In blender or food processor, place thawed raspberries in syrup. Cover; blend until smooth. Place strainer over small bowl; pour berries into strainer. Press berries with back of spoon through strainer to remove seeds; discard seeds.

4   In 1-quart saucepan, mix granulated sugar and cornstarch. Gradually add raspberry puree, mixing well. Heat to boiling. Cook until mixture is clear, stirring constantly. Cool 5 minutes. Spread over brownie layer to within ½ inch of edge. Arrange 1 cup fresh raspberries evenly over raspberry mixture. Refrigerate.

5 In medium bowl, beat cream cheese, powdered sugar and crème de cacao with electric mixer on medium speed until smooth. Beat in melted vanilla chips until smooth. Fold in whipped cream. Cover; refrigerate 45 minutes.

6 Stir topping mixture until smooth. Spread 1½ cups of the topping over raspberries. Pipe or spoon on remaining topping. Refrigerate at least 1 hour until firm.

7 Before serving, sprinkle grated chocolate in 1-inch border around outside edge of torte. Garnish center with whole raspberries and mint leaves. Cover and refrigerate any remaining torte.

High Altitude (3500–6500 ft): Add ⅓ cup Pillsbury BEST® all-purpose flour to dry brownie mix; increase water to ⅓ cup.

1 Serving: Calories 430; Total Fat 24g (Saturated Fat 11g; Trans Fat 0g); Cholesterol 60mg; Sodium 180mg; Total Carbohydrate 48g (Dietary Fiber 2g) Exchanges: ½ Starch, 2½ Other Carbohydrate, ½ High-Fat Meat, 4 Fat; Carbohydrate Choices: 3

Tuxedo Brownie Torte

Mocha Macaroon Torte

Chocolate Mousse Fantasy Torte

Christine Vidra   Maumee, OH
Bake-Off® Contest 34, 1990
$10,000 Winner

Prep Time: 20 Minutes
Start to Finish: 3 Hours 35 Minutes
16 servings

BASE
1 box (19.5 oz) Pillsbury® Brownie
   Classics traditional fudge
   brownie mix
2 teaspoons instant coffee granules
   or crystals
½ cup butter or margarine, softened
2 tablespoons water
2 eggs

TOPPING
1½ cups semisweet chocolate chips (9 oz)
1 oz unsweetened baking chocolate
1 teaspoon instant coffee granules or
   crystals
¼ cup water
2 tablespoons butter or margarine
1 cup whipping cream

GARNISH
½ oz unsweetened baking chocolate,
   melted

1   Heat oven to 350°F. Grease
9- or 10-inch springform pan with
shortening. In large bowl, beat
base ingredients with electric
mixer on medium speed 1 minute.
Spread batter in pan. Bake 36 to 42
minutes or until set. Cool in pan on
cooling rack 1 hour. Remove side of
pan; cool completely, about 1 hour.

2   In 1-quart saucepan, cook
all topping ingredients except
whipping cream over low heat,
stirring constantly, until mixture
is smooth. Remove from heat. Cool

15 minutes, stirring occasionally.
Meanwhile, in small bowl, beat
whipping cream on high speed
until soft peaks form.

3   Fold warm chocolate mixture
into whipped cream. With pastry
tube fitted with decorative tip, pipe
topping mixture evenly over cooled
base, or spread topping over base.
Drizzle ½ ounce melted chocolate
over topping. Refrigerate at least
1 hour until topping is set. Before
serving, let torte stand at room
temperature about 30 minutes.
Cover and refrigerate any remaining torte.

High Altitude (3500–6500 ft): Decrease
butter in base to ⅓ cup.

1 Serving: Calories 370; Total Fat 22g (Saturated Fat 12g;
Trans Fat 0g); Cholesterol 60mg; Sodium 160mg;
Total Carbohydrate 40g (Dietary Fiber 2g) Exchanges:
½ Starch, 2 Other Carbohydrate, 4 ½ Fat; Carbohydrate
Choices: 2½

Mocha Macaroon Torte

Pamela Kenney Basey   Denver, CO
Bake-Off® Contest 40, 2002

Prep Time: 20 Minutes
Start to Finish: 3 Hours 35 Minutes
12 servings

CRUST AND FILLING
1 roll (16.5 oz) Pillsbury® Create 'n
   Bake® refrigerated double chocolate
   chip & chunk cookies
1 package (8 oz) cream cheese,
   softened
1 egg
½ cup coconut
¼ cup sugar
2 tablespoons brewed coffee
1 teaspoon vanilla
⅓ cup semisweet chocolate chips

TOPPING
¼ cup sugar
¼ cup chopped pecans
1 cup semisweet chocolate chips

SERVE WITH, IF DESIRED
French vanilla ice cream or vanilla
   frozen yogurt
Chocolate-covered coffee beans

1   Heat oven to 350°F. Cut cookie
dough in half crosswise; cut each
section in half lengthwise. Press
dough in bottom of ungreased
10- or 9-inch springform pan.

2   Bake 12 to 18 minutes or
until light golden brown. Cool
10 minutes. While crust is cooling,
in medium bowl, beat cream cheese
with electric mixer on medium speed
until light and fluffy. Add egg; beat
until smooth. On low speed, beat in
coconut, ¼ cup sugar, the coffee and
vanilla. With spoon, stir in ⅓ cup
chocolate chips. Spoon and carefully
spread mixture over crust. Sprinkle
with topping ingredients.

3   Bake 30 to 45 minutes longer
or until filling is set and edges are
golden brown. Cool 10 minutes.

4   Run knife around side of pan to
loosen; carefully remove side. Cool
1 hour. Refrigerate until chilled,
1 to 2 hours. Serve with ice cream
garnished with coffee beans. Cover
and refrigerate any remaining torte.

High Altitude (3500–6500 ft): Bake crust
16 to 20 minutes. After sprinkling with
topping, bake 35 to 50 minutes.

1 Serving: Calories 450; Total Fat 26g (Saturated
Fat 12g; Trans Fat 0g); Cholesterol 45mg; Sodium
200mg; Total Carbohydrate 48g (Dietary Fiber 1g)
Exchanges: 1½ Starch, 1½ Other Carbohydrate, 5 Fat;
Carbohydrate Choices: 3

Fudgy Orange Cappuccino Torte

Sharla Jack Springfield, OH
Bake-Off® Contest 35, 1992
$10,000 Winner

Prep Time: 30 Minutes
Start to Finish: 2 Hours 40 Minutes
16 servings

BROWNIE

1 box (19.5 oz) Pillsbury® Brownie
   Classics traditional fudge
   brownie mix
½ cup vegetable oil
¼ cup water
¼ cup orange-flavored liqueur or orange
   juice
2 eggs
1 teaspoon grated orange peel
4 oz sweet dark chocolate or semisweet
   baking chocolate, coarsely chopped

FILLING

1 cup sweetened condensed milk
   (not evaporated)
6 oz sweet dark chocolate or semisweet
   baking chocolate, chopped
2 egg yolks, slightly beaten
2 tablespoons orange-flavored liqueur
   or orange juice
¾ cup finely chopped nuts

TOPPING

1½ cups whipping cream
¾ cup powdered sugar
⅓ cup unsweetened baking cocoa
2 tablespoons orange-flavored liqueur
   or orange juice
1 teaspoon grated orange peel
⅛ teaspoon salt

GARNISH, IF DESIRED

Orange slices, twisted
Orange leaves

1 Heat oven to 350°F. Grease bottom of 9- or 10-inch springform pan. In large bowl, mix all brownie ingredients except 4 ounces chocolate; beat 50 strokes by hand. Stir in chocolate. Spread in pan. Bake 40 to 45 minutes or until center is set. Cool completely.

2 In 2-quart saucepan, mix condensed milk and 6 ounces chocolate. Cook over low heat, stirring constantly, until chocolate is melted and mixture is smooth. Remove from heat. Stir 2 tablespoons hot mixture into egg yolks. Gradually stir yolk mixture into hot mixture in saucepan. Cook over medium heat 3 minutes, stirring constantly. Remove from heat. Stir in 2 tablespoons liqueur and the nuts. Refrigerate until just cool, about 25 minutes. Spread filling mixture over top of cooled brownies. Refrigerate at least 1 hour until filling is set.

3 Run knife around side of pan to loosen; remove side of pan. To serve, place brownie on serving plate. In large bowl, beat topping ingredients until stiff peaks form. Pipe or spoon topping mixture evenly over chilled filling. Garnish with orange slices and leaves. Cover and refrigerate any remaining torte.

High Altitude (3500–6500 ft): Heat oven to 375°F. Add ½ cup Pillsbury BEST® all-purpose flour to dry brownie mix. Bake 35 to 45 minutes.

1 Serving: Calories 520; Total Fat 29g (Saturated Fat 11g; Trans Fat 0g); Cholesterol 85mg; Sodium 160mg; Total Carbohydrate 59g (Dietary Fiber 3g) Exchanges: ½ Starch, 3 ½ Other Carbohydrate, ½ High-Fat Meat, 5 Fat; Carbohydrate Choices: 4

Key Lime Pecan Tart (page 318)

Glazed Apple Cream Pie

Rema Conger   Tulsa, OK
Bake-Off® Contest 37, 1996

Prep Time: 30 Minutes
Start to Finish: 3 Hours 10 Minutes
8 servings

CRUST
1 box (15 oz) Pillsbury® refrigerated pie
   crusts, softened as directed on box

FILLING
½ cup granulated sugar
½ cup milk
½ cup whipping cream
¼ cup butter or margarine
2 tablespoons cornstarch
2 tablespoons milk
1 teaspoon vanilla

APPLE LAYER
2 tart baking apples, peeled, cut into
   thin slices (2 cups)
1 tablespoon Pillsbury BEST® all-
   purpose flour
¼ teaspoon ground cinnamon

GLAZE
½ cup powdered sugar
1 tablespoon milk
¼ teaspoon vanilla
1 tablespoon butter or margarine,
   softened

1   Heat oven to 400°F. Make
pie crusts as directed on box for
Two-Crust Pie, using 9-inch glass
pie plate.

2   In 2-quart saucepan, mix granulated sugar, ½ cup milk, the whipping cream and ¼ cup butter. Cook
over medium-low heat, stirring
occasionally, until hot and butter is
melted.

3   In small bowl, mix cornstarch
and 2 tablespoons milk until smooth.
Add to mixture in saucepan; cook
7 minutes, stirring constantly, until
thickened. Remove from heat; stir
in 1 teaspoon vanilla. Set aside.

4   In medium bowl, mix apple
layer ingredients. Pour filling
mixture into crust-lined pie plate.
Arrange apple layer evenly over
filling. Top with second crust; seal
edge and flute. Cut slits in several
places in top crust.

5   Bake 30 to 40 minutes or until
apples are tender and crust is golden
brown. Cool 30 minutes.

6   In small bowl, mix glaze ingredients until smooth. Pour and
spread glaze evenly over warm pie.
Refrigerate pie 1 hour 30 minutes
before serving. Cover and refrigerate
any remaining pie.

High Altitude (3500–6500 ft): No change.

1 Serving: Calories 460; Total Fat 26g (Saturated Fat 13g;
Trans Fat 0g); Cholesterol 45mg; Sodium 290mg;
Total Carbohydrate 54g (Dietary Fiber 0g) Exchanges:
½ Starch, 3 Other Carbohydrate, 5 Fat; Carbohydrate
Choices: 3 ½

Apple Berry Pie

Bessie E. Miller   Tampa, FL
Bake-Off® Contest 32, 1986

Prep Time: 30 Minutes
Start to Finish: 1 Hour 20 Minutes
6 to 8 servings

CRUST
1 box (15 oz) Pillsbury® refrigerated pie
   crusts, softened as directed on box

FILLING
3 cups chopped, peeled apples
½ cup sugar
¼ cup chopped pecans or walnuts
¼ cup raisins
3 tablespoons Pillsbury BEST®
   all-purpose flour
½ teaspoon ground cinnamon
¼ teaspoon ground nutmeg
2 tablespoons butter or margarine, melted
1 can (16 oz) whole berry cranberry sauce

1   Heat oven to 425°F. Make
pie crusts as directed on box for
Two-Crust Pie, using 9-inch glass
pie plate. Cut second crust into
6 or 8 wedges; set aside.

2   In large bowl, mix filling
ingredients. Spoon into crust-lined
pie plate. Arrange pie crust wedges
over berry mixture, points of
wedges meeting in center. (Do not
overlap.) Fold outer edge of each
wedge under bottom crust; flute.

3   Bake 40 to 50 minutes or until
crust is golden brown and apples are
tender. Cover edge of pie crust with
strip of foil during last 10 to 15
minutes of bake time if necessary to
prevent excessive browning.

High Altitude (3500–6500 ft): No change.

1 Serving: Calories 630; Total Fat 26g (Saturated Fat 9g;
Trans Fat 0g); Cholesterol 20mg; Sodium 340mg;
Total Carbohydrate 97g (Dietary Fiber 2g) Exchanges:
½ Starch, ½ Fruit, 5½ Other Carbohydrate, 5 Fat;
Carbohydrate Choices: 6½

Apple Berry Pie

Apple Pie '63

Apple Pie '63

Julia Smogor Cedar Rapids, IA
Bake-Off® Contest 14, 1962
$25,000 Grand Prize Winner

Prep Time: 35 Minutes
Start to Finish: 2 Hours 20 Minutes
18 servings

CARAMEL SAUCE

28 caramels (half of 14-oz bag),
   unwrapped
½ cup half-and-half or evaporated
   milk

CRUST

2½ cups Pillsbury BEST® all-purpose
   flour
¼ cup sugar
1½ teaspoons salt
½ cup butter or margarine
¼ cup vegetable oil
¼ cup water
1 egg, beaten

FILLING

6 cups sliced peeled apples
   (about 6 medium)
1 cup sugar
⅓ cup Pillsbury BEST® all-purpose
   flour
1 to 2 teaspoons grated lemon peel
2 tablespoons lemon juice

TOPPING

1 package (8 oz) cream cheese,
   softened
⅓ cup sugar
1 egg
⅓ cup chopped nuts

1 Heat oven to 375°F. In 1-quart saucepan, cook caramels and half-and-half over low heat, stirring occasionally, until caramels are melted. Keep warm.

2 In medium bowl, mix 2½ cups flour, ¼ cup sugar and the salt. With pastry blender or fork, cut in butter until mixture looks like coarse crumbs. Stir in oil, water and egg. Press mixture evenly in bottom and up sides of ungreased 15 × 10 × 1-inch pan.

3 In large bowl, lightly mix filling ingredients. Spoon into crust-lined pan. Drizzle warm caramel sauce over filling.

4 In small bowl, beat all topping ingredients except nuts with electric mixer on medium speed until smooth. Spoon over filling, spreading slightly. Sprinkle with nuts.

5 Bake 35 to 45 minutes or until light golden brown. Cool completely, about 1 hour. Cut into squares. Cover and refrigerate any remaining pie.

High Altitude (3500–6500 ft): No change.

1 Serving: Calories 370; Total Fat 17g (Saturated Fat 8g; Trans Fat 0g); Cholesterol 55mg; Sodium 320mg; Total Carbohydrate 50g (Dietary Fiber 1g) Exchanges: 1 Starch, 2½ Other Carbohydrate, 3 Fat; Carbohydrate Choices: 3

Crunchy Crust Blueberry Swirl Pie

Mrs. Richard Furry LaMesa, CA
Bake-Off® Contest 23, 1972

Prep Time: 20 Minutes
Start to Finish: 2 Hours 35 Minutes
8 servings

CRUST

½ cup butter or margarine
¾ cup Pillsbury BEST® all-purpose flour
½ cup quick-cooking oats
½ cup chopped nuts
2 tablespoons sugar

FILLING

1 box (4-serving size) lemon gelatin
½ cup boiling water
1 can (21 oz) blueberry pie filling
½ cup sour cream

1 Heat oven to 400°F. In 2-quart saucepan, melt butter. Stir in remaining crust ingredients. Mix well and pat in 9-inch glass pie plate. Bake 11 to 14 minutes or until golden brown. Set aside to cool.

2 Meanwhile, in medium bowl, dissolve gelatin in boiling water; stir in blueberry filling. Refrigerate until thickened, about 1 hour. Pour into crust. Spoon sour cream by teaspoonfuls onto filling. With spatula, cut through sour cream and lightly fold filling over it, making swirls. Refrigerate 1 hour. If desired, top with whipped cream. Cover and refrigerate any remaining pie.

High Altitude (3500–6500 ft): Bake crust 13 to 15 minutes.

1 Serving: Calories 380; Total Fat 20g (Saturated Fat 10g; Trans Fat 0.5g); Cholesterol 40mg; Sodium 140mg; Total Carbohydrate 47g (Dietary Fiber 2g) Exchanges: 1 Starch, 2 Other Carbohydrate, 4 Fat; Carbohydrate Choices: 3

Melba Streusel Pie

Elaine Stoeckel Minneapolis, MN
Bake-Off® Contest 15, 1963

Prep Time: 25 Minutes
Start to Finish: 1 Hour 20 Minutes
8 servings

CRUST
1 Pillsbury® refrigerated pie crust
   (from 15-oz box), softened as
   directed on box

TOPPING
¾ cup all-purpose flour
½ cup packed brown sugar
¼ cup butter or margarine

FILLING
⅓ cup sugar
2 tablespoons cornstarch
¼ teaspoon ground cinnamon
1 bag (16 oz) frozen peaches, thawed,
   drained
1 bag (10 oz) frozen raspberries in
   light syrup, thawed
1 tablespoon lemon juice

1 Heat oven to 375°F. Place pie crust in 9-inch glass pie plate as directed on box for One-Crust Filled Pie.

2 In small bowl, mix flour and brown sugar. With fork or pastry blender, cut in butter until mixture is crumbly; set aside.

3 In large bowl, mix sugar, cornstarch and cinnamon. Stir in fruits. Sprinkle with lemon juice; mix well. Pour into crust-lined pie plate. Bake 35 to 40 minutes or until filling is partially set in center. Sprinkle evenly with topping mixture. Cover edge of crust with strips of foil to prevent excessive browning. Bake 12 to 15 minutes longer or until topping is light golden brown.

High Altitude (3500–6500 ft): Place cookie sheet on rack below pie rack to catch any spillover; heat oven to 375°F. In step 3, increase first bake time to 38 to 43 minutes; increase second bake to 14 to 17 minutes.

1 Serving: Calories 400; Total Fat 13g (Saturated Fat 6g; Trans Fat 0g); Cholesterol 20mg; Sodium 160mg; Total Carbohydrate 69g (Dietary Fiber 3g) Exchanges: ½ Starch, ½ Fruit, 3½ Other Carbohydrate, 2½ Fat; Carbohydrate Choices: 4½

Rosy Raspberry-Pear Pie

Lola Nebel Cambridge, MN
Bake-Off® Contest 39, 2000

Prep Time: 15 Minutes
Start to Finish: 4 Hours 5 Minutes
8 servings

1 box (15 oz) Pillsbury® refrigerated pie
   crusts, softened as directed on box
3 firm ripe pears, peeled, cut into
   ½-inch slices
1 tablespoon lemon juice
½ teaspoon almond extract
¾ cup sugar
3 tablespoons Pillsbury BEST®
   all-purpose flour
1 cup fresh raspberries, or frozen
   whole raspberries without syrup,
   partially thawed
1 tablespoon butter or margarine,
   melted
1 tablespoon sugar
Vanilla ice cream, if desired

1 Heat oven to 400°F. Place 1 pie crust in 9-inch glass pie plate as directed on box for One-Crust Filled Pie.

2 In large bowl, gently mix pears, lemon juice and almond extract. Stir in ¾ cup sugar and the flour. Spoon about half of pear mixture into crust-lined pie plate. Top with raspberries. Spoon remaining pear mixture over raspberries.

3 Unroll second crust on cutting board. With floured 2½-inch round cutter, cut 9 rounds from crust. Brush each with melted butter. Place 8 rounds, butter side up, in circle on outer edge of fruit, overlapping as necessary. Place 1 round in center. Sprinkle rounds with 1 tablespoon sugar. Cover crust edge with 2- to 3-inch-wide strips of foil to prevent excessive browning; remove foil during last 15 minutes of bake time.

4 Bake 40 to 50 minutes or until crust is golden brown and filling is bubbly. Cool completely, about 3 hours, before serving. Serve with ice cream.

High Altitude (3500–6500 ft): Bake 45 to 50 minutes.

1 Serving: Calories 370; Total Fat 15g (Saturated Fat 6g; Trans Fat 0g); Cholesterol 10mg; Sodium 220mg; Total Carbohydrate 59g (Dietary Fiber 3g) Exchanges: ½ Fruit, 3½ Other Carbohydrate, 3 Fat; Carbohydrate Choices: 4

Rosy Raspberry-Pear Pie

Apricot-Coconut Cream Pie

Apricot-Coconut Cream Pie

Harriet Warkentin   San Jacinto, CA
Bake-Off® Contest 33, 1988

Prep Time: 30 Minutes
Start to Finish: 4 Hours 40 Minutes
8 servings

CRUST
1 Pillsbury® refrigerated pie crust (from 15-oz box), softened as directed on box

FILLING
1 envelope unflavored gelatin
1 cup apricot nectar
2 cans (16 oz each) apricot halves, drained
½ cup sugar
¼ cup cornstarch
¼ teaspoon salt
1¾ cups milk
4 egg yolks, beaten
1 tablespoon butter or margarine
½ teaspoon vanilla
½ cup coconut, toasted*

TOPPING
1 cup whipping cream
1 tablespoon sugar
¼ teaspoon vanilla
2 to 3 tablespoons apricot preserves, melted
½ cup coconut, toasted*

1   Heat oven to 450°F. Bake pie crust as directed on box for One-Crust Baked Shell, using 9-inch glass pie plate. Cool completely, about 15 minutes.

2   Meanwhile in small bowl, sprinkle gelatin over ¼ cup of the apricot nectar; let stand to soften. Set aside. In another small bowl, cut 1 can of the apricot halves into small pieces. Set aside. In blender or food processor, place remaining can apricot halves and remaining ¾ cup apricot nectar. Cover; blend or process until smooth.

3   In 2-quart saucepan, mix ½ cup sugar, the cornstarch and salt Stir in milk and blended apricot mixture. (Mixture will look curdled. Cook over medium heat, stirring constantly, until mixture heats to boiling and is slightly thickened. Boil 2 minutes, stirring constantly. Remove from heat. Blend a small amount of hot mixture into egg yolks. Return egg yolk mixture to saucepan; mix well. Over medium heat, heat to boiling, stirring constantly. Boil 2 minutes, stirring constantly.

4   Remove from heat; stir in butter, ½ teaspoon vanilla and the gelatin mixture. Fold in ½ cup toasted coconut. Refrigerate about 30 minutes or until slightly thickened. Fold in apricot pieces. Spoon into crust. Cover; refrigerate about 45 minutes or until mixture is partially set.

5   In large bowl, beat whipping cream until soft peaks form. Add 1 tablespoon sugar and ¼ teaspoon vanilla; beat until stiff peaks form. Gently fold in apricot preserves. Pipe or spoon whipped cream mixture over cooled filling. Garnish with remaining ½ cup toasted coconut. Refrigerate 3 to 4 hours or until set. Cover and refrigerate any remaining pie.

To toast coconut, spread on cookie sheet; bake at 375°F about 5 minutes or until light golden brown. Or, spread in a thin layer in microwavable glass pie plate. Microwave on Medium (50%) 4½ to 8 minutes or until light golden brown, tossing with fork after each minute.

High Altitude (3500–6500 ft): No change.

1 Serving: Calories 460; Total Fat 24g (Saturated Fat 14g; Trans Fat 0g); Cholesterol 145mg; Sodium 260mg; Total Carbohydrate 55g (Dietary Fiber 2g) Exchanges: ½ Starch, 3 Other Carbohydrate, ½ High-Fat Meat, 4 Fat; Carbohydrate Choices: 3½

That's a Lot of Mouths to Feed!

For some of us, learning to cook is a gradual process, something we pick up slowly; for others it is a trial by fire. "When I married my husband in 1958," Harriet Warkentin told Pillsbury, "I not only married him but also took over a family of five children ranging in age from fifteen months to eleven years. I went from cooking for myself to cooking and caring for a large family." Tasty desserts like Harriet's Apricot-Coconut Cream Pie smoothed that transition, and "a year and a half later we had a beautiful baby girl."

Lemon Cloud Pie

Jerry Ordiway   Jamesville, NY
Bake-Off® Contest 11, 1959
$3,000 Winner

Prep Time: 45 Minutes
Start to Finish: 6 Hours 45 Minutes
8 servings

CRUST

1 Pillsbury® refrigerated pie crust
(from 15-oz box), softened as
directed on box

FILLING

1 cup sugar
3 tablespoons cornstarch
1 cup water
⅓ cup lemon juice
2 egg yolks, slightly beaten
4 oz cream cheese, cubed, softened
1 teaspoon grated lemon peel
½ cup whipping cream

TOPPING

½ cup whipping cream, whipped

1   Heat oven to 450°F. Bake pie crust as directed on box for One-Crust Baked Shell, using 9-inch glass pie plate. Cool completely, about 15 minutes.

2   Meanwhile, in 2-quart saucepan, mix sugar and cornstarch. Stir in water, lemon juice and egg yolks. Cook over medium heat, stirring constantly, until mixture boils and thickens. Boil 1 minute. Add cream cheese and lemon peel, stirring until cream cheese is melted and mixture is smooth. Cool to room temperature.

3   In large bowl, beat ½ cup whipping cream until soft peaks form; fold into lemon mixture. Spoon filling mixture evenly into crust. Cover surface with plastic wrap; refrigerate at least 6 hours or overnight before serving.

4   Just before serving, spoon or pipe whipped cream over filling. Cover and refrigerate any remaining pie.

High Altitude (3500–6500 ft): In step 2, boil mixture 2 to 3 minutes.

1 Serving: Calories 380; Total Fat 22g (Saturated Fat 12g; Trans Fat 0g); Cholesterol 105mg; Sodium 170mg; Total Carbohydrate 43g (Dietary Fiber 0g) Exchanges: 3 Other Carbohydrate, 4½ Fat; Carbohydrate Choices: 3

"Orange-Kist" Coconut Cream Pie

Eugenia Ward   Amherst, WI
Bake-Off® Contest 34, 1990
$2,000 Winner

Prep Time: 50 Minutes
Start to Finish: 3 Hours 50 Minutes
8 servings

CRUST

1 Pillsbury® refrigerated pie crust
(from 15-oz box), softened as
directed on box

FILLING

1 cup granulated sugar
3 tablespoons cornstarch
1 cup water
¼ cup orange juice
¼ cup butter or margarine
1 tablespoon grated orange peel
3 egg yolks
½ cup coconut, toasted*
½ cup sour cream
½ cup whipping cream, whipped

TOPPING

½ cup whipping cream
2 tablespoons powdered sugar
¼ cup coconut, toasted*
2 tablespoons sliced almonds,
toasted**

1   Heat oven to 450°F. Bake pie crust as directed on box for One-Crust Baked Shell, using 9-inch glass pie plate. Cool completely, about 15 minutes.

2   In 2-quart saucepan, mix granulated sugar and cornstarch. Stir in water, orange juice, butter, orange peel and egg yolks. Cook over medium heat about 5 minutes, stirring constantly, until mixture thickens and boils. Remove from heat. Refrigerate 1 hour. Stir in ½ cup toasted coconut and sour cream. Fold in whipped cream. Spoon into crust.

3   In small bowl, beat ½ cup whipping cream and the powdered sugar until stiff peaks form. Spread over coconut filling. Garnish with ¼ cup toasted coconut and almonds. Refrigerate 1 to 2 hours before serving. Cover and refrigerate any remaining pie.

*To toast coconut, spread on cookie sheet; bake at 375°F 5 to 7 minutes or until light golden brown, stirring occasionally. Or, spread in thin layer in microwavable pie plate. Microwave on Medium (50%) 6 to 8 minutes or until golden brown, tossing with fork after each minute.

**To toast almonds, spread on cookie sheet; bake at 375°F 5 to 6 minutes or until light golden brown, stirring occasionally. Or, spread in thin layer in microwavable pie plate. Microwave on High 6 to 7 minutes or until light golden brown, stirring frequently.

High Altitude (3500–6500 ft): No change.

1 Serving: Calories 470; Total Fat 30g (Saturated Fat 16g; Trans Fat 0.5g); Cholesterol 140mg; Sodium 190mg; Total Carbohydrate 49g (Dietary Fiber 0g) Exchanges: 1 Starch, 2 Other Carbohydrate, 6 Fat; Carbohydrate Choices: 3

Italian Cream Pie with Strawberry Sauce

Jean Gottfried   Upper Sandusky, OH
Bake-Off® Contest 42, 2006
$10,000 Splenda® Pure Magic Award
Winner

Prep Time: 50 Minutes
Start to Finish: 3 Hours 50 Minutes
12 servings

CRUST

1 Pillsbury® refrigerated pie crust
(from 15-oz box), softened as
directed on box

FILLING

1 cup skim (fat-free) milk
1 envelope unflavored gelatin
¼ cup sugar blend for baking
1½ cups part-skim ricotta cheese
(12 oz)
½ teaspoon vanilla
1 cup frozen (thawed) fat-free whipped
topping
2 containers (6 oz each) very vanilla
nonfat yogurt

STRAWBERRY SAUCE

¼ cup sugar blend for baking
1 tablespoon cornstarch
1 bag (10 oz) organic frozen whole
strawberries, thawed
1 tablespoon lemon juice

1   Heat oven to 450°F. Unroll
pie crust; place in 8- or 9-inch
springform pan, pressing crust
up side of pan to top edge.
(Do not overwork or let crust
get too warm.) Prick bottom
and side of crust with fork. Bake
9 to 11 minutes or until lightly
browned. Cool completely, about
30 minutes.

2   Meanwhile, in 1-quart
saucepan, place ½ cup of the milk.
Sprinkle gelatin over milk; let
stand 5 minutes to soften. Stir in
remaining ½ cup milk and ¼ cup
sugar blend. Cook on low heat,
stirring frequently, until gelatin is
completely dissolved (do not boil).
Pour milk mixture into blender.
Add ricotta cheese and vanilla.
Cover; blend until pureed. Pour
into large bowl; stir in whipped
topping and yogurt.

3   Remove side of pan; remove
crust from pan and place crust on
serving plate. To create collar for
crust, wrap piece of string around
outside of crust to measure; cut
sheet of waxed paper length of
string plus 3 inches. Fold waxed
paper in half lengthwise; fold in
half again. Wrap around outside of
crust; staple collar together to

secure around crust. Pour filling
into cooled baked crust. Refrigerate
until set, 2 to 3 hours.

4   In 1½-quart saucepan, mix
¼ cup sugar blend and the cornstarch. Stir in thawed strawberries.
Cook over medium heat, stirring
constantly, until slightly thickened. Remove from heat. Stir in
lemon juice. Refrigerate until
serving time.

5   To serve, remove waxed paper
collar. Cut into wedges; place
on individual dessert plates.
Top servings with strawberry
sauce. Store dessert and sauce in
refrigerator.

High Altitude (3500–6500 ft): No change.

1 Serving: Calories 200; Total Fat 7g (Saturated Fat 3g;
Trans Fat 0g); Cholesterol 10mg; Sodium 135mg;
Total Carbohydrate 29g (Dietary Fiber 0g) Exchanges:
1 Starch, 1 Other Carbohydrate, 1½ Fat; Carbohydrate
Choices: 2

Almond Macaroon-Cherry Pie

Rose Anne LeMon   Sierra Vista, AZ
Bake-Off® Contest 32, 1986

Prep Time: 20 Minutes
Start to Finish: 1 Hour
8 servings

CRUST
1 Pillsbury® refrigerated pie crust (from 15-oz box), softened as directed on box

FILLING
1 can (21 oz) cherry pie filling
¼ to ½ teaspoon ground cinnamon
⅛ teaspoon salt, if desired
1 teaspoon lemon juice

TOPPING
1 cup coconut
½ cup sliced almonds
¼ cup sugar
⅛ teaspoon salt, if desired
¼ cup milk
1 tablespoon butter or margarine, melted
¼ teaspoon almond extract
1 egg, beaten

1   Heat oven to 400°F. Place pie crust in 9-inch glass pie plate as directed on box for One-Crust Filled Pie.

2   In large bowl, mix filling ingredients; spoon into crust-lined pie plate. Cover edge with 2- to 3-inch-wide strips of foil to prevent excessive browning.

3   Bake 20 minutes. Meanwhile, in medium bowl, mix topping ingredients. Spread topping evenly over pie.

4   Bake 15 to 30 minutes longer or until crust and topping are golden brown, removing foil during last 10 to 15 minutes of bake time.

High Altitude (3500–6500 ft): No change.

1 Serving: Calories 330; Total Fat 16g (Saturated Fat 7g; Trans Fat 0g); Cholesterol 35mg; Sodium 160mg; Total Carbohydrate 45g (Dietary Fiber 2g) Exchanges: 1 Starch, 2 Other Carbohydrate, 3 Fat; Carbohydrate Choices: 3

Lemon Truffle Pie

Patricia Kiewiet   LaGrange, IL
Bake-Off® Contest 35, 1992

Prep Time: 1 Hour 10 Minutes
Start to Finish: 3 Hours 10 Minutes
10 servings

CRUST
1 Pillsbury® refrigerated pie crust (from 15-oz box), softened as directed on box

LEMON LAYER
1 cup sugar
2 tablespoons cornstarch
2 tablespoons Pillsbury BEST® all-purpose flour
1 cup water
2 egg yolks, beaten
1 tablespoon butter or margarine
½ teaspoon grated lemon peel
¼ cup lemon juice

CREAM CHEESE LAYER
1 cup white vanilla baking chips or chopped white chocolate baking bar (6 oz)
1 package (8 oz) ⅓-less-fat cream cheese (Neufchâtel), softened

TOPPING
½ cup whipping cream
1 tablespoon sliced almonds, toasted*

1   Heat oven to 450°F. Bake pie crust as directed on box for One-Crust Baked Shell, using 9-inch glass pie plate. Cool completely, about 15 minutes.

2   Meanwhile, in 2-quart saucepan, mix sugar, cornstarch and flour. Gradually stir in water until smooth. Cook over medium heat, stirring constantly, until mixture

Daddy's Little Girl

Many Bake-Off® Contest finalists credit their mothers or grandmothers for influencing them to become great cooks. Rose Anne LeMon shared a family cooking tradition passed down a different line. Rose Anne's father was a restaurant owner and her grandfather was a chef, inspiring her interest in cooking at an early age. And what an inspiration! Rose Anne's culinary creativity produced a festive cherry pie with a unique crunchy macaroon topping.

boils. Reduce heat to low; cook 2 minutes, stirring constantly. Remove from heat. Stir about ¼ cup hot mixture into egg yolks until well blended. Stir egg yolk mixture into mixture in saucepan. Cook over low heat, stirring constantly, until mixture boils. Cook 2 minutes, stirring constantly. Remove from heat. Stir in butter, lemon peel and lemon juice.

3 Place ⅓ cup hot lemon mixture in 1-quart saucepan; cool remaining lemon mixture 15 minutes. Into hot mixture in saucepan, stir vanilla baking chips. Cook and stir over low heat just until chips are melted.

4 In small bowl, beat cream cheese with electric mixer on medium speed until fluffy. Beat in melted vanilla chip mixture until well blended. Spread in crust. Spoon lemon mixture evenly over cream cheese layer. Refrigerate until set, 2 to 3 hours, before serving.

5 Just before serving, in small bowl, beat whipping cream with mixer on high speed until stiff peaks form. Pipe or spoon whipped cream over pie. Garnish with toasted almonds. Cover and refrigerate any remaining pie.

*To toast almonds, bake uncovered in ungreased shallow pan in 350°F oven about 10 minutes, stirring occasionally, until golden brown. Or cook in ungreased heavy skillet over medium-low heat 5 to 7 minutes, stirring frequently until browning begins, then stirring constantly until golden brown.

High Altitude (3500–6500 ft): No change.

1 Serving: Calories 430; Total Fat 23g (Saturated Fat 14g; Trans Fat 0g); Cholesterol 75mg; Sodium 240mg; Total Carbohydrate 49g (Dietary Fiber 0g) Exchanges: ½ Starch, 3 Other Carbohydrate, ½ High-Fat Meat, 3½ Fat; Carbohydrate Choices: 3

Lemon Tuffle Pie

Cheesecake Cherry Pie

Mrs. Henri L.J. deSibour, Jr.   Royal Oak, MI
Bake-Off® Contest 8, 1956

> **Prep Time:** 25 Minutes
> **Start to Finish:** 5 Hours 25 Minutes
> 8 servings

CRUST
½ cup butter or margarine
2 tablespoons sugar
Dash salt
1 cup Pillsbury BEST® all-purpose
   or unbleached flour

FILLING
1 can (21 oz) cherry fruit pie filling

TOPPING
2 packages (3 oz each) cream cheese,
   softened
⅓ cup sugar
½ teaspoon vanilla
1 egg

1   Heat oven to 350°F. In small bowl, beat butter, 2 tablespoons sugar and the salt with electric mixer on medium speed until light and fluffy. Add flour; mix well. Press mixture in bottom and up sides of ungreased 9-inch glass pie plate. Spread filling evenly over crust. Bake 15 minutes.

2   Meanwhile, in small bowl beat topping ingredients with electric mixer on medium speed until smooth. Spoon topping mixture by tablespoonfuls over filling around edge of pie; carefully spread over filling leaving a 3-inch circle in center of pie. Seal topping to edge of crust. Bake 25 to 30 minutes longer or until topping is light golden brown and set. Cool 30 minutes. Refrigerate 3 to 4 hours. Cover and refrigerate any remaining pie.

High Altitude (3500–6500 ft): In step 2, bake 30 to 35 minutes.

1 Serving: Calories 370; Total Fat 20g (Saturated Fat 12g; Trans Fat 0.5g); Cholesterol 80mg; Sodium 170mg; Total Carbohydrate 44g (Dietary Fiber 1g) Exchanges: ½ Starch, 2½ Other Carbohydrate, ½ High-Fat Meat, 3 Fat; Carbohydrate Choices: 3

Strawberry Devonshire Pie

Grayce Berggren
State College, PA
Bake-Off® Contest 16, 1964

> **Prep Time:** 1 Hour
> **Start to Finish:** 5 Hours 30 Minutes
> 8 servings

CRUST
1 Pillsbury® refrigerated pie crust (from
   15-oz box), softened as directed on
   box

FILLING
1 envelope unflavored gelatin
¼ cup water
⅓ cup sugar
⅛ teaspoon salt
1 cup sour cream
2 tablespoons milk
2 egg yolks, slightly beaten
1 cup whipping cream, whipped

TOPPING
2 tablespoons sugar
1 tablespoon cornstarch
1 box (10 oz) frozen strawberries
   in unsweetened juice, thawed,
   drained, liquid reserved

1   Heat oven to 450°F. Bake pie crust as directed on box for One-Crust Baked Shell, using 9-inch pie pan. Cool completely, about 15 minutes.

2   Meanwhile in small bowl, sprinkle gelatin over water; let stand to soften. In 2-quart saucepan, mix ⅓ cup sugar, the salt, sour cream, milk and egg yolks. Cook over medium heat, stirring constantly, 10 to 15 minutes or until very hot. DO NOT BOIL. Stir in softened gelatin. Cover surface with plastic wrap; refrigerate 45 to 60 minutes or until slightly thickened. Fold in whipped cream. Spoon into crust. Refrigerate until set, about 2 hours.

3   Meanwhile in 1-quart saucepan, mix 2 tablespoons sugar and the cornstarch. Gradually stir in reserved strawberry liquid. Cook over medium heat, stirring constantly, until mixture thickens and boils. Boil 1 minute. Stir in strawberries. Cool to room temperature. Spoon strawberry mixture evenly over filling. Refrigerate until set, about 2 hours. Cover and refrigerate any remaining pie.

High Altitude (3500–6500 ft): No change.

1 Serving: Calories 340; Total Fat 23g (Saturated Fat 12g; Trans Fat 0.5g); Cholesterol 105mg; Sodium 170mg; Total Carbohydrate 31g (Dietary Fiber 0g) Exchanges: 1 Starch, 1 Other Carbohydrate, 4 ½ Fat; Carbohydrate Choices: 2

"Peacheesy" Pie

Janis Risley   Melbourne, FL
Bake-Off® Contest 16, 1964
$25,000 Grand Prize Winner

Prep Time: 30 Minutes
Start to Finish: 2 Hours 20 Minutes
8 servings

CRUST
1 box (15 oz) Pillsbury® refrigerated pie
   crusts, softened as directed on box

FILLING
½ cup sugar
2 tablespoons cornstarch
1 to 2 teaspoons pumpkin pie spice
2 tablespoons light corn syrup
2 teaspoons vanilla
1 can (29 oz) peach slices, drained,
   3 tablespoons liquid reserved

TOPPING
⅓ cup sugar
1 tablespoon lemon juice
2 eggs, slightly beaten
½ cup sour cream
1 package (3 oz) cream cheese, softened
2 tablespoons butter or margarine

1   Heat oven to 425°F. Place 1 pie crust in 9-inch glass pie plate as directed on box for One-Crust Filled Pie. In medium bowl, mix all filling ingredients except peach liquid; set aside.

2   In 1-quart saucepan, mix 2 tablespoons of the reserved peach liquid, ⅓ cup sugar, the lemon juice and eggs. Cook over medium heat, stirring constantly, until mixture boils and thickens. Boil 1 minute, stirring constantly. Remove from heat.

3   In small bowl, beat sour cream and cream cheese with electric mixer on medium speed until smooth.

Gradually beat in hot egg mixture until well blended; set aside.

4   Spoon filling into crust-lined pie plate. Dot with butter. Spoon topping mixture evenly over filling.

5   Unroll second crust on work surface. With floured 3-inch round cutter, cut out 8 rounds from crust. Brush tops of rounds with remaining 1 tablespoon reserved peach liquid. Arrange pie crust rounds over topping.

6   Bake 10 minutes. Reduce oven temperature to 350°F; bake 35 to 40 minutes longer or until crust is golden brown. After 15 to 20 minutes of baking, cover crust edge with strips of foil to prevent excessive browning. Cool completely, about 1 hour. Cover and refrigerate any remaining pie.

High Altitude (3500–6500 ft): In step 6, increase second bake time to 45 to 50 minutes.

1 Serving: Calories 380 ; Total Fat 18g (Saturated Fat 9g; Trans Fat 0g); Cholesterol 85mg; Sodium 190mg; Total Carbohydrate 50g (Dietary Fiber 1g) Exchanges: 1 Starch, 2½ Other Carbohydrate, 3½ Fat; Carbohydrate Choices: 3

Toffee Banana Cream Pie

Charlene Margesson   Brentwood, CA
Bake-Off® Contest 35, 1992

Prep Time: 30 Minutes
Start to Finish: 2 Hours 30 Minutes
8 servings

CRUST
1 Pillsbury® refrigerated pie crust
   (from 15-oz box), softened as
   directed on box

FILLING
2 packages (3 oz) cream cheese,
   softened
½ cup butterscotch-caramel-fudge
   topping
3 cups sliced bananas
2 bars (1.4 oz each) chocolate-covered
   English toffee candy, chopped
1⅓ cups whipping cream
2 tablespoons brown sugar
1 teaspoon vanilla

GARNISH
Banana slices

1   Heat oven to 450°F. Bake pie crust as directed on box for One-Crust Baked Shell, using 9-inch glass pie plate. Cool completely, about 15 minutes.

2   In small bowl, beat cream cheese and topping with electric mixer on medium speed until smooth. Spread in crust. Arrange 3 cups sliced bananas over cream cheese mixture. Reserve 2 tablespoons of the chopped candy bars; sprinkle remaining candy bars over bananas.

3   In small bowl, beat whipping cream, brown sugar and vanilla with electric mixer on high speed until stiff peaks form. Spread over pie. Refrigerate at least 2 hours before serving. Just before serving, garnish with reserved chopped candy bar and banana slices. Cover and refrigerate any remaining pie.

High Altitude (3500–6500 ft): No change.

1 Serving: Calories 490; Total Fat 30g (Saturated Fat 17g; Trans Fat 1g); Cholesterol 75mg; Sodium 290mg; Total Carbohydrate 51g (Dietary Fiber 2g) Exchanges: ½ Fruit, 3 Other Carbohydrate, ½ High-Fat Meat, 5 Fat; Carbohydrate Choices: 3 ½

Culinary Dreams

Through the years, finalists have said, if they won the contest, they would:

- Attend cooking schools in China and France
- Build a chocolate factory
- Start a cooking program at an elementary school
- Open a kitchen or cookbook store
  - Travel around the world to experience and learn about food from other countries

Cappuccino Cheesecake Pie with Pecan Sauce

Jim Wick, Jr.   Longwood, FL
Bake-Off® Contest 34, 1990

> **Prep Time:** 40 Minutes
> **Start to Finish:** 3 Hours 30 Minutes
> 10 to 12 servings

CRUST

1 Pillsbury® refrigerated pie crust (from 15-oz box), softened as directed on box

FILLING

3 packages (8 oz each) cream cheese, softened
1¾ cups packed dark brown sugar
4 eggs
2 tablespoons strong brewed coffee (room temperature)

SAUCE

1 cup packed dark brown sugar
1 cup whipping cream
½ cup butter or margarine
¼ cup strong brewed coffee (room temperature)
2 tablespoons coffee-flavored liqueur or strong coffee
1 cup pecan halves

GARNISHES, IF DESIRED

Whipped cream
Pecan halves

1 Heat oven to 350°F. Place pie crust in 9-inch deep-dish or 10-inch glass pie plate as directed on box for One-Crust Filled Pie—except roll crust slightly larger to fit pan.

2 In large bowl, beat cream cheese and 1¾ cups brown sugar until smooth. Add eggs 1 at a time, beating well after each addition. Add 2 tablespoons coffee; blend well. Pour into crust-lined pie plate. Cover crust edge with strips of foil to prevent excessive browning; remove foil during last 15 minutes of bake time.

3 Bake 45 to 50 minutes or until edges are set and golden brown (center will not appear set). Cool completely. Refrigerate until thoroughly chilled and cheesecake is set, about 2 hours.

4 In 2-quart saucepan, heat all sauce ingredients except pecans to boiling over medium heat, stirring occasionally. Reduce heat; simmer 5 minutes, stirring occasionally. Stir in 1 cup pecan halves. To serve, pour warm sauce over each serving of pie. Garnish with whipped cream and pecan halves. Cover and refrigerate any remaining pie.

High Altitude (3500–6500 ft): Bake 50 to 55 minutes.

1 Serving: Calories 840; Total Fat 55g (Saturated Fat 29g; Trans Fat 1.5g); Cholesterol 215mg; Sodium 410mg; Total Carbohydrate 75g (Dietary Fiber 0g) Exchanges: ½ Starch, 4½ Other Carbohydrate, 1 High-Fat Meat, 9½ Fat; Carbohydrate Choices: 5

Greek Walnut Pie

Maria E. Irvine   San Leandro, CA
Bake-Off® Contest 41, 2004

> **Prep Time:** 25 Minutes
> **Start to Finish:** 4 Hours 15 Minutes
> 12 servings

PIE

1 box (15 oz) Pillsbury® refrigerated pie crusts, softened as directed on box
2½ cups finely chopped walnuts
¼ cup packed brown sugar
2 tablespoons granulated sugar
1½ teaspoons ground cinnamon
¾ cup butter or margarine, melted, cooled
¾ cup honey
1 tablespoon lemon juice

TOPPING

1 cup whipping cream
1 teaspoon granulated sugar
1 teaspoon vanilla

1 Heat oven to 325°F. Spray 9-inch glass pie plate with cooking spray. Make pie crusts as directed on box for Two-Crust Pie—except use sprayed pie plate.

2 In medium bowl, mix walnuts, brown sugar, 2 tablespoons granulated sugar and the cinnamon. Pour and evenly spread ¼ cup of the cooled melted butter over bottom of pie crust. Spread walnut mixture evenly over butter. Drizzle another ¼ cup butter over nut mixture.

3 Top with second crust; seal edge and flute. Cut large slits in several places in top crust. Drizzle remaining ¼ cup butter evenly over top crust.

4 Bake 45 to 55 minutes or until golden brown. About 5 minutes before removing pie from oven, in 1-quart saucepan, cook honey and

lemon juice over medium heat, stirring frequently, until mixture has a watery consistency.

5 Place pie on cooling rack. Slowly pour hot honey mixture evenly over top of hot pie, making sure it seeps into slits in top crust. Cool at least 3 hours before serving.

6 Just before serving, in small bowl, beat topping ingredients with

electric mixer on high speed about 2 minutes or until stiff peaks form. Spoon topping onto individual servings of pie.

High Altitude (3500–6500 ft): Bake 55 to 65 minutes.

1 Serving: Calories 590; Total Fat 43g (Saturated Fat 16g; Trans Fat 0.5g); Cholesterol 60mg; Sodium 240mg; Total Carbohydrate 46g (Dietary Fiber 2g) Exchanges: 3 Other Carbohydrate, ½ High-Fat Meat, 8 Fat; Carbohydrate Choices: 3

Greek Walnut Pie

Holiday Fruit and Nut Pie

Gudren Farah Lake Oswego, OR
Bake-Off® Contest 35, 1992

> **Prep Time:** 30 Minutes
> **Start to Finish:** 2 Hours 20 Minutes
> 8 servings

CRUST
1 Pillsbury® refrigerated pie crust (from 15-oz box), softened as directed on box

FILLING
¾ cup sugar
¾ cup dark corn syrup
3 eggs
1 tablespoon butter or margarine, melted
2 teaspoons grated orange peel
⅓ cup orange juice
1 cup chopped dates
½ cup raisins
½ cup sliced almonds
½ cup coconut
1 jar (6 oz) maraschino cherries, drained, halved (½ cup)

TOPPING
1 cup whipping cream
1 to 2 tablespoons powdered sugar

1 Heat oven to 375°F. Place pie crust in 9-inch pie plate as directed on box for One-Crust Filled Pie.

2 In large bowl, mix filling ingredients. Spoon into crust-lined pie plate. Bake 35 to 50 minutes or until filling is set and light golden brown. Cover pie with foil during last 15 minutes of bake time to prevent excessive browning. Cool 1 hour.

3 In small bowl, beat whipping cream and powdered sugar until stiff peaks form. Pipe or spoon around edge of pie. Cover and refrigerate any remaining pie.

High Altitude (3500–6500 ft): No change.

1 Serving: Calories 610; Total Fat 24g (Saturated Fat 12g; Trans Fat 0g); Cholesterol 120mg; Sodium 190mg; Total Carbohydrate 91g (Dietary Fiber 3g) Exchanges: ½ Starch, 5½ Other Carbohydrate, ½ High-Fat Meat, 4 Fat; Carbohydrate Choices: 6

Candy Bar Pie

Tracey Chrenko Owosso, MI
Bake-Off® Contest 35, 1992

> **Prep Time:** 25 Minutes
> **Start to Finish:** 5 Hours 5 Minutes
> 10 servings

1 Pillsbury® refrigerated pie crust (from 15-oz box), softened as directed on box
5 bars (2.07 oz each) milk chocolate-covered peanut, caramel and nougat candy, unwrapped
4 packages (3 oz each) cream cheese, softened
½ cup sugar
2 eggs
⅓ cup sour cream
⅓ cup creamy peanut butter
3 tablespoons whipping cream
⅔ cup milk chocolate chips

1 Heat oven to 450°F. Make pie crust as directed on box for One-Crust Filled Pie using 9-inch glass pie plate. Bake 5 to 7 minutes or until very lightly browned. Cool 10 minutes. Reduce oven temperature to 325°F.

2 Meanwhile, cut candy bars in half lengthwise; cut into ¼-inch pieces. Set aside. In small bowl, beat cream cheese and sugar with electric mixer on medium speed until smooth. Add eggs 1 at a time, beating well after each addition. Beat in sour cream and peanut butter until mixture is smooth. Arrange candy bar pieces in partially baked crust. Spoon cream cheese mixture over candy bar pieces. Cover crust edge with strips of foil to prevent excessive browning; remove foil during last 15 minutes of bake time.

3 Bake at 325°F 30 to 40 minutes or until center is set. Cool completely, about 2 hours.

4 In 1-quart saucepan, heat whipping cream over low heat until very warm. Remove from heat; stir in chocolate chips until melted and mixture is smooth. Spread over top of pie. Refrigerate 2 to 3 hours before serving. Cover and refrigerate any remaining pie.

High Altitude (3500–6500 ft): Bake crust 6 to 8 minutes. Bake pie 35 to 45 minutes.

1 Serving: Calories 560; Total Fat 36g (Saturated Fat 18g; Trans Fat 0g); Cholesterol 95mg; Sodium 320mg; Total Carbohydrate 48g (Dietary Fiber 1g) Exchanges: 1 Starch, 2 Other Carbohydrate, 1 High-Fat Meat, 5½ Fat; Carbohydrate Choices: 3

Candy Bar Pie

The Oven Holds Many Secrets

One of the delights of cooking is the almost magical transformation food goes through—from raw flour to rich mellow bread, from ordinary eggs to a soaring soufflé. Mary McClain marvels at the mysteries of the pecan pie she adapted to win a cash prize in the 16th Bake-Off® Contest. "What happens to the extra 'sweet' of the pecan pie in its old form, and the fact that the cream cheese and pecans seem to change places—only the oven knows, I guess."

Mystery Pecan Pie

Mary McClain   North Little Rock, AR
Bake-Off® Contest 16, 1964
$1,000 Winner

> Prep Time: 15 Minutes
> Start to Finish: 3 Hours
> 8 servings

CRUST
1 Pillsbury® refrigerated pie crust (from 15-oz box), softened as directed on box

CREAM CHEESE LAYER
1 package (8 oz) cream cheese, softened
⅓ cup sugar
¼ teaspoon salt
1 teaspoon vanilla
1 egg

PECAN LAYER
3 eggs
¼ cup sugar
1 cup corn syrup
1 teaspoon vanilla
1¼ cups chopped pecans

1   Heat oven to 375°F. Place pie crust in 9-inch glass pie plate as directed on box for One-Crust Filled Pie.

2   In small bowl, beat cream cheese layer ingredients with electric mixer on low speed until well blended and smooth. Set aside.

3   In another small bowl, beat 3 eggs with electric mixer on medium speed. Add remaining pecan layer ingredients except pecans; beat until well blended.

4   Spread cream cheese mixture in crust-lined pie plate. Sprinkle with pecans. Gently pour egg mixture over pecans. Cover crust edge with 2- to 3-inch-wide strips of foil to prevent excessive browning; remove foil during last 15 minutes of bake time.

5   Bake 35 to 45 minutes or until center is set. Cool completely, about 2 hours, before serving. Cover and refrigerate any remaining pie.

High Altitude (3500–6500 ft): Bake 40 to 50 minutes.

1 Serving: Calories 570; Total Fat 32g (Saturated Fat 11g; Trans Fat 0g); Cholesterol 140mg; Sodium 330mg; Total Carbohydrate 64g (Dietary Fiber 1g) Exchanges: ½ Starch, 4 Other Carbohydrate, ½ High-Fat Meat, 5½ Fat; Carbohydrate Choices: 4

Luscious Almond Caramel Pie

Bettie Sechrist   Montgomery, AL
Bake-Off® Contest 34, 1990

> Prep Time: 20 Minutes
> Start to Finish: 4 Hours
> 10 servings

CRUST
1 Pillsbury® refrigerated pie crust (from 15-oz box), softened as directed on box

FILLING
¼ cup unsalted butter, butter or margarine, softened
2 teaspoons Pillsbury BEST® all-purpose flour
1 package (7 oz) almond paste, cut into small pieces
2 eggs
1 jar (12.5 oz) caramel topping (1 cup)
3 tablespoons Pillsbury BEST® all-purpose flour
1 cup sliced almonds

TOPPING
1 to 2 cups whipping cream
2 to 3 tablespoons powdered sugar

1   Heat oven to 400°F. Place pie crust in 9-inch glass pie plate as directed on box for One-Crust Filled Pie.

2   In small bowl, beat butter, 2 teaspoons flour, the almond paste and eggs with electric mixer on medium speed until well blended. (Mixture will not be smooth.) Spoon mixture evenly into crust-lined pie plate. Bake 17 to 20 minutes or until filling is set and light golden brown.

3   Reserve ⅓ cup of the caramel topping. In small bowl, blend remaining caramel topping and 3 tablespoons flour, using wire whisk. Stir in almonds. Carefully spoon over filling in pie plate. Bake 9 to 12 minutes longer or until golden brown. Cool on cooling rack 30 minutes. Refrigerate 2 to 3 hours.

4 In large bowl, beat whipping cream and powdered sugar until stiff peaks form. Pipe or spoon whipped cream around edge of chilled pie, leaving 4-inch circle in center. Just before serving, drizzle about 2 teaspoons of the reserved caramel topping over each piece. Cover and refrigerate any remaining pie.

High Altitude (3500–6500 ft): No change.

1 Serving: Calories 480; Total Fat 28g (Saturated Fat 11g; Trans Fat 0g); Cholesterol 85mg; Sodium 220mg; Total Carbohydrate 49g (Dietary Fiber 2g) Exchanges: 1 Starch, 2½ Other Carbohydrate, ½ High-Fat Meat, 4½ Fat; Carbohydrate Choices: 3

New Orleans Praline Pie

Amelia S. Meaux Crowley, LA
Bake-Off® Contest 32, 1986

  Prep Time: 45 Minutes
  Start to Finish: 4 Hours 5 Minutes
  8 to 10 servings

CRUST
1 Pillsbury® refrigerated pie crust (from 15-oz box), softened as directed on box
¾ cup chopped pecans
¼ cup packed brown sugar
2 tablespoons butter or margarine, softened

FILLING
2 packages (8 oz each) cream cheese, softened
½ cup firmly packed brown sugar
1 tablespoon lemon juice
1 teaspoon vanilla
1 teaspoon brandy extract, if desired
2 eggs

TOPPING
1 cup whipping cream
¼ cup packed brown sugar
Chopped or whole pecans

1 Heat oven to 425°F. Place pie crust in 9-inch glass pie plate as directed on box for One-Crust Filled Pie. In small bowl, mix ¾ cup pecans, ¼ cup brown sugar and the butter until crumbly. Sprinkle in bottom of crust-lined pie plate. Bake about 7 minutes or until lightly browned and brown sugar mixture is slightly melted. Set aside.

2 In large bowl, beat filling ingredients with electric mixer on medium speed until light and fluffy. Carefully spread over partially baked filled crust. Bake 20 to 25 minutes longer or until filling is set and light brown around edges. Cover edge of pie crust with strip of foil during last 10 to 15 minutes of bake time if necessary to prevent excessive browning. Cool; refrigerate 1 hour.

3 In small bowl, beat cream until stiff peaks form. Add ¼ cup brown sugar; blend at low speed until thoroughly combined. Spoon or pipe over cooled filling. Garnish with pecans. Refrigerate about 2 hours or until serving time. Cover and refrigerate any remaining pie.

High Altitude (3500–6500 ft): In step 2, bake 25 to 30 minutes.

1 Serving: Calories 650; Total Fat 49g (Saturated Fat 24g; Trans Fat 1g); Cholesterol 160mg; Sodium 340mg; Total Carbohydrate 44g (Dietary Fiber 1g) Exchanges: 3 Other Carbohydrate, 1 High-Fat Meat, 8 Fat; Carbohydrate Choices: 3

Chocolate–Peanut Butter Cookie Pie

Jenny Monfred Wintersville, OH
Bake-Off® Contest 38, 1998

  Prep Time: 15 Minutes
  Start to Finish: 1 Hour 50 Minutes
  16 servings

1 roll (16.5 oz) Pillsbury® Create 'n Bake® refrigerated chocolate chip cookies with walnuts
3 cups powdered sugar
1 cup peanut butter
2 tablespoons butter or margarine, softened
¼ cup water
1 cup milk chocolate chips, melted
16 pecan halves, if desired

1 Heat oven to 350°F. In bottom of ungreased 10- or 9-inch springform pan, break up cookie dough. With floured fingers, press dough evenly in bottom of pan. Bake 14 to 18 minutes or until golden brown. Cool 15 minutes.

2 In medium bowl, mix powdered sugar, peanut butter, butter and water until well blended. (If necessary, add additional water 1 teaspoon at a time until mixture is smooth.) Drop spoonfuls of mixture over baked cookie crust; press evenly to cover crust.

3 Spread melted chocolate chips over peanut butter mixture. If desired, carefully swirl chocolate with fork. Garnish with pecan halves. Refrigerate about 1 hour or until chocolate is set.

High Altitude (3500–6500 ft): No change.

1 Serving: Calories 390; Total Fat 19g (Saturated Fat 6g; Trans Fat 1g); Cholesterol 10mg; Sodium 180mg; Total Carbohydrate 49g (Dietary Fiber 1g) Exchanges: 1 Starch, 2 Other Carbohydrate, ½ High-Fat Meat, 3 Fat; Carbohydrate Choices: 3

Classic German Chocolate Pie

Jean Hurst   Sherwood, AZ
Bake-Off® Contest 33, 1988

> **Prep Time:** 35 Minutes
> **Start to Finish:** 4 Hours 35 Minutes
> 8 servings

CRUST
1 Pillsbury® refrigerated pie crust (from 15-oz box), softened as directed on box

FILLING
4 oz sweet baking chocolate, cut up
⅓ cup butter or margarine
¾ cup sugar
2 tablespoons Pillsbury BEST® all-purpose flour
3 eggs, separated
1 teaspoon vanilla

TOPPING
½ cup sweetened condensed milk (not evaporated)
1 egg
1 cup coconut
½ cup chopped pecans
1 teaspoon vanilla

1   Heat oven to 375°F. Place pie crust in 9-inch glass pie plate as directed on box for One-Crust Filled Pie.

2   In 3-quart saucepan over low heat, melt chocolate and butter, stirring until smooth. Remove from heat. Add sugar, flour, 3 egg yolks and 1 teaspoon vanilla; stir until well blended. In small bowl, beat 3 egg whites until stiff peaks form. Fold into chocolate mixture. Pour into crust-lined pie plate.

3   Bake 24 to 30 minutes or until filling is set. Remove from oven to cool while preparing topping. Set oven control to broil. In small bowl, mix topping ingredients. Drop by teaspoonfuls over baked filling; spread carefully. Broil with top 6 to 8 inches from heat 2 to 3 minutes or until coconut begins to brown. Watch carefully; DO NOT BURN CRUST. Cool on cooling rack 30 minutes. Refrigerate 2 to 3 hours before serving. Cover and refrigerate any remaining pie.

High Altitude (3500–6500 ft): Bake 33 to 39 minutes.

1 Serving: Calories 540; Total Fat 31g (Saturated Fat 15g; Trans Fat 0g); Cholesterol 135mg; Sodium 250mg; Total Carbohydrate 58g (Dietary Fiber 2g) Exchanges: 1 Starch, 3 Other Carbohydrate, ½ High-Fat Meat, 5 Fat; Carbohydrate Choices: 4

Chocolate Pecan Caramel Pie

Karen Ann Pionke   Delafield, WI
Bake-Off® Contest 32, 1986

> **Prep Time:** 35 Minutes
> **Start to Finish:** 3 Hours 30 Minutes
> 8 to 10 servings

CRUST
1 Pillsbury® refrigerated pie crust (from 15-oz box), softened as directed on box

CARAMEL SAUCE
1 teaspoon butter or margarine
1 teaspoon Pillsbury BEST® all-purpose flour
⅛ teaspoon salt, if desired
⅓ cup half-and-half
¼ cup granulated sugar
¼ cup firmly packed brown sugar

FILLING
⅔ cup granulated sugar
½ teaspoon salt
⅓ cup butter or margarine, melted
1 cup light corn syrup
3 eggs
1 cup pecan halves or chopped pecans
2 oz unsweetened baking chocolate, melted

SERVE WITH, IF DESIRED
Ice cream or whipped cream

1   Heat oven to 375°F. Place pie crust in 9-inch glass pie plate as directed on box for One-Crust Filled Pie.

2   In 1-quart saucepan, melt 1 teaspoon butter over medium heat. Stir in 1 teaspoon flour and ⅛ teaspoon salt. Gradually stir in half-and-half. Add ¼ cup granulated sugar and the brown sugar; mix well. Cook over medium heat, stirring constantly, until mixture boils and thickens; boil 1 minute. Set aside.

3   In large bowl, mix ⅔ cup sugar, ½ teaspoon salt, ⅓ cup butter, the corn syrup and eggs; beat well. Stir ½ cup of filling mixture into caramel sauce; blend well. Set aside. Stir pecans and chocolate into remaining filling mixture; blend well. Pour into crust-lined pie plate. Pour caramel sauce evenly over filling. Cover crust edge with strips of foil to prevent excessive browning; remove foil during last 15 minutes of bake time.

4   Bake 40 to 55 minutes or until outer edge of filling is set and center is partially set. Cool on cooling rack 1 hour; refrigerate 1 hour before serving. Serve with ice cream or whipped cream. Cover and refrigerate any remaining pie.

High Altitude (3500–6500 ft): No change.

1 Serving: Calories 620; Total Fat 31g (Saturated Fat 12g; Trans Fat 0g); Cholesterol 110mg; Sodium 370mg; Total Carbohydrate 80g (Dietary Fiber 2g) Exchanges: ½ Starch, 4½ Other Carbohydrate, ½ High-Fat Meat, 5½ Fat; Carbohydrate Choices: 5

Vienna Chocolate Pie

Dorothy Wagoner   Lufkin, TX
Bake-Off® Contest 11, 1959

Prep Time: 15 Minutes
Start to Finish: 45 Minutes
8 servings

CRUST
1 Pillsbury® refrigerated pie crust
   (from 15-oz box), softened as
   directed on box

FILLING
1½ cups sugar
3 tablespoons Pillsbury BEST®
   all-purpose flour
¾ teaspoon instant coffee granules
¼ teaspoon ground cinnamon
Dash salt
4 eggs
½ cup buttermilk*
1½ teaspoons vanilla
½ cup butter or margarine, softened
2 oz unsweetened baking chocolate,
   melted
¼ cup slivered almonds

1   Heat oven to 400°F. Place pie crust in 9-inch glass pie plate as directed on box for One-Crust Filled Pie.

2   In medium bowl, mix sugar, flour, instant coffee, cinnamon and salt. In large bowl, beat eggs with electric mixer on high speed until light in color. Beat in dry ingredients. Add buttermilk, vanilla, butter and chocolate; mix well. (Filling may look curdled.) Pour into crust-lined pie plate. Sprinkle with slivered almonds.

3   Bake 25 to 30 minutes or until center is set and crust is deep golden brown. Cover edge of crust with strips of foil after 15 to 20 minutes of bake time to prevent excessive browning.

* To substitute for buttermilk, use 1 teaspoon vinegar or lemon juice plus milk to make ½ cup.

High Altitude (3500–6500 ft): Bake 40 to 45 minutes.

1 Serving: Calories 490; Total Fat 27g (Saturated Fat 13g; Trans Fat 0g); Cholesterol 140mg; Sodium 260mg; Total Carbohydrate 57g (Dietary Fiber 1g) Exchanges: 1 Starch, 3 Other Carbohydrate, ½ Medium-Fat Meat, 4½ Fat; Carbohydrate Choices: 4

Memories in Every Bite

Dorothy Wagoner described the path to creating her chocolate pie as "searching for a flavor to match a memory." Dorothy's father had emigrated from Germany when he was a young man. "Dad had a vivid memory," Dorothy said, "and through the stories of his childhood I could picture Grandmother's kitchen, the many wonderful things she baked and the dark, luxurious pastries that were Dad's favorite."

Experimenting with recipes, Dorothy tried different flavor combinations, combining her own memories of foods from her mother, who died when Dorothy was twelve, with her father's memories of his mother's pastries. "My mother was a wonderful cook and loved to bake. Saturday was baking day, and our big old kitchen would be filled with the fragrance of bread and sweet rolls, and always pie." Finally, Dorothy came up with her Vienna Chocolate Pie— a true labor of love and a dessert destined to make wonderful new memories.

Chocolate Silk Pecan Pie

Leonard Thompson San Jose, CA
Bake-Off® Contest 32, 1986
$2,000 Winner

Prep Time: 25 Minutes
Start to Finish: 3 Hours 5 Minutes
10 servings

CRUST

1 Pillsbury® refrigerated pie crust (from 15-oz box), softened as directed on box

PECAN FILLING

2 eggs
⅓ cup granulated sugar
½ cup dark corn syrup
3 tablespoons butter or margarine, melted
⅛ teaspoon salt, if desired
½ cup chopped pecans

CHOCOLATE FILLING

1 cup hot milk
¼ teaspoon vanilla
1 bag (12 oz) semisweet chocolate chips (2 cups)

TOPPING

1 cup whipping cream
2 tablespoons powdered sugar
¼ teaspoon vanilla
Chocolate curls, if desired

1 Heat oven to 350°F. Place pie crust in 9-inch glass pie plate as directed on box for One-Crust Filled Pie.

2 In small bowl, beat eggs with electric mixer on medium speed until well blended. Add granulated sugar, corn syrup, butter and salt; beat 1 minute. Stir in pecans. Pour into crust-lined pie plate. Cover crust edge with 2- to 3-inch-wide strips of foil to prevent excessive browning; remove foil during last 15 minutes of bake time.

3 Bake 40 to 55 minutes or until center of pie is puffed and golden brown. Cool 1 hour.

4 Meanwhile, in blender or food processor, place chocolate filling ingredients. Cover; blend about 1 minute or until smooth. Refrigerate until mixture is slightly thickened but not set, about 1 hour 30 minutes.

5 Gently stir chocolate filling; pour over cooled pecan filling in crust. Refrigerate at least 1 hour or until firm before serving.

6 Just before serving, in small bowl, beat whipping cream, powdered sugar and ¼ teaspoon vanilla with mixer on high speed

meet len thompson

Len Thompson's original name for what became his Bake-Off® Contest entry didn't bode well for its chances. Len had started a pecan pie for Thanksgiving, "but I made one little mistake, using a pan with holes in the bottom. Everything turned out fine—except there was a black cloud of smoke pouring out of the oven. Half the filling leaked out. And we were supposed to go to Thanksgiving dinner that day! My wife suggested I put chocolate pudding in there, so I did, topped it off with a little whipped cream, and named it 'Disaster Pie.' People really liked it, so I improved it."

After he revised the recipe, Len's wife suggested that he enter it in the Bake-Off® Contest. Says Len, "I only sent in one entry, and lo and behold . . ." Chocolate Silk Pecan Pie won a $2,000 prize and was on its way to becoming a contest classic.

Len considers his journey to the Bake-Off® Contest as rewarding as the outcome. Despite baking in childhood, the demands of raising four children and navigating a successful engineering career meant he had to postpone perfecting his baking skills until retirement. "Getting to the Bake-Off® Contest is a challenge, and if you like challenges, it's a tremendous one, and I do like challenges."

until stiff peaks form. Spoon or pipe whipped cream over filling. Garnish with chocolate curls. Cover and refrigerate any remaining pie.

High Altitude (3500–6500 ft): No change.

1 Serving: Calories 530; Total Fat 32g (Saturated Fat 16g; Trans Fat 0g); Cholesterol 85mg; Sodium 160mg; Total Carbohydrate 56g (Dietary Fiber 2g) Exchanges: ½ Starch, 3 Other Carbohydrate, ½ High-Fat Meat, 5½ Fat; Carbohydrate Choices: 4

Black-Bottom Peanut Butter Pie

Claudia Shepardson   South Yarmouth, MA
Bake-Off® Contest 42, 2006

Prep Time: 25 Minutes
Start to Finish: 3 Hours 25 Minutes
8 servings

CRUST
1 Pillsbury® refrigerated pie crust (from 15-oz box), softened as directed on box

FUDGE LAYER
1¼ cups dark or semisweet chocolate chips
½ cup whipping cream
2 tablespoons butter or margarine, melted

FILLING
1¼ cups milk
1 container (6 oz) French vanilla fat-free yogurt
1 box (4-serving size) white chocolate instant pudding and pie filling mix
3 tablespoons butter or margarine
1 bag (10 oz) peanut butter chips (1⅔ cups)

TOPPING
4 peanut butter crunchy granola bars (2 pouches from 8.9-oz box), crushed (¾ cup)*

1   Heat oven to 450°F. Make pie crust as directed on box for One-Crust Baked Shell, using 9-inch glass pie plate. Cool on cooling rack 15 minutes.

2   Meanwhile, in 1-quart heavy saucepan, mix fudge layer ingredients. Cook over low heat, stirring constantly, until chips are melted. Remove from heat; stir until smooth. Reserve ¼ cup fudge mixture in small microwavable bowl for drizzle; set remaining mixture aside to cool.

3   In large bowl, beat milk, yogurt and pudding mix with electric mixer on high speed about 3 minutes or until smooth and thickened. Set aside.

4   In another small microwavable bowl, microwave 3 tablespoons butter and the peanut butter chips uncovered on High 45 seconds. Stir; if necessary, continue to microwave in 10-second increments, stirring after each, until chips are melted and mixture is smooth. On low speed, gradually beat peanut butter mixture into pudding mixture until combined; beat on high speed until filling is smooth and fluffy, scraping side of bowl occasionally.

5   Spread cooled fudge layer mixture evenly into crust. Carefully spoon and spread filling over fudge layer. Sprinkle crushed granola bars evenly over top. Refrigerate until set, 3 to 4 hours.

6   To serve, microwave reserved fudge mixture uncovered on High 15 to 20 seconds or until drizzling consistency. Drizzle over top of pie. Cover and refrigerate any remaining pie.

To easily crush granola bars, do not unwrap; use rolling pin to crush bars.

High Altitude (3500–6500 ft): No change.

1 Serving: Calories 690; Total Fat 40g (Saturated Fat 18g; Trans Fat 0g); Cholesterol 45mg; Sodium 520mg; Total Carbohydrate 72g (Dietary Fiber 4g) Exchanges: 1 Starch, 4 Other Carbohydrate, 1 High-Fat Meat, 6 Fat; Carbohydrate Choices: 5

Fudge Crostata with Raspberry Sauce

Paula Cassidy Boston, MA
Bake-Off® Contest 34, 1990
$10,000 Winner

Prep Time: 50 Minutes
Start to Finish: 3 Hours 10 Minutes
12 servings

CRUST
1 box (15 oz) Pillsbury® refrigerated pie
   crusts, softened as directed on box

FILLING
1 cup semisweet chocolate chips
½ cup butter or margarine
⅔ cup sugar
1 cup ground almonds
1 egg
1 egg yolk

SAUCE
1 bag (12 oz) frozen raspberries
   without syrup, thawed
¾ cup sugar
1 teaspoon lemon juice

GARNISH, IF DESIRED
Sweetened whipped cream
Chocolate curls
Whole raspberries

1 Place cookie sheet on middle oven rack in oven to preheat; heat oven to 375°F. Make pie crusts as directed on box for Two-Crust Pie, using 10-inch tart pan with removable bottom or 9-inch glass pie plate.

2 In 1-quart saucepan, melt chocolate chips and 2 tablespoons of the butter over low heat, stirring constantly, until smooth. In medium bowl, mix remaining 6 tablespoons butter and ⅔ cup sugar with wire whisk until light and fluffy. Stir in almonds, 1 egg, the egg yolk and melted chocolate until well blended. Spread mixture evenly into crust-lined pie plate.

3 Unroll second crust on cutting board. With sharp knife or pizza cutter, cut crust into ½-inch-wide strips. Arrange strips in lattice design over filling. Trim and seal edge. Cover crust edge with 2- to 3-inch-wide strips of foil to prevent excessive browning; remove foil during last 15 minutes of bake time.

4 Place tart on preheated cookie sheet in oven; bake 45 to 50 minutes or until crust is golden brown. Cool completely, about 1 hour 30 minutes.

5 Meanwhile, in blender or food processor, place raspberries. Cover; blend on high speed until smooth. Place strainer over 1-quart saucepan; pour berries into strainer. Press berries with back of spoon through strainer to remove seeds; discard seeds. Stir in ¾ cup sugar and the lemon juice. Heat mixture to boiling, stirring constantly. Reduce heat to medium-low; boil 3 minutes, stirring constantly. Cool; refrigerate until serving time.

6 Just before serving, garnish crostata with whipped cream, chocolate curls and whole raspberries. Serve with raspberry sauce. Cover and refrigerate any remaining crostata.

High Altitude (3500–6500 ft): No change.

1 Serving: Calories 470; Total Fat 26g (Saturated Fat 11g; Trans Fat 0g); Cholesterol 60mg; Sodium 210mg; Total Carbohydrate 54g (Dietary Fiber 3g) Exchanges: 1 Starch, 2½ Other Carbohydrate, 5 Fat; Carbohydrate Choices: 3½

Grands!® Little Pies

S. Lea Mead   San Mateo, CA
Bake-Off® Contest 40, 2002
$10,000 Winner

> **Prep Time:** 20 Minutes
> **Start to Finish:** 55 Minutes
> 16 servings

¾ cup Pillsbury BEST® all-purpose flour
½ cup packed brown sugar
1 teaspoon ground cinnamon
½ cup butter or margarine
½ cup chopped nuts, if desired
1 can (16.3 oz) Pillsbury® Grands!® Flaky Layers refrigerated original or buttermilk biscuits
1 can (21 oz) apple, blueberry or cherry pie filling
1 to 1½ cups whipping cream
Cinnamon-sugar

1 Heat oven to 350°F. In medium bowl, mix flour, brown sugar and cinnamon. With pastry blender or fork, cut in butter until mixture looks like coarse crumbs. Stir in nuts.

2 Separate dough into 8 biscuits. Split each biscuit in half to make

16 rounds. With floured fingers, flatten each to form 4-inch round. Press each biscuit round in ungreased 2¾ × 1¼-inch muffin cup.

3 Spoon 2 tablespoons pie filling into each biscuit-lined cup. Sprinkle each with about 2 tablespoons flour mixture. (Cups will be full.)

4 Bake 15 to 22 minutes or until golden brown. Cool 5 minutes. Remove from muffin cups; place on cooling rack. Cool 10 minutes.

5 In small bowl, beat whipping cream with electric mixer on high speed until stiff peaks form. Top each serving with whipped cream; sprinkle with cinnamon-sugar. Cover and refrigerate any remaining pies.

High Altitude (3500–6500 ft): Bake 17 to 22 minutes.

1 Serving: Calories 280; Total Fat 15g (Saturated Fat 8g; Trans Fat 2g); Cholesterol 30mg; Sodium 320mg; Total Carbohydrate 34g (Dietary Fiber 0g) Exchanges: 1 Starch, 1 Other Carbohydrate, 3 Fat; Carbohydrate Choices: 2

White Chocolate Pecan Mousse Pie

Jeannette Allman   Mesa, AZ
Bake-Off® Contest 34, 1990

> **Prep Time:** 45 Minutes
> **Start to Finish:** 5 Hours 20 Minutes
> 12 servings

FILLING
2 tablespoons butter or margarine
2 cups chopped pecans
6 oz (1 cup) white vanilla baking chips or chopped white chocolate baking bar
¼ cup milk
2 cups whipping cream
⅓ cup sugar
1 teaspoon vanilla

CRUST
1 Pillsbury® refrigerated pie crust (from 15-oz box), softened as directed on box

GARNISH
1 tablespoon grated chocolate or ¼ cup chocolate-flavor syrup, if desired

1 In 10-inch skillet, melt butter over medium heat. Stir in pecans. Cook about 6 minutes, stirring constantly, until pecans are golden brown. Cool at room temperature 1 hour.

2 Meanwhile in 1-quart saucepan, melt white chips and milk over low heat, stirring constantly with wire whisk. Cool at room temperature 1 hour.

3 Heat oven to 450°F. Bake pie crust as directed on box for One-Crust Baked Shell, using 10-inch springform pan or 9-inch glass pie plate. Cool completely, about 15 minutes.

4 In large bowl, beat whipping cream with electric mixer on high speed until stiff peaks form. Fold in sugar, vanilla, pecans and melted white chips. Spoon into crust. Refrigerate 4 hours before serving. Just before serving, garnish with grated chocolate or chocolate syrup. Cover and refrigerate any remaining pie.*

* Pie can be frozen. Let stand at room temperature 30 to 45 minutes before serving.

High Altitude (3500–6500 ft): No change.

1 Serving: Calories 440; Total Fat 36g (Saturated Fat 15g; Trans Fat 0.5g); Cholesterol 50mg; Sodium 130mg; Total Carbohydrate 27g (Dietary Fiber 1g) Exchanges: 1 Starch, 1 Other Carbohydrate, 7 Fat; Carbohydrate Choices: 2

Chocolate Dream Pie

Lirene Alexander   Tampa, FL
Bake-Off® Contest 12, 1960

> **Prep Time:** 40 Minutes
> **Start to Finish:** 3 Hours 40 Minutes
> 10 servings

CRUST
1 Pillsbury® refrigerated pie crust (from 15-oz box), softened as directed on box

FILLING
½ cup sugar
¼ cup cornstarch
⅛ teaspoon salt
1 cup milk
1 cup semisweet chocolate chips (6 oz)
2 egg yolks, slightly beaten
1 package (3 oz) cream cheese, cubed, softened
1½ cups whipping cream
1 teaspoon vanilla

1   Heat oven to 450°F. Make pie crust as directed on box for One-Crust Baked Shell, using 9-inch glass pie plate. Cool completely, about 15 minutes.

2   In 2-quart saucepan, mix sugar, cornstarch and salt. Gradually stir in milk. Add chocolate chips and egg yolks. Cook over medium heat, stirring constantly, until mixture is thickened. Remove from heat. In medium bowl, with electric mixer at medium speed, beat cream cheese until smooth. Cover surface with plastic wrap. Refrigerate until just cool, about 1 hour.

3   In large bowl with electric mixer, beat whipping cream and vanilla on high speed until soft peaks form. Reserve 1 cup whipped cream for topping. Fold remaining whipped cream into cooled chocolate mixture. Spoon evenly into crust. Refrigerate 2 hours or overnight. Spoon or pipe reserved whipped cream over filling. Cover and refrigerate any remaining pie.

High Altitude (3500–6500 ft): No change.

1 Serving: Calories 400; Total Fat 26g (Saturated Fat 14g; Trans Fat 0.5g); Cholesterol 95mg; Sodium 170mg; Total Carbohydrate 37g (Dietary Fiber 1g) Exchanges: 1 Starch, 1½ Other Carbohydrate, 5 Fat; Carbohydrate Choices: 2½

Cranberry Cheesecake Tart

James Sloboden   Puyallup, WA
Bake-Off® Contest 34, 1990
$2,000 Winner

> **Prep Time:** 30 Minutes
> **Start to Finish:** 5 Hours 30 Minutes
> 10 servings

CRUST
1 Pillsbury® refrigerated pie crust (from 15-oz box), softened as directed on box

FILLING
1 can (16 oz) whole berry cranberry sauce
½ cup chopped pecans
6 tablespoons sugar
1 tablespoon cornstarch
12 oz cream cheese, softened
2 eggs
½ cup sugar
1 tablespoon milk

TOPPING
1 cup sour cream
½ teaspoon vanilla
2 tablespoons sugar

1   Heat oven to 450°F. Bake pie crust as directed on box for One-Crust Baked Shell, using 10-inch tart pan with removable bottom or 9-inch glass pie plate. Cool completely, about 15 minutes. Reduce oven temperature to 375°F.

2   In medium bowl, mix cranberry sauce, pecans, 6 tablespoons sugar and the cornstarch; spread in crust.

3   In medium bowl, beat cream cheese, eggs, ½ cup sugar and the milk with electric mixer on medium speed until smooth. Spoon evenly over cranberry mixture. Bake at 25 to 30 minutes or until set.

4   In small bowl, mix topping ingredients. Spoon evenly over filling. Bake 5 minutes longer. Cool slightly. Refrigerate 3 to 4 hours or until set. Cover and refrigerate any remaining tart.

High Altitude (3500–6500 ft): No change.

1 Serving: Calories 490; Total Fat 28g (Saturated Fat 13g; Trans Fat 0.5g); Cholesterol 100mg; Sodium 240mg; Total Carbohydrate 54g (Dietary Fiber 0g) Exchanges: ½ Starch, 3 Other Carbohydrate, ½ High-Fat Meat, 5 Fat; Carbohydrate Choices: 3½

Bananas Foster Tart

Brenda Elsea   Tucson, AZ
Bake-Off® Contest 38, 1998
$2,000 Winner

Prep Time: 30 Minutes
Start to Finish: 1 Hour
10 servings

CRUST

1 Pillsbury® refrigerated pie crust
(from 15-oz box), softened as
directed on box

FILLING

2 medium bananas, cut into
¼-inch-thick slices
4½ teaspoons light rum*
2 teaspoons grated orange peel
⅔ cup chopped pecans
⅔ cup packed brown sugar
¼ cup whipping cream
¼ cup butter or margarine
½ teaspoon vanilla

SERVE WITH, IF DESIRED

Vanilla ice cream

1   Heat oven to 450°F. Bake pie crust as directed on box for One-Crust Baked Shell, using 9-inch tart pan with removable bottom or 9-inch glass pie plate. Cool 5 minutes.

2   In small bowl, gently mix bananas and rum to coat. Sprinkle orange peel evenly in bottom of crust. Arrange bananas in single layer over peel. Sprinkle with pecans.

3   In 2-quart heavy saucepan, mix brown sugar, whipping cream and butter. Cook and stir over medium-high heat 2 to 3 minutes or until mixture boils. Cook 2 to 4 minutes longer, stirring constantly, until mixture has thickened and is deep golden brown. Remove from heat; stir in vanilla. Spoon warm filling over bananas and pecans. Cool 30 minutes. Serve tart warm or cool with ice cream. Cover and refrigerate any remaining tart.

* To substitute for the rum, mix ½ teaspoon rum extract with 4 teaspoons water.

High Altitude (3500–6500 ft): No change.

1 Serving: Calories 290; Total Fat 17g (Saturated Fat 7g; Trans Fat 0g); Cholesterol 20mg; Sodium 130mg; Total Carbohydrate 31g (Dietary Fiber 1g) Exchanges: ½ Starch, 1½ Other Carbohydrate, 3½ Fat; Carbohydrate Choices: 2

Apple-Nut Lattice Tart

Mary Lou Warren   Medford, OR
Bake-Off® Contest 32, 1986
$40,000 Grand Prize Winner

Prep Time: 30 Minutes
Start to Finish: 3 Hours 25 Minutes
8 servings

CRUST

1 box (15 oz) Pillsbury® refrigerated pie
crusts, softened as directed on box

FILLING

3 to 3½ cups thinly sliced, peeled
apples (3 to 4 medium)
½ cup granulated sugar
3 tablespoons golden raisins
3 tablespoons chopped walnuts or
pecans
½ teaspoon ground cinnamon
¼ to ½ teaspoon grated lemon peel
2 teaspoons lemon juice

GLAZE

¼ cup powdered sugar
1 to 2 teaspoons lemon juice

1   Place cookie sheet on middle oven rack in oven to preheat; heat oven to 400°F. Make pie crusts as directed on box for Two-Crust Pie, using 10-inch tart pan with removable bottom or 9-inch glass pie plate.

2   In large bowl, mix filling ingredients to coat. Spoon into crust-lined pie plate.

3   Unroll second crust on cutting board. With sharp knife or pizza cutter, cut crust into ½-inch-wide strips. Arrange strips in lattice design over filling. Trim and seal edge. Cover crust edge with 2- to 3-inch-wide strips of foil to prevent excessive browning; remove foil during last 15 minutes of bake time.

4   Place tart on preheated cookie sheet in oven; bake 40 to 55 minutes or until apples are tender and crust is golden brown. Cool tart on cooling rack 1 hour.

5   In small bowl, blend glaze ingredients, adding enough lemon juice for desired drizzling consistency. Drizzle glaze over slightly warm tart. Cool completely, about 1 hour. Remove side of pan before serving.

High Altitude (3500–6500 ft): No change.

1 Serving: Calories 350; Total Fat 16g (Saturated Fat 5g; Trans Fat 0g); Cholesterol 5mg; Sodium 220mg; Total Carbohydrate 51g (Dietary Fiber 0g) Exchanges: ½ Starch, ½ Fruit, 2½ Other Carbohydrate, 3 Fat; Carbohydrate Choices: 3 ½

The Greatest Prize of All

When Bake-Off® Contest participants return from the competition, they sometimes find their recipe has preceded them. The finalists hear from friends and neighbors—and even people they've never met before—about how much they've enjoyed the winning recipe.

Vesta Frizzel, a finalist three times in the Bake-Off® Contest, found one of her winners was a favorite in a senior citizens' home. "Winning was a pleasurable experience, she says, "but learning that the dish is a special treat for others touches my heart!"

Key Lime Pecan Tart

Sue Tyner Tustin, CA
Bake-Off® Contest 42, 2006

> **Prep Time:** 25 Minutes
> **Start to Finish:** 2 Hours 35 Minutes
> 12 servings

CRUST
2 cups honey graham cereal squares, finely crushed (¾ cup)
6 pecan crunch crunchy granola bars (3 pouches from 8.9-oz box), finely crushed (heaping 1 cup)*
½ cup chopped pecans, ground
2 tablespoons sugar
7 tablespoons butter or margarine, melted

FILLING
¼ cup Key lime or regular lime juice
½ package (1½ teaspoons) unflavored gelatin
1 package (8 oz) cream cheese, softened
1 box (4-serving size) lemon instant pudding and pie filling mix
3 containers (6 oz each) Key lime pie fat-free yogurt
½ cup sugar
½ cup chopped pecans

1 Heat oven to 350°F. In medium bowl, mix crust ingredients. Press in bottom and up side of ungreased 11- or 10-inch tart pan with removable bottom. Bake 10 minutes. Cool 10 minutes. Place in freezer while making filling.

2 In 1-cup microwavable measuring cup or small bowl, place lime juice. Stir in gelatin. Microwave on High about 30 seconds, stirring occasionally, until gelatin is dissolved; set aside.

3 In large bowl, beat cream cheese with electric mixer on medium speed until light and fluffy. Add gelatin mixture and pudding mix; beat until smooth, scraping bowl frequently. Add 1 container of yogurt at a time, beating well after each addition. Gradually beat in ½ cup sugar until smooth.

4 Spread filling evenly in crust; sprinkle with pecans. Refrigerate at least 2 hours before serving. Cut into wedges to serve. Cover and refrigerate any remaining tart.

* To easily crush granola bars, do not unwrap; use rolling pin to crush bars.

High Altitude (3500–6500 ft): No change.

1 Serving: Calories 390; Total Fat 22g (Saturated Fat 10g; Trans Fat 0g); Cholesterol 40mg; Sodium 350mg; Total Carbohydrate 41g (Dietary Fiber 1g) Exchanges: 1 Starch, 2 Other Carbohydrate, 4 Fat; Carbohydrate Choices: 3

Coffee Crunch Chocolate Tart

Vesta Frizzel   Independence, MO
Bake-Off® Contest 32, 1986

> **Prep Time:** 25 Minutes
> **Start to Finish:** 3 Hours 15 Minutes
> 12 servings

CRUST
1 Pillsbury® refrigerated pie crust (from 15-oz box), softened as directed on box

CRUMB LAYER
½ cup crisp coconut cookie crumbs (3 to 4 cookies)
2 tablespoons Pillsbury BEST® all-purpose flour
2 tablespoons packed brown sugar
1 to 2 teaspoons instant coffee granules or crystals
1 tablespoon butter or margarine

FILLING
1 cup powdered sugar
1 package (3 oz) cream cheese, softened
1½ teaspoons vanilla
2 oz unsweetened baking chocolate, melted
2 cups whipping cream
6 to 8 dark roasted or chocolate-covered coffee beans or crushed coconut cookies, if desired

1 Heat oven to 450°F. Place pie crust in 10-inch tart pan with removable bottom or 9-inch glass pie plate; press in bottom and up side of pan. Trim edges if necessary. Generously prick crust with fork.

2 In small bowl, mix cookie crumbs, flour, brown sugar and instant coffee. Using fork or pastry blender, cut in butter until mixture is crumbly. Sprinkle over bottom of pie crust–lined pan. Bake 12 to 16 minutes or until light golden brown. Cool completely, about 15 minutes.

3 In large bowl, beat powdered sugar, cream cheese and vanilla with electric mixer on medium speed until well blended. Add chocolate; beat until smooth. Gradually add whipping cream, beating on high until firm peaks form. Spread filling into cooled baked shell. Refrigerate 2 to 3 hours. Remove side of pan; garnish with coffee beans or crushed coconut cookies. Cover and refrigerate any remaining tart.

High Altitude (3500–6500 ft): No change.

1 Serving: Calories 330; Total Fat 23g (Saturated Fat 14g; Trans Fat 0.5g); Cholesterol 55mg; Sodium 125mg; Total Carbohydrate 26g (Dietary Fiber 0g) Exchanges: ½ Starch, 1½ Other Carbohydrate, 4 ½ Fat; Carbohydrate Choices: 2

Glazed Pineapple Pecan Tart

Linda Raschke Holland, OH
Bake-Off® Contest 37, 1996

Prep Time: 40 Minutes
Start to Finish: 3 Hours 5 Minutes
12 servings

CRUST
1 Pillsbury® refrigerated pie crust (from 15-oz box), softened as directed on box

FILLING
¾ cup granulated sugar
½ cup butter or margarine, softened
1 package (8 oz) cream cheese, softened
1 cup crushed pineapple in juice, pureed if desired*
2 eggs
½ cup Pillsbury BEST® all-purpose flour
½ cup chopped pecans, toasted**

GLAZE
¾ cup powdered sugar
¼ cup crushed pineapple in juice, pureed if desired*
1 tablespoon chopped pecans, toasted**

1 Heat oven to 450°F. Bake pie crust as directed on box for One-Crust Baked Shell, using 10-inch tart pan with removable bottom or 9-inch pie pan. Reduce oven temperature to 325°F.

2 Meanwhile, in large bowl, beat sugar, butter and cream cheese with electric mixer on medium speed until light and fluffy. Add 1 cup pineapple and the eggs; blend well. Add flour and ½ cup pecans; blend well. Pour into crust; spread evenly.

3 Bake at 325°F 45 to 55 minutes or until top is light golden brown and center is set. Cool 10 minutes.

4 In small bowl, mix powdered sugar and ¼ cup pineapple. Spoon evenly over warm tart; sprinkle with 1 tablespoon pecans. Cool 20 minutes. Refrigerate about 1 hour or until completely cooled. Cover and refrigerate any remaining tart.

Two (8 oz) cans crushed pineapple equal 1½ cups.

**To toast pecans, spread on cookie sheet. Bake at 350°F 5 to 10 minutes or until golden brown, stirring occasionally. Or, spread in thin layer in microwavable glass pie plate. Microwave uncovered on High 4 to 7 minutes or until golden brown, stirring frequently.*

High Altitude (3500–6500 ft): In step 3, bake 55 to 65 minutes.

1 Serving: Calories 380; Total Fat 24g (Saturated Fat 11g; Trans Fat 0.5g); Cholesterol 80mg; Sodium 190mg; Total Carbohydrate 38g (Dietary Fiber 0g) Exchanges: 1 Starch, 1½ Other Carbohydrate, 4½ Fat; Carbohydrate Choices: 2½

Let Your Stomach Lead You

Sudden cravings can be the source of inspiration for a cook. "I was craving peanut butter cups and thought about how to make the ultimate creation using peanut butter and chocolate," recalls Laura Stensberg. Although she normally cooks low-fat, her taste for something rich and indulgent led her to create this decadent tart. The Bake-Off® Contest judges must have found her recipe satisfied a craving, too, because they awarded it $10,000. Laura says it's the perfect dessert to make a weekend more special, yet only requires a few steps and ingredients.

Peanut Butter Truffle Tart

Laura Stensberg   Marshfield, WI
Bake-Off® Contest 42, 2006
$10,000 Category Winner

Prep Time: 25 Minutes
Start to Finish: 3 Hours
16 servings

1 roll (16.5 oz) Pillsbury® Create 'n Bake® refrigerated peanut butter cookies
6 peanut butter crunchy granola bars (3 pouches from 8.9-oz box), crushed (1 heaping cup)*
2 bags (12 oz each) semisweet chocolate chips (4 cups)
1 cup whipping cream
½ cup crunchy peanut butter
⅓ cup chopped peanuts or 1 package (2 oz) nut topping

1   Heat oven to 350°F. In large bowl, break up cookie dough. Stir or knead in crushed granola bars until well mixed. Press dough in bottom and up side of ungreased 10-inch tart pan with removable bottom or 13 × 9-inch pan. Bake 12 to 17 minutes or until light golden brown.

2   With back of spoon, press down crust on bottom and side; bake 3 to 5 minutes longer or until deep golden brown. Press down crust again with spoon. Cool 3 minutes.

3   Meanwhile, in large microwavable bowl, microwave chocolate chips and whipping cream uncovered on High 1 minute. Stir; microwave 1 to 2 minutes longer, stirring every 30 seconds to prevent chocolate from burning, until completely melted and smooth. In small microwavable bowl, microwave peanut butter uncovered on High about 1 minute or until melted; stir.

4   Spread warm peanut butter in bottom of crust. Pour chocolate mixture over peanut butter mixture. Sprinkle peanuts evenly over top. Refrigerate at least 2 hours until serving time. For easier cutting, let tart stand at room temperature 15 minutes before serving. Cover and refrigerate any remaining tart.

To easily crush granola bars, do not unwrap; use rolling pin to crush bars.

High Altitude (3500–6500 ft): No change.

1 Serving: Calories 510; Total Fat 30g (Saturated Fat 13g; Trans Fat 1g); Cholesterol 20mg; Sodium 230mg; Total Carbohydrate 51g (Dietary Fiber 3g) Exchanges: 1 Starch, 2½ Other Carbohydrate, ½ High-Fat Meat, 5 Fat; Carbohydrate Choices: 3½

11 | OTHER DESSERTS

Hot Buttered Rum and Apple Cobbler (page 340)

Raspberry-Mango Shortcakes

Nancy Flesch Kent, OH
Bake-Off® Contest 37, 1996

Prep Time: 50 Minutes
Start to Finish: 50 Minutes
8 shortcakes

SHORTCAKES
½ cup coconut
¼ cup granulated sugar
½ teaspoon ground ginger
1 can (16.3 oz) Pillsbury® Grands!®
   refrigerated buttermilk biscuits
2 tablespoons butter or margarine,
   melted

FRUIT MIXTURE
2 cups fresh or frozen (partially thawed)
   raspberries
1½ cups chopped peeled fresh mangoes
   or 1 jar or can (16 oz) mangoes or
   peaches, drained, chopped
2 tablespoons granulated sugar

TOPPING
1 cup whipping cream
2 tablespoons packed brown sugar
¼ teaspoon ground ginger

1 Heat oven to 375°F. In small bowl, mix coconut, ¼ cup granulated sugar and ½ teaspoon ginger.

2 Separate dough into 8 biscuits. Dip top and sides of each biscuit into melted butter; dip top and sides into coconut mixture. Place biscuits, coconut side up, 2 inches apart on ungreased cookie sheet. Sprinkle any remaining coconut mixture over tops of biscuits.

3 Bake 14 to 18 minutes or until biscuits and coconut are light golden brown. Cool 5 minutes.

4 Meanwhile, in medium bowl, gently stir together all fruit mixture ingredients. In small bowl, beat all topping ingredients with electric mixer on high speed until stiff peaks form.

5 To serve, split warm biscuits; place bottom halves on dessert plates. Spoon generous ⅓ cup fruit mixture over each biscuit half; top each with ¼ cup topping and biscuit top. Store fruit and topping in refrigerator.

High Altitude (3500–6500 ft): No change.

1 Shortcake: Calories 420; Total Fat 22g (Saturated Fat 12g; Trans Fat 3.5g); Cholesterol 40mg; Sodium 650mg; Total Carbohydrate 49g (Dietary Fiber 3g) Exchanges: 1½ Starch, ½ Fruit, 1 Other Carbohydrate, 4½ Fat; Carbohydrate Choices: 3

Creamy Peach Biscuit Puffs

Patricia Lee Henry Anaheim, CA
Bake-Off® Contest 28, 1978

Prep Time: 25 Minutes
Start to Finish: 40 Minutes
10 pastries

PASTRIES
⅓ cup granulated sugar
¼ to ½ teaspoon pumpkin pie spice
1 package (8 oz) cream cheese,
   softened
⅓ cup canned peaches, well drained
   (reserve syrup) and chopped
1 can (12 oz) Pillsbury® Golden Layers®
   refrigerated flaky biscuits
1 to 2 tablespoons peach syrup

GLAZE
¾ cup powdered sugar
1 to 2 tablespoons peach syrup

1 Heat oven to 375°F. In medium bowl, mix granulated sugar and pumpkin pie spice; reserve 1 tablespoon. Add cream cheese to remaining sugar mixture; beat with electric mixer on medium speed until smooth and creamy. Stir in peaches.

2 Separate biscuit dough into 10 biscuits; press or roll each between pieces of waxed paper to a 5-inch round. Spoon about 2 tablespoons peach mixture onto center of each biscuit. Pull edges of dough to top center; twist firmly and pinch to seal. Place on ungreased cookie sheet. Brush top of each with peach syrup; sprinkle with reserved sugar mixture.

3 Bake 10 to 15 minutes or until tops are golden brown. In small bowl, stir glaze ingredients until smooth and thin enough to drizzle; drizzle over warm pastries. Remove from cookie sheet while warm. Serve warm or cool.

High Altitude (3500–6500 ft): No change.

1 Pastry: Calories 250; Total Fat 12g (Saturated Fat 6g; Trans Fat 1.5g); Cholesterol 25mg; Sodium 430mg; Total Carbohydrate 31g (Dietary Fiber 0g) Exchanges: 1 Starch, 1 Other Carbohydrate, 2½ Fat; Carbohydrate Choices: 2

Banana Dessert Wraps

Heather Snedic   Lisle, IL
Bake-Off® Contest 41, 2004

Prep Time: 20 Minutes
Start to Finish: 40 Minutes
4 servings

½ **cup coconut**
½ **cup chopped pecans**
1 **Pillsbury® refrigerated pie crust
 (from 15-oz box), softened as
 directed on box**
¼ **cup sugar**
½ **teaspoon ground cinnamon**
¼ **teaspoon ground nutmeg**
4 **firm ripe bananas (5 to 6 inch)**
⅓ **cup semisweet chocolate chips**
1 **jar (12.25 oz) caramel topping, heated**
Whipped cream, if desired
1 **cup vanilla ice cream**

1   Heat oven to 350°F. Spread coconut and pecans separately on cookie sheet. Bake 5 to 8 minutes, stirring occasionally, until light golden brown; set aside.

2   Increase oven temperature to 450°F. Remove pie crust from pouch; unroll on work surface. With rolling pin, roll crust until 12 inches in diameter.

3   In small bowl, mix sugar, cinnamon and nutmeg. Reserve 1 tablespoon sugar mixture; sprinkle remaining sugar mixture evenly over crust. Cut crust into 4 wedge-shaped pieces.

4   Place 1 banana lengthwise on each crust wedge, about ¾ inch from curved edge (if banana is too long, trim ends so it fits within crust, at least ¼ inch from each edge). Push about 1 rounded tablespoon chocolate chips, points first, into top and sides of each banana.

5   Bring curved edge and point of each crust wedge up over banana to meet; pinch seam and ends to seal, shaping crust around banana.

Sprinkle tops of wrapped bananas with reserved 1 tablespoon sugar mixture; place on ungreased cookie sheet.

6   Bake at 450°F 10 to 14 minutes or until golden brown. Immediately remove from cookie sheet. Cool 5 minutes.

7   To serve, drizzle or spread about 2 tablespoons warm caramel topping on each dessert plate. Top each with baked banana, whipped cream and if desired, additional caramel topping. Sprinkle coconut and pecans over top of each. Serve with ice cream.

High Altitude (3500–6500 ft): After toasting coconut and pecans, increase oven temperature to 425°F. In step 6, bake wrapped bananas 15 to 19 minutes.

1 Serving: Calories 940; Total Fat 37g (Saturated Fat 15g; Trans Fat 0g); Cholesterol 25mg; Sodium 580mg; Total Carbohydrate 147g (Dietary Fiber 7g) Exchanges: 2 Starch, 2 Fruit, 5 Other Carbohydrate, 7 Fat; Carbohydrate Choices: 10

Quick Crescent Blintzes

Mrs. Robert H. Levine   Omaha, NE
Bake-Off® Contest 20, 1969

> Prep Time: 20 Minutes
> Start to Finish: 35 Minutes
> 16 blintzes

FILLING
1 egg
1 cup (8 oz) dry cottage cheese*
1 package (3 oz) cream cheese, softened
1 tablespoon sugar
½ teaspoon vanilla

BLINTZES
2 cans (8 oz each) Pillsbury® refrigerated crescent dinner rolls
2 tablespoons butter or margarine, melted

TOPPINGS, IF DESIRED
Sour cream
Choice of preserves or fruit toppings

1   Heat oven to 375°F. In small bowl, mix all filling ingredients; set aside.

2   Separate crescent dough into 8 rectangles. Press perforations of each rectangle to seal into 1 piece. Cut each rectangle in half crosswise to form 16 squares. Place about 1 tablespoon of filling on each square; fold dough in half and seal edges of squares with fork. On ungreased cookie sheets, place about 2 inches apart. Brush blintzes with melted butter.

3   Bake 12 to 15 minutes until golden brown. Serve warm with sour cream and a choice of preserves or fruit toppings.

* Dry cottage cheese works best, but creamed cottage cheese may be used if it is rinsed with water and well drained on a paper towel.

High Altitude (3500–6500 ft): No change.

1 Blintz: Calories 160; Total Fat 10g (Saturated Fat 4g; Trans Fat 1.5g); Cholesterol 25mg; Sodium 250mg; Total Carbohydrate 12g (Dietary Fiber 0g) Exchanges: ½ Starch, ½ Other Carbohydrate, ½ High-Fat Meat, 1 Fat; Carbohydrate Choices: 1

Fudgy Peanut Butter Banana Parfaits

Robin Wilson   Altamonte Springs, FL
Bake-Off® Contest 42, 2006

> Prep Time: 15 Minutes
> Start to Finish: 1 Hour 50 Minutes
> 2 servings

4 Pillsbury® Ready to Bake!™ Big Deluxe Classics® refrigerated peanut butter cup cookies (from 18-oz package)
¼ cup whipped cream cheese (from 8-oz container)
3 tablespoons powdered sugar
2 tablespoons creamy peanut butter
1 container (6 oz) banana thick & creamy low-fat yogurt
½ cup frozen (thawed) whipped topping
1 bar (2.1 oz) chocolate-covered crispy peanut-buttery candy, unwrapped, finely crushed*
¼ cup hot fudge topping

1   Heat oven to 350°F. On ungreased cookie sheet, place cookie dough rounds 2 inches apart. Bake 14 to 18 minutes or until edges are golden brown. Cool 3 minutes; remove from cookie sheet. Cool completely, about 15 minutes.

2   Meanwhile, in medium bowl, beat cream cheese, powdered sugar, peanut butter and yogurt with electric mixer on low speed until blended. Fold in whipped topping and crushed candy with rubber spatula.

3   In small microwavable bowl, microwave fudge topping on High 25 to 30 seconds or until melted and drizzling consistency. Crumble 1 cookie into each of 2 (12- to 14-ounce) parfait glasses.** Top each with about ⅓ cup yogurt mixture; drizzle each with 1 tablespoon fudge topping. Repeat layers. Refrigerate at least 1 hour but no longer than 4 hours before serving.

* To easily crush candy bar, unwrap, break into pieces and place in mini food processor; process with on-and-off motions until crushed. Or place unwrapped candy bar in small resealable plastic bag; use rolling pin to crush bar.

** Any 12- to 14-ounce tall parfait, dessert or wine glasses can be used.

High Altitude (3500–6500 ft): No change.

1 Serving: Calories 1030; Total Fat 50g (Saturated Fat 21g; Trans Fat 3.5g); Cholesterol 40mg; Sodium 740mg; Total Carbohydrate 124g (Dietary Fiber 4g) Exchanges: 2 Starch, 6 Other Carbohydrate, 2 High-Fat Meat, 6½ Fat; Carbohydrate Choices: 8

Fudgy Peanut Butter Banana Parfaits

Banana Crème Pastries

Jaimie Caltabellatta   Midland Park, NJ
Bake-Off® Contest 42, 2006

Prep Time: 15 Minutes
Start to Finish: 35 Minutes
2 servings

1 can (4 oz) Pillsbury® refrigerated
    crescent dinner rolls (4 rolls)
2 tablespoons finely chopped walnuts
1 tablespoon granulated sugar
1 teaspoon milk
1 container (6 oz) banana crème low-fat
    yogurt
1 snack-size container (3.5 oz) banana
    pudding
1 medium banana, sliced
Whipped cream topping (from aerosol
    can), if desired
Powdered sugar, if desired

1   Heat oven to 375°F. Spray cookie sheet with cooking spray. Unroll dough; separate into 4 triangles. On cookie sheet, make 2 kite shapes by placing longest sides of 2 dough triangles together; press edges to seal.

2   In small bowl, mix walnuts and granulated sugar. Lightly brush dough with milk; sprinkle each evenly with walnut mixture.

3   Bake 8 to 12 minutes or until bottoms are golden brown. Meanwhile, in another small bowl, mix yogurt and pudding until well blended. Stir in banana.

4   Remove pastries from oven. Immediately turn pastries over with pancake turner; gently fold each in half along sealed seam, walnut mixture side out. Remove from cookie sheet; place on cooling rack. Cool completely, about 15 minutes.

5   To serve, place pastries on individual dessert plates; fill each with about ¾ cup yogurt mixture. Garnish each with dollop of whipped cream topping; sprinkle with powdered sugar.

High Altitude (3500–6500 ft): No change.

1 Serving: Calories 500; Total Fat 20g (Saturated Fat 5g; Trans Fat 3.5g); Cholesterol 5mg; Sodium 560mg; Total Carbohydrate 70g (Dietary Fiber 3g) Exchanges: 1 Starch, 1 Fruit, 2 Other Carbohydrate, ½ Skim Milk, ½ High-Fat Meat, 3 Fat; Carbohydrate Choices: 4½

Almond-Toffee-Mocha Squares

Beverly Starr   Nashville, AR
Bake-Off® Contest 41, 2004

Prep Time: 20 Minutes
Start to Finish: 2 Hours 50 Minutes
16 brownies

BROWNIES
1 box (19.5 oz) Pillsbury® Brownie
    Classics® fudge toffee or traditional
    fudge brownie mix
1 teaspoon instant coffee granules
    or crystals
½ cup butter or margarine, melted
¼ cup water
2 eggs
½ cup finely chopped chocolate-
    covered English toffee candy bars
    (two 1.4-oz bars)
½ cup slivered almonds, toasted*

TOPPING
4 oz cream cheese (half of 8-oz
    package), softened
⅓ cup packed brown sugar
1 teaspoon instant coffee granules
    or crystals
1½ cups whipping cream
1 teaspoon vanilla
1 cup chopped chocolate-covered
    English toffee candy bars (four 1.4-
    oz bars)
½ cup slivered almonds, toasted*

1   Heat oven to 350°F. Grease bottom only of 13 × 9-inch pan with shortening or cooking spray. In large bowl, beat brownie mix, 1 teaspoon coffee granules, the butter, water and eggs with electric mixer on low speed 1 minute. Gently stir in ½ cup chopped candy bars and ½ cup almonds. Spread batter in pan.

Open House, Open Kitchen

Put out the welcome mat. When Beverly Starr says her home has an "open door policy," she means it. Anywhere from seven to eighteen people enjoy Sunday dinner each week at her house. And it's not unusual for several high school boys to call and ask if they can come over to bake cookies. Beverly specializes in brownies: "I've served 'millions' of them to all ages," she says.

2 Bake 24 to 28 minutes or until edges are firm. DO NOT OVERBAKE. Cool completely in pan on cooling rack, about 1 hour.

3 In medium bowl, beat cream cheese, brown sugar and 1 teaspoon coffee granules on medium speed until smooth. On high speed, beat in whipping cream and vanilla until soft peaks form.

4 Spread cream cheese mixture over cooled brownies. Sprinkle 1 cup chopped candy bars and ½ cup almonds over top. Refrigerate at least 1 hour before serving. Cut into 4 rows by 4 rows, or for smaller bars, cut into 6 rows by 4 rows. Store covered in refrigerator.

To toast almonds, bake uncovered in ungreased shallow pan in 350°F oven 6 to 10 minutes, stirring occasionally, until light brown.

High Altitude (3500–6500 ft): Follow High Altitude directions on brownie mix box. Bake 28 to 32 minutes.

1 Brownie: Calories 300; Total Fat 18g (Saturated Fat 9g; Trans Fat 0.5g); Cholesterol 55mg; Sodium 150mg; Total Carbohydrate 30g (Dietary Fiber 1g) Exchanges: 1 Starch, 1 Other Carbohydrate, 3½ Fat; Carbohydrate Choices: 2

Almond-Toffee-Mocha Squares

Fluffy Lemon-Raspberry Treat

Kathryn Friedl Lawton, OK
Bake-Off® Contest 42, 2006

Prep Time: 20 Minutes
Start to Finish: 2 Hours 25 Minutes
24 servings

1 roll (16.5 oz) Pillsbury® Create 'n Bake® refrigerated sugar cookies
1 bag (12 oz) white vanilla baking chips (2 cups)
1 cup organic frozen raspberries (from 10-oz bag), thawed
1 container (1 lb) Pillsbury® Creamy Supreme® lemon frosting
1 package (8 oz) cream cheese, softened
1 teaspoon lemon extract
1 container (8 oz) frozen whipped topping, thawed
1 teaspoon vegetable oil, if desired

1 Heat oven to 350°F. Grease 13 × 9-inch pan with shortening or cooking spray. In pan, break up cookie dough; press evenly in bottom to form crust.

2 Bake 13 to 18 minutes or until golden brown. Immediately sprinkle 1 cup of the baking chips evenly over crust. Let stand 5 minutes. Spread evenly with back of spoon. Cool completely, about 30 minutes.

3 Meanwhile, in small bowl, stir ½ cup of the raspberries with fork until broken up and slightly mashed; refrigerate. In large bowl, beat frosting, cream cheese and lemon extract with electric mixer on medium-high speed about 2 minutes or until well blended. Fold in whipped topping; refrigerate.

4 Spread mashed raspberries over cooled crust. Place in freezer 15 minutes. Spread frosting mixture over raspberries. Refrigerate until set, about 1 hour.

5 To serve, in small bowl, mash remaining ½ cup raspberries with fork. Spread raspberries over frosting mixture. In small resealable freezer plastic bag, place remaining 1 cup baking chips and the oil; seal bag. Microwave on High 1 minute. Squeeze bag to mix; microwave in 10-second increments, squeezing after each, until chips are melted and smooth. Cut small hole in one bottom corner of bag; squeeze bag to drizzle mixture over top of dessert. Cut into squares. Store covered in refrigerator.

High Altitude (3500–6500 ft): No change.

1 Serving: Calories 300; Total Fat 16g (Saturated Fat 8g; Trans Fat 2g); Cholesterol 15mg; Sodium 160mg; Total Carbohydrate 38g (Dietary Fiber 0g) Exchanges: 1 Starch, 1½ Other Carbohydrate, 3 Fat; Carbohydrate Choices: 2½

"Marble-ous" Peanut Butter Dessert

Florence Stull Danville, OH
Bake-Off® Contest 21, 1970

Prep Time: 30 Minutes
Start to Finish: 3 Hours 10 Minutes
15 servings

CRUST
½ cup packed brown sugar
½ cup peanut butter
¼ cup butter or margarine, softened
1 cup Pillsbury BEST® all-purpose flour

FILLING
1 package (8 oz) cream cheese, softened
½ cup granulated sugar
¼ cup peanut butter
1 teaspoon vanilla
2 pasteurized eggs
1 cup whipping cream, whipped, sweetened
1 cup semisweet chocolate chips (6 oz)

1 Heat oven to 350°F. In small bowl, beat brown sugar, ½ cup peanut butter and the butter with electric mixer on medium speed until light and fluffy. Beat in flour until crumbly. Sprinkle crumb mixture into ungreased 12 × 8-inch (2-quart) or 13 × 9-inch (3-quart) glass baking dish. Bake 10 to 15 minutes or until golden brown. Cool 10 minutes.

2 Reserve half of crumb mixture (about 1 cup) for topping. Lightly press remaining crumb mixture in bottom of baking dish.

3 In small bowl, beat cream cheese, granulated sugar, ¼ cup peanut butter and the vanilla on medium speed until smooth and creamy. Add 1 egg at a time, beating well after each. Fold in whipped cream. Pour over crumb mixture in baking dish.

4 In 1-quart saucepan, melt chocolate chips over low heat, stirring frequently, until melted and smooth. Drizzle chocolate over cream cheese mixture. With table knife, gently cut through both mixtures to marble. Sprinkle with reserved crumb mixture; press in slightly. Freeze at least 2 hours or until serving time. Let stand at room temperature 15 minutes before serving. Cut into squares.

High Altitude (3500–6500 ft): No change.

1 Serving: Calories 370; Total Fat 24g (Saturated Fat 12g; Trans Fat 0.5g); Cholesterol 70mg; Sodium 150mg; Total Carbohydrate 31g (Dietary Fiber 2g) Exchanges: 2 Other Carbohydrate, 1 High-Fat Meat, 3 Fat; Carbohydrate Choices: 2

"Marble-ous" Peanut Butter Dessert

Granola-Apple Mini Cheesecakes

Nick Dematteo   Sunnyside, NY
Bake-Off® Contest 41, 2004

Prep Time: 25 Minutes
Start to Finish: 2 Hours 5 Minutes
24 mini cheesecakes

1 box (8.9 oz) roasted almond crunchy granola bars (12 bars)
¼ cup butter or margarine, melted
3 packages (8 oz each) cream cheese, softened
¾ cup sugar
1 teaspoon vanilla
3 eggs
1 can (21 oz) apple pie filling

1 Heat oven to 350°F. Place foil baking cup in each of 24 regular-size muffin cups. Break 8 of the granola bars into pieces; place in gallon-size resealable food-storage plastic bag or food processor; seal bag and crush with rolling pin or process until fine crumbs form.

2 In medium bowl, mix crumbs and melted butter until well combined. Place scant tablespoon crumb mixture in each lined muffin cup; press in bottom of cup to form crust.

3 In large bowl, beat cream cheese and sugar with electric mixer on medium speed until creamy. Beat in vanilla and eggs until well combined. Cut or break remaining 4 granola bars into ½-inch pieces; stir into cream cheese mixture. Spoon scant ¼ cup mixture over crust in each cup.

4 Bake 20 to 25 minutes or until set. Cool in pans on cooling rack 15 minutes. Top each cheesecake with 1 tablespoon apple pie filling. Refrigerate until chilled, about 1 hour, before serving. Store cheesecakes in refrigerator.

High Altitude (3500–6500 ft): No change.

1 Mini Cheesecake: Calories 220; Total Fat 14g (Saturated Fat 9g; Trans Fat 0.5g); Cholesterol 65mg; Sodium 135mg; Total Carbohydrate 20g (Dietary Fiber 0g) Exchanges: 1 Starch, ½ Other Carbohydrate, 2½ Fat; Carbohydrate Choices: 1

Well if the Pan Fits...

New Yorkers know cheesecake. And Nick Dematteo is no exception. An actor, singer and songwriter, this Big Apple cook worked in a kitchen he describes as "way too small" to come up with the individual mini cheesecakes that earned him a trip to the Bake-Off® Contest in Hollywood.

Cookie Cheesecake Squares

Grace M. Wold   Phoenix, AZ
Bake-Off® Contest 19, 1968

Prep Time: 20 Minutes
Start to Finish: 50 Minutes
12 servings

1 roll (16.5 oz) Pillsbury® Create 'n Bake® refrigerated sugar cookies
¾ cup strawberry preserves
1 package (8 oz) cream cheese, softened
¼ cup sugar
1 container (8 oz) sour cream
½ teaspoon vanilla
1 egg

1 Heat oven to 375°F. Cut dough into ¼-inch slices.* Press slices in bottom of ungreased 13 × 9-inch pan to form crust. Bake 10 to 15 minutes or until light golden brown. (Cookie dough will appear puffy when removed from oven.) Gently spread evenly with preserves.

2 In large bowl, beat cream cheese and sugar with electric mixer on medium speed until fluffy. Add remaining ingredients; beat until well blended. Pour mixture over preserves, spreading to edges.

3 Bake 28 to 33 minutes or until knife inserted in cheese layer comes out clean. Cool. Store covered in refrigerator.

To slice dough easily, place in freezer 10 minutes before cutting.

High Altitude (3500–6500 ft): Stir or knead 2 tablespoons Pillsbury BEST® all-purpose flour into dough before pressing into pan.

1 Serving: Calories 360; Total Fat 19g (Saturated Fat 9g; Trans Fat 2.5g); Cholesterol 65mg; Sodium 180mg; Total Carbohydrate 43g (Dietary Fiber 0g) Exchanges: 1 Starch, 2 Other Carbohydrate, 3½ Fat; Carbohydrate Choices: 3

Cherry-Crescent Cheesecake Cups

Glen Ocock Appleton, WI
Bake-Off® Contest 22, 1971

Prep Time: 20 Minutes
Start to Finish: 45 Minutes
8 servings

CUPS
1 package (8 oz) cream cheese, softened
1 egg
1 cup powdered sugar
¼ cup chopped almonds
½ to 1 teaspoon almond extract
1 can (8 oz) Pillsbury® refrigerated
  crescent dinner rolls

TOPPING
1 cup cherry pie filling
1 to 2 tablespoons amaretto or
  cherry-flavored brandy
1 tablespoon butter or margarine

1 Heat oven to 350°F. Grease 8 regular-size muffin cups with shortening or cooking spray. In medium bowl, beat cream cheese and egg with electric mixer on medium speed until smooth. Beat in powdered sugar, almonds and almond extract until well blended.

2 Separate dough into 4 rectangles; firmly press perforations to seal. Press or roll each into 8 × 4-inch rectangle. Cut each rectangle in half crosswise, forming 8 squares. Press each square in bottom of muffin cup, leaving corners of each square extended over side of cup.

3 Place about ¼ cup cream cheese mixture into each dough-lined cup. Bring 4 corners of each square together in center of cup; firmly press points together to seal.

4 Bake 18 to 23 minutes or until golden brown. Immediately remove from muffin cups. In 1-quart saucepan, cook all topping ingredients over low heat, stirring occasionally, until bubbly and butter melts. Serve over warm desserts. Store desserts in refrigerator.

High Altitude (3500–6500 ft): Bake 20 to 25 minutes. Cool 5 to 10 minutes before removing from muffin cups.

1 Serving: Calories 350; Total Fat 20g (Saturated Fat 10g; Trans Fat 2g); Cholesterol 60mg; Sodium 320mg; Total Carbohydrate 37g (Dietary Fiber 1g) Exchanges: 1 Starch, 1½ Other Carbohydrate, ½ High-Fat Meat, 3 Fat; Carbohydrate Choices: 2½

Black Forest Cheesecake Dessert Cups

Kyle O'Malley Brigantine Beach, NJ
Bake-Off® Contest 42, 2006

Prep Time: 55 Minutes
Start to Finish: 2 Hours 50 Minutes
24 dessert cups

1 box (19.5 oz) Pillsbury® Brownie
  Classics traditional fudge brownie mix
½ cup vegetable oil
¼ cup water
4 eggs
1 cup semisweet chocolate chips (6 oz)
2 packages (8 oz each) cream cheese,
  softened
½ cup granulated sugar
1 container (6 oz) vanilla thick & creamy
  low-fat yogurt
1 can (21 oz) cherry pie filling
1 aerosol can whipped cream topping
1 large sprig fresh mint, if desired

1 Heat oven to 350°F. Place paper baking cup in each of 24 large muffin cups (2¾ inches in diameter and 1¼ inches deep). Make brownie mix as directed on box using oil, water and 2 of the eggs. Divide batter evenly among muffin cups (about 2 tablespoons per cup). Bake 15 minutes.

2 Meanwhile, in small microwavable bowl, microwave chocolate chips on High 1 minute. Stir and microwave in 15-second increments, stirring after each, until chips are melted and smooth; set aside. In large bowl, beat cream cheese with electric mixer on medium speed until smooth. Beat in sugar, remaining 2 eggs and the yogurt until blended. Add melted chocolate; beat until well blended.

3 Divide chocolate mixture evenly over warm brownie layer in cups (about 3 tablespoons per cup), filling each to top of cup. Cups will be full.

4 Bake 22 to 26 minutes longer or until set. Cool in pans 20 to 30 minutes. Carefully remove dessert cups from pan (cream cheese mixture will be soft); place on serving platter. Refrigerate at least 1 hour before serving.

5 To serve, remove paper; top each dessert cup with 1 tablespoon pie filling (including 2 or 3 cherries) and 1 tablespoon whipped cream topping. If desired, arrange cupcakes on pedestal cake plate covered with linen napkin. Garnish platter or plate with mint sprig. Store in refrigerator.

High Altitude (3500–6500 ft): Stir ½ cup Pillsbury BEST® all-purpose flour into dry brownie mix. Increase water to ⅓ cup. Makes 30 dessert cups.

1 Dessert Cup: Calories 330; Total Fat 18g (Saturated Fat 8g; Trans Fat 0g); Cholesterol 65mg; Sodium 150mg; Total Carbohydrate 36g (Dietary Fiber 2g) Exchanges: 1 Starch, 1½ Other Carbohydrate, 3½ Fat; Carbohydrate Choices: 2½

Royal Marble Cheesecake

Royal Marble Cheesecake

Isaac Feinstein   Atlantic City, NJ
Bake-Off® Contest 16, 1964

Prep Time: 35 Minutes
Start to Finish: 12 Hours
16 servings

CRUST
¾ cup Pillsbury BEST® all-purpose flour
2 tablespoons sugar
Dash salt
¼ cup butter or margarine
1 cup semisweet chocolate chips (6 oz),
  melted

FILLING
3 packages (8 oz each) cream cheese,
  softened
1 cup sugar
¼ cup Pillsbury BEST® all-purpose flour
2 teaspoons vanilla
6 eggs
1 cup sour cream

1   Heat oven to 400°F. In small bowl, mix ¾ cup flour, 2 tablespoons sugar and the salt. With pastry blender or fork, cut in butter until mixture resembles coarse crumbs. Stir in 2 tablespoons of the melted chocolate; reserve remaining chocolate for filling. Press crumb mixture in bottom of ungreased 9-inch springform pan.

2   Bake 10 minutes or until very light brown. Remove pan from oven. Reduce oven temperature to 325°F.

3   Meanwhile, in large bowl, beat cream cheese and 1 cup sugar with electric mixer on medium speed until light and fluffy. Beat in ¼ cup flour and the vanilla until well blended. On low speed, add 1 egg at a time, beating just until blended after each addition. Beat in sour cream. Place 1¾ cups filling mixture in medium bowl; stir in reserved melted chocolate.

4   Pour half of plain filling over crust. By spoonfuls, top with half of chocolate filling. Cover with remaining plain filling, then with spoonfuls of remaining chocolate filling. With table knife, swirl chocolate filling through plain filling. Place cheesecake in center of oven. Place shallow pan half full of water on bottom oven rack under cheesecake.

5   Bake at 325°F 1 hour to 1 hour 15 minutes or until set but center of cheesecake still jiggles when moved. Cool on cooling rack 10 minutes. Run knife around edge of pan to loosen cheesecake. Cool at least 2 hours. Refrigerate at least 8 hours or overnight before serving. Carefully remove side of pan. Store cheesecake in refrigerator.

High Altitude (3500–6500 ft): In step 5, bake cheesecake at 325°F 1 hour 15 minutes to 1 hour 25 minutes. Remove from oven; immediately run knife around edge of pan to loosen cheesecake.

1 Serving: Calories 370; Total Fat 26g (Saturated Fat 15g; Trans Fat 0.5g); Cholesterol 145mg; Sodium 190mg; Total Carbohydrate 29g (Dietary Fiber 0g) Exchanges: 2 Other Carbohydrate, 1 High-Fat Meat, 3½ Fat; Carbohydrate Choices: 2

Stocking 100 kitchens

The kitchen equipment list for finalists in a past contest included: 437 mixing bowls, 309 rubber spatulas, 238 wooden spoons, 172 measuring spoon sets, 168 measuring cup sets, 147 glass measuring cups, 117 cookie sheets, 90 skillets and 89 cooling racks.

Apple-Crescent Cheesecake

Eugene Majewski Elmhurst, IL
Bake-Off® Contest 22, 1971

Prep Time: 25 Minutes
Start to Finish: 3 Hours 20 Minutes
10 servings

FILLING
⅓ cup sugar
½ teaspoon ground cinnamon
3 cups thinly sliced, peeled cooking
   apples (3 medium)
3 packages (3 oz each) cream cheese,
   softened

¼ cup sugar
2 tablespoons milk
½ teaspoon vanilla
1 egg

CRUST
1 can (8 oz) Pillsbury® refrigerated
   crescent dinner rolls

GLAZE
½ cup apricot preserves
1 tablespoon water

1 Heat oven to 400°F. In medium
bowl, mix ⅓ cup sugar and the
cinnamon. Stir in apples until
coated; set aside.

2 In small bowl, beat cream
cheese, ¼ cup sugar, the milk,
vanilla and egg with electric mixer
on medium speed until smooth;
set aside.

3 Unroll dough; separate into
8 triangles. In ungreased 9-inch
springform pan or 9-inch round
cake pan, arrange triangles; press
in bottom and about 1½ inches
up side. Spoon cheese mixture
into crust.

4 Drain any liquid from apples; arrange apples over cheese mixture. In small bowl, mix preserves and water; drizzle over apples.

5 Bake 20 minutes. Reduce oven temperature to 350°F; bake 30 to 35 minutes longer or until crust is deep golden brown and center is firm to the touch. Cool completely, about 30 minutes. Refrigerate at least 1 hour 30 minutes before serving.

High Altitude (3500–6500 ft): In step 5, increase second bake time to 35 to 40 minutes.

1 Serving: Calories 290; Total Fat 14g (Saturated Fat 7g; Trans Fat 1.5g); Cholesterol 50mg; Sodium 260mg; Total Carbohydrate 37g (Dietary Fiber 0g) Exchanges: 1 Starch, 1½ Other Carbohydrate, 2½ Fat; Carbohydrate Choices: 2½

Peanut Butter–Chocolate Creme Cheesecake

Melissa Henninger   Northport, AL
Bake-Off® Contest 36, 1994

Prep Time: 25 Minutes
Start to Finish: 3 Hours 25 Minutes
16 servings

CRUST

1½ cups finely crushed creme-filled chocolate sandwich cookies (about 18)
6 tablespoons sugar
3 tablespoons unsweetened baking cocoa
¼ cup butter or margarine, melted

FILLING

3 packages (8 oz each) cream cheese, softened
1 cup creamy peanut butter
1 container (1 lb) Pillsbury® Creamy Supreme® vanilla frosting
1½ cups coarsely chopped creme-filled chocolate sandwich cookies (about 16)

TOPPING

4 packages (1.6 oz each) or 8 chocolate-covered peanut butter cups (0.6 oz each), unwrapped, broken into pieces
¼ cup milk
1½ cups frozen (thawed) whipped topping
3 tablespoons unsweetened baking cocoa
2 tablespoons sugar

GARNISH, IF DESIRED

1 chocolate-covered peanut butter cup, cut into 6 wedges
1 creme-filled chocolate sandwich cookie, cut into 6 wedges

1 In blender, food processor or large bowl, mix all crust ingredients. Press in bottom of ungreased 9- or 10-inch springform pan; set aside.

2 In large bowl, beat cream cheese with electric mixer on medium speed until smooth and creamy. Add peanut butter; beat until light and fluffy. Fold in frosting. Pour half of batter over crust; sprinkle evenly with 1½ cups chopped cookies. Cover with remaining batter. Refrigerate until set, about 2 hours.

3 In small microwavable bowl, microwave broken peanut butter cups and milk on High 1 minute 30 seconds to 3 minutes, stirring once halfway through cooking.* Stir until smooth; pour over top of cheesecake. Refrigerate until set, about 1 hour.

4 In large bowl, gently mix whipped topping, 3 tablespoons cocoa and 2 tablespoons sugar until well blended. Remove side of pan. Pipe or spoon 12 circular mounds around edge of cheesecake; garnish with candy and cookie wedges. Store cheesecake in refrigerator.

*_To melt peanut butter cups on stove top, in 1-quart saucepan, heat peanut butter cups and milk over low heat 2 to 3 minutes, stirring frequently, until candy is melted and mixture is smooth._

High Altitude (3500–6500 ft): No change.

1 Serving: Calories 620; Total Fat 40g (Saturated Fat 20g; Trans Fat 2g); Cholesterol 55mg; Sodium 410mg; Total Carbohydrate 55g (Dietary Fiber 3g) Exchanges: 1 Starch, 2½ Other Carbohydrate, 1 High-Fat Meat, 6 Fat; Carbohydrate Choices: 3½

Pecan Pie–Ginger Cheesecake

Kathy Ault   Edmond, OK
Bake-Off® Contest 40, 2002
$2,000 Winner

Prep Time: 20 Minutes
Start to Finish: 4 Hours 10 Minutes
12 servings

CRUST
1 Pillsbury® refrigerated pie crust (from 15-oz box), softened as directed on box

FILLING
1 package (8 oz) cream cheese, softened
6 tablespoons granulated sugar
½ teaspoon vanilla
1 egg
¼ cup finely chopped crystallized ginger

TOPPING
2 tablespoons Pillsbury BEST® all-purpose flour
¼ cup butter, melted
¾ cup packed brown sugar
1 teaspoon vanilla
2 eggs
2 cups pecan halves or pieces

1   Heat oven to 350°F. Place pie crust in 9-inch glass pie plate or 9-inch deep-dish glass pie plate as directed on box for One-Crust Filled Pie.

2   In small bowl, beat cream cheese, granulated sugar, ½ teaspoon vanilla and 1 egg with electric mixer on medium speed, scraping bowl occasionally, until smooth. Stir in ginger. Spoon and spread filling in crust-lined pie plate.

3   In medium bowl, mix flour and butter. Stir in brown sugar, 1 teaspoon vanilla and 2 eggs until well mixed. Stir in pecans. Carefully spoon mixture evenly over filling.

4   Bake 40 to 50 minutes or until center is set and crust is golden brown. Cool on cooling rack 1 hour.

5   Refrigerate until thoroughly chilled, about 2 hours, before serving. Store cheesecake in refrigerator.

High Altitude (3500–6500 ft): No change.

1 Serving: Calories 410; Total Fat 28g (Saturated Fat 10g; Trans Fat 0g); Cholesterol 85mg; Sodium 180mg; Total Carbohydrate 35g (Dietary Fiber 2g) Exchanges: ½ Starch, 2 Other Carbohydrate, ½ High-Fat Meat, 4½ Fat; Carbohydrate Choices: 2

Peaches and Cream Crescent Dessert

Marilyn Blankschien   Clintonville, WI
Bake-Off® Contest 28, 1978

Prep Time: 15 Minutes
Start to Finish: 45 Minutes
12 servings

1 can (8 oz) Pillsbury® refrigerated crescent dinner rolls
1 package (8 oz) cream cheese, softened
½ cup sugar
¼ to ½ teaspoon almond extract
1 can (21 oz) peach pie filling*
½ cup Pillsbury BEST® all-purpose flour
¼ cup packed brown sugar
3 tablespoons butter or margarine, softened
½ cup sliced almonds or chopped nuts

1   Heat oven to 375°F. Separate dough into 2 long rectangles. Place in ungreased 13 × 9-inch pan; press in bottom to form crust. Seal perforations. Bake 5 minutes.

2   In small bowl, beat cream cheese, sugar and almond extract with electric mixer on medium speed until smooth. Spread over partially baked crust. Spoon pie filling evenly over cream cheese mixture.

The Laws of Baking Do Not Apply

An attorney, Kathy Ault created a fabulous cheese cake that seems to defy the laws of baking. "The recipe transforms when you bake it. The top filling sinks to the bottom and the filling on the bottom rises," Kathy testifies. Kathy got her start in the kitchen in Girls Scouts and 4-H, and says, "I can't remember not being interested in cooking. My husband and I built our house with two dishwashers because I cook so much."

3 In medium bowl, mix flour and brown sugar. Using fork or pastry blender, cut in butter until mixture is crumbly. Stir in almonds; sprinkle crumb mixture over pie filling.

4 Bake 25 to 30 minutes or until golden brown. Cool completely. Store in refrigerator. Cut into squares.

* Cherry or apple pie filling can be substituted for peach filling.

High Altitude (3500–6500 ft): In step 4, bake 28 to 33 minutes.

1 Serving: Calories 310; Total Fat 15g (Saturated Fat 7g; Trans Fat 1.5g); Cholesterol 30mg; Sodium 230mg; Total Carbohydrate 39g (Dietary Fiber 1g) Exchanges: 1 Starch, 1½ Other Carbohydrate, 3 Fat; Carbohydrate Choices: 2½

Pumpkin Bread Pudding with Ginger Cream

Candice Merrill   Pasadena, CA
Bake-Off® Contest 38, 1998

> **Prep Time:** 15 Minutes
> **Start to Finish:** 1 Hour 45 Minutes
> 9 servings

PUDDING
3 eggs
1¼ cups sugar
1½ teaspoons ground cinnamon
½ to 1½ teaspoons ground nutmeg
¼ cup butter or margarine, melted
1½ teaspoons vanilla
1 container (8 oz) plain dry bread crumbs (1¾ cups)
2 cups milk
1 cup canned pumpkin (not pumpkin pie mix)
½ cup raisins

GINGER CREAM
1 cup whipping cream
3 tablespoons sugar
½ teaspoon ground ginger

1 Heat oven to 350°F. Spray 8- or 9-inch square pan with cooking spray. In large bowl, beat eggs until well blended. Add 1¼ cups sugar, the cinnamon, nutmeg, butter and vanilla; beat with electric mixer on medium speed until smooth. Add bread crumbs, milk and pumpkin; mix well. Let stand 10 minutes.

2 Add raisins to batter; mix well. Spread evenly in pan. Bake 37 to 47 minutes or until knife inserted 1½ inches from edge comes out clean. Cool 30 minutes.

3 In small bowl, beat whipping cream, gradually adding 3 tablespoons sugar and ginger until soft peaks form. To serve, cut pudding into squares. Serve warm or cool topped with ginger cream. Store covered in refrigerator.

High Altitude (3500–6500 ft): Heat oven to 375°F. Bake 35 to 45 minutes.

1 Serving: Calories 430; Total Fat 17g (Saturated Fat 10g; Trans Fat 0.5g); Cholesterol 120mg; Sodium 240mg; Total Carbohydrate 60g (Dietary Fiber 2g) Exchanges: 1 Starch, 3 Other Carbohydrate, ½ Medium-Fat Meat, 3 Fat; Carbohydrate Choices: 4

Caramel Apple Pudding

Clifton G. Mandrell   Russell, KY
Bake-Off® Contest 9, 1957

> **Prep Time:** 20 Minutes
> **Start to Finish:** 1 Hour 25 Minutes
> 6 servings

¾ cup Pillsbury BEST® all-purpose flour
½ cup granulated sugar
1 teaspoon baking powder
1 teaspoon ground cinnamon
¼ teaspoon salt
1½ cups coarsely chopped, peeled apples (1½ medium)
½ cup slivered almonds
½ cup milk
¾ cup packed brown sugar
¼ cup butter or margarine
¾ cup boiling water
Vanilla ice cream or whipped cream, if desired

1 Heat oven to 375°F. Grease 8-inch square (2-quart) glass baking dish or 1½-quart casserole with shortening or cooking spray. In medium bowl, mix flour, granulated sugar, baking powder, cinnamon and salt. Add apples, almonds and milk; stir until well blended. Spread mixture in baking dish.

2 In small bowl, mix brown sugar, butter and boiling water until butter is melted. Pour over batter in baking dish.

3 Bake 45 to 50 minutes or until golden brown. Cool at least 15 minutes before serving. Serve with ice cream.

High Altitude (3500–6500 ft): No change.

1 Serving: Calories 390; Total Fat 14g (Saturated Fat 6g; Trans Fat 0g); Cholesterol 20mg; Sodium 250mg; Total Carbohydrate 63g (Dietary Fiber 2g) Exchanges: 1½ Starch, 2½ Other Carbohydrate, 2½ Fat; Carbohydrate Choices: 4

Swedish Apple Mini Dumplings

Swedish Apple Mini Dumplings

Stella Riley Bender   Colorado Springs, CO
Bake-Off® Contest 36, 1994

Prep Time: 20 Minutes
Start to Finish: 1 Hour 10 Minutes
4 servings

½ cup packed brown sugar
½ teaspoon ground cinnamon
¼ teaspoon ground cardamom
2 teaspoons vanilla
1 Pillsbury® refrigerated pie crust (from
   15-oz box), softened as directed on box
1 tablespoon butter or margarine, softened
1 small Granny Smith apple, peeled,
   cored and cut into 8 slices
¼ cup raisins
1½ cups apple juice
3 tablespoons sugar
2 tablespoons red cinnamon candies
¼ cup half-and-half

1   Heat oven to 375°F. Spray
8-inch square (2-quart) glass baking
dish with cooking spray. In small
bowl, mix brown sugar, cinnamon,
cardamom and vanilla; set aside.

2   Remove pie crust from pouch;
unroll on work surface. Spread butter
over crust; sprinkle with brown
sugar mixture. Cut crust into 8
wedges; place apple slice crosswise in
center of each wedge. Starting with
pointed end, fold crust wedge over
apple; fold corners of wide end of
wedge over apple, forming dumpling
and sealing completely. Place seam
side down and sides touching in
baking dish. Sprinkle with raisins.

3   In 1-quart saucepan, heat apple
juice, sugar and cinnamon candies
to boiling over medium heat. Cook
1 minute, stirring frequently, until
candies are melted. Carefully pour
over dumplings.

4   Bake 30 to 40 minutes or until
crust is light golden brown, apples
are tender and sauce thickens. Cool
10 minutes before serving. Spoon
dumplings into serving dishes;
spoon sauce over dumplings. Serve
warm with half-and-half.

High Altitude (3500–6500 ft): Bake 35 to
40 minutes.

1 Serving: Calories 540; Total Fat 19g (Saturated Fat 8g;
Trans Fat 0g); Cholesterol 20mg; Sodium 260mg; Total
Carbohydrate 91g (Dietary Fiber 0g) Exchanges: 6 Other
Carbohydrate, 4 Fat; Carbohydrate Choices: 6

Easy Crescent-Apple Cobbler

Kevin Bellhorn   Richmond, MI
Bake-Off® Contest 24, 1973

Prep Time: 20 Minutes
Start to Finish: 1 Hour 15 Minutes
6 servings

4 cups sliced peeled cooking apples
   (4 medium)
½ cup granulated sugar
3 tablespoons Pillsbury BEST®
   all-purpose flour
2 teaspoons ground cinnamon
1 can (8 oz) Pillsbury® refrigerated
   crescent dinner rolls
½ cup packed brown sugar
2 tablespoons butter or margarine, melted
Whipped cream or vanilla ice cream,
   if desired

1   Heat oven to 375°F. In large
bowl, mix apples, granulated sugar,
flour and 1 teaspoon of the cinnamon.

2   Separate crescent dough into
4 rectangles. Press 2 rectangles in
bottom of ungreased 8- or 9-inch
square pan. Spread apple mixture over
dough. Place remaining 2 rectangles
over apples, gently stretching to cover.

3   In small bowl, mix brown sugar
and remaining teaspoon cinnamon;
sprinkle over dough. Drizzle with
butter.

4   Bake 30 to 40 minutes or until
deep golden brown and center is no
longer doughy. Cool 15 minutes before
serving. Serve with whipped cream.

High Altitude (3500–6500 ft): No change.

1 Serving: Calories 370; Total Fat 12g (Saturated Fat 5g;
Trans Fat 2g); Cholesterol 10mg; Sodium 330mg;
Total Carbohydrate 62g (Dietary Fiber 2g) Exchanges:
1 Starch, 3 Other Carbohydrate, 2½ Fat; Carbohydrate
Choices: 4

Marriage Leads to New Family Traditions

In many families, cooking is an activity shared by mothers and
daughters—and sometimes mothers-in-law. Stella Riley Bender
credits the mothers in her life as inspiration for her wonderful
dumplings: "A long time ago my Swedish-born mother-in-
law taught me how to make her apple dumplings," Stella
says. "I adapted her recipe to smaller portions, or 'mini-
dumplings,' and I can thank my own mother for the idea
of adding cinnamon candy—she always spices up her
applesauce with a handful."

Country French Apple Crescent Casserole

Sharon Richardson Dallas, TX
Bake-Off® Contest 34, 1990
$10,000 Winner

> **Prep Time:** 25 Minutes
> **Start to Finish:** 1 Hour 5 Minutes
> 8 servings

DUMPLINGS
2 tablespoons sugar
½ to 1 teaspoon ground cinnamon
1 can (8 oz) Pillsbury® refrigerated crescent dinner rolls
1 large apple, peeled, cut into 8 slices

SAUCE
½ cup sugar
½ cup whipping cream
1 tablespoon almond extract or amaretto
1 egg

TOPPING
½ cup sliced almonds
Additional ground cinnamon

1 Heat oven to 375°F. In small bowl, mix 2 tablespoons sugar and ½ to 1 teaspoon cinnamon. Separate dough into 8 triangles; sprinkle sugar mixture evenly over each. Gently press sugar mixture into each triangle, flattening each slightly.

2 Place apple slice on shortest side of each triangle; tuck in edges around apple slice. Roll up, starting at shortest side and rolling to opposite point. Seal all seams. Place point side down in ungreased 9-inch round baking dish or pie plate, placing long side of 7 filled crescents around outside edge of dish and 1 in center.

3 Bake 15 to 20 minutes or until golden brown.

4 Remove baking dish from oven. In small bowl, beat all sauce ingredients with wire whisk until well blended. Spoon sauce evenly over partially baked rolls. Sprinkle with almonds and additional cinnamon.

5 Bake 13 to 18 minutes longer or until deep golden brown. If necessary, cover with foil during last 5 minutes of baking to prevent excessive browning. Serve warm. Store in refrigerator.

High Altitude (3500–6500 ft): In step 5, bake 16 to 21 minutes. Cover with foil during last 5 minutes of baking.

1 Serving: Calories 280; Total Fat 14g (Saturated Fat 5g; Trans Fat 1.5g); Cholesterol 45mg; Sodium 230mg; Total Carbohydrate 32g (Dietary Fiber 1g) Exchanges: 1 Starch, 1 Other Carbohydrate, 3 Fat; Carbohydrate Choices: 2

Hot Buttered Rum and Apple Cobbler

Margi Mulkey Boise, ID
Bake-Off® Contest 30, 1982

> **Prep Time:** 20 Minutes
> **Start to Finish:** 1 Hour 10 Minutes
> 8 servings

COBBLER
1 cup Pillsbury BEST® all-purpose flour
¾ cup sugar
2 teaspoons baking powder
¼ teaspoon salt
¼ cup butter or margarine, softened
½ cup milk
1 can (21 oz) apple pie filling
⅓ cup raisins
½ cup frozen (thawed) apple juice concentrate (from 12-oz can)
½ cup water

TOPPING
1 tablespoon sugar
1 teaspoon cornstarch
¼ cup frozen (thawed) apple juice concentrate (from 12-oz can)
1 tablespoon butter or margarine
½ to 1½ teaspoons rum extract

GARNISH, IF DESIRED
Whipped cream

1 Heat oven to 375°F. Grease 12 × 8-inch (2-quart) glass baking dish or 11 × 7-inch pan with shortening or cooking spray. In small bowl, mix flour, ½ cup of the sugar, the baking powder, salt, ¼ cup butter and the milk with electric mixer on low speed until moistened, scraping bowl

---

Returning to the Bake-Off® Contest

If the Bake-Off® Contest had an award for persistence, Margi Mulkey would have been a top candidate to win. Margi's trip to the Bake-Off® Contest in 1982 wasn't her first. She'd competed earlier—twenty-seven years before at the 7th contest, held at the Waldorf-Astoria Hotel in New York City. Of course, lots of other important things happened in those intervening years, including Margi's son growing up, getting married and making Margi a grandmother.

occasionally. Beat on high speed 1 minute. Spread in baking dish.

2 Spoon pie filling evenly over batter; sprinkle with raisins. Sprinkle with remaining ¼ cup sugar; pour ½ cup apple juice concentrate and the water over sugar.

3 Bake 40 to 50 minutes or until golden brown and toothpick inserted in cake portion comes out clean, covering with foil during last 10 minutes of baking if necessary to prevent excessive browning.

4 In 1-quart saucepan, blend 1 tablespoon sugar, the cornstarch, ¼ cup apple juice concentrate and 1 tablespoon butter over medium heat, stirring constantly, until thickened. Stir in rum extract. Pour and spread evenly over hot cobbler. Serve warm topped with whipped cream.

High Altitude (3500–6500 ft): No change.

1 Serving: Calories 480; Total Fat 8g (Saturated Fat 5g; Trans Fat 0g); Cholesterol 20mg; Sodium 280mg; Total Carbohydrate 100g (Dietary Fiber 2g) Exchanges: 1 Starch, 5½ Other Carbohydrate, 1½ Fat; Carbohydrate Choices: 6½

Peach-Berry Cobbler

Oliver C. Duffina Washington, DC
Bake-Off® Contest 13, 1961

> **Prep Time:** 20 Minutes
> **Start to Finish:** 1 Hour 20 Minutes
> 6 servings

FRUIT MIXTURE
¼ cup granulated sugar
¼ cup packed brown sugar
1 tablespoon cornstarch
½ cup water
1 tablespoon lemon juice
2 cups sliced peeled fresh peaches (3 medium) or frozen (thawed) unsweetened sliced peaches
1 cup fresh or frozen blueberries

TOPPING
1 cup Pillsbury BEST® all-purpose flour
½ cup granulated sugar
1½ teaspoons baking powder
½ teaspoon salt
½ cup milk
¼ cup butter or margarine, softened
2 tablespoons granulated sugar
¼ teaspoon ground nutmeg

1 Heat oven to 375°F. In 3-quart saucepan, mix ¼ cup granulated sugar, the brown sugar and cornstarch. Stir in water. Cook over medium heat 7 to 9 minutes, stirring constantly, until thickened. Stir in lemon juice, peaches and blueberries. Pour into ungreased 8-inch square (2-quart) glass baking dish.

2 In medium bowl, mix flour, ½ cup granulated sugar, the baking powder and salt. With electric mixer on medium speed, beat in milk and butter until smooth. Spoon over fruit mixture. Sprinkle with 2 tablespoons granulated sugar and the nutmeg.

3 Bake 40 to 45 minutes or until golden brown. Cool at least 15 minutes before serving. Serve warm or cool.

High Altitude (3500–6500 ft): No change.

1 Serving: Calories 350; Total Fat 9g (Saturated Fat 5g; Trans Fat 0g); Cholesterol 20mg; Sodium 390mg; Total Carbohydrate 66g (Dietary Fiber 2g) Exchanges: 1 Starch, ½ Fruit, 3 Other Carbohydrate, 1½ Fat; Carbohydrate Choices: 4½

Chocolate-Cherry Crisp

Amy Heyd Cincinnati, OH
Bake-Off® Contest 39, 2000

> **Prep Time:** 10 Minutes
> **Start to Finish:** 1 Hour 35 Minutes
> 10 servings

1 box (15.8) Pillsbury® Brownie Classics double chocolate brownie mix
1 cup quick-cooking oats
½ cup chopped walnuts, if desired
½ cup butter or margarine, melted
2 cans (21 oz each) cherry pie filling
Vanilla ice cream
Fresh mint sprigs, if desired

1 Heat oven to 350°F. Reserve chocolate syrup packet from brownie mix for topping. In large bowl, mix brownie mix, oats and walnuts. Stir in butter until mix is moistened (mixture will be dry).

2 Spoon pie filling evenly into ungreased 8-inch square (2-quart) glass baking dish. Sprinkle brownie mixture over pie filling.

3 Bake 30 to 40 minutes or until edges are bubbly. Cool 45 minutes before serving. Spoon crisp into dessert bowls. Top each serving with ice cream; drizzle with chocolate syrup from packet. Garnish with mint sprigs.

High Altitude (3500–6500 ft): No change.

1 Serving: Calories 500; Total Fat 19g (Saturated Fat 10g; Trans Fat 1.5g); Cholesterol 40mg; Sodium 210mg; Total Carbohydrate 78g (Dietary Fiber 5g) Exchanges: 1½ Starch, 3½ Other Carbohydrate, 3½ Fat; Carbohydrate Choices: 5

Ruby Razz Crunch

Achsa Myers   Fort Collins, CO
Bake-Off® Contest 8, 1956
$2,000 Winner

Prep Time: 25 Minutes
Start to Finish: 1 Hour 30 Minutes
9 servings

FILLING
1 box (10 oz) frozen raspberries
    with syrup, thawed, drained,
    reserving liquid
1 bag (16 oz) frozen rhubarb, thawed,
    drained, reserving liquid
½ cup granulated sugar
3 tablespoons cornstarch

GARNISH
½ cup whipping cream, whipped
2 tablespoons granulated sugar
1 to 3 drops red food color, if desired

CRUST AND TOPPING
1¼ cups Pillsbury BEST® all-purpose flour
1 cup packed brown sugar
1 cup quick-cooking oats
1 teaspoon ground cinnamon
½ cup butter or margarine, melted

1 Heat oven to 325°F. Reserve 2 tablespoons raspberries for topping. In measuring cup, mix reserved raspberry and rhubarb liquids; if necessary, add water to make 1 cup.

2 In 2-quart saucepan, mix ½ cup granulated sugar and the cornstarch; stir in reserved liquids. Cook over medium heat, stirring constantly, until thickened. Remove from heat. Stir in remaining raspberries and rhubarb; set aside.

3 Line cookie sheet with waxed paper. In small bowl, gently mix whipped cream, 2 tablespoons granulated sugar, reserved

raspberries and food color. Drop in 9 mounds onto lined cookie sheet; freeze until firm.

4 In large bowl, mix flour, brown sugar, oats and cinnamon. Stir in butter until crumbly. Press ⅔ of crumb mixture in bottom of ungreased 9-inch square pan. Spoon filling mixture over crust, spreading evenly. Sprinkle with remaining crumb mixture.

5 Bake 45 to 55 minutes or until topping is golden brown and filling bubbles around edges. Cool slightly, about 10 minutes, before serving. Cut into 9 squares; top each serving with mound of frozen garnish.

High Altitude (3500–6500 ft): Heat oven to 350°F. In step 4, before adding filling and topping, prebake crust 12 minutes. In step 5, bake 50 to 55 minutes.

1 Serving: Calories 430; Total Fat 15g (Saturated Fat 9g; Trans Fat 0.5g); Cholesterol 40mg; Sodium 90mg; Total Carbohydrate 69g (Dietary Fiber 4g) Exchanges: 1 Starch, 3½ Other Carbohydrate, 3 Fat; Carbohydrate Choices: 4½

Cherry Cream Crunch

Joyce Herr   Rogers, AR
Bake-Off® Contest 14, 1962

Prep Time: 25 Minutes
Start to Finish: 3 Hours 15 Minutes
12 servings

BASE AND TOPPING
1 cup Pillsbury BEST® all-purpose flour
½ cup packed brown sugar
½ teaspoon ground cinnamon
Dash salt
½ cup butter or margarine, softened
1 teaspoon vanilla
1 cup coconut
½ cup quick-cooking oats
½ cup chopped walnuts

FILLING
1 can (14 oz) sweetened condensed
    milk (not evaporated)
1 tablespoon grated lemon peel
¼ cup lemon juice
Dash salt
2 eggs, slightly beaten
1 can (21 oz) cherry or blueberry pie
    filling

1 Heat oven to 375°F. In large bowl, beat flour, brown sugar, cinnamon, dash salt, the butter and vanilla with electric mixer on low speed until crumbly. Stir in coconut, oats and walnuts. Press 2½ cups of the crumb mixture into bottom of ungreased 12 × 8-inch (2-quart) glass baking dish or 13 × 9-inch pan; reserve remaining crumb mixture for topping.

2 Bake base 12 minutes or until light golden brown. Meanwhile, in medium bowl, mix all filling ingredients except pie filling.

3 Spread filling evenly over partially baked base. Carefully spoon pie filling evenly over condensed milk mixture. Sprinkle reserved crumb mixture over top.

4 Bake 15 to 18 minutes longer or until top is golden brown. Cool 30 minutes. Refrigerate at least 2 hours before serving. Cut into squares. Store covered in refrigerator.

High Altitude (3500–6500 ft): In step 2, bake base 14 minutes. In step 4, bake 19 to 22 minutes.

1 Serving: Calories 400; Total Fat 18g (Saturated Fat 10g; Trans Fat 0.5g); Cholesterol 65mg; Sodium 160mg; Total Carbohydrate 54g (Dietary Fiber 2g) Exchanges: 2 Starch, 1½ Other Carbohydrate, 3½ Fat; Carbohydrate Choices: 3½

Cherry Cream Crunch

Cranberry-Pear Cobbler

Marsha Michael   Bloomington, MN
Bake-Off® Contest 38, 1998

Prep Time: 10 Minutes
Start to Finish: 50 Minutes
10 servings

FRUIT MIXTURE
2 cans (15 oz each) pear halves or slices, drained, liquid reserved
½ cup sweetened dried cranberries
½ cup applesauce
¼ teaspoon ground cinnamon

TOPPING
½ cup sugar
½ teaspoon ground cinnamon
1 can (12 oz) Pillsbury® Golden Layers® refrigerated buttermilk flaky biscuits
2½ teaspoons butter or margarine

SERVE WITH, IF DESIRED
Vanilla ice cream or whipped cream

1   Heat oven to 450°F. Cut pears into 1-inch chunks. In ungreased 11×7-inch or 8-inch square (2-quart) glass baking dish, arrange pear chunks. Sprinkle with cranberries. In small bowl, mix applesauce and ¼ teaspoon cinnamon. Spoon over fruit.

2   Bake 8 to 10 minutes or until hot and bubbly. Remove from oven. Reduce oven temperature to 400°F.

3   In small bowl, mix sugar and ½ teaspoon cinnamon. Separate dough into 10 biscuits. Dip each biscuit into reserved pear liquid; coat all sides with sugar-cinnamon mixture. Arrange biscuits over hot fruit in 2 rows of 5 biscuits each. Top each biscuit with about ¼ teaspoon butter.

4   Bake 15 to 20 minutes or until biscuits are golden brown. Cool 10 minutes before serving. Serve warm with ice cream.

High Altitude (3500–6500 ft): No change.

1 Serving: Calories 230; Total Fat 5g (Saturated Fat 1.5g; Trans Fat 1.5g); Cholesterol 0mg; Sodium 370mg; Total Carbohydrate 43g (Dietary Fiber 2g) Exchanges: 1 Starch, 1 Fruit, 1 Other Carbohydrate, ½ Fat; Carbohydrate Choices: 3

Incredible Peach Cobbler

Becky Beus   Kuna, ID
Bake-Off® Contest 39, 2000

Prep Time: 15 Minutes
Start to Finish: 1 Hour 25 Minutes
15 servings

½ cup butter or margarine
1 box (15.6 oz) Pillsbury® cranberry quick bread & muffin mix
2 tablespoons grated orange peel
2 cans (29 oz each) peach slices in light syrup, drained, 1 cup liquid reserved
1 egg
⅓ cup sweetened dried cranberries
⅓ cup sugar
Vanilla ice cream, if desired

1   Heat oven to 375°F. Place butter in ungreased 13 × 9-inch pan. Place in oven until butter is melted; remove from oven.

2   Meanwhile, in large bowl, place quick bread mix, 1 tablespoon of the orange peel, 1 cup reserved peach liquid and the egg; stir 50 to 75 strokes with spoon until mix is moistened. Drop mixture by spoonfuls over butter in pan; spread slightly without stirring. Arrange peaches over mixture. Sprinkle with cranberries.

3   In small bowl, mix sugar and remaining 1 tablespoon orange peel; sprinkle over fruit.

4   Bake 45 to 50 minutes or until edges are deep golden brown. Cool 20 minutes before serving. Serve warm with ice cream.

High Altitude (3500–6500 ft): Add 1 tablespoon Pillsbury BEST® all-purpose flour to dry quick bread mix.

1 Serving: Calories 260; Total Fat 9g (Saturated Fat 4.5g; Trans Fat 1g); Cholesterol 30mg; Sodium 190mg; Total Carbohydrate 41g (Dietary Fiber 2g) Exchanges: 1 Starch, 1½ Other Carbohydrate, 1½ Fat; Carbohydrate Choices: 3

Applescotch Crisp

Frank Donelson   Bloomington, IL
Bake-Off® Contest 22, 1971

Prep Time: 15 Minutes
Start to Finish: 1 Hour 5 Minutes
8 servings

TOPPING
⅔ cup Pillsbury BEST® all-purpose flour
½ cup quick-cooking oats
½ cup chopped nuts
¼ cup granulated sugar
½ teaspoon salt
1 teaspoon ground cinnamon
1 box (4-serving size) butterscotch or vanilla pudding and pie filling mix (not instant)
½ cup butter or margarine, melted

FRUIT MIXTURE
4 cups sliced peeled cooking apples (4 medium)
½ cup packed brown sugar
1 tablespoon Pillsbury BEST® all-purpose flour
¼ cup milk
½ cup water

1 Heat oven to 350°F. In medium bowl, mix all topping ingredients until crumbly; set aside.

2 In large bowl, mix all fruit mixture ingredients. Pour into ungreased 9-inch square pan. Sprinkle topping over fruit mixture.

3 Bake 45 to 50 minutes or until apples are tender and topping is golden brown. Serve warm or cool.

High Altitude (3500–6500 ft): Heat oven to 375°F.

1 Serving: Calories 370; Total Fat 17g (Saturated Fat 8g; Trans Fat 0.5g); Cholesterol 30mg; Sodium 310mg; Total Carbohydrate 51g (Dietary Fiber 2g) Exchanges: 1 Starch, ½ Fruit, 2 Other Carbohydrate, 3 Fat; Carbohydrate Choices: 3½

Sour Cream Apple Squares

Luella Maki   Ely, MN
Bake-Off® Contest 26, 1975
$25,000 One of Two Grand Prize Winners

> **Prep Time:** 15 Minutes
> **Start to Finish:** 50 Minutes
> 12 to 15 squares

2 cups Pillsbury BEST® all-purpose flour
2 cups packed brown sugar
½ cup butter or margarine, softened
1 cup chopped nuts
1 to 2 teaspoons ground cinnamon
1 teaspoon baking soda
½ teaspoon salt
1 cup sour cream
1 teaspoon vanilla
1 egg
2 cups finely chopped peeled apples (2 medium)
Sweetened whipped cream, if desired

1 Heat oven to 350°F. In large bowl, beat flour, brown sugar and butter with electric mixer on low speed until crumbly. Stir in nuts. In ungreased 13 × 9-inch pan, press 2¾ cups of the crumb mixture.

2 To remaining crumb mixture, add cinnamon, baking soda, salt, sour cream, vanilla and egg; blend well. Stir in apples. Spoon evenly over crumb crust in pan.

3 Bake 25 to 35 minutes or until toothpick inserted in center comes out clean. Serve with whipped cream.

High Altitude (3500–6500 ft): Heat oven to 375°F.

1 Square: Calories 410; Total Fat 18g (Saturated Fat 8g; Trans Fat 0.5g); Cholesterol 50mg; Sodium 290mg; Total Carbohydrate 57g (Dietary Fiber 2g) Exchanges: 1 Starch, 3 Other Carbohydrate, 3½ Fat; Carbohydrate Choices: 4

Viennese Streusel Cookie Torte

Pat Neaves   Kansas City, MO
Bake-Off® Contest 38, 1998

> **Prep Time:** 15 Minutes
> **Start to Finish:** 1 Hour 50 Minutes
> 10 servings

TORTE
1 roll (16.5 oz) Pillsbury® Create 'n Bake® refrigerated sugar cookies
½ cup raspberry preserves
½ cup white vanilla baking chips
1 box (4-serving size) vanilla instant pudding and pie filling mix

STREUSEL
3 tablespoons Pillsbury BEST® all-purpose flour
3 tablespoons sugar
2 tablespoons butter or margarine
1 egg white, beaten
⅓ cup sliced almonds

1 Heat oven to 350°F. Spray 10- or 9-inch springform pan with cooking spray. Remove half of cookie dough from wrapper; refrigerate remaining half until needed. Place dough between 2 sheets of lightly floured waxed paper; roll to form 10-inch round. Refrigerate while preparing remainder of torte.

2 With floured fingers, press remaining half of dough evenly in bottom of pan. Spread preserves over dough; sprinkle with vanilla baking chips and pudding mix. Remove dough round from refrigerator. Peel off top sheet of waxed paper. Carefully invert dough over mixture in pan; remove waxed paper. Press edges to fit.

3 In small bowl, mix flour and sugar until well blended. With pastry blender or fork, cut in butter until mixture resembles coarse crumbs. Brush top of dough with egg white; sprinkle with flour mixture and almonds.

4 Bake 40 to 50 minutes or until edges are golden brown. Run knife around side of pan to loosen torte. Cool 45 minutes. Carefully remove side of pan. Serve warm.

High Altitude (3500–6500 ft): After pressing remaining half of dough in bottom of pan, bake 5 to 10 minutes and continue as directed.

1 Serving: Calories 420; Total Fat 17g (Saturated Fat 6g; Trans Fat 2.5g); Cholesterol 20mg; Sodium 320mg; Total Carbohydrate 62g (Dietary Fiber 0g) Exchanges: 1 Starch, 3 Other Carbohydrate, 3½ Fat; Carbohydrate Choices: 4

Streusel Pecan Pie Squares

Debbie A. Porteur   Hollister, CA
Bake-Off® Contest 29, 1980
$15,000 Winner

> Prep Time: 15 Minutes
> Start to Finish: 1 Hour
> 15 servings

CRUST
3 cups Pillsbury BEST® all-purpose flour
¾ cup packed brown sugar
1½ cups cold butter or margarine

FILLING
¾ cup packed brown sugar
1½ cups corn syrup or maple-flavored
   syrup
1 cup milk
⅓ cup butter or margarine, melted
1 teaspoon vanilla
4 eggs
1½ cups chopped pecans

TOPPING
Whipped cream or ice cream, if desired

1   Heat oven to 400°F. In large bowl, mix all crust ingredients until crumbly. Reserve 2 cups crumbs for filling and topping. Press remaining crumbs in bottom and ¾ inch up sides of ungreased 15 × 10 × 1-inch pan. Bake 10 minutes.

2   In large bowl, mix ¼ cup of the reserved crumbs and all filling ingredients except pecans. Stir in pecans. Pour over partially baked crust; bake 10 minutes.

3   Reduce oven temperature to 350°F. Sprinkle remaining 1¾ cups reserved crumbs over filling; bake 20 to 25 minutes longer or until filling is set and crumbs are golden brown. Serve with whipped cream.

High Altitude (3500–6500 ft): No change.

1 Serving: Calories 590; Total Fat 32g (Saturated Fat 16g; Trans Fat 1.5g); Cholesterol 115mg; Sodium 230mg; Total Carbohydrate 69g (Dietary Fiber 2g) Exchanges: 2 Starch, 2½ Other Carbohydrate, 6 Fat; Carbohydrate Choices: 4½

Caramel-Pear-Pecan Flan

Tillie Astorino   North Adams, MA
Bake-Off® Contest 32, 1986

> Prep Time: 30 Minutes
> Start to Finish: 3 Hours 30 Minutes
> 8 servings

CRUST
1 Pillsbury® refrigerated pie crust
   (from 15-oz box), softened as
   directed on box
½ cup chopped pecans

FILLING
1 package (8 oz) cream cheese,
   softened
¾ to 1 cup caramel topping
2 eggs
1 can (29 oz) pear halves, well drained,
   sliced*
1½ cups frozen (thawed) whipped
   topping
3 tablespoons chopped pecans

1   Place pie crust in 10-inch microwavable tart pan or 9-inch microwavable pie plate as directed on box for One-Crust Filled Pie. Press ½ cup pecans on bottom and side of crust. Microwave on High 6 or 8 minutes, rotating pan ½ turn every 2 minutes. Crust is done when surface appears dry and flaky.

2   In small bowl, beat cream cheese, ½ cup of the caramel topping and the eggs with electric mixer on medium speed until smooth and creamy. Pour into cooked crust.

3   Arrange pear slices in single layer over cream cheese mixture. For tart pan, microwave on High 6 to 9 minutes (for pie plate, 9 to 11 minutes), rotating pan ¼ turn every 3 minutes. Pie is done when center is almost set (cream cheese mixture will firm up as it cools and chills). Cover loosely with waxed paper; cool on flat surface 1 hour. Refrigerate at least 2 hours or until serving time.

4   Just before serving, top with whipped topping. Drizzle with remaining ¼ to ½ cup caramel topping; sprinkle with 3 table-spoons pecans. Store flan in refrigerator.

Six to 10 canned pear halves, arranged with rounded sides up and narrow ends pointing toward center, can be substituted for the sliced pears. If desired, score pears by making ⅛-inch-deep decorative cuts on pear halves.

High Altitude (3500–6500 ft): No change.

1 Serving: Calories 460; Total Fat 28g (Saturated Fat 12g; Trans Fat 0g); Cholesterol 90mg; Sodium 320mg; Total Carbohydrate 47g (Dietary Fiber 3g) Exchanges: 1 Starch, 2 Other Carbohydrate, 5 ½ Fat; Carbohydrate Choices: 3

Caramel-Pear-Pecan Flan

Almond Brickle Dessert

Louise Bork Garfield Heights, OH
Bake-Off® Contest 18, 1967
$1,000 Winner

Prep Time: 20 Minutes
Start to Finish: 55 Minutes
9 servings

½ **cup slivered almonds**
⅓ **cup sugar**
½ **cup butter or margarine**
¼ **cup honey**
1 **tablespoon milk**
1¾ **cups Pillsbury BEST® all-purpose flour**
⅔ **cup sugar**
2 **teaspoons baking powder**
½ **cup butter or margarine, softened**
⅓ **cup milk**
1 **teaspoon almond extract**
2 **eggs**

1 Heat oven to 350°F. Grease 9-inch square pan with shortening or cooking spray. In small saucepan, mix almonds, ⅓ cup sugar, ½ cup butter, the honey and 1 tablespoon milk. Cook over medium heat 9 to 11 minutes, stirring constantly, until mixture boils; boil and stir 2 minutes longer. Remove from heat; set aside.

2 In large bowl, beat 1 cup of the flour, ⅔ cup sugar, the baking powder, ½ cup butter, ⅓ cup milk, the almond extract and eggs with electric mixer on low speed until moistened; beat on medium speed 3 minutes. Stir in remaining ¾ cup flour; mix well. Spread batter in pan. Spoon almond mixture over batter; spread evenly to cover.

3 Bake 25 to 35 minutes or until toothpick inserted in center comes out clean.

High Altitude (3500–6500 ft): No change.

1 Serving: Calories 450; Total Fat 25g (Saturated Fat 14g; Trans Fat 1g); Cholesterol 100mg; Sodium 270mg; Total Carbohydrate 51g (Dietary Fiber 1g) Exchanges: 1 Starch, 2½ Other Carbohydrate, 5 Fat; Carbohydrate Choices: 3½

Peanut Butter Cookie Pizza

Adeline Carr Atladena, CA
Bake-Off® Contest 20, 1969

Prep Time: 15 Minutes
Start to Finish: 1 Hour 50 Minutes
12 servings

CRUST
1 **roll (16.5 oz) Pillsbury® Create 'n Bake® refrigerated cookies (any flavor)**

BUTTER-CREAM FILLING
½ **cup peanut butter**
1 **package (3 oz) cream cheese, softened**
3 **tablespoons sugar**
3 **tablespoons butter or margarine, softened**
2 **tablespoons milk**
2 **teaspoons vanilla**
⅛ **teaspoon salt**

TOPPINGS
1 **banana, sliced**
½ **cup toasted sliced almonds or chopped peanuts**
⅓ **cup flaked coconut**

1 Heat oven to 375°F. Slice cookie dough into ¼-inch slices. Arrange slices on bottom of ungreased 14- or 12-inch pizza pan; press together to form a crust. Bake 8 to 10 minutes until golden brown. Cool completely, about 1 hour.

2 Meanwhile, in small bowl, beat all filling ingredients with electric mixer on medium speed until light and fluffy. Spread over crust. Refrigerate at least 30 minutes before topping.

3 Top pizza with banana, almonds and coconut. Cut into wedges. Serve with ice cream if desired.

High Altitude (3500–6500 ft): Stir or knead 2 tablespoons Pillsbury BEST® all-purpose flour into dough before pressing into pan. Bake crust 10 to 12 minutes.

1 Serving: Calories 350; Total Fat 22g (Saturated Fat 7g; Trans Fat 2g); Cholesterol 30mg; Sodium 230mg; Total Carbohydrate 34g (Dietary Fiber 1g) Exchanges: 2 Other Carbohydrate, 1 High-Fat Meat, 3 Fat; Carbohydrate Choices: 2

Peanut Butter Cookie Pizza

Fruity Almond Dessert Pizza

Rosemary Leicht Bethel, OH
Bake-Off® Contest 38, 1998

Prep Time: 15 Minutes
Start to Finish: 45 Minutes
8 servings

1 can (13.8 oz) Pillsbury® refrigerated
  classic pizza crust
⅓ cup cream cheese or light cream
  cheese, softened
¼ cup apricot preserves
1 large apple, peeled, thinly sliced
¼ cup Pillsbury BEST® all-purpose
  or unbleached flour
¼ cup packed brown sugar
2 tablespoons butter or margarine
¼ cup blanched almonds, coarsely
  chopped

1 Heat oven to 425°F. Grease 12-inch pizza pan or 13 × 9-inch pan with shortening or cooking spray. Unroll dough; place in pan. Starting at center, press out dough with hands. Spread cream cheese evenly over dough. Spread with preserves. Arrange apple slices over preserves.

2 In small bowl, mix flour and brown sugar. With pastry blender or fork, cut in butter until mixture resembles coarse crumbs. Stir in almonds. Sprinkle mixture evenly over apples.

3 Bake 15 to 20 minutes or until edges are golden brown. Cool 10 minutes. Cut into wedges. Serve warm.

High Altitude (3500–6500 ft): Bake 15 to 18 minutes.

1 Serving: Calories 290; Total Fat 10g (Saturated Fat 4.5g; Trans Fat 0g); Cholesterol 20mg; Sodium 410mg; Total Carbohydrate 44g (Dietary Fiber 0g) Exchanges: 1½ Starch, 1½ Other Carbohydrate, 2 Fat; Carbohydrate Choices: 3

As Fate Would Have It

Some Bake-Off® Contest finalists decide to enter the contest on a whim and are successful; for others it's a lifelong dream. A finalist at the 42nd contest, Bobbie Keefer of Byers, Colorado, recalled, "I dreamt of going to the Bake-Off® when my friends wanted to be Miss America." Another finalist in 2006, Michael Weaver of San Francisco, finally won a place at the contest after entering for 30 years. For Suzanne Conrad of Findlay, Ohio, the first time was a charm. The first time she entered she became a finalist—and the $1 million grand prize winner of the 41st Bake-Off® Contest—with her recipe for Oats 'n Honey Granola Pie.

Metric Conversion Guide

Volume

U.S. Units	Canadian Metric	Australian Metric
¼ teaspoon	1 mL	1 ml
½ teaspoon	2 mL	2 ml
1 teaspoon	5 mL	5 ml
1 tablespoon	15 mL	20 ml
¼ cup	50 mL	60 ml
⅓ cup	75 mL	80 ml
½ cup	125 mL	125 ml
⅔ cup	150 mL	170 ml
¾ cup	175 mL	190 ml
1 cup	250 mL	250 ml
1 quart	1 liter	1 liter
1½ quarts	1.5 liters	1.5 liters
2 quarts	2 liters	2 liters
2½ quarts	2.5 liters	2.5 liters
3 quarts	3 liters	3 liters
4 quarts	4 liters	4 liters

Weight

U.S. Units	Canadian Metric	Australian Metric
1 ounce	30 grams	30 grams
2 ounces	55 grams	60 grams
3 ounces	85 grams	90 grams
4 ounces (¼ pound)	115 grams	125 grams
8 ounces (½ pound)	225 grams	225 grams
16 ounces (1 pound)	455 grams	500 grams
1 pound	455 grams	½ kilogram

Measurements

Inches	Centimeters
1	2.5
2	5.0
3	7.5
4	10.0
5	12.5
6	15.0
7	17.5
8	20.5
9	23.0
10	25.5
11	28.0
12	30.5
13	33.0

Temperatures

Fahrenheit	Celsius
32°	0°
212°	100°
250°	120°
275°	140°
300°	150°
325°	160°
350°	180°
375°	190°
400°	200°
425°	220°
450°	230°
475°	240°
500°	260°

NOTE: The recipes in this cookbook have not been developed or tested using metric measures. When converting recipes to metric, some variations in quality may be noted.

Helpful Nutrition and Cooking Information

Nutrition Guidelines

We provide nutrition information for each recipe that includes calories, fat, cholesterol, sodium, carbohydrate and fiber. Individual food choices can be based on this information.

Criteria Used for Calculating Nutrition Information

- The first ingredient was used wherever a choice is given (such as ⅓ cup sour cream or plain yogurt).

- The first ingredient amount was used wherever a range is given (such as 3- to 3½-pound cut-up broiler-fryer chicken).

- The first serving number was used wherever a range is given (such as 4 to 6 servings).

- "If desired" ingredients and recipe variations were not included (such as sprinkle with brown sugar, if desired).

- Only the amount of a marinade or frying oil that is estimated to be absorbed by the food during preparation or cooking was calculated.

Ingredients Used in Recipe Testing and Nutrition Calculations

- Ingredients used for testing represent those that the majority of consumers use in their homes: large eggs, 2% milk, 80%-lean ground beef, canned ready-to-use chicken broth and vegetable oil spread containing not less than 65 percent fat.

- Fat-free, low-fat or low-sodium products were not used, unless otherwise indicated.

- Solid vegetable shortening (not butter, margarine, nonstick cooking sprays or vegetable oil spread as they can cause sticking problems) was used to grease pans, unless otherwise indicated.

Equipment Used in Recipe Testing

We use equipment for testing that the majority of consumers use in their homes. If a specific piece of equipment (such as a wire whisk) is necessary for recipe success, it is listed in the recipe.

- Cookware and bakeware without nonstick coatings were used, unless otherwise indicated.

- No dark-colored, black or insulated bakeware was used.

- When a pan is specified in a recipe, a metal pan was used; a baking dish or pie plate means ovenproof glass was used.

- An electric hand mixer was used for mixing only when mixer speeds are specified in the recipe directions. When a mixer speed is not given, a spoon or fork was used.

Cooking Terms Glossary

Beat: Mix ingredients vigorously with spoon, fork, wire whisk, hand beater or electric mixer until smooth and uniform.

Boil: Heat liquid until bubbles rise continuously and break on the surface and steam is given off. For rolling boil, the bubbles form rapidly.

Chop: Cut into coarse or fine irregular pieces with a knife, food chopper, blender or food processor.

Cube: Cut into squares ½ inch or larger.

Dice: Cut into squares smaller than ½ inch.

Grate: Cut into tiny particles using small rough holes of grater (citrus peel or chocolate).

Grease: Rub the inside surface of a pan with shortening, using pastry brush, piece of waxed paper or paper towel, to prevent food from sticking during baking (as for some casseroles).

Julienne: Cut into thin, matchlike strips, using knife or food processor (vegetables, fruits, meats).

Mix: Combine ingredients in any way that distributes them evenly.

Sauté: Cook foods in hot oil or margarine over medium-high heat with frequent tossing and turning motion.

Shred: Cut into long thin pieces by rubbing food across the holes of a shredder, as for cheese, or by using a knife to slice very thinly, as for cabbage.

Simmer: Cook in liquid just below the boiling point on top of the stove; usually after reducing heat from a boil. Bubbles will rise slowly and break just below the surface.

Stir: Mix ingredients until uniform consistency. Stir once in a while for stirring occasionally, often for stirring frequently and continuously for stirring constantly.

Toss: Tumble ingredients (such as green salad) lightly with a lifting motion, usually to coat evenly or mix with another food.

Index

Let these collections from
the Pillsbury Bake-Off® library
inspire you to make your own
prize-winning creations.